WALTER BLAIR

UNIVERSITY OF CHICAGO

NATIVE AMERICAN HUMOR

CHANDLER PUBLISHING COMPANY

An Intext Publisher · Scranton, Pennsylvania 18515

PREFACE

Nearly two and a half decades after this book appeared scholars have persuaded me—more impressive, they have persuaded a publisher—that its continuing usefulness justifies its republication.

During the years since 1937 historians have greatly enlarged our knowledge of American humor. I have decided nevertheless to let Parts I-VII of my Introduction, my selections and my Notes reappear unchanged. One justification is that while new findings have added details and modified some of my beliefs they have not persuaded me that I should substantially change my Introduction or supplant original selections. Another justification is that this procedure makes reprinting at a reduced price possible. Still another is that I was enabled to add to the bibliography studies setting forth important recent findings. Finally, I added to my Introduction Part VIII, which continues the history of older humorous traditions and discriminates new modes which appear likely in time to replace them.

I was unable to resist an invitation to have reproduced some of my works of art. On the cover is a picture of my imaginary visit (dressed in a suit borrowed from W. D. Howells) with Mark Twain in Elmira. At intervals in the text are drawings the creation of which helped me through several faculty meetings. If these do not exactly delight with their beauty, my hope is that somehow they will interpret and edify.

WALTER BLAIR

PREFACE TO THE FIRST EDITION

This book attempts to trace the mutations of nineteenth-century humorous treatments of American characters. The introduction discusses aspects of the evolution of writing of this sort, the notes comment upon it, the bibliography lists primary sources and helpful studies of it, and the selections are examples of the humor itself. It seemed worth while to center attention upon this type of writing not only because its materials and methods are highly characteristic of "American humor" but also because, as literature, at its best it is delightfully rich and even at its worst it has many elements of interest.

The introduction obviously derives much from recent studies by such scholars as Misses Tandy and Rourke, Messrs. Chittick, Meine, De Voto, and others. A whole series of gaps, however, must be filled by other investigators before a complete history of this important type of American writing can be written. Consequently, this study, more fragmentary than I would wish, is simply a series of essays on phases of a history not yet discernible in its entirety. I have tried to give these essays coherence by ordering them chronologically and by making all of them deal chiefly with certain nineteenth-century developments in American humor which may be grouped as follows:

(1) *The changing attitudes of humorists towards comic native characters.* A first step, brought about in complicated ways, was a slow process—the discovery of these figures by writers who, for various reasons, were contemptuous of the bumpkins they portrayed. At a later time, for a variety of reasons, more tolerant humorists portrayed sympathetically characters they regarded as good and, still later, some authors presented admiringly even rascally figures. Finally sympathy broadened until, after many decades of the depiction of only comic phases of low life, some writers perceived and revealed the pathetic elements as well.

(2) *The changes in humorous technique.* Along with an enriching of portraiture which resulted from broadening sympathy came the change, for example, from portrayal of simple types to more individualized depiction and the display of more widely varied characters. While these developments continued, between 1855 and 1900, some authors moved back toward greater simplification of characterization. There were other significant changes— in narrative technique, in the use of the vernacular, in the imaginative depiction of comic worlds—mutations the causes of which I have attempted to discover and effects of which I have tried to suggest.

(3) *The changing attitudes of readers towards this humor.* Readers, like authors, were at first rather contemptuous of native figures

and had comparatively little interest in them unless the fable about them dealt with politics. As time passed, however, although readers still admired crackerbox commentators upon national affairs (even lifting some such sages to pedestals), they became increasingly interested in humorous depictions as characterizations and social studies or simply as provokers of laughter. Meanwhile, from a despised position, the humorists climbed, by degrees, to a place fairly high in popular esteem. These changes of attitude, which came about in interesting ways, were reflected in the appraisals of the critics and the success of the writers.

In addition to outlining these interactive developments, I have tried to indicate how humor at various times stood in relation to some of the currents of other American literature and how at all times individual humorists stood in the history of humor. The greatest of them, Mark Twain, has been considered in his relationship with his predecessors and contemporaries in a way which perhaps will make him more understandable than heretofore both as a humorist and as a literary figure. Also, though none of these writers, probably, will stir laughter today as that writer once did, I have tried to show that some of them at least may have an interest not merely historical for modern readers.

The bibliography, a somewhat more extensive one than any other which has appeared, will, it is hoped, have value for those who wish to further their study of these writings. . . .

Such were the tasks attempted. Errors which have crept in have done so despite valiant efforts of helpful friends. My colleagues, Messrs. Napier Wilt and Clarence H. Faust, listened patiently when I talked about my notions, carefully read my record of them, and showed me how to eliminate various faults. My erstwhile collaborator, Mr. Franklin J. Meine, generously gave me access to his fine library, corrected my mistakes, and checked my bibliography. Professor Harry Hayden Clark, editor of the series in which this volume appears, kindly suggested corrections and revisions. Professor Percy H. Boynton, after reading the proofs, gave helpful assistance. And, as my documentation suggests, numerous authors helped by writing useful books and articles.

[1937]

CONTENTS

ILLUSTRATIONS FROM PUBLICATIONS

INTRODUCTION

Walter Blair

INTRODUCTION

I. The Requisites for "American Humor"

The term, "American humor," like many another term in general use, is more easily understood than defined. As it is usually employed, it does not mean all humor produced in America, since much humor originating in this country is not in any way marked by its place of origin. Nor does it mean humor with characteristics discoverable in the comedy of no other land, since apparently there is no such humor. It means humor which is *American* in that it has an emphatic "native quality"[1]—a quality imparted by its subject matter and its technique. Its subject matter is national in the sense indicated in 1838 by a writer who was hailing the beginnings of this type of writing. Said this writer, an English critic:

Humour is national when it is impregnated with the convictions, customs, and associations of a nation. . . . National American humour must be all this transferred into shapes which produce laughter. The humour of a people is their institutions, laws, customs, manners, habits, characters, convictions,—their scenery whether of the sea, the city, or the hills,—expressed in the language of the ludicrous. . . .[2]

Its technique, which will be characterized hereafter, is of a sort which develops effectively such subject matter. The phrase, "native American humor," suggests as well as any the usual implication of the term.

American humor—in this sense of the term—did not come into widespread existence until about 1830, more than two hundred years after John Smith wrote the first American book. In other words, though the colonists were more prolific of humor than is generally supposed,[3] the beginnings of this type of writing

---

[1] The phrase is that of Will D. Howe, in *The Cambridge History of American Literature* (New York, 1918), II, 150.

[2] H. W., "Slick, Downing, Crockett, Etc.," *The London and Westminster Review*, XXXII, 138–139 (December, 1838).

[3] For studies of humorous writings during the years before 1800, see Carl Holli-

came late. And they were long coming because most American authors failed for a long time to perceive the richest comedy about them or to discover a technique which revealed that comedy.

In part, of course, the perception of comedy depended upon the attitude of the writers. Many details in the native scene which seemed comic to the people of the nineteenth century belonged to the seventeenth and eighteenth centuries as well. Furthermore, quite early, some of the colonists saw and recorded some of these details. One is forced to conclude—not very profoundly, perhaps —that many early writers failed to develop American humor because they were too earnest, too serious about subjects which later proved amusing.

Proof of this is discoverable in the writings of two colonial authors, Francis Higginson and John Smith, who were so serious in their treatment of typical details that, though their works now provoke laughter, they themselves did not realize that their materials were amusing. By contrast, two rare frivolous souls of colonial times, Sarah Kemble Knight and William Byrd, in their treatment of typical details, foreshadowed American humor.

Undoubtedly comedy unperceived by the author is implicit in *New England's Plantation* (1630) by Francis Higginson. In his rhapsodic account of newly opened territory, similar to those produced by writers on every American frontier, eager to share with others the blessings of a land of milk and honey, Higginson wrote enthusiastically of New England's fertility, its plentiful game and fish, its salubrious climate. Corn, he said, grew amazingly: "Thirty, forty, fifty, sixty [fold increases] are abundant here. Yea, Joseph's increase in Egypt are outstript. . . . Our planters hope to have more than a hundredfold this year." Root vegetables flourish astonishingly, "both bigger and sweeter than ordinarily is found in England." And the wild beasts—"bears, and they say some lions also . . . several sorts of deer, some whereof bring three or four young ones at once, which is not ordinary in England . . . wolves, foxes, beavers, otters, martens, great wild

day's book, *The Wit and Humor of Colonial Days, 1607–1800* (Philadelphia, 1912); the same author's article, "Colonial Laughter," *English Journal*, XXIV, 125–136 (February, 1935); Henry Clay Lukens, "American Literary Comedians," *Harper's*, LXXX, 783–788 (April, 1890); Stephen Leacock, *The Greatest Pages of American Humor* (Garden City, 1936), pp. 1–24.

cats, and a beast called a molke, as big as an ox"—furnish food a-plenty and precious furs. Even the fish in the sea are plentiful "almost beyond believing . . . our fishermen take many hundreds together . . . their nets take more than they are able to haul to land . . . they fill two boats at a time. . . ."

But the climax is Higginson's enthusiasm for the climate of New England, concerning which most people today are likely to have some reservations. ". . . there is hardly," he exclaims, rapturously, "a more healthful place in the world. . . ."

Many that have been weak and sickly in old England, by coming hither have been thoroughly healed, and grown healthful and strong. None can more truly speak hereof . . . than myself. . . . My friends that knew me can well tell how very sickly I have been, and continually in physic, being much troubled with tormenting pain . . . and abundance of melancholic humors. But since I came hither . . . I thank God I have had perfect health, and freed from pain . . . and whereas beforetime I clothed myself with double clothes and thick waistcoats to keep me warm, even in the summer time, I do now go as thin clad as any. . . . a sup of New-England's air is better than a whole draught of Old England's ale.[1]

To us, though not to Higginson, this is amusing. The unconscious comedy of the ecstatic passage was effectively demonstrated by Higginson himself, however, when, during the very year his moving tribute to the healthfulness of New England appeared, the poor man sickened and died.[2] His demise conveniently and irrefutably proves that his unconscious humor was the humor of exaggeration, often called typically American.[3] In early writings of colonists who, like Higginson, whistled to keep up their spirits or sought to persuade other settlers to join them by reporting the richness of the new world—in natural resources,

[1] *New England's Plantation, or a short and true description of the Commodities of that Country*, reprinted in the *Massachusetts Historical Society Collections*, Vol. I. Since similar passages might be cited from the writings of Alsop, Morton, Ward and half a dozen authors of the same period, it will be evident that Higginson is fairly representative.

[2] Thomas Wentworth Higginson, *Life of Francis Higginson* (New York, 1891), p. 128.

[3] H. W., in the review cited (p. 3, footnote 2), as early as 1838, said: "The curiosity of the public regarding the peculiar nature of American humour seems to have been easily satisfied with the application of the all-sufficing word exaggeration." Though American humor has other qualities as well, exaggeration is a device very frequently employed.

in the spiritual grace and the bravery of its inhabitants—time after time comedy was missed by similarly narrow margins.[1]

Later Americans, more sympathetic to comedy, more detached, and hence more perceptive of incongruities, were to discover the comic possibilities of such an attitude as the booster's enthusiasm displayed by Higginson.[2] Here, for example, is how an Arkansan, in 1845, made capital of subject matter akin to Higginson's:

Strangers, if you'd asked me how we got our meat in Arkansaw, I'd a . . . given you a list of varmints that would make a caravan, beginning with the bar, and ending off with the cat . . . a bird . . . is too trifling. I never did shoot at but one, and I'd never forgive myself for that, had it weighed less than forty pounds. . . . You see, the thing was so fat that it couldn't fly far; and when he fell out of the tree, after I shot him, on striking the ground he bust open behind, and the way the pound gobs of tallow rolled out of the opening was perfectly beautiful.

. . . Arkansaw . . . the creation state, the finishing-up country —a state where the *sile* runs down to the centre of the 'arth, and government gives you title to every inch of it. Then its airs—just breathe them, and they will make you snort like a horse. It's a state without a fault, it is.[3]

Other writers in the nineteenth century were to find comedy in harrowing adventures similar to those which, from the time of Captain John Smith, had been celebrated by colonists and frontiersmen. As Henry Adams has shown, Smith, like Higginson,

[1] There are a few exceptions, notably Franklin's tales about prodigious American sheep and leaping whales and some passages in the writings of the Rev. Samuel Andrew Peters, which are embryonic American tall tales. Franklin's fanciful yarns are printed in his *Works*, ed. Jared Sparks (Boston, 1847), VII, 289–290, and Peters' invention is displayed in *A General History of Connecticut* . . . (London, 1781).

[2] Early in the nineteenth century, they were smiling at the Kentucky preacher who, describing eternal bliss, suggested that heaven was "a regular Kentuck of a place" or they were telling tales about game so plentiful that the hunter killed great numbers of animals with a single shot of his gun. (See the almanac story, p. 199 of this book.) Mark Twain's Beriah Sellers is the greatest achievement in this type of humor, but during the twentieth century, Americans were still amused by the Californian who arose at a funeral "to say a few words about the climate of California," and in 1936, the rhymed boast of the Rotarian club about the glories of a small town amused those who viewed the picture, "Mr. Deeds Goes to Town."

[3] *The Big Bear of Arkansas, and Other Tales, Illustrative of Characters and Incidents in the South and Southwest* (Philadelphia, 1845), pp. 16–17.

was an unconscious creator of comedy. When that blustering, mustachioed Elizabethan soldier-of-fortune retold his tale of captivity, the number and the ferocity of his Indian captors provide comedy of exaggeration not unlike that in Falstaff's famous yarn to Prince Hal. Hence, when one compares the first version of Smith's yarn with the second, laughter, unforeseen by the bold captain, results:

Eight guards, which had been sufficient in 1608, were multiplied into thirty or forty tall fellows in 1624. What was enough for ten men at the earlier time would feed twenty according to the later version . . . a few months after the event, a people was described, savage, but neither cruel nor bloodthirsty . . . kind and even magnanimous toward their captive. . . . Yet in 1624, throughout his long imprisonment, he was . . . expecting every hour to be put to one death or another.[1]

But two centuries were to pass before a perception of the outlandish and grotesque qualities of American wilderness adventures made possible the display of their fantastic comedy in a whole series of sketches consciously, not unconsciously, humorous.[2]

Two colonial authors came nearer than Higginson and Smith, however, to cultivating the most fertile field for nineteenth-century American humor—American character. From the seventeenth century, comedy had lurked in the mingling of people of many civilizations, of many classes, on one sparsely settled continent; and the attempts of these people to adjust themselves to totally new ways of living and the sensing by every man of the amazing differences between himself and his neighbors had provided the stuff of rich comedy.[3] But though some colonial writers

---

[1] Henry Adams, *Historical Essays* (New York, 1891), pp. 53–54.

[2] Indians much more ferocious than those who menaced Smith were the comic redmen who, in 1853, seized Sal Fink: ". . . she war captered in the most all-sneaken manner by about fifty Injuns, an' carried by 'em to Roast Flesh Hollow, whar the blood drinkin' wild varmints detarmined to skin her alive, sprinkle a leetle salt over her, an' devour her before her own eyes. . . ." *Crockett Almanac* (Philadelphia, New York, Boston and Baltimore, 1852). For other fantastic yarns about the redmen or the beasts of the wilderness, see *The Spirit of the Times* of the forties and fifties, or read the chapter called "Hunters and Fishermen" in *Humor of the Old Deep South*, ed. Arthur Palmer Hudson (New York, 1936), pp. 98–125.

[3] As Andrew Lang says, in "Western Drolls," *Lost Leaders* (London, 1889), p. 186: "The contrasts, the energy, the mixture of races in America, the overflowing young

were stern with their neighbors for differing from them,[1] and though some interestedly recorded the fact that many races lived in America, effective comic portraiture did not evolve in America, with minor exceptions,[2] until the eighteenth century. Then, two authors contemptuous of folk they saw on their travels, Madam Knight, a light-hearted lady traveling from Boston to New York, and William Byrd, a sophisticated Southern aristocrat on a surveying party, partially, at least, developed the comedy of American character.

The sprightly Sarah Kemble Knight, recording some of her adventures in her *Private Journal of a Journey from Boston to New-York* (1704–1705),[3] is frivolous enough, amused enough, to limn an admirable picture of a gawky Connecticut Yankee and his awkward Joan whom she saw in a merchant's house. The man was

. . . a tall country fellow, w*th* his alfogeos full of Tobacco; for they seldom Loose their Cudd, but keep Chewing and Spitting as long as they'r eyes are open,—he advanc't to the midle of the Room, makes an Awkward Nodd, and spitting a Large deal of Aromatick Tincture, he gave a scrape with his shovel like shoo . . . Hugging his own pretty Body with his hands under his arms, Stood staring rown'd him, like a Catt let out of a Baskett. At last, . . . he opened his mouth and said: have You any Ribinen for Hatbands to sell I pray? The Questions and Answers about pay being past, the Ribin is bro't and opened. Bumpkin Simpers, cryes its confounded Gay I vow; and beckning to the door, in comes Jone Tawdry, dropping about 50 curtsees, and stands by him: hee shows her the Ribin.

life of the continent, doubtless give its humorists the richness of its vein." George Edward Woodberry makes the same point in *America in Literature* (New York, 1903), pp. 157–158, as he considers Western humor, and F. L. Pattee, in *American Literature Since 1870* (New York, 1915), p. 24, points out: "The incongruities of the new world— the picturesque gathering of peoples like the Puritans, the Indians, the cavaliers, the Dutch, the negroes and the later immigrants; the makeshifts of the frontier, the vastness and the richness of the land, the levelling effects of democracy, the freedom of life, and the independence of spirit—all have tended to produce a laughing people."

[1] Particularly were they stern about differences of religious belief. A famous example is Bradford's consideration of his neighbors led by Thomas Morton, in *History of Plymouth Plantation* (Boston, 1856), pp. 236–243.

[2] Perhaps more than a minor exception is Thomas Morton, who in his *New English Canaan* (1637) naughtily and frivolously derided the speech, the costumes, the religious attitudes of the Plymouth colonists. Compare Chapter XIV of his book with the passage by Bradford cited above.

[3] First published by Theodore Dwight, in 1825, and more recently made available in reprints, ed. W. R. Deane (1858) and G. P. Winship (1920).

Law you, sais shee, *its right Gent,* do You, take it, tis *dreadfull pretty.*

The vividly pictured Jonathan and Joan, the backgrounds of their lives, their peculiarities of gesture, of manner, and particularly of speech, foreshadowed what was to be the stuff of America's favorite comedy a century after they were created. Similarly, William Byrd, in his *History of the Dividing Line betwixt Virginia and North Carolina* (1728),[1] hinted at the sort of humor later to be popular when he pictured the poor whites of Lubberland:

The Men, for their Parts, just like the Indians, impose all the Work upon the poor Women. They make their Wives rise out of their Beds early in the Morning, at the same time they lye and Snore, till the Sun has run one third of his course, and disperst all the unwholesome Damps. Then, after Stretching and Yawning for half an Hour, they light their Pipes, and, under the protection of a cloud of Smoak, venture out into the open Air; tho', if it happens to be never so little cold, they quickly return Shivering into the Chimney corner. When the Weather is mild, they stand leaning with both their arms upon the corn-field fence, and gravely consider whether they had best go and take a small Heat at the Hough [hoe]: but generally find reasons to put it off till another time.

Such passages look forward to the myriad picturings in detail of the Jonathans and Lubbers of their country which were to be a leading source of humor in the coming century. The varied men and women whose characters, whose very accents, were molded by the country and the times, and the social and political backgrounds of those men and women, were, as S. S. Cox noted in 1875, when he tried to summarize American humor, endlessly amusing:

. . . we have in America specific objects of humor—the scheming Yankee, the big, bragging brave Kentuckian, and the first family Virginian. We have lawyers on the circuit . . .; loafers on a

---

[1] Printed first in German in 1737 and in English in 1841. The passage quoted below is from the definitive edition, ed. J. S. Bassett (1901). For comment on the passage dealing with Lubberland, see A. S. McIlwaine, *The Poor White in American Literature* (Unpublished University of Chicago Doctoral Dissertation, 1937).

spree . . .; politicians in caucus; legislators in session; travelers on cars and steamers; indeed the history of every American's life is humorous. . . .[1]

But passages like Byrd's and Madam Knight's were unusual because, of the vast majority of the colonists, at least of the serious men and women who wrote, one might say what a French scholar of English humor said of the Anglo-Saxons:

Their mental equipment was such as rather to promise future fitness [for humorous writing], than to secure actual ability. Like most early races, they would be handicapped for humorous thinking by the violence of their passions, and by their general incapacity to be detached from the urgency of their feelings and ideas.[2]

Detachment was needed before many could follow the lead of Byrd and Madam Knight. The detachment was likely at first, as in the writings of these two authors, to be colored with contempt. Later, it was to be more tolerant. But detachment and a certain amount of frivolity were requisites for the development of native American humor.

These were not the only requisites, however. Before this humor could become at all pervasive, two other things were needful— (1) a general perception of the elements in the American scene which Higginson and Smith saw but did not consciously exploit, and of the elements of American character which the Southern gentleman and the New England lady observed and wrought into brief passages of comedy;[3] and (2) the development of a technique which allowed effective and extensive comic treatments of these materials. How needful these powers of perception and this technique were is revealed by writers of the latter part of the eighteenth century and the early part of the nineteenth century— writers sufficiently detached and appropriately frivolous who were

[1] "American Humor," *Harper's Magazine*, L, 700 (April, 1875). A more detailed summary is that of V. L. O. Chittick, in *Thomas Chandler Haliburton* (New York, 1924), pp. 533–534.

[2] Louis Cazamian, *The Development of English Humour: Part I. From the Early Times to the Renaissance* (New York, 1930), pp. 28–29.

[3] It should be pointed out, perhaps, that the passages quoted are not representative of either volume as a whole. Such sketches were almost as unusual in the writings of both authors as they were in eighteenth-century American writings in general.

eager to produce comic writings but who did not articulate American humor.

These authors failed largely because, light-hearted and eager to amuse as they were, they looked to eighteenth-century English models to learn how to write.[1] And their models did not reveal to them the necessary methods of finding American comedy or of reporting it.

Suppose, for example, American writers turned to the simplest models for the simplest type of humor—the English jest books. In these they would find anecdotes beginning, "When Sidney Smith's physician . . ." or "Ben Jonson, owing a man some money . . ." or "A shrewish wife . . ." From these they would, as a rule, get enough inspiration to copy the ancient English wheezes.[2] And even jest books which made an occasional attempt to develop American humor consistently retold mossy anecdotes which had nothing to do with the native scene or native life.[3]

Equally unproductive of a stimulus to national humor, it appears, were the neo-classical models of comic or fictional treatment which Americans followed more consistently than any others.[4] A glance at the newspapers published in every part of the country between 1800 and 1830 will show that, as in an earlier period,[5] the Addisonian essay was predominant. In nearly all these papers, columns or quadrangles at the ends of columns which were not filled by records of congressional debates, stories of national happenings, and foreign news were filled with essays by English or American authors who were steeped in the *Spectator*

---

[1] They failed, that is, to be "American" humorists. There is, of course, no need either to bewail or to commend this failure.

[2] See, for example, *The American Jest-Book. Containing A curious Variety of Jests, Anecdotes, Bon Mots, Stories &c.* (Boston, 1796), in which few jests, despite the title, are American in any sense.

[3] *The Chaplet of Comus; or Feast of Sentiment, and Festival of Wit* (Boston, 1811) boasts that "the reader will find in this collection more specimens of *American humor* than in any other publication," but, only six of the first twenty-five anecdotes are even vaguely connected with America. See also Constance Rourke, *American Humor, a Study of the National Character* (New York, 1931), p. 306: "In most of the jokebooks before 1840 only the faintest traces of native humor can be discovered."

[4] This dependence has been frequently noted by critics. See particularly V. F. Calverton's *The Liberation of American Literature* (New York, 1932).

[5] Elizabeth Cook, *Literary Influences on Colonial Newspapers (1704-1750)* (New York, 1912). See also E. C. Coleman's *The Influence of the Addisonian Essay before 1810* (Urbana, 1936).

tradition.[1] Two compilations of newspaper humor, one English, one American, reveal the predominance of this type of humor on both sides of the Atlantic in the early years of the century.[2] And since only the data concerning publication on the title page, a few scattered references to localities, and a paltry number of jests which are vaguely national,[3] distinguish the American book from the contemporary volume published in London, it is evident that the copying of these models did not stimulate humor with much of an American flavor. Essays on the ancient subjects, "Duelling," "City Manners" and "Fashion"[4] in the American volume are just as localized as the character sketches which introduce us to shadowy figures named "Scepticus," "Frothy," "Pedanticus" or the like,[5] or limn a vague "Uncle Jonathan" and "Cousin Peter."[6]

Not only these portions of the newspapers but also the periodicals devoted largely to humor were American—though scarcely Americanized—versions of the *Spectator* and the *Bee*. Composed "in every city of importance" by "a band of young lawyers without cases, or young beaux with a taste for letters and some claim to wit,"[7] these might have been written by "Oliver Oldschool, Esq." of London as easily as by "Oliver Oldschool, Esq." of Philadelphia.[8] Hudson, N. Y., for example, had *The Wasp* (1801–

---

[1] Smaller gaps were usually filled with English anecdotes or passages of poetry. Newspapers examined for this period represented New York, Washington, D. C., New England, the Middle States, and the Southwest.

[2] *The Spirit of the Public Journales; or Beauties of the American Newspaper for 1805* [compiled by George Bourne] (Baltimore, 1806), which draws material from ninety-six newspapers of various parts of the country, and *The Spirit of the Public Journals for 1804* (London, 1805). Although these do not attempt exactly the same thing, they are comparable on points essential here. The American volume, at least, is representative.

[3] To be considered hereafter.

[4] There are two on this perennial favorite, one in heroic couplets.

[5] See "Characteristics," pp. 42–45; 64–70; "The Idler," pp. 75–78; "Begin in Time," pp. 92–95; "Honesty is the Best Policy," pp. 109–113.

[6] "Uncle Jonathan's Reflection," pp. 20–24. The names alone are individualized.

[7] John Bach McMasters, *A History of the People of the United States* (New York, 1900), V, 296, treating the period 1790–1800, thus characterizes the editors. Remarking that "the list is too long to cite," he names seven such publications. See also Frank Luther Mott, *A History of American Magazines, 1741–1850* (New York, 1930), p. 170.

[8] Oliver Oldschool happened to be Dennie, the editor of the Philadelphia *Port Folio*, which, as Professor Boynton has noted, typically indicated in the statement of its program that its contents were all to be composed "after the manner of" various English authors.—*Literature and American Life* (Boston, 1936), pp. 215–216.

1803), edited by Robert Rusticoat; Philadelphia had its *Tickler*, edited by Toby Scratch 'em; Boston had Roderick Rover's *The Thistle* (1807) and Tim Touchstone's *Scourge* (1811), while in the South, Baltimore produced *The Observer* and the *Scourge* (Titus Tickler, Esq., ed.), and the Richmond Literary Club held forth in *The Rainbow*.

Most of these transplanted English periodicals, quite properly, have managed to fall into obscurity. The association of John Pendleton Kennedy of Baltimore with *The Red Book* (1818–1819) gave that Addisonian publication whatever lasting importance it had—and that importance did not derive from the fact that it published native humor.[1] Washington Irving's association with the New York *Salmagundi Papers* (1807–1808) gave them a certain biographical interest and Irving's genius and the skill of his associates gave them qualities which make these papers still enjoyable; but they, like Irving's earlier "open imitations of the *Spectator* and the *Tatler*,"[2] Jonathan Oldstyle Papers (1802), were too much in the English tradition to be much concerned with American scenes, life, or character. Except here and there,[3] the subjects incessantly developed were the frail sex, fashions, assemblies, theatrical productions, and highly generalized characters.

A typical characterization is that of Pindar Cockloft, who might as well have been English as American:

. . . he is now in his fifty-eighth year—is a bachelor . . . and an oddity of the first water. Half his life has been employed in writing odes, sonnets, epigrams, and elegies. . . .

In his younger days he figured as a dashing blade in the great world; and no young fellow of the town wore a longer pig-tail, or carried more buckram in his skirts. From sixteen to thirty he was continually in love. . . . The evening of his thirtieth birthday . . . he was seized with a whim-wham that he was an old fool to be in love at this time of life. . . . From that time he gave up all particular attention to the ladies. . . .[4]

---

[1] Edward M. Gwathmey, *John Pendleton Kennedy* (New York, 1931), pp. 60–61. Like Irving's earlier *Salmagundi Papers*, the satire had certain local applications.

[2] Charles Dudley Warner, *Washington Irving* (Boston, 1881), p. 30.

[3] A few passages, notably those on American elections, on militia drills, and on travel books about America, gave the book a slightly national character.

[4] *Salmagundi Papers*, No. II, February 4, 1807.

It was characters such as these—characters portrayed in a generalized style, with no particular background in place or time—which were likely to emerge in imitations of eighteenth-century English writings.[1] Actually, the imitation of neo-classical writers caused most American humorous authors to fail to see that this country as well as England had its comic types. Hugh H. Brackenridge, who wrote, in *Modern Chivalry*, what Henry Adams called "a more thoroughly American book than any written before 1833,"[2] in 1805 admitted that when he looked around in America to find a comic figure, he had had to be satisfied with an Irish clown. He could not portray an English clown or a Scotch clown well, he said; hence he had made use of an Irishman. An American did not seem a comic possibility to him because:

The American has, in fact, yet no character; neither the clown nor the gentleman; so that I could not take one from our country, which I would much rather have done as the scene lay there.[3]

Brackenridge had learned to portray an Irishman, he implies, because the English stage had shown him such a character. But no English work had suggested to him the qualities of a Yankee, a Pennsylvania Dutchman, a Virginian, or a Kentuckian.[4]

But even when a disciple of neo-classicism had better luck than Brackenridge in discovering distinctively American comedy before 1830, he employed a technique which, admirable though it was, differed from that of typical American humor.[5] Irving's

---

[1] Later Irving and Paulding, his collaborator, under a different stimulus, were to develop more particularized characters.

[2] *History of the United States* (New York, 1890), I, 124.

[3] *Modern Chivalry*, Book III, Chapter XVII.

[4] Complaint against another influence of English fictional methods in America is made by John Neal, in *The Down-Easters, &c.&c.&c.* (New York, 1833), pp. v–vi: "To judge by our novel-writers, play-makers and poets, with here and there a partial exception . . . we have cottages and sky-larks in this country; pheasants and night-ingales, first families, youth of 'gentle blood,' and a virtuous *peasantry;* moss-grown churches, curfews and ivy-mantled towers; with a plenty of hard-hearted fathers, runaway matches—to nobody knows whom, for nobody knows what; unfaithful wives, cruel step-mothers, treacherous brothers—any thing and every thing in short which goes to the ground-work of a third-rate English or Scotch novel, and nothing—absolutely nothing—whereby a stranger would be able to distinguish an *American* story from any other, or to obtain a glimpse of our peculiar institutions, or of the state of society here . . ." This complaint, of course, has to do with the effects of Gothic romances upon American fiction.

[5] Similarly, of course, most nineteenth-century fictional depictions differed from eighteenth-century depictions: the phenomenon is not discoverable in humor alone.

portrayals of Yankees, Kentuckians, and Virginians in *Knicker-bocker's History of New York* (1809),[1] presented in the delightful style he had "formed upon the prose of Goldsmith, Sterne, Swift, Steele, and Addison, with romantic coloring from Mrs. Rad-cliffe,"[2] were as amusing and as effective as any master of an eighteenth-century style could have made them. But, since he employed an eighteenth-century style, his portrayals were gener-alized, unlocalized, relatively unconcerned with individualizing details.[3]

Its effect is about the same as the effect of Byrd's passage about the Lubbers, cited above, or of Barlowe's pleasant presenta-tion of a typical American scene, a corn-husking:

> For now, the corn-house fill'd, the harvest home,
> Th' invited neighbours to the *Husking* come;
> A frolic scene, where work, and mirth, and play,
> Unite their charms, to chace the hours away.
>
> Where the huge heap lies center'd in the hall,
> The lamp suspended from the cheerful wall,
> Brown corn-fed nymphs, and strong hard-handed beaux,
> Alternate rang'd, extend in circling rows,
> Assume their seats, the solid mass attack;
> The dry husks rustle, and the corn-cobs crack;
> The song, the laugh, alternate notes resound,
> And the sweet-cider trips in silence round.
>
> The laws of Husking ev'ry wight can tell;
> And sure no laws he ever keeps so well:
> For each red ear a general kiss he gains,
> With each smut ear she smuts the luckless swains:
> But when to some sweet maid the prize is cast,
> Red as her lips, and taper as her waist,
> She walks the round, and culls one favor'd beau,
> Who leaps, the luscious tribute to bestow.

---

[1] Book III, Chapters VI, VII; Book IV, Chapter IV.

[2] Henry Seidel Canby, *Classic Americans* (New York, 1931), p. 70.

[3] This statement remains true of the passages cited in spite of the fact that Irving pointed out in "The Author's Apology," which prefaced the 1848 edition, that his main purpose was "to embody the traditions of the city [of New York] in an amusing form; to illustrate its local humors, customs, and peculiarities; to clothe home scenes and places and familiar names with . . . imaginative and whimsical associations . . ." —in spite of the fact, in other words, that he was interested, like various romantic writers, in the local past. Scott understandably asserted that he "never read anything so closely resembling the style of Dean Swift."

Various the sport, as are the wits and brains
Of well pleas'd lasses and contending swains;
Till the vast mound of corn is swept away,
And he that gets the last ear, wins the day.[1]

This admirable sketch deals with a scene of the sort a nine-teenth-century humorist would be delighted to treat; it is vivid, and it is written in high good spirits. But a typical American humorist, writing in the style of the century which produced American humor, would be pretty sure to use even more details than does this unusually detailed eighteenth-century description—details about the farmer who held the husking, about the barn where the husking was held, about the gathering of the huskers, about individual "lasses" and "swains"—their faces, figures, costumes, actions. Some of these might not receive attention, but the later humorist would be pretty sure to record much conversation, catching the dialect, the intonations, the characteristics which revealed themselves in speech.[2] The elegant style would probably suffer, but such details as these would in part atone for the loss.[3]

Even after the writers of America became sufficiently detached, sufficiently jocose, then, before the characteristic writings of American humorists could appear, two developments were necessary: the development of perception of the comic possibilities of the American scene and American character, and the development of a fictional technique which would reveal them. Somehow, American authors had to become aware of native materials for humorous literature; somehow they had to learn to exploit them.

[1] *The Hasty Pudding* (1793), Canto III, lines 6–28. The text is from the first edition, published in 1796.

[2] G. W. Harris's "The Knobs Dance," reprinted hereafter, offers an illuminating comparison.

[3] Irving's depiction of the quilting party in "The Legend of Sleepy Hollow," *The Sketch Book* (1819), written after Irving had adopted a more particularized style of writing than is apparent in his earlier works, employs something like the detail here suggested. Except for the fact that the conversation is practically unrecorded and the fact that Irving's style is more polished than is common, this is a characteristic piece of American humor.

II. BEGINNINGS (1775–1830)

As its history reveals, the process of recognition by American writers of the literary possibilities of native characters was a lengthy one and also a fairly complicated one, made possible by numerous agencies.[1] Though some evidence concerning the process is no longer discoverable, enough evidence exists to point to a process of the sort one would expect—a slow accretion of details until at last native figures came to be generally perceived.

The Revolutionary War, it appears, first made Americans in general acquainted with their national peculiarities, and the British invaders evidently deserve credit for the discovery. The term "Yankee," in widespread use to denote an American, dates back to about 1775, when it was employed by the invaders as a term of derision.[2] "Yankee Doodle," a rollicking song which mysteriously emerged from the conflict and became less of a derisive portrayal as the Yankees themselves perversely adopted it, caught several qualities of the rustic New Englander. His simplicity,[3] his penury,[4] and his cautiousness[5] are details of a sketchy portrait made believable partly because it is presented by the Yankee himself with a number of lapses into homely dialect.[6] The song doubtless inspired other portraits set to the same tune,[7] and doubtless "Yankee Doodle" aided Americans in

[1] Primitivism as an aid to the discovery of native types is treated by J. W. Harris in *The Glorification of American Types in American Literature, 1775–1825* (University of North Carolina Typed Doctoral Dissertation, 1928). The anthropological-philosophical attitude which caused Byrd to scrutinize the Lubbers with interest also was important. This section will trace only some of the more direct processes of perception.

[2] O. G. T. Sonneck, *Report on "The Star-Spangled Banner," "Hail Columbia," "America," "Yankee Doodle"* (Washington, 1909) traces the origin of the term, pp. 80–82, and reproduces the song.

[3] He wonders at the size of a cannon, at the loud noise it makes, and sees a drum for the first time.

[4] He worries about the amount of food wasted every day in camp, wishes it might be saved, and is impressed because the soldiers eat 'lasses whenever "they're a mind to."

[5] Frightened not only by the boom of a gun but also by the sight of some graves being dug, he runs home.

[6] He uses homely similes ("men and boys as thick as hasty pudding," "a swamping gun large as a log of maple," "pumpkin shell as big as mother's basin") and other rural expressions of the sort which, later, were to be important in Yankee dialect: "I'll be bound," "a nation louder," "folks," "tarnal proud," "meeting clothes," "tearing fine," "wanted pockily," etc.

[7] Sonneck, *op. cit.*, cites some variations. See also the Tory account of the un-

their discovery of additional national figures such as Brother Jonathan and Uncle Sam.[1]

But even before 1775, at least details of the sketch had been incorporated in *Poor Richard's Almanac* (1732–1758), wherein, shadowy figure though he was, Poor Richard had embodied the Yankee characteristics of thrift, industry, and godliness in aphorisms which often had had the homely style of a typical rural New Englander.[2] And the later almanacs, read by thousands, did their full share to build up the portraits of Yankees and other native types. In several ways they added touches to growing pictures.

Simplest of all was the device employed by the *Columbian Almanac* for 1801, published in Wilmington. Here, in an anecdote, a Yankee was substituted for a vaguely sketched countryman who had appeared in an earlier telling of the tale, as one may see by comparing this version with the earlier one:

1796	1801
A countryman, seeing a lady in the street in a very odd dress, as he thought, begged her to be pleased to tell him what she called it. The lady, a little surprised at the question, called him an impudent fellow. Nay, I hope no offence, madam, cried Hodge. I am a poor countryman, just going out of town, and my wife always expects I should bring her an account of the newest fashion, which occasioned my inquiring what you call this that you wear: It is a sack, said she, in a great pet. I have heard, replied the countryman (heartily nettled at her behaviour) of a pig	A countryman, seeing a lady in the street in a very odd dress, as he thought, says to her, Madam, if I may be so bold, what do you call this? taking hold of the dress. The lady, not a little surprised at the question, called him an impudent fellow. Nay, I hope no offense, cried *Jonathan*, I am a poor countryman, just going out of town, and my *woman* always expects I should bring her an account of the newest fashions, which occasioned my asking what you call this thing that you wear. It is a sack, said the woman in a pet. *I vow*, (reply'd the countryman,

successful attack on the British in Newport, July, 1778, in Rivington's *Gazette*, October 3, 1778, "Yankee Doodle's Expedition to Rhode Island," reprinted in *A Library of American Literature*, ed. E. C. Steman and E. M. Hutchinson (New York, 1890), III, 352–353.

[1] See the two articles by Albert Mathews, "Brother Jonathan," in *Publications of the Colonial Society of Massachusetts*, VII, 94–122 (1900–1902) and "Uncle Sam," in *Proceedings of the American Antiquarian Society*, n.s. XIX, 21–65 (1908–1909).

[2] This was true despite the fact that many were of English origin, since Franklin selected them.

in a poke, but never saw a sow in a sack before.[1]

*heartily nettled at her behaviour)
I have heard of a pig in a poke, but
I'll swamp it, if ever I saw a sow in a
sack before.*[2]

The English Hodge yields his place to the Yankee Jonathan, a bit of Yankee speech is inserted, and the refurbished jest is naturalized for American consumption.

An even more notable move in the direction of Yankee portrayal was made by R. B. Thomas (1766-1846), whose *Old Farmer's Almanac*, started in 1793, and still issued annually, was perhaps the most popular publication of its kind in the early years of the century.[3] Thomas, perhaps inspired by some of the characterizations in earlier English comedies, hit upon the idea of putting the advice to rural readers, previously couched in the drawing-room language of eighteenth-century prose, into the form of salty speeches presumably made by an actual farmer. For example:

Hah! How fare ye again neighbor Spriggins? Come take a chair, light your pipe, and we'll have a bit of a tid-re-i upon farming.— How does your hay spend? do your cattle look lusty? How are Squire Thimbleberry's? Now I have but one thing against the Squire.—He will pinch his own cattle, that he may sell hay in the spring. The Squire's hay, you know, ain't of the best quality.[4]

Sometimes, too, Thomas used the still more effective device for the presentation of his ideas described by Clarence S. Brigham:

Robert B. Thomas . . . inculcated moral precepts in the minds of his readers more by allegory than by proverbs. His diatribe against the telling of idle rumors takes the form of a tale of a village gossip whom he calls "Old Betty Blab." All the characters in his little moral dramas have names suited to their failings, such as "Ben Bluster," "Captain Swash," "Goody Shipshod," . . . "Tabitha Twistem" . . . "Widow Nippet," "Captain Gripe" and "Old Screwpenny". . . .[5]

---

[1] *The American Jest-Book* (Boston, 1796), Part II, p. 219.

[2] The italics are the author's. It may be worth noting that they call attention to most of the words which represent an effort to Americanize the jest.

[3] A sale of a hundred thousand copies or more was not unusual.

[4] *The Farmer's Almanac for 1802* (Boston, 1801), January. The name "Old" was later added to the title to distinguish the publication from its many imitators.

[5] *An Account of American Almanacs and their Value for Historical Study* (Worcester, 1925), p. 5.

These little tales were notable not only for their excellence but also for their frequency. Allegorical though they were, they pointed beyond the portrayal of the genus country bumpkin to the more individualized gossips, braggarts, penny-squeezers, storytellers, drunkards, and farmers of a rural community. Many of them, especially one which Professor Kittredge singles out for high praise,[1] had real literary merit. And as Miss Tandy has pointed out, in a rather conservative estimate, they were numerous: "Thomas has at least sixty incarnations of New England humors and foibles before 1830."[2] Furthermore, at least some of them were picked up and purveyed by other almanacs.[3]

Other almanacs, though less active than Thomas's in sketching native figures, nevertheless contributed helpful touches. Low's *Almanack for 1777*, for example, reported rustic Chloe's homely recipe for catching a man:

> With meal-dust and tallow I trim up my hair,
> And spangle with ribbons so neat and so rare.[4]

And in 1816, it regaled its readers with a typical bit of American humorous exaggeration concerning a huge nose.[5] At times it reprinted Thomas's humor or originated passages in much the same vein. Fifteen years after Thomas,[6] its editor suggested planting enough vegetables to supply Boston folk. "And next fall," remarked the editor, "or sooner, we may carry to market 'a pretty considerable darnation deal' of one 'notion' or another. . . . Boston folks, tho' 'tarnal 'cute sometimes, part with their loose change and 'notions' pretty freely for our produce." September

---

[1] In his delightful study of Thomas's publication, *The Old Farmer and His Almanack* (Boston, 1904), pp. 95–96. Says Professor Kittredge: "There is undeniable merit in this unpretentious narrative. It is somewhat crude, but any attempt at polish would have defeated the author's purpose. . . . Some of the details are hardly susceptible of improvement. . . . It is a masterpiece of suggestive reticence." The story is the one of Neighbor Freeport, reprinted in this volume, pp. 199–200.

[2] *Crackerbox Philosophers* (New York, 1925), p. 13.

[3] See, for example, *Johnson & Warner's Kentucky Almanac . . . for . . . 1810* by Josiah Sharp (Lexington, 1809), which reprints the remarks to neighbor Spriggins quoted above; and Nathaniel Low's *An Astronomical Diary; or Almanac*, which at times reprints bits of Thomas's advice.

[4] "A Neglected Maiden's Lamentation. A Tale." This is only a portion of the poem.

[5] "A Long Nose."

[6] The Thomas almanac treats the subject in the 1811 issue (May) and Low's almanac in the 1826 number (April).

of the same year (1826) suggests frolics: "Now the evenings are growing long, and the girls and boys, Tom, Suke, Jemima, and all, begin to have their heads full of huskings and quiltings, red ears and sweethearts, rigadooning and trampoosing all night and 'as lazy as Ludlam's dog that laid his head against the wall to bark' all day as the old saying is. . . ."[1] *The Maryland and Virginia Almanac* (Baltimore) in its issue for 1806 published a poem made up of a whole series of Yankee phrases, chiefly similes which praised a maid who "smil'd like a basket of chips," was "as tall as a hay-pole," had "eyes as bright as a button," and lips "as sweet as molasses."[2]

Notable also was the emergence in almanacs of comic characters other than the Yankee. *Howe's Almanac for 1805* (Greenwich) had a story of a stupid Dutch justice of peace, whose dialect slightly characterized him; and a similar Dutchman, who was outwitted by a sharp Yankee, appeared in *The Kentucky Farmer's Almanac* for 1810.[3] A Virginia fire eater and a Kentuckian revealed their hot tempers in *Houghton's Genuine Almanac* (Keene, N. H.) for 1813. *Howe's Almanac* (Greenwich) for 1819 displayed a comic Quaker. And the Lexington *Farmer's Almanac* for 1830 told of an encounter between a keelboatman and a French dandy in the streets of New Orleans.

In displaying these types, however, the almanacs were merely carrying on work of the jest books which, as early as 1796, had interlarded jokes about Voltaire, the kings and queens of England, and other famous folk with tales about simple Negroes (who talked a vaguely appropriate dialect), lying Indians, shrewd Yankees, pious Quakers, and blundering New York Dutchmen.[4] The jests, albeit none of them were side-splitting, at least indicated that the traits of some of these characters were well enough established to give the jokes point.

---

[1] The old saying, as J. DeLancey Ferguson pointed out in another connection, is a bit of English folklore—*American Scholar*, IV, 41 (Winter, 1935).

[2] These apparently originated in the Portland, Maine, *Eastern Herald*, May 11, 1795, with the title, "Cant Phrases." Entitled "Yankey Phrases," they were also published in *The Spirit of the Public Journals for 1805*, pp. 114–115.

[3] This publication the next year printed Irving's "Character of a Yankee from Knickerbacker's [*sic*] History of New York."

[4] *The American Jest-Book*, Part I, pp. 3, 4, 5–6, 6–7, 22, 23, 132; Part II, pp. 35, 36, 37, 133.

More lengthy, of course, and more detailed, were the portraits of some native characters presented in stage plays before 1830. At no time in the history of comedy had playwrights failed to see the possibilities of at least some type characters whose modes of life had developed quaintness of speech, action, or thought.[1] On the English stage of the eighteenth century, comic tradesmen, sailors, countrymen, Scotchmen, and Irishmen were portrayed in many dramas later presented in America.

But the trick of presenting a similar characterization—even a type characterization—of an American, despite these precedents, was evidently not easy to learn. It is not impossible that a British officer, General Burgoyne, who had a flair for dramatic authorship, was the first to hit upon the idea when, during the Revolution, he prepared for presentation by his compatriots a farce called *The Blockade of Boston*. A contemporary account shows that the British perception which introduced the bumpkin hero of "Yankee Doodle" may also have suggested the portrayal of a Yankee rustic in a play:

The figure designed to burlesque General Washington was dressed in an uncouth style, with a large wig and a long rusty sword, attended by his orderly-sergeant in his country dress, having on his shoulder an old rusty gun, seven or eight feet long.[2]

Another Revolutionary play by a Loyalist or an invader, the scurrilous *Battle of Brooklyn*, has touches of New England portraiture in the speeches of a maid. And it is probable that another invader crossed the ocean after the war and wrote a play containing a Yankee before any American dramatist made use of the character.[3]

[1] See J. Aikin and Anna Barbauld, "On the Province of Comedy," *Miscellaneous Pieces in Prose* (3rd ed. London, 1792), pp. 6–7, 9, for a recognition by eighteenth-century critics of this point.

[2] James Thacher, *Military Journal of the Revolutionary War*. Revised edition (Boston, 1827). Though the play is lost, Henry Stanhope Lee, in "Records and Reminiscences," *New York Mirror*, XVII, 218 (June 29, 1839), quotes passages cherished by "the tenacious memory of an old lady . . . present at the representation" which reveal that the Yankees were not tenderly characterized. One song evidently addressed them as "tar-barrel law-givers, Yankeefied pigs." The first performance of the play was interrupted by news of the Yankee attack on Bunker Hill. Cf. F. J. Hudleston, *Gentleman Johnny Burgoyne* (Indianapolis, 1927), p. 88.

[3] Marston Balch, "Jonathan the First," *Modern Language Notes*, XLVI, 281–288 (May, 1931).

The first important stage Yankee from the standpoint of influence in America, however, was the creation of a Boston-born author, Royall Tyler, who, in *The Contrast* (1787), gave Jonathan a sizeable part. Tyler obviously was aided by predecessors who had created Yorkshire farmers and the admirable Tony Lumpkin in the drama, and the whimsical gentlemen in the essay.[1] Nevertheless, Tyler skilfully drew together all the touches of type-characterization available for his portrait, and probably from his own experiences, added some additional touches.[2] The play was presented in a number of American cities, and when printed, in 1790, it was purchased not only in the North but also in the South.[3]

Thereafter, a whole series of plays were written, and increasing numbers were presented until, in the thirties, the Yankee play became one of the most popular types of drama.[4] In the thirties, too, several actors became famous as portrayers of native roles, and several won fame for anecdotes they told during intermissions about folk Down East.[5] Throughout the century, these stage characters had an influence upon non-dramatic humor and were influenced by it.[6]

Simultaneously, like the almanacs, the jest books, and the dramas, the newspapers moved in the direction of native portraiture. Remarkably conservative though they were,[7] they managed to print occasional passages which in a sense bridged the gap between the portraiture of the eighteenth and the portraiture of the nineteenth century.

[1] Tandy, *op. cit.*, p. 2.

[2] For a consideration of the dialect in this play and some of those which followed, see Marie Killheffer, "A Comparison of the Dialect of the 'Biglow Papers' with the Dialect of Four American Yankee Plays," *American Speech*, III, 222–236 (February, 1928).

[3] See G. O. Seilhamer, *History of the American Theatre* (New York, 1888–1891), II, 238, 239, 275–285.

[4] Perley Isaac Reed, *The Realistic Presentation of American Characters in American Plays Prior to 1870* (Ohio State University Bulletin, Vol. XXII, May, 1918) shows the growing popularity of the type.

[5] Most notable among such monologists were Dan Marble, Yankee Hill, and Sol Smith.

[6] Plays were inspired by Sam Patch, Jack Downing, Mrs. Partington, Widow Bedott, and other Yankees who first appeared in non-dramatic writings.

[7] Even as late as 1845, many had not moved very far from the Addisonian influence, and certainly up to 1835, the majority of them, in New England, New York, Pennsylvania, as well as Washington, D. C., the South and the Southwest, depended upon frequent dips into jest books or Addisonian contributions for humor.

Helpful, for example, were a series of parodies of neo-classic pastorals and Della Cruscan poems which the same Royall Tyler who wrote *The Contrast* and his circle contributed to newspapers in the seventeen nineties and the early years of the nineteenth century. In love letters written in verse Peter Periwinkle told Tabitha Towzer of his love, or some Irish lad or lassie expressed passion, in phrases which made the highly artificial poems parodied seem ridiculous because the vernacular expressions in the mock verse provided incongruous contrasts. Thus Jonathan Jolthead proposed to the tune of "Yankee Doodle," remarking:

> Miss Sal, I's going to say, as how,
> We'll spark it here tonight,
> I kind of love you, Sal, I vow,
> And Mother said I might.[1]

And Tyler's ponderously titled "Ode Composed for the Fourth of July, Calculated for the Meridian of Some Country Towns in Massachusetts and Rye in New Hampshire" turned out to be merely a lively injunction to country folk to stock up on brandy, put on their "boughten" clothes, give Sambo, the fiddler, a drink, and proceed to drink deeply and dance gaily. Miss Tandy, who gives an admirable account of these poems,[2] lists more than twenty such rural effusions.[3]

What these verses did for neo-classic poetry, prose newspaper treatments of Yankees and some other native types did to the Addisonian essay. Parodies, in a sense, these carried a little further an ancient device—the device of attributing to a fictional letter writer the authorship of an essay and, in a few sentences or phrases, at least, molding the style to fit that of the supposed letter writer.[4] Now and then, in the early years of the century, in

---

[1] The passage is from "Jonathan's Courtship," also known as "The Country Lovers," by Thomas Green Fessenden, issued as a broadside (*ca.* 1795 and 1800) and printed, in an expurgated form, in Beer's *Farmer's Almanac* (Kingston, 1804), and in Fessenden's *Original Poems* (1806).   [2] *Op. cit.*, pp. 7–10.

[3] *Ibid.*, "Bibliography of Yankee Poems," pp. 20–23. One poem which should be added to the list appeared in a collection of patriotic songs, *The Nightingale; or Rural Songster* (Deadham, 1800), pp. 117–118, "Brother Jonathan." This appears to have been written in 1798. William Biglow's "The Country School" was probably published in 1793 instead of 1795, for it is reprinted in E. H. Smith's *Collection of American Poems* (1793), credited to the *New Hampshire Spy*.

[4] "The Letters of a Pennsylvania Farmer" of Revolutionary times in a sense represented this tradition.

place of the usual polished and elegantly cadenced essays on political subjects signed "Brutus," "Vox Populi," "Cicero," and the like, there appeared less elegant letters signed "Connecticut Farmer," "A Kentucky Man," "Jonathan," "A Virginia Slaveholder," or with a similar *nom de plume*. And, in such letters, a phrase, a sentence, or a series of sentences in a letter otherwise in the genteel coffee-house manner gave the epistle a dash or two of native flavor.

These, like the courtin' poems, were not only moderately numerous but also, it appears, popular enough to be copied and recopied by distant editors. In 1802, Sailor Jack Oakum's letter, in nautical terms, which told his "messmates" that they should vote for Jefferson, was copied from the New Jersey *Centennial of Freedom* by a Frankfort (Ky.) paper.[1] Another Frankfort paper two years later printed for its readers an advertisement, prefaced with a sonorous introduction in elegant English, in German dialect, which later or earlier appeared in a Charleston paper.[2] "Rund avay, or sdolen or sdrayed," began the advertisement, "mine large plack horse, apout fourteen, oder fifteen hands and six inches high. He has been got four plack legs . . ."

The Hartford *Courant*, for April 24, 1805, reprinted from the Charleston *Courier*, which in turn had reprinted from the Lancaster, Pennsylvania, *Journal*, a letter from Jenny Stitchem, the ignorant wife of a tailor, who couched her objections to a political situation in phrases greatly marred by bad grammar and poor spelling. "Hard working foaks," objected Jenny, "can't afford to lose so much time about pollytics when its all of no use—thats where theres no oppersition." The Hartford editor and the Charleston editor must have been amused by Jenny's character and phraseology, for the remarks she made rather definitely applied only to the political situation in Pennsylvania. Two years later, the same Hartford paper republished ten letters of rural authors about politics which had appeared first in the Albany press.[3]

---

[1] *The Palladium*, September 11, 1802.

[2] *The Spirit of the Public Journals for 1804* (London, 1805) credited it to a Charleston paper. It was also republished in *The Chaplet of Comus* (Boston, 1811), pp. 206–207.

[3] On February 24, 1808, were published two letters from a farmer, beginning "Dear Congress," which had appeared in the Albany *Gazette*, and July 13 to Septem-

These are a few typical examples of material of this sort which enjoyed more than local popularity. In addition, sketches of local life and character in the tradition of Irving were picked up by newspapers in various parts of the country. Notable among these was Oliver H. Prince's "Militia Muster," which described some Georgia bumpkins who became confused and entangled when they tried to perform military commands. First printed about 1813 in the *Monitor*, a little Georgia newspaper, this piece, said the Louisville *Public Advertiser*, when reprinting it from the Augusta *Chronicle* on June 21, 1823, was "reprinted in many of the periodical works of this country and England and has even, we understand, been translated into French." It was not until twelve years later that, after other wanderings, the sketch was printed in a famous collection of Georgia sketches (1835).[1] Clearly, localized characterizations in newspapers not only penetrated communities unacquainted with stage characterizations but also carried depictions of native types to widely separated localities.

At various intervals before 1830, the interest of newspaper editors in native portrayals of various sorts flared up, flickered, and died, only to flare up again briefly. At almost any time, had these characterizations gone a few steps farther, handled by competent authors, widespread and extensive depiction might have resulted. In 1823 and 1824, for example, Yankee type characterizations in a series of poetic monologues pictured Jonathan at the Thanksgiving table, on a steamboat, at a wedding, at a museum, a bowling alley, and at a college commencement, in newspapers scattered from New Hampshire to Maryland.[2] But

ber 14 were reprinted eight letters from Richard Saunders to the Albany *Crisis* which, says the editor, tell the truth in "a plain blunt way." These are attacks on Jefferson, written with many rustic touches.

[1] Longstreet's *Georgia Scenes*. Prince, continued the *Advertiser*, was an author "in a great measure unknown" who lived in Washington, Georgia. Probably the fact that he was not well known may be explained partly by the fact that he wrote under the pseudonym "Timothy Crabshaw." The sketch was in the tradition of Irving, but not necessarily derivative from Irving: the tolerant eighteenth-century attitude toward eccentricity, important in many a Southern writer before 1860, quite probably was reflected here. Yet the sketch had enough realism to find its way, without too much incongruity, into the pages of Thomas Hardy. See J. D. Wade, *Augustus Baldwin Longstreet* (New York, 1924).

[2] In 1823, "Jonathan's Visit to Uncle Sam's Thanksgiving" appeared in the Brooklyn, Conn., *Observer*, "Jonathan's Visit to the Steamboat" in the Providence *Journal*, and the following year, "Jonathan's Recollections" in the New York *Statesman*,

the fad died, and the portrayals ceased. Then, only a little later, a series of Yankee letters from "Joe Strickland," appearing in various newspapers, foreshadowed the coming, in the thirties, of Major Jack Downing, whose letters were to be a landmark in the development of American humor. Newspapers, always to be important as molders of this type of writing, had done their share to prepare the way for the first significant non-dramatic portrayal of a widely popular Yankee character.

The lore of national and local characterizations revealed in almanacs, jest books, plays, and bits of portraiture in the newspapers was also augmented by innumerable passages in the inundating flood of travel books which poured from presses from 1785 on. Masculine travelers of many nations and feminine travelers of England and America peered at the natives of every corner of the country, jotted down notes, and then revealed in widely purchased books what they had heard,[1] seen or guessed about the natives of America. Taking for granted, from the beginning, the correctness of the belief that Americans differed from all other people of the world, they tried to reveal how, as a people, they differed. In addition, as a student of English travel books has remarked, "there

---

"Jonathan's Visit to a Wedding" in the Baltimore *Patriot*, "Jonathan's Visit to a Bowling Alley" in the Washington, D. C., *National Journal*, and "Jonathan's Account of Commencement" in the *New Hampshire Patriot*. All of these were published by an editor who evidently had a taste for such bits in the Washington, D. C., *National Journal*, December 17, 20, 1823, and January 28, February 14, 26, March 27, 1824.

[1] Worthy, perhaps, of separate treatment as a source of native portraiture is oral lore, particularly in the form of oral tales. Numerous examples might be given to show that in many sections of the country, yarns about localized types were told, e.g.: John Neal in *Blackwood's*, XVI, 92 (July, 1824) cites the sources of certain yarns told in England by the comedian Mathews. "Mr. Jarvis, a portrait painter of New York— a man of remarkable power and drollery—" told the Yankee yarn about "that are trifle" and General Jackson; the story of the Dutch judge was secured from Judge Breckenridge, whose son, in Louisiana, "has made this very story, which he tells better than Mr. Mathews, as common in America, as an anecdote of Foote or Sheridan in this country." George Tucker, in *Valley of the Shenandoah* (New York, 1824), I, 228, tells of front-porch yarns told in the South about Yankees and Dutchmen. On the frontier in 1822, William Newnham Blane heard a story about Yankees who palmed off cat skins for currency by pinning coon tails on them. "This," he said, "like many other good stories about the Yankees, is no doubt a fiction. . . ."—*An Excursion through the United States and Canada during the Years 1822–1823* (London, 1824), pp. 175–176. Miss Tandy, *op. cit.*, pp. 11–12, cites other examples of oral tales about Yankees. Speech was flavored somewhat by such lore: on the Illinois frontier in the forties, a verb, "yankee," in general use, meant "to cheat" or "to gild." For other details concerning oral story-telling and its effects on American humor, see Section IV of this introduction.

grew up a tradition, stimulated by . . . the Americans themselves, that North, South, and West, particularly, had developed a distinct character."[1] Travelers probed for sectional differences.

Their discoveries were likely to be influential, for the travel books were read by great numbers of hypersensitive Americans—with pride or horror, with indignation or with shame. The English reviews as well as the American magazines battled ferociously about the accuracy of the distinctions they drew between Americans and the people of other nations, and between Americans of different sections of the United States.

They emerged with distinctions a-plenty.[2] Southerners were "high-spirited, fiery, and impetuous, with difficulty restraining their passions. . . . In those [Southern] States, no one deigns to work, and the gentry, or wealthy planters, occupy their time in sporting, and particularly in horse-racing and cock-fighting."[3] Other sections produced people with similarly marked—and distinctive—characteristics. By 1825, one traveler, though he admitted that the folk of Kentucky were pretty much like those of Tennessee, Ohio, Illinois, and Missouri, had no trouble distinguishing between the local characteristics of New Yorkers, New Jersey people, Pennsylvanians, Marylanders, Virginians, North Carolinians, Georgians, and Louisianians.[4]

But the types which were more interesting than any others to travelers, and were to be more interesting to humorists later, were the Down East Yankees and the Kentuckians or frontiersmen. The Yankee portrayed in travel books was a lanky and awkward bumpkin who talked through his nose. Tight-lipped and shrewd, he most often appeared as a peddler who played sharp tricks and

[1] Jane Louise Mesick, *The English Traveler in America, 1785–1835* (New York, 1922), p. 300.

[2] For some of these distinctions, see John Melish, *Travels in the United States of America* (Philadelphia, 1812), I, 44, II, 205–206; Francis Hall, *Travels in Canada and the United States in 1816 and 1817* (Boston, 1818), pp. 266–268; John Woods, *Two Years Residence in the Settlement on the English Prairie in the Illinois Country* (London, 1822), p. 317; Isaac Candler, *A Summary View of America* (London, 1824), p. 451; Blane, *op. cit.*, pp. 501–502. The article by John Neal cited above (footnote 1, p. 27), pp. 91–97, not only divides Americans into three groups but elaborately proves that the groups talk differently. [3] Blane, *op. cit.*, p. 501.

[4] *European Magazine*, III, 521–523 (1825). Typical characterizations are those of "the self-satisfied, supercilious Marylander" and "the hot and peremptory Virginian, full of generous blood, which he is ready to pour out, like his generous wine, *for* anybody or *with* anybody."

revealed his tarnal cuteness in every section of the country. Professor Chittick has listed fifteen books in which he was delineated in some detail before 1830,[1] and the list might easily be considerably extended.[2] Down through the nineteenth century, his portrait, repeated again and again, was to be continuously amusing to American readers.[3]

As he first emerged into national consciousness, largely through the medium of travel books, the frontiersman, the second of these very popular sectional figures, was chiefly renowned as a heavy drinker and a lusty fighter. The Kentuckians, as generic frontiersmen were called, were characterized by F. A. Michaux in 1804 in a fashion which was to be popular during many decades:

> The inhabitants of Kentucky . . . are, almost all, originally from Virginia, and particularly from the more remote parts of that state . . . [They therefore usually] retain the manners of the Virginians. With them, a passion for gaming and spiritous liquors is carried to excess, and sanguinary conflicts are frequently the consequence. They meet often at the taverns, particularly during the sessions of the courts of justice, when they pass whole days there. Horses, and law-suits, are the usual subjects of their conversation.[4]

In 1807, Charles William Janson added a few interesting details. Southerners, he reported, were likely to be "slingers" or "eleveners," the former being drinkers who needed a sling of whisky on awakening, the latter drinkers who started their daily stint of imbibing before eleven in the morning. The barbarians, he added, were much given to "gouging, chewing off ears and butting."[5]

During the next year, Christian Schultz, Jr., recorded a specimen of the tall talk of the roistering Westerners. He says:

[1] *Op. cit.*, p. 333. In addition, several books after 1830 which picture this character are listed.

[2] Other books which pictured the peddler, for example, are Karl Bernhard, *Travels through North America, during the Years 1825 and 1826* (Philadelphia, 1828); Adam Hodgson, *Letters from North America* . . . (London, 1824); William Faux, *Memorable Days in America* . . . (London, 1823), and Peter Neilson, *Recollections of a Six Years' Residence in the United States* . . . (Glasgow, 1830).

[3] For a brilliant consideration of the portrayal of this character, see Constance Rourke, *op. cit.*, Chapters I and II.

[4] *Travels to the Westward of the Alleghany Mountains* (London, 1805), pp. 239–240. This book was published in Paris in 1804.

[5] *The Stranger in America* (London, 1807), p. 300.

In passing two boats next to mine [anchored at Natchez], I heard some very warm words; which my men informed me proceeded from some drunken sailors, who had a dispute respecting a *Choctaw* lady. Although I might fill half a dozen pages with the curious slang made use of . . ., yet I prefer selecting a few of the most billiant expressions. . . . One said, "I am a man; I am a horse; I am a team. I can whip any man *in all Kentucky*, by G—d." The other replied, "I am an alligator, half man, half horse; can whip any man *on the Mississippi*, by G—d." The first one again, "I am a man; have the best horse, best dog, best gun, and the handsomest wife in all Kentucky, by G—d." The other, "I am a Mississippi snapping turtle: have bear's claws, alligator's teeth, and the devil's tail; can whip *any man*, by G—d." This was too much for the first, and at it they went like two bulls . . .[1]

Now the portrait was practically complete. Roaring his frontier tall talk,[2] which echoed in American idiom the cadences of boastful medieval heroes,[3] the mighty-muscled Kentuckian could appear in newspapers[4] and (incongruously) in sermons,[5] in a popular song,[6] a popular play.[7] A native type who was to be extensively

---

[1] Letter dated April 13, 1808, *Travels on an Inland Voyage* (New York, 1810), II, 145–146.

[2] See W. F. Thompson, "Frontier Tall Talk," *American Speech*, IX, 187–199 (October, 1934); V. L. O. Chittick, "Ring-Tailed Roarers," *The Frontier*, XIII, 257–258 (May, 1933); Richard H. Thornton, *An American Glossary* (London, 1912), II, 969–970.

[3] Dorothy Dondore, "Big Talk! The Flyting, the Gabe, and the Frontier Boast," *American Speech*, VI, 45–55 (October, 1930).

[4] As early as 1813, some Eastern newspapers could designate Mississippi rivermen as "half-horse half-alligator creatures" without bothering to expound the meaning of the term.

[5] It is a great temptation to quote at length the admirable colloquy between Dred Drake and his roistering companions, quoted in a sermon printed by Parson Weems in 1813—"The Drunkard's Looking Glass," now available in *Three Discourses* (New York, 1929), pp. 178–179. The pamphlet containing the sermon may have been published, as Emily E. F. Skeel remarks in introducing it, earlier than 1813, as the edition of that year is allegedly "Second" and "Greatly Improved." Eight or nine editions were printed between 1813 and 1843. The pamphlet was doubtless widely distributed, as it deserved to be.

[6] "The Hunters of Kentucky," roared by an actor costumed as a keelboatman in theaters throughout the country, became to the frontiersmen what "Yankee Doodle" had been to the New Englander.

[7] James K. Paulding's *The Lion of the West* (1830) in which Hackett, as Nimrod Wildfire, won wide fame. Paulding's purpose, as he himself observed, was "to embody certain peculiar characteristics of the west in one single person, who should thus represent, not an individual, but the species."—*New York Mirror*, VIII, 191 (December 18, 1830). For details concerning this drama, unfortunately unpublished and now no longer available for publication, see N. F. Adkins, "James K. Paulding's *Lion of the West*," *American Literature*, III, 249–258 (November, 1931).

exploited in American humor during the nineteenth century had been established.[1]

Thus the data in travel books, as in almanacs, plays, and newspaper depictions, established a valuable group of type portrayals. Even as the sketches neared completion, however, voices were uplifted concerning their falsity. Mathew Carey, after wide travel in the Southwest, protested against portrayals of Kentuckians based on insufficient evidence. Too many had judged the frontiersmen, he suggested, by considering merely river boatmen, "some of whom appear to pride themselves on the roughness and rudeness of their manners—'half horse, half alligator,' &c. But it would be quite as just to characterize the inhabitants of New York from the conduct of the boatmen or porters who ply at the ferries on the Hudson . . . as the people of Kentucky from the boatmen of the Ohio and Mississippi."[2] Charles Fenno Hoffman asserted that a ring-tail roarer Kentuckian was "anything but a fair specimen of the western population; for though you meet with some such extravagant character in almost every hamlet, you might as well form your idea of the New England yeomanry from the Yankee pedlars . . . as conceive that the mass of the population over the mountains are of this 'half-horse and half-alligator' species."[3]

Others before Hoffman had seen that the Yankee peddler was not a typical New Englander. As early as 1809, Carey had written under the heading, "A Miserable Prejudice—Yankee Tricks," an attack on the tendency to judge Down Easters on the basis of the practices of itinerant peddlers.[4] In 1819,[5] and again in 1823,[6] travelers had rebuked the Westerners who "judging from the character of a few, uncharitably condemn the whole."[7] In 1827, a Virginia

---

[1] Blane, op. cit., p. 136, reproduced the *customary* boatman's boast; and in 1829, so sure was an author of the reader's familiarity with the formula that he did not bother to write it all out, saying merely: ". . . Mike made proclamation—'I am a salt river roarer; and I love the wimming, and how I'm chockfull of fight,' &c . . ." —*Western Monthly Review*, July, 1829. For an excellent treatment of this characterization of the Westerner in American humor, see Constance Rourke, op. cit.

[2] *Miscellaneous Essays* . . . (Philadelphia, 1830), pp. 396-399.

[3] *A Winter in the Far West* (London, 1835), II, 221.

[4] *Port Folio*, December, 1809, p. 533, quoted in op. cit., pp. 377-378.

[5] Estwick Evans, *A Pedestrious Tour* . . . (1819), reprinted in Thwaites, *Early Western Travels*, VIII, 253.

[6] G. W. Ogden, *Letters from the West* (New Bedford, 1823), p. 11.

[7] The quotation is from Evans, *loc. cit.* See also Timothy Flint's *Recollections of the Last Ten Years*, pp. 32-33, and Cooper's *Notions of the Americans*, I, 190-191, II, 123-126.

newspaper viewed the prejudice "with pain."[1] By 1828, Carey was rejoicing (somewhat prematurely, perhaps) that the prejudice against New Englanders was no longer held "by men of liberal minds—although it still lingers among a few of the low and the vulgar,"[2] and by 1844, a reviewer was referring to the Yankee peddler as "that very apochryphal personage."[3]

Despite such complaints, the generic portraits were valuable and influential aids to fiction writers. True, they were not of much assistance to most of the authors who attempted humorous portrayals in fiction before 1820. When Royall Tyler turned from the writing of the drama which had so skilfully portrayed Jonathan to the writing of a novel, the best he could do was garnish the story with a few effective atmospheric touches.[4] Upon him, as upon others, the tradition of eighteenth-century fiction rested too heavily.[5] Even John Neal, who lifted his voice to complain, in 1824, that "with two exceptions, or at most three, there is no American writer who would not pass just as readily for an English writer"[6]—even he was bogged down by the Gothic tradition in two of his novels;[7] and in 1825, even he was unable to see that his countrymen offered opportunities to the humorist.[8] Irving, who

---

[1] The Fredericksburg Arena, quoted in the Massachusetts Spy, October 3, 1827.

[2] Op. cit., pp. 397–398.

[3] North American Review, LVIII, 211 (January, 1844). The reviewer, however, with a sigh, confesses that it seems to be impossible to correct "the mythical and highly imaginative notions of the men of the North" revealed in jests by the "Southern brethren."   [4] The Algerine Captive (1797).

[5] Following the pattern of Arbuthnot's History of John Bull, for example, Jeremy Belknap in The Foresters (Boston, 1792) managed to distinguish between the inhabitants of states very vaguely only by giving their allegorical embodiments distinctive names; following the pattern of the Quixotic novel, the anonymous author of The Yankee Traveler (Concord, 1817) did even less with native portraiture than Brackenridge had; following the example of Godwin and the Gothic romancers, Charles Brockden Brown justified the statement made in his own book, Clara Howard that "our books are almost wholly the productions of Europe." These books are typical of those which show any influence of American origin.

[6] Blackwood's Magazine, XVI, 305 (September, 1824). The exceptions were Paulding, Neal, and Brown. In the preface to The Down-Easters, &c.&c.&c. (New York, 1834), I, vi, he made about the same complaints, but cited as exceptions, not Brown, not Irving, whose books, he said, were "not American," but Cooper, Flint, Miss Ledgwick [sic], and Paulding.

[7] Brother Jonathan (1825) and The Down-Easters (1833).

[8] Americans, he asserted, "have nothing outrageous in their nature; little or no raw material, of their own, for generous, broad, rich, caricature; no humour, no delicious drollery; little or nothing, in themselves, or their habits, for good-natured misrepresentation."—Blackwood's Magazine, XVII, 48 (January, 1825).

amusingly portrayed Yankees and Kentuckians in *Knickerbocker's History* (1809) and Paulding who turned the same trick in *The Diverting History of John Bull and Brother Jonathan* (1812) were not exceptions notable enough to disprove the rule.

Both, significantly, were to do the same thing differently—and better—thereafter. In Irving's very next book—*The Sketch Book* (1819), the laughable sketch, "The Legend of Sleepy Hollow," represented a marked change: here was a vivid scene, here were individualized characters. What had happened during the decade between the two books? Professor Pattee, answering this question, says: "He had come into contact with Scott. The transition from Irving the classicist to Irving the romanticist had been caused by that great Jupiter of the North which had deflected from their orbit all the fiction writers of a generation."[1]

And other writers, in various ways, were influenced by Scott or the changing forces in fiction for which he stood. Scott, like several of his contemporaries, was active in the creation of a fictional technique which stressed the relationship between characters and their background, which attempted to individualize, to localize, to particularize more than had previous fictional techniques. A reviewer of *Waverley* in 1814 pointed out the change. The earlier writers, he said, painted very vague romantic characters:

> The novelists next endeavoured to exhibit a general view of society. The characters of Gil Blas and Tom Jones are not individuals so much as specimens of the human race; and these delightful works have been, are, and ever will be popular, because they present lively and accurate delineations of the workings of the human soul . . . .
>
> From this species the transition to a third was natural. The first class was theory—it was improved into a *generic* description, and that again led the way to a more particular classification—a copying not of man in general, but of men of a peculiar nation, profession, or temper, or to go a step further—of *individuals*.
>
> Thus Alcander and Cyrus could never have existed in human society . . . . Tom Jones might have been a Frenchman, and Gil Blas an Englishman . . . while . . . the characters of the most popular novels of later times were Irish, Scotch, or French, and not

---

[1] *The Development of the American Short Story* (New York, 1923), pp. 7–8.

in the abstract, *men*.—The general operations of nature are cir-
cumscribed to her effects on an individual character . . . .[1]

In essentials, the statement was correct. The most popular
authors of England were no longer saying, with Fielding, "I describe not men, but manners; not an individual, but a species . . ."
Instead they were proud of their detailed presentation of real
individuals against local backgrounds. As a recent student of the
change says,

Though general nature remained the approved object of the
writer's representation, it came to be thought that this general
nature was best arrived at by localizing the characters—that is
to say, by giving them the special sort of imaginative solidity
which derives from the sense of their being actual persons in an
actual environment. And even though the persons and environ-
ments were typical rather than singular, and the novel of the day
was more a genre picture than a study of individuals, there was
still a feeling that there was *some* particular locus for the action.
Indeed, the feeling for locality was more intense for typical places
than for rare ones; the most real scenes, for the fiction reader of the
day, were those which corresponded most readily with what he
recognized as common in actual life. In any case, the sense of
locality was what the novelist was certainly required to satisfy.[2]

Thus Scott's reputation to a great extent was based upon his
ability truly to depict Scottish character,[3] and Maria Edgeworth
won fame for her local color depictions: thirty years after its appearance, *Castle Rackrent* (1800) was hailed as "the first very successful delineation of Irish character."[4]

No contemporary fiction writer on either side of the Atlantic
was more popular in the United States than Sir Walter Scott.[5]

---

[1] *Quarterly Review*, XI, 354–355 (July, 1814).

[2] Houghton Wells Taylor, *The Idea of Locality in English Criticism of Fiction, 1750–
1830* (Typed Doctoral Dissertation, University of Chicago, 1934), pp. 121–122.

[3] Reviews which indicate this include, for example, the review of *Guy Mannering*,
Quarterly Review, XII, 501–509 (January, 1815) and the review of *Tales of My Landlord*,
Edinburgh Review, XXVIII, 196–199 (March, 1817).

[4] *Edinburgh Review*, LII, 412 (January, 1831).

[5] George Harrison Orians, *The Influence of Walter Scott upon America and American
Literature before 1860* (Urbana, 1929); Grace Warren Landrum, "Notes on the Reading
of the Old South," *American Literature*, III, 60–71 (March, 1931) and "Sir Walter
Scott and His Literary Rivals in the Old South," *American Literature*, II, 256–276
(November, 1930).

Second to him, perhaps, in popularity was Maria Edgeworth, with Bulwer third.[1] It would be surprising indeed if the changes in fictional methods reflected in their writings were not influential in the United States. American critics perceived the change in fiction, first in England, later in America. E. T. Channing, in 1819, noted that

. . . there is an extremely popular kind of fictitious writing, which makes the fable subservient to the development of national character, or of the manners, usages, prejudices and conditions of particular classes . . . sketches . . . represent classes . . . [and] distinctive characters [derived] from limited external influences.[2]

Charles Brockden Brown, he perceived, had "not even attempted to draw a peculiar American character."[3] Eight years later, another American reviewer remarked that, as a result of the new influence, "the old school of novels underwent a complete French Revolution in England, and, by a natural consequence, in this country."[4]

During less than a decade, while critics fought over the question of "the suitability of American life and history as material for . . . fiction,"[5] the change had been clear, if not in all American novels, at least in a number of them. Not only Irving but others as well between 1819 and 1827 began to use the new fictional method. Cooper's *The Spy* in 1821 displayed such native figures as the peddler and the Negro, displayed, too, as W. H. Gardner immediately noted, a "particular talent . . . in . . . hitting off the humors of low life." In this book, Gardner continued, "we are brought to hear a spirited dialogue, replete with comic humor,

[1] See Miss Landrum's articles, cited above, and Mesick, *op. cit.*, pp. 218–219. See also contemporary comments in magazines and newspapers.

[2] *North American Review*, IX, 65 (June, 1819).

[3] *Ibid.*, p. 68. Channing had some doubts about the possibility of individualization in American fiction, because America had no "well-defined classes," but he pointed to sketches "of domestic manners, national customs and individual singularities" which already had been successful.

[4] *American Quarterly Review*, II, 34 (September, 1827).

[5] William Charvat, *The Origins of American Critical Thought, 1810–1835* (Philadelphia, 1936), p. 140. As Dr. Charvat indicates, the struggle had complicated ramifications. For additional details concerning the contest, only one phase of which is touched here, see G. H. Orians, "The Romance Ferment after *Waverley*," *American Literature*, III, 408–431 (January, 1932). For details concerning the continuation of the conflict, see Benjamin T. Spencer, "A National Literature, 1837–1855," *American Literature*, VIII, 125–159 (May, 1936).

rich with the direct language of untutored men . . . . These are . . .
also . . . the characteristics of the great Scottish antiquary. . . ."[1]
In *The Pioneers* (1823), *Lionel Lincoln* (1825), and *The Last of the
Mohicans* (1826), stock Yankees were well depicted. Miss Sedgwick
wrote her *New England Tale* (1822), dedicated to Maria Edgeworth, to whose writings one critic noted she paid the tribute of
imitation,[2] although another thought he saw Scott's influence in
the book.[3] She followed this with *Redwood* (1824) in which, Bryant
remarked, "the national peculiarities are hit off with great dex-
terity. . . . the actors . . . are made to look and act like people in
the world about us . . . varied with exceeding art and judgment."[4]
And during the year Bryant's criticism appeared (1825), Jared
Sparks reviewed ten recent American novels imitative of Scott and
Miss Edgeworth.[5] He suggested the pattern of such works, particularly calling attention to the fact that "the actors . . . have
not only a human but also a national, and often a provincial
character . . . exemplified in modes of speech . . . . In these various ways," he concluded, "a new and fertile field has been opened
to the modern novelist."[6] The early chapters of Neal's *Brother
Jonathan, or the New Englanders* (1825), before its characters were
swallowed by melodrama, might have been cited as another example of the change. Two years later Mrs. Hale's *Northwood* was
commended for following the admirable example of the British
local colorists.[7]

In 1832, when a critic protested against American writers following authors "such as Scott and Bulwer" who had distinguished
"the lower classes of society" thus transplanting "flowers of speech
that naturally bloom in the dunghill and sewer to the . . . boudoir
and the drawing room,"[8] the protest was in vain. Already, in the
West an annual had been praised for publishing "characteristic

---

[1] *North American Review*, XV, 276 (July, 1822).

[2] *The Museum*, I, 468 (November 18, 1822).

[3] *The Literary Gazette*, VI, 721 (November 16, 1822).

[4] *North American Review*, XX, 256 (April, 1825).

[5] The novels were *The Refugee, Hobomok, Peep at the Pilgrims in 1636, The Witch of
New England, Saratoga, Adsonville, A Winter in Washington, Tales of an American Landlord,
O'Halloran,* and *Goslington Shadow.* Most of them were not only localized but also,
like Scott's novels, historical.

[6] "Recent American Novels," *North American Review*, XXI, 82–83 (July, 1825).

[7] *American Quarterly Review*, II, 46 (September, 1827).

[8] "Yankeeisms," *New England Magazine*, III, 378–379 (November, 1832).

and genuinely Western" fiction, embodying faithfully "the unique and amusing backwoods dialect";[1] and a magazine starting its career had promised its readers "original tales, characteristic of the western people."[2] In the South, where critics "emphasized excellences" in Scott's "portrayal of humble characters"[3] Kennedy, Simms, and Tucker before long were to follow the fashion, and a critic would soon be urging writers to bear in mind that "the success of Scott and Edgeworth as delineators of real life . . . is in proportion to the fidelity with which they copy the *diction* of whatever rank they introduce—of the vulgar, no less than the exalted," and to follow their example.[4]

The preparations for American humor were now complete. Such agencies as almanacs, jest books, dramas, newspapers, and travel books had made Americans aware of native materials. Writers of fiction, encouraged to view low characters with tolerant amusement, following the example of British authors, had discovered a method of portrayal. The humorists would exploit these materials and details which they discovered by employing a similar technique, adapted to their purposes. In some portrayals, they would surpass the fiction writers, too many of whom were satisfied with drawing characters dimly[5] or with repeating stock characterizations of Yankees and Westerners.[6] Indigenous to the section they portrayed, drawing from life, making the first extensive use of the spicy American vernacular,[7] the best humorists were to uncover new riches of character Down East and in the Southwest.

---

[1] *Western Monthly Review*, II, 366 (November, 1828).

[2] *Illinois Monthly Magazine*, I, 3 (October, 1830).

[3] Grace Warren Landrum, *op. cit.*, *American Literature*, II, 273 (November, 1930).

[4] *Southern Literary Messenger*, III, 692 (November, 1837).

[5] Miss Sedgwick and Mrs. Hale among the better novelists, and scores of lesser fiction writers.

[6] Cooper, though he splendidly characterized Natty Bumpo, drew type Yankees; and Simms, capable of limning the delightful Porgy, depicted such stage Down Easterners as Jared Bunce in *Guy Rivers* and Watson in *Border Beagles* as well as a number of stock Kentuckians. Bird's Yankee in *Sheppard Lee* (Philadelphia, 1836), II, 132, and his Ralph Stackpole in *Nick of the Woods* (1837) were type characters. Few fictional depictions of Westerners or Yankees were much better.

[7] H. L. Mencken, *The American Language*. Fourth edition (New York, 1936), pp. 71–73.

III. Down East Humor (1830–1867)

Humor with an emphatic native quality, which amusingly displayed localized characters and characteristics as well as various American social and political foibles, and which realized at least some of the possibilities of a typical technique, became widely popular during the years between 1825 and 1833.[1] During that period, both the East and the West were represented by humor of more than sectional appeal.

Just why these particular years should be the time of this development, it is difficult to say. Newspapers edited by a new class

[1] A few of the "mileposts" which might be cited during those years are:

1825—The first stage Yankee of national, even international, and fairly lasting appeal was created—Jonathan Ploughboy in Woodworth's *The Forest Rose*, highly successful in both America and England.—O. S. Coad, *op. cit.*

1826—Joe Strickland's (Arnold's) Yankee letters, appearing in various newspapers, established the tradition of a rustic character writing a series of humorous letters in the vernacular.

1828—Neville's "The Last of the Boatmen" introduced Mike Fink into humorous literature. "The Last of the Boatmen" was widely reprinted and thus established what Professor Pattee called "the Mike Fink school of short fiction."—*The Development of the American Short Story* (New York, 1923), p. 60. As early as 1830, a phrase in "Amos Kendall," published in the New York *Spectator* and republished in the Maysville (Ky.) *Eagle*, January 12, indicated Mike's fame had reached the East. In 1832, Miss Mitford reprinted the story in an English collection of American tales. By 1828, too, Davy Crockett, now in Congress, had become a widely known figure in newspaper comedy. The West as well as the East had produced popular humor.

1830—Nimrod Wildfire, Western tall talker, was portrayed in a popular stage play.— A. H. Quinn, *A History of American Drama to the Civil War* (New York, 1923), p. 293. The first of a long line of almanacs—*The American Comic Almanac for 1831*—employing humor representing many sections, was published.—C. L. Nichols, "Notes on Almanacs of Massachusetts," *Proceedings of the American Antiquarian Society*, XXII, 38 (1912). An immediate hit, it was followed by a host of imitators.—C. S. Brigham, *op. cit.*, pp. 11–12. Seba Smith's Jack Downing letters created a typical figure of American humor who appealed to a national audience and established lasting traditions in American humorous writing.

1832—Augustus Baldwin Longstreet began to publish, in a newspaper, the sketches which were later to appear in a very important book in Southwestern humor, *Georgia Scenes*.

1833—Two works, *Life and Writings of Major Jack Downing* and *Sketches and Eccentricities of Colonel Davy Crockett*, one representing the Eastern, the other the Western tributaries of American humor, in book form, were widely circulated, widely influential. In three books—*The Life and Adventures of Doctor Diodemus Duckworth, Travels in America*, and a *Yankee Among the Nullifiers*, Asa Greene capitalized on the popularity of native humor, and John Neal's *The Downeasters* not only made a strong plea for localized portraiture but also comically portrayed a Yankee, a Kentucky roarer, and a Virginia aristocrat. The publication of the new humor in book form had begun auspiciously.

of writers for a new class of readers were doubtless important. So, too, was the dramatic triumph of Andrew Jackson, Old Hickory, the first real representative of the common people, which made agrarians and frontiersmen, who, for a long time, were to contribute the characters of popular comedy, bulk large in the national consciousness. The fact that sectional feeling, simmering since the Constitutional Convention, now boiled to fever heat and added to Americans' awareness of the differences between Yankees and Westerners and Southern planters and city men was also important. It seems probable, too, that the literary portrayal of Americans which, paradoxically enough, had been stimulated by the British about 1775, now was newly encouraged by local colorists across the Atlantic. Whatever the reasons, Americans were now able to look at their countrymen and their native scene with enough disinterested amusement to find comedy—were now able to record that comedy with some success. About 1830, American humor, losing its nebulous quality, becomes a graspable phenomenon.

The year 1830, among the various ones which might be chosen as a starting point, merits special attention because during that year both Down East humor and frontier humor were well represented, in American almanacs and newspapers then (and thereafter) hospitable to native comedy, and because that year marked the birth date of Jack Downing, the leader of a century-long parade of similar popular comic native figures.[1]

Seba Smith (1792–1868), Jack's creator, in 1830 was the editor of a new-born newspaper which was struggling for breath—the Portland (Me.) *Daily Courier*. Not only was this the first daily published in its section; in addition, it was independent, nonpartisan, in a day of hot political warfare. As Smith later indicated, the local political situation and the plight of the newspaper led to Jack's advent:

The Maine Legislature met in. Portland . . . and the two political parties were so evenly balanced, and partisan feeling ran so high, that it was six weeks before they got fairly organized and proceeded with the business of legislation. The political papers were hot and

---

[1] From the day of Downing's appearance to 1935, when Will Rogers died, America was at no time without at least one homespun humorous philosopher.

furious, and there was no small excitement throughout the State, which even spread . . . to other portions of the country.

At this juncture . . ., the author of these papers, wishing to show the ridiculous position of the legislature in its true light, and also, by something out of the common track of newspaper writing, to give increased interest and popularity to his little daily paper, bethought himself of the plan to bring a green, unsophisticated lad from the country into town with a load of axe-handles, hoop poles, and other notions, for sale, and while waiting the movements of a dull market, let him blunder into the halls of the legislature, and after witnessing for some days their strange doings, sit down and write an account of them to his friends at home in his own plain language.[1]

The idea proved to be a good one—so good that Jack did not permanently relinquish his pen until twenty-nine years after the first letter appeared. But the idea was not so novel, of course, as Smith implied. Typically, he benefited by past developments. Nearly all the ingredients of his character portrayal had appeared earlier. This rustic visitor commenting on the town or city to which he had traveled had counterparts in a whole series of plays [2] and in newspaper sketches which had appeared as early as 1805.[3] His comments on local political squabbles had been prepared for by Joe Strickland's adventures in Albany in 1827.[4] And his travels, once Jack had left Portland, were not entirely unlike those recorded by and of Yankee peddlers.[5] Less precedent is discoverable for Jack's intimate association with such famous political leaders as Presidents Jackson and Polk. For this Miss

[1] Preface to *My Thirty Years out of the Senate* (New York, 1859), p. 5.

[2] Beginning with *The Contrast* (1787). See also *The Politician Out-Witted* (1788), *Jonathan Postfree* (1806), *Love and Friendship* (1809), and *The Forest Rose* (1825).

[3] "City Life" and "Town Dress" in *The Spirit of the Public Journals for 1805*, pp. 51–54, 93–95. Of situations in American humor, this was one of the most popular. At the end of the century, countrymen still puffed out gaslights in hotels.

[4] Wyman, *op. cit.*, pp. 33–34. These were reprinted in Maine papers, where Smith might have seen them. Thirty years later, Smith revealed his acquaintance with at least the name of the character. However, he might have read Strickland's letters after 1830; some MS. letters owned by Mr. Franklin J. Meine and signed Joe Strickland were apparently written for a New York paper as late as 1835.

[5] "The Boston *New England Galaxy* for 1827–28 prints a letter series called 'Travels of a Tin Pedlar' . . . and quotes in one number a humorous sketch from the Savannah *Mercury* called 'The Yankee in Georgia.'"—Chittick, *op. cit.*, p. 365. Fugitive bits about peregrinating Yankees were frequent.

Wyman finds suggestions in "Smollett's roving heroes," Captain Farrago's Irish squire in *Modern Chivalry*, Sancho Panza, and Gil Blas,[1] though it seems at least equally possible that some of the tales ascribed to Davy Crockett were the direct source.[2]

Add to the list of Smith's literary models the name of Sterne[3] and, at a later date, perhaps the name of Lowell,[4] and it may seem strange that readers of the Downing letters found in them enough that was new to amuse them. But Jack was a decided hit: by 1834, the publishers of his letters could allege that Jack's writings "were copied into every paper all over the land, and his name was in everybody's mouth. Next to General Jackson he was decidedly the most popular man in the United States."[5]

Seba Smith had many followers. His influence is particularly clear in many letters written beginning in 1833, for their authors stole not only Jack's character but also his name.[6] In various newspapers appeared spurious accounts in Yankee phrases of Jack's adventures in politics. The letters of one imitator, Charles Augustus Davis of New York City, published in the New York *Advertiser*, equalled and perhaps exceeded in fame those written by Smith.[7] One imitator was active as late as the days of the Civil War, his letters appearing in the New York *Weekly Caucasian*.[8]

Other Yankee letter writers, less specific about their disciple-

---

[1] *Op. cit.*, pp. 32–33.

[2] *Sketches and Eccentricities* (New York, 1833) reprints one of the newspaper narratives about a democratic visit with the President ascribed to Davy.

[3] The grandfather who talks of his military exploits in Jack's introductory autobiographical sketch (1833) has no slight resemblance to Uncle Toby.

[4] Miss Wyman, *op. cit.*, pp. 60–61, notes the resemblance between Lowell's "Leaving the Matter Open" and Downing's letter of October 25, 1849. Quite conceivably both, however, had still earlier sources among the allegories considered by George E. Hastings in "John Bull and his American Descendents," *American Literature*, I, 40–68 (March, 1929) and by Albert Mathews in "Uncle Sam," *Proceedings of the American Antiquarian Society*, n.s. XIX, 22 (April, 1908).

[5] Preface to the second edition (Boston, 1834).

[6] For comments on the widespread use of Downing's signature, see "Uncle Sam's Peculiarities," *Bentley's Miscellany*, IV, 43 (1838).

[7] Miss Wyman, *op. cit.*, pp. 67–93, has accomplished the task of distinguishing between the real and the spurious letters. For criticism of Davis's letters, see also Tandy, *op. cit.*, pp. 32–38. Davis's letters were collected in a book, *Letters of J. Downing, Major, Downingville Militia, Second Brigade, to his Old Friend Mr. Dwight of the N. Y. Daily Advertiser* (New York, 1834), which went through ten American editions before 1836 and which was published in London in 1835.

[8] Published in book form under the title of *The Letters of Major Jack Downing of the Downingville Militia* (New York, 1864).

ship, may have been inspired by Jack Downing or some other Yankee writer of the day, Joe Strickland of Vermont, for example, or Enoch Timbertoes of Massachusetts.[1] However, the works of Strickland, Downing, and Timbertoes stimulated a definite taste for drollery with a Yankee flavoring. In 1833, one author took advantage of the fad by putting many pages of such material into a fictionized political pamphlet[2] and into a burlesque travel book.[3] Paper-covered collections labeled Yankee tales had a remunerative sale, and jest books, almanacs, and the columns of newspapers increased the number of jokes in which Yankees figured.

During the forties, and on into the fifties, the liking for such writings flourished. Scores of letters in dialect signed with various countrified names were printed in newspapers and periodicals.[4] The word "Yankee" appeared in the titles of a number of comic periodicals, all of which made frequent use of stories about New England peddlers, schoolmasters, and yokels.[5] A periodical called *Uncle Sam* published a series of humorous skits which were garnered in a strangely heterogeneous volume, one-third of which was devoted to illiterate Yankee letters.[6] In 1856, the *American Agricul-*

---

[1] I have been unable to discover in which paper Timbertoes' letters originally appeared, although I suspect it was a Boston newspaper.

[2] [Asa Greene], *A Yankee Among the Nullifiers: an Autobiography:* by Elnathan Elmwood, Esq. (New York, 1833) is a sombre, thin comic book, chiefly devoted to proving, by various means, the folly of nullification. Several tales about the hero, a Yankee, and about Yankee tricksters, some burlesque political speeches, and an Arbuthnotian allegory are intended to amuse.

[3] [Asa Greene], *Travels in America*, by George Fibbleton, Esq., Ex-Barber to His Majesty, the King of Great Britain (New York, 1833) burlesques such travel books as those by Mrs. Trollope and Hamilton. Strickland, Timbertoes, and Downing are introduced as characters with whom the ex-barber has conversations.

[4] One periodical, the New York *Spirit of the Times*, although it printed comparatively little Yankee humor, contained during one year (1846), letters signed Obediah Squash, Obediah Oldfort, Jotham Green, Simon Sharp, Joe Bramby, Pardon Jones, Bob Waddam and Down East. Benjamin P. Shillaber, writing his autobiography, recalled that in Boston, readers in the forties were aware of such rustic commentators as Job Sass, a Walpole farmer created by George E. Foxcraft in the Boston *Herald;* K. N. Pepper in the New York *Knickerbocker;* Uncle Toby (Rev. Tobias H. Miller); Ethan Spike of Hornsby—originated by Matthew F. Whittier, the poet's brother—and numerous others. One Yankee character, on becoming a candidate for the presidency, Shillaber recalls, was mentioned almost as frequently in the press as the real candidates.—"Experiences During Many Years," *New England Magazine*, n.s. IX, 154–155 (October, 1893).

[5] *Yankee Miscellany* (Boston, 1839–?); *Yankee Blade* (Portland and Boston, 1845–1890); *Yankee Doodle* (New York, 1846–1847); *Yankee Notions* (New York, 1852–1872).

[6] *Comic Lectures on Everything in General and Nothing in Particular* (New York, [1846?]) is composed of one part burlesque Negro sermons, one part German dialect sermons,

turalist began to print a series of popular Yankee letters which continued until 1868 and in which Tim Bunker wrote edifying little tales suggesting, among other things, the value of subsoiling, county fairs, and feeding cattle with oil meal.[1] These are only a few straws which show which way the wind blew. Between 1830 and 1870, in other words, a group of humorous portrayers of New England and its inhabitants were constantly busy. Some of these writers, because they rose to greater popularity than others and because they represent the chief tendencies and achievements in the development of this humor, deserve special attention. These include:

Seba Smith (1792–1868), the creator of Jack Downing.

Thomas Chandler Haliburton (1796–1865), creator of Sam Slick, an itinerant Yankee peddler whose deeds were celebrated, beginning in 1836, in books which together ran through two hundred editions published in Canada, the United States, and England. Though the books about Sam Slick were less influential than those about Downing,[2] it is probable that Sam was, between 1836 and 1860, "the best known character in the field of ludicrous 'down east' sayings and doings."[3]

James Russell Lowell (1819–1891), author of *The Biglow Papers*, issued in two series, "a complete success from the beginning."[4]

and one part Yankee letters. Though the last deal chiefly with courtin', they also treat Millerites, lectures on animal magnetism, schoolteachers, etc. The style and materials foreshadow Artemus Ward. The book may have been written by George H. Williams, editor of *Uncle Sam*.

[1] Published as *The Tim Bunker Papers, or Yankee Farming* (New York, 1858). In spite of their somewhat startling mission, these letters have a realistic flavor, a vividness, a businesslike quality, and an unconscious puritanical streak which make them attractive. They are written in a pleasantly restrained dialect which has the rhythms of actual speech.

[2] *Sam Slick's Almanac*, ed. P. J. Cozans (New York, 1856, 1857, 1858); S. A. Hammett's *Piney Woods Tavern; or, Sam Slick in Texas* (Philadelphia, 1858); *High Life in New York by Jonathan Slick* (New York, 1843), by Mrs. Ann S. Stephens; the anonymous Sam Slick, Jr.'s *Courtship and Adventures of Jonathan Homebred* (New York, 1860), and a curious broadside, *Sam Slick, the Yankee Pedlar*, published in England about 1860, are the only works which make capital of Sam's wide appeal, and none of these is greatly influenced by Slick's writings.

[3] V. L. O. Chittick, "Ring-tailed Roarers," in *The Frontier*, XIII, 263 (May, 1933). The same author's *Thomas Chandler Haliburton* (New York, 1924) is not only an excellent study of Slick's creator but also an authoritative consideration of various phases of American humor.

[4] J. R. Dennett, in *The Nation*, III, 387 (November 15, 1866). The first series, in covers, sold fifteen hundred copies during one week and went through at least ten editions in America by 1876.

Frances M. Whitcher (1811–1852), creator of Widow Spriggins, Widow Bedott, and Aunt Maguire, who chatted at length, to the delight of many, in the Albany *Argus*, *Neal's Saturday Gazette* (Philadelphia), and *Godey's Lady's Book*. All these characters, but particularly Widow Bedott, were highly regarded by readers of the forties, fifties, and sixties.[1]

Benjamin P. Shillaber (1814–1890), whose Mrs. Partington won, in the forties, a fame lasting well into the nineties.[2]

Two questions about these writings which seem to call for consideration are: What was the contemporary appeal of these popular humorous works? And what, if any, is their appeal today?

Seba Smith's Downing letters evidently appealed in several ways to Americans during the first sixty years of the nineteenth century. For one thing, Jack commented amusingly upon political affairs—at first, upon those of the Maine legislature, later, upon those of the nation at large. Their impudence was amusing. When the mythical Jack told how he became an intimate associate of President Jackson, chatting familiarly with him, reaching his arm under the old man's tired shoulder to shake hands for him at a reception, or when he portrayed Webster, Polk, Scott, and other men of the day in irreverently familiar terms, newspaper readers chuckled. They smiled, too, at satirical touches concerning the spoils system, the controversy about Mrs. Eaton, and other matters currently discussed.[3]

---

[1] Editor Neal in September, 1846, wrote: ". . . the world is full of Bedott. Our readers talk of nothing else, and despise 'Neal' if the Widow be not there. An excellent critic . . . said . . . that he regarded them [the Bedott papers] as the best Yankee papers yet written, and such indeed is the general sentiment."—*The Widow Bedott Papers*. New Edition (New York, 1883), p. x. These papers swelled the circulation of Neal's paper, and three years after Mrs. Whitcher's death sold, in book form, "something over a hundred thousand copies." —James Derby, *Fifty Years Among Publishers and Authors* (New York, 1886), pp. 413–416. Fifteen years after the author's death, a New York publishing firm thought it a good risk to bring out her earliest writings, contributed to a newspaper in 1845, as a book called *Widow Spriggins, Mary Elmer and Other Sketches* (1867). In addition, Widow Bedott had a successful career on the stage.

[2] James Derby, *op. cit.*, pp. 407–411.

[3] Says Francis Lieber, in *The Stranger in America* (London, 1835), I, 252: "The interest of these letters lies partly in the simple and blunt, yet forcible and not infrequently convincing manner, in which certain intricate questions . . . are treated in them . . ." Davis, if he was more popular than Smith, as some evidence indicates, gained preference because his political satire was more apt, more biting, than that of Smith. Evidence that not only Jack Downing but also Strickland and Timbertoes, were popular because of their political satire is discoverable in *Travels in America by George Fibbleton*, pp. 134–142, 166–169, 202–207.

Amusing, too, in the period, were the Yankees who appeared in the various letters—those quaint and laughable rustics of the state of Maine. And the language of the letters, idiomatic, racy, full of comic metaphors and similes, awkwardly apt adjectives, nouns, and phrases—this, too, as a critic pointed out in 1844,[1] seemed comic to readers of the day. Cousin Joel's reason for shouting "Hurrah for General Scott!" when he had promised to vote for Pierce, for example, was funny. To yell for Pierce, he said, "makes me feel so much like digging small potatoes and a few in a hill. But when I get right hungry for a hurrah, I give it to Gineral Scott, and I feel there's refreshment and nourishment in that, something like real meat; it makes me feel as it used to when we gin the loudest hurrahs for Gineral Jackson."[2] The strange earthiness of such metaphors and similes, the blithe disrespect for elegance, seemed ludicrous to a group of readers whose reading was still largely made up of heavily rhetorical language thoroughly divorced from the speech of country people.[3]

Sam Slick, Jack's most famous successor in the thirties, likewise amused by employing comic rustic speech in the dialogues he carried on with the highly literate Squire of Haliburton's stories; but Slick's chief appeals were slightly different. Paying no attention, evidently, to the political materials in Sam Slick's conversations, which might have offended or at least might have bored them,[4] Americans nevertheless were glad enough to purchase

---

[1] Professor Felton, in his review of *The Attaché*, *North American Review*, LVIII, 215 (January, 1844) remarked: ". . . the originality and truth of the Major's character, the sagacity of his observations, the felicity and idiomatic point of his language, and the argumentative wit of his illustrations . . . gave a wide and immediate popularity to his letters, almost unexampled in America."

[2] *My Thirty Years out of the Senate* (New York, 1859), p. 394. Somewhat more poetic, but comic in the same way, was a description of timberland in northern Maine: "And, my stars! sich great whapping pine trees, as straight as a candle, as tall as a liberty-pole, and standing all round as thick as the bean-poles in our garden, I guess you never see."—*John Smith's Letters* (New York, 1839), p. 99.

[3] The language of Timbertoes, Strickland, and Davis's Jack Downing was even more ludicrous. See the *New England Magazine*, III, 377 (November, 1832), which accuses the former two writers of cramming "into the mouth of one man, all the queer, cant phrases they ever heard . . . doubling the stock to boot out of their own invention, and then sending the crambo out to the world, as a caricature of Yankeeisms"; and the *Morning Courier and New York Enquirer*, July 16, 1845, which points out the broadly comic nature of the language employed by Davis.

[4] Haliburton, a Canadian, invented his hero, he said, to advocate, in a "popular style, under the garb of amusement," the development of natural resources in Nova

Sam's books as soon as they were issued.[1] Perhaps their enthusiasm was augmented by comments of the English critics, then (as now) much respected in this country, who rejoiced to find an author had broken away from eighteenth-century traditions,[2] or who were much impressed by "the novelty of the subjects, persons and dialect"[3] and the "apt, homely and quaint illustrations . . . employed."[4] At any rate, the American critics indicated similar reasons for Sam's success. The *New York Mirror* commended Sam as "a shrewd and sagacious observer,"[5] and the *Knickerbocker* critic said:

> The clock-maker [Sam Slick] has lost none of his shrewdness, his acute observation, nor his sparkling humor . . . he has more genuine wit than is to be found in all the "down-east" letters which have been inflicted on the public *ad nauseam* . . . Mr. SLICK's originality is the originality of *thought*, less than of *manner* . . . while he equals LACON in saying "many things in a few words," he never sacrifices truth to the external form of sententiousness. In his descriptions he is never striking at the expense of verisimilitude; nor does he permit his observation of character to be diverted from its naturalness by over-cumulative features in his picture, which destroys so many otherwise clever limnings.[6]

Notable in the last criticism is a hint of interest in the veracity of portraiture, but this matter is not generally stressed. From the

Scotia and the building of a railroad from Halifax to Windsor—V. L. O. Chittick, *Thomas Chandler Haliburton*, p. 179. In addition, as Sam remarked in a prefatory letter to the first series and a sketch in the second series (p. 319), Sam sternly criticized the Nova Scotians, the English, and Yankees. For a detailed statement of Haliburton's concept of the achievement of his critical papers, see the final chapter, "Valedictory Address," in *The Attaché*.

[1] *The Clockmaker* went through three series (1836, 1838, 1840) and *The Attaché; or Sam Slick in England* went through two (1843, 1844) all of which were printed in America the year of their appearance in England (except the first, published in America in 1837) and all of which were reprinted and widely sold in the United States. Even Slick's sternest critic admits that the sketches were not only widely circulated but also widely praised.

[2] John Wilson, in *Blackwood's*, XLII, 677 (November, 1837) is pleased with the divergence of Haliburton from what he calls "the Washington Irving style, which to us tastes like a composition of treacle and water, sickly and sweet, the feeble effusion of feelings which no man ever felt but after a dose of molasses . . ."

[3] *The Spectator*, X, 306 (April 1, 1837).

[4] *The Athenium*, pp. 902–904 (November 14, 1840).

[5] XVI, 85, September 8, 1838. The only adverse comment is that "Mr. Slick is occasionally a little coarse in his language and descriptions."

[6] *Knickerbocker*, XXII, 382 (October, 1843)—review of *The Attaché*.

admired passages cited by these critics, as from their specific comment, one gathers that the popularity of the books about Sam Slick was great chiefly because readers enjoyed the aphoristic wisdom of Sam, which Haliburton emphasized by italicization; the individualized portrait of the peddler; the thumbnail characterizations which dotted many pages; and the humorous tales Sam told to drive home his points. Though none of these features originated with Haliburton,[1] the combination evidently gave an impression of appealing novelty. And one suspects that the variety of Sam's adventures—he could reminisce about visits to the South Sea Islands, Italy, Java, Persia, and practically every part of the United States in his tales—augmented his attractiveness for readers of the day.

Various elements which made Sam Slick and Jack Downing popular in the forties gave to the Yankees of Lowell's first series of *The Biglow Papers* (1846–1848) such popularity that Lowell, hitherto little appreciated, was astonished.[2] Like Slick and Downing, Hosea, the chief character in these papers, was an unschooled Yankee with wise and amusing things to say about politics. Like Downing, he inaugurated his career as a writer whose efforts were appreciated and printed by a newspaper editor.[3] Laughable turns of Yankee speech and illiterate spelling, portraits of politicians which had the amusing quality of well-executed caricatures, crackerbox wit and political commentary attracted readers. The ingredients, as a passage in one of the poems indicates, were exactly the same as those used in the letters of Enoch Timbertoes:

[1] The humorous aphorisms, of course, trace back at least to Franklin. Sam's craftiness as a peddler was a motif which had been stressed for decades in travel books, jest books, newspapers and even humorous books. Many touches in Sam's character were clearly derived from Jack Downing. (See *Thomas Chandler Haliburton*, pp. 327–384). Haliburton probably invented some of the anecdotes Sam told, but far more of them he picked up in story-telling sessions with fellow-lawyers, in newspaper columns, and in periodicals. (*Ibid.*, pp. 182–183).

[2] Lowell says in the Preface to *The Biglow Papers: Second Series* (Boston, 1867), p. vii: "The success of my experiment soon began not only to astonish me, but to make me feel the responsibility of knowing that I held in my hand a weapon instead of the mere fencing-stick I had supposed . . . I found the verses . . . copied everywhere; I saw them pinned up in workshops; I heard them quoted and their authorship debated . . ."

[3] The first paper appeared in the Boston *Courier*, June 17, 1846, and others were published in that paper and the *Anti-Slavery Standard* until September, 1848. The first series was published in book form in 1848.

Then you can call me "Timbertoes,"—thet's wut the
people likes;
Sutthin' combinin' morril truth with phrases sech ez
strikes . . .[1]

In general, it seems likely that Lowell's first series of papers had
about the same contemporary appeal the Downing letters and
the Slick papers had. Such reviewers as were not hostile [2] stressed
the appeal of the political satire, "the droll and felicitous portraiture of the Yankee character and dialect . . . the quaint drollery
of the illustrations," merely hinting at any other appeals.[3] Some
note was made of the added drollery of the sprightly light verse
in which Hosea wrote.[4]

Before Lowell's Biglow appeared on the scene, readers had
been able to enjoy Sam Slick in spite of his political attitudes and
some Yankee papers in which there was no tinge of politics. J. W.
McClintock had written one such popular book in 1841,[5] William E. Burton had written another probably in 1847,[6] and Ann

[1] No. VIII, "A Second Letter from B. Sawin, Esq.," First Series. It may or may
not be a coincidence that a character in Davis's *Letters of J. Downing, Major*, bore the
name of Zekel Bigelow and that Hosea's father was called Ezekiel Biglow. Zekel, like
Ezekiel, wrote a letter introducing the author. Another predecessor to whom Lowell
refers, but for whom he has no praise, is Sam Slick.

[2] The critical reception on the whole, as Lowell notes, was not very enthusiastic.
One hostile review, signed P. P., in the New York *Spirit of the Times*, XIX, 73 (April 7,
1849) asserted that "our author out-Yankeys the Yankee, and gives us specimens of
orthography that certainly do not belong to New England, or in fact any other
[section], short of Yorkshire." Since the periodical published much more exaggerated
dialect sketches, and since it had many subscribers in the South, the reviewer may
not have been entirely disinterested.

[3] The quoted phrases are from F. Bowen, "Humorous and Satirical Poetry,"
North American Review, LXVIII, 187 (January, 1849). Bowen has a little to say about
the accuracy of the dialect and the portraiture. *The Literary World*, III, 872 (December 2, 1848) calls the papers "squibs on the Mexican War and the Southern
Slavery Question," cites the poem about John P. Robinson as "the hit of the volume,"
and complains about the book's irreverence and its faulty dialect. *The New Englander*,
VII, 63–72 (February, 1849) contains a review which is very similar, although here
the dialect is praised. See also "J. R. Lowell" in George W. Bungay, *Off-Hand Takings;
or Crayon Sketches* (New York, 1854), pp. 394–399, and the *Nation*, III, 387 (November,
1866) for details concerning the contemporary attitude.

[4] Bowen, *op. cit.*, p. 188. Hosea, versifying Birdofredum's letters, hits upon such
inspired rhymes as "come on't," "thumb on't" and "sum on't"; "innercent" and
"sinner sent"; "harnsome" and "darn some," etc.

[5] *Johnny Beedle's Courtship, Sleigh Ride, and Marriage* (New York, 1841) is, as its
title indicates, pretty largely concerned with domestic phases of Yankee life.

[6] *Waggeries and Vagaries* (Philadelphia, [1847?]) contains a widely reprinted tall
tale and several Yankee sketches.

Stephens wrote sketches about Jonathan Slick which were very popular in the New York *Express* and Neal's *Brother Jonathan*, and which later, in book form, went through three editions.[1] In the 1850's, however, two Yankee characters leaped to an amazing popularity which did not depend at all upon political touches.

One of these was the Widow Bedott whose adventures, first recorded in magazines in the forties by Frances M. Whitcher, appearing in book form in 1855, went through twenty-three editions before the end of 1864, and were reissued in a new and popular edition in 1883, selling prodigiously through the years. The other was Mrs. Partington, created by B. P. Shillaber, whose sayings, gathered from the pages of the Boston *Post* and the *Carpet Bag*, in book form attracted thirty thousand buyers in a short time and, continuing in a second volume in 1859, sold ten thousand copies before publication.[2] In 1884, after Mrs. Partington's literary labors had produced a whole series of books, her creator was still receiving frequent requests for her autograph from her admirers.[3]

Neither of these New England ladies was concerned in the least with political affairs. Part of their appeal doubtless derived from their novelty. They were the first feminine American comic figures to be portrayed at length, and the technique for their portrayal differed from the letters which characterized Jack Downing, the dialogues which pictured Sam Slick, and the letters or poems which Lowell had used in *The Biglow Papers*, for they revealed themselves chiefly in monologues. Each had a characteristic vice: Mrs. Bedott wrote poetry which was bad to the point of being a parody on poetry, and Mrs. Partington could hardly open her mouth without employing a malapropism. But evidently the chief appeal of each was simply as a character and commentator on other characters.

The object of the author of *The Widow Bedott Papers*, as Alice B. Neal remarked, "whether she depicted the verbosity of the self-sufficient preacher, or portrayed the vulgar coquetries of the incon-

---

[1] In the list of contributors to *Brother Jonathan*, the name of Jonathan Slick was printed in the largest type. *High Life in New York* . . . by Jonathan Slick, Esq., of Weathersfield, Conn., was published in New York in 1843 and 1854, and in Philadelphia in 1859. Therein, Jonathan told of his adventures in the big city. Miss Stephens, who hailed from Portland, had a flair for Yankee dialect, vivid descriptions, and scenes in which the scent of onions was important.

[2] Bungay, *op. cit.*, p. 372.   [3] Derby, *op. cit.*, p. 411.

solable widow—whether she held up to view the would-be literary circle, or narrated the gossip of the sewing society . . . was

> the gift to gie 'em
> To see themsels as others see 'em!"[1]

Gossipy, somewhat malicious, simple but rather pretentious, the widow talks naturally, digressively, about herself and her neighbors, revealing her character by what she says. Her neighbors, too, are taken off in neat little sketches and anecdotes as the pattern of her existence is revealed in her leisurely chatter. Teas, Thanksgiving feasts, donation parties, sewing circles, courtin's, phrenology lectures, and bickerings with peddlers are the mundane events she celebrates.

Similarly admired as a character was Mrs. Partington. Commended by such influential critics as Oliver Wendell Holmes and Henry Ward Beecher, her sayings were praised not only because they were witty but also because they characterized her; said one critic: "There is a wise and humane blending of humor, philosophy, and benevolence, in the short utterances to which this writer has given vitality."[2] Said another critic:

> The character of the oracular old dame is sustained with dramatic harmony throughout the whole of her unique comments; she never by any chance relapses into orthodox English; and always hides beneath her eccentricity of expression the largest and warmest soul of grandmotherly kindness. Her biographer and "honest chronicler" has succeeded to a charm in giving the veracious history of her life . . . He is certainly a master. . . .[3]

Shillaber himself, in the preface to *Life and Sayings of Mrs. Partington, and Others of the Family* (Boston, 1854), indicates the chief appeal of his work derives from character portrayal. Sydney Smith of England, he confesses, invented the dame's name.

But the *character* we claim as ours; and whether it had been embodied in Mrs. Smith, or Brown, instead of Mrs. Partington, would have been immaterial. Those sayings are *ours*, and we venture to affirm that Sydney Smith would not lay claim to them. . . . Be-

---

[1] Introductory to *The Widow Bedott Papers*, p. xii.

[2] Bungay, *op. cit.*, p. 373.

[3] *Harper's*, IX, 136 (June, 1854). See also *Peterson's Magazine*, XXV, 409 (June, 1854).

cause, forsooth, he had spoken of Mrs. Partington's sweeping back the Atlantic with her broom, would he claim the illustrious PAUL, the roguish ISAAC, and the jocose ROGER, and the great PHILAN-THROPOS, and the poetical WIDESWORTH, as his progeny? We trow not. . . . The character has been drawn from life. The Mrs. Partington we have depicted is no fancy sketch, and no Malaprop imitation, as some have thought. . . . We need no appeal to establish this fact.[1]

These comments seem to indicate a slight shift in the attitude toward Yankee humor. When Down East humor originated, critics were evidently so pleased with its novelty that they made slight demands upon it. If it smartly satirized contemporary political affairs, if it contained comic portraits and funny touches of dialect, that was enough. But by the fifties, an additional possibility was recognized—the possibility of authentic though comic portraiture. Increasing stress is placed upon the lifelikeness of the characterization. Some exceptions to this statement are not hard to discover; yet if one surveys all the comment upon the Yankee humor, such a trend is evident. A climax in such a trend is certainly quite clear to one who examines the critical comment upon *The Biglow Papers* when the second series appeared in 1867.

William Dean Howells states the attitude clearly when he finds reasons for admiring both series of the papers which contrast strikingly with those suggested in the earlier reviews. "It is not as mere satire, however," he suggests, "that *The Biglow Papers* are to be valued. The First and Second Series form a creative fiction of unique excellence." And his review is largely concerned with the vividness of background, and the truth to life of Lowell's character portrayal.[2] Similarly J. R. Dennett, in the *Nation*, notes that the papers are admirable because they present "characters so life-like and, in the main, so true to nature—so good as individuals and as types that we know not where in literature to look for . . . others that excel them . . ."[3] In addition, reviews after the appearance of the second volume of Lowell's humorous papers —the reviews of Howells and Dennett, for example—are much

---

[1] "Prefatory," pp. vii–viii. The italics are Shillaber's.
[2] *Atlantic Monthly*, XIX, 124–125 (January, 1867).
[3] *Nation*, III, 387 (November 15, 1866).

concerned with the admirable way Lowell has caught the authentic accents of New England talk.

Why this change in emphasis? A dogmatic answer to this question is, of course, impossible; but some reasons may be suggested. For one thing, here and there in the criticisms which had treated comic Yankee literature in the thirties, forties, and fifties, various passages had touched upon the value of authentic—not merely comic—New England language as an aid to character portrayal, and upon the value of characterization in American humor. As early as 1834, Lieber, for example, had had something to say on these points.[1] In 1844, furthermore, C. C. Felton had devoted almost all the pages of a review of two books by Haliburton to a consideration of the authenticity of the characterization by dialect and other means of Sam Slick, unfavorably comparing him as a character with Jack Downing.[2] Elsewhere, similar points had been briefly touched upon.

Moreover, interest in the language of Americans, long a subject of controversy, had been greatly stimulated beginning in the forties and fifties by philological students. John Russell Bartlett's *Dictionary of Americanisms*, first issued in 1848, had gone into its third edition in 1860, and other studies had appeared.[3] Bartlett had devoted some space in his scholarly introduction not only to the condemnation of literary American writing but also to praise of writings in the vernacular by American humorists,[4] and Charles A. Bristed had spoken slightingly of one Yankee portrayer whose rendition of the vernacular was faulty, but had praised highly the language of Jack Downing and *The Biglow Papers*.[5]

Furthermore, English critics had, upon the publication of

---

[1] *The Stranger in America*, I, 252.

[2] *North American Review*, CXXII, 211–227 (January, 1844).

[3] J. O. Halliwell-Philips, *A Dictionary of Archaisms and Provincialisms, Containing Words Now Obsolete in England, All of Which are Familiar and in Common Use in America*, originally published in 1847, which went into a second edition in 1850; Charles A. Bristed, "The English Language in America," *Cambridge Essays* (London, 1855); Alfred L. Elwyn, *Glossary of Supposed Americanisms* (Philadelphia, '1859). For an account of the lengthy argument concerning the use of Americanisms, see H. L. Mencken, *op. cit.;* for documents in the argument, see those collected by M. M. Matthews in *The Beginnings of American English* (Chicago, 1931).

[4] *Dictionary of Americanisms* (New York, 1848), pp. v, xxvii. Yankee humorists to whom he refers in this edition include Sam Slick and Jack Downing. In the 1859 edition, he adds *The Widow Bedott Papers* and *The Biglow Papers* to his list of sources.

[5] *Op. cit.*, pp. 66–67.

Lowell's papers in England, greeted them with an enthusiasm sure to be echoed by Americans, once England had given the signal. Thomas Hughes, in his introduction to the 1859 English edition, spoke lovingly of the characterization and did not hesitate to place Lowell's name alongside such names as Aristophanes, Cervantes, Molière, and Swift. Reviewers of the English edition were also enthusiastic. F. G. Stephens, in *Macmillan's Magazine*, spoke of one character in the papers as "totally new . . . as original in his way as Becky Sharp is in hers," and continued: "Individuality and truth of portraiture, those grand elements of fiction, are to be found in abundance in *The Biglow Papers*, from the personages who introduce the nine poems to the reader, to the varied characters who appear in their progress." Numerous illustrations followed.[1] *Chambers's Journal* was likewise enthusiastic about the veracity and the vividness of Lowell's portraiture.[2]

Finally, Lowell himself had in a way prepared for a kind reception of his second series. No longer was he an obscure author; his professorship at Harvard, his editorship (1857–1861) of the *Atlantic Monthly*, and his writings had established him as a leader in literature. In a review of the second edition of Bartlett's *Dictionary* in the *Atlantic*, Lowell had championed the use of common-folk-talk in literature, saying:

No language, after it has faded into *diction*, none that cannot suck up feeding juices from the mother-earth of a rich common-folk-talk, can bring forth a sound and lusty book. True vigor of expression does not pass from page to page, but from man to man, where the brain is kindled and the lips are limbered by downright living interests and by passions in the very throe. Language is the soil of thought; and our own especially is a rich leaf-mould, the slow growth of ages . . .[3]

He had published the papers of the second series in the *Atlantic Monthly*, which gave them added prestige.[4] And in his "Introduction" to the second series, revealing the artistry back of his

[1] *Macmillan's Magazine*, I, 206–210 (January, 1860).

[2] XXXVII, 293–296 (May 10, 1862).

[3] *Atlantic Monthly*, IV, 638–639 (November, 1859). Lowell's attitude on the related subject of nationalism, it should be noted, was not constant. See the article by Orians cited above, *American Literature*, VIII, 148–151 (May, 1936).

[4] They appeared in issues between January, 1862 and May, 1866.

creations and insisting upon the dignity and usefulness of dialect, he also prepared the way for a new appraisal of his work.

The preface said wise and impressive things about the use of the American language, suggesting its value as an antidote to the greatest fault in current writings, "a studied want of simplicity." Americans had a dangerous tendency "to look on our mother-tongue as a dead language, to be sought in the grammar and dictionary rather than the heart." He cited examples of bloated diction in contemporary literature.[1] For "directness, precision, and force," they should turn to the language of the "divinely illiterate," for "our popular idiom is racy with life and vigor and originality, bucksome . . . to our new occasions, and proves itself no mere graft by sending up new suckers from the old root in spite of us." "The first real postulate of an original literature," Lowell continued, "is that a people should use their language instinctively and unconsciously, as if it were a lively part of their growth and personality, not as the mere torpid boon of education and inheritance. . . . It may well be that the life, invention, and vigor shown by our popular speech, and the freedom with which it is shaped to the instant want of those who use it, are of the best omen for our having a swan at last." The essay ended with a series of illustrations of the point that American speech was not vulgar, since it had many honorable antecedents in the speech of England.[2]

[1] On pp. xii–xvii, he cites examples of stretching and swelling. He might well have cited Seba Smith, capable of writing strikingly, even beautifully, in dialect, but writing non-dialect passages such as "It was but a few minutes, however, before the extreme violence of the wind began to abate and they were enabled to pursue their labors" (meaning "Soon the wind stopped blowin' so hard and they sot to wuk"), and "Pond Village is situated upon the margin of one of those numerous and beautiful sheets of water that gem the whole surface of New England, like the stars in the evening sky, and received its appellation to distinguish it from three other villages in the same town, which could not boast of a similar location."—*Way Down East* . . . (New York, 1854), pp. 208, 339. In 1936, A. P. Herbert still fought against such diction in *What a Word!*

[2] Much of the material in the essay had appeared in the 1859 review of Bartlett's *Dictionary.* An interesting development in Lowell's attitude toward dialect is discoverable in his letters. The first series started as badly spelled, broadly comic renditions of speech, but moved toward less exaggerated forms. "As for Hosea," wrote Lowell, November 13, 1847, in a letter, "I am sorry that I began by making him such a detestable speller. There is no fun in bad spelling itself. . . . You see I am getting him out of it gradually."—*Letters of James Russell Lowell,* ed. Charles Eliot Norton (New York, 1894), I, 296. In the later papers, there is obviously an attempt at scientific accuracy in recording a dialect which, as Lowell said, was "homely" to him.

the Union, with a slight mixture of odd phrases from Nova
Scotia."[1] Some years before Haliburton started to depict his
comic hero, an American critic treating the use of the vernacular
in literature had pointed out the error which the Canadian was
likely to make:

One error . . . is usually avoided by our own writers, into
which foreigners fall very readily; that . . . of confounding together the peculiarities of different sections of the Union, for these
peculiarities are extremely well marked in many instances, and
the cant and slang, as well as the simple idioms of the *centaur*
of Kentucky, are as different from those of the . . . tin ware vender
of New England, as the Ohio flat boat of the one is different from
the pedlar's cart of the other.[2]

Haliburton made exactly this mistake.

Along with this mingling of the language of the East and the
Southwest went a characterization which was something of a mon-
strosity. Haliburton, alone among the popular creators of Down
East humor, chose to depict the threadworn type character of a
Yankee peddler, hence Sam was "a libel on Yankee character," as
Lowell called him, "and a complete falsification of Yankee modes
of speech."[3] He was, as Dennett noted,[4] "the British tourist's and
Sam Slick Yankee . . . morbidly inquisitive and an impossible
compound of shrewdness, conceit, ignorance, all the dialects
spoken between Maine and Texas, together with enough exclusively English book-English to show him born not of observation
but of books." But he was more than that: he was a character
who was a combination of two distinctly different type characters,
the foxy, soft-spoken Yankee peddler and the forthright, tall-talk-
ing, ring-tailed roarer from old Kaintuck. As a passage from *The
Attaché*, printed hereafter, reveals, his costume, at one time the
homespun of a traveling merchant, at another time was the buckskin of a frontiersman.[5] Adding to the confusion, his author, a
staunch Tory, frequently made Sam say things which no Yankee
farmer, even the most conservative, would have been likely to say

[1] F. Bowen, in the *North American Review*, LXVIII, 188 (January, 1849).
[2] *New England Magazine*, III, 377 (November, 1832).
[3] "Introduction" to *The Biglow Papers: Second Series*, p. lxxiii. Generously,
Lowell conceded that such a person might have existed in Nova Scotia.
[4] *Nation*, III, 387 (November, 1866).   [5] "Natur," reprinted on pp. 232–236.

These various forces, then—and perhaps the s
attitudes—prepared the way for an estimate of
Biglow Papers which would give an important place
tion of the dialect employed and, related to this, th
zation. By 1867, in other words, Down East humo
judged by standards which, in 1830, had seemed re
important. To modern readers, it will seem that the s
the direction of more lasting methods of evaluation. M
satire in the writings of this whole group of humorists p
Yankees has lost its value to everybody save the histo
cept for a few touches which happen to satirize huma
still perceivable,[1] the whole appeal of the political and
satire in the papers is gone. The sentchtious statements a
witty comments which were so diverting to readers of 1
in the thirties no longer seem very amusing. More importa
the reader of today is the continued appeal of the languag
this literature—if that language happens to be vivid, hon
strongly flavored with the soil, alive. More important, too, is
depiction of background and the characterization of human bein
whom we can understand and in whom we can believe.

How, according to the standards evolved by 1867—the stand
ards for evaluation which still seem valid, does the humor of Seba
Smith and his followers fare? One of the most popular of all the
humorists, Haliburton, fares badly indeed by such a test. The
reader of today, turning the pages of books about Sam Slick, finds
himself often on the verge of a weary yawn: one may say, putting
it mildly, that these books are no longer even slightly amusing.
The wise saws which Haliburton proudly italicized cannot make
amends for a soggy language. Even in the early forties some of
Sam's admirers noted an admixture of cockneyisms with his
speech,[2] and an unfriendly critic who was able to present evidence
that he knew Yankees intimately perceived that "the jargon
which he uses is a hodgepodge of provincialisms from every state

[1] Lowell fares better than the rest here. We can understand, still, "The Pious
Editor's Creed" and "John P. Robinson" as political portraiture. The letter of Jack
Downing printed on pp. 223–228 is still understandable to a nation which is in the
habit of seeing the wrong men become candidates for the presidency. Some other
passages of political or social satire, though not many, retain their interest.

[2] *Knickerbocker*, XXII, 382 (October, 1843).

about politics; and Sam was outfitted with a background of travel and accomplishments too complex even to be comic.[1] Too, the thumbnail sketches of minor figures in Haliburton's books about Slick, so amusing in the forties, today prove to be grotesque caricatures, only slightly more comic than Sam.

The other four writers of Down East humor fare better than Haliburton does when they are tested as creators of believable humorous characters and writers of racy dialect. No one today will laugh boisterously at them, probably, but modern readers will at least find some charm in them.

The Widow Bedott and Mrs. Partington become, to be sure, wearying to one who reads many of their monologues. One is bored before long by the doggerel poetry of the former and by the malapropisms of the latter character. But, sampled briefly, their remarks amusingly display their characters, other characters, and the life of the day. Mrs. Whitcher is below Mrs. Gaskell, but some of the same quality one finds in *Cranford*, in spite of all the horseplay, enters into *The Widow Bedott Papers*. Here are the churchly ladies of a community, here is how they thought and how they talked. Here, too, are their neighbors. And Shillaber, born and reared in New Hampshire, knew intimately the minutiae of his Yankee heroine's life. Hence, aside from her impossible mistakes in words, Mrs. Partington speaks a believable language, and she is a character. Her mind works in a lifelike fashion—puritanical, narrow, domestic, but withal sentimentally genial. Her enthusiasm for gardening, domestic animals, patent medicines, and Calvinism, and her muddled but well-intentioned interest in current events, give her individuality. With her are a group of type characters, Dr. Spooner, Old Roger, and Widesworth, "representing," as Shillaber says,[2] "the profound, the jolly, and the sentimental," who are fairly diverting. More amusing is her nephew, Ike, "an imitation of the universal 'human boy' . . . roguish without being malicious, ever alert in mischief, acting from impulses as irrepressible as those of an untamed

---

[1] Chittick, *Thomas Chandler Haliburton*, pp. 339–342. Professor Chittick, *op. cit.*, pp. 383–384, correctly points out that though Haliburton "set no fashions in American humor . . . affected no change in the traditional character of the 'genuine' Yankee," he did much for the international reputation of American humor.

[2] *Knitting-Work . . . Wrought by Ruth Partington* (Boston, 1859), p. iii.

colt"[1]—revealing some of the comedy of boyhood later to be richly developed by Mark Twain.

Better than either of these, however, is the Yankee humor of the first and the last of the group in this field of writing—Seba Smith and James Russell Lowell.

Authentic descriptions and characterizations of the sort which gave permanent appeal crept quite incidentally into the Downing letters. At first, apparently, it was enough to give the screeds verisimilitude by using three devices: a letter form, the type characterization of their writer, and Yankee dialect. The epistolary style was far more natural in newspapers of the day than it is now, since items in newspapers customarily assumed that form.[2] And the letters were written by a recognizable character—a countryman who, despite his naïveté, was thrifty, a shrewd trader, with an observing eye on the main chance. This character was rendered believable partly because he couched his letters in language which was real—having the real tang of Yankee speech as his creator had known it from childhood. Further, his phrases were more than quaint expressions; as Smith himself pointed out, they were revelations of a way of thinking.[3]

Then, as the letters grew in number, the author added details—lastingly diverting touches of portraiture and background. Jack's relatives began to send notes which, with a foreword to the collected letters, made Downingville a familiar village peopled by inhabitants so well drawn that Smith could later make a good case for his claim that he had characterized the Yankee effectively.[4] Downingville exists as

---

[1] *New England Magazine*, n.s. IX, 153 (October, 1893).

[2] Circulars to collectors of customs, from the Secretary of the Treasury, letters from the Secretary of State to the President, and from the President to various people, letters announcing candidacies for office or defending actions of the legislature, letters from abroad reporting foreign affairs or from distant parts of the United States reporting on local affairs—these, unadorned and unexplained, gave the sturdy readers of that period their undiluted news. Hence Jack's reports of his adventures in Portland, in Washington, and elsewhere, were in the style of the other columns in the papers.

[3] Said Smith: "Genuine Yankee delineations do not consist in mere out of the way modes of expression, but in subtle quaintness of thought, which under the simplest language conveys a homely truth or a statesman-like idea."—*Emerson's Magazine and Putnam's Monthly*, VI, 666 (June, 1858). For contemporary comment on Jack's language, see the *Morning Courier and New York Enquirer*, February 27, 1844, and July 16, 1845, and Bartlett's *Dictionary of Americanisms* (New York, 1848), p. v.

[4] *Emerson's Magazine and Putnam's Monthly*, VI, 666 (June, 1858).

a snug, tidy sort of village, situated in a valley . . . scooped out between two large rugged hills that lie to the east and the west, having a thick forest of trees to the north, and a clear pond of water, with a sandy beach to the south . . . just about in the middle of Down East. . . . It has a school-house and a tavern, and a minister, and a doctor, and folks that work at most all sorts of trades.[1]

Today, a hundred years after Jack wrote, one can still glimpse that village, can still see its inhabitants at work, "hoeing about among the potatoes, and chopping wood, and making big stone walls" if they were men, or, if they were women, going on "afternoon visits where they went sociable without stays, and took their knitting work and got home before milking time." For relaxation, Downingville folk had sleigh-rides, huskings, or quiltings with "everybody in Downingville . . . trying the double shuffle and the cutting out jigg"; or neighbors dropped in of evenings to hear the old hero retelling yarns of the Revolution, or Debby reading the evening paper—drinking a mug of cider and digging teeth "into the mellow side of a great sweet apple" while they listened.

Smith had skill not only in descriptive touches but also in characterization. Members of the Downing tribe are more than mere theatrical characters. Uncle Joshua, lazy, good-natured, a keen student of politics who'd "rather stand and dispute about politiks any time, than work on his farm," demonstrates his sense of drama, his "cuteness," in several episodes. Mrs. Downing, writing a letter after churning all morning, though her hand shakes so she can "hardly hold her pen still," can nevertheless record at length her impressions of the housekeeping of a new bride. Aunt Keziah bustles about to prepare for guests, washing every inch of her house from garret to cellar, putting green bushes into fireplaces, baking huge quantities of pumpkin pies and navy beans, putting "on two feather beds on top of the straw bed, and a brand-new calico quilt that she made the first summer after she was married, and never put it on a bed before." Quietly and briefly sketched, in language as tangy as new-picked fruit, these and other lifelike figures continue to have charm.

[1] To perceive the value of dialect to Smith compare this with the description of Pond Village given in footnote 1, p. 54.

The Biglow Papers have something of the same flavor, especially after some papers in the second series turn aside from politics long enough to give the characters a vivid background. Hosea has the earmarks of a Yankee, the common-sense shrewdness, the keen perception, and he realistically speaks a language such as his neighbors speak.[1] But, unlike Jack Downing, he is not a politician but a farmer; and phrases and illustrations which are drawn from farming come naturally to his tongue. Countrybred, he knows that

> 'Taint a knowin' kind o' cattle
> That is ketched with mouldy corn.

It is natural for him to think of a recruiting sergeant as one who follows his bell-wethers, to feel that a real argument against war is that "the hay's to mow," to assert that editors who crow "like a cockerel three months old" are likely to sprout "like a peach that's got the yellers."[2] And just as natural is his familiarity with scriptural texts and even God Almighty:

> Ez fer war, I call it murder,—
>   There you hev it plain an' flat;
> I don't want to go no furder
>   Than my Testyment fer that;
> God hez sed so plumb an' fairly,
>   It's ez long ez it is broad,
> An' you've gut to git up airly
>   Ef you want to take in God.[3]

References to "the angel that writes all our sins in a book," "a marciful Providunce," and "our Maker's orig'nal idee" sprinkle the pages of Biglow's writings. Such touches prove that, as George Augustus Sala remarked:

Mr. Lowell is the Yankee *pur sang*—the bred and born New Englander. . . . New England has entered into Mr. Lowell's very soul. The scriptural phraseology, the nasal twang, the stiff-necked complacency, the iron will, the dogmatism and intolerance and

---

[1] For comment on the dialect, see Dennett, *op. cit.*, p. 387; F. T. in the *Cornhill Magazine*, XXXI, 70 (January, 1875); and G. E. Woodberry, "James Russell Lowell," *Century*, XLIII, 114–115 (November, 1891).

[2] All these phrases are from his first poem. Other poems add more touches of this sort.   [3] *First Series*, No. I.

sincerity of the Pilgrim Fathers, are all latent in the "Biglow Papers" under a diaphonous veil of burlesque humor.[1]

Useful in the fiction is Homer Wilbur, described by Lowell as "my parson-editor with his pedantry and verbosity, his amiable vanity and superiority to the verses he was editing." He is useful, however, chiefly as a foil: learned, pedantic, his bookish comment is an incongruous setting for the homely, unschooled speech of young Hosea.[2] But Lowell's best characterization is Birdofredum Sawin, whose letters are translated into verse by Hosea. A country boy stirred to enlist for the Mexican war by the rattle of a drum, Sawin reports from time to time on his disillusionment, his grotesque suffering, and his moral disintegration. A comic study in degeneration, embodying, as Lowell put it, "that half-conscious *un*morality which I had noticed as the recoil in gross natures from . . . puritanism,"[3] Sawin is a delightful rascal.[4] And because all three characters represent different levels of intelligence, different codes of morality, there is a certain richness in the variety of their reactions. Hence, by treatment of them individually and by contrasts between them, Lowell bodies forth three characters— characters who are not, to be sure, realistically rounded, but who, nevertheless, have enough of the breath of life in them to continue amusing. They gain depth and reality because of the background against which they are displayed. As Howells pointed out,

. . . we enjoy the very woods and fields in Hosea Biglow's quaintly and subtly faithful feeling for them. However, we are not suffered to forget Mr. Lowell's creed, that human nature is the nature best worth celebrating. The landscape is but the setting for Jalaam —shrewd, honest, moral, angular—Hosea Biglow municipalized. The place should be on the maps, for it has as absolute existence as any in New England, and its people by slight but unerring touches are made as real. . . .[5]

[1] Introduction to *The Biglow Papers* (London, 1866), pp. iv-v.

[2] As Bret Harte says in "A Few Words About Mr. Lowell," *New Review*, V, 195 (February, 1891): "It was part of Mr. Lowell's art to contrast this rude working-Christian Biglow with the older-fashioned Puritan Parson Wilbur, still wedded to his creed and his books."

[3] Introduction to *Second Series*, p. vii.

[4] For effective criticism of the characterization of Sawin, see Tandy, *op. cit.*, pp. 43–64, and F. G. Stephens, *op. cit.*, pp. 206–210.

[5] *Atlantic Monthly*, XIX, 124 (January, 1867).

Dialect, the characterization achieved by dialect and by other means, and the vividly sensed background of New England town and countryside thus give the humorous writings of Lowell a lasting appeal.

Yankee humor, then, in the period between 1830 and 1867, consistently employing dialect—an earmark of much American humor,[1] moved in the general direction of increased emphasis upon two elements at first incidental: accurate rendition of dialect and the authentic depiction of localized background and individualized characters. A richly varied narrative technique also developed, including the letter written by the character depicted, versification by a rustic poet, straightforward narrative employing much dialogue, and the dramatic prose monologue.

Developing in the same period, the humor of the Old Southwest, next to be considered, was unlike Down East humor in that, from the first, it had only incidental associations with political disputes, and from the first its authors stressed its authenticity. Like Yankee humor in its use of much vernacular language and a variety of narrative methods, it differed from Yankee humor, as will be indicated, because its subject matter necessarily was very different and because its artistry was more perceivably influenced by the art of oral narratives.

IV. Humor of the Old Southwest (1830–1867)

Contemporaneous with the humor of life Down East, the robust humor of the Old Southwest revealed the comedy of background, custom, and character in Tennessee, Georgia, Alabama, Louisiana, Mississippi, Arkansas, and Missouri. In these states, ways of living differed greatly among the inhabitants not only because many peoples mingled but also because various stages of civilization naturally were juxtaposed in stretches between settled sections and frontiers. Here, therefore, flourished striking contrasts which furnished excellent stuff for humor. Using these materials, a boisterous band of humorists produced a body of amusing narrative unsurpassed by any group in American literature.

[1] As Joel Chandler Harris remarked, "The fact remains that the vernacular, as distinct from literary form and finish, is the natural vehicle of the most persistent and most popular variety of American humor: hence the employment of what is frequently called dialect."—*The World's Wit and Humor: American* (New York, 1906), I, xxii.

A few biographical facts about some of the members of this group will suggest some interesting generalizations. Typical and important were:

Augustus Baldwin Longstreet (1790–1870), author of *Georgia Scenes*, published in newspapers (1832–1835) and in book form (1835)—lawyer, legislator, judge, and editor.[1]

Madison Tensas, M.D. (pseudonym—real name unknown), who summarized part of his life thus: "I was scarcely sixteen, yet I was a student of medicine, and had been, almost a printer, a cotton-picker, a ploughboy, gin-driver, gentleman of leisure, cabin-boy, cook, scullion, and runaway. . . ." The sentence is from his *Odd Leaves of a Louisiana "Swamp Doctor"* (1843).

Johnson J. Hooper (1815–1863) of Alabama, author of *Adventures of Simon Suggs*, published in part in newspapers and periodicals before it appeared in book form (1845)—lawyer, political office holder, and editor of various newspapers.[2]

Sol Smith (1801–1869) who, according to a friend, was successful as "editor, actor-manager, preacher and lawyer." His books were *Theatrical Apprenticeship* (1845) and *Theatrical Journey Work* (1854).

Thomas Bangs Thorpe (1815–1878), whose work was collected from periodicals to take book form in *The Mysteries of the Backwoods* (1846) and *The Hive of the Bee Hunter* (1854)—painter, soldier, newspaper editor.

William T. Thompson (1812–1882) of Georgia whose *Major Jones's Courtship* (1843), *Chronicles of Pineville* (1845) and *Major Jones's Sketches of Travel* (1847) were collections of newspaper stories —soldier, printer, law student, and journalist.

Joseph M. Field (1810–1856), St. Louis actor, actor-manager, and journalist, whose newspaper and periodical sketches made up *The Drama in Pokerville* (1847).

John S. Robb, also of St. Louis, journeyman printer and, later, editor, whose newspaper and periodical sketches went into *Streaks of Squatter Life* (1847).[3]

---

[1] See John Donald Wade, *Augustus Baldwin Longstreet* (New York, 1924).

[2] See Marion Kelley, *The Life and Writings of Johnson Jones Hooper* (Unpublished Master's Dissertation, Alabama Polytechnic Institute, 1934).

[3] For data concerning Thompson, Thorpe, Field, and Robb, as well as others of the group, see Franklin J. Meine's admirable *Tall Tales of the Southwest* (New York, 1930). For treatments of Robb, Smith, and Field, see Carl Brooks Spotts, "The Development of Fiction on the Missouri Frontier," *Missouri Historical Review*, XXIX, 100–108, 186–194 (1935).

Joseph G. Baldwin (1815–1864), who wrote of his experiences as a young frontier lawyer in *Flush Times of Alabama and Mississippi*.[1]

George W. Harris (1814–1869) of Tennessee, jeweler's apprentice, river boat captain, silversmith, political writer, postmaster, hunter, inventor, and a frequent contributor to periodicals of humorous writings, some of which appeared in *Sut Lovingood* (1867).[2]

Even such brief notes as these show what a remarkable species these men were. Before they became authors, most of them had knocked around from place to place, from job to job, seeing much of the teeming life of the sections they portrayed. They were not scholars who emerged from libraries, blinking as they carried manuscripts into the light of day.[3] They were lawyers who wrote their stories between swings around the circuit, journalists who scratched out their yarns on desks around which eddied the life of a newspaper office, soldiers and doctors who jotted down their tales during lulls in strenuous activity.

Their literary training, as one would expect, was varied; and one soon discovers that they patterned their work upon the writings of various schools. And the characters whom they pictured were of many kinds: though they knew the ring-tailed roarer of the sort repeated frequently during the century, these men, steeped in the life of their sections, preferred as a rule to limn more individualized characters. Nevertheless, one will discover several qualities common to the writings of all of them.

For one thing, writing with an eye cocked towards the East, where sooner or later their books were published, and to which they wanted to "interpret" their section, they were all, consciously or unconsciously, local colorists, eager to impart the flavor of their particular locality. There was no gradual development of this desire, as there was in the East. From the beginning, their humor, as Mr. Meine, who knows it better than any modern scholar, has

---

[1] See George F. Mellen, "Joseph Glover Baldwin," *Library of Southern Literature* (New Orleans, n. d.), I, 175–181.

[2] A monograph on Harris is being prepared by Mr. Meine. Unless Harris's writings were collected many years after they were written, it is highly probable that the date 1867 indicates a reprint rather than a first edition. He contributed to *The Spirit of the Times* as early as 1845, and at least three of the Sut Lovingood yarns were written in the fifties.

[3] For additional comment on this point, see W. P. Trent, "Retrospect of American Humor," *Century*, LXIII, 50–52 (November, 1901).

pointed out, "was provincial, wholly local"[1]—localized in space and time. Tied up with this aim was a desire to write truthfully, authentically.

The title page of the first and most influential book of South-western 'humor emphasized the fact that it contained "*Georgia Scenes, Characters, Incidents, &c. in the First Half Century of the Republic,*" emphasized the fact, too, that these scenes were authentic, since they were "By a *Native* Georgian."[2] In his preface, the author, A. B. Longstreet, indicated that he was eager to present to his countrymen a vivid account of an interesting phase of history: in his book, he spoke of "Georgia language"[3] and "Georgia humor."[4] As he talked about the book, the author stressed his desire to write authentically about a particular place at a particular time:

> The design of the "Georgia Scenes" has been wholly misapprehended by the public. It has been invariably received as a mere collection of fancy sketches, with no higher object than . . . entertainment . . . whereas the aim of the author was to supply a chasm in history which has always been overlooked—the manners, customs, amusements, wit, dialect, as they appear in all grades of society to an ear and eye witness to them. But who ever tells us the comments of the wits and the ways of the common walks of life, in their own dialect, upon the victors and the vanquished in the public games? Could we hear them, we would find a rich fund of amusement in their remarks upon the dresses of their characters, the horses, their mode of driving, and their blunders; upon the pugilistic combatants, their appearance, their muscle, their remarks, and gruntings and groanings . . .; their own private games, quarrels, and fights, and the manner in which they were conducted . . . I have chosen the first fifty years of our republic . . . To be sure . . . I have not confined myself to strictly veracious historic detail; but there is scarcely one word from the beginning to the end of the book which is not strictly *Georgian* . . . "The Gander Pulling" actually occurred at the very place where I locate it. The names of the persons who figure in it are such as were well known in Richmond County at that time, and the language which I put in the mouths of my actors was just such as was common at

---

[1] *Op. cit.,* p. xvi.
[2] Printed in Augusta in 1835, in New York in 1840 and thereafter.
[3] 1840 edition, p. 72.   [4] *Ibid.,* p. 200.

such exhibitions. . . . Again, take "The Wax Works." The exhibition actually came off in Waynesboro, Burke County, Ga. Every character introduced actually existed . . . performing precisely the part ascribed to him . . . "The Fight" . . . is a description of a combat which was not uncommon in almost every county in Georgia, at almost every one of which there was a Ransy Sniffle, a little more ludicrous in form and figure, and made rather more conspicuous in this fight than the real Ransys were. In person, however, he answered very well to many of the poorer class whom all Georgians have seen in the sterile pine woods of that State. These may serve as examples of how far the sketches were actually true and how far fanciful.[1]

The preface similarly asserted that the sketches "consist of nothing more than fanciful *combinations* of *real* incidents and characters; and throwing into those scenes . . . some personal incident or adventure of my own, real or imaginary, as it would best suit my purpose; usually *real* but happening at different times and under different circumstances from those in which they are here represented."[2] "I have not always," he continued, "taken this liberty. Some of the scenes are as literal as the frailties of memory would allow them to be." Longstreet asserted to his friends that he hoped that through his writings "we may be seen and heard by our posterity two hundred years hence just as we are."[3]

William Tappan Thompson, a disciple of Longstreet,[4] shared his attitude toward writing and attempted similarly to display the Georgia Crackers as "a genus of bipedulus animals *sui generis* . . ."[5] His first book, *Major Jones's Courtship* (1844) was an attempt, he said in his preface, "to depict some of the peculiar features of the Georgia backwoodsman." His second book, *Major Jones's Chron-*

---

[1] Quoted in Bishop O. P. Fitzgerald, *Judge Longstreet. A Life Sketch* (Nashville, 1891), pp. 164–166. The italics are Longstreet's.

[2] The italics are Longstreet's.

[3] Review by William T. Thompson, *Southern Literary Messenger*, VI, 573 (July, 1840). See also the review in *The New-Yorker*, IX, 157 (May 23, 1840). At one point in his book (p. 47), Longstreet voiced regret that fidelity to history forced him to record profanity.

[4] Associated with Longstreet as a newspaper editor, he admired his predecessor heartily, and was flattered when a book of his was attributed to the author of *Georgia Scenes*—Wade, *op. cit.*, pp. 165–166.

[5] The phrase is used by "Uncle Solon" in "Sketches of Piney Woods Character," *Spirit of the Times*, XXI, 79 (April, 1851). The writer links Longstreet's and Thompson's books as accurate portrayals of Georgians.

icles of Pineville (1845) contained, the Preface asserted, "other stories illustrative of similar character . . . [designed] to present a few more interesting specimens of the genus Cracker." The Cracker, he continues, has "strongly marked" lineaments, easy for even a beginner to catch. The author has tried "to catch his 'manners living as they rise' . . . to afford the student of human nature a glance at characters not often found in books, or anywhere else, indeed, except in just such places as '*Pineville*,' Georgia."

Though Longstreet and Thompson indicated more clearly than others their literary theories, obviously humorists who followed them had in mind the same localized and realistic portrayal. Wrote T. B. Thorpe of a book whose very title indicated concern with locality: "An effort has been made, in the course of these sketches, to give those personally acquainted with the scenery of the Southwest, some idea of the country, of its surface, and vegetation."[1] The purpose of Baldwin's *Flush Times in Alabama and Mississippi* was largely "to illustrate the periods, the characters, and the phases of society, some notion of which is attempted to be given in this volume."[2] John S. Robb stresses the value of the originality of the Western life he portrays to the humorist:

The west abounds with incident and humor . . . . It would indeed seem that the nearer sundown, the more original the character and odd the expression, as if the sun, with his departing beams, had shed a new feature upon the back-woods inhabitants. This oddity and originality has often attracted my attention and contributed to my amusement . . .[3]

The preface to the most famous collection of humorous tales from the Southwest stressed the fact that the book "furnished most valuable and interesting reminiscences of the pioneers of the far West—sketches of thrilling scenes and adventures in that then comparatively unknown region, and the extraordinary characters occasionally met with—their strange language and habi-

---

[1] *The Mysteries of the Backwoods; or Sketches of the Southwest including Characters, Scenery and Rural Sports* (Philadelphia, 1846), p. 8. "Mysteries" here apparently refers to occupations. Reviewers mentioned the historical value of Thorpe's writings frequently.

[2] Published in New York, 1853, p. v.

[3] *Streaks of Squatter Life and Far Western Scenes. A Series of Humorous Sketches Descriptive of Incident and Character in the Wild West* (Philadelphia, 1846), p. viii. He mentions Thorpe, Hooper, Field, and Sol Smith as predecessors.

tudes . . ." and the subtitle of the book called attention to the
fact that the sketches were "Illustrative of Characters and Incidents in the Southwest."[1] The very titles of the stories had local
flavoring—"Jones' Fight, a Story of Kentucky by an Alabamian,"
"That Big Dog Fight at Myers's, a Story of Mississippi by a Missis-
sippian," and so on. And the popularity of this volume led to the
compilation of a similar volume "Illustrative of Scenes, Characters, and Incidents, throughout 'the Universal Yankee Nation.' "[2]
Henry Watterson, learned in the lore of the South and its humor,
speaks of the "local tone" of these writings, pointing out that
scenes portrayed by Thompson "might possibly be laid in Tennessee or Alabama, but not in Virginia or Mississippi" and that
"Sut Lovingood belongs to a class which is but little known in
the South. The gulf between him and Simon Suggs," he continues,
"is impassable. He is no relation to Major Jones, or even to Ransy
Sniffle [portrayed by Longstreet]."[3]

These local colorists, in their attempt to satisfy what a discerning editor called "the eager curiosity to know more of the
distinguishing traits of character of the denizens of . . . the West
and Southwest,"[4] typically amassed many details concerning the
life about them. As Bernard De Voto points out, as a part of his
excellent study of their writings,

No aspect of the life in the simpler America is missing from this
literature. The indigo tub and the bearskin rug are here, as well
as the frontier gentry's efforts to speak French. In the solitude of
the upper rivers, trappers practice their ferocity . . . in the solitude
of hither-Illinois, Ole Bull meditates on his art. Jackson, Van
Buren, Harrison, Benton, Taylor, Tyler, Douglas, and such worthies entertain the electorate; so do such humbler worthies as Big
Bear of Arkansas, Kit Kuncker, Dick McCoy, Billy Warrick, and
Cousin Sally Dilliard. The panorama of religion passes: camp
meetings, christenings, Millerism, Mormonism, spiritualism. So
does the comedy of the land—claim jumpers, false locators, Regu-
lators, auctions, surveyors, roof-raisings, husking bees—and of the
law courts, the bench and bar, sheriffs, muster days, legislatures,

[1] *The Big Bear of Arkansas* . . . (New York, 1843).
[2] *A Quarter Race in Kentucky* . . . (New York, 1846).
[3] *Oddities in Southern Life and Character* (Boston, 1882), pp. viii, 134, 415.
[4] Preface to *The Big Bear of Arkansas*, p. xi.

election campaigns. The folk boil over in Texas and the literature swarms with dragoons and infantry, recruits, West Pointers, and Rangers. Itinerants pass by, those strange travellers from abroad, peddlers, actors, singers, mesmerists, prophets, temperance agitators, physicians, census takers, circus clowns, bear leaders, accordionists. The folk labor at their vocations in the fields and the woods, the doggeries, the still-houses, the swamps, the bayous; at the spinning wheel, the loom, the churn. They frolic always, and if Betsy Smith, the fair offender, isn't married to John Bunce, why, jedge, "we oughter been, long ago." . . . Cataloguing is futile. Here is the complete life of the frontier.[1]

Alike in making their writings local, authentic, and detailed, these humorists were also alike in imparting to their stories a zest, a gusto, a sheer exuberance. In part, of course, the materials handled by them made for racy narration: one could not write of the staccato gambolings of frontiersmen in a tranquil style. A writer in a periodical of 1851, though he caricatured the liveliness of the frontier, caught something of its galloping tempo when he said:

"Out West" is certainly a great country . . . there is one little town in "them diggins" which . . . is "all sorts of a stirring place." In one day, they recently had two street fights, hung a man, rode three men out of town on a rail, got up a quarter race, a turkey shooting, a gander pulling, a match dog fight, had preaching by a circus rider, who afterwards ran a footrace for apple jack all round, and, as if this was not enough, the judge of the court, after losing his year's salary at single-handed poker, and licking a person who said he didn't understand the game, went out and helped to lynch his grandfather for hog stealing.[2]

[1] *Mark Twain's America* (Boston, 1932), p. 98. *Georgia Scenes*, most influential of the humorous books of the section, typically dealt with country and ballroom dancing, horse swapping, racing, fox-hunting, the militia drill, the shooting-match, the fight, the gander-pull, the debating society meeting, and the gossipy matrons of Georgia.

[2] *Spirit of the Times*, XXI, 205 (June 28, 1851). Compare Baldwin's note on conditions in *Flush Times of Alabama and Mississippi* (New York, 1853), pp. 84–85: "The pursuits of industry neglected, riot and debauchery filled up the vacant hours . . . . Even the little boys caught the taint of the general infection of morals; and I knew one of them . . . to give a man ten dollars to hold him up to bet at the table of a faro-bank . . . . The groceries—*vulgice*—doggeries, were in full blast in those days, no village having less than a half-dozen all busy all the time: gaming and horse-racing were polite and well patronized amusements. I knew of a Judge to adjourn two courts (or court twice) to attend a horse-race, at which he officiated judicially and ministerially, and with more appropriateness than in the judicial chair. Occasionally the scene was diversified by a murder or two . . ."

This sprightly passage manages to indicate why a picture of folk "out West" never could be as idyllic as a picture of the folk in "Down East" Downingville or Jalaam.

But more important as a cause for gusto perhaps was the manner of the origination of much of this humor. Definitely, much of this literature had its origin in the greatest American folk art—the art of oral story-telling. The fact is worthy of attention because the oral tale had an important influence upon the matter of most Western tales and upon the manner of many of them.

An Englishman in 1889 perceived more clearly than many Americans the importance of oral story-telling. "All over the land [in America]," said Andrew Lang, "men are eternally 'swopping stories' at bars, and in the long endless journeys by railway and steamer. How little, comparatively, the English 'swop stories'! . . . The stories thus collected in America are the subsoil of American literary humour, a rich soil in which the plant . . . grows with vigour and puts forth fruit and flowers."[1]

The art of oral narrative noted by the British critic, not unknown in New England, where it influenced the almanacs of Robert B. Thomas[2] and some of the periodical literature,[3] and not foreign to other sections of the United States[4] or even to Canada,[5] flourished particularly in the West and the Southwest. Evidence of this fact is missing from many travel books, presumably because many of the genteel folk who visited America did not consort with the tellers of tales; but visitors who kept their ears open and many an American left records of the widespread art. As Lang suggests, the telling of yarns was particularly well adapted to travelers by stagecoach or boat. James Hall and his party, floating down the Ohio on a flatboat in the twenties, were

[1] "Western Drolls" in *Lost Leaders* (London, 1889), pp. 186–187. See also De Voto, *op. cit.*, pp. 92–94.

[2] Neighbor Freeport in the sketch reproduced hereafter (pp. 199–200) was famed as a story-teller. The tall tales from the almanac, reproduced pp. 199, 201–202 are probably recorded oral tales.

[3] See, for example, "Big Connecticut Pumpkins," *Spirit of the Times*, XXI, 350 (September 13, 1851).

[4] See footnote 1, p. 27, which cites tales told in various sections.

[5] Haliburton was the only notable humorist to win fame as a portrayer of a famous Yankee comic figure who drew much upon oral story-telling. See V. L. O. Chittick, *Thomas Chandler Haliburton*, pp. 182–183. In *The Attaché*, II, 18, Sam Slick tells of collecting material in fireside conversations.

delighted, he records, by a visit from a weatherbeaten old keel-boatman called "Pappy," whose "affected gravity, drawling accent, and kind, benevolent manner . . . marked him as . . . a humorist." Pappy entertained the travelers by telling "merry and marvelous tales."[1] James P. Beckwourth, drifting down the Missouri, about 1824, with a group of soldiers, "had a jovial time of it, telling stories, cracking jokes, and frequently making free with Uncle Sam's 'O be joyful' . . . The soldiers listened with astonishment to the wild adventures of the mountaineers, and would, in turn, engage our attention with recitals of their own experience."[2] A British captain on an Ohio river steamboat in the thirties heard, so he said, fine stories of "high life in Kentucky" and an oral account of a yarn Longstreet had told in *Georgia Scenes*.[3] Tall tales, exuberant combinations of fact with outrageous fiction which came to be thought of as typical of much oral narrative in the West, whiled away the time of a group with which J. S. Buckingham rode in a stagecoach between Wheeling and Zanesville in the forties. His companions, he said, exercised their wit "in the exaggerated strain so characteristic of Western manners":

The unhealthy condition of some of the Western rivers, the Illinois in particular, was the subject of their discourse; when one asserted, that he had known a man to be so dreadfully affected with the ague, from sleeping in the fall on its banks, that he shook . . . all the teeth out of his head. This was matched by another, who said there was a man from his State, who had gone to Illinois to settle, and the ague seized him so terribly hard, that he shook off all his clothes . . . and could not keep a garment whole, for it unravelled the very web, thread by thread, till it was all destroyed! The climax was capped, however, by the declaration of a third, that a friend of his who had settled on the banks of the Illinois, and built a most comfortable dwelling . . . was seized with an ague, which grew worse and worse, until its fits . . . at length shook the whole house about his ears, and buried him in its ruins! Such is the kind of wit in which the Western people

---

[1] *Letters from the West* (London, 1828), pp. 181–182.

[2] T. D. Bonner, *The Life of James P. Beckwourth*, ed. Bernard De Voto (New York, 1930), p. 55.

[3] *Echoes from the Backwoods* (London, 1849), pp. 28–30. The Longstreet story was "Georgia Theatrics," but the author did not indicate any acquaintance with the written version.

especially delight, and which the Southern and Western newspapers feed and encourage, by racking their invention for the supply of new extravaganzas.[1]

But travelers by boat and stagecoach were not the only tellers of tales. William Tappan Thompson, down in Florida to campaign against the Seminoles in 1836, assembled around the campfire with other soldiers after tattoo, to listen to comic yarns.[2] George Wilkins Kendall, a contributor to Southwestern humorous literature, told of tales related by campfires on an expedition to Santa Fé—"long yarns about border forays, buffalo hunts, and brushes with Indians on the prairies" in the course of one of which an old-timer innocently asserted that, on one occasion, he saw "between two and three million" buffaloes. In Texas, Kendall heard widely told tall tales about a mythical White Steed of the Prairies.[3] This was in 1841. Four years later, when Hall visited Texas, stories about the same handsome steed were still going the rounds.[4] In country stores in Illinois,[5] in the gunsmith's shop or Larkin Snow's mill in Fisher's River in North Carolina,[6] in a log hotel in Kansas territory,[7] by a bear hunters' campfire in Tennessee,[8] the story-teller told his yarns.

History has fortunately informed most of us of at least one great story-teller of the frontier, Abraham Lincoln. The coonskin tales which he collected came to him everywhere he went, it seems, until he left Springfield—at Anderson Creek ferry, in the log store at New Salem, on a raft drifting down the great river, and in taverns at night when he foregathered with other lawyers

[1] J. S. Buckingham, *The Eastern and Western States of America* (London, [n. d.]), pp. 271–273.   [2] *John's Alive* (Philadelphia, 1883), p. 176.

[3] *Narrative of the Texan Santa Fé Expedition*, ed. Milo M. Quaife (Chicago, 1929), pp. 87, 91–93, 108–110. The book was first published in 1844.

[4] *The Wilderness and Warpath* (New York, 1846), pp. 160–170.

[5] Charles B. Johnson, *Illinois in the Fifties* (Champaign, 1918), pp. 58–61.

[6] [H. E. Taliaferro], *Fisher's River (North Carolina) Scenes and Characters* (New York, 1859), pp. 51, 58. Uncle Davy, the gunsmith, "had a great fund of long-winded stories and incidents, mostly manufactured by himself—some few he had 'hearn'—and would bore you or edify you, as it might turn out, from sun to sun, interspersing them with a dull, gutteral, lazy laugh. He became quite a proverb in the line of big story-telling. True, he had many obstinate competitors, but he distanced them all . . . Uncle Davy's mind was trained in a sort of horse-mill track, and would pass from one story to another with great naturalness and ease."

[7] G. Douglas Brewerton, *The War in Kansas* (New York, 1855), p. 240.

[8] Joseph S. Williams, *Old Times in West Tennessee* (Memphis, 1873), p. 115.

in swings around the circuit. The lawyers, in particular, cherished good stories in which the vernacular figured prominently. Wrote Philip Paxton, in 1853:

The origin and perpetuity of many of our queer and out-of-the-way phrases, may be traced to the semi-annual meetings of the gentlemen of the bar at the courts of our Southern and Western States.

These gentlemen, living as they do in the thinly inhabited portion of our land, and among a class of persons generally very far their inferiors in point of education, rarely enjoying anything that may deserve the name of intellectual society, are apt to seek for amusement in listening to the droll stories and odd things always to be heard at the country store or bar-room. Every new expression and queer tale is treasured up, and new ones manufactured against the happy time when they shall meet their *brothers-in-law* at the approaching term of the district court.

If ever pure fun, broad humor, and "Laughter holding both his sides," reign supreme, it is during the evening of these sessions. Each one empties and distributes his well filled budget of wit and oddities, receiving ample payment in like coin, which he pouches, to again disseminate at his earliest opportunity.[1]

Of the ten Southwestern humorists listed above, four—Longstreet, Hooper, Smith, and Baldwin—were all, at one time or another, lawyers. Longstreet was one of a jolly group of tellers of tales on the circuit which included Oliver H. Prince, author of the laughable "Militia Drill";[2] A. S. Clayton, believed by some to have had a hand in Davy Crockett's racy writings;[3] the humorous Judge Dooley, and others. Many years later, a contemporary wistfully recalled hilarious evenings in an old tavern where "assembled at night the rollicking boys of the Georgia bar . . . Humor and wit, in anecdotage and repartee, beguiled the hours."[4]

---

[1] *A Stray Yankee in Texas* (New York, 1853), pp. 113–114. For an excellent characterization of circuit story-telling in Georgia, see R. M. Johnston, "Middle Georgia in Rural Life," *Century*, XLIII, 739–740 (March, 1892).

[2] See footnote 1, p. 26.

[3] John D. Wade, "Authorship of Davy Crockett's Autobiography," *Georgia Historical Quarterly*, VI, 265–268 (September, 1922). See also Constance Rourke, "Davy Crockett: Forgotten Facts and Legends," *Southwest Review*, XIX, 149–161 (January, 1934).

[4] W. H. Sparks, *The Memories of Fifty Years*. Third edition. (Philadelphia and Macon, 1872), p. 483. See also Edward Mapes, *Lucius Q. C. Lamar*, p. 39, quoted by Tandy, *op. cit.*, p. 75.

Presumably other lawyer-humorists, like Longstreet, heard scores of yarns at night-time gatherings of the bench and bar. Certainly Ovid Bolus and Cave Burton, described by Baldwin, were typical tellers of tales. Certainly Johnson J. Hooper averred that he secured at least one of his stories, "Shifting the Responsibility," while "attending court in the adjoining county of Randolph" from "a friend who is fond of jokes of all sorts, and who relates them almost as humorously as 'His Honour . . .'"[1] and at least four of his yarns bear the earmarks of circuit origin.[2]

But neither Hooper nor the others of the period needed to go to gatherings of lawyers to hear amusing tales. On a hunting trip, Hooper listened to a series of anecdotes told by the guide, and when they stopped overnight, their host entertained them with a tall tale. A visit with old Kit Kuncker yielded another yarn.[3] Joseph M. Field testified that one of his tales—his best, in fact—was a patchwork of oral narratives about a frontier hero which he had heard in barrooms or by firesides in five cities over a period of fifteen years.[4] T. B. Thorpe's description of a tale-telling session aboard a Mississippi steamboat is vivid enough to convince one that he was no stranger to the art of the oral story-teller.[5] It seems reasonably probable that all the humorists of the old Southwest could, if they chose, learn something about narrative materials and method from oral story-tellers.

What they learned about materials to some extent limited and to some extent enlarged the subject matter with which the humorists dealt. Since fireside story-telling in the Southwest, as elsewhere, was largely a rugged masculine pastime, no subtle psychological depictions were likely to develop as a result of its influence. Certain important elements of life were likely to be neglected: there was no equivalent here for Mrs. Partington or Widow Bedott. Longstreet and Thompson were the only two outstanding humorists who concerned themselves much with the tenderer do-

---

[1] Printed in *Polly Peablossom's Wedding*, ed. T. A. Burke, and recently reprinted in *Tall Tales of the Southwest*, pp. 299–301.

[2] "The Bailiff that 'Stuck to His Oath,'" "Jim Bell's Revenge," "Mrs. Johnson's Post Office Case," and "The Fair Offender," in *The Widow Rugby's Husband* (Philadelphia, 1851), pp. 64–86.   [3] These will be cited later, p. 86.

[4] "Mike Fink, the Last of the Boatmen," St. Louis *Reveille*, June 14 and June 21, 1847, unfortunately too long for publication in this volume.

[5] "The Big Bear of Arkansas," reprinted hereafter.

mestic scenes. And despite Longstreet's exceptional desire to portray "all grades of society,"[1] he and others who were concerned with subject matter like that of the oral tale were more concerned with the lower social groups than the higher ones. Masculine pastimes, such as hunting, fishing, gambling, drinking, and fighting, and the trades of the doctor, the editor, the lawyer, the politician, the actor, the boatman, and the soldier received attention to the neglect of some other phases of life. Too, a large amount of the humor, as C. Alphonso Smith suggests,[2] derived from physical discomfort, which often, apparently, was more hilariously amusing than it is today.

But despite these limitations suggested by oral art, the vistas of adventure and character opened by tale-spinners were wide enough to give the Southwestern literature richness. As Mr. De Voto's catalogue indicates, interesting materials were not lacking. The hairbreadth adventures, the feverish competition of sports and commercial enterprise, the heterogeneous minglings of characters in the new country gave the humor, as George E. Woodberry noted, a picturesque quality: "It was as if all the world had gone on a picaresque journey by general consent in various quarters, and at the chance roundup for nightly rest and refreshment fell to telling what, and especially whom, they had met with."[3] Tales which told what happened in the bustling section, sometimes factually, sometimes in a hilariously exaggerated fashion, and character sketches of the highly varied figures who lived in the settled districts or on the frontier or who moved restlessly from place to place had plenty of variety.

It is more difficult to generalize about the effect of the oral tale upon the manner of these humorists. The chief general effect has been indicated—a zestful exuberance entered into the narratives. Stories he heard told in the Western country, John Neal noted, had "a decided character"—"*live* stories I should call them," he said. They were "brimful of energy and vivacity . . ."[4]

---

[1] Fitzgerald, *op. cit.*, p. 164. Longstreet did treat the upper classes more than most of his contemporaries.

[2] "Johnson Jones Hooper," *Library of Southern Literature* (New Orleans, 1909), VI, 2490.   [3] *America in Literature* (New York, 1903), p. 159.

[4] "Story-Telling," *New York Mirror*, XVI, 321 (April 6, 1839). "Of all the stories I meet with," testified Neal, "none are so delightful to me as those I *over*-hear on board a steamboat or a stage-coach." He cited several thus overheard.

But some of the humorists, naturally, were more affected by the oral art than others.

It was to be expected that Longstreet, the first of the group, despite his appreciation of "the comments of the wits . . . in their own dialect, upon the victors and the vanquished in the public games," would be influenced particularly by the methods of earlier narrators. Quite correctly, his latest biographer points out that Addisonian echoes were quite frequent in *Georgia Scenes*.[1] In the *Spectator* tradition, though rather more heavily, he moralizes about the vices he portrays. Fighting, baby talk, drunkenness, modern dancing, duelling, horse racing, and the undomestic wife are reprimanded severely.[2] Several of his sketches later appeared in a book labeled, not inappropriately, *Stories With a Moral*. Humor, he asserted, should improve the reader by correcting his errors or leading him to reflect upon them; he saw ridicule as a weapon against vice.[3] More important than this attitude was the essay-like quality of much of the material. "The Dance," "The Song," "The Charming Creature as a Wife," "The Mother and Her Child," and "The Ball" are Americanized *Spectator* papers. In the last of these, such characters as Misses Mushy, Feedle and Deedle and Messrs. Boozle and Noozle play parts in a fable which proves the folly of duelling.

The style often echoes eighteenth-century writings. "Some passages," Poe remarked, "in a certain species of sly humor, wherein intense observation of character is disguised by simplicity of relation, put us forcibly in mind of the Spectator."[4] In at least half of the volume, the language has the cadences, the rhetorical quality, at best the elegance, of the older essays. The character, "designated," Longstreet says ponderously, "by the appellation of Ned Brace," is introduced in lines reminiscent of the older style:

This man seemed to live only to amuse himself with his fellow-beings, and he possessed the rare faculty of deriving some gratification of his favorite propensity from almost every person whom he met, no matter what his temperament, standing, or disposition.

[1] Wade, *Augustus Baldwin Longstreet*, pp. 157–160.
[2] Percy H. Boynton, *Literature and American Life* (Boston, 1936), pp. 437–438.
[3] *Master William Mitten* (Macon, 1864), p. 185.
[4] *Southern Literary Messenger*, II, 289 (March, 1836).

Of course he had opportunities enough of exercising his uncommon gift, and he rarely suffered an opportunity to pass unimproved. The beau in the presence of his mistress, the fop, the pedant, the purse-proud, the over-fastidious and sensitive, were Ned's favorite game. These never passed him uninjured, and against such he directed his severest shafts. With these he commonly amused himself, by exciting in them every variety of emotion, under circumstances peculiarly ridiculous.

And so on. Ned Brace, thus characterized, is a contemporary of Pindar Cockloft, an Addisonian humorist, a link between the humor of the eighteenth and the nineteenth centuries[1]—and the manner is unmistakably reminiscent. Thompson, reviewing the book, noted, "As to the *style*, except where the author quotes the language of his characters, it is *throughout* remarkably pure, flowing and beautiful";[2] and he cited several passages of a similar sort. Longstreet's liking, doubtless, was for the essay.

To modern taste, these passages are the least admirable in the book; and one regrets their frequency—not because they are bad but because Longstreet's predecessors did such things better. We are much more amused by the talk of the characters, especially when, as is often the case, it is valuable in humorous characterization. The adolescent bellicosity of the hero of "Georgia Theatrics," Hiram Baugh's elaborate alibi for his poor shot and Billy Curlew's acute and sly humor in "The Shooting-Match" (though the latter is sometimes too derivative from commonplace oral tale formulae); the learned talk of yerbs and curses by the old women in "A Sage Conversation"; the boastful bargaining of the Yellow Blossom from Jasper in "The Horse-Swap"—perfect for portraiture—are in Longstreet's best vein. So, too, are his vivid descriptions of some of the characters—Ransy Sniffle, for example, and the animals in his tales. "Of geese and ganders," Poe observed, "he is the La Bruyère, and of good-for-nothing horses, the Rochefoucault."[3] And at its best, with the sometimes lengthy rhetorical introduction out of the way, Longstreet's narration moves along

---

[1] The ability of a cultured, well-balanced gentleman to perceive eccentricity, carefully cultivated by many of the humorists of the South, was important particularly in the earlier humorous writings.

[2] *Southern Literary Messenger*, VI, 572 (July, 1840).

[3] *Southern Literary Messenger*, II, 287 (March, 1836).

swiftly, in the manner of a well-told anecdote which leads up to an explosive conclusion.

Of course, various fictional creations of the time made use of some of these same devices, and Longstreet was not unacquainted with the literature of his day. As Poe pointed out, one scene in Longstreet's book is quite reminiscent of a scene by Miss Edgeworth.[1] But Longstreet had learned the art of the oral tale. An "inimitable story-teller," a contemporary recalled, at circuit tale-swapping sessions he was "usually the center of a listening, laughing, admiring crowd. His tone, gesture, and play of feature gave his narratives a peculiar zest and charm."[2] Stories incorporated in *Georgia Scenes* he told with "indescribably amusing mimicry."[3] And since mimicry of speech (particularly for purposes of characterization), humorous depictions of men and beasts, and the development of a story with a point are important in the art of oral story-telling, it seems fairly reasonable to suggest that what was best in *Georgia Scenes* was at least in part derived from the method of the oral tale.

Even more than Longstreet, Baldwin, in his writing, is influenced by the older essay style; four-fifths of his book takes that form. In *The Flush Times in Alabama and Mississippi*, the lawless life of the new country, the strange ways of its inhabitants, are presented in a generalized style. Primarily an essayist, outside of reports of court room speeches, Baldwin makes little use of direct discourse. At times, this is a handicap, as when, in an essay about a liar, the author lyricizes about the liar's artistry amusingly but fails to do the thing most needful—give us a specimen, in the man's own words, of the lie told "from the delight of invention and the charm of fictitious narrative."[4] Or consider another sketch entirely concerned with a story-teller, "Cave Burton, Esq., of Kentucky." In a generalized passage, Baldwin dilates upon the way Cave tells yarns. But when the time comes for Cave to tell one of his interminable narratives, Baldwin says, "We can only

---

[1] *Southern Literary Messenger*, II, 289. "The Turn Out" reminded him of Miss Edgeworth's "Barring Out."

[2] R. H. Rivers, quoted by Fitzgerald, *op. cit.*, pp. 169–170.

[3] John B. Gordon, *Reminiscences of the Civil War* (New York, 1905), p. 93.

[4] "Ovid Bolus, Esq.," *The Flush Times in Alabama and Mississippi* (New York, 1853), pp. 1–19.

give it *our* way, and only such parts as we can remember, leaving out most of the episodes, the casual explanations and the slang; which is almost the play of Hamlet with the Prince of Denmark omitted."[1] Of course it is. And too often, Baldwin, omitting specific detail of this sort, falls short of heights he might have achieved.

This, of course, does not entirely condemn him, since he has other abilities. Despite the fact that he writes in a style at times too leisurely, too polished, for an account of the brisk frontier and its rough inhabitants, he is a diverting essayist. Observant, he laughingly perceives the comic topsy-turvy quality of law in a relatively lawless country. He enjoys himself hugely as he writes the record of the strange assortment of men, ranging from rascals to statesmen, who inhabit Alabama and Mississippi. There are at least touches of admirable characterization. And he accomplishes his purpose as he himself announces it: he does record— as a highly readable contemporary historian—the chief aspects of those two states during the flush times.[2]

The oral anecdote affects his writings but little. Some of the details of Ovid Bolus's yarns, though they are presented in indirect discourse, have the flavor of frontier oral humor. And some of the practical jokes Baldwin tells about have plots of the sort which pleased fireside audiences—tales of how a young lawyer was befooled by an old lawyer, how a horse thief persuaded a drunken sheriff to allow him to escape, how a lover of oysters was kept talking until his friends in an adjacent room had eaten three barrels of the bivalves, how a slick lawyer outwitted a tricky publisher. And now and then, a paragraph in the midst of a lengthy exposition takes the form of a pointed anecdote: there are three such in "Ovid Bolus, Esq."

To some extent, then, oral literature molded the work of Longstreet and Baldwin. Other humorists of the period and of the section, however, were influenced in a much more tangible fashion either by the fireside yarn or by writings which had been

---

[1] *The Flush Times in Alabama and Mississippi*, p. 162.

[2] Miss Tandy, *op. cit.*, p. 83, concludes her illuminating criticism of Baldwin with an excellent summary: "Baldwin is the amateur story teller, the professional lawyer and historian. His talent and wit are carelessly displayed. Nevertheless his pictures of the era of inflation are faithful and valuable."

flavored and fashioned by it. Even while Longstreet's sketches were appearing in newspapers, writings very directly affected by oral humor were beginning to find their way into print—stories in varied publications about comic legendary heroes of the frontier, and stories about Southwestern happenings by yarn spinners who simply put campfire talk in ink for newspapers or for the periodical which was the most important influence of the day in American humor.

"The narratives of the frontier circle, as they draw around their evening fire," said Flint, "often turn upon the exploits of the old race of men, the heroes of the past days, who wore hunting shirts, and settled the country."[1] Of such men,[2] predecessors of Paul Bunyan,[3] anecdotes translated from fireside talk into printed form began to appear in newspapers in the late twenties. Davy Crockett (1786–1836), for example, shrewd politician, great hunter, fighter, drinker, and tall talker, had been the source of many tales, some printed, some orally circulated, after 1828, when he entered Congress. An idea of the way oral tales clustered about him is given by an English captain who, traveling through Kentucky, heard many a story of the comically godlike hero of the canebrakes:

Every thing here [he said] is Davy Crockett. He was a member of Congress. His voice was so loud it could not be described—it was obliged to be drawn as a picture. He took hailstones for "Life Pills" when he was unwell—he picked his teeth with a pitchfork . . . fanned himself with a hurricane . . . He had a farm, which was so rocky, that, when they planted the corn, they were obliged to shoot the grains into the crevices with muskets . . . He could . . . drink the Mississippi dry—shoot six cord of bear in one day . . .[4]

[1] *Recollections of the Last Ten Years* (Boston, 1836), p. 161.

[2] Captain Sam Brady, Pennsylvania Regulator; the Wetzel family, Indian exterminators in West Virginia; Kit Carson of Texas, mountain man; Jim Bridger of Utah, trapper and guide; Wild Bill Hickok of the cattle frontier were examples.

[3] Paul Bunyan, giant lumberman about whom some of the finest tall tales of all were told, is not represented in this volume simply because none of the yarns about him were printed until this present century. The best collection is Esther Shephard, *Paul Bunyan* (Seattle, 1924).

[4] R. G. A. Levinge, *Echoes from the Backwoods; or, Scenes in Transatlantic Life* (London, 1849), II, 12. This is only a portion of Levinge's report. He quotes two stanzas of a ballad in which Crockett's boast is set forth in rhyme.

Passages like this, wherein the humor of Western "tall talk," of exaggeration, reached fantastic heights, appeared in a long series of popular "Crockett" almanacs (1835–1856) which were widely circulated.[1] And tales closer to fact, told by Crockett himself or by others who assumed the role of Crockett, printed in a series of books,[2] had a wide sale.[3] These books, at their best, told in the toothsome vernacular of the people and the happenings of the frontier: in the second volume of the series, a Western critic pointed out in 1834, "the events are such . . . as we have seen acted over and over, and heard repeatedly recited by the firesides of our hardy backwoodsmen."[4]

Into the magazines, newspapers, and books, too, beginning in 1828 and on down to the end of the century, came transcriptions of oral tales about Mike Fink (1770?–1823?), whose picturesque and picaresque career carried him from Pittsburgh, where he was born, along with the shifting frontier until he died violently in Missouri. Mike, the king of the keelboatmen on the Mississippi and Ohio, talked tall, fought mightily, shot with uncanny skill, and manifested great affection for women, whisky, and adventure in a series of at least thirty yarns, republished widely, many of which pretty clearly derived from oral narratives.[5] The first two lengthy accounts of his career, published in Cincinnati in 1828 and 1829, were admittedly based on tales told respectively by a

---

[1] A fine bibliography of these is available in Constance Rourke, *Davy Crockett* (New York, 1934), pp. 251–258. The same volume (pp. 259–270) contains the best study of the tangled problem of the authorship of the *Sketches and Eccentricities* and the books attributed to Crockett which are listed in the next footnote.

[2] *Sketches and Eccentricities of Col. David Crockett* (New York, 1833), published in Cincinnati the same year as *The Life and Adventures of Colonel David Crockett of West Tennessee*, followed by *A Narrative of the Life of David Crockett, of the State of Tennessee* . . . (Philadelphia, 1834); *An Account of Col. Crockett's Tour to the North and Down East* . . . (Philadelphia, 1835); and *Col. Crockett's Exploits and Adventures in Texas* (Philadelphia, 1836). The best parts of the last three of these are available in *The Autobiography of David Crockett*, ed. Hamlin Garland (New York, 1923).

[3] The first went through at least twelve editions in the thirties, and the others were probably even more popular.

[4] *Western Monthly Magazine*, II, 278 (May, 1834). The reviewer, it is interesting to note, scouted the idea that Crockett was a humorist. "But the colonel," he said, "is 'barking up the wrong tree,' when he sets up for a man of humor. Whatever he may be in conversation . . . it is not that quality which will give him fame as a writer. The dullest parts of his book are those intended to produce a laugh . . ."

[5] See Walter Blair and Franklin J. Meine, *Mike Fink, King of Mississippi Keelboatmen* (New York, 1933), pp. 273–277, for a list of the stories. In print, many of the tales were definitely given the form of oral yarns.

steamboat pilot and a fur-trader;[1] one anecdote hinted at but not
recounted in the second of these bobbed up, with full details, in
an almanac published in 1839 in Nashville,[2] and another which
had merely been sketched was told, with many added details, in a
St. Louis newspaper in 1847.[3] And the story of Mike's death
escaped becoming fixed in print so well that when eleven versions
of it at length appeared, they differed concerning where he died,
why he died, and who killed him.[4]

Newspapers all over the country published humorous tales
about Crockett, Fink, or others celebrated in oral lore during the
thirties and forties, the New Orleans *Picayune* and *Delta* and the
St. Louis *Reveille* being particularly productive in the Southwest.
These were important in the development of oral humor in print.
But more important than any other publication was a weekly
paper appearing in New York—*The Spirit of the Times* (1831–
1861), edited by William T. Porter (1809–1858).

This unique periodical, a "Chronicle of the Turf, Agriculture,
Field Sports, Literature and the Stage," as its subtitle proclaimed,
had a racy masculine flavor. One who sought out its editor, if he
had poor luck at the editorial office, did well to move a few doors
away to Frank Monteverde's saloon, the unofficial editorial sanctum. In the cosy anteroom, there would be clustered around the
tall figure of Porter a crowd of jockeys, trainers, doctors, race-track
patrons, hunters in fustian jackets and corduroy pantaloons, artists,[5] authors,[6] dandies, actors—all "discussing the merits of the
drama, the turf, and the chase, interrupted only by the monotonous clang of domino pieces."[7] These men were a sampling of
the magazine's varied readers and its contributors. Scattered over
the face of the earth "from Hudson's Bay to the Caribbean Sea,

[1] "The Last of the Boatmen," *Western Souvenir* (Cincinnati, 1828), and "Mike
Fink, the Last of the Boatmen," *Western Monthly Review*, July, 1829, pp. 15–19.

[2] *Crockett Almanac for 1840* (Nashville, 1839) reveals how Mike shot at a target
held by his wife. The earlier narrator felt "compelled to omit the anecdote altogether."

[3] "Trimming a Darky's Heel," St. Louis *Reveille*, January 25, 1847.

[4] See Blair and Meine, *op. cit.*, pp. 176–239, for an examination of the various
versions of the story of his death.

[5] Such as Henry Inman, Robert Clark, Charles Elliot.

[6] Fitz-Greene Halleck, William Gaylord Clark, and any contributors to the *Spirit*
who happened to be in New York, such as T. B. Thorpe, Albert Pike, G. W. Kendall.

[7] Francis Brinley, *Life of William T. Porter* (New York, 1860), pp. 86–100, gives
a lengthy account of the *Spirit* crowd at Monteverde's.

from the shores of the Atlantic to the Pacific,"[1] subscribers included men of many backgrounds and many occupations—soldiers and sailors at every American post,[2] farmers, planters, lawyers, doctors, newspaper editors, and so forth. Reasonably common interests, apparently, were an affection for sports of all kinds—horse-races, cock-fights, hunting, and fishing, an enthusiasm about fine dogs, fine horses, and fine cattle, and a love for good comic stories.

From some of these readers came the "original contributions" to the *Spirit*, small in number during the early years of the publication, but increasing until, in 1846, Porter proudly announced: "Last week's 'Spirit of the Times' contained nearly SEVEN PAGES of ORIGINAL MATTER, from the pens of no less than *thirty-three correspondents!*"[3] These came from every section of the country, but particularly from the old Southwest. And they came from men of many sorts—army officers,[4] "country gentlemen, planters, lawyers, &c. 'who live at home at ease,' "[5] denizens of the frontier with "exteriors 'like the rugged Russian bear' . . . gifted with . . . good sense and knowledge of the world . . . fond of whiskey . . . characterized by . . . their fondness for story-telling."[6] Their stories, which "refer," said Porter, "to characters and scenes of recent date—to men who have not only succeeded 'Mike Fink, the Last of the Boatmen,' but 'Col. Nimrod Wildfire,' and originals of his stamp,"[7] had the qualities of Southwestern humor which have been suggested: they were local, authentic, detailed, zestful;[8] they

---

[1] Brinley, *op. cit.*, pp. 78–79. This is to be taken literally.

[2] In the issue of the *Spirit* for February 22, 1851 (XXI, 1), Porter said: "We are not aware of a single Military or Naval station of the United States, in any clime, where the 'Spirit of the Times' is not to be found."

[3] *Spirit of the Times*, XVI, 277 (August 15, 1846).

[4] In the issue of the *Spirit* for August 22, 1846 (XVI, 303), Porter stated with pride that fourteen correspondents had received army promotions "since the glorious achievements on the Rio Grande."   [5] *The Big Bear of Arkansas*, p. xii.

[6] *Ibid.*, p. ix.   [7] *Ibid.*, p. xii.

[8] Porter often commented on the way these stories "illustrated," as he said in the preface to *A Quarter Race in Kentucky*, "character and incident in the south and south-west." In the *Turf Register* for April, 1841, Porter asserted that American sporting literature was better than that of England, because there was an exhaustless fund of adventure. To this, to "incidents of travel over prairies and mountains hitherto unknown by the white man, the singular variety of manners in the different States, springing from differences of origin, in climate and product, peculiarities unhackneyed by a thousand tourists, to this is attributed the greater freshness and raciness of American sketches."

were distinctly masculine, and they dealt largely with the lower classes.[1]

Perhaps because, as a recent commentator suggested, "they had the wit to realize that something old in talking might look new in writing,"[2] or perhaps—as seems more probable—because they saw in the oral tale the only artistic form dealing to their satisfaction with the problems they had to solve, the contributors to the *Spirit* more clearly than any other group embodied in their writings the matter and the manner of the oral story. Now and then a subscriber would write gleefully about hearing a story from the lips of a contributor, sadly pointing out that the written version was inferior to the oral version.[3] Tales which showed changes characteristically associated with oral transmission appeared frequently. In 1841, a yarn which had appeared in a New England almanac at the beginning of the century was sent in, not from New England, but from Buffalo, where the correspondent's grandfather had told it, changed in many details.[4] A little later, a man in East Baton Rouge, trying to top the yarn of the Buffalo narrator, sent in his yarn about a similar incident, including details which had been in the New England version but not in the Buffalo version, and adding new details.[5] Thus the magazine became a medium for the swapping of tall tales—and this sort of thing happened frequently. Furthermore, time after time, an author would indicate where he had listened to the story he told—on a

[1] The quotation on the title page of *The Big Bear* collection, aptly selected by Porter, was Dogberry's "This is your charge; you shall comprehend all vagrom men."

[2] Arthur Palmer Hudson, "Introduction" to *Humor of the Old Deep South* (New York, 1936), pp. 16-17.

[3] See "Familiar Epistle from Mississippi," *Spirit of the Times*, XV, 63 (April 5, 1845): "Mr. P[orter]—Sam has been here for a few days past setting up with 'Jim and Bill,' and when he was fairly through last night we made him *tell* the story about 'That Big Dog Fight at Ned Myers's,' and then after two or three whiskey punches he was prevailed upon . . . to give the *true* account of the 'Tooth Pulling' as related by 'Uncle Johnny.' It is unfortunate for you that Sam lives such a long way off—he *tells* a story much better than he writes it—he gives the *action*, the pantomimic part of a good anecdote inimitably; without being a buffoon he is certainly one of the most delightful *raconteurs* in the state." Both of the stories mentioned were by P. B. January, "a country gentleman of Mississippi" and a highly admirable story-teller, according to the testimony of Porter. Both, too, were reprinted in *The Big Bear* collection. See also the reference to Harris as a story-teller, p. 96.

[4] The almanac story is reprinted in this book, p. 199. The Buffalo version appears in the *Spirit of the Times*, XI, 205 (July, 1841).

[5] *Ibid.*, XI, 288 (August 21, 1841).

steamboat on the Mississippi[1] or on the Ohio River,[2] on a boat on the Chattahoochee in Florida,[3] in an old log cabin in Louisiana wherein a party of hunters had taken shelter for the night,[4] by a Missouri hunter's campfire,[5] or by the fireside after a coon hunt in Texas.[6]

How large the circulation of Porter's periodical was during its best days in the middle forties it is impossible to say, but it was probably more than forty thousand, a huge subscription list for that time.[7] Not only did its stories reach many subscribers directly; in addition, they were widely reprinted: the Rutland (Vermont) *Herald* estimated that "the original communications of the 'Spirit' furnish matter for half the papers in the Union,"[8] and the Boston *Times* asserted that Porter, as editor of his periodical, had "done more to develop and foster the humorous genius of his countrymen than any man alive."[9]

That the oral humor of the Crockett tales, the Fink tales, the *Spirit of the Times*, and kindred publications affected the writings of many Southwestern humorists seems reasonably sure. Of the ten listed above, at least three—T. B. Thorpe, Joseph M. Field, and John S. Robb—told tales about Mike Fink, tales which were evidently based upon oral lore.[10] And all of the ten except Longstreet wrote material which appeared in Porter's magazine.[11]

[1] "Driving a Parson Ashore"—reprinted from the *Spirit*—in *Stray Subjects* (Philadelphia, 1848), p. 110.

[2] *Spirit of the Times*, XVI, 374 (October 3, 1846).

[3] *Ibid.*, XXI, 55 (March 22, 1851).   [5] *Ibid.*, XXI, 194 (June 14, 1851).

[4] *Ibid.*, XVI, 331 (September 5, 1846).   [6] *Ibid.*, XXI, 19 (March 1, 1851).

[7] Definite statistics are not available. However, in 1856, well past the peak of the magazine's popularity, when Porter allowed his name to be associated with another periodical, *Porter's Spirit of the Times*, by the time the new publication reached its eighth number, it was "backed by a circulation of 40,000 copies."—Brinley, *op. cit.*, p. 266.

[8] Quoted in the *Spirit of the Times*, XVI, 618 (February 20, 1847).

[9] *Ibid.*, XI, 540 (January 2, 1840).

[10] T. B. Thorpe, "The Disgraced Scalp-lock," *Spirit of the Times*, July 16, 1842, reprinted frequently; J. M. Field, "The Death of Mike Fink," St. Louis *Reveille*, October 21, 1844, and "Mike Fink, the Last of the Boatmen," *Reveille*, June 14, 21, 1847; John S. Robb, "Trimming a Darky's Heel," *Reveille*, January 25, 1847. Field's stories are based in part upon oral narratives of Charles Keemle, a former trapper, in part, says Field, upon many tales heard in many places. Robb's story is a version of a story merely hinted at as early as 1823.

[11] None of the stories written by Baldwin have been identified, although Porter testifies that he was a contributor. It would be interesting to discover how much Baldwin modified his style when he wrote for the racy pages of the *Spirit*.

Evidence of the influence of the oral tale upon the writings of these men is plentiful.

Consider Hooper's book, *Widow Rugby's Husband*,[1] for example. Almost every tale in it might well be preceded by the quotation which prefaces "The Res Gestae of a Poor Joke" (pp. 142–145)— "We tell the tale as 'twas told to us." A series of little yarns told by a guide are reported in "Dick McCoy's Sketches of His Neighbors" (pp. 35–40); "A Night at the Ugly Man's" (pp. 41–51) is a tall tale told by a host, full, as Mr. De Voto has pointed out, of oral lore, some of it particularly linked with Crockett;[2] four stories are pretty clearly derived from yarn-spinning sessions on the law circuit;[3] "A Ride with Old Kit Kuncker" (pp. 86–96) is a reported oral yarn; "The Evasive Soap Man" (pp. 109–111) is made up chiefly of the spiel of a peddler, and "Captain McSpadden" (pp. 112–120) is a tall tale recounted by an Irishman. Less specifically acknowledged sources in oral tales are discoverable in three of the other sketches in the volume.

It is at least possible, furthermore, that without the example of the Crockett tales, the Fink stories, and the yarns in the *Spirit*, Hooper never would have written his masterpiece, *Adventures of Simon Suggs* (1845). This is a notable American contribution to the literature of roguery as defined by Frank W. Chandler.[4] Hooper's book is an admirable account of a crafty rascal, Simon Suggs, who gorgeously lived up to his motto, "It is good to be shifty in a new country," by cheating or hoodwinking as many of his Alabama neighbors as possible. A series of chapters are given unity because they all reveal hawk-nosed, watery-eyed Simon Suggs brilliantly duping people. They are given variety because the backgrounds and the characters change as the hero—"as clear

[1] First published as *A Ride with Old Kit Kuncker* (Tuscaloosa, 1849), but generally known by the title given above, published in Philadelphia in 1851, since no copy of the first edition has been discovered.

[2] De Voto, *op. cit.*, pp. 93–94. Crockett makes much of his ugliness, alleging that he can bring a coon from a tree by grinning at it. Hooper's hero is so ugly that flies avoid lighting on his face even when he is a baby, so ugly that his wife has to practice before she can manage to kiss him, so ugly that a whole crowd of men who have been told to give their knives to any man uglier than they are shower knives upon him.

[3] "The Bailiff that 'Stuck to His Oath'" (pp. 64–70), "Jim Bell's Revenge" (pp. 71–79), "Mrs. Johnson's Post Office Case" (pp. 80–82), and "A Fair Offender" (pp. 83–86).

[4] *The Literature of Roguery* (Boston, 1907), I, 2–6.

cut a figure as is to be found in the whole field of American humor"[1]—moves around the frontier, cheating his father at cards, collecting money on false pretenses from an over-anxious claim-filer, passing himself off as a rich uncle in Augusta, cozening the godly folk at a camp meeting by simulating repentance. They are humorous because they ludicrously display a series of comic upsets of poetic justice shrewdly arranged by a downright rascal who, in Hooper's words, "lives as merrily and comfortably as possible at the expense of others" by taking advantage of the frailties of human nature.

Three forces, conceivably, may be back of this book: the influence of European picaresque fiction, the influence of life on the frontier, and the influence, direct or indirect, of oral literature. How much Hooper knew of the literature of Europe which detailed the adventures of rogues it is impossible to say, and it is likewise impossible to presume that, even if he knew this literature, he would have been any quicker to imitate it than most of his countrymen were.[2] But it is possible to perceive that with nothing except a knowledge of life on the frontier and acquaintance with Southwestern humor, Hooper could have learned how to draw Simon Suggs.

For in the United States the frontier was to a large degree responsible for such a character as Hooper's shifty hero. As Miss Hazard has suggested, "To find the American picaro we must follow the American pioneer; the frontier is the natural habitat of the adventurer. The qualities fostered by the frontier were the qualities indispensable to the picaro: nomadism, insensibility to danger, shrewdness, nonchalance, gaiety."[3] As Watterson said of Suggs, "His adventures as a patriot and a gambler, a moralizer

[1] C. Alphonso Smith, "Johnson Jones Hooper," *Library of Southern Literature* (New Orleans, 1909), VI, 2491.

[2] Teague, in *Modern Chivalry*, is hardly worthy of the tradition. Birdofredum Sawin came later. The best American predecessor of Simon is discoverable in Henry Junius Nott's *Novelettes of a Traveller* (1834) wherein the South Carolina author displayed the farcical adventures of Thomas Singularity. Singularity, as Professor Wauchope pointed out, is "a sharper 'deadbeat' and unscrupulous rascal—a lineal descendant of the earlier picaresque romances."—*The Writers of South Carolina* (Columbia, S. C., 1910), p. 59. But Nott's book is pretty generalized, pretty pallid, and rather dull.

[3] Lucy L. Hazard, "The American Picaresque," *The Trans-Mississippi West* (Boulder, 1930), p. 198.

and cheat, could not have progressed in New England, and would have come to a premature end anywhere on the continent of Europe."[1] And in the oral literature of the frontier—literature which idolized Mike Fink for swigging a gallon of whisky without showing effects, for flaunting justice at the St. Louis court house, for stealing from his employer, for maltreating his spouse, and for cheating a gullible farmer, restraints which limited the stuff of other American fiction had disappeared.[2] Professor Boynton discerningly calls attention to the change:

> In all the accounts of the real figures of the frontier in South and Southwest the point is in one respect utterly different from that of the older North and East. The conscious literature was consciously edifying; it was not only polite but also moral. The Saxon insistence on ethical motivation was seldom relaxed at any section of the Atlantic seaboard. But the unconscious, or un-literary, literature of the backwoodsman, plainsman, riverman, was frankly unethical, amoral. The prevailing practice is summed up in Simon Suggs's favorite saw, "It is good to be shifty in a new country" . . . Crockett boasted of his shiftiness as proudly as of his shooting prowess. Ovid Bolus is presented . . . with great gusto . . . as a natural liar. . . . If it is pertinent to refer to these tales as savoring of folk literature, it is pertinent to suggest that guile prevails in all of it, and that Reynard the Fox and Brer Rabbit move on the same plane as Simon Suggs. On the open, fluid frontier the ethics implicit in these stories is the ethics of success . . .[3]

The most notable precedent for Hooper's volume is the literature, oral and printed, about Fink and—to some extent—Crockett. Their tales, too, are told in loosely linked yarns, since oral narrative fosters episodes and anecdotes rather than thoroughly integrated plots. Their histories reveal wandering heroes who, like Suggs, despise book larnin', who know that mother wit is the best asset of a man in a new territory, and who consistently display their

---

[1] "The South in Light and Shade," in *The Compromises of Life* (New York, 1903), p. 78. Simon receives high praise from Watterson: "He is to the humor of the South what Sam Weller is to the humor of England, and Sancho Panza is to the humor of Spain . . . he stands out of the canvas whereon an obscure local Rubens has depicted him as lifelike and vivid as Gil Blas of Santillane."

[2] Blair and Meine, *op. cit.*, p. x.

[3] *Op. cit.*, pp. 614–615.

common sense in their dealings with others. And the book about Simon, like the first book about Crockett, is a campaign biography.

Thompson's Major Jones letters are, of course, in the literary tradition of the Downing letters, and their greatest merit, it may be, is that they approach, in their limning of Pineville, the Down East Yankee's depiction of community and domestic existence: graphically they portray the interior life of Georgia.[1] As Watterson says, they "possess a value as contemporaneous pictures beyond and above their humor, abundant as that is."[2] The major is a believable figure, and those who appear in his tales are likewise convincing. In addition, Thompson is a capable story-teller.[3] His capability as a teller of tales, and a dialect more flavorsome than that even of the admirable Major, however, are better displayed in the yarns which were brought together in book form in 1872,[4] although some of them were written in the fifties[5]—such tales as "A Coon Hunt in a Fency Country" and "Beginning to Practice."

These are "mock oral tales," that is, reproductions in print of yarns told in the vernacular by a narrator of the sort who might delight a fireside audience. The influence of the unwritten form of the *raconteur* here is indeed a strong one. Whereas the loose commentary of the letter or the highly mannered style of most short stories of the time encouraged diffuseness, this form encouraged, among other things, directness. Oral tales, as Neal pointed out, were likely to be told "with a straightforwardness and simplicity . . . irresistibly impressive."[6] An oral story-teller could not hold his audience if he employed the leisurely and heavily rhetorical manner of even some of the best nineteenth-century narratives. Vivid phrases, drawn from the racy vernacular, here were likely to replace rambling descriptions; a striking

---

[1] De Voto, *op. cit.*, p. 257.

[2] *The Compromises of Life*, p. 72. For additional comment on Thompson, see Watterson's *Oddities of Southern Life and Character*, pp. 134–135, wherein the provincial qualities of the fiction are stressed.

[3] Robert Cecil Beale, *The Development of the Short Story in the South* (Charlottesville, 1911), p. 38.

[4] *Major Jones's Courtship* . . . [and] *Thirteen Humorous Sketches* (New York, 1872).

[5] "A Coon Hunt in a Fency Country" appeared in the collection, *Polly Peablossom's Wedding* (1851), and "The Hoosier and the Salt Pile," ascribed to another author, in Burton's *Cyclopedia of Wit and Humor* (New York, 1858).

[6] *New York Mirror*, XVI, 321 (April 6, 1839).

figure of speech or a single well-chosen verb quickly recorded an action,[1] and the narrative moved along. Thumbnail sketches of characters and the use of much direct quotation which caught peculiarities of speech were bound up with the art.[2]

Some of these qualities are displayed in "A Coon Hunt in a Fency Country." The setting is meager; the characters are introduced simply as "the two greatest old coveys in our settlement for coon-huntin"; and after their fondness for liquor is revealed, the story moves forward rapidly, consistently holding interest. Vivid phrases catch the action: "After takin a good startin horn, they went out on their hunt, with their lightwood torch a blazin, and the dogs a barkin and yellin like they was crazy." They paused now and then to drink one another's health "until they begun to feel first-rate"; and a little later "they begun to be considerable tired and limber in their jints." Then Tom, "kerslash! . . . went into the water up to his neck. Bill heard the splash, and he clung to the fence with both hands like he thought it was slewin round to throw him off." Nothing could seem more artless and at the same time be more vivid, lively, direct, or more in keeping, than such phrases as these. The tale ends, as an anecdote should, with a point. In this and similar tales, palpably derived from the art of the fireside yarns, perfectly fulfilling their purpose, Thompson was at his best.

Whether or not this story appeared in the *Spirit*, it was typical of many yarns which did appear there. Typically, the stories in Porter's publication told of amusing characters who had their comic experiences while traveling, while attending to some sort of business in town, while enjoying a boisterous frolic or—most frequently—while on a hunt. But incidentally, to demonstrate the sophistication, the culture, of the author, and, even more im-

---

[1] Note the opening paragraph of "The Hoosier and the Salt Pile," reproduced hereafter, wherein travel by rail "whar people are whirled along 'slam bang to eternal smash,' like they wer so many bales and boxes" is compared with travel by stagecoach, which allows one to enjoy "the rattle of the wheels over the stones . . . the lunging and pitching into the ruts and gullies, the slow pull up the steep hills."

[2] In "The Hoosier and the Salt Pile," the second paragraph quickly and vividly pictures seven characters, including "a dandy gambler, with a big diamond breastpin and more gold chains hangin round him than would hang him; an old hardshell preacher . . . with the biggest mouth and the ugliest teeth I ever seed," and "a cross old maid, as ugly as a tar-bucket." The conversation in later paragraphs is highly characteristic of the various characters.

portant, to go one step farther in catching the pleasant quality of a fireside yarn, many of the correspondents of the periodical put their mock oral tales into an evocative framework. The circumstances of the telling of the tale were set forth, often with appreciative detail. Perhaps the yarn was told after an exciting hunt and a big meal, with all the company comfortable around the fire. A typical passage would describe the situation:

Our saddles furnished a glorious pillow, and our buffalo skins a glorious bed . . . You may talk about your soirées, and your déjeuners, and all that sort of . . . social refinement, but let me tell you . . . for true-hearted benevolence, for that freedom of expression that conveys and leaves no sting, for an unreserved intercourse . . . commend me to a hunting-party in a half-faced camp.[1]

Then the teller of the tale would be described. In the story just quoted, he was a broad-shouldered, gigantic bear-hunter named Tom Wade. Then, in the words of the narrator thus introduced, the tale itself—a reported oral yarn—would be presented. The story-teller would begin slowly, philosophizing, perhaps, as if he had no intention of telling a tale, but incidentally introducing his characters and meandering up to the beginning of the events he described. With the introduction out of the way, the story itself moved rapidly through its big scene or scenes to its conclusion. At the end, the fireside scene of the opening paragraphs might again receive attention.

This box-like structure, a common enough device in fiction, was probably the best humorous narrative method employed in the Southwest. It was not new: one might allege that it derived from Chaucer, Boccaccio, or the *Arabian Nights*. One might even point to more recent antecedents, Scott's "Wandering Willie's Tale" in *Red Gauntlet* (1824), Downing's passage about his grandfather (1833), or Haliburton's enclosed Sam Slick monologues.[2]

---

[1] "Tom Wade and the Grizzly Bear," by Phil, *Spirit of the Times*, XXI, 194 (June 14, 1851). For other tales which are told in this fashion in the *Spirit*, see those cited in footnotes 1–6, p. 85, and several in each of the collections edited by Porter and Haliburton.

[2] The framework form was adopted by Haliburton, probably, so that the sketches might be written from the viewpoint of a Canadian, although Sam was always quoted at length. Like the writer of the Southwest, Haliburton too was no doubt eager to display cultural superiority.

But it seems reasonable to guess that its best qualities in Southwestern humor simply derived from oral story-telling. However it came into being, it proved to be one of the best devices for telling a humorous story of the sort then and later prevalent.

Most important, it was admirable because it effectively characterized the story-teller, through direct description, through indirect description (i.e., the depiction of the effect he had upon his listeners), and through a long and highly characteristic dramatic monologue in which, revealingly, the imagination of the yarn-spinner was displayed. The vividness of the presentation of the narrator gave the narrative illusive power. It was also admirable because, as it was used, it seemed artless. The realistic setting given at the beginning, the detailed description of scene and narrator, gave an impression of naturalness just as it does when Kipling or Conrad presents a tale in such a framework. And from the standpoint of comic appeal, the method was particularly rich in its underlining of three types of incongruity:

(1) Incongruity between the grammatical, highly rhetorical language of the framework on the one hand and, on the other, the ungrammatical racy dialect of the narrator.

(2) Incongruity between the situation at the time the yarn was told and the situation described in the yarn itself. Far less amusing than the contrast provided by the first type of incongruity, this contrast was nevertheless important for comedy, since it helped to remove the happenings described by the tale-teller from the realm of harassing reality, to render them less disturbing, more amusing. Recounted in the atmosphere of the quiet, peaceful fireside, even the most harrowing episodes of a frontier tale might become comic.

(3) Incongruity between realism—discoverable in the framework wherein the scene and the narrator are realistically portrayed, and fantasy, which enters into the enclosed narrative because the narrator selects details and uses figures of speech, epithets, and verbs which give grotesque coloring.

Such was the artistry particularly developed by the *Spirit of the Times*—an artistry discoverable in tales by Madison Tensas, Johnson J. Hooper, Sol Smith, T. B. Thorpe, John S. Robb, George W. Harris, and dozens of others. Such was the art which at its best is revealed in a story thus introduced by William T. Porter: "Our readers must on no account fail to read an article . . . under the head of the 'Big Bear of Arkansas' . . . the best sketch of backwoods life, that we have seen in a long while."[1]

This tale, the masterpiece of T. B. Thorpe, begins with a vivid description of the heterogeneous crowd on a Mississippi steamboat, men of many sections and of many levels of society, crowded together in the cabin of the "Invincible." They were startled by the voice of the yarn-spinner booming from the social hall, uttering fragments of his boast. Then—

. . . the "Big Bar" walked into the cabin, took a chair, put his feet on the stove, and looking back over his shoulder, passed the general and familiar salute of "Strangers, how are you?" . . . in a moment every face was wreathed in a smile. There was something about the intruder that won the heart on sight. He appeared to be a man enjoying perfect health and contentment: his eyes were as sparkling as diamonds and good-natured to simplicity. Then his perfect confidence in himself was irresistibly droll.

The Big Bear started to talk, meanderingly at first, long enough for one to become acquainted with him. Then he launched, naturally, into a fantastic tall tale—the tale of how he battled to conquer a huge bear—a creation bear, and how, after epic struggles, the bear died. "'Twould astonish you," said the yarn-spinner, "to know how big he was: I made a *bed-spread of his skin*, and the way it used to cover my bar mattress, and leave several feet on each side to tuck up, would have delighted you." The yarn ended, and in the cabin there was deep silence, as Thorpe cogitated about the story. The yarn-spinner broke the silence by jumping up and suggesting a nightcap. Thus the simple story ends.

But during the course of its telling, Thorpe takes advantage of its possibilities for incongruity. In the framework, there are pedestrian sentences such as: "Starting from New Orleans in one of these boats, you will find yourself associated with men from every state in the Union, and from every portion of the globe; and a man of observation need not lack for amusement or in-

---

[1] *Spirit of the Times*, XI, 37 (March 27, 1841). The story was first printed in this issue.

struction in such a crowd, if he will take the trouble to read the
book of character so favourably opened before him."[1] With such
ponderous phraseology still ringing in one's ears, one appreciates
the refreshing contrast furnished by the illiterate narrator's "Strangers, the dog knows a bar's way as well as a horse-jockey knows a
woman's: he always barks at the right time, bites at the exact
place, and whips without getting a scratch." Similar incongruity
is furnished by the juxtaposition of the interruptions by the
Hoosier, the timid little man, and the Englishman, with the Big
Bear's remarks before and after them. And the framework not
only throws into relief the comic qualities of the Westerner's talk
but also makes the scene vivid, reveals the quaint personality of
the yarn-spinner, and moves the possibly distressing details of
the contest with the bear out of the realm of harassing realism
into the realm of comedy.

The comedy, furthermore, is developed fully because, side by
side with the realistic depiction of a commonplace scene—a steamboat cabin jammed with a jostling crowd, there is told a tale colored
by details which belong not in realism but in fantasy. Here the
world of fact is a revealing background for a wildly imagined world
—a world in which potato hills grow so large that they are mistaken
for Indian mounds, in which a bear becomes so hot that steam
spurts out of a bullet hole in his body, in which a bear walks over
a fence, "looming up like a black mist, he seems so large." This
fantastic world is one of mythical splendors and poetic mysteries:

. . . he walked straight towards me. I raised myself, took deliberate aim, and fired. Instantly the varmint wheeled, gave a yell,
and walked *through the fence* like a falling tree would through a
cobweb. I started after . . . I heard the old varmint groaning
in a thicket near by, like a thousand sinners, and by the time I
reached him he was a corpse. Stranger, it took five niggers and
myself to put that carcase on a mule's back, and old long-ears
waddled under his load, as if he was foundered in every leg of his
body, and with a common whopper of a bar, he would have
trotted off, and enjoyed himself . . . It was in fact a creation bar,
and if he had lived in Samson's time, and had met him, in a fair

---

[1] Compare the opening sentences of "The Hoosier and the Salt Pile," by Thompson, rather clearly influenced by Thorpe's famous sketch.

fight, it would have licked him in the twinkling of a dice-box. But strangers, I never liked the way I hunted, *and missed him.* There is something curious about it, I could never understand,—and I never was satisfied at his giving in so easy at last. Perhaps, he had heard of my preparations to hunt him the next day, so he jist come in, like Captain Scott's coon,[1] to save his wind to grunt with in dying; but that ain't likely. My private opinion is, that that bar was an *unhuntable bar, and died when his time come.*

Rich in detail, in contrast, in fancy, Thorpe's sketch is a delightfully humorous achievement. And it reveals a splendidly realized character—a character who is memorable because the reader learns not only how he looked, how he talked, how others reacted to him, but also how his mind worked, and, more important, how his imagination worked. The framework and the reported narrative combine to make possible this splendid achievement.[2]

Such is the artistry of Thorpe at its best. Unfortunately the tale is not typical of him. More often, he wrote passably good but essentially dull essays about various aspects of the frontier—about bee-hunters or buffalo hunts or the like. Only in "The Disgraced Scalp-lock," "A Piano in Arkansaw," "Bob Herring, the Arkansas Bear Hunter," and perhaps in other stories discoverable solely in old newspapers and periodicals, does Thorpe forsake his heavily literary style and employ the more direct artistic methods of oral narrative. And in no other tale known to be by him, does he approach the level of his masterpiece.

Other contributors to the *Spirit* used the highly effective framework technique more frequently.[3] It is quite tellingly employed by many anonymous contributors as well as by John S. Robb, for example, in "The Standing Candidate" and Madison Tensas in "A Tight Race Considerin'."[4]

[1] The reference is to Captain Martin Scott who, legend had it, made a coon give up by looking at him, so certain was his aim. The legend also was attached to Boone and Crockett (see p. 282), though it is impossible to know who was the original hero.

[2] Some of these comments parallel—except for emphasis and terminology—Mr. De Voto's comments on Jim Baker's blue-jay story—*op. cit.*, p. 251. Mr. De Voto's suggestive criticism is the only one I have seen dealing with the value of the framework technique for humorous narrative.

[3] In Porter's collections of favorite stories, *The Big Bear of Arkansas* and *Quarter Race in Kentucky*, there are twenty-one framework narratives and thirty-two which do not use the framework. Of the latter, seven are letters or mock oral tales in the vernacular.   [4] Reprinted in this volume, pp. 299–307.

But the author who most consistently uses the framework narrative method to portray his chief character is George W. Harris. His book, *Sut Lovingood* (1867), the product of a man who himself was an adept at oral story-telling[1]—a book which is typical of Southwestern humor because it is full of local color, exuberant, masculine, "the nearest thing to the undiluted oral humor of the Middle West that has found its way into print"[2]— has never had the widespread appreciation it deserves, partly, perhaps, because its artistry has never been sufficiently appreciated, partly because its faults have been overemphasized by over-squeamish critics.[3] Nevertheless, this volume which, in a sense, may be thought of as a picaresque novel in the form of anecdotes within a framework, represents a highly artistic use of the formula employed by Thorpe in his masterpiece.

Harris's tales have all the qualities made possible by this technique. So artless do they seem that even such a discerning critic as Watterson takes for granted that any reader will observe that in Sut's yarns there is "little attempt at technical literary finish, either in description or proportion . . . ; the author is seemingly satisfied to aim merely at his point, and, this reached, to be satisfied to leave it work out its own moral and effect."[4] Yet a careful study will reveal that there is sufficient artistry splendidly to reveal Sut's character and to underline various incongruities. In the framework, Sut is revealed by direct description—a "queer looking, long legged, short bodied, small headed,

[1] See Charlie's letter from "Out West," in which he tells how Harris came charging down the street to tell a "cock and bull story" about a steamboat explosion. "The story is very good," he concludes, "particularly when you hear it told by S—l [Harris's pen name] . . ."—*Spirit of the Times*, XVIII, 73 (April 8, 1848).

[2] Napier Wilt, *Some American Humorists* (New York, 1929), p. 130.

[3] The book has three faults: (1) Sut employs a dialect which some readers think too hard to translate. (2) Sometimes the details about the plights of the victims or details incidental to the tales are coarse, in bad taste, and unfunny. (3) The repetition in his tales of the motif of physical discomfort is so frequent that it becomes monotonous. None of these faults, in my opinion, should damn the book. Sut's dialect is mastered after a little effort. Harris suggested that those who were troubled by the second fault would be those who had a wholesome fear of the devil, and ought to, and those who hadn't a great deal of faith that their reputation would stand much of a strain; and "fur a gineral skeer—speshully for the wimen," quoted the words, "Evil to him that evil thinks." The point is well taken: the stories are no coarser than highly admired stories by some of the greatest writers. And the richness of the detail may well atone for the monotonous resemblances between situations.

[4] *Oddities of Southern Life and Character*, p. 415.

white haired, hog eyed" youth, who comes into view at the beginning or the conclusion of various sketches—reining up his bownecked sorrel in front of Pat Nash's grocery or Capehart's Doggery to tell a yarn to a crowd of loafing mountaineers, weaving along the street after a big drunk or a big fight, or stretching his skinny body at full length by a cool spring at noon. Indirectly, too, by showing the reactions of those who listen to Sut's tales, Harris reveals his hero's character. A rat-faced youth who is conquered by Sut's badinage (p. 21),[1] "George" (Harris), who claims that a part of a tale is not true (p. 120), or who tolerantly encourages Sut's yarns, even when he is awakened to hear them (p. 122), the book agent who is insulted and frightened by Sut's onslaught (p. 244), others affected in various ways by Sut's talk, help us to understand the manner of person he is.

Sut's character is also revealed, moreover, by the tales he tells about himself, tales which display "his keen delight for Hallowe'en *fun*,—there is no ulterior motive (except occasionally Sut's desire to 'get even'), no rascality, no gambling, no sharping as in *Simon Suggs*. . . . Sut is simply the genuine naïve roughneck mountaineer riotously bent on raising hell."[2] They indicate his chief passions—telling stories, eating good food, drinking "corkscrew kill-devil whisky," hugging pretty girls, and "breeding scares among darned fools" by playing pranks. Just as revealing are his dislikes: Yankee peddlers, Yankee lawyers, Yankee scissor-grinders—any kind of Yankees, sheriffs, most preachers, learned men who use big words or flowery language, tavern keepers who serve bad food, and reformers. His idea of what is funny shows us what kind of person he is: a comic situation, according to this son of the soil, is usually one in which a character of the sort he hates, or preferably a large number of characters, get into highly uncomfortable circumstances.[3] Comic to him, too, are the procreative and bodily functions, the animal qualities in humans and the human qualities in animals.

[1] Page references here and hereafter are to the 1867 edition. In some excerpts given later on, the dialect will be simplified for purposes of illustrating points.

[2] Meine, *op. cit.*, p. xxiv.

[3] A host of wasps or bees which interfere with the business or social activities of various people, a wild bull on a rampage, lizards surreptitiously introduced into the pantaloons of a preacher, who thereupon disrupts a camp meeting—these and similar agencies are likely to be the inciting forces in Sut's little comedies.

The language he employs in his monologues helps reveal his character—a language polished little by book larnin', Rabelaisian, close to the soil, but withal poetic in an almost Elizabethan fashion.[1] The very figures of speech he employs have more than comedy to recommend them. They are conceits, comic because they are startlingly appropriate and inappropriate at the same time, devices for characterization because they arise with poetic directness from the life Sut knows. Consider these passages, redolent of Sut's knowledge of nature and of liquor groceries:

Bake dwelt long on the *crop* of dimes to be *gathered from that field;* [saying] that he'd make *more than there were spots on forty fawns in July,* not to speak of the *big gobs* of reputation he'd bear away, *shining* all over his clothes, *like lightning bugs on a dog fennil top.* (p. 62)

. . . her skin was as *white as the inside of a frogstool,* and her *cheeks and lips as rosy as a perch's gills in dogwood blossom time*—and such a smile! why, when it struck you fair and square it felt just *like a big horn of unrectified old Monangahaley, after you'd been sober for a month, attending a ten horse prayer meeting twice a day, and most of the nights.* (p. 76)

Wirt had changed his *grocery range,* and the spirits at the new *log-lick* had more *scrimmage seed* and *raise-devil* into it than the old *boiled drink* he was used to, and three horns *hoisted his tail,* and *set his bristles about as stiff* as eight of the other *doggery juice* would. So when court sat at nine, Wirt was about as far ahead as *cleaving,* or *half past that.* The *hollering stage of the disease* now struck him, and he roared one good *ear-quivering roar* . . . (p. 249)

[Of a man howling in fear and pain:] The noise he made sounded *like a two-horse mowing-machine, driven by chain-lightning, cutting through a dry cane brake on a big bet.* (pp. 268–269)

Recited in Sut's drawl, with far more touches of dialect than are here revealed, in fact, in "the wildest of East Tennessee jargon,"[2] these passages and others in Sut's stories contrast amusingly

---

[1] In Sut's speech better than elsewhere, one may see what George H. McKnight meant when, in Chapter X of *Modern English in the Making* (New York, 1928), he spoke of Shakespeare's language being enriched by common speech. "The effect produced," he said, "is like that of the renewed metaphors to be heard in modern times in the speech of the frontier, where, free from the blighting influence of learning, forms of language are created afresh."   [2] Watterson, *The Compromises of Life,* p. 66.

with the rhetorical framework language. Harris seemed to realize the possibilities of ludicrous antitheses in language, for he liked to put Sut's talk alongside of flowery passages[1] or of learned language in which big words predominated.[2] Humorous, too, is the contrast between the circumstances under which Sut tells his tale and the harrowing scenes he describes. Incidentally, most of the happenings about which Sut tells never could be amusing unless they were removed by several steps from reality.

But the great incongruity in the tales, only partly exploited by Harris, is that between the realistically depicted world of the framework and the fantastically comic world created by Sut in the highly colored, highly imaginative enclosed narrative. His is a world in which the religious life of the Smoky Mountains is grotesquely warped until all its comedy is emphasized, a cosmos wherein the squalor in which the Lovingoods live—squalor without alleviation, without shame—somehow becomes very jolly. It is a world in which the crowds at a camp meeting, a frolic, or a quarter race[3] are revealed in postures and garbs as amusing as those of the earthy and lively figures that throng a canvas by Peter Breughel. Startlingly, it is a world in which scent, sound, form, color, and motion are not only vividly lifelike but also hilariously comic. Here is a mare in that strange country, whose rider has just shouted "Get up!":

Well she did "get up," right then and there, and staid up long enough to light twenty feet further away, in a broad trembling squat, her tail hid between her thighs, and her ears dancing past

---

[1] *Sut Lovingood*, pp. xiii, xiv, 114–115, 244.

[2] *Ibid.*, pp. 19, 21, 29, 48–49, 65, 75, 87, 159, 210, 231, 232, 243–244, 264, 276. An example is this passage on p. 232:

"'. . . an' that very nite he tuck Mary, fur better, fur wus, tu hev an' to hole to him, his heirs, an'—'

'Allow me to interrupt you,' said our guest; 'you do not quote the marriage ceremony correctly.'

'Yu go to *hell*, mistofer; yu bothers me.'

This outrageous rebuff took the stranger all aback, and he sat down.

'Whar wer I? Oh yes, he married Mary tight an' fas', an' next day he were abil to be about . . .'"

[3] Harris's masterpiece, among all the stories I have seen, a number of which have not appeared in book form, is "Bill Ainsworth's Quarter Race," in the Knoxville *Press and Messenger*, June 4, 1868. Mr. Meine, who courteously allowed me to read his photostat of the story, is preparing it and others for a forthcoming collection.

each other, like scissors cutting. The jolt of the lighting set the clock [which her rider was carrying and which prodded her unmercifully] to striking. Bang-zee-bang-zee-whang-zee. She listened powerful attentive to the three first licks, and they seemed to go through her as quicksilver would through a sifter. She waited for no more, but just gave her whole soul to the one job of running from under that infernal Yankee, and his hive of bumble bees, rattle snakes, and other awful hurting things, as she took it to be. (p. 40)

Here is a bull on a rampage in the public market:

. . . just a-tearing, a thirteen hundred pound black and white bull, with his tail as straight up in the air as a telegraph pole, and a chestnut fence rail tied across his horns with hickory withes. He was a-toting his head low, and every lick he made . . . he'd blow whoff, outen his snout . . . He'd say whoff! and a hundred and sixty pound nigger would fly up in the air like unto a grasshopper, and come back spread like a frog . . . Whoff! again, and a boy would turn ten somersaults towards the river. Whoff! and an Amherst woman lit a-straddle of an old fat fellow's neck, with a jolt that jumped his tobacco out of his mouth and scrunched *him*, while she went on down hill on all fours in a fox trot . . . A little bald-headed man, dressed in gold specks and a gold-headed walking stick, was a-passing . . . he looked like he was a-ciphering out a sum . . . in his head . . . Whoff! and the specks lit on the roof of the market house, and the stick, gold end first, sat in a milk can sixty feet off. As to bald head himself, I lost sight of him, while the specks were in the air; he just disappeared from mortal vision somehow, sort of like the breath from a looking-glass. (pp. 126–127)

In such passages as these, in passages which use conceits even more grotesque than those quoted above,[1] in passages of imaginative exaggeration,[2] of strangely linked entities,[3] the world of Sut's

---

[1] For example, this description of a clever man (p. 38): "Why he'd have held his own in a pond full of eels, and have swallowed the last darned one of them, and then set the pond to turning a shoe-peg mill."

[2] Sut's maw, for example, when frightened, "out-run her shadow thirty yards in coming half a mile," (p. 68), and of a man's big nose, Sut remarked that "the skin off of it would have covered a saddle, and was just the right color for the job, and the holes looked like the bow-ports of a gun boat"—and several lines of exaggeration of a similar sort follow.

[3] The incongruous catalogue delights Sut. One example: a horse, running in-

stories, tremendously different from the world where Sut's whisky flask flashes in the sun, takes its queer shape to delight the reader. And from the passages about Sut, and from his imaginative tales, emerges a character, coarser and earthier, perhaps, than any other in our literature during the nineteenth century, but at the same time, understandably true to life, an ingratiating mischief-maker, America's Till Eulenspiegel,¹ in his own right a poet and a great creator of comedy.

In *Sut Lovingood*, the antebellum humor of the South reaches its highest level of achievement before Mark Twain. The author of this book, like his contemporaries, was a man of the world who became an author almost by accident. Like them, he wrote tales full of authentic local color, zestful yarns which blossomed from the rich subsoil of oral humor. Encouraged by the *Spirit of the Times* and other publications, he learned to employ the best method for telling a story developed by members of a highly artistic group, making the most of the framework technique for setting forth a mock oral tale, making the most, too, of the mock oral tale itself, with its colloquial richness, its disarming directness, its vivid comic detail. If his writings were better than the rest, they were better because he had more sense of incongruities, more exuberance, more imagination, and because he had greater genius than his contemporaries for transferring the unique artistry of the oral narrative to the printed page.

efficiently, suggests this: "The gait . . . was an assortment made up of dromedary gallop, snake sliding, side winding, and old Virginia jig, touched off with a sprinkle of quadrille . . ." (p. 291).

¹ Eulenspiegel, too, liked to get people tangled up in conflicts, enjoyed particularly disrupting churchly gatherings by discomforting priests, and played tricks which were gross, coarse, and sometimes brutal. Sut's story, "Well! Dad's Dead!"—in the Knoxville *Press and Messenger*, November 19, 1868, has the theme but none of the details of the anecdote about Eulenspiegel's burial: "He was strange in his life, he wants to be so after his death"; like several of Sut's yarns, it poetically combines the macabre and the grotesque. Enid Welsford, in *The Fool—His Social and Literary History* (London, 1935), p. 47, summarizes Eulenspiegel's career in words which might apply equally well to Sut's career: he "indulges in an occasional wit-combat, but his main purpose is 'to live joyously for nothing,' he makes mischief for the fun of the thing, and slips away before he can be made to suffer the consequences. There is something elvish about him . . ." Nevertheless, it is very improbable that Harris ever heard of Sut's medieval predecessor.

V. Literary Comedians (1855–1900)

Americans who had a taste for comic writings were better supplied from about 1860 down to the end of the century than at any previous time. The books of the regional humorists of New England and the Southwest were at hand in editions which kept up with the public demand. *The Biglow Papers* became a classic, frequently reissued. The Partington papers went on and on, and in the eighties *The Widow Bedott Papers* appeared in a new edition. Haliburton's books were available in editions down into the same decade. New editions of *Georgia Scenes* appeared in 1860, 1884, 1894, and 1897, one of *Major Jones* in 1872, one of *Flush Times* in 1876, and Sut Lovingood's yarns were not out of print down to the end of the century, or, in fact, down to 1937.

But Americans did not have to read this older humor only. On bookshop shelves, side by side with these volumes, were those of a new crop of humorists with wider audiences than the exploiters of Down East and frontier comedy had ever won. A glance at some of those who were famous after the war shows what manner of men they were:

George Horatio Derby (1823–1861), John Phoenix or Squibob according to his title pages, was a West Point graduate who fought in the Mexican War and later went West to serve as a surveyor, military engineer, and journalist, and to write *Phoenixiana* (1855) and *The Squibob Papers* (1859).[1]

Charles Farrar Browne (1834–1867), author of books about Artemus Ward which appeared 1862–1869, before he became a humorist and lecturer, was a journeyman printer.[2]

David Ross Locke (1833–1888), whose books (1865–1882) celebrated Petroleum Vesuvius Nasby, was another journeyman printer who turned to the writing of humor.[3]

Robert H. Newell (1836–1901), newspaper and magazine editor, was the author of novels and volumes of poetry as well as the *Orpheus C. Kerr Papers* (1862–1868).[4]

---

[1] See "Introduction" by John Kendrick Bangs to *Phoenixiana* (New York, 1903) and F. L. Pattee, *A History of American Literature since 1870* (New York, 1915), pp. 31–33.

[2] An admirable study is Don C. Seitz, *Artemus Ward* (New York, 1919). E. P. Hingston, Browne's manager, tells the story of Browne's life in *The Genial Showman* (London, 1870).   [3] Cyril Clemens, *Petroleum Vesuvius Nasby* (Webster Groves, 1936).

[4] Tandy, *op. cit.*, pp. 118–120.

Charles H. Smith (1826–1903), who signed the name Bill Arp to his books (1866–1892), was a mail carrier, a Georgia lawyer, a soldier, a judge, a state senator, and a plantation owner.[1]

Henry Wheeler Shaw (1818–1895), pseudonym, Josh Billings, left Hamilton College at the end of his first year to go West with an expedition which soon disbanded, was a farmer, coal operator, steamboat captain, real estate agent, and auctioneer before he wrote humorous books and almanacs (1865–1881).[2]

Melville D. Landon (1839–1910), who wrote his books in the guise of Eli Perkins between 1871–1891, graduated from Union College, served in the United States treasury and the Confederate Army, was a cotton planter in Arkansas and Louisiana, traveled abroad, and wrote a history of the Franco-Prussian War.[3]

James M. Bailey, the Danbury *News* Man (1841–1894), was a carpenter and Civil War soldier before he became an editor and humorist; his first book was published in 1873, his last in 1880.[4]

Charles Heber Clark (1841–1915) was an office boy, a soldier, and a Philadelphia reporter before he became a journalist and the author of humorous works (1874–1882) signed Max Adeler.[5]

Robert J. Burdette (1844–1914) was a soldier during the Civil War, taught school, served as a mail clerk, went to Cuba on a blockade-runner, and then became a journalist famed as the Burlington *Hawkeye* Man, whose books appeared between 1877 and 1900.[6]

Edgar W. Nye—Bill Nye—(1850–1896), after a brief period in school, was a farmer, a miller, a schoolteacher, a journalist, a lawyer, and a justice of the peace before he became famous as the author of humorous books published between 1881 and 1896.[7]

Finley P. Dunne (1868–1936), a journalist, was the creator of Mr. Dooley (1898).[8]

---

[1] *Ibid.*, pp. 104–118.

[2] F. S. Smith, *Life and Adventures of Josh Billings* (New York, 1883) and Cyril Clemens, *Josh Billings, Yankee Humorist* (Webster Groves, 1935).

[3] Melville D. Landon, *Thirty Years of Wit* (New York, 1891) is in part a meandering autobiography.

[4] Melville D. Landon, *Kings of the Platform and Pulpit* (Chicago, 1890), pp. 239–262.

[5] W. M. Clemens, *Famous Funny Fellows* (New York, 1882), pp. 34–40.

[6] Clara B. Burdette, *Robert J. Burdette, His Message* (Pasadena and Philadelphia, 1922).

[7] *Bill Nye, His Own Life Story, Continuity by Frank Wilson Nye* (New York, 1926).

[8] Obituary notices in Chicago *Tribune* and Chicago *Daily News*, April 25, 1936, and Charles H. Dennis, "The Origin of Mr. Dooley," Chicago *Daily News* (April 27, 1936).

This group of humorists is representative of a still larger group, some of whom are perhaps equally entitled to a place on the list.[1] But these are representative of the host of writers famed as humorists after the middle of the century. A historian of American journalism in 1873 truly said, "We need not count the names of our wits and humorists on the ends of our fingers . . . We are a nation full of such characters . . . always in abundance . . ." [2]

Professor Pattee has spoken of these humorists who so abundantly supplied the American demand as a "new school."[3] In a sense, the term is deserved, for they are distinguishable from the earlier humorists. But in another sense, as another critic has observed, "they are plainly in the main channel of American humor." [4] In other words, America by 1850 had discovered most of the things it was going to laugh at, and thereafter authors played variations on themes already announced.

Their affiliations with the earlier group are not hard to see. The synopses of their biographies reveal that they, like the Southwestern humorists, were men of the world—often of almost fantastically wide experiences—who happened to wander into humorous writing. As their biographies also show, ten of the twelve intermittently or consistently wrote in the guise of comic characters. Browne's character Artemus Ward in part paralleled Seba Smith's Jack Downing, to whom Browne admitted indebted-

[1] Some of the more prominent ones include Joseph C. Aby (Hoffenstein), Charles F. Adams (Yawcob Strauss), George W. Bagby (Mozis Addums), William P. Brannen (Vandyke Brown), W. W. Clark (Gilhooley), Roger F. Coffin, Edward E. Edwards, Eugene Field, George B. Goodwin (Dennis Muldoon), A. Miner Griswold (Fat Contributor), Jay C. Goldsmith (The P. I. Man), John Habberton, Charles G. Halpine (Miles O'Reilley), Marrietta Holley (Josiah Allen's Wife), Charles Hoyt, Stanley Huntley (Spoopendyke), W. J. Lampton (Topnoody and Waxem), George T. Lanigan, Charles G. Leland (Hans Breitmann), W. H. Levinson (Professor Julius Caesar Hannibal), C. B. Lewis (M. Quad), Henry Clay Lukens (Erratic Enrique), J. W. Morris (K. N. Pepper), George W. Peck (Peck's Bad Boy), Marcus M. Pomeroy (Brick Pomeroy), Samuel W. Small (Old Si), G. A. Townsend (Gath), J. T. Trowbridge, Thomas Small Weaver (Job Shuttle), Charles H. Webb (John Paul), P. H. Welch, Henry Ten Eyck White (The Tribune Man), William Albert Wilkins (Hiram Green), John H. Williams (B. Dadd). This list is incomplete.

[2] Frederick Hudson, *Journalism in the United States from 1690–1872* (New York, 1873), p. 696.

[3] *Op. cit.*, p. 28.

[4] Will D. Howe, "Early Humorists," *Cambridge History of American Literature* (New York, 1918), II, 158. He speaks only of Derby, Shaw, Locke, and Browne in this connection.

ness.[1] Eli Perkins is a name derived from Artemus Ward's *Travels*. Bill Arp very evidently continues the tradition of another Georgia humorist, W. T. Thompson, to whom a critic has wisely compared him,[2] with a few dashes of Benjamin Franklin-T. C. Haliburton aphoristic wisdom.[3] Nasby is reminiscent not only of Artemus Ward, his direct inspiration, but also of Lowell's Birdofredum Sawin; and Orpheus C. Kerr,[4] as he writes about political life in Washington and about his adventures in the war, recalls Seba Smith's Jack Downing and John Smith. Josh Billings won his fame by writing aphorisms of the sort discoverable in ancient almanacs. Mr. Dooley is a crackerbox philosopher with an Irish accent.

Derby, Landon, Burdette, Bailey, Clark, and Nye may seem at first glance to be rather different from the older humorists; but a study of their writings will show that they differ chiefly in being more versatile than the earlier writers who have been considered—that they have taken over the ways of earlier writers, not only of New England and the Southwest, but of other sections as well.

Every now and then in the writings of Phoenix, for example, one finds an outrageous tall tale, such as the yarn about the reader so affected by reading Phoenix's newspaper that he exploded with mirth.[5] In such passages there are echoes, of course, of the tall talk of many frontiersmen and some of the Down Easters.[6] The tall tale, in brief form or told at length, adorns the pages of these writers. Landon's Eli Perkins, for example, zestfully repeats a tall tale which first celebrated deep mud in 1828 and which has grown even more impressive as Eli tells it, with augmented detail, in

[1] M. A. D. Howe, "Some American Humorists," *Bookman*, VI, 28 (September, 1897).

[2] Tandy, *op. cit.*, p. 116.

[3] Franklin might have originated such a sentence as, "A family that sleep late will always be behind in the farm work."—*Bill Arp's Scrap Book* (Atlantic, 1884), p. 227.

[4] The name is a pun on "office seeker."

[5] *Phoenixiana*. Thirteenth edition (New York, 1889), p. 134.

[6] Here there is also perhaps an echo of "The Height of the Ridiculous," (1830) or of some lines in "Urania, a Rhymed Lesson" by Holmes. The suspicion that there may be such an echo makes one rather dubious about the generalization that Phoenix introduced the laughter of the West to the nation. He wrote in California, to be sure; but like most California authors, he was born elsewhere, and no section had a patent on tall tales.

1890.[1] Eli tells of cyclones, rapid changes of climate, floods, rain storms, and great shots in various parts of the country.[2] Lecturing on lying, he was proud to be called by Bill Nye, "Eliar Perkins."[3] Nye was likewise inclined to draw the long bow for humorous purposes. One of the very popular features of his lectures was a series of stories which he told about cyclones. Graphically, he told how one cyclone picked up some angleworms from a can: ". . . it picked up those angleworms and drove them head first through his new grindstone without injuring the worms or impairing the grindstone."[4] His first book contained five such yarns; his second, *Forty Liars and Other Lies*, contained the same number, and here and there throughout his works brief passages of tall talk aroused laughter. Passages in Burdette's writing are typified by "The Romance of the Carpet," which tells of the decades spent by a man who tried in vain to beat a carpet enough to satisfy his wife. "My grandfather owned a little white horse that would get up from a meal at Delmonico's to kick the President of the United States," remarked James M. Bailey.[5] His writings were full of similar passages. Charles Heber Clark told of a century plant which spurted so in its growth that in two weeks:

It had a trunk as thick as my leg, and the branches ran completely over three sides of the house; over the window shutters, which were closed so tightly that we had to chop the century plant away with a hatchet; over the roof, down the chimneys, which were so filled with foliage that they wouldn't draw; and over the grapevine arbor, in such a fashion that we had to cut away vines and all to get rid of the intruder.[6]

Or he told of a fat woman who sat down on a man, flattening him so badly that "they merely slid him into a crack in the ground when they buried him."[7]

Not only the tall tale—which appeared in the writings of

---

[1] The early version is in James Hall, *Letters from the West* (London, 1828), pp. 346–348. The later version is in *Thirty Years of Wit* (New York, 1891), p. 101. Eli presents it as a tale told him by a Kentucky clergyman.

[2] *Thirty Years of Wit*, pp. 92–105.

[3] *Kings of the Platform and Pulpit*, p. 311.

[4] *Ibid.*, p. 324.

[5] *Life in Danbury* (Boston, 1873), p. 25.

[6] *Out of the Hurly-Burly* (Philadelphia, 1874), p. 55.

[7] *Ibid.*, pp. 95–98.

others than those here considered[1]—but also other literary forms popular in American humor before the middle of the century made their appearance in the pages of these authors. Letters of the sort used by Jack Downing and Major Jones,[2] dramatic monologues of the sort employed by Mrs. Whitcher and the Southwestern humorists,[3] anecdotes in the older tradition[4] were frequently employed.

Important, too, in the humor of the period, was the essay, descending from the eighteenth and early nineteenth century essays, to be sure, but now strangely and wonderfully changed. The essay had not, of course, died out as a vehicle for humor as soon as Seba Smith invented Jack Downing. The form was important in the humor of Longstreet and Baldwin. As a historian of the magazines of America has remarked, essays which "varied from dullness to slapstick" were consistently prominent in American magazines.[5] Upon this form, as well as the forms more typically employed by regional humorists before the war, the authors of the second part of the century drew for inspiration, replacing the quietly urbane jesting, however, with the louder and less subtle humor which had come to be regarded as typically American. In the humorous writings of almost any author of the period, one might come upon an "essay" of the metamorphosed sort not unlike Bill Nye's "Spring," the first paragraph of which reads:

Spring is now here. It has been here before, but not so much so, perhaps, as it is this year. In spring the buds swell up and bust. The "violets" bloom once more, and the hired girl takes off the double window and the storm door. The husband and father puts up the screen doors, so as to fool the annual fly when he tries to make his spring debut. The husband and father finds the screen

[1] Of Artemus Ward, Petroleum V. Nasby, Orpheus C. Kerr, Bill Arp, Josh Billings, and Mr. Dooley, for example. The best book of tall tales published during the period was Fred H. Hart's *The Sazerac Lying Club*. Fifth edition (San Francisco, 1878).

[2] For further elaboration of this point, see Walter Blair, *The Background of Bill Nye in American Humor* (Unpublished Doctoral Dissertation, University of Chicago, 1931), pp. 19–28.

[3] *Ibid.*, pp. 28–31.

[4] *Ibid.*, pp. 31–49.

[5] Frank Luther Mott, *A History of American Magazines, 1741–1850* (New York, 1930), p. 41.

doors and windows in the gloaming of the garret. He finds them by feeling them in the dark with his hands. He finds the rafters, also, with his head. When he comes down, he brings the screens and three new intellectual faculties sticking out on his brow like the button on a barn door.[1]

An imaginative reader may perhaps see a kinship between this material and that of Addison or Lamb, though doubtless the older writers would be shocked by their descendants.

Such were some of the likenesses of the newer humor to the older. But the newer group differed from the older in several ways. For one thing, they were more highly honored and esteemed than the native humorists of an earlier time. Lowell, apologetic about his *Biglow Papers*, typified the attitude of the better people toward "mere humor" before the war. Joseph C. Neal felt called upon defiantly to reassure Mrs. Whitcher in 1846 that humorists were "useful as moralists, philosophers, and teachers . . ."[2] And though it was not true that Longstreet was actually ashamed of his authorship of *Georgia Scenes*,[3] the legend that he was ashamed is probably indicative of a general feeling that he should have been.

Revealing is a passage in William Garrett's *Reminiscences of Public Men in Alabama* (Atlanta, 1872), which indicates not only how his contemporaries but also Johnson J. Hooper felt about *Simon Suggs:*

Thousands and tens of thousands of readers have laughed over it, and the grotesque situations and characters introduced; but probably not one of them all has had his reverence for virtue increased by the perusal. While Mr. Hooper gained celebrity as a humorist, he lost something of a higher value in public estimation. . . . He confessed and regretted that his writings had established that character [of a mere story-teller] in the public estimation, and that he felt its depressing influence whenever he desired, or aimed, to soar above it, to a higher rank before the

---

[1] *Remarks* (Chicago, 1891), p. 337. In this, Nye's most typical collection, of a hundred and eighty-two divisions, forty-three are essays. All of the humorists listed above used the essay more or less, Josh Billings employing the form more than any of the others.

[2] *The Widow Bedott Papers*, p. x.

[3] Wade, *Augustus Baldwin Longstreet*, p. 214. At times, however, Longstreet was evidently disturbed about the frivolity of the pieces, calling them "literary bagatelles, the amusement of idle hours."—*Ibid.*, p. 213.

public. His ambition had been . . . to enjoy the respect of men; but he had unfortunately obtained a reputation which cut off all such hopes. It was an evil day to his fortunes and to his happiness when he embarked in that class of literature, or otherwise became a *chronic* story-teller for his companions. . . . Here let him stand as a beacon-light, to give warning of the rock on which the manly ambition of his youth perished.[1]

And a dramatic story tells how Hooper, hailed as the famous author of *Simon Suggs* by members of the state legislature, huddled down in his seat, horribly ashamed.

The attitude is a little extreme, but it is more representative than one might suppose. In the South and in the North, the "better people" did not as a rule go for native humor.[2] The attitude did not die suddenly, of course. Late in the century, William Mathews pointed with dismay at the frivolity of American comedy,[3] and Edmund Clarence Stedman shuddered at the thought of the popularity of newspaper humor.[4] Mark Twain would have to be feted by Oxford before many Americans could suspect his greatness.

But Mathews was able to find an exception to his indictment of humorists. Consider, he suggested, the high achievements of Locke:

Who has forgotten the powerful aid rendered to the North in our late civil war by "Petroleum V. Nasby," of the "Confederate Cross-Roads?" Though he assumed the cap and bells, Rabelais

---

[1] Pp. 526–529.

[2] Exceptions occur to one, of course. Lowell's *Biglow Papers*, after they were stamped with the approval of English critics and associated with Brahmin prestige, could be admired. And Baldwin's *Flush Times* is genteel enough to be something of an exception—more praiseworthy than Longstreet or Thompson, *The Southern Literary Messenger*, XIX, 779 (December, 1853), seems to suggest, because of "graces of style which belong peculiarly to him." And—"In the way of illustrating his subject by allusions to the earlier and later classics, no writer we know approaches Mr. Baldwin—he seems to have the whole range of ancient and modern literature at his command. 'The Virginians in a New Country' is worthy of Goldsmith in its easy and quiet satire and its smooth descriptions. . . ." George F. Mellen, in *The Library of Southern Literature*, I, 179–180 represents the same attitude, complimenting Baldwin for quoting many classics.

[3] *Wit and Humor: Their Use and Abuse* (Chicago, 1888).

[4] Letter to Bayard Taylor, September 16, 1873, in Laura Stedman and G. M. Gould, *Life and Letters of Edmund Clarence Stedman* (New York, 1910), I, 447. Particularly to blame for a "*horrible* degeneracy of public taste," he said, "were Hay, Harte, Josh Billings and the Danbury *News* Man."

was not more terribly in earnest. . . . His rib-tickling irony cheered the patriots, as well as confounded the Copperheads and Rebels. President Lincoln found relief from the weary anxieties of office in reading the letters of this Toledo blade. Grant declared that he "couldn't get through a Sunday without one;" and Secretary Boutwell publicly attributed the overthrow of the Rebels to three great forces,—the Army and Navy, the Republican Party, and the Letters of Petroleum V. Nasby.[1]

Lowell likewise had high praise for Nasby.[2] And doubtless, the affection of Lincoln for lowly American humorists did much, as has been suggested, to win for them higher esteem.[3] In fact, the day by day commentary of the Civil War humorists on the affairs of the war, often enthusiastically appreciated because it deftly embodied war-time hatred, became a feature as important as news. In a sense, the humorous writings were news. Thus Nasby, Kerr, the reincarnated Jack Downing, and Arp gave a terrific impetus to newspaper humor.

Then, too, England seemed, surprisingly enough, to be inclined to hail Artemus Ward as a genius,[4] and to give America's literary comedians far more praise than they had received in America.[5] This, of course, was impressive. And as the century waned, though sober critics were not often inclined to write profound reviews of American humorous books, and histories of American literature patronized most of our humorists, magazines were willing to print portraits of humorists and brief articles about

[1] "Pleasantry in Literature," *The Great Conversers and Other Essays* (1874), Eighth edition. (Chicago, 1898), pp. 164–165.

[2] Preface to *The Biglow Papers, Second Series*, p. lxxiv: ". . . I am sure that political satire will have full justice done it by that genuine and delightful humorist, the Rev. Petroleum V. Nasby."

[3] Pattee, *op. cit.*, pp. 26–28. According to Charles Sumner, Lincoln said of the Nasby letters: "For the genius to write these things I would gladly give up my office." Introduction to *The Struggles of Petroleum V. Nasby* (Boston, 1872), p. 15.

[4] Surprisingly, that is, in the opinion of many American readers. For details concerning England's adulation of Browne, see Seitz, *op. cit.*, pp. 184–222. On the hundredth anniversary of Browne's birth, April 26, 1934, the London *Times Literary Supplement* thought it appropriate to run a long leading article on Artemus Ward, recalling his triumphs and savoring his comedy. The anniversary was not generally observed in the United States.

[5] H. R. Haweis, George Augustus Sala, and Robert Ford wrote enthusiastically about American humorists in books, and magazine articles were numerous. For English comment on Artemus Ward, see the extensive bibliography in Seitz, *op. cit.*, pp. 319–338.

them. Agnes Repplier, in 1894, interested to note that an American humorist could win more adulation than an English humorist, remarked:

Perhaps it is our keener sense of humor which prompts Americans to show more honor to her humorists than England often grants. Perhaps it is merely because we are in the habit of according all our men of letters a larger share of public esteem than a more critical or richly endowed nation would think their labors merited. Perhaps our humorists are more amusing than their English rivals. Whatever may be the cause, it is undoubtedly true that we treat Mr. Stockton with greater deference than England treats Mr. Anstey. We have illustrated articles about him in our magazines, and incidents of his early infancy are gravely narrated, as likely to interest the whole reading public.[1]

Perhaps, too, Miss Repplier might have added, Americans were impressed by the monetary success of the humorists of the post-war period. For, beginning with Ward, the first comic man to make a really good living from humor alone, here was something relatively rare in the nineteenth century—a rather large group of authors who attracted many readers and who earned impressive returns from their books.

Sales which earlier had seemed impressive bulked small beside the sales of books during this period. Of *Flush Times*, *The Southern Literary Messenger* noted in February, 1854: "We are glad to know that this volume has already passed to a seventh edition and that the demand still increases for it. The sale will reach 20,000 copies before six months have expired from the date of its publication."[2] But eight years later, the first edition of Artemus Ward's first book, sold outright, was forty thousand copies.[3] Two decades after Ward's phenomenal success with his first volume, when a minor humorist named Stanley Huntley published *Spoopendyke*, "over 300,000 copies of the work were manufactured and disposed of within three months of its first appearance," and several revised and enlarged editions followed.[4] And these fig-

[1] "Humor: English and American," *Cosmopolitan*, XVI, 367–368 (January, 1894). Of course, as the phrase probably would have had it, Stockton was more than a "mere" humorist: he was a fictionist.   [2] XX, 125.

[3] Seitz, *op. cit.*, p. 120. See also Derby, *op. cit.*, p. 242.

[4] Will M. Clemens, *op. cit.*, p. 201.

ures are representative. Stimulated by the nation-wide reprinting of humor in newspapers, by wide-flung periodical circulation of jests, by the interest aroused by personal appearances of lecturer-humorists, and by the snowballing enthusiasm for comic books, the sale of humorous volumes mounted to extraordinary heights.[1]

A pretty good humorist could make a very good living by devoting all his energies to making people laugh. Jocosely, the authors of humorous books indicated that they were interested chiefly in making a living. By 1855, one humorist was frankly proclaiming that: "This book, like Hodge's razors, was 'made to sell' . . ."[2] Ward, in his first book, wrote a short preface telling his readers, at the door of his tent, that they could not expect to go in without paying, but that they could pay without going in.[3] And after the war, it was for some time conventional for a humorist to remark that he wrote not for humanity or for the truth, but to replenish his pocketbook.[4]

Thus these writers flouted claims such as Longstreet's assertion that he was recording history or Lowell's plea that his comic creations battled for the right.[5] It took rather longer, however, for even these frankly professional humorists to get away from the amateur pose—if it was a pose—which had caused many an antebellum writer not to acknowledge authorship of humorous writings.[6] Even in 1874, Clark did not put his own name on the title page of *Out of the Hurly-Burly:* the book was "by Max Adeler,"

---

[1] Walter Blair, "The Popularity of Nineteenth-Century American Humorists," *American Literature*, III, 175–193 (May, 1931). At the end of the century, Bill Nye probably sold a hundred thousand copies of each of his first three books, about five hundred thousand copies of his comic history of the United States, and almost as many copies of *Remarks*—Letter from F. W. Nye, Bill Nye's son, to the writer, February 19, 1930.

[2] Mortimer Thompson, *Doesticks, What He Says* (New York, 1855), p. vii.

[3] *Artemus Ward: His Book* (New York, 1862), p. vii.

[4] See Locke's "Prefis" to *Ekkoes from Kentucky* (New York, 1867); "Foreword" to *Josh Billings Hiz Sayings* (New York, 1865); *Out of the Hurly-Burly* (Philadelphia, 1874), p. 6; Robert J. Burdette, *The Rise and Fall of the Mustache* (New York, 1877), p. iii.

[5] Major Jones, however, had anticipated their confessions of avarice by saying, in 1844: ". . . my book was made jest a purpose to sell and make money."

[6] Neither Smith nor Davis laid claim to the Downing letters on a title page; *Georgia Scenes* was "by a native Georgian"; and the title pages of the first and second series of *The Biglow Papers* did not contain Lowell's name, although the introduction to the second series was signed with his initials. About two-thirds of the sketches in *The Big Bear of Arkansas* were anonymous; not even the editor knew who wrote some of them.

and as late as 1898, *Mr. Dooley in Peace and War* emerged from the presses without any author's name, although Dunne carefully signed the preface with his initials. Long before this "Brick" Pomeroy had signed not only his semi-pseudonym but also his real name to a book,[1] Melville D. Landon had been pretty clearly indicated as the real name of Eli Perkins in a Preface,[2] and Bailey and Burdette had used their own names on title pages. When Bill

TWO ARTEMUS WARDS

The frontispiece of *Artemus Ward: His Travels* (1865) (left) shows the character who was called "the Genial Showman." A later illustration in the same book (right) shows another Artemus, identifiable as Charles F. Browne. See pp. 113–114.

Nye came along, he trade-marked all of his books with at least his last name.

But no matter how coy some of these authors pretended to be about their names, unlike many earlier humorists, they saw to it that the personality of the author came to be associated with his pen name. The transition is pretty clearly illustrated in *Artemus Ward, His Travels* (New York, 1865). Artemus Ward, of course,

[1] *Sense* (New York, 1868).   [2] *Saratoga in 1901* (New York, 1872).

originally was a character invented by Browne—a traveling show-man who displayed animals and wax figures here and there in America. On the title page of this book, Artemus is pictured somewhat as he was in Browne's first book—fat, bald-headed, round-nosed. But on page 116 appears a picture, according to the caption, of Artemus strolling around the farm. Here, however, Artemus is skinny, has a high-bridged hawk nose and a drooping mustache. (The illustrations are reproduced on p. 113.) The second Artemus is obviously not the traveling showman but Charles Farrar Browne, the comic lecturer caricatured in *Vanity Fair* as early as May 24, 1862. The character of Artemus Ward, in other words, merged with that of his creator, and, in time, people used the name Browne or Ward interchangeably, having no feeling that the comic writer differed from the comic figure he had created.[1] His lecture advertisements read, "Artemus Ward Will Speak a Piece,"[2] and frequently he signed his pen name to his correspondence.

This sort of identification happened frequently. In *Famous Funny Fellows*, a book about humorists, a page contains pictures of Robert J. Burdette, S. L. Clemens, Charles Bertrand Lewis, W. T. Thompson, and Charles Heber Clark; but though Bur-dette's name is given under his picture, the other pictures are la-beled M. Quad, Mark Twain, Major Jones, and Max Adeler. Important, perhaps, in bringing about the identification of an author with his pen name were the appearance of many of the comic writers on the lecture platform[3] and the reproduction of pic-tures of authors in the frontispieces of their books, common in the seventies and eighties.

This meant, of course, a great deal so far as individualization of comic characters was concerned. It meant a significant con-trast between earlier and later humorous characters. Since Artemus Ward was not distinct from C. F. Browne, the characteri-

---

[1] See Seitz, *op. cit.*, pp. 92–93, 101, 103, 104, for evidence of contemporary use of the two names synonymously. A review of Ward's *Travels*, in the *North American Review*, CII, 588 (April, 1866), criticized the merging of Browne and Ward.

[2] Reproduced in *Kings of the Platform and Pulpit*, p. 23.

[3] Of the twelve listed at the beginning of the section, at least eight—C. F. Browne, D. R. Locke, Charles H. Smith, Henry W. Shaw, Melville D. Landon, Robert J. Burdette, James M. Bailey, and Edgar W. Nye—were popular as lecturers. And there were scores of others active in the field.

zation became blurred, and Ward was often out of character.[1] Other "characters" similarly—with a few exceptions[2]—lacked distinctness. J. M. Steadman has noticed how the character of Bill Arp in time came to be identified with that of Charles H. Smith: "Dialect was gradually used less and less, and Bill Arp became more like his creator in his language, thoughts, feelings and experiences."[3] What W. D. Howells said of Ward and Nasby applied to most of them:

. . . they are neither of them without wit; and for the present they have a sort of reality; but they are of a stuff wholly different from Hosea Biglow, who is the type of a civilization, and who expresses, in a genuine vernacular, the true feeling, the racy humor, and the mother-wit of Yankee land . . . . Nasby . . . is only a moralized merry-andrew.[4]

In a sense, a new sort of "framework" stressing incongruity was provided by the humorist himself—as he appeared on the lecture platform, as his picture or cartoon adorned his comic writings. The term, "literary comedians," applied by one of the writers to his brethren,[5] was not inaccurate: they acted a part.

The part Ward played on the lecture platform—a role very similar to that played by other humorists of the period—was well described by the London *Spectator:*[6]

The character he likes best to fill is that of a sort of intellectual Hans—the world simpleton of the old German stories—in the act of confiding himself to the public. In the German stories Hans only makes a practical fool of himself in all sorts of impossible ways. But Artemus Ward intellectualizes him, shows the inner absurdity of his thoughts with pathetic earnestness. . . . He yields a literal

---

[1] Pattee, *op. cit.*, pp. 36–37, points out several instances when Ward spoke out of character, expressing Browne's thoughts.

[2] Hans Breitmann, the members of M. Quad's Lime Kiln Club, and Mr. Dooley, for example, were exceptions.

[3] "Charles Henry Smith," in *Dictionary of American Biography* (New York, 1935), XVII, 249.

[4] *Atlantic Monthly*, XIX, 124 (January, 1867).

[5] Henry Clay Lukens, "American Literary Comedians," *Harper's* LXXX, 783–797 (April, 1890). Lukens as a professional humorist wrote under the name of Erratic Enrique.

[6] November 24, 1866. See also Stephen Leacock, *The Greatest Pages of American Humor* (Garden City, 1936), p. 97, where the actual C. F. Browne is compared with the very different Artemus Ward of the lecture platform.

obedience to every absurd suggestion of thought and language, just as Hans does to the verbal directions of his wife and mother, and gets into intellectual absurdity just as Hans gets into practical absurdity. This, with the melancholy earnest manner of a man completely unconscious that there is anything grotesque in what he says, conveys an effect of inimitable humor.

Josh Billings, similarly, in demeanor "was as solemn as an owl. No one ever saw him shed a tear or crack a smile."[1] This solemnity of mien, combined with ridiculous mental and grammatical gyrations, was the chief stock in trade of many a melancholy lecturer. At the end of the century, between 1883 and 1895, Bill Nye, standing tall and bald-headed before his listeners, assumed a "solemnity of look and sepulchral voice when he was saying something he knew would be humorous. At such times he had a queer sort of cross-eyed glint leftward."[2] In earlier humor, the setting for such drollery had been established by a characterization which set forth the moral earnestness of a Hosea Biglow or the naïveté of a Major Jones, or by a framework which pictured a solemn-visaged Mrs. Partington or an impressively sober liar like the Big Bear of Arkansas. Now only the bare necessities for comedy remained—the simple Hans, whose talk revealed "amiable idiocy."[3] The device was not particularly American: the French *trouvères* had used it, and Chaucer, and that fine humorist created by Shakespeare, John Falstaff.[4] It was in the tradition of the court jester.[5]

[1] Cyril Clemens, *Josh Billings* . . ., p. 110. See also the quotation from the London *Quarterly*, *op. cit.*, pp. 14–16.

[2] W. L. Visscher, *Ten Wise Men and Some More* (Chicago, 1909), p. 96.

[3] The phrase is that of Stephen Leacock, *op. cit.*, p. 155. He uses it in connection with Mark Twain and other humorists. Note also Hall's description of "Pappy," p. 71.

[4] Cazamian, *op. cit.*, pp. 107–108, talks of the use of the device by *trouvères* and by Chaucer. Chaucer, it will be remembered, innocently asserted:

My wit is short, ye may wel understonde . . .

and enhanced the comedy of the *Canterbury Tales* by assuming the role of a dull fellow. Falstaff, in *Henry IV*, *2* (V, i, 89–93) admirably described his method and that of the American humorist when he said: "O, it is much that a lie with a slight oath and a jest with a sad [i.e., serious] brow will do with a fellow that never had the ache in his shoulders."

[5] Says H. W. Boynton, in "American Humor," *Atlantic*, XC, 414 (September, 1902): "We like to think that our popular humorists are first of all queer fellows. Jesters like Bill Nye have not been slow to recognize this taste in their audience, and the absurd toggery of the clown has been deliberately employed to enhance the relish

The audience, of which these professional humorists were naturally more vividly aware than their predecessors had been, perhaps influenced the humor in another way. Before the war, Easterners had delighted in Down East humor for its realistic qualities and Western humor for its informative and historical values,[1] while Westerners had enjoyed Western wit and, looking nostalgiacally Eastward, had also enjoyed the portraits of Yankees back home. But now, in a period which saw local color writing flourish in fiction, inconsistently, perhaps, some demanded national scope in humor. Said a reviewer of Artemus Ward's *Travels* in 1866, speaking of American humorous editors:

Let them seek to embody the wit and humor of all parts of the country, not only of one city where their paper is published; let them force Portland to disgorge her Jack Downings and New York her Orpheus C. Kerrs, for the benefit of all. Let them form a nucleus which will draw to itself all the waggery and wit of America.[2]

Lowell's claim that "we cannot produce a national satire or character, because there is no butt visible to all parts of the country at once"[3] was disproved by literary comedians whose comedy was unlocalized. A sense of locality—except of the general American scene—was not important in the works of a majority of these writers.[4]

of their screamingness. In fact, our professional funny man of humor is a pretty close modern equivalent of the Old World Fool; a creature of motley who is admitted to have some sense about him, but must appear under a disguise if he wishes to be taken seriously. More than one of Shakespeare's Fools possess the illuminating kind of humor; but the jest is what they are valued for. It would not be very hard, perhaps, to show that in America this idea of silly-funny man has survived with especial distinctness, and that upon this survival the quality of our alleged American humor really depends."

[1] Note, for example, the review of Thorpe's *The Hive of the Bee Hunter*, in *Godey's Lady's Book*, August, 1854, which remarks: "His sketches should be carefully laid aside after having been carefully read, for the benefit of a future generation, when his revelations will probably be referred to in order to decide important questions of American history."   [2] *North American Review*, CII, 591-592 (April, 1866).

[3] "A Great Public Character," *Prose Works* (Boston, 1892), II, 278.

[4] Of the twelve listed at the beginning of the section, only two—Bill Arp and Mr. Dooley—were regional in the sense the older humorous figures were regional. Even the domestic sketches, which were perhaps the most realistic writings of the school, were not particularly localized. These are considered by J. L. Ford, in *Munsey's Magazine*, XXV, 488 (July, 1901). Ford errs in thinking Bailey originated the type. Its origin is in eighteenth-century essays on house-cleaning and moving, and the form has pretty well crystallized in Cozzens' *Sparrowgrass Papers* (New York, 1857).

Less concerned with characterization and localization than their forerunners had been, the literary comedians were more concerned with continuously amusing their readers. A laugh a sentence or at least a laugh every paragraph was their aim. "Today," wrote a humorist in 1902, "the joke, or the humorous article, is funny all the way through. In other days it was enough to write on and on, with minute and detailed description, leading up to the comic *dénouement* in the last two lines. Now the risibilities of the reader must be aroused with the opening line, or the rest of the story goes unread."[1] Helpful in achieving almost continuous amusement was the narration of comic happenings, representative, as often as not, of the humor of physical discomfiture—a standby of many an earlier humorist. But the employment of amusing verbal devices, which the earlier humorists had as a rule used rather sparingly, now became more important than ever before.

When, in the earlier writings of the group,[2] a humorist used cacography, he far outdid Longstreet, say, or Baldwin, each of whom used it once—and briefly—in his book. He outdid Hosea Biglow, Jack Downing, or Major Jones by a notable margin, going to extremes only minor earlier humorists, such as Enoch Timbertoes and Joe Strickland, had gone to. Earlier humorists had used queer vernacular expressions and amusing similes. So did the later humorists. And to these they added dozens of other tricks with words and sentences most of which would have been impossible in the remarks of highly individualized characters of an earlier time.

[1] W. D. Nesbit, "The Humor of Today," *Independent*, LIV, 1302 (May 29, 1902). Nesbit was "Josh Wink" of the Baltimore *American*.

[2] Cacography, sparingly used in the *Spectator*, was employed in a scattered batch of letters in American newspapers as early as the first decade of the nineteenth century. There was the letter signed "Jenny Stitchem," for example, which appeared in 1805 in the Lancaster, Pa., *Journal*, the Charleston *Courier*, and the Hartford, Connecticut *Courant*. Joe Strickland, Enoch Timbertoes, and other early Yankee letter writers spelled badly. Henry J. Finn's *American Comic Annual* (Boston, 1830), pp. 216–220, contained one badly spelled screed, attributed to Sam Patch. In the forties, the device bobbed up now and then in the comic periodicals—in the letters of Stoke Stout and Billy Warwick to the *Spirit of the Times* in 1843, the letters of Solomon Piper to *Uncle Sam* in 1844, and several letters to *Yankee Doodle* (1846–1847). James W. Morris perhaps popularized the device most in the fifties, with his K. N. Pepper letters and poems in *Knickerbocker*, beginning in 1853, published in the very popular volume *The K. N. Pepper Papers* (New York, 1859). On the other side of the Atlantic, Thomas

A favorite device, which a shrewd Scotch analyst of American humor perceived was frequently employed, was anticlimax.[1] Artemus Ward revealed to Eli Perkins how important anticlimactic sentences were to him during a visit to Perkins' farm about which the host tells in a magazine article:

One day the negroes were grinding their hoes on an old dilapidated grindstone, which wabbled and swayed up and down, being worn by time and hard usage into an eccentric ellipse. When the eyes of Artemus sighted the rickety grindstone, he settled into a long and hearty laugh. Then, tired of laughing, he eased himself down upon his elbows, but did not cease his intermittent chuckling. "There!" he gasped, as he wabbled his hand and arm through something meant for a parabola; "there is wit personified —or thingified. When you can express an eccentric anti-climax instead of a rounded sentence, then you will have something funny."

"People laugh at me," the humorist once said to me, "more because of my eccentric sentences than on account of the subject-matter. . . . There is no wit in the *form* of a well-rounded sentence. If I say Alexander the Great conquered the world and then sighed because *he could not do it some more*, there is a funny mixture."[2]

Artemus Ward, however, had no patent on the use of the anticlimactic sentence. Before him, Derby had used it extensively in "Musical Review Extraordinary,"[3] in such sentences as: "The symphonic opens upon the wide and boundless plains, in longitude 115° W., latitude 35° 21' 03" N., and about sixty miles from the west bank of the Platte River." It is a constant device in the writings of most of the others—for example:

Hood made use of the device, as did Thackeray. Such was the background of the misspelling bee which reached its climax during the sixties, when Ward, Mozis Addums, Bill Arp, Nasby, Billings and others won fame by using it. These writers continued to prosper, though one of them, Bill Arp, reformed his spelling in 1866. But the fad waned. Harte spoke contemptuously of the device in a review of a book by Ward in *The Golden Era*, December 27, 1863, and in the seventies, Horace Greeley denounced it in lectures and Mozis Addums became more restrained. The later humorists avoided it or used it very sparingly.

[1] John Nichol, *American Literature, an Historical Sketch*. Second edition (Edinburgh, 1885), p. 405, says of American humor of the period: ". . . it relies mainly on exaggeration, and a blending of jest and earnest, which has the effect, as in their negro melodies, of singing comic words to a sad tune. Nine-tenths of it relies on the figures of hyperbole, antithesis, and anticlimax."

[2] Melville Landon, "Traveling with Artemus Ward," *Galaxy*, XII, 443 (September, 1871).   [3] Reprinted hereafter.

Locke's *Swingin' Round the Cirkle*, as the title page proclaims, is by "Petroleum V. Nasby, Late pastor uv the Church uv the New Dispensation, Chaplain to his excellency the President, and p.m. at Confederate x roads, kentucky."

Says Orpheus C. Kerr: "This heroic young officer, now attracting so much attention, drew his first breath among the peaceful scenes of home, from which the captious might have augured anything but a soldier's destiny for him. While yet very young, he was remarkable for his proficiency in making dirt pies, and went to school with the sons of the late Mr. Jones."

Bill Arp achieves an anti-anticlimax: "I like an affectionate familiarity between parents and children, though I want it understood I'm the boss of the family, that is, when Mrs. Arp is away from home."

Josh Billings says: "When i see people ov shallow understandings, extravagantly clothed, i always feel sorry—for the clothes."

"As good an example of anti-climax as I know of occurred over in New Jersey the other day," says Eli Perkins. "A good old colored clergyman was describing a storm, and he pictured it something like this: 'The winds howled like the roaring of Niagara; the thunder rumbled and grumbled and pealed like Vesuvius laboring with an earthquake; the lurid lightnings flashed through the sky like—like—sixty!'"

Examples might be quoted indefinitely. The end of the century found Bill Nye still making use of anticlimax in such a sentence as "Spring comes with joyous laugh, and song, and sunshine, and the burnt sacrifice of the over-ripe boot and the hoary overshoe."

This type of sentence, of course, perpetuates humor of a sort discoverable in the framework story of the earlier period. There is an amusing contrast similar to that between the ornate language of Parson Wilbur and the vernacular of Hosea Biglow, between the rhetorical language of Longstreet, Baldwin, Hooper, or Thorpe and the homely speech of their low characters. But in the later humor, the speech is not of two characters but of one—and its purpose cannot be characterization, since only a deliberate jester would combine, say, the first nine words of the sentence of Nye quoted above with the remaining part of the sentence. It is typical of the new school, too, in that it puts into a sentence or two what would previously have required two or more paragraphs. The humor of the later group, in other words, is that of phraseology rather than of character.

The use of anticlimax is only one of the devices found in the writings of many members of this group of literary comedians. They liked to juxtapose incongruous predicates, as in Nye's "The man of the house pulls tacks out of himself and thinks of days gone by, when you and I were young, Maggie"; or incongruous nouns, like Nasby's list of examinations for Negroes, "in Latin, embroidery, French, German, English, Grammar, and double entry book keepin"; or proper names which came strangely together, like Mr. Dooley's "gran' procission iv lithry men,—Tinnyson an' Longfellow an' Bill Nye an' Ella Wheeler Wilcox an' Tim Scanlon." They liked to misquote the Scriptures or the classics,[1] to use extraordinary or mixed figurative language, to state euphemistically an unpleasant truth,[2] to pun, to coin words,[3] and to employ malapropisms. One is not surprised to find that Eli Perkins, analyzing the humor, puts great stress on deformity—of sentences, words, quotations, grammar, and logic.[4]

When, now and then, a comic writer managed to concoct a sentence in which a whole group of the devices stimulated amusement, he doubtless was delighted. Thus Artemus Ward probably was greatly pleased when he wrote such a sentence as, "Gents, it greeves my hart in my old age, when I'm in 'the Sheer & yeller leef' (to cote from my Irish frend Mister McBeth) to see the Show

[1] This is reminiscent, of course, of the burlesque sermons of Sut Lovingood, "Dow, Jr.," the author of "The Harp of a Thousand Strings," and others. In 1888, Mathews complained: "Another illegitimate use of wit too common today, is the process of applying passages from the Scripture to trivial or ludicrous events."—*Wit and Humor, Their Use and Abuse*, p. 123. Artemus Ward furnishes an example in: "Be still, my sole, be still, & you, Hart, stop cuttin up!"

[2] Thus Baldwin told (*Flush Times*, p. 128) how Simon Suggs, Jr., as judge of a quarter race, adjudged one horse winner by three and a half inches; "and such was the sense of the winner of Simon's judicial expertness and impartiality, that immediately after the decision was made, he took Simon behind the grocery and divided the purse with him." Thus Derby tells how the father of Joseph Bowers, "who engaged in business as a malefactor . . . finally ended his career of usefulness, by falling from a cart in which he had been standing, addressing a numerous audience, and in which fall he unfortunately broke his neck." Professor Pattee, who cites the passage (*op. cit.*, p. 30), correctly points out that this device is used "freely by later humorists."

[3] Says Josh Billings, "The hawk is a karniverous foul, and a chickeniverous one too, every chance he kan git." Says Artemus Ward, "He also writes well, his composition bein' seldom marred by ingrammaticisms."

[4] *Kings of the Platform and Pulpit*, pp. 195, 200, 201, 202.

biznis is pritty much plade out."[1] Here the author uses: (1) cacography, particularly amusing because it is associated with some elegant phrases; (2) anticlimax; (3) Shakespearian quotation in an incongruous context; and (4) plays on words. Nasby must have been similarly delighted with the sentence: ". . . I shel withdraw from public life, and start a grocery, and in that umble callin will flote peecefully down the stream uv time, until my weather-beaten bark strikes on the rocks of death, gettin my licker in the meantime (uv wich I consume many) at wholesale prices";[2] for here is a sentence which amuses with (1) cacography; (2) anticlimax; (3) a device which Professor Beers calls "an unusual collocation of words,"[3] and which is really a form of incorrect grammar; and (4) a mixed metaphor. Bill Nye achieved a sentence which embodies (1) anticlimax, (2) the incongruous catalogue, (3) mixed metaphor when he wrote: "Where prosperous cities now flaunt to the sky their proud domes and floating debts, the rank jimson weed nodded in the wind and the pumpkin pie of to-day still slumbered in the bosom of the future."[4]

As early as 1855, a humorist, analysing the qualities of his book, had by chance summarized the qualities of the whole school of literary comedians. His book was, he said, simply a collection of "sketches of various persons, places, and events . . . some are bad, and some are worse; but all have a claim to originality in treatment, although the same things may have been better said by better people . . . although many of the thoughts are not novel in themselves, but are merely whimsically put, and not a few of the whims are borrowed . . . They are dressed up in a lingual garb so quaint, eccentric, fantastic, or extravagant, that each lender will be sadly puzzled to recognize his own. It is undoubtedly this trick of phrase, this affectation of a new-found style, which has caused their widespread notoriety."[5]

---

[1] *Artemus Ward: His Book*, p. 100.   [2] *The Struggles of Petroleum V. Nasby*, p. 101.

[3] The phrase, "licker . . . (uv wich I consume many)," is much like Ward's "I never knew that there were so many of me," which Beers cites in his analysis of Ward's humor in *Initial Studies in American Letters* (New York, 1891), p. 192. Beers finds that American humor is characterized by "extravagance, surprise, audacity, and irreverence," and cites (*op. cit.*, pp. 191–193) the use, in Ward, of cacography, bad grammar, the violation of logic, the unusual collocation of words, "a whimsical understatement and affectation of simplicity," and, in Mark Twain, the device "of putting a painful situation euphemistically."   [4] *Remarks*, p. 115.

[5] Mortimer Thompson, *Doesticks What He Says* (New York, 1855), pp. v–vi.

This new, wild emphasis upon verbal comedy brought into being some comic appeals previously little developed. Such acrobatics of language are of course, in a sense, burlesques of language; and in burlesque particularly these writers (Bret Harte leading all the rest) excelled. During this period, dialect humor—making capital of Negro dialect and foreign dialect—blossomed as never before. And during this period, burlesques abounded—of the oratory of the day, of history, of fiction, of the elegant style of the essay, of obituary poetry.[1] Ruthlessly, these irreverent comic men battled against the sentimental literature which became so popular during the nineteenth century.

Possibly their chief service was their victorious onslaught upon the sentimentality which flowered in early nineteenth-century American literature. This, at least, was the opinion of Charles Dudley Warner, who wrote:

In that seething time [1830–1860], the lighter literature took a sentimental tone, and either spread itself in manufactured fine writing, or lapsed into a reminiscent and melting mood. In a pretty affectation, we were asked to meditate upon the old garret, the deserted hearth, the old letters, the old well-sweep, the dead baby. . . . Even the newspapers caught the pathetic tone. . . . I need not say how suddenly and completely this affectation was laughed out of sight by the coming of the "humorous" writer, whose existence is justified by the excellent service performed in clearing the tearful atmosphere. His keen and mocking method . . . puts its foot on every bud of sentiment, holds few things sacred, and refuses to regard anything in life seriously . . . it has no mercy for any sham.[2]

As Professor Beers remarked of such humorists, "they . . . supplied a wholesome criticism upon sentimental excesses, and the whole world is in their debt for many a hearty laugh."[3]

But despite this admirable accomplishment, these later humorists are less amusing to the reader today than are the best of their predecessors. Perhaps they tried too hard. It may be that quantity production gave their japes a machine-made quality too easily

[1] See Walter Blair, "Burlesques in Nineteenth-Century American Humor," *American Literature*, II, 236–247 (November, 1930).

[2] *Washington Irving* (Boston, 1881), pp. 18–19.

[3] *Op. cit.*, p. 195.

perceived.[1] Or possibly, when some critics pointed out that Artemus Ward appealed only—or at least appealed most—when people heard him, they pointed out a vital fact about these lecturer-humorists.[2] Perhaps a critic in *The Living Age* was correct when he said of the American humor of the period:

Quiet or effervescent, quick-firing or meandering, it belongs properly to talk, and not to written speech. Spontaneity and the play of personality is its essence. It is good for this trip only; or, at best, for casual repetition: the printed page soon stales it and turns it sour.[3]

It may be that it was too topical: burlesques of style no longer are likely to be very amusing when the style itself is forgotten, and comments upon current events are less hilarious when the events are not remembered. And finally, it may be that when the humorists of the latter half of the century became more attached to the humor of words and phrases than they were to the humor of regional character, they gave over to their contemporaries—the local colorists—the most enduring stuff of American humor.

VI. The Local Colorists (1868–1900)

During the late sixties and the early seventies, the general reading public perceived a trend in literature called the local color movement—the extensive portrayal in fiction of various sections of the country and their inhabitants. Recognition of the movement was brought about by the sensational success of several books appearing within a brief span of years—Harriet Beecher Stowe's *Oldtown Folks* (1869) and *Sam Lawson's Fireside Stories* (1871),[4] excellent depictions of New England; Bret Harte's *The Luck of Roaring Camp and Other Sketches*, which caused a flurry of

---

[1] As early as 1874, William Mathews was sneering at "mechanical jokers who turn out jokes as the patent bread manufacturer turns out loaves . . ."—*The Great Conversers, and Other Essays*, p. 161.

[2] Said H. R. Haweis, in *American Humorists* (New York, 1882), p. 120: ". . . much of Artemus Ward was simply flat without Artemus . . ." Says Gerald Massey, in "Yankee Humour," *Quarterly Review*, CXXII, 225 (January, 1867): "To us it seems that the drollery [of Artemus Ward] would be better spoken than written. It wants the appropriate facial and nasal expression to make it complete." See also Robert S. Ford, *American Humorists Recent and Living* (London, 1897), pp. 16–17.

[3] "The Spirit of American Humor," *Living Age*, CCLXV, 687 (July, 1910).

[4] Later called *Oldtown Fireside Stories*.

interest as they appeared in magazines beginning in 1868 and which were hailed as masterly portrayals of life in California when they appeared in book form in 1870; and *The Hoosier School-master* (1871), Edward Eggleston's novel picturing backwoods Hoosiers.

By 1872, therefore, William Dean Howells was saying, "Gradually, but pretty surely, the whole varied field of American life is coming into view in American fiction. . . ."[1] This was only the beginning. Hundreds of local stories appeared during the next decade, and hardly a corner of the nation lacked fictional portrayers.[2] The flood swept on during the nineties: in 1894, Edward E. Hale, Jr., remarked: "Everybody writes 'local' stories nowadays; it is as natural as whooping-cough. There is no need of encouragement: to tell the truth, a little restraint would do no harm."[3] When the century ended, restraint was at last coming into evidence.

Some consideration of a part of the vast mass of local color writing is needful in a study of native American humor in the nineteenth century because much of the fiction of the local colorists is humorous. These authors, furthermore, represented the continuation of certain tendencies inaugurated by the writers of Down East humor and Southwestern humor during the period down to the end of the war.

One important tendency of the earlier humorists, as several students have pointed out, was the tendency toward realism.[4] Professor Wilt thus characterizes this development of fictional method:

The authors [of Southwestern and Yankee humor] were trying to create natural American characters and to give pictures of the American scene. Aside from the humor and satire, the value of the Jack Downing-Major Jones-Sut Lovingood type of writing lies in these very facts. In these informal and sometimes despised

---

[1] "Recent Literature," *Atlantic Monthly*, XXX, 487 (October, 1872).

[2] See the excellent survey of the movement by J. H. Morse, "The Native Element in American Fiction," *Century*, IV, 288–298, 362–375 (June, July, 1883).

[3] "Signs of Life in Literature," *The Dial*, XVII, 12 (July 1, 1894).

[4] F. L. Pattee, *A History of American Literature since 1870*, p. 43; J. L. King, *Doctor George William Bagby* (New York, 1927), p. 62; Franklin J. Meine, *Tall Tales of the Southwest*, pp. xxix–xxx; Louis Wann, "Introduction" to *The Rise of Realism* (New York, 1933), pp. 9–10.

books we have genuine American characters, not the slightly disguised figures taken from the English fiction which appear in all
but the very best novels of the period, for their authors were freed
from the sentimentality and elegance that dominated the more
ambitious writers. In short, these humorists were our first realists.[1]

The literary comedians, not unaware of this tendency, to some
extent continued it. "The humorist," said Eli Perkins, "takes an
ordinary scene . . . and describes it true to life. That's all." He
cited the writings of Lowell, the Danbury *News* Man, and M.
Quad.[2] The domestic sketches of Burdette and others pictured
with recognizable truth the life of the middle-class American in
the village, the suburb, or the city: typical was Max Adeler's
Out of the Hurly-Burly or Life in an Odd Corner, which a German critic
perceived was a display of almost every facet of life in an Eastern
American village.[3] The story of Pitman's running for the legislature in this volume is full of realistic, even naturalistic, detail.[4]
Bill Nye's writings contain much of the local color of the frontier,
the farm, and the city.[5] Nevertheless, the professional humorists
usually were more interested in doing clever tricks with words,
sentences, and paragraphs than they were in authentically de-
picting American life. In a sense, therefore, American humor split
after the Civil War, with the professional funny men continuing
the tradition of amusing expression and another group, the local
color writers, continuing the tradition of local portrayal.

For, like the earlier humorists—particularly those of the Southwest—and like the later humorists in certain moods, the local
colorists usually regarded themselves as truthful depicters of the
life of a section of America during a certain period. The secret of
the American local color story, Harte averred, "was the treatment
of characteristic American life, with absolute knowledge of its
peculiarities and sympathy with its methods; with no fastidious
ignoring of its actual expression, or the inchoate poetry that may
be found even hidden in its slang; with no moral determination

---

[1] *Op. cit.*, p. xi.

[2] *Thirty Years of Wit . . .*, pp. 69–85.

[3] Karl Knortz, *Geschichte der Nordamerikanischen Literatur* (Berlin, 1891), II, 175–
176.   [4] Pp. 363–386.

[5] Blair, *The Background of Bill Nye in American Humor*, pp. 44–49. See particularly
"The Farmer and the Tariff," in *Sparks*.

except that which may be the legitimate outcome of the story itself; with no more elimination than may be necessary for the artistic conception, and never from the fear of the 'fetish' of conventionalism." [1] Thus he described not only his own art but that of others as he conceived it. Edward Eggleston, though he regarded Harte as a writer of romantic tales, thought of himself as an occupant of "the field of provincial realism" [2] whose novels were distinguished from other fiction by "the prominence which they give to social conditions; . . . the individual characters are here treated to a greater degree than elsewhere as parts of a study of society—as in some sense the logical result of environment." [3] The preface to Mrs. Stowe's *Oldtown Folks* contained these sentences:

My object is to interpret to the world the New England life and character in that particular time of its history which may be called the seminal period. . . . In doing this work, I have tried to make my mind as still and passive as a looking-glass, or a mountain lake, and then to give you merely the images reflected there. I desire that you should see the characteristic persons of those times, and hear them talk. . . . My studies for this object have been . . . taken from real characters, real scenes, and real incidents. [4]

Said Constance Fenimore Woolson, "All I write is founded, and intended to be founded, upon actual realities." [5] And so on. With only a few exceptions, the local colorists might have been echoing Longstreet's remarks about *Georgia Scenes*. [6]

Whether they were realists or not (and for the most part, they were not), because the local color writers thus duplicated the aims of the humorists, the suspicion that perhaps the earlier writers influenced the later ones is a natural one. The suspicion is strengthened when one notes how certain humorists comfortably took their places alongside the sectional fiction writers in the affection

[1] "The Rise of the 'Short Story,'" *Cornhill*, n.s. VII, 8 (July, 1899). In the preface to *The Luck of Roaring Camp* . . ., dated December 24, 1869, Harte, styling himself "a humble writer of romance," said his motive was "to illustrate an era of which California history has preserved the incidents more often than the character of the actors . . . an era still so recent that in attempting to revive its poetry, I am conscious also of awakening the more prosaic recollections of . . . survivors."

[2] Preface to the Library Edition of *The Hoosier Schoolmaster*, dated 1892.

[3] *Forum*, X, 286 (November, 1890).

[4] *Oldtown Folks*, Riverside Edition (Boston, 1899), pp. xxiii–xxiv.

[5] Quoted by Pattee in *The Development of the American Short Story*, p. 252.

[6] Quoted above, pp. 65–66.

of the reading public. Longstreet's book, for example, and numerous others by his contemporaries and followers, as has been noted, appealed to the same group which greatly admired the local fictionists. In 1875, when the later movement was well under way, S. S. Cox suggested that the admirable collection of humorous books published by T. B. Peterson and Brothers—a collection which included a large share of the Down East humor and the Southwestern humor, "if purged of their grossness, and artistically inwoven with some genial purpose, would better represent our national idiosyncrasies . . . and novel parlance, than any other portion of our literature."[1] Henry Watterson's collection of Southern pre-war and post-war humorous stories, which he called "the most graphic chronicles of the nether side of Southern life,"[2] had a wide sale after its issuance in 1882. And when Professor Beers wrote of the new school of fictionists in 1891, no sense of contrast prevented him from treating Charles G. Leland—or Hans Breitmann—in the same paragraph which evaluated Eggleston, Harris, Cable, and Miss Murfree.[3]

One author who very clearly shows a relationship between the older humor and the newer local color writing is Richard Malcolm Johnston. Like his fellow Georgian, Longstreet, Johnston was a lawyer who learned the art of telling humorous tales on the circuit. "During his career as a lawyer," pointed out a contemporary, "practising in five or six adjoining counties, much of his time was passed at county-seat taverns, where numbers of lawyers would gather together and relate their observations of Cracker life, their personal experiences among the countrymen of middle Georgia, court-house scenes, and the like. These tavern stories, together with his own intimate acquaintance with the people in the old-field schools and as a lawyer, supplied a rich mine of matter for literary work. . . ."[4] Like Longstreet, he believed that an author

---

[1] "American Humor," *Harper's*, L, 699 (April, 1875).

[2] *Oddities in Southern Life and Character*, p. viii. Included in this excellent volume, with the writings of such post-war figures as Bill Arp, Richard M. Johnston, and Joel Chandler Harris, were those of such pre-war humorists as Longstreet, Baldwin, Crockett, Hooper, Thompson, and others.   [3] *Op. cit.*, pp. 202–203.

[4] Charles W. Coleman, Jr., "The Recent Movement in Southern Literature," *Harper's*, LXXIV, 843 (May, 1887). See also Watterson, *Oddities in Southern Life and Character*, pp. 329–330, and the brief but very suggestive treatment of the importance of oral story-telling to Georgia humor in Johnston's article cited in footnote 1, p. 73.

should take the "utmost pains in the study of naturalness, and
that an artist can create interesting concretes only if he can re-
enact scenes from human life."[1] His stories, which began to appear in 1857, written "after the Longstreet pattern,"[2] when first
published between covers in 1864, had a title, *Georgia Sketches
by an Old Man*, reminiscent of Longstreet's book. Much of the
method of story-telling in the vernacular, and at least one definite
scene in a story[3] appear to stem directly from the writings of
William Tappan Thompson. Republished later, with some changes,
in 1871, 1874, 1883, and 1892, as *Dukesborough Tales*, these writings
and others by Johnston in the same vein—writings obviously
molded according to the model of the older humorists—were accepted without any sense of discomfort as contributions to the
local color movement.

Bret Harte actually asserted that the local color story derived
from American humor. Harte knew a good deal about American
humor: as a parodist, he competed successfully with literary comedians; he lectured on native humor and wrote about it. He traced
it back, to be sure, only to Haliburton, whom he considered the
first to use Yankee dialect. But he savored its fine qualities, perceived the excellence of the Southwestern practitioners,[4] and be-
moaned the turn humor took as practiced by the literary comedians: "it seemed," he said of this last group, "as if they were losing
the faculty of story-telling in the elaboration of eccentric character
—chiefly used as a vehicle for smart sayings, extravagant incident,
or political satire."[5] Nevertheless, humor furnished a suggested
path of escape from English literary tradition:

. . . while the American literary imagination was still under the
influence of English tradition, an unexpected factor was develop-

---

[1] *Critic*, XII, 126 (March 17, 1888). Again, he says, "As long as the people in my
stories have no fixed surroundings, they are nowhere to me; I cannot get along with
them at all."

[2] F. L. Pattee, *American Literature since 1870*, p. 299. See also R. C. Beale, *op. cit.*,
p. 53, which calls attention to the influence of Longstreet upon specific stories.

[3] Compare "The Great Attraction" in *Major Jones' Chronicles of Pineville* (Philadelphia, 1845) with Chapter IV of "The Expensive Treat of Colonel Moses Grice,"
Dukesborough Tales (New York, 1892), pp. 256–260. The basic situation is an even
older one in frontier humor.

[4] "American Humor," in *The Lectures of Bret Harte* (Brooklyn, 1909), p. 22.

[5] "The Rise of the 'Short Story,'" *Cornhill*, n.s. VII, 3 (July, 1899).

ing to diminish its power. It was *Humour*—of a quality as distinct and original as the country and civilisation in which it was developed. It was at first noticeable in the anecdote or 'story,' and, after the fashion of such beginnings, was orally transmitted. It was common in the bar-rooms, the gatherings in the 'country store,' and finally at public meetings in the mouths of 'stump orators.' . . . It at last received the currency of the public press. But wherever met it was so distinctly original and novel, so individual and characteristic, that it was at once known and appreciated abroad as 'an American story.' Crude at first, it received a literary polish in the press, but its dominant quality remained. It was concise and condensed, yet suggestive . . . delightfully extravagant—or a miracle of understatement. It voiced not only the dialect, but the habits of thought of a people or locality. It gave a new interest to slang . . . . It was a foe to prolixity of any kind, it admitted no fine writing or affectation of style. It went directly to the point. It was burdened by no conscientiousness; it was often irreverent; it was devoid of all moral responsibility. . . . By degrees it developed character with its incident, often, in a few lines, gave a striking photograph of a community or a section, but always reached its conclusion without an unnecessary word. . . . It was the parent of the American 'short story.'[1]

Harte's statement, of course, simplifies too much. Local color writers learned their art from many masters. The tradition of the Scott-Edgeworth-Bulwer influence of the twenties persisted with growing strength down to the seventies: in America during that period, "a gradually increasing number of reviews dealt with local color in fiction."[2] Recognition of the local color movement was merely the perception of a development which had been going on for a long time. Harte himself owed much to Irving and Dickens,[3] and the same may be said for others of the school. In Eg-

---

[1] "The Rise of the 'Short Story,' " *Cornhill*, n.s. VII, 3 (July, 1899).

[2] Mary Elizabeth Hamilton, *The Development of the Conception of Local Color in Fiction* (Unpublished Master's Dissertation, University of Chicago, 1925). The first use of the term, "local color," Miss Hamilton discovered occurs in a review of Mrs. Emma Southworth's *Love's Labor Won* in Knickerbocker, LX, 173 (August, 1862), although the concept was clearly formulated long before this date. A rapid survey of magazines which I made revealed that at least twenty-five reviews of Southern stories, twelve of Western stories, and thirty-eight of New England stories commended fictionists for accurate sectional portrayals between August, 1832 and August, 1869.

[3] The *Atlantic*, XXI, 128 (January, 1868) called attention to Harte's penchant for imitating Dickens, as many passages in Harte's stories do. See Pattee, *The Development of the American Short Story*, pp. 224–234, for an analysis of the sources of Harte's artistry.

gleston's opinion, a translation of Taine's *Art in the Netherlands* in 1871 impelled him to make fictional use of humble Hoosiers.[1] Cable learned some of his art, he thought, from such French authors as Hugo, Mérimée, and About, and more of it from Dickens, Thackeray, Poe, and Irving.[2] Thomas Hardy's art had a share in shaping the craftsmanship of several authors. In short, to say that American humor was the only ancestor of local color is to disregard not only the way of biology but also the way of art.

But oversimplified though it is, Bret Harte's statement does point to a significant truth: American humor was an influential force in the development of local color writing of the post-war period. Especially to some of the authors who were pioneers in the great surge of this sort of writing, the earlier humor was a valuable aid.

It was significant, for example, that Harte himself, so far as he was conscious of an art shaping his art, was able to point only to American humor. Furthermore, one who analyzes only the story which skyrocketed him to fame, "The Luck of Roaring Camp," will find it easy to understand why he placed emphasis upon this element of his writing. In spirit and in manner, this tale is in the tradition of American humor. It is an anecdote which leads surely and unwaveringly to a final line of dialogue. Exaggeration is represented in the passage about gamblers so imperturbable that they continued their little game in Tuttle's Grocery while two men noisily killed one another in the front room. Irreverence of the sort that made comic camp meetings or even the exploitation of folk at camp meetings hilarious in the older humor is duplicated in what Harte called the "reckless irreverence of Roaring Camp"—an irreverence which caused the miners to make bets, at proper odds, on the outcome of a woman's struggle with death, caused them also to plan an outrageous burlesque of a christening. A charming interlude is Kentuck's report of the infant's conversation with a blue jay—an example of the sort of fantastic tall tale-telling which had given America "The Big Bear of Arkansas" and many another imaginative sketch. "I

---

[1] Preface to *The Hoosier Schoolmaster*, Library Edition.
[2] Letter to F. L. Pattee, quoted in Lucy Leffingwell Cable Bickle, *George W. Cable, His Life and Letters* (New York, 1928), p. 47.

crep' up the bank just now," said Kentuck, "and dern my skin if he wasn't a talking to a jay-bird as was a sittin' on his lap. There they was, just as free and sociable as anything you please, a jawin' at each other just like two cherry-bums."

The last phrase was a comic simile, useful to native humorists ever since 1795, useful to Harte elsewhere in the same story when a miner noted that the baby was "no bigger nor a derringer." From the earlier humorists and the literary comedians Harte learned other tricks of phrasing. Euphuistic language to convey an unpleasant truth told how "Stumpy, in other climes, had been the putative head of two families; in fact, it was owing to some legal informality in these proceedings that Roaring Camp—a city of refuge—was indebted to his company." The incongruous catalogue beloved by professional humorists and Sut Lovingood was represented in the strange assortment of gifts presented to the child, including a tobacco-box, an embroidered handkerchief, a slingshot, a Bible, and a pair of surgeon's shears; it was represented in a more condensed form in the phrases of Stumpy's christening speech: "I proclaim you Thomas Luck, according to the laws of the United States and the State of California, so help me God." Anticlimax was present in the sentence which told how Sandy Tipton sympathetically considered the suffering of Sal, "and, in the contemplation of her condition, for a moment rose superior to the fact that he had an ace and two bowers in his sleeve."

Further analysis is hardly necessary, though one might go on to cite other proof elsewhere as here that Harte learned much from humorous predecessors—a passage in a poem which derives directly from *Phoenixiana*,[1] satirical thrusts in the manner of Yankee Hill,[2] the repetition of characters drawn from the "Pike" literature which was the California version of the literature of the old Southwest,[3] a masculinity of temper which was highly reminiscent of

---

[1] Compare the passage on p. 113 of *Phoenixiana* which tells how "an old villain . . . punched me in the abdomen; I lost my breath, closed my eyes, and remembered nothing further," with the passage in "The Society Upon Stanislaus," reprinted hereafter.

[2] Rourke, *American Humor*, pp. 225–226.

[3] The non-indigenous California authors derived much of their comedy from the old Southwest, calling the imported comic figures "Pikes." For an admirable consideration of the Pikes and their appearance in Harte, see G. R. MacMinn, "'The

the male comedy of the South.[1] Small wonder, then, that Harte's contemporaries, with the recent humor fresh in their memories, classified the new literary sensation not as a fictionist but as a humorist.[2]

No such specific acknowledgment of a relationship to American humor is made by Edward Eggleston; but the link between his writings and earlier comic writings is, if anything, clearer than the relationship in Harte. The preface to the first edition of *The Hoosier Schoolmaster* asserts that Indianans were jealous when the author was a boy because "the manners, customs, thoughts, and feelings of New England country people filled so large a place in books, while our life, not less interesting, not less romantic, and certainly not less filled with grotesque material, had no place in literature." Possibly they were jealous of Seba Smith, who, in 1854, published a volume containing a story which may have suggested a series of incidents in the Hoosier's first book,[3] almost certainly they were jealous of Lowell, whom the author had corresponded with a year or two before he wrote his novel,[4] whom he mentioned to his brother when planning the book,[5] and whom he was still admiring twenty-one years later when he wrote the preface to the library

Gentleman from Pike' in Early California," *American Literature*, VIII, 160–169 (May, 1936). See also Eggleston's preface to the library edition of *The Hoosier Schoolmaster*, which points out how the heroes of the earlier humor "wended their way to California, to appear in Mr. Bret Harte's stories as 'Pikes.'" Also valuable is Professor Pattee's chapter, "The Discovery of Pike County," in *American Literature since 1870*, pp. 83–98.

[1] The review of *The Luck* in the *Atlantic*, XXV, 633–635 (May, 1870) noted the masculine temper and suggested that most women would not enjoy the sketches unless they were gifted with an unusual sense of humor.

[2] In Sala's anthology, *Yankee Drolleries; Haweis's American Humorists* (London, 1882); Eli Perkins's *Kings of the Platform and Pulpit* (Chicago, 1891); Robert Ford's *American Humorists Recent and Living* (London, 1897), and other books about and anthologies of American humor, Harte was treated as a typical humorist. See also Pattee, *Development of the American Short Story*, p. 246, which notes that "Harte entered the East as a humorist as certainly as did Mark Twain" and that *Appleton's* summary of 1870 literature listed *The Luck* with humorous and unclassified publications.

[3] The book was *Way Down East*, editions of which appeared in 1854 in four cities, one of them Cincinnati, and later editions of which were published in 1855, 1859, 1860, and 1866, before Eggleston began his career as a novelist. For Smith's possible influence, see Wyman, *op. cit.*, p. 162.

[4] Preface to Library Edition. See also Edward Eggleston, "Folk Speech in America," *Century*, XXVI, 875 (October, 1894).

[5] "He cited the Dutch painters, and justified his choice of what seemed an unliterary theme, involving rude characters and a strange dialect perversion, by reference to Lowell's success with the Biglow papers."—George Cary Eggleston, *The First of the Hoosiers* (Philadelphia, 1903), p. 297.

edition of his novel.[1] It is worth noting, too, that an early piece by Eggleston was a comment on politics in Hoosier dialect, published in an Indianapolis newspaper.

But in this same preface, he mentioned another group of humorists who, though unacknowledged, were probably of more importance as influences in his work than the New Englanders. He had postponed the attempt to write in the Hoosier dialect, he said, "probably because the only literary use that had been made of the allied speech of the Southwest had been in the books of the primitive humorists of that region. I found it hard to dissociate in my own mind the dialect from the somewhat coarse boisterousness which seemed inseparable from the works of these rollicking writers." Evidently one author of rollicking Southwestern humor, however, did not fall under the ban. For when Eggleston listed the carefully selected humorous books in the library of a character whose literary taste he admired greatly, he noted that to the list of masterpieces the man had "added the Georgia Scenes of Mr. Longstreet, insisting that they were quite equal to Don Quixote."[2] To this great Southwestern author Eggleston paid the tribute of imitation in *The Hoosier Schoolmaster:* talkative Mrs. Means might have walked from the pages of the earlier book to those of the later one, as might Granny Sanders, who talked learnedly of herbs; Longstreet's description of the turn-out might well have suggested the thirteenth chapter, "A Struggle for the Mastery." But authors presumably less admired by Eggleston were also helpful. If the Hardshell preacher who spoke in Chapter XII of the same book is not a descendant of the orator who delivered "The Harp of a Thousand Strings," he is surely a descendant of an imitator of that orator, and old Jack Means, young Bud Means, Pete Jones, and old John Pearson would have been hard indeed for any one to create who did not know the humor of the old Southwest. In *The End of the World*, Jonas talked the language of Artemus Ward, and the inefficient "steam doctor" was a repetition of a favorite character of frontier comedy.

---

[1] The folk-speech of New England, after its use by Lowell, he said, "had acquired a standing that made it the classic *lingua rustica* of the United States."

[2] The library was that of the wise Backwoods philosopher in *The End of the World* (New York, 1872), p. 43. Other books were those of Cervantes, Le Sage, Molière, Swift, and Boz. Rabelais was rejected.

But even more influences of the older humor are evident in Eggleston's masterpiece, *The Circuit Rider*. Chapters I and II, treating respectively a corn shucking and a frolic, characteristically present subject matter much favored by the earlier humorists. In Chapter V, Kike utters a defiance phrased in the rhythms of frontier tall talk: "I ain't afeard of the devil nor none of his angels; and I reckon you're one of the blackest. It'll cost you more burnt barns and dead hosses and cows and hogs and sheep than what you make will pay for." Chapter VII repeats the ancient frontier comedy of the illiterate candidate on an electioneering trip which came into fashion with Davy Crockett, and a story of fun with a Methodist minister is reminiscent of tales of how Mike Fink and his bully boys broke up camp meetings. Chapter VIII contains a reference to the way Davy Crockett grinned a coon out of a tree.[1] Religious matters intervene, and it is not until Chapter XXIII that an old-fashioned New England peddler revives an episode straight out of the older humor, but meanwhile numerous characters in the tradition have acted important parts in the story—Mr. Brady, Job Goodwin, and Captain Lumsden, among others, and still others were to appear later.

But more important was the derivative quality of many portions of Eggleston's work. "On the whole," as Miss Dondore has pointed out,[2] "in its strength and its weaknesses, Eggleston's method resembles most nearly that of the humorists. They 'aired' the crudities of the middle western civilization to excite the laughter of a more sophisticated public; in the idiosyncrasies of the border type that surrounded them they found a literary soil. . . . In exploiting such material the chief danger, of course, was that of caricature—a danger Eggleston himself evidences in his vain and shallow Mrs. Plausaby, his chronic invalid, Mr. Minorkey, his reminiscent New Englander, Miss Matilda Hawkins, or his Backwoods Philosopher. The strength of the humorists' characterization lay largely in their ability to produce awkward but virile and good natured types; their strength he excelled in his portraits of bashful Bud Means . . . of the crotchety cobbler; or of herculean, indolent, adventurous, and stalwart pioneers who first braved the

---

[1] Also mentioned in *The End of the World*, p. 110.
[2] *The Prairie and the Making of Middle America* (Cedar Rapids, 1926), pp. 306–307.

fastnesses of the Great Valley." Small wonder, therefore, that the illustrations of the early editions of Eggleston's books took the form of caricatures almost as broad as any which had illustrated earlier comic volumes.

It is not easy to say exactly which New England local colorist should be ranked with Harte and Eggleston as the most important figure from that section in the early years of the movement. Several authors might be candidates for the honor—Rose Terry Cooke, Elizabeth Stuart Phelps, John T. Trowbridge, Henry Ward Beecher, Edward Everett Hale, or still others. But earlier than any other in the field, as representative as any, and probably more popular than any other, was Mrs. Stowe. Her first local color story, "A New England Sketch,"[1] won a prize and was printed in 1834, long before the term "local color" was in general use. Here, taking up the manner of Miss Sedgewick, but showing a finer flair for dialect, revealing an interest in morality which might have derived from Miss Edgeworth but which was for Lyman Beecher's daughter more probably simply a natural enthusiasm, she showed real skill in sketching New England character. Other sketches followed and were gathered, with her first, in *The May Flower* (1843), a volume of fictional depictions of New Englanders which only on occasion rose above the stiff portraiture of current magazine fiction. By 1851, when *Uncle Tom's Cabin* appeared, Mrs. Stowe apparently had learned something about characterization from Dickens. But her art reached its greatest heights when, after years of occasional writing about New England, she produced *Oldtown Folks* and *Sam Lawson's Fireside Stories*.

Currents which had eddied through fiction for more than three decades had shaped Mrs. Stowe's art by this time. Whether American humor had had any influence upon her artistry it is difficult to say, but it is interesting to note that the second of these volumes, her richest work in humor, used the framework technique beloved by Sam Slick and the Southwestern humorists, and both volumes derived much from oral story-telling. The story-teller was Professor Stowe: "the characters and incidents of these two books were

[1] Published in Judge Hall's *Western Monthly*, this tale was later called "Uncle Lot." Of course other local stories had appeared before this, but their authors were not active during the great post war period of local color writing.

largely built upon the foundations of Professor Stowe's memory and the experience of his boyhood."[1] He was "an inimitable mimic and story-teller," says his wife's biographer. "No small proportion of her success . . . is to be attributed to him," and he prints a letter written from Natick in 1839 in which the professor reproduced New England background, character, and the rhythms of Yankee talk. The stories in the second book, he continues, "are told as they came from Mr. Stowe's lips, with little or no alteration."[2] The statement is not quite correct: the stories were so altered that they consistently took on the flavor of the character of their fictional narrator. Nevertheless, the art of Professor Stowe's oral narratives offered Mrs. Stowe many helpful hints.

Such were the forces which shaped the works of the pioneers in the school of regional writers. Later local color writers were taught their art not only by those from whom Harte, Eggleston, and Stowe learned to write but by other local colorists as well;[3] and to trace any phases of their art back to humor is of course usually impossible. One catches glimpses of the possible influence of humor in some of Miss Murfree's tales of the Southern mountaineers; Page acknowledges the influence upon his writings of George W. Bagby, the creator of Mozis Addums and the celebrator of the Old Virginia Gentleman;[4] in the work of Joseph Kirkland, passages which tell of youthful hunters swapping tall yarns, of Zury's persecution for infidelity, of how Zury's neighbors "'low he's puttin' on scallops," or of Zury's campaign speech, are obviously derivative;[5] and various passages in other local colorists' works would not have been out of place in the earlier humor. But only one other writer among the local colorists derives his artistry as directly from the early humorists as did Harte and Eggleston— Joel Chandler Harris.

Of Harris's affiliation with the humorists there can be no doubt.

[1] Introductory note to the Riverside edition of *Oldtown Folks*, p. vii.
[2] Charles E. Stowe, *The Life of Harriet Beecher Stowe* (Boston, 1889), pp. 439–443. The material in the letter later was used in Chapter XXXII of *Oldtown Folks*.
[3] Hamlin Garland, for example, not only recalled reading *The Hoosier Schoolmaster*, which he characterized as a "milestone in his literary progress," as a serial, but he also read widely among the regional fiction before he started his career.
[4] Preface to *The Old Virginia Gentleman and Other Sketches* (New York, 1910).
[5] *Zury, the Meanest Man in Spring County* (Boston, 1887), pp. 151–154, 379–384, 522–528.

True, he started his career on a plantation newspaper the proprietor of which lived up to his name of Joseph Addison Turner by aping Addison and Steele; but his fame as a humorous depicter of character did not come until after a period on the paper edited by William Tappan Thompson, editor of the Savannah *News*, who doubtless aided him during his apprenticeship.[1] Uncle Remus was created as a commentator on current events, rather than as a story-teller, to replace "Old Si" when Si's creator, Sam W. Small, left the newspaper which employed Harris.[2] Between the appearance of the first and the second of the "Negro Folklore" papers which introduced Uncle Remus as a story-teller, Harris wrote two editorials revealing a pretty thorough knowledge of some of the earlier humor, disparaging Sam Slick as a caricature and Jack Downing as a lay figure, but praising Major Jones as "a character study unsurpassed in our literature" and Hosea Biglow as "a serious literary study of the typical Yankee."[3] But more important as evidence of an influence are the tales themselves: Uncle Remus reveals his character thoroughly in exactly the manner of the earlier humorous figures—by extensive monologues and by tall tales within a framework,[4] tall tales the very fantasy of which is an excellent device for character depiction. Billy Sanders, a character created by Harris and highly popular, is obviously a reincarnation of Bill Arp, whose originator Harris met in 1878.[5] Two compilations edited by Harris indicated an abiding enthusiasm for the earlier humor and an appreciation of its qualities,[6] and even more generally than Harte, Harris was at first classified as a humorist.

[1] Robert Lemuel Wiggins, *The Life of Joel Chandler Harris* (Nashville, 1918), pp. 112–113. [2] *Ibid.*, pp. 124–128.

[3] The first of the folklore sketches appeared July 20, 1879, the second November 16 of the same year in the Atlanta *Constitution*. The two editorials referred to appeared in the same paper headed "Georgia Crackers: Types and Shadows," and "The Puritan and the Cracker," September 28, 1879 and October 5, 1879.

[4] Miss Tandy, *op. cit.*, p. 95, briefly notes the similarity of technique.

[5] See the letter in the *Weekly Constitution*, July 2, 1878. For a consideration of Billy Sanders, see *Joel Chandler Harris, Editor and Essayist*, ed. Julia Collier Harris (Chapel Hill, 1931), pp. 191–241. Bill Arp quite possibly gave Harris a model even earlier, for while Harris was still on Turner's paper he published a letter in Cracker dialect, signed Obediah Skinflint, to Lincoln, telling the President "that unless he evacuates Washington in less time 'than a sheep can skin a 'simmon tree,' Jeff Davis will break his pitcher at the cistern."—Julia Collier Harris, *The Life and Letters of Joel Chandler Harris* (Boston, 1918), p. 46.

[6] *Georgia Stories* (New York, 1896) and *The World's Wit and Humor—American*. See also the letter written to E. L. Burlingame, December 28, 1893, which reveals

The fiction thus linked with the earlier humor varied as much in quality as did the humor itself. Regardless of its origin, considering it solely as humorous fiction, those who read it today will find that two local colorists, more than any others among its creators, merit attention as creators of comedy rather than as historical landmarks. Critical readers of today will probably find least appealing the writings of Edward Eggleston and Bret Harte. The former, for all his talk about the crudeness of Southwestern humorists, was far below the best of them in artistry, while the latter is revealed, after the decades which have passed since he began his career, as a trickster whose tricks are too obvious, as a character portrayer whose characters are too evidently formulae rather than people. W. D. Howells, pointing out that Eggleston's first book was weakest when its author attempted pathos or dealt with religion,[1] touched on a real barrier to appreciation of all his books today. The sentimentality of an incorrigible sentimentalist and the preaching of an irrepressible moralizer enter far too often into Eggleston's books, blurring or cluttering up the story.[2] And these qualities in the author are probably responsible for the creation of as melodramatic a set of black-hearted villains as one may find outside of dime novels or melodrama. By contrast, Harte's characters are too virtuous; for he, of course, had no villains: that was part of his formula. Hence, one reading through many of Harte's pages begins to yearn before long for the introduction of someone totally depraved—some prostitute, thief, gambler, or drunkard within whose breast is a heart *not* of gold. However, some of Harte's poems continue to be amusing, and his tales, before one discovers the formula, are mildly diverting. The best passages in Eggleston are fair humor. Both of these writers, in short, are more important historically than they are aesthetically: they both called attention to unexploited riches of American life for the fictionist; both bridged the gap between humor and "more respectable" fiction, and both to some extent battered old prejudices against fiction.[3]

enthusiasm for *Georgia Scenes, Major Jones' Courtship, Simon Suggs*, and Johnston's writings, quoted in Julia Collier Harris, *op. cit.*, pp. 316–317.

[1] *Atlantic*, XXIX, 363–364 (March, 1872).

[2] For justification of this characterization, see George Cary Eggleston, *op. cit.*

[3] Religion in Eggleston's books probably won them places in libraries kept pretty

Much more enduring is the appeal of other local colorists whose writings have elements of comedy—Sarah Orne Jewett, whose quiet sketches are hardly robust enough to classify as American humor, but sure to endure as literature; Rose Terry Cooke, who wrote tales in which humor was an occasional grim incidental intrusion; Rowland E. Robinson, who caught the dry comedy of Vermont; Mary E. Wilkins Freeman, who better than any other in the period, perhaps, reproduced the sharp comedy and the tragic irony of New England repression; Mary N. Murfree, more memorable for her description than her humorous passages; George W. Cable, who learned from his masters some tricks of sly Gallic humor; Thomas Nelson Page, whose comedy is touched with sadness because of his deep nostalgia for the days before the war. The semi-humorous writings of these and perhaps the writings of others among the many who created local color studies will continue to appeal. But because they were essentially and not incidentally humorous, some of the diverting writings of Harriet Beecher Stowe and Joel Chandler Harris demand more thorough consideration than these in any study of American humor. These authors, typical local colorists in many ways, are important not only as historical figures but also as depicters of two delightful characters who deserve high places among the creations of American humorists—Sam Lawson and Uncle Remus.

In 1872, T. S. Perry, having recently read *Sam Lawson's Fireside Stories*, suggested that perhaps Mrs. Stowe's great popularity was not "due entirely to her wonderful success with *Uncle Tom's Cabin*. To her youngest readers that book must be already a thing of the past; but we fancy that it is because she has succeeded in catching certain traits of American life that she is widely read. Besides, with all her faults, she is a humorist. . . . Sam Lawson . . . is an extremely amusing person . . . an admirable copy of an original that can be found in almost any New England village."[1] Others saw in this book admirable qualities. The reviewer in *Scribner's* remarked:

clear of fiction by religious folk. For the importance of Harte's assault upon Victorianism, see George R. Stewart, Jr., *Bret Harte—Argonaut and Exile* (Boston, 1931), pp. 167–168, 330–331. The golden hearts of Harte's prostitutes and gamblers probably helped them a great deal when they sought admission into respectable society.

[1] "American Novels," *North American Review*, CXV, 370 (October, 1872).

He [Sam Lawson] is, to our way of thinking, the best drawn Yankee in print. The perfection of the characterization . . . is in danger of being overlooked in consequence of regarding him too exclusively as the story-teller. But in every tale . . . he really reveals himself. His shrewdness, his humor, his patience, his tenderness, his uncouthness, his simplicity, all are revealed in every sentence he speaks.[1]

And Howells thought Mrs. Stowe had never surpassed the work in these tales which, he said, "have lured us to read them again and again by their racy quaintness and the charm of the shifty Lawson's character and manner." A whole Yankee village-world, he pointed out, "the least important figure of which savors of the soil and 'breathes full East'" is conjured up by the tales. "The virtues of fifty years and more ago, the little local narrowness and intolerance, the lurking pathos, the hidden tenderness of a rapidly obsolescent life, are all here, with the charm of romance in their transitory aspects. . . ."[2]

To merit this high praise, Mrs. Stowe effectively adapted for her own end the framework form which served the Southwestern humorists so well. As usual there was the contrast between the language of the framework and that of the story-teller.

The framework vividly described and lucidly explained Sam, "a tall, shambling, loose-jointed man, with a long, thin visage, prominent watery blue eyes, very fluttering and seedy habiliments, who occupied the responsible position of first do-nothing-in-ordinary in our village of Oldtown . . . a man who won't be hurried, and won't work, and will take his ease in his own way, in spite of the whole protest of his neighborhood. . . ."

The framework, in addition, concretely bodied forth the varied aspects of the New England scene. At times it was a gloomy country with "an iron-bound shore" against which the Atlantic "dashed its moaning waters." Again, sunlight made the scene idyllic, and the river, dotted with "white flocks of water-lilies," had "grassy green banks" shaded by "graceful elm draperies"; or golden light fell on a huckleberry pasture, "embroidered with star-moss and wintergreen, or foamy patches of mossy frostwork" with

[1] *Scribner's Monthly*, III, 761 (April, 1872).
[2] *Atlantic*, XXIX, 365-366 (March, 1872).

fire-lilies rising "in jets of flame." Or the scene narrowed down to a circle of light from the hearth, and Sam, comfortable and cozy, dipped his thin nose into a mug of cider during pauses in his tale. The shifting background assumed shapes appropriate for the varied yarns spun by Lawson.

But though the scenes of the framework, vivid and often homely, properly set the scene for Sam's yarning, the tales themselves created another New England. Winds in the enclosed tales went "a-screechin' round the chimbley," with power enough to fetch a woman. The huckleberry patch he depicted was so hot in August that "you could fairly hear the huckleberries a sizzlin' and cookin' in the bushes, and the locust kept a gratin' like a hot saw." For this elvish observer, Oldtown was a place wherein comedy intruded unwelcomed into the serious lives of comic people—the amusing Mis' Amaziah Pipperidge, for example, "a widder with snappin' black eyes, and a hook nose,—kind o' like a hawk . . . one o' them up-and-down commandin' sort o' women, that feel they have a call to be seein' every thing that goes on in the parish," or others who are equally comic as his salty phrases reveal them. These folk behaved amusingly: a flirtatious woman "went off switchin' and mincin'" or an angry man "bounced right over in his bed." Sam's stories, meandering along like "a dreamy, slow-moving river through a tangled meadow-flat," recalled ghostly visitors, seekers for buried treasures, Yankee lads a-courtin', the comic fellow who pretended he was the devil, the ram on the rampage which upset the meetin', and preachers who involuntarily inspired laughter.

Both the stories and the framework served to "make tremendously alive Sam Lawson." [1] Better than any frontier yarn-spinner, he was individualized by contrast, for all around him were the glum New Englanders, pondering deep problems of theology and going about their tasks tight-lipped, very different indeed from complacent, jolly Sam, his philosophical problems tolerantly settled, his life—despite stern disapproval—joyously, irresponsibly lazy. [2] He was a simple fellow at times. A poor hand at deception,

---

[1] Pattee, *Development of the American Short Story*, p. 248.
[2] See the comment of O. F. Matthiessen, "New England Stories," in *American Writers on American Literature* (New York, 1930), pp. 400–401.

he was unable to hide some of his secrets: unconsciously he revealed that he took part in the disreputable treasure hunt and that the girl he thought was his for the asking would not have him after all. And he saw no irony in the fact that a rich man, much better than a poor one, could preach powerful sermons about the evils of money. But he had his elements of shrewdness. He knew how to pretend piety when he had it not; he could look innocent enough as he revealed how gossipy women spread a secret; and he knew intimately the quirks of the pawky New Englanders. He kept his watery eyes busy, and what he saw and the glib way he told what he saw made fine Yankee comedy.

Various figures of the South are very well depicted in the writings of Joel Chandler Harris; but his masterpieces, overshadowing the rest, are the books which portray Uncle Remus, especially *Uncle Remus: His Songs and Sayings* (New York, 1880) and *Nights with Uncle Remus* (Boston, 1883). Here, employing essentially the same technique as Mrs. Stowe and some of the humorists of the old Southwest for his portrayal of the Southern Negro, he won fuller appreciation than any of his predecessors. From their appearance, his writings about Uncle Remus were recognized as classics.

It may be that his artistry was more quickly noted than that of the others because he depicted members of a different race, or because his success contrasted so brilliantly with the dismal failure of most of those who had tried to picture the Negro before he turned his hand to the task.[1] It may have been because to the incongruities of the earlier stories using the framework, all useful in his tales—incongruity of language, of settings, of fictional methods—he added another in his animal legends which may have been more easily perceived, "that incongruity," as he described it, "of animal expression that is just human enough to be humorous."[2]

[1] See John Herbert Nelson, *The Negro Character in American Literature* (Lawrence, 1926), which contains (pp. 107–119) the best criticism of Harris's work in this field, and Benjamin G. Brawley, *The Negro in Literature and Art* (Atlanta, 1910).

[2] Letter from Harris to Frederick S. Church, regarding the illustrations for Harris's first book, quoted in Julia Collier Harris, *op. cit.*, pp. 148–149. Church did not succeed in interpreting what Harris called "the roaring comedy of animal life," although A. B. Frost, later, was brilliantly successful. The comedy was not new, for some of the Southwestern humorists had already made use of it. But Harris used it consistently in his legends.

And it is likely that the enthusiasm for portrayals of Southern types, which culminated in the eighties, had much to do with Harris's immediate success.

Regardless of the reason for the success of these books, they deserved praise because, with all their restraint, they effectively revealed a variety of incongruities, thus providing delightful comedy, and because in three ways they illuminated Negro life and character.

In the framework, objectively presented, Uncle Remus became a living figure as bits of description, presented at intervals, culminated in a vivid portrait. Not only did Harris display the physical aspect of the man: especially well, he caught his activities and gestures—the way he smiled or shook his head, the way he adjusted his spectacles before he threaded a needle, the way he "settled himself back in his seat with an air of melancholy resignation," or "rubbed his hands together contemplatively . . . chuckling to himself in a very significant manner." Little by little, his life, past and present, in all its aspects, was presented. Better than anywhere else in fiction one learns here of the ways of life on the old plantation;[1] more clearly than anywhere are set forth the racial relationships of the pre-war South. Thus the lifelike representation of Uncle Remus, typical of his race and yet highly individualized against his background, makes one understand the Negro.

But even more revealing are the monologues within the framework, for they show Uncle Remus's ways of thinking, of looking at things. Recorded, with loving accuracy,[2] by a man who savored the flavor of folk speech,[3] this character's talk, as had been the dialect of many American humorous figures, consistently was enriched by figurative language drawn directly from the speaker's experience. But the peculiar poetic gift of his race gave it a quality

[1] F. P. Gaines, *The Southern Plantation* (New York, 1924), pp. 75–77.

[2] There is pretty general agreement as to the accuracy of the dialect. Professor Nelson, *op. cit.*, p. 113, points out that this accuracy extends through page after page, volume after volume.

[3] When he was writing the Aunt Minerva stories in Negro dialect, Harris wrote to Burlingame: ". . . I am very fond of writing this dialect. It has a fluency all its own; it gives new coloring to statement, and allows a swift shading in narrative that can be reached only in the most painful and roundabout way."—Julia C. Harris, *op. cit.*, pp. 403–404.

of its own: it had rhythms sometimes almost metrical in their regularity; it employed, as the spirituals do, the somehow mournful device of repetition;[1] comically, it employed onomatopoeia.[2] Its most notable quality, however, was its indirectness: here, for example, is how the old man revealed that Brer Rabbit stole the fish which Brer Wolf had left lying on the ground:

"Dar wuz de fishes, en dar wuz Brer Rabbit, en w'en dat de case w'at you speck a sorter innerpen'ent man like Brer Rabbit gwin do? I kin tell you dis, dat dem fishes ain't stay whar Brer Wolf put um at, en w'en Brer Wolf come back dey wuz gone."[3]

In this revelatory language, Uncle Remus registered his opinions of things in general and things in particular. The section of *Uncle Remus: His Songs and Sayings* called "His Sayings" presents a commentator on all sorts of subjects;[4] but even in the Brer Rabbit stories, a consistent philosophy is disclosed. Brer Tarrypin, in "Mr. Rabbit Finds His Match at Last," had, Uncle Remus revealed, played a mean trick:

"But, Uncle Remus," said the little boy, dolefully, "that was cheating."

"Co'se, honey. De creeturs 'gun ter cheat, en den fokes tuck it up, en hit keep on spreadin'. Hit mighty ketchin', en you mine yo' eye, honey, dat somebody don't cheat you 'fo' yo' ha'r git gray ez de ole nigger's."

In similar passages, the old man's whole simple philosophy is revealed.

But in addition to the objective portrait, and in addition to the old man's commentaries, there are, of course, the stories—folk-tales of the Negro race, having originated after the fashion

---

[1] A beautiful example occurs in "Mr. Fox Tackles Old Man Tarrypin," wherein there is an intricate pattern of incremental repetition in the opening lines.

[2] In the tale referred to in footnote 1, this page, Uncle Remus lovingly repeats three times a word which catches the sound of Brer Tarrypin's trip to the bottom of the pool. "Kerblunkity-blink!" he says, giving the phrase "gutteral sonorousness." See also Brer Bullfrog's song in "Mr. Bear Catches Old Mr. Bullfrog."

[3] In "How Mr. Rabbit Saved His Meat." A pleasant variant is Brer Rabbit's worried suggestion to the buzzard, on whose back he is dangerously perched at the top of a tree: "Don't flop yo' wings . . . kaze den ef you duz, sum'n 'ill drap fum up yer . . ." Numerous examples might be cited: Professor Smith cites one in "Dialect Writers," *Cambridge History of American Literature*, II, 352.

[4] These are in the tradition, of course, of the literary comedians.

of cherished oral tales. The world which their creators have invented is a dream world of which the hero is "the weakest and most harmless of all animals," and yet that hero, Brer Rabbit, is, as Harris says, "victorious in contests with the bear, the wolf, and the fox. It is not virtue that triumphs, but helplessness; it is not malice, but mischievousness."[1] The anthropomorphosis which the animal characters undergo is just as illuminating as the fables. As Professor Nelson says:

The ideals of the animals are the negro's; their prying dispositions, their neighborliness, their company manners, their petty thefts, their amusements are all the negro's; Brer Rabbit likes the same kind of food, the same brand of fun, as his interpreter does: he has the same outlook on life. Even the hopeless incongruity of this animal world—the rabbit and the fox owning cows, and hurting their "hands," and feeling an elementary kind of responsibility for their families—is part and parcel of the negro spirit. It is a product of his primitive outlook on life, of a poetical feeling that takes no account of the hard logic of consistency.[2]

Hence, the animals "had der camp-meetin' times en der bobby cues w'en de wedder wuz 'greeable," and Brer Rabbit, leaving Miss Meadows and the gals after a social call, "paid um his 'specks, en tip his beaver, en march off, he did, des ez stiff en ez stuck up ez a fire-stick."

In the field of humorous depiction, then, the local color writers achieved their greatest success in the writings of Mrs. Stowe and Joel Chandler Harris. One other notable achievement of these portrayers should, perhaps, be noted. This achievement was suggested by Harris when, in the preface to his first volume, he asserted "that a volume in dialect must have its solemn, not to say melancholy, features." In 1880, this was a typical rather than an unusual suggestion. Tenderly nostalgic as they looked back to vanished or vanishing ways of living, the local colorists had, from the beginning, been eager to follow Dickens in the sympathetic revelation of the sadder elements in humble life. For the first time, therefore, pathos or even tragedy became a part of many

[1] Preface to Harris's first book. See also Pattee, *American Literature since 1870*, pp. 304–305.
[2] *Op. cit.*, p. 116.

passages of American humor. Too often, that pathos—as in Harte or in Eggleston—was likely to be associated with sentimentality; but in some writings—those of Mrs. Stowe or Harris at their best, for example,—the perception of this element in life made for a fuller and more human portraiture.

By 1880, the way had been prepared for the masterpiece of American humor. Its creator had already made his sensational appearance upon the scene. In 1884, Mark Twain was to give the world *The Adventures of Huckleberry Finn*.

VII. MARK TWAIN

It is impossible, of course, to discover any author who furnishes a better climax to a consideration of American humor than Mark Twain. It would also be difficult to discover any author who furnishes better opportunities for a summary. For Mark Twain was trained as a writer in the old Southwest during the days of the flowering of its humor; his first recovered published sketch appeared in a comic periodical published in Boston by a writer of Down East humor; he rose to fame as a literary comedian, and his masterpieces were created in the field of local color.

No one in the early days of Clemens's fame would have argued against the assertion that he emerged to prominence as a literary comedian, or, as the phrase had it, "a funny man." The reviewer in the *Nation* found in *Innocents Abroad* (1869) "all the prominent characteristics of our peculiar school of humorists— their audacity, their extravagance and exaggeration."[1] A few years later, Howells was noting "the grotesque exaggeration and broad irony" of *Roughing It* (1872),[2] which, as a scholar has recently asserted, "was looked upon as a funny book, of the journalistic sort."[3] Other books which followed did not change the opinion of a number of critics about his proper classification: in 1891, Professor Beers of Yale thought it proper to mention him as one of a group including Artemus Ward, Nasby, Billings, Kerr, and Nye, "the most eminent by all odds" of them, but much like Ward:

[1] IX, 195 (September 2, 1869).
[2] *Atlantic*, XXIX, 754 (June, 1872).
[3] Minnie M. Brashear, *Mark Twain, Son of Missouri* (Chapel Hill, 1934), p. 7.

Mark Twain's drolleries have frequently the same air of innocence and surprise as Artemus Ward's, and there is a like suddenness in his turns of expression, as where he speaks of "the calm confidence of a Christian with four aces." If he did not originate, he at any rate employed very effectively that now familiar device of the newspaper "funny man," of putting a painful situation euphemistically, as when he says of a man who was hanged that he "received painful injuries which terminated in his death." He uses to the full extent the American humorist's favorite resources of exaggeration and irreverence. An instance of the former quality may be seen in his famous description of a dog chasing a coyote, in *Roughing It*, or in his interview with the lightning-rod agent. . . .[1]

"He was often very funny," remarked Barry Pain, in 1910, "and he knew every trick of the trade."[2]

He did, indeed; going through his pages one may discover any number of the devices of the literary comedians—in abundance in his earlier works and scattered through his later ones—puns, malapropisms, misquotations of the Bible or the classics (like the famous mistreatment of Shakespeare in *Huckleberry Finn*), sentences which juxtapose incongruities, understatements. Sometimes, as in Chapter XVII of *A Tramp Abroad*, a series of comic sentences huddled together on a page:

. . . a most prodigious fire-breathing dragon used to live in that region, and made more trouble than a tax collector. He was as long as a railway train. . . . [comic similes] His breath bred pestilence and conflagration, and his appetite bred famine. [Exaggeration] He ate men and cattle impartially, and was exceedingly unpopular. [Anticlimax and understatement]. . . . So the most renowned knights came from the four corners of the earth and retired down the dragon's throat one after the other. [Anticlimax]

The manner was unmistakable in such passages. Too, he assumed for purposes of humor, like the doctor in *Innocents Abroad*, and like typical funny men, the character of what Mark called "an

[1] *Initial Studies in American Letters*, p. 201. Mark Twain was the author, says this critic, of *Innocents Abroad, Roughing It, A Tramp Abroad*, and "others not so good." Those not so good included, interestingly enough, *Tom Sawyer, Huckleberry Finn*, and *Life on the Mississippi*.

[2] "The Humour of Mark Twain," *London Bookman*, XXXVIII, 107 (June, 1910).

inspired idiot." [1] "The most conspicuous intellectual trait of Mr. Clemens," observed an English critic, "seems to me to be an almost preternatural shrewdness, thinly veiled under the assumption of simplicity. . . ." [2] On the lecture platform, he assumed the manner of the conventional comic lecturer, acting out the customary role. A member of the audience attending his first lecture described:

His slow deliberate drawl, the anxious and perturbed expression of his visage, the apparently painful effort with which he framed his sentences, and, above all, the surprise that spread over his face when the audience roared with delight or rapturously applauded the finer passages. . . .

The commentator went on to say that this was something previously entirely unknown, original; [3] but that seems doubtful, for every part of the description applied equally well to Ward on the lecture platform. [4]

It seems quite possible, in fact, that Mark learned a great deal about the art of the humorous lecture from Ward. He cited Ward as a great artist in "the dropping of a studied remark apparently without knowing it" and in the handling of the pause, [5] and on at least one occasion, he suggested before a lecture: "Would you mind, now, just to please me, letting me introduce myself, as Artemus used to do?" [6]

Understandably, therefore, it became conventional to suggest that Mark learned from Ward not only the way to speak but also

[1] "The doctor," said Mark, "asks the questions, generally, because he can keep his countenance, and look more like an inspired idiot, and throw more imbecility into the tone of his voice than any man that lives."

[2] Nichol, *op. cit.*, p. 426.

[3] Noah Brooks, "Mark Twain in California," *Century*, n.s. XXV, 98–99 (November, 1898).

[4] See the comment in the London *Spectator*, November 24, 1866, part of which has been quoted. This speaks of the impression created by Ward "that his confusions of thought and speech are all inevitable on his own part" and of his "hesitating, anxious way . . . often conveying a sense of difficulty. . . . A general effect of having to grope for his language . . . always hovers about his manner." J. E. Preston-Murdock spoke of Ward's "inimitable drawl," and the lecture reproduced in *Kings of the Platform and Pulpit* attempted to reproduce this feature of his lecture, by spacing the words. Like Mark, too, he feigned surprise at unseemly outbursts of mirth.

[5] "How to Tell a Story," *Literary Essays* (New York, 1899), pp. 11–12.

[6] W. H. Merrill, "When Mark Twain Lectured," *Harper's Weekly*, L, 199 (February 10, 1906).

the way to write humorously. "The imitation is discoverable," suggested Robert Ford, "in the joke forms peculiar to both. Each writer . . . begins in a serious—or apparently serious—mood, and produces his comic effects—or the best of them—by giving the most ludicrous and unexpected turns to his sentences."[1] Conceivably, he might have cited such a passage as this, written by Clemens when, above the pseudonym of Thomas Jefferson Snodgrass, he used the sort of cacography employed by Ward:

It mought be that some people think your umble sarvent has "shuffled off this mortal quile" and bid an eternal adoo to this subloonary atmosphere—nary time. He ain't dead, but sleepeth. That expreshun are figerative, and go to signerfy that he's pooty much quit scribblin.[2]

Place alongside this a passage by Ward:

Gentz—Hears two you old fellers . . . I spose you have bin a wonderin whare upon arth the undersined was . . . and prehaps the sollum thawt has struck you that i had taken my departer from this mundane spear and as Hamleck sez, "Shoveled orf this mortal Koil," and seazed two be no moore. Likeliz not yu hav bin temptid moren once to rite a obitchuary . . . But surs my time hasent arrovan yet.[3]

The resemblance is unmistakable. But if there is any influence here, it is Clemens who is the tutor; for the Snodgrass letter appeared April 10, 1857, and the Ward letter is dated "May the 25 18&58." It is probable, however, that neither author particularly influenced the writings of the other. Both were following a well established tradition in American humor. But though there is probably no literal indebtedness on Mark's part to Ward, Clemens owes much to the method of the literary comedians.

His debt to Down East humor may, similarly, be one merely to tradition; though a closer relationship with an individual work seems highly possible. The first printed sketch by Sam Clemens which has been discovered appeared in the *Carpet-Bag*, edited by B. P. Shillaber, in the issue of May 1, 1852,[4] in the same issue

---

[1] Robert Ford, *American Humorists Recent and Living* (London, 1897), pp. 32–33.
[2] *The Adventures of Thomas Jefferson Snodgrass*, ed. C. Honce (Chicago, 1928), p. 31.
[3] Quoted in Seitz, *Artemus Ward*, p. 39.
[4] "The Dandy Frightening the Squatter," discovered by Franklin J. Meine, who

which contained a Partington paper detailing the mischievous activity of Ike Partington in school. This humorous paper was well known in the West: it had two agents in St. Louis; it was widely quoted by river town newspapers; it was a permanent exchange of the Hannibal *Journal*, into which some of its jests were copied.[1] Sam Clemens, printer's devil, may have put some of them in type, or later, when the Partington books appeared, he may have read one or two of them.

At any rate, when Clemens, in *Tom Sawyer*, portrayed the amusing Aunt Polly, a better feminine characterization than any created by his Southwestern humorous predecessors, he drew one quite reminiscent of Shillaber's Mrs. Partington. There is a physical resemblance. One who looks at a picture of Shillaber's heroine is immediately struck by the fact that she looks exactly like Aunt Polly. The fact must have been noted by someone in 1876, for, inexplicably, labeled "Contentment" and presumably representing Tom's aunt, the pleasing illustration which had revealed the dame in *The Life and Sayings of Mrs. Partington* (1854) turned up in the first edition of *Tom Sawyer* on page 274.[2] But the resemblance is more than physical. Like Aunt Polly, Ruth Partington was a widow, burdened with the task of caring for an orphaned nephew. Like Aunt Polly, it develops in the series of books about her, she cared for the boy's health by administering frequent doses of patent medicine in which she had great faith. Aunt Polly, said Mark, "was one of those people who are infatuated with patent medicines." Mrs. Partington had said of such nostrums: ". . . there's so much virtue in 'em that everybody . . . will be made over new, and there'll be no excuse for dying. . . ." Aunt Polly had trouble because doctors changed their treatments frequently. So with Ike's aunt. "Things change so," she complained, "that I don't know how to subscribe for any disease now-a-days."

reprinted it in *Tall Tales of the Southwest*, pp. 447–448. Its attribution to Clemens is generally accepted. See George Hiram Brownell, "Mark Twain's First Published Literary Effort," *American Book Collector*, III, 92–95 (1933).

[1] De Voto, *op. cit.*, p. 89. Mr. De Voto notes that "between March 4 and June 3, 1852, with five weekly issues missing, the *Carpet-Bag* is quoted [by the *Journal*] four times. This is perhaps the average frequency."

[2] Mr. Franklin J. Meine discovered this interesting point. The picture is reproduced in this book, p. 517.

Mrs. Partington and Aunt Polly, both Calvinists, believed that they should sternly punish their nephews for their frequent mischievous adventures. (Ike, like Tom, had a particular flair for torturing cats.)[1] Often, though, both tender-hearted women failed to do their duty, and then rebuked themselves. And typically both Tom and Ike pulled the wool over the eyes of their innocent aunts:

"Dear me," said she [Mrs. Partington], dropping into a chair, "I am afraid your predestination will not be a good one, if you go on so; and little boys who tease their aunts don't go to heaven, by a great sight." Ike was much subdued by this, and, taking advantage of her momentary abstraction and three doughnuts, he whistled for Lion and went out to play.[2]

. . . she [Aunt Polly] took him [Tom Sawyer] into the closet and selecting a choice apple, delivered it to him, along with an improving lecture upon the added virtue and flavor a treat took to itself when it came without a sin through virtuous effort. And while she closed with a happy Scriptural flourish, he "hooked" a doughnut. Then he skipped out.[3]

Since these traits of Mrs. Partington are thus faithfully reproduced in the depiction of Aunt Polly, it may seem rather surprising that Mark told his biographer that Tom's aunt was really a portrayal of the author's mother. The statement was probably, so far as Mark's recollection went, quite true. But one sentence in the biography by Paine makes one wonder how accurate Mark's recollections were. Speaking of his mother's tenderness, he said: "She would drown the young kittens, when necessary, but warmed the water for the purpose."[4] It makes one wonder because, in 1854, Shillaber had recorded that Ike's aunt, confronted with a similar unpleasant chore, prepared for its performance by pouring hot water in the tub to take the chill off. "It would be cruel," she said, "to put 'em in stone-cold."[5] Such repetition may have been an example of fiction appropriated to autobiography, like

---

[1] "It is interesting to observe that her nephew Ike and his experience with the dog and cat and with 'spirits' is a striking prototype of Tom Sawyer in his relationship to his Aunt Polly."—Will D. Howe, *op. cit.*, p. 155.

[2] *Knitting-Work* (Boston, 1859), p. 301.

[3] *The Adventures of Tom Sawyer*, Chapter III.

[4] Albert Bigelow Paine, *Mark Twain, a Biography* (New York, 1912), I, 36.

[5] The story is reprinted hereafter, pp. 267–268.

the Davy Crockett story which Clemens appropriated to himself[1] or Crockett's own use of "Georgia Theatrics" from Longstreet's volume. The details of the portrait of Tom's aunt may have been an example of the sort of "unconscious plagiarism" which caused Mark to borrow from Holmes.[2] The whole resemblance may have been a coincidence. It is impossible to say. The conclusion must be, however, that Mark here, as elsewhere,[3] had links with the traditions of the pre-war Down East humor.

But most important of all was the influence in Mark's writing of the humor of the old Southwest. He grew up with that humor. It adorned the newspaper and periodical exchanges which came to his brother's newspaper, for which he set type. He heard oral versions of it in Hannibal where he lived as a boy and on the river steamboats where he worked as a young man. It followed him to the Pacific Coast, where it was published, sometimes in its old forms, sometimes in newly adapted forms, in the newspapers. To it, he was greatly indebted. Specifically, perhaps, in general, certainly, he was indebted to Crockett, Longstreet, and those who followed them. Passages in Mark's writings time after time are reminiscent of this older Southwestern humor. A paragraph in *Tom Sawyer* which tells how Tom behaved when a fellow student stole his sweetheart offers an example. Tom rehearsed, alone, the defiant remarks he would make upon meeting his rival. And, says Mark:

. . . he went through the motions of thrashing an imaginary boy—pummeling the air, and kicking and gouging. "Oh, you do, do you? You holler 'nough, do you? Now, then, let that learn you!" And so the imaginary flogging was finished to his satisfaction.[4]

The humor of the paragraph is, of course, exactly the same as that in Longstreet's "Georgia Theatrics," wherein another imaginative youngster ruthlessly had licked an imaginary opponent.[5] Mark as an old man told his biographer that he had known

[1] De Voto, *op. cit.*, p. 79.

[2] *Mark Twain's Autobiography* (New York, 1924), I, 238–242.

[3] *A Connecticut Yankee in King Arthur's Court* has, as Mr. De Voto has remarked, affiliations with the Jack Downing letters. See also Miss Rourke's *American Humor*, p. 215.

[4] Chapter XVIII.   [5] Reprinted hereafter, pp. 287–289.

Georgia Scenes for a long time.[1] Did he recall the book when he wrote the passage? Did he, perhaps, recall oral tellings of the same tale?[2] Regardless of how this question is answered, it must be conceded that the paragraph and its point derive from the Longstreet tradition. Many passages show that he turned to the same materials as did the earlier humorists, looking at those materials with the same attitudes, and using the same patterns and methods.

So far as material went, Mark's "Dandy Frightening the Squatter," the *Carpet-Bag* tale of 1852, might be regarded as a mosaic of materials earlier used. It told of a fop outwitted by a rustic: the theme had inspired a Kentucky almanac story as early as 1828.[3] The rustic called the swaggering dude's bluff when threatened with physical violence: the same theme had been developed by J. M. Field in a tale published in *A Quarter Race in Kentucky* (1846) and in Field's *The Drama in Pokerville* (1847).[4] The sketch told how a man went ashore from a steamboat to manhandle an inhabitant: the situation had been unfolded, with variations, in a volume published in 1851,[5] and Clemens's tale was, in plot, very like one going the rounds of newspapers just before his yarn was published.[6] Hints for the passage about Huck's trip to the circus might have come to Mark from tales by W. T. Thompson, G. W. Harris, or Richard Malcolm Johnston.[7] G. W. Harris might have suggested, in one of his sketches, the

---

[1] Wade, *Augustus Baldwin Longstreet*, p. 168.

[2] As indicated in footnote 3, p. 70, an oral version of the story was told on an Ohio steamboat in the thirties.

[3] *Farmer's Almanac for . . . 1829 . . .* (Lexington, 1828), p. 17.

[4] "Kicking a Yankee."

[5] Falconbridge [Jonathan Kelly], *Dan Marble* (New York, 1851), pp. 145–149. The story is assigned to Marble, who is said to have told it in 1842. The most important variation consists in the fact that the passenger defeated his opponents.

[6] Fred W. Lorch suggests that "A Scene on the Ohio," published in the Bloomington *Herald*, February 13, 1849, and credited to *The Elephant*, might have suggested Sam's version.—*American Literature*, III, 309–313 (November, 1931).

[7] "The Great Attraction" by Thompson is suggested by Mr. De Voto, though I am inclined to favor "The Expensive Treat of Col. Moses Grice," which came out in magazine form shortly before the book appeared. The latter tale, by Johnston, was used in *Mark Twain's Library of Humor* (New York, 1888), edited by others but probably with the aid of Clemens. George W. Harris used details in the story in a sketch published in 1868 which Mark probably did not see. To complete the record, it may be worth noting that the same anecdote is told as a happening of his childhood by E. W. Howe in his autobiography, *Plain People* (New York, 1929), pp. 45–47.

more refined episode about the boys in the loft who played jokes on the teacher in Chapter XXI of *Tom Sawyer*.[1] The passage in *Innocents Abroad* in which Clemens scornfully recorded that Lake Como was not nearly so wide as the Mississippi and that the Italian lake would seem a "bedizened little courtier" in the "august presence of Lake Tahoe"[2] and the passage about the Arno being "a historical creek with four feet of water . . . a very plausible river if they would pump some water into it"[3] were definitely foreshadowed, in 1841, by T. B. Thorpe, when he remarked: "Imagination in Europe is not up to reality in America. . . . The 'Big Bear of Arkansas,' if he should see the Thames, would designate it as 'that creek, thar.'"[4] Mark's explanation that his whole career was affected by his having a contagious disease revealed the same sort of comic thinking which led Madison Tensas to assert that *his* whole career depended on the fact that when Tensas was ten years old, a young woman wore "No. 2 shoes, when common sense and the size of her foot whispered 'fives.' "[5] Perhaps, as Mr. De Voto suggests, Mark was specifically indebted to other passages in the writings of Field, Thompson, Hooper, and Sol Smith.[6] However, whether his indebtedness was specific in any particular instance or not, there is

---

[1] "A Razor-Grinder in a Thunder Storm." The tone of the later passage is quite reminiscent of Sut, who would have delighted in all of its details, but who would have added more. Clemens undoubtedly knew the Lovingood yarns when they first appeared in the West and when they were published in book form; and Harris was represented in Mark's *Library of Humor*.

[2] First edition, Chapter XX, pp. 201, 204.

[3] First edition, Chapter XXIV, p. 247.

[4] *Spirit of the Times*, XI, 331 (September 11, 1841). Interesting, too, is the suggestion of Gerald Massey, in an article, "Yankee Humor," in the *Quarterly*, CXXII, 212–237 (January, 1867), reprinted in *Every Saturday*, III, 330–338 (March, 1867): "The geography [of America] has been too much for the brain. Thus we meet with a Yankee in England who is afraid of taking his usual morning walk lest he should step off the edge of the country. Another, who had been in Europe, when asked if he had crossed the Alps, said he guessed they did come over some risin ground." Of course, however, travel books which made use of this point of view preceded *Innocents Abroad*. In 1855, for example, one American traveler not only mistook the Thames for a creek but also had much fault to find with European art.—*Mr. Dunne Brown's Experiences in Foreign Parts* (Boston, 1857), pp. 19, 51–53.

[5] *Odd Leaves* . . ., p. 27.

[6] *Op. cit.*, pp. 252–257. Mr. De Voto thus summarizes: "So far as there is any validity in literary ideas, so far as notions of influence can be accepted, these writers, with the tradition to which they belonged, gave Mark Twain a means of perception and evocation, and gave him also the material to which he applied it."—*Ibid.*, p. 257.

no denying that in many passages of his works the subject matter and the attitudes of Mark Twain are definitely in the tradition of Southwestern humor.

The greatest gift of Southwestern humor to Mark, however, was the gift of a narrative method. This method is evident in his "Jumping Frog" story of 1865. The tale was an old one when he told it, even then "a classic of the mining-camps, rehearsed around campfires and in convivial gatherings."[1] It had been told, with variations, of course, at least twice in California newspapers.[2] But when Mark told that tale, he made it his own, and he made it his own because he applied to its telling the very effective framework technique whose efficacy had been discovered by numerous writers for the *Spirit of the Times*. Only one previous incarnation of a version of the yarn—so far as is known—had employed that technique, and, significantly, that telling of the story had appeared in Porter's paper.[3] In Mark's story, Simon Wheeler, "fat and bald-headed," with "an expression of winning gentleness," was given the honor of unfolding the narrative, which was repeated in Simon's own words—words which revealed the way his mind worked, the way he looked on life, the way he imagined. The technique—in its use of various types of incongruity, in its revelation—was in essentials exactly the technique of T. B. Thorpe's "Big Bear of Arkansas," of the Sut Lovingood yarns, of dozens of frontier masterpieces.

It was a technique which Mark fully appreciated. In "How to Tell a Story," he cited as a beautiful example a tale thus told by Riley "in the character of a dull-witted old farmer." The way of telling it, he noted, revealed the character of the narrator perfectly: "The simplicity and innocence and sincerity and unconsciousness of the old farmer are perfectly simulated, and the result is a performance which is thoroughly charming and delicious. This is art—and fine and beautiful, and only a master can compass it . . ."[4] Such a technique, Clemens pointed out to Joel

---

[1] Noah Brooks, *op. cit.*, p. 91.

[2] Brooks, in 1898, recorded that Samuel Seabrough claimed it. Seabrough's version (1858) and another, dated 1853, have been reprinted in Oscar Lewis, *The Origin of the Celebrated Jumping Frog of Calaveras County* (San Francisco, 1931).

[3] Henry P. Leland's "Frogs Shot without Powder," in the *Spirit of the Times*, May 26, 1855, reprinted in De Voto, *op. cit.*, pp. 340–342.

[4] *Literary Essays*, p. 11. He was talking, he specified, of oral story-telling, wherein

Chandler Harris, was responsible for what was best in the Uncle Remus stories. Harris had modestly protested that "the matter and not the manner . . . attracted public attention and won the consideration of people of taste in the North . . ."[1] Mark scoffed at the notion:

> My dear Mr. Harris,—You can argue *yourself* into the delusion that the principle life is in the stories themselves and not in the setting; but you will save labor by stopping with that solitary convert, for he is the only intelligent one you will bag. In reality the stories are only alligator pears—one merely eats them for the sake of the salad-dressing. Uncle Remus is most deftly drawn, and is a lovable and delightful creation; he, and the little boy, and their relations with each other, are high and fine literature, and worthy to live, for their own sakes; and certainly the stories are not to be credited with *them*. But enough of this; I seem to be proving to the man that made the multiplication table that twice one are two.[2]

He appreciated the framework. He appreciated, too, the monologue revealing character whether it was enclosed in a framework or not. Hence, as many testify, he could, by appreciative reading, make crystal-clear the obscure monologues by Robert Browning.[3] Hence he could create *Huckleberry Finn*, in which every paragraph revealed the yarn-spinner's character.

Clemens could assume, for the length of an essay, or for part of a book, or for a platform appearance, the role of a literary comedian; but essentially, all his life long, he was a teller of humorous anecdotes in the manner of Southwestern humorists, usually in a framework of description or narration. Mr. De Voto properly characterized the technique when he said:

> He took the humorous anecdote, combined it with autobiographical reminiscence, and so achieved the narrative form best adapted to his mind. . . . *The Innocents Abroad* is Mark's discovery of the

the speaker supplied the framework, in part: he cited Dan Setchell, Artemus Ward, Bill Nye, and Riley. When the story was printed, Riley supplied a framework introducing the character as, presumably, he did when he spoke.

[1] Julia C. Harris, *The Life and Letters of Joel Chandler Harris*, p. 168.

[2] *Mark Twain's Letters* (New York, 1917), pp. 401–402. The letter is dated August 10, 1881.

[3] William L. Phelps, "Mark Twain," *Yale Review*, XXV, 291–310 (Winter, 1936).

method. . . . Descriptive passages interrupt the narrative from time to time but its steady progress is accomplished by means of stories. . . . The same framework produces *Roughing It*, *A Tramp Abroad*, *Life on the Mississippi*, and *Following the Equator*.[1]

The picaresque method—the method with emphasis upon anecdotal narrative—developed in Southwestern humor was the art which he could best appreciate and employ. Of the larger patterns of fictional form created by a Nathaniel Hawthorne or a Henry James he might be unaware, but he knew, as he said, "that a man might tell that Jumping Frog Story fifty times without learning how to tell it."[2]

Like Richard Malcolm Johnston, therefore, Clemens was a Southwestern humorist whose abilities were properly appreciated and encouraged in the period of flourishing local color writing. He climbed to his first fame, of course, as a literary comedian; but there was something in the spirit of the times, something in addition to the appreciation of his comedy, which brought appreciation of what he had to offer. Consider the case of J. Ross Browne (1821–1875), his predecessor, a man whose earlier life ran a course parallel to the life of Clemens.[3] In *Yusef* (1853) and in *Adventures in the Apache Country* (1869), this author, whose attitudes and artistry were shaped by very similar currents to those which molded Mark's artistry, wrote books which had all the tricks of humor, all the journalistic appeals of Mark's very similar *Innocents Abroad* and *Roughing It*.[4] But Browne won slight recognition and dropped out of sight, while Mark not only succeeded sensationally but also forged ahead to write his master-

[1] *Op. cit.*, pp. 244–246.

[2] Clara Clemens, *My Father Mark Twain* (New York, 1931), p. 46.

[3] Both spent their boyhood on the Western frontier. Both, as young men, traveled through the United States. Both were active in commerce on the Mississippi—Browne on flatboats, Clemens on steamboats. Both were on the Pacific Coast during the days of the mining frontier, were trained in the frontier school of humor and on the humorous lecture platform. Both wrote of their impressions not only of Europe but also of the far West. See Francis J. Rock, *J. Ross Browne: a Biography* (Washington, D. C., 1929).

[4] See F. J. Rock, *op. cit.*, pp. 52–72. *Yusef*, like Mark Twain's book about Europe, satirizes travel literature, and Browne's other book has the same attitude as *Roughing It*. Still another book by Browne has its counterpart in *A Tramp Abroad*. Father Rock's conclusion is: "It is enough to suppose that Mark Twain became subject to the same frontier influences as Browne and developed the same point of view and the same methods of expression as the older writer."

pieces. Probably Browne could have written nothing like those masterpieces, but unlike Clemens, he was never urged to try.

Those masterpieces quite conceivably were encouraged by the appreciation of Mark Twain as a local colorist. As early as 1872, Howells was calling attention to the admirable depiction of life in Nevada discoverable in *Roughing It*.[1] The local color of *Life on the Mississippi* won for it the honor of serial publication in the *Atlantic*. The phrases used by Howells in praising *Tom Sawyer* were duplicated, in substance, in dozens of reviews of local color depictions: the book gave, he said, "incomparably the best picture of life in that region as yet known to fiction."[2] It is noteworthy that *The Adventures of Huckleberry Finn* was published at what Professor Pattee called "the high tide" of "the greatest flood of dialect literature that America has ever known," along with a surge of such writings which made the years 1883 and 1884 memorable.[3] By 1897, a critic was announcing that Clemens deserved fame, not because he was a great humorist or because he was a great artist, but because:

He has recorded the life of certain southwestern portions of our country, at one fleeting stage in their development, better than it is possible it will ever be done again. . . . His tenacious memory . . . microscopic imagination, and his real interest in the serious side of life make his pictures . . . both absolutely accurate and surprisingly comprehensive.[4]

Many of his attitudes were those of the local colorist. He looked back to a time in the past which seemed to him particularly charming, lovingly re-creating its details from memory. He wanted to be accurate in giving the flavor of those idyllic days.[5] His accuracy, typical in the 1880's, extended, so far as he could make it extend, to even the recording of the dialects of the sec-

---

[1] *Atlantic*, XXIX, 734 (June, 1872).

[2] *Atlantic*, XXXVII, 621 (May, 1876).

[3] *American Literature since 1870*, pp. 306–307. It is questionable whether Huck would have been permitted to come into being if Harte's M'liss and various other unconventional figures had not come into American literature before him.

[4] Charles Miner Thompson, "Mark Twain as an Interpreter of American Character," *Atlantic*, LXXIX, 448 (April, 1897).

[5] The effect of nostalgia upon a humorist's manner is admirably illustrated in the story by George W. Harris cited in footnote 3, p. 99. This most boisterous of humorists, looking back to the forties in 1867, created an idyll.

tion.[1] And in his depictions there were elements of tenderness far more characteristic of the local colorists than of the earlier humorists.

Mark Twain, in short, who as a personality could not help but be a humorist,[2] as a literary artist whose works were channeled by such currents, could not help but be an American humorist. His works are, in a sense, a summary of nineteenth-century native American humor. They are a climax, as well, to its development. They had, to be sure, its faults; but more important, in their best passages, they revealed the development of its artistry in the works of a genius.

His sins, which were many, were likely to be those of a literary comedian. He sometimes strained for too many laughs and therefore got none, assuming unnatural poses of idiocy, pouring out too many sentences hopefully constructed to create hilarity, forcing his materials into forms too fantastic to be amusing, allowing burlesque and caricature to intrude even into the pages of his best books. In the earlier books, only occasional passages hinted at his real abilities. But his sins diminished, though they did not disappear, as he moved from the role of the literary comedian to the accomplishment of a literary artist—in passages (for his greatness must be perceived in passages, or not at all) in *The Gilded Age*, *Tom Sawyer*, *Huckleberry Finn*, *Pudd'nhead Wilson*, *Life on the Mississippi*, and the underrated *Tom Sawyer Abroad*.

In the best parts of these volumes, more richly than any earlier humorist, he revealed background. Farm and woodland—the natural setting—had been vividly depicted in *The Biglow Papers;* the country folk at work and play had moved through the background of the writings of such diverse humorists as Seba Smith and G. W. Harris; and W. T. Thompson had explored the value of a community as a background. In Mark's pages, the scenic background was faultlessly described; and folk toiling and frolicking, whole communities as well as individuals, came to life. The dwellings of the characters, only slightly appreciated by earlier

[1] See Katherine Buxbaum, "Mark Twain and American Dialect," *American Speech*, II, 233–236 (February, 1927).

[2] Edward Wagenknecht, *Mark Twain, the Man and His Work* (New Haven, 1935), pp. 69–73. See also Friedrich Schönemann, *Mark Twain als literarische Persönlichkeit* (Jena, 1926).

humorists—the unforgettable Grangerford interior or "the House Beautiful" of Chapter XXXVIII of *Life on the Mississippi*, for example—minutely described, offered a new kind of delight.

His characterization, too, in his best anecdotal pieces of narration, marked a culmination. Smith, Lowell, Shillaber, Mrs. Whitcher, Thompson, Hooper, and G. W. Harris, and others each might create one, two, or three animated humorous characters, but Mark could throng his pages with laughable figures who breathed the breath of life. He could make them exist vividly through many pages, as he did with Huck, Tom, Jim, Colonel Sellers and Pudd'nhead Wilson, or he could give them vital creation in a few phrases as he did, in a few pages of *Huckleberry Finn*, when he depicted Boggs, Colonel Sherburn, and the village loafer who re-enacted the killing of Boggs. Or he could sketch them quickly in a framework, and then let them talk so revealingly that their mere way of telling a story made them intimate acquaintances of the reader. Mark Twain accomplished a wide range of character portrayal visioned but not achieved by earlier humorists.

But Mark, like those who preceded him in humor, was not only a fictionist: he was, in addition, a humorous fictionist. Satire of mankind in general and of American mankind in particular flashed as brilliantly on his best pages as it had in the pages of Seba Smith, James Russell Lowell, Johnson J. Hooper, and Petroleum V. Nasby. Like the humorous group of the Southwest, he recognized and developed the comedy of hilarious situation, writing with such high spirits that his most successful narratives had an exuberant zestfulness. Like most American humorists, he knew and exploited the incongruities between learned language and the vernacular. Like them, too, he realized the possibilities of laughter created by contrasts between realistic passages and fantastic ones, winning even greater success than they had because of his greater skill in perceiving, imagining, and recording what was essentially the same sort of detail. His gorgeous imagination made possible the recording of the fanciful flights of the Mississippi raftsmen, Jim Baker, and Huckleberry Finn, all perfectly in character and all wildly delightful.

His genius showed itself, too, in the creation of that type of

poetry with which American humor had experimented since the
beginning—the poetry of folk speech. "He imparted to the
printed page," said Brander Matthews, "the vivacity of the
spoken word, its swiftness and its apparently unpremeditated
ease."[1] Matthews referred to passages written by Clemens in his
own character; but, even more notably, perhaps, the same quality was imparted to spoken dialogue. No signs of laborious phrasing were evident in the drawling speech of Simon Wheeler, Jim
Baker, or Huck Finn—they just talked. But their talk, it should
be noted, had the precision, the imagination, of poetic art: almost every critical word was exactly the right one, nearly every
phrase reproduced the rhythms of conversation and evoked the
most effective imagery for purposes of laughter. And the daringly
chosen verbs, the metaphors, the conceits—verbal devices used
often enough by the earlier humorists—were shaped by Mark's
artistry to lift the boldly colored talk of his characters, at its best,
to new heights of splendor.

American humor, then, gave Mark Twain his materials, his
methods, and his inspiration. His success was merely the working
out of its attempted achievements on the level of genius.[2] Its
masterpiece, as well as Mark Twain's, was *Huckleberry Finn.*

VIII. AFTERMATH: TWENTIETH-CENTURY HUMORISTS

The end of the nineteenth century did not, of course, abruptly
halt the flow of humor in the older traditions.

Common-sensible characters—unlearned but sharp-minded,
experienced, and witty—literary descendants of old-time Yankees or of some literary comedians—continued to appeal to
many.[3] Kin Hubbard (1868–1930) began in 1905 to picture and
quote Abe Martin, a Hoosier bumpkin, first in the Indianapolis
News, later in many newspapers and in annual almanacs. So
popular were Abe's commentaries that even after Hubbard's

[1] "Mark Twain and the Art of Writing," *Essays on English* (New York, 1924),
p. 248.
[2] De Voto, *op. cit.*, pp. 240–241, applies this generalization to frontier humor. I
would agree that frontier humor is the greatest force in the shaping of his artistry
and that his humor is the greatest expression of the school. But his alliances with
other creators of American humor, it seems to me, also deserve emphasis.
[3] See Walter Blair, *Horse Sense in American Humor* (Chicago, 1942), pp. 256–273;
295–318.

death numerous newspapers reprinted selections daily. Robert Quillan's "Poor Pa" and "Aunt Het" and Stanley Link's "Chin Chow" were syndicated daily features in similar styles. Will Rogers (1879–1935), who started as a cowboy monologuist, turned writer and assumed the rôle of an unlettered commentator on public affairs in newspaper pieces, magazine articles, and books which possibly attracted more contemporary readers than writings of any successors had.[1] James Whitcomb Riley (1849–1916) and Edgar A. Guest (1881–1959) won large followings with rustic verses after the manner of Hosea Biglow, and though he was far from rustic Ogden Nash at times wrote weirdly metred and rhymed poems backing up the horse-sense dictum voiced in his "I'll Take a Bromide, Please," "It is well to remember that the mighty platitude is made up of little drops of experience, little grains of truth." As late as 1958 with *Only in America*, and 1959 with *For 2¢ Plain*, Harry Golden proved that a collection of pawky newspaper columns clearly in the old tradition could make the best-seller list and stay there for many months.[2]

Stories or yarns which in substance and form resembled those fashionable in the past often were highly successful. Don Marquis (1878–1937), who from 1906 to 1909 was an assistant editor of *Uncle Remus Magazine* in Atlanta, learned his trade not only from Joel Chandler Harris but also from Mark Twain.[3] His most famous characters were a cockroach and a cat, Archy and Mehitabel, humanized animals with resemblances to Bre'r Rabbit and Baker's jays. The cockroach Archy told tall tales in which feats of physical prowess occurred frequently. The boast of the tarantula who vanquished Freddy the rat echoes ancient frontier challenges:

> . . . he would stand in
> the middle of the floor and taunt

[1] Rogers enlarged his audience by appearing on the stage and in motion pictures and by broadcasting monologues on national radio hookups.

[2] Several reviewers remarked that the author was in the tradition of Nye, Twain, Dunne and Rogers.

[3] Christopher Morley, noticing similarities in backgrounds and techniques, called Marquis "our closest spiritual descendant of Mark Twain."—Introduction, *The Best of Don Marquis* (Garden City, 1946), p. xiv.

us ha ha he would say where i
step a weed dies do
you want any of my game i was
raised on red pepper and blood i am
so hot if you scratch me i will light
like a match you better
dodge me when i m feeling mean and
i don t feel any other way i was nursed
on a tobasco bottle if i was to slap
your wrist in kindness you
would boil over like job and heaven
help you if i get angry give me
room i feel a wicked spell coming on[1]

Marquis's "Old Soak," Clem Hawley, engaged in vernacular monologues which often became tall tales.[2] Irvin S. Cobb (1876–1944), who as a boy delighted in Sut Lovingood's yarns and as a beginning humorist made Mark Twain his model,[3] recounted his own adventures in the comic style of Twain's travel books and wrote many popular short stories featuring old Judge Priest, a julep-nourished Kentuckian like unto Huck's Colonel Grangerford. One of the most frequently anthologized short stories during the 1930's and 1940's was one by Stephen Vincent Benét (1898–1943), "The Devil and Daniel Webster" (1937), one of a number of the author's mock oral tales.[4] Wilbur Schramm wrote similar yarns for the *Atlantic Monthly* and the *Saturday Evening Post*.[5]

A number of twentieth-century authors wrote, usually in the vernacular, about tall-tale heroes such as Old Stormalong, Mike Fink, Davy Crockett, Febold Feboldson, Pecos Bill, John Henry, Joe Magarac and other comic demigods. Most made use

---

[1] *lives and times of archy and mehitabel* (Garden City, 1935), pp. 43–44. Because of physical limitations, Archy, who used Marquis's typewriter, was incapable of capitalizing or punctuating.

[2] *The Old Soak* (1921) and *The Old Soak's History of the World* (1924), both published in Garden City.

[3] Fred G. Neuman, *Irwin S. Cobb, His Life and Letters* (Emaus, Pa., 1938), p. 37; Max Eastman, *The Enjoyment of Laughter* (New York, 1936), p. 337.

[4] Others included "A Tooth for Paul Revere," "Johnny Pye and the Fool-Killer," "The Sobbin' Women," "Daniel Webster and the Sea-Serpent" and "Doc Mellhorn and the Pearly Gates."

[5] Collected in *Windwagon Smith and Other Yarns* (New York, 1947).

of legendary lore but augmented it with inventions of their own.[1] And a number of more scientific folklorists recorded in the field oral stories recounted in Texas (J. Frank Dobie and Mody C. Boatright), in Arkansas (Vance Randolph), in New York (Harold W. Thompson) and elsewhere.[2]

Literary comedians continued to attract readers. Robert J. Burdette, who had started his career in the nineteenth century, lived until 1914. Charles Heber Clark lived until 1915. And since Finley Peter Dunne lived until 1936, most of his writings in the personality of Mr. Dooley actually appeared during the present century. George Ade (1866–1944) collected into a book in 1899 *Fables in Slang*, pieces which had first appeared in the Chicago *Record*. Its remarkable success led to the syndication of new fables and the appearance in books of ten other collections (some often reprinted) by 1920. Ade used many of the comic ways of saying things literary comedians had exploited, adding the device of emphasizing slang, clichés, and unusual phrasings by capitalizing them. John Kendrick Bangs (1862–1922), Oliver Herford (1863–1935), and Gelett Burgess (1866–1951) were probably as famous and, despite remarkable versatility, were as much in the tradition.

Well into the 1920's the conductors of humorous newspaper columns—a group which had many close ties with the literary comedians—were increasingly popular. Their productions, often supplemented by similar ones from contributors, were miscellaneous, ranging from puns, comically shaped sentences, and witty aphorisms to pieces of some length—society verse, comic narratives, humorous essays. A newspaper in any city was likely to have its humorous columnist, though the most famous worked in Chicago and New York—Bert Leston Taylor (1866–1921), Don Marquis (1878–1937), Franklin P. Adams (1881–1960), Keith Preston (1884–1927), Heywood Broun (1888–1939) and Christopher Morley (1890–1957). Columns such as these men

---

[1] For bibliographies see Walter Blair, *Tall Tale America: A Legendary History of Our Humorous Heroes* (New York, 1944), pp. 257–262; Harold W. Felton (ed.), *Legends of Paul Bunyan* (New York, 1947), pp. 379–406; Daniel C. Hoffman, *Paul Bunyan, Last of Frontier Demigods* (Philadelphia, 1952), pp. 193–200.

[2] For a bibliography, see Richard M. Dorson, *American Folklore* (Chicago, 1959), pp. 282–300.

conducted gradually became unfashionable and tended to be replaced by those made up of serious commentary, gossip, or feature stories. Gossip columnists (Walter Winchell, for instance) often enlivened their reports with puns, word coinages, satirical gibes, smart cracks. And feature-story columns could be turned into books very like the products of older humorists. H. Allen Smith, for instance, in the 1940's produced three books which as individual chapters and as wholes conformed to patterns of older humorous books.[1] Anecdotes were loosely strung together by explanatory or narrative links, in the mode of Mark Twain's travel books.[2] Verbal tricks like those of the older literary comedians abound. And since the characters whom Smith celebrates often are bizarre figures, anecdotes about them frequently have the guise of tall tales with urban settings.[3]

In local color stories and in some novels, notably in *Huckleberry Finn*, native American humor during the nineteenth century had invaded reputable fiction. In the twentieth century humorous fiction, promulgating and modifying older traditions, was plentiful and prosperous. The influence of Mark Twain's masterpiece was clear in such varied books as O. Henry's *The Gentle Grafter* (1908), Don Marquis's *Danny's Own Story* (1912), Ring Lardner's *You Know Me Al* (1916), William Faulkner's *Wild Palms* (1939),[4] J. D. Salinger's *The Catcher in the Rye* (1945), William Saroyan's *The Adventures of Wesley Jackson* (1946), Saul Bellow's *The Adventures of Augie March* (1953) and Robert Lewis Taylor's *The Travels of Jaimie McPheeters* (1958) as well as in many novels which differ far more from *Huck* in tone.[5] Other comic fictional works varied greatly. Max Shulman wrote several wild fantasies embodying without stint the prankish sentences,

---

[1] *Low Man on a Totem Pole, Life in a Putty Knife Factory, Lost in the Horse Latitudes* (Garden City, 1941, 1943, 1944).

[2] Smith's selections and introductory remarks in his anthology of humor, *Desert Island Decameron* (Garden City, 1945) show that he has great admiration for Mark Twain.

[3] Though usually more subdued, the "Profiles" of *The New Yorker* are very similar.

[4] The "Old Man" narrative. See Malcolm Cowley, "Editor's Note," *The Portable Faulkner* (New York, 1951), p. 540.

[5] See Walter Blair, *Mark Twain and "Huck Finn"* (Berkeley, 1960), pp. 6–8.

the puns, the malapropisms, the incongruous juxtapositions typical of literary comedians. Sinclair Lewis at his most satirical constantly used grotesque descriptions of characters, scenes, and actions, and employed mimicry in his dialogue, all highly reminiscent of those in older American satire.[1] Booth Tarkington wrote very popular books about the Hoosier youngster, Penrod Schofield, and his playmates, quite in the mood and manner of *Tom Sawyer*.[2] Erskine Caldwell, Jesse Stuart, Mac Hyman, and on occasion William Faulkner exploited comedy like that in old-time Southern humorists' portrayals of shiftless poor whites.[3] John Steinbeck's light books about California's paisanos,[4] though they dealt with folk of mixed "Spanish, Indian, Mexican and assorted Caucasian bloods," showed similar delight in human fecklessness. At the opposite end of the social scale, J. P. Marquand satirized genteel New Englanders, Peter DeVries Eastern suburbanites.

As a rule these fiction writers devoted only a part of their energies to being comic, and few customarily wrote "pieces" for magazines and later collected them in books. They were not therefore called—nor were they—"humorists" in the older sense of the word. Yet they stole away portions, sometimes large, sometimes small, of the vast audience which writing humorists once had reached. Workers in other media met the demands for humor of even larger segments of the population. Pictorial humorists produced comic strips and animated cartoons enjoyed by millions. Comedians heard on some of America's 200,000,000 radio sets or seen on some of America's 50,000,000 television sets in the late 1950's entertained similarly large—or even larger—mass audiences.[5]

As newspaper columns and humorous sections changed or dis-

---

[1] These are most obvious in the ferociously satirical *Elmer Gantry* (1927).

[2] Sales of four of these exceeded a million.

[3] See Shields McIlwaine, *The Southern Poor White from Lubberland to Tobacco Road* (Norman, 1939); Stuart's *Taps for Private Tussie* (1943); Hyman's *No Time for Sergeants* (1954); Faulkner's "Spotted Horses," first published as a short story, later expanded and included in *The Hamlet* (1940).

[4] *Tortilla Flat* (1935), *Cannery Row* (1945), *Sweet Thursday* (1954).

[5] Writers for radio and television scripts, some highly capable, were practically unknown except in the trade.

appeared and as humor magazines dwindled in number,[1] some homespun wits, some tellers of yarns and tall tales, some old-school literary comedians survived as writing humorists.[2] An exceptional Harry Golden—aided by the timely appeal of some of his preachments—could score a remarkable success. But writers in the older tradition in general could not attract the vast fairly homogeneous audience which had read nineteenth-century humorists. A great share of the public satisfied its appetite for comedy in mass media—or in fiction of the less subtle sort.

The magazine which was more responsible than any other medium for the rise of a new type of humor even before its start in 1925 disavowed interest in rural and small-town readers who had been so important as part of the humorists' audience in the past:

THE NEW YORKER [said the Prospectus] will be the magazine which is not edited for the old lady in Dubuque. It will not be concerned in what she is thinking about. . . . THE NEW YORKER is a magazine avowedly published for a metropolitan audience and thereby will escape an influence which hampers most national publications. It expects a considerable national circulation, but this will come from persons who have a metropolitan interest.

Harold Ross, the author of the Prospectus, as editor, dominated the course of the magazine's development over the years until his death in 1951.[3] Not surprisingly, therefore, the announcement, as one of Ross's biographers remarks, "for conciseness and

[1] At the start of the century three reputable humor magazines were doing well—*Puck*, *Life*, and *Judge*. These, respectively, disappeared in 1918, 1936 and 1939. Meanwhile a single new one, *The New Yorker*, had been founded (in 1925) and has continued.

[2] The older humor survived in much pictorial humor. Crockett Johnson's "Barnaby" (very popular in the 1930's), Walt Kelley's "Pogo," and Al Capp's "Li'l Abner" perpetuated the tall tale in the comic strips, Walt Disney's and other producers' humanized animals and UFA's "Mr. Magoo" in animated cartoons. "Li'l Abner's" Dogpatchers, moreover, are kissing cousins of the squalid white trash of traditional Southern humor. "Skeezix," "Dagwood and Blondie," "the Gumps," and others are comic strips with appeals akin to those of old-time literary domestic sketches. On radio and television Jack Benny, Bob Hope, and George Gobel have many of the traits of the lecturing literary comedians.

[3] See Dale Kramer, *Ross and "The New Yorker"* (Garden City, 1952), and James Thurber, *The Years with Ross* (Boston, 1959). Kramer quotes the Prospectus, pp. 61–63.

prophecy has probably never been equaled in editorial manifestoes."[1] And not surprisingly the magazine attracted and sponsored four writers who by general agreement have been outstanding "modern humorists." Despite the urban flavor of their humor, or it may be because of it, each eventually achieved wide popularity.

Clarence Shepard Day (1874–1935), Robert Benchley (1889–1945), James Grover Thurber (1894–) and Sidney Joseph Perelman (1904–) all rose to prominence in the 1920's and were still being appreciatively read in the 1950's. And though they did not entirely break with the past—no humorist is likely to do this— they wrote humor based upon assumptions quite different from those of older humorists and employed techniques contrasting with older techniques.

Day, the son of a Wall Street broker, worked in the Stock Exchange after graduating from Yale in 1896. While serving in the navy during the Spanish-American War, he was crippled by arthritis. After the war, despite crippled hands, he became a cartoonist whose deft impressionistic drawings in some ways foreshadowed those of some imaginative moderns. He also became a journalist and a writer of sketches, essays, and books.[2] Not, however, until he wrote a series of family reminiscences, first for *Harper's Magazine*, later for *The New Yorker* and other magazines, did he find his best and most popular vein. *God and My Father*, *Life with Father*, and *Life with Mother* (New York, 1932, 1935, 1937) were best sellers (the second was a Book-of-the-Month Club choice); a dramatization based upon them had a prodigiously long run as a play and reincarnation as a successful motion picture.

Father, as Day pictures him, could have been an old-fashioned horse-sense philosopher if he had had a rural upbringing and had learned to say wise things in a witty way. Like Hosea Biglow and Josh Billings, he has arrived at firm opinions about what is right on the basis of sound experience and keen thinking. He

---

[1] Kramer, *op. cit.*, p. 61.

[2] *This Simian World, The Crow's Nest, Thoughts without Words, After All* (New York, 1920, 1921, 1928, 1936).

courageously takes stands and announces them. His spirit is weighed down by those who carry on "all the chuckle-headed talk and rascality in business and politics":

He was always getting indignant about them, and demanding that they be stamped out. . . . And twice a day, regularly, he would have a collision, or bout, with the newspaper; it was hard to see why God had made so many damned fools and democrats. . . . I would try to persuade him . . . to accept the world as it was and adapt himself to it, since he could scarcely expect to . . . change the whole earth single-handed. Father listened to this talk with suspicion. . . . If he ever was tempted to give in, it was only in his weak moments; a minute later he was again on the warpath, like a materialistic Don Quixote.

God Himself does not awe this rugged individualist: "he seemed to envisage a God in his own image. A God who had small use for emotionalism and who prized strength and dignity. . . . Father and God . . . usually saw eye to eye."[1]

The similarity of Father to ancient rustic oracles is obvious enough. But the tone contrasts sharply with that of authors who pictured similar characters in the past. The earlier authors—a Mark Twain portraying a Pudd'nhead Wilson, say—admired such characters and approved their attitudes. Day is fond of Father but regards him as a quaint figure of a bygone era; he questions his standards, laughs at his judgments, gently satirizes his outmoded ways. In story after story Father is surrounded by an irresponsible flutter-brained family who do not know what they are doing, who bumble and blunder. But time after time Father fails to get what he wants while the family flounders to triumph. Mother in particular, conniving, not overcareful with truth, incorrigibly unsystematic, in general amoral, constantly outwits him. The contrast is particularly clear in "Father and His Hard-Rocking Ship."[2] Here an old Yankee trick is assigned to Mother as she fights a battle in the continuous war with Father about household accounts. The hero of the Yankee story had cheated his victim because he was shrewd enough to devise the trick. Mother, on the contrary, manages to get away with

[1] "God and My Father," *Clarence Day Omnibus* (Garden City, 1945), pp. 9-10.
[2] *Ibid.*, 114-119.

the operation because she is illogical enough to stumble upon this way of outwitting her bewildered spouse.[1] And Day leaves no doubt about his preference for Mother's way of doing things.

Benchley, Thurber, and Perelman depict different characters but similarly rebel against ancient standards. Speaking of this group, "The literary comedians . . . presented themselves as Perfect Fools," says Bernard De Voto, "whereas our comedians present themselves as Perfect Neurotics."[2] "There is no other difference," De Voto claims. This may be true; but the difference is revolutionary. He points out an important element of kinship which he supports by noticing that older humorists and modern ones make much use of "erratic association" and citing Max Adeler's "My First Political Speech" as an earlier version of Robert Benchley's famous "The Treasurer's Report."

Robert Benchley, after graduating from Harvard, turned to journalism and eventually became an important contributor to *The New Yorker*, to other magazines and newspapers, to the profits of publishers of his collected pieces in fifteen books, and even to those of moving picture companies which filmed nearly fifty "shorts" in which he delivered monologues.[3]

Each of Benchley's books shows that he constantly assumes the role of "a Perfect Neurotic." The character he pretends to be time after time is prevented from doing a number of harmless things he would like to do—leave a party when he wants to, smoke a cigarette, wear a white suit, waltz, make faces, pick flowers, and so on, *ad infinitum*. The frustrations have given this character, so the collected pieces show, a mess of phobias and complexes which he shows at work on innumerable occasions. A reader is not surprised to find this assumed character ticking off one after another the symptoms of dementia praecox and finding that he has all of them.

---

[1] Characters like Father and Mother became stock figures in many family reminiscences, some doubtless influenced by Day. See Walter Blair, "Laughter in Wartime America," *College English*, XXXIV, 179–185 (April, 1945). The 1950's saw Auntie Mame, a wilder and more irresponsible version of Mother, winning similar illogical victories.

[2] "The Lineage of Eustace Tilley," *Saturday Review of Literature*, XVI, 20 (September 25, 1937).

[3] For a list of books and shorts see Nathaniel Benchley, *Robert Benchley* (New York, 1955), pp. 256–258.

"Some of this," writes his son in a biography,[1] "was exaggerated, but not as much as might be supposed. Benchley was a highly subjective writer, and most of what he wrote was conditioned by his feelings about himself." This modern humorist, then, exaggerates—as did the oldtime humorists who told tall tales. But whereas the oldsters exaggerated the difficulties which they had to overcome and their ability to cope with them, Benchley exaggerates the smallness of the difficulties he has to overcome and his inability to cope with them. And the author's own troubles are like those of his comic character. J. Bryan III subtitles his profile of the humorist "A Study in Professional Frustration," and indicates Benchley's conception of himself is of a man constantly humiliated and defeated by trifles:

 . . . he sees himself . . . not [as] the master of high comedy, but the victim of low tragedy. King Lear loses a throne; Benchley loses a filling. Romeo breaks his heart; Benchley breaks his shoelace. They are annihilated: he is humiliated. And to his humiliations there is no end. His whole life has been spent as the dupe of "the total depravity of inanimate things" . . . the minute perplexities loom so hugely that he shrinks from even attempting a solution.[2]

Benchley's humor constantly makes use of such humiliations and the failure of the assumed character to handle trifling problems. Not surprisingly he has spoken of working in "the dementia praecox field" and has voiced a preference for humor that has "a mad quality." As Bryan notices, "Every page of his books is riddled with these pitfalls for sanity. Madness so dominates the landscape of his humor that a second reading is necessary to recognize its other features."[3]

Now mild or temporary or even violent and permanent aberrations were far from unusual in the older humor. Artemus

[1] Nathaniel Benchley, *op. cit.*, pp. 1–2. See also Walter Blair, *Horse Sense in American Humor*, pp. 280–283.

[2] *Saturday Evening Post*, CCXII, 11 (September 23, 1939). "It is the inanimate enemies who have me baffled," says his alter ego. "The hundred and one little bits of wood and metal that go to make up the impedimenta of our daily life . . . each and every one bent on my humiliation. . . . "—*No Poems* (Garden City, 1932), p. 315. The character's fellow humans, however, are equally disconcerting.

[3] *Saturday Evening Post*, CCXII (October 7, 1939), 68. See also Robert Strunsky, "The Benchley Case," *Saturday Review*, XIV, 14 (May 9, 1936).

Ward, it will be recalled, was described as one yielding "a literal obedience to every absurd suggestion of thought and language"; many literary comedians—including Mark Twain—made people laugh, as Stephen Leacock notices, at their "amiable idiocy." But the difference between the assumed character and the character of his creator was an important incongruity. Charles Farrar Browne played up the differences between himself, sane, logical, sound in his attitudes, and Artemus Ward, mildly mad, illogical, unsound in his attitudes. The contrast made for irony, and the irony often made for satire. Just as Clemens stood apart from Pap Finn while Pap lauded racial discrimination and by standing apart attacked an attitude which Clemens abhorred, or as Locke stood apart from the copperhead Nasby with whom he violently disagreed and thereby attacked copperheadism, many literary comedians made the "I" in their writings obviously, comically, and satirically different from his creator.

The new emphasis was not on differences but on resemblances. Benchley, as his son says, exaggerates; but he exaggerates what he believes are his own qualities. And the expectation is that instead of feeling superior to the comic character whose qualities are enlarged versions of Benchley's own characteristics, the reader will identify with that character, will sympathize with him. "The fellow," he will say, "suffers from much the same frustrations, the same fears, the same incompetency I suffer from." And he will join the assumed character in being irritated by all the self-confident people he encounters—clerks, advertising men, efficiency experts, go-getters, clubwomen, scholars, scientists—all those well-adjusted (and quite probably self-deceived) clods. Clarence Day's Father is a character who definitely belongs to the enemy forces; Benchley would align himself with Mother.

James Grover Thurber was born and reared in Columbus, Ohio, was educated at the Ohio State University, and worked on several newspapers before beginning in 1927 an association with *The New Yorker* which continues at the present writing. Thurber's important books, all collections of pieces previously published in magazines, include: *The Owl in the Attic* (1931), *The Seal in the Bedroom* (1932), *My Life and Hard Times* (1933), *The Middle-*

Aged Man on the Flying Trapeze (1935), *Let Your Mind Alone!* (1937), *My World—and Welcome to It* (1942), *The Thurber Carnival* (1945), *The Thurber Album* (1952), *Thurber Country* (1953) and *Alarms and Diversions* (1957), all published in New York.

Thurber's discussion of the nature of humor shows immediately his kinship with Benchley:

The things we laugh at are awful while they are going on, but get funny when we look back. And other people laugh because they've been through it too. . . . I think humor is the best that lies closest to the familiar, to that part of the familiar which is humiliating, distressing, even tragic. Humor is a kind of emotional chaos told about calmly and quietly in retrospect. There is always a laugh in the utterly familiar. . . . People can laugh out of a kind of mellowed self-pity as well as out of superiority.

Human dignity, the humorist believes, is not only silly but a little sad. So are dreams and conventions and illusions. The fine brave fragile stuff that men live by. They look so swell, and go to pieces so easily.[1]

The humiliation, the distress, the emotional chaos, as has been suggested, are all reminiscent of the misadventures of the "I" in Benchley's pieces. The identification of the reader with the suffering character is specifically indicated. Thurber adds the shrewd comment that the events are "told about calmly and quietly in retrospect"—a statement which, incidentally, also applies to Benchley's way of telling about his emotional experiences.

A fine illustration is a portion of Thurber's story of what happened in Columbus, Ohio, the day the dam broke:

The only possible means of escape for us was to flee the house, a step which grandfather sternly forbade, brandishing his old army sabre in his hand. "Let the sons -- ------- come!" he roared. Meanwhile hundreds of people were streaming by our house in wild panic, screaming "Go east! Go east!" We had to stun grandfather with the ironing board. Impeded as we were by the inert form of the old gentleman—he was taller than six feet and weighed almost a hundred and seventy pounds—we were passed, in the first half mile, by practically everybody else in the

[1] Quoted in Max Eastman, *The Enjoyment of Laughter* (New York, 1936), pp. 341–343.

city. Had grandfather not come to, at the corner of Parsons Avenue and Town Street, we would unquestionably have been overtaken and engulfed by the roaring waters—that is, if there had *been* any roaring waters.[1]

Quel dommage! But what calm, what quietude, the author manifests in writing about the events! There is no mention of the narrator's attitude: with Hemingwayesque restraint, he writes not about the emotion but the happenings which produce it. And an important disparity is that between the harrowing happenings and the objectivity which marks their description.

The fact that this is a passage in what playfully purports to be an autobiography, *My Life and Hard Times*, at least based upon personal experiences,[2] suggests that Thurber, like Benchley, tends to identify himself, in essential ways, with his first-person narrator. And the author's description of "humorists" shows that they qualify to write Thurberian humor by living as their characters do:

They lead . . . an existence of jumpiness and apprehension. . . . [They] have a genius for getting into minor difficulties: they walk into the wrong apartments, they drink furniture polish for stomach bitters, they drive their cars into the prize tulip beds of haughty neighbors. . . .

Such a writer moves restlessly wherever he goes, ready to get the hell out at the drop of a pie-pan or the lift of a skirt. His gestures are the ludicrous reflexes of the maladjusted; his repose is the momentary inertia of the nonplussed. . . . He talks largely about small matters and smally about great affairs.[3]

This characterizes not only "the humorist"; it also characterizes the protagonists in Thurber's pieces and their adventures. In his guise of pictorial artist, Thurber portrays similar characters: his men "are frustrated, fugitive beings; at times they seem

---

[1] *My Life and Hard Times* (New York, 1933), p. 39.
[2] The chaos of course is greatly exaggerated, and the fanciful elaboration is at least part of the fun. For a less exaggerated account of the author's youthful years and more factual characterizations of his family, see *The Thurber Album* (New York, 1952), written in a much more emotional and a less playful mood. Here, however, Thurber's father's difficulties with "the manufactured" and "the mechanical," pp. 110–111, are shown as much like his son's.
[3] "Preface" to *My Life and Hard Times*.

vaguely striving to get out of something without being seen (a room, a situation, a state of mind), at other times they are merely perplexed and too humble or meek to move."[1] Like Benchley's characters they are baffled not only by people but also by inanimate objects. Thurber tells how irritated Wolcott Gibbs was when as a *New Yorker* editor he received a piece which began, "Mr. West had never been very good at machinery." "Here," says Thurber, "was the little man, a genus sometimes called, around the office, the Thurber husband, popping up for the thousandth time, and it was too much for the Gibbsian nerves." And he quotes Gibbs' assertion that too many writers trying to break into the magazine, "unfortunately influenced by Mr. Thurber, [have] come to believe that the ideal . . . piece is about a vague, little man helplessly confused by a menacing and complicated civilization."[2]

Benchley testifies to S. J. Perelman's leadership in "the dementia praecox field."[3] He has pictured his alter ego in a guise much like those of Benchley and Thurber: he too is frustrated and put upon; he too is helpless in a hostile world. Even more than they he is victimized by free association: "The color drained from my face, entered the auricle, shot up the escalator, and issued from the ladies' and misses' section into the housewares department," he reports. Or—

That Philomene was a manic-depressive in the downhill phase was, of course, instantly apparent to a boy of five. Several boys of five, who happened to be standing around and were by way of being students of psychology, stated their belief to me in just those words: "Manic-depressive, downhill phase."[4]

His assumed character's distinctions are two: First, he tries to swagger, to brazen things out. A man of less than ordinary presence, he deceives himself into believing that he is a handsome dog. "I am a fairly typical Yankee," he modestly asserts, "who looks like Gary Cooper, sings like Frank Sinatra and dances

---

[1] E. B. White, in *Is Sex Necessary?* (New York, 1929), pp. 195–196.

[2] *The Years With Ross* (Boston, 1959), pp. 129–130.

[3] His best books include *Dawn Ginsberg's Revenge* (1929), *Strictly from Hunger* (1933), *Crazy Like a Fox* (1944), *Perelman's Home Companion* (1955), *The Most of S. J. Perelman* (1958), all published in New York.

[4] *Crazy Like a Fox*, pp. 124, 4–5.

like Fred Astaire."[1] Again in the third person, he describes himself as "this man, who by sheer poise and magnetism had surmounted the handicap of almost ethereal beauty."[2] A man of limited intelligence, he tries to impress one with his learning. He dots his pages with showy French, German and Italian phrases— *mise en scène, danse à ventre, maladie du temps, Walpurgisnacht, wandervögel, schrecklichkeit, volte-face, corpo di Bacco*—with exotic names for pieces of clothing or strange dishes, with scientific jargon.

Secondly (it may be as a result of his preoccupation with language), the character Perelman assumes has been brainwashed by mass media. Not only does he believe the advertisements concocted by Madison Avenue slickers; he also accepts as actuality the fantastic world of current magazine fiction, the movies, even television. The delight and the horror of his style is that it constantly takes off into the Never-Never Land of the mass media. As a result, after reading an advertisement he follows with complete trust the suggestions it makes. After reading a story or seeing a motion picture he concocts fantasies which are even more absurd than those which have unfolded before him. Sometimes these are little dramas;[3] more often they are cliché-bedecked phrases or sentences which mottle whatever he writes: "Diamonds of the finest water gleamed at the throats of women whose beauty put the gems to shame," he avers, "and if each was not escorted by a veritable Adonis, he was at least a Greek." Again, "Not a muscle flickered in my lean jaw . . . as our little procession moved past the group of cattlemen lounging outside the Golden Girl Saloon, and their pithy comments had long since died away before I permitted myself a muttered 'Swine.' " And again, of an inexperienced actress who appears in a Broadway play, "Slowly the disbelief faded from the faces of the critics and was replaced by a placidity, a tenderness so intense that it could only be called slumber."[4]

As in reading Benchley and Thurber, the reader sees in

---

[1] *Perelman's Home Companion*, p. 159.
[2] *The Most of S. J. Perelman*, p. 415.
[3] For some excellent examples, *ibid.*, pp. 110–114, 254–258, 409–414, 439–444, 474–479, 508–513, 536–541.
[4] *The Dream Department*, p. 39; *Perelman's Home Companion*, p. 199; *Crazy Like a Fox*, p. 202.

Perelman's assumed character a man in many ways like himself. In some ways, Perelman's vision of what we all tend to be is the most frightening of all. His is a comic version of Huxley's *Brave New World* or Orwell's *1984.*

He is not the only writer in this group whose comic representatives are allied with more serious fictions. Peter DeVries many years ago pointed out an extraordinary resemblance between Thurber's little man and that famous creation of T. S. Eliot, J. Alfred Prufrock—"the same dominating sense of Predicament . . . the same immersion in weary minutiae, the same self-disparagement, the same wariness . . . the same fear, in summary, that someone—in Thurber's case a brash halfback or maybe even a woman—will 'drop a question on his plate.'"[1] The comparison might be extended to include many characters in the best modern fiction, the figure Sean O'Faolain, for instance, sees as "the anti-Hero":

He is always represented as groping, puzzled, cross, mocking, frustrated, isolated in his manful or blundering attempts to establish his own personal, suprasocial codes. (One of his clearest of recent avatars in Britain was Kingsley Amis's *Lucky Jim*). . . . Whether he is weak, brave, brainy or bewildered he is always out on his own. Which is why, in those fateful twenties, writers quite deliberately began . . . to dig out private caves, or air-raid shelters, of their own, and there started to compose private satires, laments, fantasies and myths in the effort to fill the vacuum left by the death of the social Hero with asocial rebels, martyrs, misfits, minor prophets, or, in short, with aberrants and anti-Heroes.[2]

The relationship between Thurber's humor and this serious view of humanity becomes clear when one compares Thurber's personal nonhumorous statement about his own view of Man:

---

[1] "James Thurber: The Comic Prufrock," *Poetry,* LXIII (December, 1943), 151–152.

[2] *The Vanishing Hero* (Boston, 1957), pp. xxix-xxx. Compare Edmund Fuller: "From . . . disillusionment we get that terrible spate of novels now current in which man is seen specifically as an ironic biological accident, inadequate, aimless, meaningless, isolated, inherently evil, thwarted, self-corrupting, morally answerable to no one, clasped in the vise of determinisms economic or biological . . . He inhabits a universe which is the creation of irrational and possibly malignant forces."—*Man in Modern Fiction* (New York, 1958), pp. 11–12.

For some curious reason Man has always assumed that he is the highest form of life in the universe. There is, of course, nothing with which to sustain this view. Man is simply the highest form of life on his own planet. His superiority rests on a thin and chancy basis: he has the trick of articulate speech and out of this, slowly and laboriously, he has developed the capacity of abstract reasoning. Abstract reasoning, in itself, has not benefited Man so much as instinct has benefited the lower animals. . . . In giving up instinct and going in for reasoning, Man has aspired higher than the attainment of natural goals; he has developed ideas and notions; he has monkeyed around with concepts. The life to which he was naturally adapted he has put behind him; in moving into the alien and complicated sphere of Thought and Imagination he has become the least well-adjusted of all the creatures of the earth, and hence the most bewildered. . . . Man . . . is surely farther away from the Answer than any other animal this side of the ladybug.[1]

The humor of Thurber and his contemporaries is, I suggest, a comic representation of Man in this grim situation. Grim, yes. But native American humor has always dealt comically with worries and tribulations—the struggles of a democratic nation to get going, frontier hardships, wartime tragedies, the upheavals accompanying the shift from an agrarian, rural society to an industrial, urban society. In that sense, Day, Benchley, Thurber, and Perelman write in an old and honorable tradition. Also their assumptions and beliefs are in tune with attitudes of their era. But the different nature of their assumptions and the great change in their beliefs have led them to write humor strikingly different indeed from that of the past.

[1] *I Believe*, ed. Clifton Fadiman (New York, 1938), pp. 296–298. Thurber's animals seem to have benefited from living by instinct: they are happier, much less frustrated, than his humans. When Thurber humanizes his animals he shows them getting into bad fixes, and the moral is, "If you live as humans do, it will be the end of you."—*Fables for Our Time*, p. 10.

SELECTED BIBLIOGRAPHY

SELECTED BIBLIOGRAPHY

(The most generally useful works are asterisked.)

GENERAL ASPECTS AND VARIOUS PHASES

[Anon.] "American Humour," *North British Review*, XXXIII, 247–60 (November, 1860). (The author, after pointing out that American humor is characterized by exaggeration, as was old Norse humor, rather inconsistently cites *The Biglow Papers* as the "greatest American book of humour.")

[Anon.] "American Humour," *British Quarterly*, LII, 324–51 (October 1, 1870). (Contains a number of errors of fact. Points out the importance of the dramatic monologue in American humor.)

[Anon.] "American Humour," *Eclectic Magaine*, XXXIII, 137–44 (September, 1854).

[Anon.] "The Spirit of American Humor," *Living Age*, CCLXV, 686–9 (July 11, 1910). (American humor, says the author, "belongs properly to talk, and not to written speech.")

Bangs, J. K. "A Word Concerning American Humor," *Book Buyer*, XX, 205–8 (April, 1900). (Asserts a change toward more subtle humor took place at the end of the nineteenth century.)

Bentzon, T. L. "Les Humoristes Américains: I, Mark Twain; II, Ward, Billings, Breitmann," *Revue des Deux Mondes*, C, 313–25, 837–62 (1872).

Blair, Walter. "Burlesques in Nineteenth-Century American Humor," *American Literature*, II, 236–47 (November, 1930). (Spread-eagle oratory, romantic history, sentimental fiction were widely burlesqued by the humorists.)

Blair, Walter. *Horse Sense in American Humor from Benjamin Franklin to Ogden Nash.* Chicago, 1942. (Traces the rise and decline of humor as rhetoric based on common sense.)

Blair, Walter. "The Popularity of Nineteenth-Century American Humorists," *American Literature*, III, 175–94 (May, 1931). (Reveals the various ways humorous writings received wide publication.)

Blair, Walter. "Laughter in Wartime America," *College English*, VI, 361–7 (April, 1945). (Notes changing attitudes and characters.)

Boynton, H. W. "American Humor," *Atlantic*, XC, 414–20 (September, 1902). (Explains the "petering out" of American humor on the ground that it had tended to become too dependent upon mere joking. Suggestive.)

Bradley, Sculley, "Our Native Humor," *North American Review*, CCXLII, 351–62 (Winter, 1937).

Bragdon, Claude, "The Purple Cow Period," *Bookman*, LXIX, 475–8 (July, 1929).

Charpentier, John. "Humeur Anglais et Humeur Américain. A Propos du Centenaire de Mark Twain," *Mercure de France*, CCLXIV, 475–501 (December 15, 1935). (A comedy of misunderstanding.)

Chesterton, C. "Salt of America," *Living Age*, CCXCV, 243–6 (October 27, 1917). (Democracy and irreverence are called characteristic of American humor.)

Chesterton, G. K. "American Humour and Bret Harte," *Critic*, XLI, 170–4 (August, 1902). (Asserts that Harte's humor was not typically American.)

Clemens, Cyril, "Benjamin Shillaber and His Carpet Bag," *New England Quarterly*, XIV, 519–37 (September, 1941).

Cox, S. S. "American Humor," *Harper's Magazine*, LXXX, 690–702, 847–59 (April, May, 1875). (See comment on next entry.)

Cox, S. S. *Why We Laugh*. New York, 1876. (Reprints and augments the magazine articles cited above, supporting the view that American humor is typically exaggerative. The writings of many authors are analyzed. Large portion of the book deals with legislative humor.)

De Voto, Bernard, "Lineage of Eustace Tilley," *Saturday Review of Literature*, XVI, 3–4 (September 25, 1937). (Relates modern humor to that of the past, arguing that there has been no great change.)

Eastman, Max. "Humor and America," *Scribner's*, C, 9–13 (July, 1936). (The distinct flavor of American humor derives from "the primitive strain of imagination and the mature enjoyment of nonsense." Suggestive and stimulating. Reprinted in *The Enjoyment of Laughter*, New York, 1936.)

Ellsworth, W. W. "Old-time Humor," in *Golden Age of Authors*. New York, 1919, pp. 211–20. (Notes changes in the comic appeals.)

Evans, E. P. "Zur Charakteristik des amerikanischen Humors," in *Beiträge zur amerikanischen Litteratur- und Kulturgeschichte*. Stuttgart, 1898, pp. 69–105.

Ferguson, J. DeLancey, "On Humor as One of the Fine Arts," *South Atlantic Quarterly*, XXXVIII, 177–86 (April, 1939).

Ferguson, J. DeLancey. "The Roots of American Humor," *American Scholar*, IV, 41–9 (Winter, 1935). (Claims that American humor is "the free growth on American soil of a literary heritage as old as the race," citing what seem to him medieval counterparts of tall tales and comic figures of speech. See Miss Constance Rourke's counter claims, cited below.)

Ford, J. L. "A Century of American Humor," *Munsey*, XXV, 482–90

(July, 1901). (A loose and frequently inaccurate development of the thesis that "every humorous writer who has won distinct recognition from the American people has been a philosopher as well as a mere fun maker.")

Hamer, John. *American Humour*. London, 1901.

Hancock, Ernest L. "The Passing of the American Comic," *Bookman*, XXII, 78–84 (September, 1905).

Haweis, H. R. *American Humourists*. London, 1882. New York, 1889. (Treatments, usually shallow but occasionally illuminating, of Irving, Holmes, Lowell, Browne, Clemens, and Harte.)

*Howe, M. A. D. "Some American Humorists," *Bookman*, VI, 24–34 (September, 1897). (Seba Smith, C. F. Browne, B. P. Shillaber, Henry W. Shaw, John Godfrey Saxe, each treated briefly.)

*Howe, Will D. "Early Humorists," in *Cambridge History of American Literature*. New York, 1918, II, 148–59. (Competent and suggestive.)

Hudson, Frederick. *Journalism in the United States 1690–1872*. New York, 1873. (Contains numerous references to journalistic humor.)

Hunter, Edwin Ray. *The American Colloquial Idiom*, 1830–1860. Unpublished Doctoral Dissertation, University of Chicago, 1925, pp. xvi–xxv. (The pages cited indicate the value of American humor of the period for social history and dialect study. The chief sources for the entire dissertation are humorous works.)

Johnson, Burges. "New Humor," *Critic*, XL, 331–8, 526–32 (April, June, 1902). (Deprecates the idea that there is anything particularly new in American humor after 1900.)

Johnston, Charles. "The Essence of American Humor," *Atlantic*, LXXXVII, 195–201 (February, 1901). (Stresses the universality of the best humor.)

Johnston, Charles. *Why the World Laughs*. New York, 1912. (An unsuccessful study of the rise of humor in its racial and national aspects.)

Kirke, Edmund. "Wit and Humor—Old and New," *North American Review*, CXLVIII, 33–46 (January, 1889).

*Lang, Andrew. "American Humour" and "Western Drolls," in *Lost Leaders*. London, 1889, pp. 70–7, 181–8. (Intelligent criticism, which calls attention to "the rusticity and puritanism," the lack of "reverence and sympathy" in American humor, and which stresses the importance of the oral "sub-soil" of comic anecdotes.)

*Lukens, Henry Clay. "American Literary Comedians," *Harper's*, LXXX, 1783–97 (April, 1890). (Encyclopedically compact and informative, although not particularly good in its analysis.)

MacMinn, G. R. " 'The Gentleman from Pike' in Early California Humor," *American Literature*, VIII, 160–9 (May, 1936). (A thoroughly documented study of California's most famous humorous type.)

*[Massey, Gerald] "Yankee Humour," *Quarterly*, CXXII, 212–37

(January, 1867). Reprinted in *Every Saturday*, III, 330–8, in March of the same year. (Suggests that exaggeration and "knowing unconsciousness" are typical traits, offering numerous examples.)

Matthews, Brander. "American Humor," in *The American of the Future and Other Essays*. New York, 1910, pp. 161–76. ("Geniality and imaginative exaggeration" are "the chief essential qualities" of American humor.)

Matthews, Brander. "The Comic Periodical Literature of the United States," *American Bibliopolist*, VII, 199–201 (August, 1875).

Meine, Franklin J. "*The Carpet-Bag*," *The Collector's Journal*, IV, 411–3 (October-November-December, 1933). (Interesting comment on a "transitional" periodical which "offered a stimulus and vehicle for such young budding geniuses as Artemus Ward, Mark Twain and John Phoenix, whose contributions . . . anticipated the humor of the latter half of the nineteenth century.")

Meine, Franklin J. "*Vanity Fair*," *The Collector's Journal*, IV, 461–3 (January-February-March, 1934). (An authoritative comment on a leading comic periodical which had many notable contributors.)

Mencken, H. L. *The American Language*. Fourth Edition. New York, 1936, pp. 71–3, 224. (On the extensive use of the vernacular by the humorists.)

Murrell, William. *A History of American Graphic Humor. Vol. I. (1741–1865)*. New York, 1933. (Interesting details about various comic illustrations in humorous works and periodicals.)

Nesbit, W. D. "The Humor of To-day," *Independent*, LIV, 1300–4 (May 29, 1902). (A practicing humorist, "Josh Wink," contrasts old and new humor.)

Pattee, F. L. *The First Century of American Literature 1770–1870*. New York, 1935, pp. 213–29, 471–88. (Suggestive.)

Reed, Perley Isaac. "The Realistic Presentation of American Characters in Native American Plays Prior to 1870," *Ohio State University Bulletin*, Vol. XXII (May, 1918). (A dissertation, elaborately documented.)

Repplier, Agnes. "Humor: English and American," *Cosmopolitan*, XVI, 361–9 (January, 1894).

Roth, G. L. "The American Theory of Satire, 1790–1820," *American Literature*, XXIX, 399–407 (January, 1958). (A scholarly survey.)

*Rourke, Constance. *American Humor, A Study of the National Character*. New York, 1931. (An important study, particularly effective in its study of traditional portrayals of the Yankee, the Frontiersman, and the comic Negro and in its analysis of the fantastic qualities of much American humor.)

Rourke, Constance. "Examining the Roots of American Humor," *American Scholar*, IV, 249–52, 254 (Spring, 1935). (A reply to the article by Professor Ferguson, cited above, this alleges that the differences between English and American humor "have to do with creative fancy.")

Shanly, Charles Dawson. "Comic Journalism," *Atlantic*, XIX, 167–73 (February, 1867).

*Tandy, Jennette. *Crackerbox Philosophers in American Humor and Satire*. New York, 1925. (An admirable survey of the homely native philosophers in America, indispensable for the study of any phase of its subject. Well documented.)

Thompson, Harold W. "Humor," *Literary History of the United States*. New York, 1948, II, 728–57.

Thurber, James. "Reply to Ohioana Award," *Library Journal*, LXXIX, 273–5 (February 15, 1954).

Thurber, James. "The Saving Grace," *Atlantic Monthly*, CCIV, 61–4 (November, 1959). (Humorously deplores the decay of humor.)

*Trent, W. P. "Retrospect of American Humor," *Century*, LXIII, 45–64 (November, 1901). (A helpful summary.)

*W., H. "Slick, Downing, Crockett, Etc.," *London and Westminster Review*, XXXII, 136–45 (December, 1838). (Praises American humorists for breaking away from British traditions—for becoming "national" and "original.")

Wallace, Frederick T. "Humor and Its Uses," in *Men and Events of Half a Century*. Cleveland, 1887, pp. 181–6.

Weeks, Edward, "The American Sense of Humor," *Scribner's-Commentator*, X, 91–5 (May, 1941).

Weiss, Stanley. "A Brief History of American Jest Books," *Bulletin of the New York Public Library*, XLVII, 273–89 (April, 1943).

Weiss, Stanley. "Some Comic Histories of the United States," *Bulletin of the New York Public Library*, XLI, 303–12 (April, 1938).

Whipple, E. P. "American Literature in the First Century of the Republic," *Harper's Magazine*, LII, 526–7 (March, 1876). (Contemporary view by a competent critic of the humor of Browne, Derby, Locke, Clemens, and Harte.)

STUDIES OF AMERICAN ALMANACS

Brigham, Clarence. *An Account of American Almanacs and Their Value for Historical Study*. Worcester, 1925.

Fitts, James H. "The Thomas Almanacs," in *Historical Collections of the Essex Institute*, XII, 243–70 (October, 1874).

*Kittredge, George Lyman. *The Old Farmer and His Almanack*. Boston, 1904. (Charming and informative.)

Nichols, Charles L. "Notes on the Almanacs of Massachusetts," in *Proceedings of the American Antiquarian Society*, n.s., XXII, 15–134 (April, 1912).

Paltsits, Victor Hugo. *The Almanacs of Roger Sherman 1750–1761*. Worcester, 1907.

Robinson, Henry M. "The Almanac," *Bookman*, LXXV, 218–24 (June-July, 1932). (A good brief account.)

Rourke, Constance. *Davy Crockett*. New York, 1934, pp. 251–8. (A good bibliography of the Crockett almanacs, important in American humor.)

STUDIES OF DOWN EAST HUMOR (1830–1867)

[Anon.] "American Humour," *Cornhill Magazine*, XIII, 28–43 (January, 1866). (Particularly concerned with Lowell and Holmes.)

[Anon.] "Yankeeisms," *New England Magazine*, III, 377–81 (November, 1832). (Notes the tendency towards dialect characterizations, rebukes foreigners who mingle Yankee speech with Kentucky speech, and bewails the vulgarity of portrayals of low types.)

Bungay, George W. "B. P. Shillaber" and "J. R. Lowell," in *Off-Hand Takings: or Crayon Sketches*. New York, 1854, pp. 372–6, 394–9.

Crandall, Arthur G. *New England Joke Lore*. New York, 1922.

Derby, J. C. *Fifty Years among Authors, Books and Publishers*. New York, 1886, pp. 407–40, 538–44. (A publisher's reminiscences of B. P. Shillaber, Miriam B. Whitcher, and other humorists.)

Dorson, Richard M. *Jonathan Draws the Long Bow*. Cambridge, 1946. (The tall tale in old New England humor.)

Howells, William D. "Our National Humorists," *Harper's Magazine*, CXXXIV, 442–5 (February, 1917).

Roth, G. L. "New England Satire on Religion, 1790–1820," *New England Quarterly*, XXVIII, 246–54 (June, 1955).

Stephens, F. G. "American Humorous Poetry," *Macmillan's*, I, 203–11 (January, 1860). (Deals with John G. Saxe, O. W. Holmes, and J. R. Lowell, particularly praising Lowell.)

STUDIES OF SOUTHERN AND SOUTHWESTERN HUMOR (1830–1860)

Adkins, N. F. "James K. Paulding's *Lion of the West*," *American Literature*, III, 249–58 (November, 1931). (Well documented and exhaustive.)

Adkins, N. F. "A Study of James K. Paulding's *Westward Ho!*," *American Collector*, III, 221–9 (March, 1927).

[Anon.] "Review of *The Americans at Home*," *British Quarterly Review*, XXI, 60–78 (January, 1855). (Enthusiastically praises this collection, chiefly made up of humor from the Southwest, pointing out the superiority of the material to popular American fiction. Calls attention to the persistence of English customs among the people of "the byeways, backwoods, and prairies.")

Blair, Walter. "Traditions in Southern Humor," *American Quarterly*, V, 132–42 (Summer, 1953). (Stresses sporting tradition.)

*Boatright, Mody. *Folk Laughter on the American Frontier*. New York, 1949. (Relates oral to printed humor.)

Brinley, Francis. *Life of William T. Porter*. New York, 1860. (A biography of the editor of *The Spirit of the Times*, the most important of all publishing media for humor of the frontier. Valuable.)

Budd, Louis J. "Gentlemanly Humorists of the Old South," *Southern Folklore Quarterly*, XVII, 232–40 (December, 1953).

Chittick, V. L. O. "Ring-Tailed Roarers," *The Frontier*, XIII, 257–63 (May, 1933). (A vigorous and authentic study of the humorous literature of the frontier, 1830–1860.)

Crothers, Samuel McChord. "A Community of Humorists," in *The Pardoner's Wallet*. Boston, 1905, pp. 176–98. (An illuminating characterization of the comedy of a frontier community.)

Current-Garcia, Eugene. "Newspaper Humorists in the Old South, 1835–1855," *Alabama Review*, II, 102–21 (April, 1949).

*De Voto, Bernard. *Mark Twain's America*. New York, 1932, pp. 79–98, 141–58. (One of the best summaries of the important facts about frontier humor.)

Dondore, Dorothy. "Big Talk! The Flyting, the Gabe, and the Frontier Boast," *American Speech*, VI, 45–55 (October, 1930). (Traces the tradition of frontier tall talk.)

Dondore, Dorothy. *The Prairie and the Making of Middle America*. Cedar Rapids, 1926, pp. 236–9, 253–4, 306–7, 347–55, 447. (Stresses the relationship between the oral tall tale and Western humor.)

Eaton, Clement. "The Humor of the Southern Yeoman," *Sewanee Review*, XLIX, 173–83 (April-June, 1941).

Flanders, B. H. "Humor in Ante-Bellum Georgia," *Emory University Quarterly*, I, 149–59 (October, 1945).

Harris, Joel Chandler. "Georgia Wit and Humor," in *Stories of Georgia*. New York, 1896, pp. 240–51. (An appreciative and intelligent discussion.)

Holliday, Carl. *A History of Southern Literature*. New York, [n.d.], pp. 157–68. (Treats Davy Crockett, A. B. Longstreet, W. T. Thompson, J. J. Hooper.)

Johnston, Charles. "Old Funny Stories of the South and West," *Harper's Weekly*, LVII, 21 (January 4, 1913). (Anecdotes of the fifties.)

Jordan, P. D. "Humor in the Backwoods, 1820–1840," *Mississippi Valley Historical Review*, XXV, 25–38 (June, 1938).

Link, Samuel Albert. "Southern Humorists: Longstreet, Baldwin, Hooper, W. T. Thompson, Davy Crockett and Others," in *Pioneers of Southern Literature*. Nashville: 1900, II, 465–545.

Lynn, Kenneth S. *Mark Twain and Southwestern Humor*. Boston, 1960. (Overemphasizes political aspects.)

McIlwaine, Shields. *The Southern Poor-White from Lubberland to Tobacco Road.* Norman, 1939, pp. 40–74.

*Meine, Franklin J., ed. *Tall Tales of the Southwest.* New York, 1930. (The introduction and the bibliographical notes in this anthology offer the best of all treatments of the humor of the old Southwest.)

Moses, Montrose J. *The Literature of the South.* New York, 1910, pp. 230–40.

Parrington, V. L. *The Romantic Revolution in America 1800–1860.* New York, 1927, pp. 166–79. (Treats Longstreet and Crockett as representatives of the realistic frontier.)

Penrod, J. H. "Folklore Motifs in Old Southwestern Humor," *Southern Folklore Quarterly,* XIX, 117–24 (June, 1955).

Spotts, Carle Brooks. "The Development of Fiction on the Missouri Frontier (1830–1860)," *Missouri Historical Review,* XXIX, 17–26, 100–8, 186–96 (October-July, 1935). (On the careers of Alphonse Wetmore, John S. Robb, and Joseph M. Field.)

Thompson, W. F. "Frontier Tall Talk," *American Speech,* IX, 187–99 (October, 1934). (A study of the qualities of typical boastful speeches.)

Turner, Arlin. "Realism and Fantasy in Southern Humor," *Georgia Review,* XII, 451–57 (Winter, 1958).

Turner, Arlin. "Seeds of Literary Revolt in the Humor of The Old Southwest," *Louisiana Historical Quarterly,* XXXIX, 143–51 (1957).

*Watterson, Henry. "The South in Light and Shade," in *The Compromises of Life and Other Lectures and Addresses.* New York, 1903, pp. 59–101. (An edifying discussion of antebellum Southern humor, particularly concerned with Longstreet, Harris, Thompson, and Hooper. As in his anthology, noted below, Marse Henry shows a thorough knowledge of his subject.)

Woodberry, George E. *America in Literature.* New York, 1903, pp. 157–69. (Gives a good account of the relationship between life and humor on the frontier, and then comes to the amazing conclusion that Bret Harte, Joaquin Miller, and Lew Wallace were the great artists of the section.)

*Yates, Norris W., *William T. Porter and "The Spirit of the Times."* Baton Rouge, 1957. (Scholarly study of "the Big Bear school" of humor.)

Studies of Literary Comedians (1850–1900)

[Anon.] "Neglected Worthies," *Nation,* CVII, 165 (August 17, 1918). (Brief account of Artemus Ward and Josh Billings as wartime humorists.)

[Anon.] "Mid-Century Humorists," Springfield (Mass.) *Republican,* September 9, 1907.

Beers, Henry A. *Initial Studies in American Letters.* New York, 1891, pp. 187–95. (Keen criticism and analysis combined with a remarkable but illuminating estimation of Mark Twain.)

*Clemens, Will M. *Famous Funny Fellows, Brief Bibliographical Sketches of American Humorists.* New York, 1882. (A contemporary view of about thirty-five humorists of the period.)

Jones, Joseph, "Josh Billings' Notions of Humor," *University of Texas Studies in English.* Austin, 1943, pp. 143–61.

Masson, Thomas L. *Our American Humorists.* New and Enlarged Edition. New York, 1931. (Deals chiefly with twentieth-century writers, but contains chapters on Finley Peter Dunne and C. B. Lewis.)

Mathews, William. "Pleasantry in Literature," in *The Great Conversers and Other Essays.* Eighth Edition. Chicago, 1878, pp. 158–67. (Deplores the frivolity of American jesters and urges the writing of humor with a purpose.)

Mathews, William. *Wit and Humor: Their Use and Abuse.* Chicago, 1888.

Nichol, John. *American Literature, an Historical Sketch.* Second Edition. Edinburgh, 1885, pp. 402–48. (Sharply slaps at contemporary comic writings for their pyrotechnics, their cynicism, their lack of seriousness.)

*Pattee, F. L. "The Laughter of the West" and "The Discovery of Pike County" in *American Literature since 1870.* New York, 1915, pp. 25–44; 83–91. (A pioneer work which contains many suggestive criticisms.)

Pond, J. B. *Eccentricities of Genius.* New York, 1900. (Major Pond recalls his experiences with a number of humorous lecturers whom he managed.)

Robbins, L. H. "American Humorists," New York *Times Magazine,* pp. 8–9 (September 8, 1935). (On the development of American humor, with special reference to Browne, Nye, Holmes, Clemens, Riley, Field, Dunne, and Rogers.)

Visscher, William Lightfoot. *Ten Wise Men and Some More.* Chicago, 1909. (The ten are Prentice, Faxon, Browne, Griswold, Field, Nye, Peck, Read, Taylor, and King.)

Whicher, George Frisbie. "Minor Humorists," in *Cambridge History of American Literature.* New York, 1921, III, 21–30.

Young, Art. *Authors' Readings Compiled and Illustrated Throughout by Art Young . . . with a Biography of Each Author.* New York, 1897. (Humorists include Riley, Nye, Field, Lewis, and Opie Read.)

HUMOR IN FOLKLORE

Alvord, Thomas G. *Paul Bunyan and Resinous Rhymes of the North Woods.* New York, 1934.

Beath, Paul, and Lynn Trank. *Febold Feboldson: Tall Tales from the Great Plains.* Lincoln, 1948.

Blair, Walter. *Tall Tale America: A Legendary History of Our Humorous Heroes*. New York, 1944.

Blair, Walter, and Franklin J. Meine, eds. *Half Horse Half Alligator: The Growth of the Mike Fink Legend*. Chicago, 1956. (Reprints all the chief sources. The bibliography shows the spread of the stories.)

Blair, Walter, and Franklin J. Meine. *Mike Fink, King of Mississippi Keelboatmen*. New York, 1933. (A re-telling of numerous yarns about a frontier hero.)

Boatright, M. C. "The Tall Tale in Texas," *South Atlantic Quarterly*, XXX, 271–9 (July, 1931).

Boatright, M. C., ed. *Tall Tales from Texas*. Austin, 1934.

Botkin, B. A., ed. *A Treasury of American Anecdotes*. New York, 1957.

Boynton, Percy H. "Popular Song and Story," in *Literature and American Life*. New York, 1936, pp. 601–24. (An excellent summary and evaluation of folk-songs and folk tales. Well documented.)

Bradford, Roark. *John Henry*. New York, 1931. (Prose narrative concerning a hero of Negro ballads.)

Chappell, Louis W. *John Henry; a Folk-Lore Study*. Jena, 1933.

Daugherty, James. *Their Weight in Wild Cats*. Boston, 1936. (Tall tales about many frontier heroes, from many sources.)

Dorson, Richard M. *American Folklore*. Chicago, 1959. (Especially concerned with tales.)

Dorson, Richard M., ed., *Davy Crockett, American Comic Legend*. New York, 1939. (Almanac stories.)

*Field, J. M. "Mike Fink," St. Louis *Reveille*, October 21, 1844; June 14, 21, 1847. (The best early compilation of Mike Fink tales.)

*Hoffman, Daniel G. *Paul Bunyan, Last of the Frontier Demigods*. Philadelphia, 1952. (Traces the development of lore concerning Paul Bunyan.)

*Johnson, Guy B. *John Henry, Tracking Down a Negro Legend*. Chapel Hill, 1929.

Laughead, W. B. *The Marvelous Exploits of Paul Bunyan, as Told in Camps of Lumbermen*. New York, 1924.

Loomis, C. Grant. "The American Tall Tale and the Miraculous," *California Folklore Quarterly*, IV, 109–28 (1945).

Masterson, James R. *Tall Tales of Arkansas*. Boston, 1942.

Masterson, James R. "Travellers' Tales of Colonial Natural History," *Journal of American Folklore*, LIX, 51–67, 174–188 (1946).

Montague, Margaret P. *Up Eel River*. New York, 1927. (Tales of Tony Beaver.)

Price, Robert. *Johnny Appleseed, Man and Myth*. Bloomington, 1954. (Exhaustive account.)

Pound, Louise, ed. *American Ballads and Songs*. New York, 1922.

Rayford, J. L. "Our Own Gods Are Always Comic," *American Mercury*, LX, 491–97 (April, 1945.)

Rounds, Glen. *Ol' Paul.* New York, 1936 (Paul Bunyan tales.)

*Rourke, Constance. *Davy Crockett.* New York, 1934. (A graceful achievement of the author's stated aim, the writing of a biography in which Crockett's "purposes, his rash and engaging character, the circumstances of his many adventures, and the bold legends about him . . . all have a place.")

Shackford, James Atkins. *David Crockett: The Man and the Legend.* Chapel Hill, 1956. (A detailed biography, well documented, with some attention to the legend.)

*Shephard, Esther. *Paul Bunyan.* Seattle, 1924. (The most effective retelling of the tales about the gigantic lumberjack.)

Sherman, Stuart P. "Paul Bunyan and the Blue Ox," in *The Main Stream.* New York, 1927. (A commentary on the Bunyan legends.)

Spotts, C. B. "Mike Fink in Missouri," *Missouri Historical Review,* XXVIII, 3–8 (October, 1933).

Stevens, James, *Paul Bunyan.* Garden City, 1924.

Stevens, James. *The Saginaw Paul Bunyan.* New York, 1932.

Stewart, Bernice K., and Homer A. Watt. "Legends of Paul Bunyan, Lumberjack," in *Transactions of Wisconsin Academy of Sciences, Arts, and Letters,* XVIII, Part II, 639–51 (1916).

Whiting, B. J. "Guyascutus, Royal Nonesuch and Other Hoaxes," *Southern Folklore Quarterly,* VIII, 251–75 (December, 1944).

BIBLIOGRAPHIES

Johnson, Thomas H. "Folk Tales and Humor," *Literary History of the United States.* New York, 1948, III, 202–11; Richard M. Ludwig. *Ibid. Supplement.* New York, 1959, pp. 47–9.

Van Doren, Mark. "Early Humorists," in *Cambridge History of American Literature.* New York, 1918, II, 503–11.

Whicher, George Frisbie. "Minor Humorists," in *Cambridge History of American Literature.* New York, 1921, IV, 639–44.

ANTHOLOGIES

[Anon.] *American Wit and Humor.* New York, 1859.

[Anon.] *American Wit and Humor.* 5 vols. Philadelphia, 1904.

[Anon.] *The Chaplet of Comus.* Boston, 1811.

Avery, S. P., ed. *The Harp of a Thousand Strings. Laughter for a Lifetime.* New York, 1858, 1865. (Takes its title from the famous burlesque sermon, and prints several Sut Lovingood stories for the first time in book form. A good sampling of the humor of the fifties.)

Barr, James, ed. *The Humor of America.* New York, [1893], London, 1894. (Contains, pp. 437–62, a helpful biographical index of American humorists.)

Brown, M., ed. *Wit and Humor of Bench and Bar.* New York, 1899.

Bruére, Mrs. Martha S., and Mary R. Beard. *Laughing their Way; Women's Humor in America.* New York, 1934.

Burke, T. A., ed. *Polly Peablossom's Wedding; and Other Tales.* Philadelphia, 1851. (An important collection of Southern comic tales.)

Burton, W. E. "American Humor," in *Cyclopedia of Wit and Humor.* New York, 1858, 1866, I, 1–480. (A serviceable selection, going back to colonial times.)

Byrne, Marcus Lafayette, ed. *The Repository of Wit and Humor.* Boston and Cleveland, 1853, 1856, 1860.

Clark, Thomas D. ed. *The Rampaging Frontier.* Indianapolis, 1939.

Clemens, S. L., ed. *Mark Twain's Library of Humor.* New York, 1888. In 3 volumes, New York, 1906. (Mark Twain played an important role in compiling the first edition.)

Conroy, Jack, ed. *Midland Humor.* New York, 1947.

Folk, Robert P., ed. *The Antic Muse: American Writers in Parody.* New York, 1955.

Ford, Robert, ed. *American Humorists Recent and Living.* London, 1897. (An Englishman writes laudatory introductions to passages from nineteen humorists.)

French, Joseph L., ed. *Sixty Years of American Humor.* Boston, 1924. (Artemus Ward to Sam Hellman.)

Haliburton, T. C., ed. *Traits of American Humor, by Native Authors.* London, 1852, 1866, 1873, [n.d.]. Under the title, *Yankee Stories and Yankee Letters.* Philadelphia, [1852]. (The first edition was in three volumes. Later editions, somewhat abridged, were in one. This and the other compilation by Haliburton listed below were the best contemporary compilations.)

Haliburton, T. C., ed. *The Americans at Home; or, Byeways, Backwoods, and Prairies.* London, 1854, [n.d.], 1873; Philadelphia, [1854?]. (The first edition was in three volumes, later editions, somewhat abridged, in one. See comment on Haliburton above.)

Harris, Joel Chandler, ed. *The World's Wit and Humor: American.* 5 vols. New York, 1907.

Hilton, G. S., ed. *The Funny Side of Politics.* New York, 1899.

Hudson, Arthur Palmer, ed. *Humor of the Old Deep South.* New York, 1936. (Excellent collection from many out-of-the-way sources, of the humor of Mississippi, Tennessee, Alabama, and Louisiana, 1540–1860. Supplements the collection by F. J. Meine listed below.)

Jerdan, William, ed. *Yankee Humor, and Uncle Sam's Fun.* London, 1853. (The "Introduction," pp. 4–29, contains an interesting English appreciation.)

Knowles, F. L., ed. *Poetry of American Wit and Humor.* New York, 1899.

Landon, Melville D., ed. *Kings of the Platform and Pulpit.* Chicago, 1891. (Best source of information on humorous lecturers; contains several lectures not elsewhere accessible. Frequently reprinted.)

Leacock, Stephen. *The Greatest Pages of American Humor*. New York, 1936. (A superficial summary of the history of American humor from Puritan times to the present, with brief excerpts from a number of humorists.)

Lynn, Kenneth S., ed. *The Comic Tradition in America*. Garden City, 1958.

Mason, E. T., ed. *Humorous Masterpieces from American Literature*. 3 vols. New York, 1886.

Meine, Franklin J., ed. *Tall Tales of the Southwest*. New York, 1930. (Indispensable for its field.)

Porter, William T., ed. *The Big Bear of Arkansas and Other Sketches, Illustrative of Characters and Incidents in the South and South-West*. Philadelphia, 1845, 1855. (A rich collection made by the editor of *The Spirit of the Times*.)

Porter, William T., ed. *A Quarter Race in Kentucky*. Philadelphia, 1846, 1847. Reprinted as *Colonel Thorpe's Scenes in Arkansas*. Philadelphia, [n.d.]. (See comment on item above.)

Sala, George, ed. *Yankee Drolleries*. Three series. London, [n.d.]. (Full selections from ten humorists.)

Smith, H. Allen, ed. *Desert Island Decameron*. Philadelphia, 1947.

Tidwell, James N., ed. *A Treasury of American Folk Humor*. New York, 1956.

Watterson, Henry, ed. *Oddities in Southern Life and Character*. Boston, 1882. (Comments illuminating, selections good.)

White, E. B., and Katharine S. White, eds. *A Subtreasury of American Humor*. New York, 1941.

Wilt, Napier, ed. *Some American Humorists*. New York, 1929. (A good small collection of crackerbox philosophers, with brief biographical introductions.)

Important Nineteenth-Century Humorous Periodicals

For extended discussions see F. L. Mott's *History of American Magazines*. New York, 1930.

Arkansas Traveller. Little Rock: June 4, 1882—November 25, 1888. Chicago: December 1, 1888—[1900?].

Carpet Bag. Boston: March 29, 1851—March 25, 1853.

Comic Monthly. New York: 1859–1876.

Judge. New York: 1881–1939.

Lantern, The. New York: 1852–1853.

Life. New York: 1883–1936.

Porter's Spirit of the Times. New York: September 6, 1856—February 25, 1860.

Puck, New York: March, 1877—September, 1918.

Red Book. Baltimore: 1819–1821.

Salmagundi. New York: January 24, 1807—January 25, 1808.

The Spirit of the Times. New York: 1831–1861.

Texas Siftings. Austin; New York: 1882–[1897?].

Vanity Fair. New York: December 31, 1859—July 4, 1863.

Yankee Blade. Portland, Me.; Boston: 1845–1890.

Yankee Notions. New York: 1852–[1872?].

DOWN EAST HUMOR

(1800–1867)

JACK DOWNING ENTERING PORTLAND, 1830

This picture from *My Thirty Years Out of the Senate* (1859) reveals the first great figure of native American humor at the beginning of his career. It also shows the character who for many years represented the United States in cartoons. The costume of Uncle Sam, who replaced him as a national symbol, still derives from Jack's apparel.

THE HUMOR OF THE FARMER'S ALMANAC
(1809–1836)

AMUSING

MR. THOMAS,

We have frequently heard of the wonderful feats and extraordinary stories of *Simonds, old Kidder, and Sam Hyde;* but I believe neither of them have exceeded the following, related by G. H——ll, a mighty hunter, and known in that part of the country where he lived by the name of the VERMONT NIMROD.—It may serve to divert some of your evening readers.   A. Z.

"I was once," said he, "passing down the banks of the Hudson in search of game, and suddenly heard a crackling on the opposite bank. Looking across the river, I saw a stately buck, and instantly drew up and let fly at him. That very moment a huge sturgeon leaped from the river in the direction of my piece.—The ball went through him, and passed on. I flung down my gun—threw off my coat and hat, and swam for the floating fish, which, mounting, I towed to the bank and went to see what more my shot had done for me. I found the ball had passed through the heart of the deer, and struck into a hollow tree beyond; where the honey was running out like a river! I sprung round to find something to stop the hole with, and caught hold of a white rabbit—It squeaked just like a stuck pig; so I thrash'd it away from me in a passion at the disappointment, and it went with such force that it killed three cock partridges and a wood cock."!!!

[MY NEIGHBOR FREEPORT]

My neighbor Freeport had a knack at telling a story, cracking a joke and singing a song, and these talents made him a favourite of his townsmen. Every town meeting and training was sure to gather round him a crowd of jovial fellows, and my neighbour pretty soon added to his other acquisitions that of handsomely swigging a glass of grog. The demands for stories, jokes and songs encreased with the reward he received for them; and Freeport had not a heart to refuse either, till the tavern became his common resort. But while Freeport was so musical at the tavern his affairs got out of tune at home. His wife took a high pitch, and often gave him an unwelcome solo. Her stories had much of pith, and her sarcasms were of the keenest sort. She insisted that their affairs were going to rack and ruin. Sometimes the neighbour's cattle had broken into the corn—the rye had been ruined by laying out in the storm—the hogs had broken in and rooted up the garden—the hay was half lost for want of attention—the fences were broken down, &c. &c. And then the children—

Alas! the poor children were shoeless, coatless and heartless; for they had become the scoff and sport of their little companions by reason of their father's neglect to provide them with decent and comfortable apparel. They were unable to read, for they had no books. The sheep—here the poor woman sorely wept—were sold by the collector to pay taxes. So there was no chance for any wool to knit the children's stockings. No flax had been raised, and of course they could have no shirts. To hear all this and ten times more was not very welcome to the ears of Freeport, whose heart was naturally tender and humane, so to get rid of it, he used to return to the tavern like a sow to her wallowing. His shop bills run up fast, while his character was running down. In this way he went on about two years, till old Scrapewell and Screwpenny got his farm; for all this time these usurers had been lending him money, and thus encouraging him to pursue this dreadful course.

Old Capt. Gripe also came in for a share of poor Freeport's estate; and there was Plunket, the cobbler, he had lent him nine pence several times and now had cobbled it up to a court demand. Bob Raikins had swapped watches with him, and came in for the boot. The widow Nippet had lent him her mare twice to mill and once to a funeral, and had sold the boys an old tow jacket for a peck of whortleberries, and also given them a mess of turnips, and so she made out her account and got a writ. Tom Teazer, well known at the grog shops for a dabster at shoemaker loo, old Jeremiah Jenkins, the Jew, Stephen Staball, the butcher, and all the village moon-cursers came in for their portion of the wreck. So poor Freeport gave up vessel and cargo to these land pirates, sent his disconsolate wife again to her father with one of their babes, the rest were provided for by the town; and as for himself, miserable wretch, he became an outcast, a vagabond, and died drunk in the highway!

[OLD BETTY BLAB]

"Rumour is a pipe blown by surmises, jealousies, conjectures; and of so easy and so plain a stop, that the blunt monster with uncounted heads, the still discordant wavering multitude, can play upon it." Old Betty Blab is a dabster on this instrument; she knows exactly how to time and to key her tune to give the proper effect; she can perform in diatonic, cromatic, or enharmonic with vast variety and astonishing modulation. Sometimes you will hear her whizzing and twittering aloft, like a swallow or curlew; then in a moment she will drop into the croaking of a cormorant; then, by a sort of *twisty-cum-quirk*, she passes into the *bob-a-lincorn*, and here she excells all description. Next succeeds a touch of the affectuoso, and then this delightful solo ends in a sort of whisper, like the notes of an humble bee in a pumpkin blossom. It is impossible for me to do justice in describing her powers. In all her compositions she is a master hand in *thorough base*. Your garden must be attended to; a plenty of sauce greatly diminishes the butcher's bill.

[THE SCRAPE]

"Did you ever hear of the scrape that I and uncle Zekiel had duckin on 't on the Connecticut?" asked Jonathan Timbertoes, while amusing his old Dutch hostess, who had agreed to entertain him under the roof of her log cottage, for and in consideration of a bran new tin milk-pan. "No, I never did; do tell it," said Aunt Pumkins. "Well—you must know that I and uncle Zeke took it into our heads on Saturday's afternoon to go a gunning after ducks, in father's skiff; so in we got and sculled down the river; a proper sight of ducks flew backwards and forwards I tell ye—and by'm-by a few on 'em lit down by the mash, and went to feeding. I catched up my powder-horn to prime, and it slipped right out of my hand and sunk to the bottom of the river. The water was amazingly clear, and I could see it on the bottom. Now I could n't swim a jot, so sez I to uncle Zeke, you're a pretty clever fellow, just let me take your powder-horn to prime. And don't you think, the stingy critter would n't. Well, says I, you're a pretty good diver, 'un if you'll dive and get it, I'll give you primin. I thought he'd leave his powder-horn; but he did n't, but stuck it in his pocket, and down he went—and there he staid" —here the old lady opened her eyes with wonder and surprise,

and a pause of some minutes ensued, when Jonathan added,—
"I looked down, and what do you think the critter was doin?"
"Lord!" exclaimed the old lady, "I'm sure I don't know." "There
he was," said our hero, "setting right on the bottom of the river,
pouring the powder out of my horn into hizen."

[The Baker]

Hark! 't is the jingle of the baker's bells. Hot bread, who buys?
Have a care now, Mr. Sweetmouth, how you let this bill run up.
Wheat loaves, gingerbread, hot buns and seedcakes—these are all
very clever. But there is my aunt Sarah's brown bread, sweet,
pleasant and wholesome; don't give it up for a cartload of muffins
and jumbles. There is no discount on my aunt Sarah's cooking;
she is the personification of neatness and nicety. Give me a plate
of her nutcakes in preference to all the sweetmeats of the city.
It has become somewhat fashionable to cast off old *Rye-and-Indian*
for *Genesee, Howard-street,* &c.—also to give up heating the oven.
I imagine that this change is vastly convenient for the shoe-
peggers. "Tell the baker he may leave us half a dozen of his three
cent biscuit," said Mrs. Crispin. Now three times six are eighteen,
and eighteen times 365 are $65.70—whew! This will never do.
In our haste to get rich, we must look at both ends of the railcut.
Bread is denominated the *staff* of life, the main supporting food;
but this so important article may, as well as a whistle, come too
dear. Let your good wife, then, have her own hands in the knead-
ing trough, nor heed too much the morning music of the baker's
boy.

ᘐᘐ

JACK DOWNING'S LETTERS AND OTHER DOCKYMENTS

by Seba Smith

(1792–1868)

[JACK'S GRANDFATHER]

As I said afore, my grandfather, old Mr Zebedee Downing, was the first settler in Downingville. Bless his old heart, he's living yet, and although he is eighty-six years old, he attended a public caucus for the good of his country about two years ago, and made a speech, as you will find somewhere before you get through this book, where it tells about my being nominated for Governor of the State of Maine.

As it is the fashion, in writing the lives of great folks, to go back and tell something about their posterity, I spose I ought to give some account of my good old grandfather, for he was a true patriot, and as strong a republican as ever uncle Joshua was. He was born somewhere in the old bay State away back of Boston, and when the revolutionary war come on he went a sogering. Many and many a time, when I was a little boy, I've sot on the dye-pot in the corner till most midnight to hear him tell over his going through the *fatigue of Burgwine*. If one of the neighbors came in to chat awhile in an evening, my grandfather was always sure to go through with the fatigue of Burgwine; and if a stranger was travelling through Downingville and stopt at my grandfather's in a warm afternoon to get a drink of water, it was ten chances to one if he could get away till my grandfather had been through the whole story of the fatigue of Burgwine. He used to tell it the best to old Mr Johnson, who used to come in regularly about once a week to spend an evening and drink a mug of my grandfather's cider. And he would set so patiently and hear my grandfather through from beginning to end, that I never could tell which took the most comfort, Mr Johnson in drinking the cider, or my grandfather in going through the fatigue of Burgwine. After Mr Johnson had taken about two or three drinks he would smack his lips, and says he, I guess, Mr Downing, you would have been glad to get such a mug of cider as this in the battle of Burgwine.

Why yes, said my grandfather, or when we was on the march from Cambridge to Peekskill either, or from Peekskill to Albany, or from Albany to Saratogue, where we went through the fatigue of Burgwine. Old Schyler was our gineral, said my grandfather, bracing himself back in his chair, and he turned out to be a traitor, and was sent for, to go to Gineral Washington to be court-martialed. Then gineral Gates was sent to us to take the command, and he was a most capital officer every inch of him. He had his cocked hat on, and his regimentals, and his furbelows on his shoulders, and he looked nobly, said my grandfather. I can see him now as plain as if 'twas yesterday. He wore a plaguy great stub cue, as big as my wrist, sticking out at the back of his neck as straight as a handspike. Well, when Gates came we were all reviewed, and every thing was put in complete order, and he led us on, ye see, to take Burgwine. By daylight in the morning we were called out by the sound of the drum, and drawn up in regiments, and the word was, 'on your posts, march.' And there we stood marching on our posts without moving forward an inch; heads up, looking to the right; we did n't dare to move an eye, nor hardly to wink.

By and by along comes the old Gineral to inspect us, riding along so stately, and that old stub cue sticking out behind his head so straight, it seems as though I can see him now right here before me. And then he addressed us, like a father talking to his children. Fellow soldiers, says he, this day we are going to try the strength of Burgwine's forces; now let every man keep a stiff upper lip, go forward boldly and attack them with courage, and you 've nothing to fear. O, he addressed us completely; and then we marched off to meet the inemy. By and by we begun to hear the balls whizzing over our heads, and the inemy's guns begun to roar like thunder. I felt terribly for a minute or two, but we kept marching up, marching up, said my grandfather, rising and marching across the floor, for we had orders not to fire a gun till we got up so near we could almost reach 'em with our bagonuts; and there was a hundred drums all in a bunch rattling enough to craze a nation, and the fifes and the bugles, continued my grand-father, still marching across the floor, went tudle, tudle, tudle, tudle—O, I can hear that very tune ringing in my ears now, as plain as if 'twas yesterday, and I shall never forget it to my dying day. When we got up so near the inemy that we could fairly see the white of their eyes, the word was 'halt,' said my grandfather, suddenly halting in the middle of the floor, and sticking his head back as straight as a soldier—'make ready;' 'twas did in a moment, continued my grandfather, throwing his staff up against his shoulder,—'take aim'—'twas did in a moment, fetching his staff down straight before his eyes—'fire'—then O marcy, what a roar, said my grandfather, striking his staff down on the floor, and such a smother and smoke you could n't hardly see your hand afore you. Well in an instant the word was 'prime and load,' and as fast as we fired we fell back in the rear to let others come up and take their turn, so by the time we were loaded we were in front and ready to fire again, for we kept marching all the time, said my grandfather, beginning to march again across the floor. But the inemy stood their ground and kept pouring in upon us tremendously, and we kept marching up and firing, marching up and firing, but did n't gain forward an inch. I felt streaked enough, for the balls were whistling over our heads, and sometimes a man would drop down on one side of me and sometimes on t' other, but it would n't do for us to flinch a hair; we must march up and fire and wheel to the right and left, and keep it going. By and by the word was, 'advance columns;' then, heavens and earth, how light I felt, said my grandfather, quickening his march across the floor. I knew in a moment the inemy was retreating, and it seemed to me I could have jumped over the moon. Well, we marched forward, but still kept firing, and presently we begun to come on to the inemy's ground; and then, O marcy, such a sight I never see before and never want to again: stepping over the dead bodies, and the poor wounded wretches wallowing in their blood, mangled all to pieces, and such screeches and groans, some crying out dont kill me, dont kill me, and others begging us to kill 'em to put 'em out of misery. O, it was enough to melt the very heart of a stone, said my grandfather, wiping the tears from his eyes.

But they need n't have been afraid of being hurt, for our Gineral was one of the best men that ever lived. He had the carts brought up immediately and all the poor wounded souls carried off as fast as possible where they could be taken good care of. He would n't let one of 'em be hurt any more than he would one of his own men. But it was a dreadful hot battle; we fit and skirmished all the afternoon and took a good many prisoners, and some cannon and ammunition. When it come night the inemy retreated to their fortifications, and we camped all night on the ground with our guns in our hands, ready at a moment's warning to pitch battle again. As soon as it was daylight we were all mustered and paraded again, and round come the old Gineral to see how we looked. He held his head up like a soldier, and the old stub cue stuck out as straight as ever. I can see it now as plain as I can see my staff, said my grandfather. And O, my stars, how he addressed us; it made our hearts jump to hear him. Fellow soldiers, says he, this day we shall make Burgwine tremble. If you are only as brave as you were yesterday we shall have him and all his army before night. But Burgwine had slipped away in the night and got into a place stronger fortified. But he could n't get away; he was hemmed in all round; so we got him before it was over. We were five or six days skirmishing about it; but I cant tell you all, nor a quarter part ont.

But how was it you took Burgwine at last? said Mr Johnson, taking another drink of cider. O, he had to give up at last, said my grandfather. After we had skirmished a day or two longer, Gineral Gates sent word to Burgwine, that if he had a mind to march his army back into Canada, and leave every thing this side unmolested, he'd let him go peaceably. But Burgwine would not accept it; he sent word back that 'he was going to winter with his troops in Boston.' Well, after we had skirmished round two or three days longer, and Burgwine got into such close quarters that he could n't get away any how, he sent word to Gineral Gates that he'd accept the offer and march back to Canada; but Gates sent word back to him again, 'You said you meant to winter in Boston, and I mean to make you as good as your word.' At last Burgwine see it was no use for him to hold out any longer, so he give all his men up prisoners of war. Then we were all paraded in lines a little ways apart to see them surrender. And they marched out and marched along towards us; and it was a most noble sight to see them all dressed out in their regimentals and their bagonuts glistening in the sun enough to dazzle any body's eyes. And they marched along and stacked their arms, and they all marched through between our lines looking homesick enough. I guess we felt as well as they did if our clothes want so good.

Well that was the end of the war in the northern states. There was a little skirmishing away off to the south afterwards, but nothing to be compared to that. The battle of Burgwine was what achieved our independence; it was the capstone of the war; there never was such a gloris battle as that since the days of Cesar, nor Methuselah, no, nor clear back to Adam. I dont think there ever was, said Mr Johnson, handing me the quart mug and telling me to run and get another mug of cider; for before my grandfather could get through the fatigue of Burgwine Mr Johnson would most always get to the bottom of the mug. When I brought in the second mug, Mr Johnson took another sip and smacked his lips, and says he, Mr Downing I should like to drink a toast with you; so here's health and prosperity to the apple-trees of Downingville. Mr Downing, what will you drink to us? said he, handing the mug to my grandfather. Why, I dont keer about any cider, said my grandfather [for he is a very temperate man, and so are all the Downings remarkably temperate] but I will jest drink a little to the memory of the greatest and the bravest Gineral that this world ever see yet; so here's my respects to old Gineral Gates' stub cue. By this time my grandfather having poured out of him the whole fatigue of Burgwine; and Mr Johnson having poured into him about three pints of cider, they would both of them feel pretty considerably relieved, and Mr Johnson would bid us good night and go home.

I take it that it was hearing these stories of my grandfather's bravery told over so often in my younger days, that made me such a military character as to induce the President to appoint me to the command at Madawaska, and also to go to South Carolina to put down the Nullifiers. But I'm getting a little before my story, for I have n't got through with my grandfather yet, and my father comes before I do too. As I said afore, my grandfather was the first settler in Downingville. When he got through sogering in the revolutionary war, he took a notion he'd go and pick him out a good lot of land away down east to settle on, where there was land enough to be had jest for whistling for it, and where his boys would have a chance to do something in the world. So he took grandmother and the two boys, for father and Uncle Joshua were all the boys he had then, and packed them into a horse-waggon, and took an axe and a hoe and a shovel, and some victuals, and a bedtick to put some straw in, and a gun and some blankets and one thing another, and started off down East. He drove away into Maine till he got clear to the end of the road, and then he picked his way along through the woods and round the pond five miles further, till he got to the very spot where Downingville now is, and there he stopt and baited his horse, and while grandmother and the boys sot down and took a bit of a luncheon, grandfather went away up top of one of the hills to take a view of the country. And when he come down again, says he, I guess we may as well ontackle, for I don't believe we shall find a better place if we travel all summer. So he ontackled the old horse, and took the waggon and turned it over against a great oak tree, and put some bushes up round it and made a pretty comfortable sort of a house for 'em to sleep in a few nights, and then he took his axe and slashed away amongst the trees. But that old oak never was cut down; it's the very same one that stands out a little ways in front of grandfather's house now. And poor old grandmother as long as she lived, for she's been dead about five years, always made a practice once a year, when the day come round that they first camped under the old oak, to have the table carried out and set under the tree, and all hands, children and grand-children, had to go and eat supper there, and the good old lady always used to tell over the whole story how she slept eight nights under the waggon, and how they were the sweetest nights' rest she ever had.

Letter 1. [Jack Goes to Portland]

Portland, Monday, Jan. 18, 1830.

To Cousin Ephraim Downing, up in Downingville:

Dear Cousin Ephraim:—I now take my pen in hand to let you know that I am well, hoping these few lines will find you enjoying the same blessing. When I come down to Portland I didn't think o' staying more than three or four days, if I could sell my load of ax handles, and mother's cheese, and cousin Nabby's bundle of footings; but when I got here I found Uncle Nat was gone a freighting down to Quoddy, and Aunt Sally said as how I shouldn't stir a step home till he come back agin, which won't be this month. So here I am, loitering about this great town, as lazy as an ox. Ax handles don't fetch nothing; I couldn't hardly give 'em away. Tell Cousin Nabby I sold her footings for nine-pence a pair, and took it all in cotton cloth. Mother's cheese come to seven-and-sixpence; I got her half a pound of shushon, and two ounces of snuff, and the rest in sugar. When Uncle Nat comes home I shall put my ax handles aboard of him, and let him take 'em to Boston next time he goes; I saw a feller tother day, that told me they'd fetch a good price there. I've been here now a whole fortnight, and if I could tell ye one half I've seen, I guess you'd stare worse than if you'd seen a catamount. I've been to meeting, and to the museum, and to both Legislaters, the one they call the House, and the one they call the Sinnet. I spose Uncle Joshua is in a great hurry to hear something about these Legislaters; for you know he's always reading newspapers, and talking politics, when he can get anybody to talk with him. I've seen him when he had five tons of hay in the field well made, and a heavy shower coming up, stand two hours disputing with Squire W. about Adams and Jackson—one calling Adams a tory and a fed, and the other saying Jackson was a murderer and a fool; so they kept it up, till the rain began to pour down, and about spoilt all his hay.

Uncle Joshua may set his heart at rest about the bushel of corn that he bet 'long with the postmaster, that Mr. Ruggles would be Speaker of that Legislater they call the House; for he's lost it, slick as a whistle. As I hadn't much to do, I've been there every day since they've been a setting. A Mr. White, of Monmouth, was the Speaker the first two days; and I can't see why they didn't keep him in all the time; for he seemed to be a very clever, good-natured sort of man, and he had such a smooth, pleasant way with him, that I couldn't help feeling sorry when they turned him out and put in another. But some said he wasn't put in hardly fair; and I don't know as he was, for the first day, when they were all coming in and crowding round, there was a large, fat man, with a round, full, jolly sort of a face, I suppose he was the captain, for he got up and commanded them to come to order, and then he told this Mr. White to whip into the chair quicker than you could say Jack Robinson. Some of 'em scolded about it, and I heard some, in a little room they called the lobby, say 'twas a mean trick; but I couldn't see why, for I thought Mr. White made a capital Speaker, and when *our* company turns out, the cap'n always has a right to do as he's a mind to.

They kept disputing most all the time the first two days about a poor Mr. Roberts, from Waterborough. Some said he shouldn't have a seat because he adjourned the town meeting and wasn't fairly elected. Others said it was no such thing, and that he was elected as fairly as any of 'em. And Mr. Roberts himself said he was, and said he could bring men that would swear to it, and good men too. But, notwithstanding all this, when they came to vote, they got three or four majority that he shouldn't have a seat. And I thought it a needless piece of cruelty, for they wan't crowded, and there was a number of seats empty. But they would have it so, and the poor man had to go and stand up in the lobby.

Then they disputed awhile about a Mr. Fowler's having a seat. Some said he shouldn't have a seat, because when he was elected some of his votes were given for his father. But they were more kind to him than they were to Mr. Roberts, for they voted that he *should* have a seat; and I suppose it was because they thought he had a lawful right to inherit whatever was his father's. They all declared there was no party politics about it, and I don't think there was; for I noticed that all who voted that Mr. Roberts *should* have a seat, voted that Mr. Fowler should *not*; and all who voted that Mr. Roberts should *not* have a seat, voted that Mr. Fowler *should*. So, as they all voted *both* ways, they must have been conscientious, and I don't see how there could be any party about it.

It's a pity they couldn't be allowed to have two Speakers, for they seemed to be very anxious to choose Mr. Ruggles and Mr. Goodenow. They two had every vote except one, and if they had had *that*, I believe they would both have been chosen; as it was, however, they both came within a humbird's eye of it. Whether it was Mr. Ruggles voted for Mr. Goodenow, or Mr. Goodenow for Mr. Ruggles, I can't exactly tell; but I rather guess it was Mr. Ruggles voted for Mr. Goodenow, for he appeared to be very glad to see Mr. Goodenow in the chair, and shook hands with him as good-natured as could be. I would have given half my load of ax handles, if they could both have been elected and set up there together, they would have been so happy. But as they can't have but one Speaker at a time, and as Mr. Goodenow appears to understand the business very well, it is not likely Mr. Ruggles will be Speaker any this winter. So Uncle Joshua will have to shell out his bushel of corn, and I hope it will learn him better than to bet about politics again. Before I came from home, some of the papers said how there was a majority of ten or fifteen *National Republicans* in the Legislater, and the other party said there was a pretty clever little majority of *Democratic Republicans*. Well, now everybody says it has turned out jest as that queer little paper, called the Daily Courier, said 'twould. That paper said it was such a close rub it couldn't hardly tell which side would beat. And it's jest so, for they've been here now most a fortnight acting jest like two boys playin see-saw on a rail. First one goes up, and then 'tother; but I reckon one of the boys is rather heaviest, for once in a while he comes down chuck, and throws the other up into the air as though he would pitch him head over heels. Your loving cousin till death.

JACK DOWNING.

Cousin Nabby Describes the Unutterable Disappointment at Downingville

DOWNINGVILLE, July 8, 1833.

To the Editor of the Portland Courier.

RESPECTABLE SIR:—As Cousin Jack is always so mity budge in writing letters to you, and as he and the President showed us a most provoking trick, and run off like a stream of chalk, back to Washington, without coming here, after they had promised over and over again that they would come, and we had got all slicked up and our clean gownds on, and more good victuals cooked than there ever was in all Downingville be fore—I say, Mr. Editor, I declare it's too bad; we are all as mad as blazes about it, and I mean to write and tell you all about it, if I live; and if Cousin Jack don't like it, he may lump it; so there now.

Ye see Cousin Jack writ to us that he and the President and some more gentlemen should be here the 4th of July, and we must spring to it and brush up and see how smart we could look, and how many fine things we could show to the President. This was a Saturday before the 4th of July come a Thursday. The letter was to Uncle Joshua, the Postmaster. Most all the folks in Downingville were at the Post-Office waiting when the mail come in, for we expected to hear from Jack.

Uncle Joshua put on his spettacles and opened the mail, and hauled out the papers and letters in a bunch. In a minute I see one to Uncle Joshua with the President's name on the outside; so I knew it was from Jack, for the President always puts his name on Jack's letters. We all cried out to Uncle Joshua to open it, and let us know what was in it. But he's such a provoking odd old man, he wouldn't touch it 'till he got every one of the papers and letters sorted and put up in their places. And then he took it and set down in his armchair, and took out his tobacker box and took a chaw of tobacker, and then he broke open the seal and sot and chawed and read to himself. We all stood tiptoe, with our hearts in our mouths, and he must needs read it over to himself three times, chawing his old quid, and once in a while giving us a knowing wink, before he would tell us what was in it. And he wouldn't tell us arter all, but, says he, "You must all be ready to put the best side out Thursday morning; there'll be business to attend to, such as Downingville never see before."

At that we all turned and run, and such a hubbub as we were in from that time 'till Thursday morning, I guess you never see. Such a washing and scrubbing, and making new clothes and mending old ones, and baking and cooking. Every thing seemed to be in a clutter all over the neighborhood. Sargent Joel flew round like a ravin' distracted rooster. He called out his company every morning before sunrise, and marched 'em up and down the road three hours every day. He sent to the store and got a whole new set of buttons, and had 'em sowed on to his regimental coat, and had a new piece of red put round the collar. And had his trowses washed and his boots greased, and looked as though he might take the shine off of most anything. But the greatest rumpus was at Uncle Joshua's; for they said the President must stay there all night. And Ant Keziah was in such a pucker to have everything nice, I didn't know but she would fly off the handle.

She had every part of the house washed from garret to cellar, and the floors all sanded, and a bunch of green bushes put into all the fire places. And she baked three ovens-full of dried punkin pies, besides a few dried huckleberry pies, and cake, and a great pot of pork and beans. But the worst trouble was to fix up the bed so as to look nice; for Ant Keziah declared the President should have as good a night's lodging in her house as he had in New York or Boston. So she put on two feather beds on top the straw bed, and a bran-new calico quilt that she made the first summer after she was married, and never put it on a bed before. And to make it look as nice as the New York beds, she took her red silk gown and ripped it up and made a blanket to spread over the top. And then she hung up some sheets all round the bedroom, and the gals brought in a whole handful of roses and pinks, and pinned 'em up round as thick as flies in August.

After we got things pretty much fixed, Uncle Joshua started off to meet Cousin Jack and the President, and left Sargent Joel to put matters to rights, and told us we must all be ready and be paraded in the road by nine o'clock Thursday morning. Well, Thursday morning come, and we all mustered as soon as it was daylight and dressed up. The children were all washed, and had their clean aprons on and their heads combed, and were put under the care of the schoolmarm, to be paraded along with her scholars.

About eight o'clock, all the village got together down the road as fur as Uncle Joshua's new barn; and Sargent Joel told us how to stand, as he said, in military order. He placed Bill Johnson and Cousin Ephraim out a little ways in front, with each of 'em a great long fowling piece with a smart charge in to fire a salute, and told 'em as soon as the President hove in sight to let drive, only to be careful and pint their guns up, so as not to hurt anybody. Then come Sargent Joel and his company; and then come the schoolmarm and the children; and then come all the women and gals over sixteen with Ant Keziah at their head; and then come all the men in town that owned horses riding on horseback; and all the boys that Sargent Joel didn't think was large enough to walk in the procession got up and sot on the fences along by the side of the road.

There we stood 'till about nine o'clock, when, sure enough, we saw somebody come riding out of the woods down the hill. The boys all screamed, ready to split their throats, "Hoorah for Jackson," and Bill Johnson fired off his gun. Cousin Ephraim, who aint so easily fluttered, held on to his and didn't fire, for he couldn't see anybody but Uncle Joshua on his old gray horse. Along come Uncle Joshua, on a slow trot, and we looked and looked, and couldn't see anybody coming behind him.

Then they all begun to look at one another as wild as hawks, and turn all manner of colors. When Uncle Joshua got up so we could see him pretty plain, he looked as cross as a thunder-cloud. He rid up to Sargent Joel, and says he, "You may all go home about your business, for Jack and the President are half way to Washington by this time."

My stars! what a time there was then. I never see so many folks boiling over mad before. Bill Johnson threw his gun over into the field as much as ten rods, and hopped up and down, and struck his fists together like all possessed. Sargent Joel marched back and forth across the road two or three times, growing redder and redder, till at last he drew out his sword and fetched a blow across a hemlock stump, and snapped it off like a pipe-stem. Ant Keziah fell down in a conniption fit; and it was an hour before we could bring her tu and get her into the house. And when she come to go round the house and see the victuals she had cooked up, and go into the bedroom and see her gown all cut up, she went into conniption fits again. But she's better to-day, and has gone to work to try to patch up her gown again.

I thought I would jest let you know about these things, and if you are a mind to send word on to Cousin Jack and the President, I'm willing. You may tell 'em there aint five folks in Downingville that would hoorah for Jackson now, and hardly one that would vote for him, unless 'tis Uncle Joshua, and he wouldn't if he wasn't afraid of losing the Post-Office.

Your respected friend,

NABBY DOWNING.

How They Drafted the Militia Company in Downingville

Downingville, Nov. 6, 1831.

General Jackson—*Dear Sir*: I hope you'll excuse me, my makin' bold to write to you, bein' you are President of the United States and I only a humble farmer in the back-woods down here in Maine; but I'm a Republikan to the back-bone, so I kind of think you'll take it in good part. My neffu, Captain Jack Downing, has been here and got his company and started off for Madawaska. He said he ought to write to you before he started, but he was so arnest to get down there and give them New Brumzickers a thrashin' he didn't know how to stop. So I told him to go ahead, and I'd write and tell you all about it arter he was gone. We had the company all drafted and cut and dried for him when he got here, for the Governor of the State had given orders to draft the militia all over the state to be ready for the war down in the disputed territory.

My son Joel has gone down to the boundary war along with the rest of 'em, and we feel bad enough about it, I can tell you. He's too young to go, I know; he's a mere striplin' of a boy yet; he won't be seventeen years old till the fifth day of next May, if he should live to see it. But the poor boy may not live to see that day now; for he's taken his life in his hands, and gone to fight for his country like a man and a hero, live or die. It was a tryin' time to us, Gineral; it was a tryin' time—but I may as well tell you the story, and then you'll know.

After we heard the British had taken our land agent, and carried him off to New Brumzick, we begun to look out for a squall. It was about dark when the post brought the papers that had the account of it; so, arter supper, we all went into father's to talk the matter over. For father knows more about sich matters than anybody else in Downingville—he was out three years in the Revolution, and was in the battle of Lexington before he 'listed, and had the fore-finger of his right hand shot off in the battle of Bunker Hill, jest as he was pulling trigger, and aiming at a British officer that was hurrying up the hill, and driving his soldiers up like a fury. But father always says he didn't lose his shot by it; for when he found that finger was gone, and wouldn't pull, he tried the next finger, and the old gun went without losing his aim, and the British officer fell; and he always believed it was his shot brought him down. Though father is eighty-five years old now, and is so lame he can't walk about much, yet his mind holds out remarkably, and he can talk about these things as smart as ever he could. His house stands right aside of mine, only fur enough apart for a long shed between 'em, and he used to live in the same house with me, or rather, I lived in the same house with him, till I had so many children, and my family got so large 'twas rather worrisome to the old gentleman, and we was rather scant of room, so I built another house and moved into it, and got Cousin Debby to live with the old folks and take care of them.

So, as I said afore, arter supper we took the papers and went into father's, and I sot down and read it all over to him—how a parcel of the British come over into our disputed territory and went to cutting down our timber like smoke, so as to steal it, and carry it off in the spring, when the rivers open, away down to New Brumzick; and how our Governor, as soon as he heard about it, sent Mr. McIntire, the land agent, and a hundred and fifty men to put a stop to that stealin' business, and ketch the fellers if he could, and bring 'em off; and how Mr. McIntire took his men and marched off down there into the woods, ever so fur, into our disputed territory, and got all ready and was jest a going to ketch the fellers and bring 'em off up to Augusta, when the thieving chaps turned about and *ketched him*, and put him on a sled and hauled him off down to Fredericton, in New Brumzick, and put him in jail.

When I got along so fur, father couldn't hold still no longer; he struck his staff down on the floor jest as if it had been a training-gun, and says he:

"Joshua, there'll be trouble; you may depend upon't, there'll be trouble. If our people will stand that, they ain't made of such kind of stuff as the old Revolution folks was made of, nor nothing like it. In them days, if the British had took one of our men and hauled him off to Fredericton, and put him in jail, every man in the old Bay State, and every boy tu, that was big enough to carry a gun, would a shouldered it, and marched to New Brumzick, and Fredericton jail would a been stripped down in no time, and Mr. McIntire brought home agin."

Says I, "father, you mistake; your Revolution folks couldn't a brought Mr. McIntire home again, for he was not there in them days; it's Mr. McIntire that's in jail now."

"Yes they would," said the old gentleman, rising out of his chair, and striking his staff down on the floor harder than he did afore; "they'd a gone after Mr. McIntire, or any other man living, that had American blood in his veins, and they'd a brought him back, if they'd had to fit their way through forty New Brumzicks for him. Ain't the people waking up about it no where? ain't they going down to give them New Brumzicks a thrashing?"

I looked at my son Joel, and I see his face was all of a blaze; and he looked as if he was jest a going to burst out.

Says I, "Joel, my boy, what's the matter?"

His face grew redder, and the tears came into his eyes, and he struck his fists together, hard enough to crack a walnut.

"By king," says he, "father, I wish I was old enough to train; I want to go down there, and help give them are British what they deserve."

"By the memory of George Washington!" said my father, "I wish I was young enough to train; I should like to shoulder my gun agin, and go and teach them New Brumzickers better manners. But what are they doing at Augusta? Ain't there no stir about it yet?"

Says I, "we'll read on and see." So I looked over the papers a little more, and found the Governor had ordered ten thousand of the militia to be drafted to go down and keep the British out of our disputed territory, and prevent their stealing our pine timber.

"That looks something like it," said my father; "that's a little like the spunk of old seventy-six. The British'll have to let our disputed territory alone now, or else they'll have to come to the scratch for it. I wish I was twenty years younger, I'd go down as a volunteer."

"I wish I was only two years older," said my son Joel, "then

I should stan' a chance to be drafted; and if I wasn't drafted, I'd go, whether or no."

At that my wife and mother both fetched a heavy sigh. Mother said she thought father had been through wars enough in his day to rest in his old age, and let sich things alone. My wife, she wiped her eyes, for they was full of tears, and begged Joel not to talk so, for he was too young ever to think of sich things. And then she turned to father, and asked him if he really thought there was going to be any war.

"Yes," said father, "jest as true as the sun will rise to-morrow, there'll be a war, and that pretty soon tu, unless the New Brum-zickers back out, and give up Mr. McIntire, and let the timber on our disputed territory alone. The orders will be up here to draft the militia within two days, and I shouldn't be surprised if they should be called out before to-morrow morning."

At that my wife and the gals had a pretty considerable of a crying spell.

After we'd talked the matter all over, we went home, and went to bed; but we didn't any of us rest very well. My wife she sighed herself to sleep arter awhile; and I heard my son Joel, arter he got to sleep, muttering about guns and the British, and de-claring he would go. I had jest got into a drowse, about midnight, when I heard a heavy knock at the door. I sprung out of bed, and went and looked out of the window, and asked who was there.

"Sargent Johnson," was the reply. "We've got to stan a draft to-night. The Governor's orders got here about an hour ago. We're sending round to warn our company to meet up here, to Mr. Wil-son's tavern, at two o'clock this morning; it's near about one now, and the Captain wants Squire Downing to come over and help see about making the draft. He wants to get through with it as soon as he can, so them that's drafted may be getting ready, for they've got to set out to Bangor at eight o'clock this morning."

I told him I would come right over; and so I lit a candle and dressed myself as quick as I could, and come out into the kitchen to put on my boots, and who should I find there but my son Joel all dressed, and his cap on, ready for a start. He had heard what had been said, and it put the fidgets right into him.

Says he, "Father, I want to go over and see 'em draft." I told him he better be abed and asleep by half. But he said he couldn't sleep; and I found the boy was so arnest to go, that I finally told him he might.

We hadn't more than got dressed, before we heard the drum beat over to Mr. Wilson's tavern; so we started off and went over. When we got there, they had a fire in the large hall, and the company was most all there. The Captain had got a bowl and some black beans and white beans all ready, and he wanted me to draw for them, so they might all feel satisfied there was no partiality. There was one sargent to be drafted, and we drew him first; and it fell to Sargent Johnson. He stood it like a man; I didn't see as he trembled or turned pale a bit. He looked a little redder if anything, and kind of bit his lip as he took his gun and marched into the middle of the floor, and he turned round and looked at the company, and says he,

"I'm ready to go and fight for our country to the last drop of my blood but what we'll make the British back out of our disputed territory, and stop their thieving."

The company gave three cheers for Sargent Johnson, and then we went to drafting the privates. There was eighty in the company, and twenty was to be drafted. So they took sixty white beans and twenty black ones, and put 'em into the bowl, and held it up, so nobody couldn't look into it, and I was to draw 'em out as the orderly sargent called out the names. So when we got ready to begin, the sargent sung out,

"William Jones."

I put my hand into the bowl and drawed, and sung out,

"White bean."

"Peter Livermore," cried the sargent.

Peter Livermore started, as if he'd had a shock from an electrical machine; his legs shook a little, and he looked in the face as if he felt rather bad. I put my hand in and drawed, and sung out,

"White bean."

Peter looked better in a minute. He's a great, tall, six-foot chap, and looks as if he could almost whip a regiment of common fellers himself; and although he's something of a brag, it's generally thought when you come right up to the pinch of the game, he's a little cowardly. Peter stretched his head back, and straddled his legs a little wider, and looked round on the company, and says he,

"I swow, I thought I should a been drafted, and I almost wish I had. It would a been fun alive to a gone down there, and had a brush 'long with them are New Brumzickers. My old fowling-piece would a made daylight shine through fifty of 'em in half an hour's fighting. I swow I'm disappinted—I was in hopes I should been drafted."

The company knew Peter too well to mind much what he said; they only laughed a little, and the Sargent went on, and called out,

"John Smith, the third."

I drawed to it, and says I,

"White bean."

The Sargent called out again,

"John Downing, the second."

That was the oldest son of Uncle John Downing, the blacksmith, a smart boy, and twenty-three years old. Somehow, as soon as I heard his name, I kind of felt as if he was going to be drafted; and I put in my hand and drawed, and sure enough, I sung out,

"Black bean."

John shouldered his gun in a minute, and marched out into the middle of the floor, and took his stand beside Sargent Johnson. He looked so resolute, and marched so quick, that the company at once gave three cheers for John.

"David Sanborn," cried the Sargent.

"White bean," said I.

"Ichabod Downing," said the Sargent.

I drawed, and answered the same as before,

"White bean."

"Jeremiah Cole," called out the Sargent.

"Black bean," said I; "black bean for Jerry."

After waiting a minute, the Captain called out, "Where's Jerry Cole? Isn't Jerry here?"

"Yes, setting down behind here on a bench," answered half a dozen at once.

"Come Jerry, come forward," said the Captain; "let us see your spunk."

By and by Jerry come creeping out from behind the company, and tried to get across the floor; but his face was as white as a cloth, and he shook and trembled so he couldn't scarcely walk. He let his gun fall on the floor, and sot down in a chair that stood by the side of the room, and boo-hoo'd out a crying like a baby.

"Well done," said the Captain; "there's spunk for you. What's the matter, Jerry—can't you go?"

"Booh-hoo," said Jerry, "I ain't well—I'm very sick, Captain; I don't think I could go any way in the world."

"Well, well," said the Captain, "leave your gun, and you may run home as fast as you can go, and see your mother, and we'll get somebody else to go in your room."

At that, Jerry darted out of the door, and pulled foot for home, like a streak of lightning.

"Where's Peter Livermore," said the Captain; "he may take Jerry's place, being he was disappointed at not being drafted." And he called Peter, and told him to take Jerry's gun and stand up in the floor with the drafts. Peter colored as red as you ever see, and begun to sweat. At last, says he:

"Captain, I don't see how I can go any way in the world, my family's out of wood and meal, and a good many other things, and I couldn't leave home."

"Oh," says the Captain, "we'll take care of your family while you are gone, Peter. Come, take the gun; don't stop to parley."

"But, Captain," said Peter, the sweat beginning to roll off his face, "if I'd been drafted, Captain, I'd a gone with the greatest pleasure in the world, and shouldn't wanted no better fun. But somehow or other, it seems to me like presumption, to go throwing myself into danger, when it wasn't my lot to go. I shouldn't like to go, Captain, without I was drafted."

"Well, well," said the Captain, "you needn't go; we want no cowards to go. But who is there here, among the spectators, or among the men whose names have been called, that isn't afraid to take Jerry's gun and fill Jerry's place? If there's any one here that's willing to go, let him come forward."

At that, my son Joel sprung like a young tiger, and seized Jerry's gun, and jumped into the middle of the floor and stood up by the side of Sargent Johnson, and shouldered his gun with so much eagerness, and looked so fierce and determined, although nothing but a striplin' of a boy, that the whole company burst out in three tremendous cheers for Joel Downing. The Captain asked me if I was willing he should go. I was never so tried in my life. For my own part, bein' the boy was so brave and wanted to go so much, I should a said yes. But then I knew it would almost kill his mother. So, what to do I didn't know. But I found the boy had got his mind so fixed upon going, that if he didn't go it would about kill him. So, on the whole, I told the Captain yes, he might put his name down.

Then we went on with the drafting again and got all through without any more trouble, and got ready to go home about three o'clock. The Captain told them that was drafted that they must all be ready to march at eight o'clock in the morning, and they must be in front of the tavern at that hour, and start together for Bangor. My son Joel and I then went home, and made up a fire and routed the folks all out, and told 'em Joel was listed, and got to start at eight o'clock, to fight for our disputed territory. Sich an outcry as there was for about a half an hour I guess you never heard. My wife couldn't a cried harder if Joel had been shot dead there before her feet, though she didn't make much noise about it, for she always cries to herself. The older gals, they cried considerable louder; and some of the younger children, that didn't hardly understand what the trouble was about, sot in and screamed as loud as they could bawl.

At last says I, "There's no use in this noise and fuss; the boy's got to go, and he's got to be off at eight o'clock tu, and the sooner we set ourselves to work to get him ready the better." That seemed to wake 'em up a little. My wife went to work and picked up his clothes, and she and the gals sot down and mended his shirts and stockins, and fried up a parcel of doughnuts for him to put in his knapsack, and got him all fixed up and breakfast ready about six o'clock. We hadn't waked up old father in the night, bein' he's so old; but in the morning we let him know about it, and he wanted my son Joel to come in and see him before he went; so we went into the old gentleman's room.

"Now, Joel, my boy," said the old gentleman, "I feel proud to hear sich a good report of you. You'd a made a good soldier in the days of the Revolution. 'Twas such boys as you that drove the British from Lexington, and mowed 'em down on Bunker Hill, and went through the fatigue of Burgoine. You'll feel a little queer at first, when you see the enemy coming up to you with their guns pinted right at you; and, brave as you are, you'll feel a little streaked. But you mus'n't mind it; as soon as they've fired once, you wont feel any more of it, and wont keer any more about 'em than you would about a flock of sheep. But don't be in a hurry to fire—mind that—don't be in a hurry to fire; they told us at Bunker Hill not to fire till the enemy got up so near we could see the whites of their eyes. And 'twas a good rule; for by that means we let 'em get up so near, that when we did fire, we mowed 'em down like a field of clover, I can tell you. Be a good boy, Joel, and don't quit our disputed territory as long as there is any dispute about it."

By this time we see 'em begin to gather in the road up by the tavern, and I told Joel it was time to be off; so he took his gun, and his knapsack, which was pretty well stuffed, for each of the children had put in a doughnut or an apple, or a piece of cake, after their mother had crammed in as much as she thought he could carry, and then he marched away like a soldier up to the tavern. When they started they had to come down again by our house and go up over a rise of land t'other way about half a mile, before they got out of sight. So we all stood out in a row along by the side of the road to see 'em as they went by. Father got out as fur as the door-step and stood leaning on his staff, and mother stood behind him with her specs on, looking over his shoulder; and the rest of us, with the children, and cousin Debby, and all, went clear out to the side of the road. Pretty soon they come along by, my son Joel at the head, and the rest marching two and two. When they got along against us, little Sally run up and tucked another great apple into Joel's pocket, and my wife called out to him, "Now do pray be careful, Joel, and not get shot."

Then grandfather raised his trembling voice, and says he:

"Now, Joel, my boy, remember and don't be in a hurry to fire."

And the children called out all together, "good-by, Joel, good-by, Joel," each repeating it over three or four times. Joel looked round and nodded once, when his mother called out to him, but the rest of the time he held his head up straight and marched like a soldier. We stood and watched 'em till they got clear to the top of the hill and was jest a going out of sight, when all to once Joel stepped out one side, where we could see him, and let his old gun blaze away into the air, and in a minute more they were out of sight.

"Ah," said old father, "that sounds like Bunker Hill; that boy'll do the business for them New Brumzickers, if they don't let our disputed territory alone."

The company had not been gone more than half an hour when my neffu, Captain Jack Downing, arrived with his commission in his pocket. Jack hadn't been in Downingville before for two years, and if there wasn't a time of it among our folks I'll never guess agin. Nabby, she hopped right up and down, like a mouse treed in a flour barrel. Ephraim snapped his thumb and finger, and spit on his hands, as though he had a cord of wood to chop. Aunt Keziah, (that's my wife) she put her apron up to her eyes and cried as much as half an hour, as hard as she could cry. I found I was rather choky, but I took down my pipe and rolled out a few whifs, and so made out to smoke it off. As soon as Jack had a chance to shake hands all round and get a little breakfast, he started off like a streak of chalk to overtake the company and take command.

So I remain your true friend and fellow-laborer in the Republikan cause.

JOSHUA DOWNING.

Showing How the Major Persuaded Uncle Joshua to Take Hold and Help Elect General Pierce to the Presidency, and How Downingville Ratified the Nomination

DOWNINGVILLE, Away Down East,
In the State of Maine, July 20, 1852.

MR. GALES AND SEATON—

MY DEAR OLD FRIENDS:—We've made out to ratify at last; but it was about as hard a job as it was for the Baltimore Convention to nominate. And I'm afraid the worst on't ain't over yet; for Uncle Joshua shakes his head and says to me, in a low tone, so the rest shan't hear, "Between you and me, Major, the 'lection will be a harder job still." I put great faith in Uncle Joshua's feelins. He's a regular political weather-glass, and can always tell whether we are going to have it fair or foul a good ways ahead. So when he shakes his head, I naterally look out for a tough spell of weather. When I got home from Baltimore, says I, "Well, Uncle Joshua, you got my letter in the Intelligencer, didn't you?" And says he, "Yes."

"Well, didn't we do that business up well?" says I.

"I don't know about that," said Uncle Joshua; "I have my doubts about it."

"Why, don't you think," says I, "the nomination of Gineral Pierce will put the Democratic party on its legs again, and give it a fine start?"

Uncle Joshua looked up to me kind of quizical, and says he, "It *has* gin the party a pretty considerable of a start already, it come so unexpected." And then he sot as much as two minutes drumming his finger on the table, and didn't say nothin'.

And then he looked up again, and says he, "Major, *who is Gineral Pierce?* It ain't a *fictious* name, is it?"

"Why, Uncle Joshua," says I, "how you talk! It is Gineral Franklin Pierce, of New Hampshire."

"Gineral Franklin Pierce, of New Hampshire, is it?" says he. "Well, now, Major, are you sure there *is* such a person, or did somebody play a hoax on the Baltimore Convention?"

"Yes," says I, "Uncle, I'm as sure of it as I am that there is such a person as Uncle Joshua Downing. To make all sure of it and no mistake, I come through New Hampshire, and went to Concord, where they said he lived, and inquired all about it. The neighbors there all knew him perfectly well, and showed me the house he lives in. He wasn't at home, or I should a seen him myself, and should got his promise to keep the Downingville Post-Office for you. But you needn't be afraid but what you'll have it, for I sent a telegraph to him from Baltimore, as soon as he was nominated, to keep it for you."

Here I see by the looks of Uncle Joshua's eyes that he begun to get hold of some new ideas. Says he, "Well, Major, it is a fact, then, is it, that he was nominated in real earnest, and 'twasn't no joke?"

"Upon my word and honor," says I, "there isn't a particle of joke about it—it was all done in real arnest."

"Well, then, if you've really got a candidate," says Uncle Joshua, "I should like to know something about him. Does he belong to the Old Fogy class or Young America class?"

"I guess about half and half," says I, "and he'll be all the stronger for that, because he can draw votes on both sides."

"After all," says he, "I'm afraid it's a bad nomination. Them old pillars of the Democratic party, Gineral Cass, and Mr. Buchanan, and Governor Marcy, and Gineral Houston, and the rest, will feel so insulted and mortified at being pushed aside for strangers to take the lead, that they'll all be agin the nomination, and their friends, too, and that'll upset the whole kettle of fish."

"Don't you never fear that, Uncle Joshua," says I; "them old pillars that you speak of are all very much tickled with the nomination. Ye see, it broke the nose of Young America, and they was delighted with it. As soon as the nomination was out of the mould, before it had time to cool, they all telegraphed right to Baltimore that nothin' in the world could have happened to suit 'em better; it was a most excellent nomination, and they felt

under everlasting obligations to the Baltimore Convention. You
needn't have no fears that they'll feel any coldness towards the
nomination. They'll turn to and work for it like beavers."

"Well, how is it," said Uncle Joshua, "about that boy candidate for the Presidency that they call Young America? If his nose
is knocked out of joint he'll of course oppose the nomination, tooth
and nail."

"There's where you are mistaken again, Uncle Joshua," says
I. "On the contrary, he goes for it hotter than any of 'em; and
he telegraphed back to Baltimore, as quick as lightning could
carry it, that the nomination was jest the thing; it couldn't be
no better. Ye see, he looks upon it in the light that it chokes off
all the Old Fogies, and leaves the field clear for him next time.
He thinks so highly of the nomination, and feels so patriotic
about it, they say he is going to stump it through all the States,
and make speeches in favor of Gineral Pierce's election. You may
depend upon it, Uncle Joshua, we've got a very strong nomination—one that'll carry all afore it—and everybody is delighted
with it, and everybody's going to go for it. I didn't expect you to
hold back a moment. I thought you would have things all cut
and dried for a rousin' ratification meeting by the time I got
home."

"Well, you know, Major," said Uncle Joshua, "I always
follow Colonel Crockett's rule, and never go ahead till I know I'm
right. How foolish we should look to call a ratification meeting
here in Downingville, and be voted right plump down. You know
the Free-Soilers are very strong among us; they are strong in all
the Northern States. And you know the Baltimore Convention
fixed up a platform to stand on, that's all in favor of the Compromise and the Fugitive law, and is dead set agin the Free-Soilers.
Now, Major, you must have more understanding than to think
the Free-Soilers will ever swallow that platform; and if they don't,
we are dished."

"You are wrong again, Uncle Joshua," says I, "for the biggest
Free-Soiler in all America swallowed it right down, and didn't
make a wry face about it."

"Who do you mean?" says he.

"I mean Mr. John Van Buren," says I.

"But you don't mean," says Uncle Joshua, "that Mr. John
Van Buren accepts this platform, and is willing to stand on it."

"Yes I do, exactly so," says I, "for he got right up in Tammany Hall and made a speech about it; and he said he would go the nomination, and he'd stand the platform; at all events, he'd stand the platform for *this election*, anyhow. You needn't be at all afraid of the Free-Soilers, Uncle; they ain't so stiff as you think for, and they are as anxious to get the offices as anybody, and will work as hard for 'em. Now let us go to work and get up our ratification, and blow it out straight. The Democracy of the country expects Downingville to do its duty."

"Well, Major," says Uncle Joshua, "you've made out a better case than I thought you could. I'm willing to take hold and see what we can do. But I declare I can't help laughing when I think it's Gineral Franklin Pierce, of New Hampshire, that we've got to ratify. I wish we knew something about him; something that we could make a little flusteration about, and wake up the Democracy."

"Good gracious, Uncle Joshua," says I, "have you been Postmaster of Downingville this twenty years, and always reading the papers, and don't know that Gineral Pierce was one of the heroes of the Mexican war?"

At that, Uncle Joshua hopped out of his chair like a boy, and says he, "Major, is that a fact?"

"Yes," says I, "'tis a fact. You know Mr. Polk sent me out there as a private ambassador to look after Gineral Scott and Mr. Trist. And Gineral Pierce *was* out there; I knew all about it, and about his getting wounded."

"Good!" says Uncle Joshua, snapping his fingers; "that's lucky, then we've got something to go upon; something that the boys can hoorah about. And if we don't have too strong a team agin us we may carry the day yet. Who do you think the other party will put up?"

"Well," says I, "it's pretty likely to be Mr. Webster or Mr. Fillmore, and they can't either of 'em hold a candle to Gineral Pierce."

"Of course not," says Uncle Joshua, "if he was the hero of the Mexican war. I s'pose it was Gineral Scott's part of the war that he was in, because that's where you was. Which of the battles did he fight the bravest in, and mow down most of the Mexicans? Did he help storm that Gibralta castle at Vera Cruz?"

"No," says I, "that little matter was all over before Gineral Pierce got to Mexico."

"Well, the great battle of Cerro Gordo come next," said Uncle

Joshua; "I dare say Gineral Pierce was foremost in marching up that bloody Bunker Hill and driving off Santa Anna and his fifteen thousand troops."

"I'm sure he would a been foremost, if he'd been there," says I, "but he hadn't got into the country yet, and Gineral Scott wouldn't wait for him. It seems as if Gineral Scott is always in a hurry when there is any fightin' to do, and won't wait for nobody."

"Well, the next great battle, if I remember the newspapers right," said Uncle Joshua, "was Contreras; and after that came the bloody and hot times of Cherubusco, and the King's Mill, and Chepultepec, and marching into the City of Mexico. These was the battles, I s'pose, where Gineral Pierce fit like a lion, and became the hero of the Mexican war. But which battle did he shine the brightest in, and cut down most of the enemy?"

"The truth is," says I, "he got wounded at Contreras, and so wasn't able to take a part in them bloody affairs of Cherubusco, King's Mill, and Chepultepec."

"Then he *was* in the battle of Contreras," said Uncle Joshua, "and that can't be disputed?"

"O yes," says I, "he certainly was in the first part of it, when they was getting the battle ready, for there's where he got wounded."

"Good," said Uncle Joshua, "he was in one battle, and got wounded; that's enough to mak a handle of, anyhow. Whereabouts was his wound?"

"Well, he had several hurts," said I; "I believe in his foot and ancle, and other parts."

"Rifle balls?" said Uncle Joshua, very earnest.

"O no, nothing of that kind," says I.

"What then; sword cuts? Or did the Mexicans stick their bayonets into him?"

"No, no; nothin' of that kind, nother," says I.

"Then it must be grape or bombshells," said Uncle Joshua, "how was it?"

"No, no, 'twasn't none of them things," says I. "The fact was, when they was skirmishing round, getting ready for the battle, his horse fell down with him and lamed him very bad."

Uncle Joshua colored a little, and sot and thought. At last he put on one of his knowing looks, and says he, "Well, Major, a wound is a wound, and we can make a handle of it without being such fools as to go into the particulars of how he came by it. I say let's go ahead and ratify Gineral Pierce, and who knows but what we can make something out of this Mexican business?"

Well, Mr. Gales and Seaton, the thing was done. We ratified on the 21st of June, in the evening, and it was a tall piece of business. When I begun, I meant to give you a full account of it, with some of the speeches and resolutions; but I've made my preamble so long that I can't do it in this letter. *We had a torchlight procession.* Cousin Ephraim took his cart and oxen, and went into the woods and got a whole load of birch bark and pitch-pine knots, and all the boys in Downingville turned out and carried torches. The school-house was illuminated with fifty candles. Uncle Joshua presided, as usual. Banners were hung round the room, with large letters, giving the names of all the great battles in Mexico; and the enthusiasm was immense. When we'd got about through, and was just winding up with three tremendous cheers for the "Hero of Mexico," a message came up to Uncle Joshua from the Post-Office, stating that the telegraph had just brought news that the Whig Convention at Baltimore had nominated Gineral Scott for President. It gin the whole Convention the cold shuggers in a minute. Uncle Joshua looked very serious, and says he, "Feller-Democrats, to prevent any mistakes, I think you had better give them three last cheers over again, and put in the name of Gineral Pierce." So we did, and gin three rousin cheers for *Gineral Franklin Pierce, of New Hampshire, the Hero of Mexico.*

Downingville is wide awake, and will do her duty in November.

So I remain your old friend,

MAJOR JACK DOWNING.

THE SAYINGS OF SAM SLICK

by *Thomas Chandler Haliburton*

(1796–1865)

THE CLOCKMAKER

I had heard of Yankee clock pedlars, tin pedlars, and bible pedlars, especially of him who sold Polyglot Bibles (*all in English*) to
the amount of sixteen thousand pounds. The house of every substantial farmer had three substantial ornaments, a wooden clock, a
tin reflector, and a Polyglot Bible. How is it that an American can
sell his wares, at whatever price he pleases, where a blue-nose
would fail to make a sale at all? I will inquire of the Clockmaker
the secret of his success.

What a pity it is, Mr. *Slick*, (for such was his name) what a pity
it is, said I, that you, who are so successful in teaching these people
the value of *clocks*, could not also teach them the value of *time*. I
guess, said he, they have got that ring to grow on their horns yet,
which every four year old has in our country. We reckon hours and
minutes to be dollars and cents. They do nothing in these parts,
but eat, drink, smoke, sleep, ride about, lounge at taverns, make
speeches at temperance meetings, and talk about "*House of Assembly.*" If a man don't hoe his corn, and he don't get a crop, he says
it is all owing to the Bank; and if he runs into debt and is sued,
why he says the lawyers are a curse to the country. They are a
most idle set of folks, I tell you.

But how is it, said I, that you manage to sell such an immense
number of clocks, (which certainly cannot be called necessary articles) among a people with whom there seems to be so great a
scarcity of money?

Mr. Slick paused, as if considering the propriety of answering
the question, and looking me in the face, said, in a confidential
tone, Why, I don't care if I do tell you, for the market is glutted,
and I shall quit this circuit. It is done by a knowledge of *soft sawder*
and *human natur*. But here is Deacon Flint's, said he, I have but one
clock left, and I guess I will sell it to him.

At the gate of a most comfortable looking farm house stood
Deacon Flint, a respectable old man, who had understood the

value of time better than most of his neighbours, if one might judge from the appearance of every thing about him. After the usual salutation, an invitation to "alight" was accepted by Mr. Slick, who said, he wished to take leave of Mrs. Flint before he left Colchester.

We had hardly entered the house, before the Clockmaker pointed to the view from the window, and, addressing himself to me, said, if I was to tell them in Connecticut, there was such a farm as this away down east here in Nova Scotia, they wouldn't believe me—why there ain't such a location in all New England. The deacon has a hundred acres of dyke—Seventy, said the deacon, only seventy. Well, seventy; but then there is your fine deep bottom, why I could run a ramrod into it—Interval, we call it, said the Deacon, who, though evidently pleased at this eulogium, seemed to wish the experiment of the ramrod to be tried in the right place—Well, interval if you please, (though Professor Eleazer Cumstick, in his work on Ohio, calls them bottoms,) is just as good as dyke. Then there is that water privilege, worth 3,000 or 4,000 dollars, twice as good as what Governor Cass paid 15,000 dollars for. I wonder, Deacon, you don't put up a carding mill on it: the same works would carry a turning lathe, a shingle machine, a circular saw, grind bark, and—. Too old, said the Deacon, too old for all those speculations—Old, repeated the Clockmaker, not you; why you are worth half a dozen of the young men we see, now-a-days; you are young enough to have—here he said something in a lower tone of voice, which I did not distinctly hear; but whatever it was, the Deacon was pleased, he smiled and said he did not think of such things now.

But your beasts, dear me, your beasts must be put in and have a feed; saying which, he went out to order them to be taken to the stable.

As the old gentleman closed the door after him, Mr. Slick drew near to me, and said in an under tone, that is what I call "*soft sawder*." An Englishman would pass that man as a sheep passes a hog in a pasture, without looking at him; or, said he, looking rather archly, if he was mounted on a pretty smart horse, I guess he'd trot away, *if he could*. Now I find—Here his lecture on "*soft sawder*" was cut short by the entrance of Mrs. Flint. Jist come to say good bye, Mrs. Flint. What, have you sold all your clocks? Yes, and very low, too, for money is scarce, and I wished to close the concarn; no, I am wrong in saying all, for I have just one left. Neighbor Steel's wife asked to have the refusal of it, but I guess I won't sell it; I had but two of them, this one and the feller of it, that I sold Governor Lincoln. General Green, the Secretary of State for Maine, said he'd give me 50 dollars for this here one—it has composition wheels and patent axles, it is a beautiful article—a real first chop—no mistake, genuine super-fine, but I guess I'll take it back; and beside, Squire Hawk might think kinder harder, that I did not give him the offer. Dear me, said Mrs. Flint, I should like to see it, where is it? It is in a chest of mine over the way, at Tom Tape's store, I guess he can ship it on to Eastport. That's a good man, said Mrs. Flint, jist let's look at it.

Mr. Slick, willing to oblige, yielded to these entreaties, and soon produced the clock—a gawdy, highly varnished, trumpery looking affair. He placed it on the chimney-piece, where its beauties were pointed out and duly appreciated by Mrs. Flint, whose admiration was about ending in a proposal, when Mr. Flint returned from giving his directions about the care of the horses. The Deacon praised the clock, he too thought it a hand-some one; but the Deacon was a prudent man, he had a watch—he was sorry, but he had no occasion for a clock. I guess you're in the wrong furrow this time, Deacon, it ain't for sale, said Mr. Slick; and if it was, I reckon neighbor Steel's wife would have it, for she gives me no peace about it. Mrs. Flint said, that Mr. Steel had enough to do, poor man, to pay his interest, without buying clocks for his wife. It's no concarn of mine, said Mr. Slick, as long as he pays me, what he has to do, but I guess I don't want to sell it, and besides it comes too high; that clock can't be made at Rhode Island under 40 dollars. Why it ain't possible, said the Clockmaker, in apparent surprise, looking at his watch, why as I'm alive it is 4 o'clock, and if I hav'nt been two hours here—how on airth shall I reach River Philip to-night? I'll tell you what, Mrs. Flint, I'll leave the clock in your care till I re-turn on my way to the States—I'll set it a going and put it to the right time.

As soon as this operation was performed, he delivered the key to the Deacon with a sort of serio-comic injunction to wind up the clock every Saturday night, which Mrs. Flint said she would take care should be done, and promised to remind her husband of it, in case he should chance to forget it.

That, said the Clockmaker, as soon as we were mounted, that

I call 'human natur!' Now that clock is sold for 40 dollars—it cost me just 6 dollars and 50 cents. Mrs. Flint will never let Mrs. Steel have the refusal—nor will the Deacon learn until I call for the clock, that having once indulged in the use of a superfluity, how difficult it is to give it up. We can do without any article of luxury we have never had, but when once obtained, it is not 'in human natur' to surrender it voluntarily. Of fifteen thousand sold by myself and partners in this Province, twelve thousand were left in this manner, and only ten clocks were ever returned—when we called for them, they invariably bought them. We trust to 'soft sawder' to get them into the house, and to 'human natur' that they never come out of it.

Natur'

In the course of the journey, the conversation turned upon the several series of the "Clockmaker" I had published, and their relative merits. Mr. Slick appeared to think they all owed their popularity mainly to the freshness and originality of character incidental to a new country.

"You are in the wrong pew here, Squire," said he; "you are, upon my soul. If you think to sketch the English in a way any one will stop to look at, you have missed a figur', that's all. You can't do it, nohow you can fix it. There is no contrasts here, no variation of colors, no light and shade, no nothin'. What sort of a pictur' would straight lines of anything make? Take a parcel of sodjers, officers and all, and stretch 'em out in a row, and paint 'em, and then engrave 'em, and put it into one of our annuals, and see how folks would larf, and ask, 'What boardin'-school gall did that? Who pulled her up out of standin' corn, and sot her up on eend for an artist?' they'd say.

"There is nothin' here to take hold on. It's so plaguy smooth and high polished, the hands slip off; you can't get a grip of it. Now, take Lord First Chop, who is the most fashionable man in London, dress him in the best cut coat, best trowsers, French boots, Paris gloves, and grape-vine-root cane, don't forget his whiskers, or mous-stache, or breast-pins, or gold chains, or anything; and what have you got?—a tailor's print-card, and nothin' else.

"Take a lady, and dress her in a'most a beautiful long habit, man's hat, stand-up collar and stock, clap a beautiful little cow-hide whip in her hand, and mount her on a'most a splendiferous white hoss, with long tail and flowin' mane, a rairin' and a cavortin' like mad, and a champin' and a chawin' of its bit, and a makin' the froth fly from its mouth, a spatterin' and white-spottin' of her beautiful trailin' skirt, like anything. And what have you got?—why, a print like the posted hand-bills of a circus.

"Now spit on your fingers, and rub Lord First Chop out of the slate, and draw an Irish laborer, with his coat off, in his shirt-sleeves, with his breeches loose and ontied at the knees, his yarn stockings and thick shoes on; a little dudeen in his mouth, as black as ink and as short as nothin': his hat with devilish little rim and no crown to it, and a hod on his shoulders, filled with bricks, and him lookin' as if he was a singin' away as merry as a cricket:—

'When I was young and unmarried, my shoes they were new,
But now I am old and am married, the water runs troo.'

Do that, and you have got sunthin' worth lookin' at, quite pic-turesquee, as Sister Sall used to say. And because why? *You have got sunthin' nateral.*

"Well, take the angylyferous dear a horseback, and rub her out (well, I won't say that nother, for I'm fond of the little crittur s, dressed or not dressed for company, or any way they like), yes, I like woman-natur', I tell *you*. But turn over the slate, and draw on t'other side on't an old woman, with a red cloak, and a striped petticoat, and a poor pinched-up, old, squashed-in bonnet on, bendin' forrard, with a staff in her hand, a leadin' of a donkey that has a pair of yellow willow saddle-bags on, with colored vegetables and flowers, and red beet-tops, a goin' to market. And what have you got? Why, a pictur' worth lookin' at, too. Why?—*because it's natur'.*

"Now look here, Squire: let Copley, if he was alive, but he ain't; and it's a pity, too, for it would have kinder happified the old man, to see his son in the House of Lords, wouldn't it? Squire Copley, you know, was a Boston man; and a credit to our great nation, too. P'rhaps Europe never has never dittoed him since.

"Well, if he was above ground now, alive, and stirrin', why take and fetch him to an upper crust London party; and sais you, 'Old Tenor,' sais you, 'paint all them silver plates, and silver dishes, and silver coverlids, and what nots; and then paint them lords with their *stars*, and them ladies' (Lord, if he would paint them with their garters, folks would buy the pictur, cause that's nateral), 'them ladies with their jewels, and their sarvants with their liveries, as large as life, and twice as nateral.'

"Well, he'd paint it, if you paid him for it, that's a fact; for there is no better bait to fish for us Yankees, arter all, than a dollar. That old boy never turned up his nose at a dollar, except when he thought he ought to get two. And if he painted it, it wouldn't be bad, I tell *you*.

"'Now,' sais you, 'you have done high life, do low life for me, and I will pay you well—I'll come down hansum, and do the thing genteel, you may depend. Then,' sais you, 'put in for a background that noble, old Noah-like lookin' wood, that's as dark as comingo. Have you done?' sais I.

"'I guess so,'" says he.

"'Then put in a brook jist in front of it, runnin' over stones, and foamin' and a bubblin' up like anything.'

"'It's in,' says he.

"'Then jab two forked sticks in the ground ten feet apart, this side of the brook,' sais you, 'and clap a pole across atween the forks. Is that down?' sais you.

"'Yes,' sais he.

"'Then,' sais you, 'hang a pot on that horizontal pole, make a clear little wood fire onderneath; paint two covered carts near it. Let an old hoss drink at the stream, and two donkeys make a feed off a patch of thistles. Have you stuck that in?'

"'Stop a bit,' says he, 'paintin' an't quite as fast done as writin'. Have a little grain of patience, will you? It's tall paintin', makin' the brush walk at that price. Now there you are,' sais he. 'What's next? But, mind I've most filled my canvas; it will cost you a pretty considerable penny, if you want all them critters in, when I come to cypher all the pictur up, and sumtotalize the whole of it.'

"'Oh! cuss the cost!' sais you. 'Do you jist obey orders, and break owners, that's all you have to do, Old Loyalist.'

"'Very well,' sais he, 'here goes.'

"'Well, then,' sais you, 'paint a party of gipsies there; mind their different colored clothes, and different attitudes, and different occupations. Here a man mendin' a harness, there a woman pickin' a stolen fowl, here a man skinnin' a rabbit, there a woman with her petticoat up, a puttin' of a patch in it. Here two boys a fishin', and there a little gall a playin' with a dog, that's a racin' and a yelpin', and a barkin' like mad.'

"'Well, when he's done,' sais you, 'which pictur do you reckon is the best now, Squire Copley? speak candid, for I want to know, and I ask you now as a countryman.'

"'Well' he'll jist up and tell you, 'Mr. Poker,' sais he, 'your fashionable party is the devil, that's a fact. Man made the town, but God made the country. Your company is as formal, and as stiff, and as oninterestin' as a row of poplars; but your gipsy scene is beautiful, because it's nateral. It was me painted old Chatham's death in the House of Lords; folks praised it a good deal; but it was no great shakes, *there was no natur' in it.* The scene was rael, the likenesses was good, and there was spirit in it, but their damned uniform toggery spoiled the whole thing—it was artificial, and wanted life and natur. Now, suppose such a thing in Congress, or suppose some fellow skiver'd the speaker with a bowie knife, as happened to Arkansaw, if I was to paint it, it would be beautiful. Our free and enlightened people is so different, so characteristic and peculiar, it would give a great field to a painter. To sketch the different style of man of each state, so that any citizen would sing right out; Heavens and earth, if that don't beat all! Why, as I am a livin' sinner, that's the Hoosier of Indiana, or the Sucker of Illinois, or the Puke of Missouri, or the Bucky of Ohio, or the Red Horse of Kentucky, or the Mudhead of Tennessee, or the Wolverine of Michigan, or the Eel of New England, or the Corn Cracker of Virginia! That's the thing that gives inspiration. That's the glass of talabogus that raises your spirits. There is much of elegance, and more of comfort in England. It is a great and a good country, Mr. Poker, but there is no natur in it.'

"It is as true as gospel," said Mr. Slick, "I'm tellin' you no lie. It's a fact. If you expect to paint them English, as you have the Blue-Noses and us, you'll pull your line up without a fish, oftener than you are a-thinkin' on; that's the reason all our folks have failed. 'Rush's book is jist molasses and water, not quite so sweet as 'lasses, and not quite so good as water, but a spilin' of both. And why? His pictur was of polished life, where there is no natur. Washington Irving's book is like a Dutch paintin', it is good, because it is faithful; the mop has the right number of yarns, and each yarn has the right number of twists (altho' he mistook the mop of the grandfather for the mop of the man of the present day) and the pewter plates are on the kitchen dresser, and the other little notions are all there. He has done the most that could be done for them, but the painter dasarves more praise than the subject.

"Why is it every man's sketches of America takes? Do you suppose it is the sketches? No. Do you reckon it is the interest we create? No. Is it our grand experiment? No. They don't care a brass button for us, or our country, or experiments nother. What is it, then? It is because they are sketches of natur. Natur in every grade and every variety of form; from the silver plate, and silver fork, to the finger and huntin' knife. Our artificial Britishers laugh at; they are bad copies, that's a fact; I give them up. Let them laugh, and be darned; but I stick to my natur, and I stump them to produce the like.

"Oh, Squire, if you ever sketch me, for goodness gracious sake, don't sketch me as an Attaché to our embassy, with the Legation button on the coat, and black Jube Japan in livery. Don't do that; but paint me in my old waggon in Nover Scotier, with Old Clay before me, you by my side, a segar in my mouth, and natur all round me. And if that is too artificial; oh, paint me in the backwoods, with my huntin' coat on, my leggins, my cap, my belt, and my powder-horn. Paint me with my talkin' iron in my hand, wipin' her, chargin' her, selectin' the bullet, placin' it in the greased wad and rammin' it down. Then draw a splendid oak openin' so as to give a good view, paint a squirrel on the tip top of the highest branch of the loftiest tree, place me off at a hundred yards, drawin' a bead on him fine, then show the smoke, and young squire squirrel comin' tumblin' down head over heels lumpus', to see whether the ground was as hard as dead squirrels said it was. Paint me nateral, I beseech you; for I tell you now, as I told you before, and ever shall say, there is nothin' worth havin' or knowin', or hearin', or readin', or seein', or tastin', or smellin', or feelin', and above all and more than all, nothin' worth affectionin' but *Natur*."

PASSAGES FROM THE BIGLOW PAPERS

by James Russell Lowell

(1819–1891)

What Mr. Robinson Thinks

(A few remarks on the following verses will not be out of place. The satire in them was not meant to have any personal, but only a general, application. Of the gentleman upon whose letter they were intended as a commentary Mr. Biglow had never heard, till he saw the letter itself. The position of the satirist is often-times one which he would not have chosen, had the election been left to himself. In attacking bad principles, he is obliged to select some individual who has made himself their exponent, and in whom they are impersonate, to the end that what he says may not, through ambiguity, be dissipated *tenues in auras*. For what says Seneca? *Longum iter per præcepta, breve et efficace per exempla.* A bad principle is comparatively harmless while it continues to be an abstraction, nor can the general mind comprehend it fully till it is printed in that large type which all men can read at sight, namely, the life and character, the sayings and doings, of particular persons. It is one of the cunningest fetches of Satan, that he never exposes himself directly to our arrows, but, still dodging behind this neighbour or that acquaintance, compels us to wound him through them, if at all. He holds our affections as hostages, the while he patches up a truce with our conscience.

Meanwhile, let us not forget that the aim of the true satirist is not to be severe upon persons, but only upon falsehood, and, as Truth and Falsehood start from the same point, and sometimes even go along together for a little way, his business is to follow the path of the latter after it diverges, and to show her floundering in the bog at the end of it. Truth is quite beyond the reach of satire. There is so brave a simplicity in her, that she can no more be made ridiculous than an oak or a pine. The danger of the satirist is, that continual use may deaden his sensibility to the force of language. He becomes more and more liable to strike harder than he knows or intends. He may be careful to put on his boxing-gloves, and yet forget, that, the older they grow, the more plainly may the knuckles inside be felt. Moreover, in the heat of contest, the eye is insensibly drawn to the crown of victory, whose tawdry tinsel glitters through that dust of the ring which obscures Truth's wreath of simple leaves. I have sometimes thought that my young friend, Mr. Biglow, needed a monitory hand laid on his arm,— *aliquid sufflaminandus erat.* I have never thought it good husbandry to water the tender plants of reform with *aqua fortis*, yet, where so much is to do in the beds, he were a sorry gardener who should wage a whole day's war with an iron scuffle on those ill weeds that make the garden-walks of life unsightly, when a sprinkle of Attic salt will wither them up. *Est ars etiam maledicendi*, says Scaliger, and truly it is a hard thing to say where the graceful gentleness of the lamb merges in downright sheepishness. We may conclude with worthy and wise Dr. Fuller, that "one may be a lamb in private wrongs, but in hearing general affronts to goodness they are asses which are not lions."—H. W. [HOMER WILBUR])

> Guvener B. is a sensible man;
>   He stays to his home an' looks arter his folks;
> He draws his furrer ez straight ez he can,
>   An' into nobody's tater-patch pokes;—
>   But John P.
>   Robinson he
>   Sez he wunt vote fer Guvener B.
>
> My! aint it terrible? Wut shall we du?
>   We can't never choose him, o' course,—thet's flat;
> Guess we shall hev to come round, (don't you?)
>   An' go in fer thunder an' guns, an' all that;
>   Fer John P.
>   Robinson he
>   Sez he wunt vote fer Guvener B.
>
> Gineral C. is a dreffle smart man:
>   He's ben on all sides thet give places or pelf;
> But consistency still wuz a part of his plan,—
>   He's ben true to *one* party,—an' thet is himself;
>   So John P.
>   Robinson he
>   Sez he shall vote fer Gineral C.

Gineral C. he goes in fer the war;
  He don't vally principle more 'n an old cud;
Wut did God make us raytional creeturs fer,
    But glory an' gunpowder, plunder an' blood?
      So John P.
      Robinson he
Sez he shall vote fer Gineral C.

We were gittin' on nicely up here to our village,
  With good old idees o' wut's right an' wut aint,
We kind o' thought Christ went agin war an' pillage,
    An' thet eppyletts worn't the best mark of a saint;
      But John P.
      Robinson he
Sez this kind o' thing's an exploded idee.

The side of our country must ollers be took,
  An' Presidunt Polk, you know, *he* is our country;
An' the angel thet writes all our sins in a book
    Puts the *debit* to him, an' to us the *per contry;*
      An' John P.
      Robinson he
Sez this is his view o' the thing to a T.

Parson Wilbur he calls all these argimunts lies;
  Sez they're nothin' on airth but jest *fee, faw, fum;*
An' thet all this big talk of our destinies
    Is half on it ignorance, an' t' other half rum;
      But John P.
      Robinson he
Sez it aint no sech thing; an', of course, so must we.

Parson Wilbur sez *he* never heerd in his life
  Thet th' Apostles rigged out in their swaller-tail coats
An' marched round in front of a drum an' a fife,
    To git some on 'em office, an' some on 'em votes,
      But John P.
      Robinson he
Sez they didn't know everythin' down in Judee.

Wal, it's a marcy we've gut folks to tell us
  The rights an' the wrongs o' these matters, I vow,—
God sends country lawyers, an' other wise fellers,

> To drive the world's team wen it gits in a slough;
>   Fer John P.
>   Robinson he
> Sez the world'll go right, ef he hollers out Gee!

(The attentive reader will doubtless have perceived in the fore-going poem an allusion to that pernicious sentiment,—"Our country, right or wrong." It is an abuse of language to call a certain portion of land, much more, certain personages elevated for the time being to high station, our country. I would not sever nor loosen a single one of those ties by which we are united to the spot of our birth, nor minish by a tittle the respect due to the Magistrate. I love our own Bay State too well to do the one, and as for the other, I have myself for nigh forty years exercised, however unworthily, the function of Justice of the Peace, having been called thereto by the unsolicited kindness of that most excellent man and upright patriot, Caleb Strong. *Patriæ fumus igne alieno luculentior* is best qualified with this,—*Ubi libertas, ibi patria.* We are inhabitants of two worlds, and owe a double, but not a divided, allegiance. In virtue of our clay, this little ball of earth exacts a certain loyalty of us, while, in our capacity as spirits, we are admitted citizens of an invisible and holier fatherland. There is a patriotism of the soul whose claim absolves us from our other and terrene fealty. Our true country is that ideal realm which we represent to ourselves under the names of religion, duty, and the like. Our terrestrial organizations are but far-off approaches to so fair a model, and all they are verily traitors who resist not any attempt to divert them from this their original intendment. When, therefore, one would have us to fling up our caps and shout with the multitude,—"*Our country, however bounded!*" he demands of us that we sacrifice the larger to the less, the higher to the lower, and that we yield to the imaginary claims of a few acres of soil our duty and privilege as liegemen of Truth. Our true country is bounded on the north and the south, on the east and the west, by Justice, and when she oversteps that invisible boundary-line by so much as a hair's-breadth, she ceases to be our mother, and chooses rather to be looked upon *quasi noverca.* That is a hard choice, when our earthly love of country calls upon us to tread one path and our duty points us to another. We must make as noble and becoming an election as did Penelope between Icarius and Ulysses. Veiling our faces, we must take silently the hand of Duty to follow her.

Shortly after the publication of the foregoing poem, there appeared some comments upon it in one of the public prints which seemed to call for some animadversion. I accordingly addressed to Mr. Buckingham, of the Boston Courier, the following letter:—

JAALAM, November 4, 1847.

"To the Editor of the Courier:

"RESPECTED SIR,—Calling at the post-office this morning, our worthy and efficient postmaster offered for my perusal a paragraph in the Boston Morning Post of the 3d instant, wherein certain effusions of the pastoral muse are attributed to the pen of Mr. James Russell Lowell. For aught I know or can affirm to the contrary, this Mr. Lowell may be a very deserving person and a youth of parts (though I have seen verses of his which I could never rightly understand); and if he be such, he, I am certain, as well as I, would be free from any proclivity to appropriate to himself whatever of credit (or discredit) may honestly belong to another. I am confident, that, in penning these few lines, I am only forestalling a disclaimer from that young gentleman, whose silence hitherto, when rumor pointed to himward, has excited in my bosom mingled emotions of sorrow and surprise. Well may my young parishioner, Mr. Biglow, exclaim with the poet,—

'Sic vos non vobis' etc.;

though, in saying this, I would not convey the impression that he is a proficient in the Latin tongue,—the tongue, I might add, of a Horace and a Tully.

"Mr. B. does not employ his pen, I can safely say, for any lucre of worldly gain, or to be exalted by the carnal plaudits of men, *digito monstrari*, etc. He does not wait upon Providence for mercies, and in his heart mean *merces*. But I should esteem myself as verily deficient in my duty (who am his friend and in some unworthy sort his spiritual *fidus Achates*, etc.), if I did not step forward to claim for him whatever measure of applause might be assigned to him by the judicious.

"If this were a fitting occasion, I might venture here a brief dissertation touching the manner and kind of my young friend's poetry. But I dubitate whether this abstruser sort of speculation (though enlivened by some apposite instances from Aristophanes) would sufficiently interest your oppidan readers. As regards their satirical tone, and their plainness of speech, I will only say, that, in my pastoral experience, I have found that the Arch-Enemy loves nothing better than to be treated as a religious, moral, and intellectual being, and that there is no *apage Sathanas!* so potent as ridicule. But it is a kind of weapon that must have a button of good-nature on the point of it.

"The productions of Mr. B. have been stigmatized in some quarters as unpatriotic; but I can vouch that he loves his native soil with that hearty, though discriminating, attachment which springs from an intimate social intercourse of many years' standing. In the ploughing season, no one has a deeper share in the well-being of the country than he. If Dean Swift were right in saying that he who makes two blades of grass grow where one grew before confers a greater benefit on the state than he who taketh a city, Mr. B. might exhibit a fairer claim to the Presidency that General Scott himself. I think that some of those disinterested lovers of the hard-handed democracy, whose fingers have never touched anything rougher than the dollars of our common country, would hesitate to compare palms with him. It would do your heart good, respected Sir, to see that young man mow. He cuts a cleaner and wider swarth than any in this town.

"But it is time for me to be at my Post. It is very clear that my young friend's shot has struck the lintel, for the Post is shaken (Amos ix. 1). The editor of that paper is a strenuous advocate of the Mexican war, and a colonel, as I am given to understand. I presume that, being necessarily absent in Mexico, he has left his journal in some less judicious hands. At any rate, the Post has been too swift on this occasion. It could hardly have cited a more incontrovertible line from any poem than that which it has selected for animadversion, namely,—

'We kind o' thought Christ went agin war an' pillage.'

"If the Post maintains the converse of this proposition, it can hardly be considered as a safe guide-post for the moral and religious portions of its party, however many other excellent qualities of a post it may be blessed with. There is a sign in London on which is painted—'The Green Man.' It would do very well as a portrait of any individual who would support so unscriptural a thesis. As regards the language of the line in question, I am bold to say that He who readeth the hearts of men will not account any dialect unseemly which conveys a sound and pious sentiment. I could wish that such sentiments were more common, however uncouthly expressed. Saint Ambrose affirms, that *veritas a quocunque* (why not, then, *quomodocunque?*) *dicatur, a spiritu sancto est.* Digest also this of Baxter:—'The plainest words are the most profitable oratory in the weightiest matters.'

"When the paragraph in question was shown to Mr. Biglow, the only part of it which seemed to give him any dissatisfaction was that which classed him with the Whig party. He says, that, if resolutions are a nourishing kind of diet, that party must be in a very hearty and flourishing condition; for that they have quietly eaten more good ones of their own baking than he could have conceived to be possible without repletion. He has been for some years past (I regret to say) an ardent opponent of those sound doctrines of protective policy which form so prominent a portion of the creed of that party. I confess, that, in some discussions which I have had with him on this point in my study, he has displayed a vein of obstinacy which I had not hitherto detected in his composition. He is also (*horresco referens*) infected in no small measure with the peculiar notions of a print called the Liberator, whose heresies I take every proper opportunity of combating, and of which, I thank God, I have never read a single line.

"I did not see Mr. B.'s verses until they appeared in print, and there *is* certainly one thing in them which I consider highly improper. I allude to the personal references to myself by name. To confer notoriety on an humble individual who is laboring quietly in his vocation, and who keeps his cloth as free as he can from the dust of the political arena (though *væ mihi si non evangelizavero*), is no doubt an indecorum. The sentiments which he attributes to me I will not deny to be mine. They were embodied, though in a different form, in a discourse preached upon the last day of public fasting, and were acceptable to my entire people (of whatever political views), except the postmaster, who dissented *ex officio*. I observe that you sometimes devote a portion of your paper to a religious summary. I should be well pleased to furnish a copy of my discourse for insertion in this department of your instructive journal. By omitting the advertisements, it might easily be got within the limits of a single number, and I venture to insure you the sale of some scores of copies in this town. I will cheerfully render myself responsible for ten. It might possibly be advantageous to issue it as an *extra*. But perhaps you will not esteem it an object, and I will not press it. My offer does not spring from any weak desire of seeing my name in print; for I can enjoy this satisfaction at any time by turning to the Triennial Catalogue of the University, where it also possesses that added emphasis of Italics with which those of my calling are distinguished.

"I would simply add, that I continue to fit ingenuous youth for college, and that I have two spacious and airy sleeping apartments at this moment unoccupied. *Ingenuas didicisse*, etc. Terms, which vary according to the circumstances of the parents, may be known on application to me by letter, post paid. In all cases the lad will be expected to fetch his own towels. This rule, Mrs. W. desires me to add, has no exceptions.

"Respectfully, your obedient servant,
"HOMER WILBUR, A.M.

"P.S. Perhaps the last paragraph may look like an attempt to obtain the insertion of my circular gratuitously. If it should appear to you in that light, I desire that you would erase it, or charge for it at the usual rates, and deduct the amount from the proceeds in your hands from the sale of my discourse, when it shall be printed. My circular is much longer and more explicit, and will be forwarded without charge to any who may desire it. It has been very neatly executed on a letter sheet, by a very deserving printer, who attends upon my ministry, and is a creditable specimen of the typographic art. I have one hung over my mantelpiece in a neat frame, where it makes a beautiful and appropriate ornament, and balances the profile of Mrs. W., cut with her toes by the young lady born without arms. H.W."

I have in the foregoing letter mentioned General Scott in connection with the Presidency, because I have been given to understand that he has blown to pieces and otherwise caused to be destroyed more Mexicans than any other commander. His claim would therefore be deservedly considered the strongest. Until accurate returns of the Mexican killed, wounded, and maimed be obtained, it will be difficult to settle these nice points of precedence. Should it prove that any other officer has been more meritorious and destructive than General S., and has thereby rendered himself more worthy of the confidence and support of the conservative portion of our community, I shall cheerfully insert his name, instead of that of General S., in a future edition. It may be thought, likewise, that General S. has invalidated his claims by too much attention to the decencies of apparel, and the

habits belonging to a gentleman. These abstruser points of states-
manship are beyond my scope. I wonder not that successful
military achievement should attract the admiration of the multitude. Rather do I rejoice with wonder to behold how rapidly this
sentiment is losing its hold upon the popular mind. It is related of
Thomas Warton, the second of that honored name who held the
office of Poetry Professor at Oxford, that, when one wished to
find him, being absconded, as was his wont, in some obscure ale-
house, he was counselled to traverse the city with a drum and fife,
the sound of which inspiring music would be sure to draw the
Doctor from his retirement into the street. We are all more or less
bitten with this martial insanity. *Nescio quâ dulcedine . . . cunctos
ducit.* I confess to some infection of that itch myself. When I see a
Brigadier-General maintaining his insecure elevation in the saddle
under the severe fire of the training-field, and when I remember
that some military enthusiasts, through haste, inexperience, or an
over-desire to lend reality to those fictitious combats, will sometimes discharge their ramrods, I cannot but admire, while I
deplore, the mistaken devotion of those heroic officers. *Semel in-
sanivimus omnes.* I was myself, during the late war with Great
Britain, chaplain of a regiment, which was fortunately never called
to active military duty. I mention this circumstance with regret
rather than pride. Had I been summoned to actual warfare, I
trust that I might have been strengthened to bear myself after
the manner of that reverend father in our New England Israel,
Dr. Benjamin Colman, who, as we are told in Turell's life of him,
when the vessel in which he had taken passage for England was
attacked by a French privateer, "fought like a philosopher and a
Christian, . . . and prayed all the while he charged and fired." As
this note is already long, I shall not here enter upon a discussion
of the question, whether Christians may lawfully be soldiers. I
think it sufficiently evident, that, during the first two centuries of
the Christian era, at least, the two professions were esteemed incompatible. Consult Jortin on this head.—   H.W.)

The Debate in the Sennit, Sot to a Nusry Rhyme

to mr. Buckenam.

mr. editor, As i wuz kinder prunin round, in a little nussry sot
out a year or 2 a go, the Dbait in the sennit cum inter my mine.
An so i took & Sot it to wut I call a nussry rime. I hev made sum

onnable Gentlemun speak that dident speak in a Kind uv Poetikul
lie sense the seeson is dreffle backerd up This way

ewers as ushul

HOSEA BIGLOW

"Here we stan' on the Constitution, by thunder!
    It's a fact o' wich ther's bushils o' proofs;
Fer how could we trample on 't so, I wonder,
    Ef't worn't thet it's ollers under our hoofs?"
        Sez John C. Calhoun, sez he;—
            "Human rights haint no more
            Right to come on this floor,
        No more'n the man in the moon," sez he.

"The North haint no kind o' bisness with nothin',
    An' you've no idee how much bother it saves;
We aint none riled by their frettin' an frothin',
    We're *used* to layin' the string on our slaves,"
        Sez John C. Calhoun, sez he;—
            Sez Mister Foote,
            "I should like to shoot
        The holl gang, by the gret horn spoon!" sez he.

"Freedom's Keystone is Slavery, thet ther's no doubt on,
    It's sutthin' thet's—wha'd'ye call it?—divine,—
An' the slaves that we ollers *make* the most out on
    Air them north o' Mason an' Dixon's line,"
        Sez John C. Calhoun, sez he;—
            "Fer all thet," sez Mangum,
            "'Twould be better to hang 'em,
        An' so git red on 'em soon," sez he.

"The mass ough' to labour an' we lay on soffies,
    Thet's the reason I want to spread Freedom's aree;
It puts all the cunninest on us in office,
    An' reelises our Maker's orig'nal idee,"
        Sez John C. Calhoun, sez he;—
            "Thet's ez plain," sez Cass,
            "Ez thet some one's an ass,
        It's ez clear ez the sun is at noon," sez he.

"Now don't go to say I'm the friend of oppression,
  But keep all your spare breath fer coolin' your broth,
Fer I ollers hev strove (at least thet's my impression)
  To make cussed free with the rights o' the North,"
    Sez John C. Calhoun, sez he;—
      "Yes," sez Davis o' Miss.,
      "The perfection o' bliss
    Is in skinnin' thet same old coon," sez he.

"Slavery's a thing thet depends on complexion,
  It's God's law thet fetters on black skins don't chafe;
Ef brains wuz to settle it (horrid reflection!)
  Wich of our onnable body 'd be safe?"
    Sez John C. Calhoun, sez he;—
      Sez Mister Hannegan,
      Afore he began agin,
    "Thet exception is quite oppertoon," sez he.

"Gen'nle Cass, Sir, you needn't be twitchin' your collar,
  Your merit's quite clear by the dut on your knees,
At the North we don't make no distinctions o' color;
  You can all take a lick at our shoes wen you please,"
    Sez John C. Calhoun, sez he;—
      Sez Mister Jarnagin,
      "They wunt hev to larn agin,
    They all on 'em know the old toon," sez he.

"The slavery question aint no ways bewilderin'.
  North an' South hev one int'rest, it's plain to a glance;
No'thern men, like us patriarchs, don't sell their childrin,
  But they *du* sell themselves, ef they git a good chance,"
    Sez John C. Calhoun, sez he;-
      Sez Atherton here,
      "This is gittin' severe,
    I wish I could dive like a loon," sez he.

"It'll break up the Union, this talk about freedom,
  An' your fact'ry gals (soon ez we split) 'll make head,
An' gittin' some Miss chief or other to lead 'em,
  'll go to work raisin' promiscoous Ned,"
    Sez John C. Calhoun, sez he;—

"Yes, the North," sez Colquitt,
"Ef we Southerners all quit,
Would go down like a busted balloon," sez he.

"Jest look wut is doin', what annyky's brewin'
  In the beautiful clime o' the olive an' vine,
All the wise aristoxy is tumblin' to ruin,
  An' the sankylots drorin' an' drinkin' their wine,"
    Sez John C. Calhoun, sez he;—
      "Yes," sez Johnson, "in France
      They're beginnin' to dance
    Beelzebub's own rigadoon," sez he.

"The South's safe enough, it don't feel a mite skeery,
  Our slaves in their darkness an' dut air tu blest
Not to welcome with proud hallylugers the ery
  Wen our eagle kicks yourn from the naytional nest,"
    Sez John C. Calhoun, sez he;—
      "O," sez Westcott o' Florida,
      "Wut treason is horrider
    Then our priv'leges tryin' to proon?" sez he.

"It's 'coz they're so happy, thet, wen crazy sarpints
  Stick their nose in our bizness, we git so darned riled,
We think it's our dooty to give pooty sharp hints,
  That the last crumb of Edin on airth shan't be spiled,"
    Sez John C. Calhoun, sez he;—
      "Ah," sez Dixon H. Lewis,
      "It perfectly true is
    Thet slavery's airth's grettest boon," sez he.

A Second Letter from B. Sawin, Esq.

(Letter VIII, First Series)

I spose you wonder ware I be; I can't tell, fer the soul o' me,
Exacly ware I be myself,—meanin' by thet the holl o' me.
Wen I left hum, I hed two legs, an' they worn't bad ones neither,
(The scaliest trick they ever played wuz bringin' on me hither,)
Now one on 'em 's I dunno ware;—they thought I wuz adyin',
An' sawed it off because they said 'twuz kin' o' mortifyin';
I 'm willin' to believe it wuz, an' yit I don't see, nuther,

Wy one should take to feelin' cheap a minnit sooner 'n t' other,
Sence both wuz equilly to blame; but things is ez they be;
It took on so they took it off, an' thet's enough fer me:
There 's one good thing, though, to be said about my wooden new
    one,—
The liquor can't git into it ez 't used to in the true one;
So it saves drink; an' then, besides, a feller could n't beg
A gretter blessin' then to hev one ollers sober peg;
It 's true a chap 's in want o' two fer follerin' a drum,
But all the march I 'm up to now is jest to Kingdom Come.

I 've lost one eye, but thet 's a loss it 's easy to supply
Out o' the glory thet I 've gut, fer thet is all my eye;
An' one is big enough, I guess, by diligently usin' it,
To see all I shall ever git by way o' pay fer losin' it;
Off'cers, I notice, who git paid fer all our thumps an' kickins,
Du wal by keepin' single eyes arter the fattest pickins;
So, ez the eye 's put fairly out, I 'll larn to go without it,
An' not allow *myself* to be no gret put out about it.
Now, le' me see, thet is n't all; I used, 'fore leavin' Jaalam,
To count things on my finger-eends, but sutthin' seems to ail 'em:
Ware 's my left hand? O, darn it, yes, I recollect wut 's come on 't;
I haint no left arm but my right, an' thet 's gut jest a thumb on 't;
It aint so hendy ez it wuz to cal'late a sum on 't.
I 've hed some ribs broke,—six (I b'lieve),—I haint kep' no ac-
    count on 'em;
Wen pensions git to be the talk, I 'll settle the amount on 'em.
An' now I 'm speakin' about ribs, it kin' o' brings to mind
One thet I could n't never break,—the one I lef' behind;
Ef you should see her, jest clear out the spout o' your invention
An' pour the longest sweetnin' in about an annooal pension,
An' kin' o' hint (in case, you know, the critter should refuse to be
Consoled) I aint so 'xpensive now to keep ez wut I used to be;
There 's one arm less, ditto one eye, an' then the leg thet's wooden
Can be took off an' sot away wenever ther' s a puddin'.

I spose you think I 'm comin' back ez opperlunt ez thunder,
With shiploads o' gold images an' varus sorts o' plunder;
Wal, 'fore I vullinteered, I thought this country wuz a sort o'
Canaan, a reg'lar Promised Land flowin' with rum an' water,
Ware propaty growed up like time, without no cultivation,

An' gold wuz dug ez taters be among our Yankee nation,
Ware nateral advantages were pufficly amazin',
Ware every rock there wuz about with precious stuns wuz blazin',
Ware mill-sites filled the country up ez thick ez you could cram 'em,
An' desput rivers run about a beggin' folks to dam 'em;
Then there were meetin'houses, tu, chockful o' gold an' silver
Thet you could take, an' no one could n't hand ye in no bill fer;—
Thet 's wut I thought afore I went, thet 's wut them fellers told us
Thet stayed to hum an' speechified an' to the buzzards sold us;
I thought thet gold-mines could be gut cheaper than china asters,
An' see myself acomin' back like sixty Jacob Astors;
But sech idees soon melted down an' did n't leave a grease-spot;
I vow my holl sheer o' the spiles would n't come nigh a V spot;
Although, most anywares we 've ben, you need n't break no locks,
Nor run no kin' o' risks, to fill your pocket full o' rocks.
I guess I mentioned in my last some o' the nateral feeturs
O' this all-fiered buggy hole in th' way o' awfle creeturs,
But I fergut to name (new things to speak on so abounded)
How one day you 'll most die o' thust, an' 'fore the next git
    drownded.
The clymit seems to me jest like a teapot made o' pewter
Our Prudence hed, thet would n't pour (all she could du) to suit
    her;
Fust place the leaves 'ould choke the spout, so 's not a drop 'ould
    dreen out,
Then Prude 'ould tip an' tip an' tip, till the holl kit bust clean out,
The kiver-hinge-pin bein' lost, tea-leaves an' tea an' kiver
'ould all come down *kerswosh!* ez though the dam broke in a river.
Jest so 't is here; holl months there aint a day o' rainy weather,
An' jest ez th' officers 'ould be a layin' heads together
Ez t' how they 'd mix their drink at sech a milingtary deepot,—
'T would pour ez though the lid wuz off the everlastin' teapot.
The cons'quence is, thet I shall take, wen I 'm allowed to leave
    here,
One piece o' propaty along, an' thet 's the shakin' fever;
It 's reggilar employment, though, an' thet aint thought to harm
    one,
Nor 't aint so tiresome ez it wuz with t' other leg an' arm on;
An' it 's a consolation, tu, although it doos n't pay,
To hev it said you 're some gret shakes in any kin' o' way.
'T worn't very long, I tell ye wut, I thought o' fortin-makin',—

One day a reg'lar shiver-de-freeze, an' next ez good ez bakin',—
One day abrilin' in the sand, then smoth'rin' in the mashes,—
Git up all sound, be put to bed a mess o' hacks an' smashes.
But then, thinks I, at any rate there 's glory to be hed,—
Thet 's an investment, arter all, thet may n't turn out so bad;
But somehow, wen we 'd fit an' licked, I ollers found the thanks
Gut kin' o' lodged afore they come ez low down ez the ranks;
The Gin'rals gut the biggest sheer, the Cunnles next, an' so on,—
We never gut a blasted mite o' glory ez I know on;
An' spose we hed, I wonder how you 're goin' to contrive its
Division so 's to give a piece to twenty thousand privits;
Ef you should multiply by ten the portion o' the brav'st one,
You would n't git more 'n half enough to speak of on a grave-stun;
We git the licks,—we 're jest the grist thet 's put into War's
    hoppers;
Leftenants is the lowest grade thet helps pick up the coppers.
It may suit folks thet go agin a body with a soul in 't,
An' aint contented with a hide without a bagnet hole in 't;
But glory is a kin' o' thing *I* shan't pursue no furder,
Coz thet 's the off'cers parquisite,—yourn's on'y jest the murder.

Wal, arter I gin glory up, thinks I at least there 's one
Thing in the bills we aint hed yit, an' thet 's the GLORIOUS FUN;
Ef once we git to Mexico, we fairly may persume we
All day an' night shall revel in the halls o' Montezumy.
I 'll tell ye wut *my* revels wuz, an' see how you would like 'em;
We never gut inside the hall: the nighest ever *I* come
Wuz stan'in' sentry in the sun (an', fact, it *seemed* a cent'ry)
A ketchin' smells o' biled an' roast thet come out thru the entry,
An' hearin', ez I sweltered thru my passes an' repasses,
A rat-tat-too o' knives an' forks, a clinkty-clink o' glasses:
I can't tell off the bill o' fare the Gin'rals hed inside;
All I know is, thet out o' doors a pair o' soles wuz fried,
An' not a hunderd miles away frum ware this child wuz posted,
A Massachusetts citizen wuz baked an' biled an' roasted;
The on'y thing like revellin' thet ever come to me
Wuz bein' routed out o' sleep by thet darned revelee.

They say the quarrel 's settled now; fer my part I 've some
    doubt on 't,
'T 'll take more fish-skin than folks think to take the rile clean out
    on 't;

At any rate, I 'm so used up I can't do no more fightin',
The on'y chance thet 's left to me is politics or writin';
Now, ez the people 's gut to hev a milingtary man,
An' I aint nothin' else jest now, I 've hit upon a plan;
The can'idatin' line, you know, 'ould suit me to a T,
An' ef I lose, 't wunt hurt my ears to lodge another flea;
So I 'll set up ez can'idate fer any kin' o' office,
(I mean fer any thet includes good easy-cheers an' soffies;
Fer ez to runnin' fer a place ware work 's the time o' day,
You know thet 's wut I never did,—except the other way;)
Ef it 's the Presidential cheer fer wich I 'd better run,
Wut two legs anywares about could keep up with my one?
There aint no kin' o' quality in can'idates, it 's said,
So useful ez a wooden leg,—except a wooden head;
There 's nothin' aint so poppylar—(wy, it 's a parfect sin
To think wut Mexico hez paid fer Santy Anny's pin;)—
Then I haint gut no principles, an', sence I wuz knee-high,
I never *did* hev any gret, ez you can testify;
I 'm a decided peace-man, tu, an' go agin the war,—
Fer now the holl on 't 's gone an' past, wut is there to go *for?*
Ef, wile you 're 'lectioneerin' round, some curus chaps should beg
To know my views o' state affairs, jest answer WOODEN LEG!
Ef they aint settisfied with thet, an' kin' o' pry an' doubt
An' ax fer sutthin' deffynit, jest say ONE EYE PUT OUT!
Thet kin' o' talk I guess you 'll find 'll answer to a charm,
An' wen you 're druv tu nigh the wall, hol' up my missin' arm;
Ef they should nose round fer a pledge, put on a vartoous look
An' tell 'em thet 's percisely wut I never gin nor—took!

Then you can call me "Timbertoes,"—thet 's wut the people likes;
Sutthin' combinin' morril truth with phrases sech ez strikes;
Some say the people 's fond o' this, or thet, or wut you please,—
I tell ye wut the people want is jest correct idees;
"Old Timbertoes," you see, 's a creed it 's safe to be quite bold on,
There 's nothin' in 't the other side can any ways git hold on;
It 's a good tangible idee, a sutthin' to embody
Thet valooable class o' men who look thru brandy-toddy;
It gives a Party Platform, tu, jest level with the mind
Of all right-thinkin', honest folks thet mean to go it blind;
Then there air other good hooraws to dror on ez you need 'em,
Sech ez the ONE-EYED SLARTERER, the BLOODY BIRDOFREDUM:

Them 's wut takes hold o' folks thet think, ez well ez o' the masses,
An' makes you sartin o' the aid o' good men of all classes.

There 's one thing I 'm in doubt about; in order to be Presidunt,
It 's absolutely ne'ssary to be a Southern residunt;
The Constitution settles thet, an' also thet a feller
Must own a nigger o' some sort, jet black, or brown, or yeller.
Now I haint no objections agin particklar climes,
Nor agin ownin' anythin' (except the truth sometimes),
But, ez I haint no capital, up there among ye, may be,
You might raise funds enough fer me to buy a low-priced baby,
An' then, to suit the No'thern folks, who feel obleeged to say
They hate an' cuss the very thing they vote fer every day,
Say you 're assured I go full butt fer Libbaty's diffusion
An' made the purchis on'y jest to spite the Institootion;—
But, golly! there 's the currier's hoss upon the pavement pawin'!
I 'll be more 'xplicit in my next.

Yourn,

BIRDOFREDUM SAWIN.

THE COURTIN'

God makes sech nights, all white an' still
    Fur 'z you can look or listen,
Moonshine an' snow on field an' hill,
    All silence an' all glisten.

Zekle crep' up quite unbeknown
    An' peeked in thru' the winder,
An' there sot Huldy all alone,
    'Ith no one nigh to hender.

A fireplace filled the room's one side
    With half a cord o' wood in—
There warn't no stoves (tell comfort died)
    To bake ye to a puddin'.

The wa'nut logs shot sparkles out
    Towards the pootiest, bless her,
An' leetle flames danced all about
    The chiny on the dresser.

"AN' ALL I KNOW IS, THEY WUZ CRIED IN MEETIN' COME NEX' SUNDAY"

One of two full pages of illustrations of "The Courtin'," published, with the poem, in *Harper's Weekly*, II, 681 (October 23, 1858). The artist was A. Hoppin.

Agin the chimbley crook-necks hung,
   An' in amongst 'em rusted
The ole queen's-arm thet gran'ther Young
   Fetched back from Concord busted.

The very room, coz she was in,
   Seemed warm from floor to ceilin',
An' she looked full ez rosy agin
   Ez the apples she was peelin'.

'T was kin' o' kingdom-come to look
   On sech a blessed cretur,
A dogrose blushin' to a brook
   Ain't modester nor sweeter.

He was six foot o' man, A 1,
   Clean grit an' human natur';
None could n't quicker pitch a ton
   Nor dror a furrer straighter.

He 'd sparked it with full twenty gals,
   Hed squired 'em, danced 'em, druv 'em,
Fust this one, an' then thet, by spells—
   All is, he could n't love 'em.

But long o' her his veins 'ould run
   All crinkly like curled maple,
The side she breshed felt full o' sun
   Ez a south slope in Ap'il.

She thought no v'ice hed sech a swing
   Ez hisn in the choir;
My! when he made Ole Hunderd ring,
   She *knowed* the Lord was nigher.

An' she 'd blush scarlit, right in prayer,
   When her new meetin'-bunnet
Felt somehow thru' its crown a pair
   O' blue eyes sot upun it.

Thet night, I tell ye, she looked *some!*
   She seemed to 've gut a new soul,
For she felt sartin-sure he 'd come,
   Down to her very shoe-sole.

She heered a foot, an' knowed it tu,
  A-raspin' on the scraper,—
All ways to once her feelins flew
  Like sparks in burnt-up paper.

He kin' o' l'itered on the mat,
  Some doubtfle o' the sekle,
His heart kep' goin' pity-pat,
  But hern went pity Zekle.

An' yit she gin her cheer a jerk
  Ez though she wished him furder,
An' on her apples kep' to work,
  Parin' away like murder.

"You want to see my Pa, I s'pose?"
  "Wal . . . no . . . I come dasignin'"—
"To see my Ma? She's sprinklin' clo'es
  Agin to-morrer's i'nin'."

To say why gals acts so or so,
  Or don't, 'ould be presumin';
Mebby to mean *yes* an' say *no*
  Comes nateral to women.

He stood a spell on one foot fust,
  Then stood a spell on t' other,
An' on which one he felt the wust
  He could n't ha' told ye nuther.

Says he, "I'd better call agin";
  Says she, "Think likely, Mister";
Thet last word pricked him like a pin,
  An' . . . Wal, he up an' kist her.

When Ma bimeby upon 'em slips,
  Huldy sot pale ez ashes,
All kin' o' smily roun' the lips
  An' teary roun' the lashes.

For she was jes' the quiet kind
  Whose naturs never vary,
Like streams that keep a summer mind
  Snowhid in Jenooary.

The blood clost roun' her heart felt glued
  Too tight for all expressin',
Tell mother see how metters stood,
  An gin 'em both her blessin'.

Then her red come back like the tide
  Down to the Bay o' Fundy,
An' all I know is they was cried
  In meetin' come nex' Sunday.

MRS. PARTINGTON

by B. P. Shillaber

(1814–1890)

BIOGRAPHY OF MRS. PARTINGTON, RELICT OF P.P., CORPORAL

Paul Partington, whose name is immortalized by its associa-tion with that of the universal Mrs. Partington, a portion of whose oracular sayings our book comprises, was a lineal descendant of Seek-the-Kingdom-continually Partyngetonne, who came from the old country, by water probably, somewhere in the early days of our then not very extensive civilization. At that time, people were not in the habit of putting everything into the papers, as they do now, when the painting of a front door, or the setting of a pane of glass, or the laying of an egg, is deemed of sufficient con-sequence for a paragraph; much, therefore, of interest concerning the early history of his family is merely known by the faint light which tradition has thrown upon it.

A story has come down to us from remote time, through the oracular lips of the oldest inhabitants, that "Seek-the-Kingdom-continually Partyngetonne"—abbreviated to Seek—was troubled in the old country by certain unpleasant and often-occurring re-minders of indebtedness, yclept "bills," which were always, like a summer night, falling due, and certain urgently-pressing impor-tunities, the which, added to a faith that was not too popular, by any means, at last induced him to warily scrape together such small means as he could, and incontinently retire from metro-politan embarrassment to the comparative quiet of an emigrant's life, where he might encounter nothing more annoying than the howling of wolves, or the yelling of savages,—sweet music both when contrasted with the horror comprised in the words "PAY THAT BILL!" which had long distressed him. Here the voice of the dunner was done, and Seek, under his own vine and pine-tree, worshipped God and cheated the Indians according to the dictates of his own conscience and the custom of the times.

But little, however, can be gleaned of the early supporters of the family name, save what we procure from the ancient family record, a Dudley Leavitt's Almanac, on which agricultural memo-randa had been kept, and from the memory of such members of a foregone generation as remembered the Partington mansion in Beanville,—of course before it was torn down to make way for the new Branch Railroad.

The "*new house*," as the mansion has been called for a century— (see the accompanying sketch, drawn on a piece of birch bark by a native artist)—to distinguish it from some *old* house that had at some previous time existed somewhere, was erected about the year ——, as is supposed, from the discovery of a receipted bill from Godffrey Pratt, for "Ayde in Rayse'g ye Nue Eddiffyce," which bears date as above, and likewise from the fact that a child was born to the erector of the new house the same year, which was duly chronicled in the ancient Bible, with other blessings, and the word "Howse" is distinctly to be traced among them.

It is supposed by some that the old house was upon a slight hill opposite the gentle acclivity upon which the new house stood, and fancied outlines of an ancient cellar are there discernible by those whose faith is large enough. But a younger class have set up another hypothesis: that what they suppose must have been a cellar, was in reality an apple-bin; and there is no knowing when or how the point will be determined.

The new house was a stanch piece of work, erected at a time when men were honest, and infused much of their own character into the work they put together; the beams of oak so sturdy, that Time, failing to make an impression upon them, gives up at last in despair. The interior of the mansion, in the latter day of its existence, contrasted gloomily with the modern houses, that sprang like mushrooms around it; its oak panelling and thick doors imparted an idea of strength, and the huge beam overhead, beneath which a tall man could not stand erect in the low-studded room, showed no more signs of decay than if placed there a hundred years later. It was not destitute of ornament, for around the fireplace were perpetuated, in the everlastingness of Dutch crockery, numerous scriptural scenes, more creditable to the devotional spirit that conceived, than to the art (or artlessness) that executed, them. The house was intended as a garrison, and where the clapboards had chafed off were revealed the scarfed logs, denoting where the loop-holes were, and the leaden bullets, still left there, which Paul was wont to dig out with his knife, when a boy, and make sinkers of for his fishing-lines. Many a story that venerable house could tell of ancient warfare, of the midnight attack and gallant defence; but it never told a thing.

It was in this house that Paul Partington was born and grew, amid all the luxuries that the town of Beanville afforded,—said town at that time consisting of five houses and a barn.

In this house he was married,—the most momentous act of his life, as through the hymeneal gate came upon the world the dame whose name we are delighted to honor. We find upon the fly-leaf of a treatise on calcareous manures, yet sacredly treasured, the following memorandum, in the corporal's own writing, significant of the methodical habits of the man who shed, in after life, as far as a corporal's warrant could do it, undying glory upon his country:—"Married this day, January the 3, 1808, to Ruth Trotter, by Rev. Mr. Job Snarl. Forty bushels of potatoes to Widow Green."

There is a blending of bliss and business in this entry that strikes one at the first glance. The record of the sale of the potatoes in the same paragraph announcing his marriage to Ruth might signify to some that they were held in equal regard. But we see the matter differently. The purchase of Ruth and the sale of the potatoes were the two great events of that important 3d of January, and they naturally associated themselves. So you, madam, might associate the birth of your first-born—the most blissful moment of your life—with the miserable matter of the death of a lame duck, or the blowing down of a pig-sty.

Of the courtship that preceded that marriage we can say nothing, except what we have gleaned by accident from the old lady herself. In rebuking the want of sincerity of devotion now-a-days, on the part of lovers, she once spoke of a time when *some one* would ride a hard-trotting horse ten miles every night, and back, for the sake of sitting up with her. But no name was mentioned. When it is remembered that the ancient borough of Dog's Bondage was just ten miles from Beanville, it is easy enough to guess who the individual was.

Ruth Partington—born Trotter—came amid sublunar scenes several years before the nineteenth century commenced; consequently, she is older than 1800. She was a child, by law, for eighteen years before she became a woman, and performed the duties "incumbered" upon her, as we have been informed by her, with great fidelity. We have often endeavored, in fancy, to picture the Ruth of Dog's Bondage, in the check apron and homespun gown, by the brook engaged in washing; or, basket in hand, feeding the yellow corn to hungry ducks, emblematic of that throwing forth of gems that have since been scrambled for by admiring crowds; or seeking berries in the woods, crowned with winter-green, as the meed of popular approbation surrounds her brow in the latter day of her existence; or engaged in incipient benevo-lences—as binding up the broken limbs of barn-yard favorites, or protecting the songsters of the marsh from predatory boyhood—fitting fore-heralds of that matured benevolence which embraces the world in its scope: here speaking the consoling word, and there dispensing comfort, mingled with catnip tea. In fancy, we say; the check apron, homespun gown and all, are but the stuff that dreams are made of.

There are vague reminiscences of things that have past which we catch occasionally, when souchong has released the memory of Mrs. Partington from the overriding care for the world's wel-fare that would fain keep it home, and we roam back through scenes of her early life that breathe of rurality like a hay-field in June, or a barn-yard in the month of March. We have tales of apple-parings, and attendant scenes and suppers; of huskings full of incident and red ears, and resonant with notes the sweet im-port of which Mrs. Partington can well tell; and jolly quiltings, great with tattle and tea, and moonlight walks home, with the laughter of mirth mingling with the song of the cricket in the hedge, or that of the monarch of the swamp singing his younglings to sleep in the distance, or the whippoorwill upon the bough; and stupendous candy pullings, with their customary consequences to broad shirt-collars and cheeks sweeter than molasses; and slides down-hill on the ox-sled runners, in winter, that the boys hauled up to the summit, disastrous at times to propriety and health, but full of a fun that looked at no result but its own enjoyment—the means a secondary consideration. And there gleams through this a ray that reveals early loves and dreams that had an existence for a time, to be swallowed up eventually in admiration for that embodiment of war and peace, Paul Partington, whose flaming eye and sword, upon an ensanguined muster-field, won a regard that only ended in Beanville, when the name of Trotter became merged in that of Partington.

Tradition—which, in this instance, may be partly right—tells of rivalry for the possession of the belle of Dog's Bondage. We can conceive of rivalry among the men, and envy among the women; of struggles on the one part to gain her favor, on the other part the struggle to lose it by provoking her hostility. Hostility? Herein

might arise a question as to whether so gentle a being ever entertained hostility to anything. We should be false to our object—
that of writing a true biography of Mrs. Partington—did we pretend that she was perfect. We would take this pen and inkstand,
as well as they have served us in our need, and throw them in the
grate, before we would make any such assertion. But we must say
that we never heard she had an enemy, and Tradition—that grim
old chap, that has so many bad things to say about people, and
so few that are good—never said a word about it. Doubtless
many a rustic heart beat warm beneath a homespun coat of
numberless years, and sighs redolent of feeling poured from beneath the rim of many an old bell-crowned hat of felt. But the
meteor came,—Paul swept the field,—the heart of Ruth surrendered with discretion,—and other people stood back.

Great was this for Dog's Bondage! The sun rose on the brightest
day of the year when it happened; the brook, that had frozen up
previously, immediately thawed out; two robins were seen looking round for places to build their nests, thinking it was spring,
so mild was it; the lilac buds almost "bursted" in their anxiety
to notice the occasion; and old farmers, as they talked to one another across dividing fences, spoke most sagaciously about the
extr'or'nary spell of weather. As old Roger, Mrs. P.'s cousin, remarked, when he heard the circumstance, it was a wether very
like a lamb. But, as we were saying,—

Schools were not so common at that time as now, and as there
was none nearer the Trotters than Huckleberry Lane, in the
Upper Parish, and as there was a quarrel between the Upper and
the Lower parishes, old Trotter, who belonged with the Lower,
felt bound to stand by that section,—though he knew nothing
about the quarrel,—and hence Ruth was kept at home to receive
by the fireside the domestic accomplishments nowhere else to be
learned, and drink in the oracular wisdom of the venerable
Trotter, as it fell from his lips through the aroma of pigtail tobacco
and hard cider.

Alas for Trotter! His day is done, his pipe is out, his cider has
gone, and even Dog's Bondage has become a name obsolete
among the places of the earth, that town rejoicing now in the
more euphonious title of Clover Hill, probably from the fact of
there not being a leaf of clover within seven miles of it.

And thou, Dame Trotter!—famous for pastry and poultry,
beneath whose ready skill Thanksgiving became a carnival of fat

things, whose memory yet lingers about the olden home, now in stranger hands, with the fragrance of innumerable virtues, like the spicy odor of many Christmas dinners,—thou, too, art gone, and Dog's Bondage may know thee no more forever! The Rev. Adoniram Smith, who preached her funeral sermon, drew largely upon the book of Proverbs for illustrations of her character, and said that better pumpkin pies, or a better exhibition of grace, he had never known any woman to make before.

A kind heart has characterized Mrs. Partington from her childhood up, displayed in many ways. Her benevolence got far in advance of her grammar in her early days, and in her sayings at times are detected certain inaccuracies that some people are inclined to laugh at; but if they will stop a little and see the yellow kernels of wisdom gleaming out through the thickly-surrounding verbiage, they will raise their hats in grateful respect for the bounty afforded.

The domestic history of Mrs. Partington requires a nice pen to portray it, so full was it of delicate beauty and delightful incident. Marriage meant something in old times. It was no holiday affair, donned like a garment, to be regarded as worthless when the fashion changed. It grew out of no sickly sentiment that had its existence in the yellow fever of a wretched romance, as unlike true life as a cabbage is to a rose; or the sere of autumn,—a more fitting simile,—to the vernal spring. It was a healthy, hearty, happy old institution in those days, was matrimony, and people jogged along together in the harness of its duties, as harmoniously as the right hand and the left, that help each other and yet don't seem to know it, so natural is the service rendered,—as if they were born to it. And as the right hand or the right eye sympathizes with the left, so did the twain thus united sympathize. Duty and affection leaned upon each other, and inseparably strove to make the home hearth cheerful. It became pleasure to carry the sweet drink to the thirsty man, in the field a-mowing; or to bear the basket of luncheon to the woods where the red-browed man was chopping wood for winter; or to patiently hold the light in the long winter evenings when the yokes were to be mended or the harness repaired. And it became pleasure when the goodman went to town to stow his pockets with something nice for the wife at home,—a new dress or a new apron,—the remembrance of whose face would come to him when away and hasten his departure back. It was that remembrance which prompted the mare into an urgent trot on the last mile home,—though *she* couldn't see the necessity for it,—and his eye looked brighter when he saw the cheerful face at the window, looking down the road, and shook his whip at it as it smiled at him, as much as to say, let me get near you, and—and what? Ask the walls, and the bureau in the corner, and the buffet where the china was, or the milk-pans upon the dresser, what.

No jars occurred in a home that owned such a pair. Can the right hand quarrel with the left? Can the left eye cast severe glances upon the right? The home where a true marriage exists is blest, and the man who finds his domesticity cast in a mould such as we have described, may be called happy in the fullest sense of the blissful word.

It would have done all of us good to peep in upon fireside scenes at the Partington mansion. The fireplace, with its wide and hospitable arms extended, looked like an incentive to population, having family capacity revealed in its huge dimensions. It was a brave idea of Seek Partyngetonne, and when he laid the corner-stone of the Beanville structure he had visions of a posterity as numerous as the leaves of the sweet-briar bush that waved by his door. Alas! how were those visions verified, as a few generations saw the line of Seek diminishing, to find its end, at last, like the snap of a whip-lash, in one little knot.

But those scenes! It was the custom of the corporal, in the long nights of winter, to seat himself in the right corner of the old fire-place, while the dame occupied the other, and read, by the light of a mutton tallow candle, such literature as the house afforded. This was comprised in the family Bible, an old and massive volume that adorned the black bureau under the glass; a copy of army tactics, presented to Paul by a revolutionary soldier; and a copy of Dudley Leavitt's Almanac. These were read, by the light of mutton fat, aloud, while Mrs. Partington pursued her knitting in the corner, nodding at times, perhaps, as the theme was dull or familiar; but the smile always rewarded Paul's effort to amuse her, as much as if he hadn't read the same things over and over a thousand times. The small, covered earthen pitcher kept time to his reading often, and sung and sputtered upon the coals between the old-fashioned dog andirons, as if a spirit were within struggling to throw off the cover that restrained it and escape. Regularly, as the hand of the old bull's-eye watch on the nail over the mantel-piece denoted the hour of nine, was the book laid by, and the mug taken from the fire and its steaming contents poured into the white earthen bowl upon the table, which sent up a vapor that rolled upon the dark walls like a fragrant cloud, and made the room redolent with the fume of the "mulled cider" that smoothed the pillow of Paul.

It was pleasant, too, to have a neighbor come in at times and spend an evening, when the big dish of apples would be brought on, and the sparkling cider, that snapped and foamed, in an ambition to be drunk, crowned the board. And then such stories as would be told of "breakings out," and "great trainings," and "immense gunnings," in which exploits were achieved that my veracious pen would hardly dare recall! And the old Indian wars would be fought again by the light of tradition and the above-named tallow candle; and the tales be retold of revolutionary valor that signalized itself in '76. Perhaps a song would be sung commemorating old times, in the quaint melody that knew no artistic skill beyond nature's teaching.

Mrs. Partington, as the presiding genius of these scenes, shed the radiance of her presence over the circle, as the sunflower claims eminence in a garden of marigolds. Her sage voice was heard in wise counsel; and in giving the news of who was sick, or dead, or about to be married, or wasn't about to be married, but ought to be, she was at home.

The time we speak of was near the close of Paul's career, before the sad military reverse took place which broke his heart. It would be impossible, in the small space allotted us, to describe all the virtues of Mrs. Partington. It were best to make an aggregate of good, and call it all hers. The herbs that adorned the garret walls in innumerable paper bags, were not gathered for herself; the balm-of-gilead buds and rum, that occupied their position in the buffet, were not prepared for her; but at the first note of distress from a neighbor her aid was ever ready. She was the first who was sent for on important occasions, when goodwives must be wakened from their beds at midnight; and to this day half the population of Beanville speak of the benevolent face that bent over them in the first moments of their struggle with existence, and gave them a better impression of life than after-experience verified; and catnip tea and saffron became palatable when commended by a spoon held by her. She knew the age of every one in the village, and, had politicians not rendered the word hackneyed, we would say she had the "antecedents" of every one at her fingers' ends. She was as good as an almanac for chronological dates; and in the matter of historical incidents Dudley Leavitt and Mrs. P. generally came out neck-and-neck.

She had a great reverence for this same almanac, and we cannot refrain from speaking of an incident in connection with it. She put implicit faith in its predictions, and the weather-table stood like a guide-board to direct her on her meteorological march through the year. One year, however, everything went wrong. Storms took place that were not mentioned, and those mentioned never occurred. The moon's phases were all out of joint, and the good dame sat up all one cold night to watch for an advertised eclipse that didn't come off. For a long time she tried to vindicate her favorite, but at last, when a "windy day" predicted proved as mild a one as ever the sun shone on, her faith wavered, to be entirely overthrown by a cold north-easterly storm that had been set down for "pleasant." A timely discovery, that Ike had put a last year's almanac instead of the true one, alone saved the credit of that mathematical standard of natural law.

Her domestic virtues were of the most exalted kind. Cleanliness was with her a habit, and every windy day was sure to see Paul's regimentals upon a clothes-line, in the yard, dancing away with a levity altogether at variance with the rules of military propriety. A spider never dared to obtrude his presence upon the homestead; a moth never corrupted the sanctuary of woollen that her care and a little camphor had touched. The white floor of the Partingtonian kitchen was as full of knots as a map of New Hampshire is of hills, from frequent scourings, and, though she never scoured through and fell into the cellar, like the Dutch damsel we read of, it did not seem at all improbable that such an event might happen.

But her benevolence was the crowning characteristic of her life, developing itself in a thousand and more ways. It sought to make every one around her happy. She commenced taking snuff with an eye solely to its social tendencies, and her box was a continual offering to friendship. When the "last war" broke out, she headed a volunteer list of patriotic women to make shirts for the soldiers, and gave them encouragement and souchong tea to work for the brave men that were exposing themselves to peril; and she scraped Paul's only linen shirt—an heir-loom, by the way, in the family—up into lint for the wounded soldiers. A fitting spouse was she for Corporal Paul. Her reputation for benevolence was spread all over the land, like butter upon a hot Johnny-cake of her own baking, and her currant-wine for the sick got a premium for three successive years in the cattle fair.

Alas that we have not room to pursue the theme further! We must take a flying leap over many incidents and hasten on.

Matter of Fact

"Shakspeare's well enough," said Mr. Slow, "but he don't come up to my idee of po'try. There is too much of your hifalutin humbug about him. What he says don't seem to 'mount to nothing. As for Falstaff, he's a miser'ble and disreputable old fellow, and Hamlick's as mad as a bed-bug. Why didn't he knock his old father-in-law over, and done with it, and not make sich a hillibolu about it? Shakspeare isn't what he is cracked up to be, and if he doesn't improve, I wouldn't give two per cent. for his chance of immortality. Who b'leves this 'ere, for instance?

> 'Orpheus' lute was strung with poets' sinews,
> Whose golden touch could soften steel and stones,
> Make tigers tame, and huge levithians
> Forsake unsounded deeps to dance on sand!'

That's all gammon. Poets' sinews, indeed! Dare say 'twasn't nothin' but catgut; and as for its softening steel and stones, and taming tigers, and making levithians dance on the sand, that 'ere's all bosh, and too ridic'lous for any man to b'leve."

Mr. Slow looked fearfully oracular as he said this, and the subject was suspended.

The Cat and Kittens

Before Ike dropped the cat, it was a matter of much annoyance to Mrs. Partington, upon coming down stairs one morning, to find a litter of kittens in her Indian work-basket, beside her black Sunday bonnet, and upon the black gloves and handkerchief, long consecrate to grief. Ike had left the basket uncovered, during a search for some thread to make a snare to catch a pigeon with. Her temper was stirred by the circumstance, as what good, tidy housekeeper's would not have been by such an occurrence?

"I'll drownd 'em," said she, "every one of 'em! O, you wicked creatur!" continued she, raising her finger, and shaking it at the cat; "O, you wicked creatur, to serve me such a trick!"

But the cat, happy in the joys of maternity, purred gladly among her offspring, and looked upon the old lady, through her half-closed eyes, as if she didn't really see any cause for such a fuss.

"Isaac," said the dame, "take the big tub, and drownd them kittens."

There was determination in her eye, and authority in her tone, and Ike clapped his hands as he hastened to obey her.

"Stop, Isaac, a minute," she cried, "and I'll take the chill off the water; it would be cruel to put 'em into it stone-cold."

She took the steaming kettle from the stove, and emptied it into the tub, and then left the rest to Ike. But she reproached herself for her inhumanity long afterwards, and could not bear to look the childless cat in the face, and many a dainty bit did that injured animal receive from her mistress. Mrs. Partington perhaps did wrong, as who hasn't at some period of life? Perfection belongeth not to man or woman, and we would throw this good pen of ours into the street, and never take another in our fingers, could we pretend that Mrs. Partington was an exception to this universal rule.

POWER OF ATTORNEY

When the widow Ames had been notified that her share of the Paul Jones prize-money would be paid her upon presenting herself at the Dummer Bank, she debated in her own mind,—though the debate never was reported,—whether she should go herself or give a power of attorney to some one else to receive the eleven dollars and sixty-two cents that was her share. In this strait she called on Mrs. Partington, who she knew had authorized a person to settle the Beanville estate for her when the Beanville Railroad had driven her from the homestead.

"Go yourself, dear," said the old lady, bringing the poker down emphatically upon the bail of the tea-kettle, as she was clearing out the ashes from the stove; "don't trust to nobody but yourself, for,"—raising the poker,—"if you give anybody power of eternity, depend upon it you won't never see the final conclusion of it."

The poker fell again upon the harmless tea-kettle, which seemed to sing out with reproach for the outrage, and Ike, who was looking slyly into the back window, wondered if Mrs. Ames wasn't sitting on a favorite piece of spruce gum of his, and whether it wouldn't stick her to the chair so that she couldn't get up. It showed that the boy had a reflective turn of mind.

The New Dress for Ladies

"A new custom for ladies!" said Mrs. Partington, when a friend spoke to her about the proposed innovation in dress. The sound of "costume" came to her ear indistinctly, and she slightly misapprehended the word. "A new custom for ladies! I should think they had better reform many of their old customs before they try to get new ones. We're none of us better than we ought to be, and"—

"Costume, ma'am, I said," cried her informant, interrupting her; "they are thinking of changing their dress."

"Well, for my part I don't see what they want to make a public thing of it for; changing the dress used to be a private matter; but folks do so alter! They are always a changing dresses now, like the caterpillar in the morning that turns into a butterfly at night, or the butterfly at night that turns to a caterpillar in the morning, I don't know which"—

"But," again interrupted her informant, "I mean they are a going to have a new dress."

"O, they are, are they?" replied the old lady; "well, I'm sure I'm glad on it, if they can afford it; but they don't always think enough of this. A good many can't afford it—they can't! But did you hear of the new apperil for wimmin that somebody is talking about?"

"Why, my dear Mrs. P.," said he, smiling, "that is just what I was trying to get your opinion about."

"Then," returned she, "why didn't you say so in the first place? Well, I don't know why a woman can't be as vertuous in a short dress as in a long one; and it will save some trouble in wet weather to people who have to lift their dresses and show their ankles. It may do for young critters, as sportive as lambs in a pasture; but only think how I should look in short coats and trousers, shouldn't I? And old Mrs. Jones, who weighs three hundred pounds, wouldn't look well in 'em neither. But I say let 'em do just what they please as long as they don't touch my dress. I like the old way best, and that's the long and the short of it."

She here cast a glance at the profile on the wall, as if for its approval of her resolution; and an idea for a moment seemed to cross her mind that he, the ancient corporal, would not know her, were he to visit sublunar scenes and find her arrayed in the new dress; and her compressed lips showed the determination of her heart to abide by the old costume, and she solemnly and slowly took an energetic pinch of snuff, as if to confirm it.

WIDOW BEDOTT'S MONOLOGUES

by Frances M. Whitcher

(1811–1852)

HEZEKIAH BEDOTT

He was a wonderful hand to moralize, husband was, 'specially after he begun to enjoy poor health. He made an observation once when he was in one of his poor turns that I never shall forget the longest day I live. He says to me one winter evenin' as we was a settin' by the fire, I was a knittin' (I was always a wonderful great knitter) and he was a smokin' (he was a master hand to smoke, though the doctor used to tell him he'd be better off to let tobacker alone; when he was well, used to take his pipe and smoke a spell after he'd got the chores done up, and when he wa'n't well, used to smoke the biggest part o' the time). Well, he took his pipe out of his mouth and turned toward me, and I knowed something was comin', for he had a pertikkeler way of lookin' round when he was gwine to say any thing oncommon. Well, he says to me, says he, "Silly," (my name was Prissilly naterally, but he ginerally called me "Silly," cause 'twas handier, you know) Well, he says to me, says he, "Silly," and he looked pretty sollem, I tell you, he had a sollem countenance naterally—and after he got to be deacon 'twas more so, but since he'd lost his health he looked sollemer than ever, and certingly you wouldent wonder at it if you knowed how much he underwent. He was troubled with a wonderful pain in his chest, and amazin' weakness in the spine of his back, besides the pleurissy in the side, and having the ager a considerable part of the time, and bein' broke of his rest o' nights 'cause he was so put to't for breath when he laid down. Why its an onaccountable fact that when that man died he hadent seen a well day in fifteen year, though when he was married and for five or six year after I shouldent desire to see a ruggeder man than what he was. But the time I'm speakin' of he'd been out o' health nigh upon ten year, and O dear sakes! how he had altered since the first time I ever see him! That was to a quiltin' to Squire Smith's a spell afore Sally was married. I'd no idee then that Sal Smith was a gwine to be married to Sam Pendergrass. She'd ben

keepin' company with Mose Hewlitt, for better'n a year, and every
body said *that* was a settled thing, and lo and behold! all of a
sudding she up and took Sam Pendergrass. Well, that was the
first time I ever see my husband, and if any body'd a told me then
that I should ever marry him, I should a said—but lawful sakes!
I most forgot, I was gwine to tell you what he said to me that
evenin', and when a body begins to tell a thing I believe in finishin'
on't some time or other. Some folks have a way of talkin' round
and round and round for evermore, and never comin' to the pint.
Now there's Miss Jinkins, she that was Poll Bingham afore she
was married, she is the tejusest individooal to tell a story that ever
I see in all my born days. But I was a gwine to tell you what husband said. He says to me says he, "Silly," says I, "What?" I
dident say "What, Hezekier?" for I dident like his name. The
first time I ever heard it I near killed myself a laffin. "Hezekier
Bedott," says I, "well, I would give up if I had sich a name,"
but then you know I had no more idee o' marryin' the feller than
you have this minnit o' marryin' the governor. I s'pose you think
it's curus we should a named our oldest son Hezekier. Well, we
done it to please father and mother Bedott, it's father Bedott's
name, and he and mother Bedott both used to think that names
had ought to go down from gineration to gineration. But we
always called him Kier, you know. Speakin' o' Kier, he *is* a
blessin', ain't he? and I ain't the only one that thinks so, I guess.
Now don't you never tell nobody that I said so, but between you
and me I rather guess that if Kezier Winkle thinks she is a gwine
to ketch Kier Bedott she is a *leetle* out of her reckonin'. But I was
going to tell what husband said. He says to me, says he, "Silly," I
says, says I, "What?" If I dident say "what" when he said "Silly,"
he'd a kept on saying "Silly," from time to eternity. He always
did, because, you know, he wanted me to pay pertikkeler attention, and I ginerally did; no woman was ever more attentive to
her husband than what I was. Well, he says to me, says he, "Silly."
Says I, "What?" though I'd no idee what he was gwine to say,
dident know but what 'twas something about his sufferings,
though he wa'n't apt to complain, but he frequently used to remark that he wouldent wish his worst enemy to suffer one minnit
as he did all the time, but that can't be called grumblin'—think
it can? Why, I've seen him in sitivations when you'd a thought
no mortal could a helped grumblin', but *he* dident. He and me
went once in the dead o' winter in a one hoss slay out to Boon-

ville to see a sister o' hisen. You know the snow is amazin' deep
in that section o' the kentry. Well, the hoss got stuck in one o'
them are flambergasted snow-banks, and there we sot, onable to
stir, and to cap all, while we was a sittin' there, husband was took
with a dretful crick in his back. Now *that* was what I call a *per-
dickerment*, don't you? Most men would a swore, but husband
dident. He only said, says he, "Consarn it." How did we get out,
did you ask? Why we might a been sittin' there to this day fur as
I know, if there hadent a happened to come along a mess o' men
in a double team and they hysted us out. But I was gwine to tell
you that observation o' hisen. Says he to me, says he, "Silly," (I
could see by the light o' the fire, there dident happen to be no
candle burnin', if I don't disremember, though my memory is
sometimes ruther forgitful, but I know we wa'n't apt to burn
candles exceptin' when we had company) I could see by the light
of the fire that his mind was oncommon solemnized. Says he to
me, says he, "Silly." I says to him, says I, "What?" He says to me,
says he, *"We're all poor critters!"*

THE REV. MRS. SNIFFLES EXPRESSES HER SENTIMENTS IN REGARD TO THE PARSONAGE

"I say I'm disgusted with this old house; 't ain't fit for ginteel
folks to live in; looks as if 't was built in Noah's time, with its
consarned old gamble ruff and leetle bits o' winders a pokin' out
like bird cages all round. Painted yaller, too, and such a humbly
yaller; for all the world jest the color o' calomel and jollup!"

"But you are aware, Mrs. Sniffles—"

"I say 't ain't fit to live in. I'm ashamed on 't. I feel awful
mortified about it whenever I look at Miss Myerses and Miss
Loderses, and the rest o' the hansome sittiwations in the neighborhood, with their wings and their piazzers and foldin' doors, and
all so dazzlin' white. It's ridicilous that we should have to live in
such a distressid lookin' old consarn, when we're every bit and
grain as good as they be, if not ruther better."

"Nevertheless, the house is very comfortable."

"Comfortable! who cares for comfort when gintility's consarned! *I* don't. I say if you're detarmined to stay in it, you'd
ought to make some alterations in 't. You'd ought to higher the
ruff up and put on some wings, and build a piazzer in front with
four great pillars to 't, and knock out that are petition betwixt the
square room and kitchen, and put foldin' doors instid on't, and

then build on a kitchen behind, and have it all painted white, with green winder blinds. *That* would look something *like*, and then I shouldent feel ashamed to have ginteel company come to see me, as I dew now. T'other day, when Curnel Billins and his wife called, I couldent help noticin' how contemptible she looked round at the house and furniture—I actilly was so mortified I felt as if I should sink right through the floor."

"But you know, Mrs. Sniffles—"

"I say we'd ought to have new furnitur—sofys and fashionable cheers, and curtains, and mantletry ornaments, and so forth. That old settee looks like a sight. And them cheers, tew, they must a come over in the ark. And then ther ain't a picter in the house, only jest that everlastin' old likeness o' Bonyparte. I'll bet forty great apples it's five hundred years old. I was raly ashamed on 't when I see Miss Curnel Billins look at it so scornful when they called here. I s'pose she was a counterastin' it with their beautiful new picters they're jest ben a gittin up from New York, all in gilt frames. I seen one on 'em t'other day in to Mr. Bungle's shop, when I went in with Sister Tibbins to look at her portrait that he's a paintin'. I seen one o' Miss Billinses picters there. 'T was a splendid one, as big as the top o' that are table, and represented an elegant lady a lyin' asleep by a river, and ther was a little angel a hoverin' in the air over her head, jest a gwine to shoot at her with a bow and arrer. I axed Mr. Bungle what 't was sent to his shop for, and he said how 't Miss Billins wa'n't quite satisfied with it on account o' the angel's legs bein' bare, and she wanted to have him paint some pantaletts on 'em, and he was a gwine to dew it as soon as he got time. He thought 't would be a very interestin' picter when he got it fixed. I think so tew. I dew admire picters when they ain't all dirty and faded out like old Bony there. Them Scripter pieces that Sister Myers has got hangin' in her front parlor—them she painted afore she was married, strikes me as wonderful interestin', especially the one that represents Pharoh's daughter a findin' Moses in the bulrushes. Her parasol and the artificials in her bunnit is jest as natral as life. And Moses, he looks so cunnin' a lyin' there asleep, with his little coral necklace and bracelets on. O it's a sweet picter. And I like that other one, tew, that represents Pharoh a drivin' full tilt into the Red Sea after the Isrelites. How natral his coat-tails flies out. I think some Scripter pieces would be very approbriate for a minister's house. We might git Mr. Bungle to paint some for the front parlor, and our portraits to hang in the back parlor, as Miss Myers has theirn. But law me! what's the use o' my talkin' o' havin' picters or any thing else that's decent? You don't take no interest in it. You seem to be perfectly satisfied with this flambergasted old house and every thing in it."

"My former consort never desired any thing superior to it."

"Your former consort! I'm sick and tired o' hearin' about her. 'T aint by no means agreeable to have dead folks throw'd in yer face from mornin' to night. What if she was satisfied with her sittiwation? 'T ain't no sign *I* should be. I s'pose she hadent never ben used to nothin' better, but I *have*."

"But, Mrs. Sniffles, you must recollect that—"

"I say 't ain't to be put up with. I want to have some company—ben wantin' tew ever sence we was married; but as for invitin' any ginteel people a visitin' to such a distressid old shell as this is, I won't dew it—and *so*—Miss Billins and Miss Loder and *them* would say I was tryin' to cut a swell, and couldent make it out. And I don't mean to accept no more invitations amonkst them that lives in style, for it aggravates me, it does, to think how different I'm sittiwated. So you may make yer pastoral visits without *me* in future, for I've made up my mind not to go out none as long as we live in this ridicilous old house."

"But recollect, Mrs. Sniffles, this house is a parsonage—I occupy it rent free."

"I don't care if 't is a parsonage. I say the congregation might afford you a better one, and for my part, I'm disposed to make a fuss about it."

"Mrs. Sniffles, you must be aware that I am not possessed of inexhaustible means. I have never attempted to conceal from you this fact—therefore, you must also be aware that there exists an entire impossibility of my erecting a new residence on the plan which you propose. Nor is it at all probable that the congregation would be willing to make such alterations in this as you suggest. Yet, I assure you that I have not the slightest objection to your employing your *own* means in the construction of a more elegant edifice."

"My own means!"

"Yes, Mrs. Sniffles. Your dissatisfaction with the parsonage is so great, that I have for some time past been expecting you would propose building a new residence; and I repeat that such an appropriation of a portion of your funds would meet my concurrence."

"My funds!"

"Your funds, Mrs. Sniffles. It is a delicate subject and one on which I have hitherto hesitated to make inquiry, although possessing an undoubted right to do so. I have been expecting ever since our union, that you would inform me how and where your property is invested."

"My property!"

"Your property, Mrs. Sniffles. In what does it consist, if I may be permitted to inquire?"

"Land o' liberty! you know as well as I dew."

"What am I to infer from that observation?"

"Jest what you're a mind to. I ain't woth money, and I never said I was."

"Mrs. Sniffles, you are well aware that on your arrival in this place, common report pronounced you to be an individual of abundant means, and I have always labored under this impression—an impression which, allow me to remind you, yourself confirmed in a conversation which occurred between us in the parsonage grove."

"You don't mean to say 't I *told* you so, and you darsent say 't I did."

"A-hem—I mean to say that you did not deny it when I delicately alluded to the subject. On the contrary you led me to infer that such was the fact, and under that impression I was induced to accede to your proposal."

"My proposal? What do you mean to insinniwate?"

"I should have said your—your—evident inclination for a—a—matrimonial engagement. I deeply regret, Mrs. Sniffles, that you should have allowed yourself to practice upon me what I can not consider in any other light than that of a heinous and unmitigated deception. I regard it as an act quite incompatible with your religious professions."

"You dew, hey? well, you can't say 't I ever told you out and out that I was woth property; and if you was a mind to s'pose so from what I *did* say, I'm sure 't ain't my fault, nor I ain't to blame for other folkses saying I was a rich widder."

"Mrs. Sniffles, I lament exceedingly that you should view it in that light. You can but acknowledge that it was your duty when I requested information on the subject, to have given me a correct account of your property."

"I hadent no property to give ye an accont of."

"You should have told me so, Mrs. Sniffles, and not have suffered me to infer that you were in easy circumstances."

"I tell ye agin, I couldent help what you *inferred*, and s'pozen I could, which was the most to blame, me for lettin' you think I was rich, or you for marryin' me *because* you thought I was rich? For my part, I think *that* was ruther incompatible with *your* professions. *Ministers* had ought to have their affections sot above transiterry riches."

"Mrs. Sniffles, this is a—a—delicate subject, we will waive it, if you please."

"But I think the congregation ought to fix up the house."

"I will lay it before the session at the next meeting."

"Well, dew, for pity's sake. And if they agree to fix it, I'll go a journey somewhar while it's a bein' altered, and you can board round, and Sal can stay at sister Magwire's."

Extracts from Mrs. Sniffles' Diary.

SABBATH DAY EVENING.—O, what a precious season this day has been to me! My pardner has hild forth with uncommon unction. O, may he long be a burnin' and shinin' light to the world! My feelins to-day has been of the most desirable natur. O that I could say so every night! but, alas! ther is times when I feel as cold as a stun, when the face o' creation seems to frown, and evidences is wonderful dull. And then agin, I'm as bright as a dollar, and have such wonderful clear manifestations, and such oncommon near-ness—and such a sense of intarnal satisfaction. O that I could always feel as I'd ought to feel. Dear suz! I'm often reminded o' what my deceased companion, the lamented Deacon Bedott, used to remark, "We're all poor critters."

> To-day we're liable to fall,
> To-morrow up we climb,
> For 't ain't our nature to enjoy
> Religion all the time.

MONDAY.—Have ben very much exercised to-day on account of Sally Blake, our help. Her depraved natur has showed out in a very tryin' manner. But I feel to rejoice that I've ben enabled to be faithful with her. How I have wrastled day and night for that distressid child! O, that I may have grace to bear with patience and resignation the daily trials I have to undergo with her! I feel to be thankful that thus far I have ben supported and hain't sunk under it as many would a done. O that I may be enabled to feel and realize that such afflictions is sent for the trial of my faith.

THURSDAY.—O, what a responsible sittiwation is mine as President of the "F.U.D.G.E., and A. Society!" I've realized it in an overwhelmin' degree to-day. Attended the meetin' this afternoon, and some very onpleasnt circumstances occured. But I feel to be truly thankful that I had grace to presarve my uniformity in the midst of the diffikilties. I wish I could say as much for some o' the rest o' the members, especially Sall Hugle. O, the vanity and pride o' that critter! it grieves me to the heart.

SATURDAY.—My beloved Shadrack has jist informed me that the parsonage is to be repaired and made comfortable. My dear pardner has requested it to be done intirely to please me, and quite unbeknown to me. It's true it needs it bad enough, but then I never should a thought o' complainin' about it. I feel that I'm a pilgrim and a sojourneyer here, and hadent ought to be partickler, and so I told the elder when he proposed havin' the house repaired. But he insisted on 't and I consented more for his sake than my own. O that I may be truly thankful for the blessins I injoy especially for such a pardner!

> Blest be the day o' sacred mirth
> That gave my dear companion birth.
> Let men rejoice while Silly sings
> The bliss her precious Shadrack brings.

THE HUMOR OF THE OLD SOUTHWEST

1830–1867

TALL TALK

Theatrical Performance

Anonymous

I was ridin along the Mississippi in my wagon, when I came acrost a feller floating down stream, settin in the starn of his boat fast asleep. Well, I hadn't had a fight for ten days; felt as tho' I should have to kiver myself up in a salt barrel, to keep so wolfy about the shoulders. So says I, hallo stranger, if you don't mind your boat will run off and leave you. So he looked up at me slant-indicular, and I looked down on him slantindicular. He took out a chor of tobacco, and says he, I don't vallee you tantamount to that; and the varmant clapped his wings and crowed. I ris up, shuch my mane, croocked my neck, and nickered like a horse. He run his boat plump head foremost ashore. I stopped my wagon, and set my triggers. Mister, says he, I can whip my weight in wild cats, and ride straight thro' a crab apple orchard on a flash of lightning—clear meat axe disposition—the best man, if I an't, I wish I may be tetotaciously exfluncated. So we come together; he was a pretty severe colt, but no part of a priming for me. I put it to him mighty droll—in ten minutes he yelled enough, and swore I was a ripstaver! Says I, an't I the yellow flower of the forest? And I'm all brimstone but the head, and that's aquafortis! Says he, stranger, you're a beauty, and if I only know'd your name, I'd vote for you next election. Says I, my name is Nimrod Wildfire—half horse, half alligator, and a touch of the airthquake—that's got the prettiest sister, fattest horse, and ugliest dog in the district, and can out run, out jump, throw down, drag out and whip any man in all Kentuck!

Crockett's Coon Story

by James S. French

That Colonel Crockett could avail himself, in electioneering, of the advantages which well applied satire ensures, the following anecdote will sufficiently prove:

In the canvass of the congressional election of 18—, Mr. **** was the Colonel's opponent—a gentleman of the most pleasing and conciliating manners—who seldom addressed a person or a company without wearing upon his countenance a peculiarly good humored smile. The Colonel, to counteract the influence of this winning attribute, thus alluded to it, in a stump speech:

"Yes, gentlemen, he may get some votes by *grinning*, for he can *out grin* me, and you know I ain't slow—and to prove to you that I am not, I will tell you an anecdote. I was concerned myself—and I was fooled a little of the damn'dest. You all know I love hunting. Well, I discovered, a long time ago, that a 'coon couldn't stand my grin. I could bring one tumbling down from the highest tree. I never wasted powder and lead, when I wanted one of the creturs. Well, as I was walking out one night, a few hundred yards from my house, looking carelessly about me, I saw a 'coon planted upon one of the highest limbs of an old tree. The night was very *moony* and clear, and old Ratler was with me; but Ratler won't bark at a 'coon—he's a queer dog in that way. So, I thought I'd bring the lark down, in the usual way, *by a grin*. I set myself—and, after grinning at the 'coon a reasonable time, found that he didn't come down. I wondered what was the reason—and I took another steady grin at him. Still, he was *there*. It made me a little mad; so I felt round and got an old limb about five feet long—and, planting one end upon the ground, I placed my chin upon the other, and took *a rest*. I then grinned my best for about five minutes—but the damn'd 'coon hung on. So, finding I could not bring him down by grinning, I determined to have him —for I thought he must be a droll chap. I went over to the house, got my axe, returned to the tree, saw the 'coon still there, and began to cut away. Down it come, and I run forward; but damn the 'coon was there to be seen. I found that what I had taken for one, was a large knot upon a branch of the tree—and, upon looking at it closely, I saw that *I had grinned all the bark off, and left the knot perfectly smooth.*

"Now fellow-citizens," continued the Colonel, "you must be convinced that, in the *grinning line*, I myself am not slow—yet, when I look upon my opponent's countenance, I must admit that he is my superior. You must all admit it. Therefore, be wide awake —look sharp—and do not let him grin you out of your votes."

Mike Fink Beats Davy Crockett at a Shooting Match

Anonymous

I expect, stranger, you think old Davy Crockett war never beat at the long rifle; but he war tho. I expect there's no man so strong, but what he will find some one stronger. If you havent heerd tell of one Mike Fink, I'll tell you something about him, for he war a helliferocious fellow, and made an almighty fine shot. Mike was a boatman on the Mississip, but he had a little cabbin on the head of the Cumberland, and a horrid handsome wife, that loved him the wickedest that ever you see. Mike only worked enough to find his wife in rags, and himself in powder, and lead, and whiskey, and the rest of the time he spent in nocking over bar and turkeys, and bouncing deer, and sometimes drawing a lead on an injun. So one night I fell in with him in the woods, where him and his wife shook down a blanket for me in his wigwam. In the morning sez Mike to me, 'I've got the handsomest wife, and the fastest horse, and the sharpest shooting iron in all Kentuck, and if any man dare doubt it, I'll be in his hair quicker than hell could scorch a feather.' This put my dander up, and sez I, 'I've nothing to say agin your wife, Mike, for it cant be denied she's a shocking handsome woman, and Mrs. Crockett's in Tennessee, and I've got no horses. Mike, I dont exactly like to tell you you lie about what you say about your rifle, but I'm d——d if you speak the truth, and I'll prove it. Do you see that are cat sitting on the top rail of your potato patch, about a hundred and fifty yards off? If she ever hears agin, I'll be shot if it shant be without ears.' So I plazed away, and I'll bet you a horse, the ball cut off both the old tom cat's ears close to his head, and shaved the hair off clean across the skull, as slick as if I'd done it with a razor, and the critter never stirred, nor knew he'd lost his ears till he tried to scratch 'em. 'Talk about your rifle after that, Mike!' sez I. 'Do you see that are sow away off furder than the eend of the world,' sez Mike, 'with a litter of pigs round her,' and he lets fly. The old sow give a grunt, but never stirred in her tracks, and Mike falls to loading and firing for dear life, till he hadn't left one of them are pigs enough tail to make a tooth-pick on. 'Now,' sez he, 'Col. Crockett, I'll be pretticularly ableedged to you if you'll put them are pig's tails on again,' sez he. 'That's onpossible, Mike,' sez I, 'but you've left one of 'em about an inch to steer by, and if it had a-been my work, I wouldn't have done it so wasteful. I'll mend your host,' and so I lets fly, and cuts off the apology he'd left the poor cretur for decency. I wish I may drink the whole of Old Mississip, without a drop of the rale stuff in it, if you wouldn't have thort the tail had been drove in with a hammer. That made Mike a kinder sorter wrothy, and he sends a ball after his wife as she was going to the spring after a gourd full of water, and nocked half her koom out of her head, without stirring a hair, and calls out to her to stop for me to take a plizzard at what was left on it. The angeliferous critter stood still as a scarecrow in a cornfield, for she'd got used to Mike's tricks by long practiss. 'No, no, Mike,' sez I, 'Davy Crockett's hand would be sure to shake, if his iron war pointed within a hundred mile of a shemale, and I give up beat, Mike, and as we've had our eye-openers a-ready, we'll now take a flem-cutter, by way of an anti-formatic, and then we'll disperse.'

SAL FINK, THE MISSISSIPPI SCREAMER

Anonymous

I dar say you've all on you, if not more, frequently heerd this great she human crittur boasted of, an' pointed out as "*one o' the gals*"—but I tell you what, stranger, you have never really set your eyes on "*one of the gals*," till you have seen Sal Fink, the Mississippi screamer, whose miniature pictur I have here give, about as nat'ral as life, but not half as handsome—an' if thar ever was a gal that desarved to be christen—"*one o' the gals*," then this gal was that gal—and no mistake.

She fought a duel once with a thunderbolt, an' came off without a single scratch, while at the fust fire she split the thunderbolt all to flinders, an' gave the pieces to Uncle Sam's artillerymen, to touch off their canon with. When a gal about six years old, she used to play see-saw on the Mississippi snags, and arter she war done she would snap 'em off, an' so cleared a large district of the river. She used to ride down the river on an alligator's back, standen upright, an' dancing *Yankee Doodle*, and could leave all the steamers behind. But the greatest feat she ever did, positively outdid anything that ever was did.

One day when she war out in the forest, making a collection o' wild cat skins for her family's winter beddin, she war captered in the most all-sneaken manner by about fifty Injuns, an' carried by 'em to Roast Flesh Hollow, whar the blood drinkin' wild varmints detarmined to skin her alive, sprinkle a leetle salt over her, an' devour her before her own eyes; so they took an' tied her to a tree, to keep till mornin' should bring the rest o' thar ring-nosed sarpints to enjoy the fun. Arter that, they lit a large fire in the Holler, turned the bottom o' thar feet towards the blaze, Injun fashion, and went to sleep to dream o' thar mornin's feast; well, after the critturs got into a somniferous snore, Sal got into an all-lightnin' of a temper, and burst all the ropes about her like an apron-string! She then found a pile o' ropes, too, and tied all the Injun's heels together all round the fire,—then fixin' a cord to the shins of every two couple, she, with a suddenachous jerk, that made the intire woods tremble, pulled the intire lot o' sleepin' red-skins into that ar great fire, fast together, an' then sloped like a panther out of her pen, in the midst o' the tallest yellin', howlin', scramblin' and singin', that war ever seen or heerd on, since the great burnin' o' Buffalo prairie!

[Sunrise in His Pocket]

Anonymous

One January morning it was so all screwen cold that the forest trees were stiff and they couldn't shake, and the very daybreak froze fast as it was trying to dawn. The tinder box in my cabin would no more ketch fire than a sunk raft at the bottom of the sea. Well, seein' daylight war so far behind time I thought creation war in a fair way for freezen fast: so, thinks I, I must strike a little fire from my fingers, light my pipe, an' travel out a few leagues, and see about it. Then I brought my knuckles together like two thunderclouds, but the sparks froze up afore I could begin to collect 'em, so out I walked, whistlin' "Fire in the mountains!" as I went along in three double quick time. Well, arter I had walked about twenty miles up the Peak O'Day and Daybreak Hill I soon discovered what war the matter. The airth had actually friz fast on her axes, and couldn't turn round; the sun had got jammed between two cakes o' ice under the wheels, an' thar he had been shinin' an' workin' to get loose till he friz fast in his cold sweat. C-r-e-a-t-i-o-n! thought I, this ar the toughest sort of suspension, an' it mustn't be endured. Somethin' must be done, or human creation is done for. It war then so anteluvian an' premature cold that my upper and lower teeth an' tongue war all collapsed together as tight as a friz oyster; but I took a fresh twenty-pound bear off my back that I'd picked up on my road, and beat the animal agin the ice till the hot ile began to walk out on him at all sides. I then took an' held him over the airth's axes an' squeezed him till I'd thawed 'em loose, poured about a ton on't over the sun's face, give the airth's cog-wheel one kick backward till I got the sun loose—whistled "Push along, keep movin'!" an' in about fifteen seconds the airth gave a grunt, an' began movin'. The sun walked up beautiful, salutin' me with sich a wind o' gratitude that it made me sneeze. I lit my pipe by the blaze o' his top-knot, shouldered my bear, an' walked home, introducin' people to the fresh daylight with a piece of sunrise in my pocket.

GEORGIA SCENES

by *Augustus Baldwin Longstreet*

(1790–1870)

GEORGIA THEATRICS

If my memory fail me not, the 10th of June, 1809, found me, at about eleven o'clock in the forenoon, ascending a long and gentle slope in what was called "The Dark Corner" of Lincoln. I believe it took its name from the moral darkness which reigned over that portion of the county at the time of which I am speaking. If in this point of view it was but a shade darker than the rest of the county, it was inconceivably dark. If any man can name a trick or sin which had not been committed at the time of which I am speaking, in the very focus of all the county's illumination (Lincolnton), he must himself be the most inventive of the tricky and the very Judas of sinners. Since that time, however (all humor aside), Lincoln has become a living proof "that light shineth in darkness." Could I venture to mingle the solemn with the ludicrous, even for the purposes of honorable contrast, I could adduce from this county instances of the most numerous and wonderful transitions from vice and folly to virtue and holiness which have ever, perhaps, been witnessed since the days of the apostolic ministry. So much, lest it should be thought by some that what I am about to relate is characteristic of the county in which it occurred.

Whatever may be said of the *moral* condition of the Dark Corner at the time just mentioned, its *natural* condition was anything but dark. It smiled in all the charms of spring; and spring borrowed a new charm from its undulating grounds, its luxuriant woodlands, its sportive streams, its vocal birds, and its blushing flowers.

Rapt with the enchantment of the season and the scenery around me, I was slowly rising the slope, when I was startled by loud, profane, and boisterous voices, which seemed to proceed from a thick covert of undergrowth about two hundred yards in the advance of me and about one hundred to the right of my road.

"You kin, kin you?"

"Yes, I kin, and am able to do it! Boo-oo-oo! Oh, wake snakes, and walk your chalks! Brimstone and—fire! Don't hold me, Nick Stoval! The fight's made up, and let's go at it—My soul if I don't jump down his throat, and gallop every chitterling out of him before you can say 'quit'!"

"Now, Nick, don't hold him! Jist let the wildcat come, and I'll tame him. Ned'll see me a fair fight! Won't you, Ned?"

"Oh, yes; I'll see you a fair fight, blast my old shoes if I don't!"

"That's sufficient, as Tom Haynes said when he saw the elephant. Now let him come!"

Thus they went on, with countless oaths interspersed, which I dare not even hint at, and with much that I could not distinctly hear.

In mercy's name! thought I, what band of ruffians has selected this holy season and this heavenly retreat for such pandemoniac riots! I quickened my gait, and had come nearly opposite to the thick grove whence the noise proceeded, when my eye caught, indistinctly and at intervals, through the foliage of the dwarf-oaks and hickories which intervened, glimpses of a man, or men, who seemed to be in a violent struggle; and I could occasionally catch those deep-drawn, emphatic oaths which men in conflict utter when they deal blows. I dismounted, and hurried to the spot with all speed. I had overcome about half the space which separated it from me, when I saw the combatants come to the ground, and, after a short struggle, I saw the uppermost one (for I could not see the other) make a heavy plunge with both his thumbs, and at the same instant I heard a cry in the accent of keenest torture, "Enough! My eye's out!"

I was so completely horror-struck that I stood transfixed for a moment to the spot where the cry met me. The accomplices in the hellish deed which had been perpetrated had all fled at my approach—at least, I supposed so, for they were not to be seen.

"Now, blast your corn-shucking soul!" said the victor (a youth about eighteen years old) as he rose from the ground—"come cutt'n' your shines 'bout me agin, next time I come to the courthouse, will you? Get your owl eye in agin if you can!"

At this moment he saw me for the first time. He looked excessively embarrassed, and was moving off, when I called to him, in a tone emboldened by the sacredness of my office and the iniquity of his crime, "Come back, you brute, and assist me in relieving your fellow-mortal, whom you have ruined forever!"

My rudeness subdued his embarrassment in an instant; and, with a taunting curl of the nose, he replied, "You needn't kick before you're spurr'd. There a'n't nobody there, nor ha'n't been nother. I was jist seein' how I could 'a' fout." So saying, he bounded to his plough, which stood in the corner of the fence about fifty yards beyond the battle-ground.

And, would you believe it, gentle reader? his report was true. All that I had heard and seen was nothing more nor less than a Lincoln rehearsal, in which the youth who had just left me had played all the parts of all the characters in a court-house fight.

I went to the ground from which he had risen, and there were the prints of his two thumbs, plunged up to the balls in the mellow earth, about the distance of a man's eyes apart; and the ground around was broken up as if two stags had been engaged upon it.

The Fight

In the younger days of the Republic there lived in the county of —— two men who were admitted on all hands to be the very *best men* in the county, which in the Georgia vocabulary means they could flog any other two men in the county. Each, through many a hard-fought battle, had acquired the mastery of his own battalion; but they lived on opposite sides of the court-house and in different battalions, consequently they were but seldom thrown together. When they met, however, they were always friendly; indeed, at their first interview they seemed to conceive a wonderful attachment to each other, which rather increased than diminished as they became better acquainted; so that, but for the circumstance which I am about to mention, the question, which had been a thousand times asked, "Which is the best man, Billy Stallions (Stallings) or Bob Durham?" would probably never have been answered.

Billy ruled the upper battalion and Bob the lower. The former measured six feet and an inch in his stockings, and, without a single pound of cumbrous flesh about him, weighed a hundred and eighty. The latter was an inch shorter than his rival, and ten pounds lighter; but he was much the more active of the two. In running and jumping he had but few equals in the county; and in wrestling, not one. In other respects they were nearly equal. Both were admirable specimens of human nature in its finest form. Billy's victories had generally been achieved by the tremendous power of his blows, one of which had often proved decisive of his battles; Bob's by his adroitness in bringing his adversary to the ground. This advantage he had never failed to gain at the onset, and when gained he never failed to improve it to the defeat of his adversary. These points of difference have involved the reader in a doubt as to the probable issue of a contest between them. It was not so, however, with the two battalions. Neither had the least difficulty in determining the point by the most natural and irresistible deductions *a priori;* and though, by the same course of reasoning, they arrived at directly opposite conclusions, neither felt its confidence in the least shaken by this circumstance. The upper battalion swore "that Billy only wanted one lick at him to knock his heart, liver, and lights out of him, and if he got two at him he'd knock him into a cocked hat." The lower battalion retorted "that he wouldn't have time to double his fist before Bob would put his head where his feet ought to be; and that, by the time he hit the ground, the meat would fly off his face so quick that people would think it was shook off by the fall." These disputes often led to the *argumentum ad hominem,* but with such equality of success on both sides as to leave the main question just where they found it. They usually ended, however, in the common way—with a bet; and many a quart of old Jamaica (whiskey had not then supplanted rum) was staked upon the issue. Still, greatly to the annoyance of the curious, Billy and Bob continued to be good friends.

Now, there happened to reside in the county just alluded to a little fellow by the name of Ransy Sniffle: a sprout of Richmond, who, in his earlier days, had fed copiously upon red clay and blackberries. This diet had given to Ransy a complexion that a corpse would have disdained to own, and an abdominal rotundity that was quite unprepossessing. Long spells of the fever and ague, too, in Ransy's youth, had conspired with clay and blackberries to throw him quite out of the order of nature. His shoulders were fleshless and elevated; his head large and flat; his neck slim and translucent; and his arms, hands, fingers, and feet were lengthened out of all proportion to the rest of his frame. His joints were large and his limbs small; and as for flesh, he could not, with propriety, be said to have any. Those parts which nature usually supplies with the most of this article—the calves of the legs, for example—

presented in him the appearance of so many well-drawn blisters. His height was just five feet nothing; and his average weight in blackberry season, ninety-five. I have been thus particular in describing him, for the purpose of showing what a great matter a little fire sometimes kindleth. There was nothing on this earth which delighted Ransy so much as a fight. He never seemed fairly alive except when he was witnessing, fomenting, or talking about a fight. Then, indeed, his deep-sunken gray eye assumed something of a living fire, and his tongue acquired a volubility that bordered upon eloquence. Ransy had been kept for more than a year in the most torturing suspense as to the comparative manhood of Billy Stallings and Bob Durham. He had resorted to all his usual expedients to bring them in collision, and had entirely failed. He had faithfully reported to Bob all that had been said by the people in the upper battalion "agin him," and "he was sure Billy Stallings started it. He heard Billy say himself to Jim Brown that he could whip him, *or any other man in his battalion*"; and this he told to Bob, adding, "Dod darn his soul, if he was a little bigger, if he'd let any man *put upon* his battalion in such a way!" Bob replied, "If he (Stallings) thought so, he'd better come and try it." This Ransy carried to Billy, and delivered it with a spirit becoming his own dignity and the character of his battalion, and with a coloring well calculated to give it effect. These and many other schemes which Ransy laid for the gratification of his curiosity entirely failed of their object. Billy and Bob continued friends, and Ransy had begun to lapse into the most tantalizing and hopeless despair, when a circumstance occurred which led to a settlement of the long-disputed question.

It is said that a hundred game-cocks will live in perfect harmony together if you do not put a hen with them; and so it would have been with Billy and Bob had there been no women in the world. But there were women in the world, and from them each of our heroes had taken to himself a wife. The good ladies were no strangers to the prowess of their husbands, and, strange as it may seem, they presumed a little upon it.

The two battalions had met at the court-house upon a regimental parade. The two champions were there, and their wives had accompanied them. Neither knew the other's lady, nor were the ladies known to each other. The exercises of the day were just over, when Mrs. Stallings and Mrs. Durham stepped simultaneously into the store of Zephaniah Atwater, from "down East."

"Have you any Turkey red?" said Mrs. S.

"Have you any curtain calico?" said Mrs. D. at the same moment.

"Yes, ladies," said Mr. Atwater, "I have both."

"Then help me first," said Mrs. D., "for I'm in a hurry."

"I'm in as great a hurry as she is," said Mrs. S., "and I'll thank you to help me first."

"And, pray, who are you, madam?" continued the other.

"Your betters, madam," was the reply.

At this moment Billy Stallings stepped in. "Come," said he, "Nancy, let's be going; it's getting late."

"I'd 'a' been gone half an hour ago," she replied, "if it hadn't 'a' been for that impudent hussy."

"Who do you call an impudent hussy, you nasty, good-for-nothing, snaggle-toothed gaub of fat, you?" returned Mrs. D.

"Look here, woman," said Billy. "Have you got a husband here? If you have, I'll *lick* him till he learns to teach you better manners, you *sassy* heifer you!"

At this moment something was seen to rush out of the store as if ten thousand hornets were stinging it, crying, "Take care— let me go—don't hold me—where's Bob Durham?" It was Ransy Sniffle, who had been listening in breathless delight to all that had passed.

"Yonder's Bob, setting on the court-house steps," cried one. "What's the matter?"

"Don't talk to me!" said Ransy. "Bob Durham, you'd better go long yonder and take care of your wife. They're playing h——l with her there in Zeph Atwater's store. Dod etarnally darn my soul, if any man was to talk to my wife as Bill Stallions is talking to yours, if I wouldn't drive blue blazes through him in less than no time!"

Bob sprang to the store in a minute, followed by a hundred friends; for a bully of a county never wants friends.

"Bill Stallions," said Bob, as he entered, "what have you been saying to my wife?"

"Is that your wife?" inquired Billy, obviously much surprised and a little disconcerted.

"Yes, she is; and no man shall abuse her, I don't care who he is."

"Well," rejoined Billy, "it ain't worth while to go over it; I've said enough for a fight, and if you'll step out we'll settle it."

"Billy," said Bob, "are you for a fair fight?"

"I am," said Billy. "I've heard much of your manhood, and I believe I'm a better man than you are. If you will go into a ring with me we can soon settle the dispute."

"Choose your friends," said Bob; "make your ring, and I'll be in with mine as soon as you will!"

They both stepped out, and began to strip very deliberately, each battalion gathering round its champion, except Ransy, who kept himself busy in a most honest endeavor to hear and see all that transpired in both groups at the same time. He ran from one to the other in quick succession; peeped here and listened there; talked to this one, then to that one, and then to himself; squatted under one's legs and another's arms; and, in the short interval between stripping and stepping into the ring, managed to get himself trod on by half of both battalions. But Ransy was not the only one interested upon this occasion; the most intense interest prevailed everywhere. Many were the conjectures, doubts, oaths, and imprecations uttered while the parties were preparing for the combat. All the knowing ones were consulted as to the issue, and they all agreed, to a man, in one of two opinions— either that Bob would flog Billy, or Billy would flog Bob. We must be permitted, however, to dwell for a moment upon the opinion of Squire Thomas Loggins, a man who, it was said, had never failed to predict the issue of a fight in all his life. Indeed, so unerring had he always proved in this regard that it would have been counted the most obstinate infidelity to doubt for a moment after he had delivered himself. Squire Loggins was a man who said but little, but that little was always delivered with the most imposing solemnity of look and cadence. He always wore the aspect of profound thought, and you could not look at him without coming to the conclusion that he was elaborating truth from its most intricate combinations.

"Uncle Tommy," said Sam Reynolds, "you can tell us all about it if you will; how will the fight go?"

The question immediately drew an anxious group around the squire. He raised his teeth slowly from the head of his walking-cane, on which they had been resting, pressed his lips closely and thoughtfully together, threw down his eyebrows, dropped his chin, raised his eyes to an angle of twenty-three degrees, paused about half a minute, and replied, "Sammy, watch Robert Durham close in the beginning of the fight, take care of William Stallions in the middle of it, and see who has the wind at the end." As he uttered the last sentence, he looked slyly at Bob's friends and winked very significantly; whereupon they rushed, with one accord, to tell Bob what Uncle Tommy had said. As they retired, the squire turned to Billy's friends and said, with a smile, "Them boys think I mean that Bob will whip."

Here the other party kindled into joy, and hastened to inform Billy how Bob's friends had deceived themselves as to Uncle Tommy's opinion. In the meantime the principals and seconds were busily employed in preparing themselves for the combat. The plan of attack and defence, the manner of improving the various turns of the conflict, "the best mode of saving wind," etc., etc., were all discussed and settled. At length Billy announced himself ready, and his crowd were seen moving to the centre of the Court-house Square, he and his five seconds in the rear. At the same time Bob's party moved to the same point, and in the same order. The ring was now formed, and for a moment the silence of death reigned through both battalions. It was soon interrupted, however, by the cry of "Clear the way!" from Billy's seconds, when the ring opened in the centre of the upper battalion (for the order of march had arranged the centre of the two battalions on opposite sides of the circle), and Billy stepped into the ring from the east, followed by his friends. He was stripped to the trousers, and exhibited an arm, breast, and shoulders of the most tremendous portent. His step was firm, daring, and martial; and as he bore his fine form a little in advance of his friends an involuntary burst of triumph broke from his side of the ring, and at the same moment an uncontrollable thrill of awe ran along the whole curve of the lower battalion.

"Look at him!" was heard from his friends; "just look at him!"

"Ben, how much you ask to stand before that man two seconds?"

"Pshaw, don't talk about it! Just thinkin' about it's broke three o' my ribs a'ready!"

"What's Bob Durham going to do when Billy lets that arm loose upon him?"

"God bless your soul, he'll think thunder and lightning a mint-julep to it!"

"Oh, look here, men, go take Bill Stallions out o' that ring, and bring in Phil Johnson's stud-horse, so that Durham may have some chance! I don't want to see the man killed right away."

These and many other like expressions, interspersed thickly with oaths of the modern coinage, were coming from all points of the upper battalion, while Bob was adjusting the girth of his pantaloons, which walking had discovered not to be exactly right. It was just fixed to his mind, his foes becoming a little noisy, and his friends a little uneasy at his delay, when Billy called out, with a smile of some meaning, "Where's the bully of the lower battalion? I'm getting tired of waiting."

"Here he is!" said Bob, lighting as it seemed from the clouds into the ring, for he had actually bounded clear of the head of Ransy Sniffle into the circle. His descent was quite as imposing as Billy's entry, and excited the same feelings, but in opposite bosoms.

Voices of exultation now rose on his side.

"Where did he come from?"

"Why," said one of his seconds (all having just entered), "we were girting him up, about a hundred yards out yonder, when he heard Billy ask for the bully, and he fetched a leap over the court-house and went out of sight; but I told them to come on, they'd find him here."

Here the lower battalion burst into a peal of laughter, mingled with a look of admiration which seemed to denote their entire belief of what they had heard.

"Boys, widen the ring, so as to give him room to jump."

"Oh, my little flying wild-cat, hold him if you can! and, when you get him fast, hold lightning next."

"Ned, what do you think he's made of?"

"Steel springs and chicken-hawk, God bless you!"

"Gentlemen," said one of Bob's seconds, "I understand it is to be a fair fight—catch as catch can, rough and tumble; no man touch till one or the other halloos."

"That's the rule," was the reply from the other side.

"Are you ready?"

"We are ready."

"Then blaze away, my game-cocks!"

At the word, Bob dashed at his antagonist at full speed, and Bill squared himself to receive him with one of his most fatal blows. Making his calculation from Bob's velocity of the time when he would come within striking distance, he let drive with tremendous force. But Bob's onset was obviously planned to avoid this blow; for, contrary to all expectations, he stopped short just out of

arm's reach, and before Billy could recover his balance Bob had
him "all under-hold." The next second, sure enough, "found
Billy's head where his feet ought to be." How it was done no one
could tell; but, as if by supernatural power, both Billy's feet were
thrown full half his own height in the air, and he came down with
a force that seemed to shake the earth. As he struck the ground,
commingled shouts, screams, and yells burst from the lower battalion, loud enough to be heard for miles. "Hurrah, my little
hornet!" "Save him!" "Feed him!" "Give him the Durham physic
till his stomach turns!" Billy was no sooner down than Bob was
on him, and lending him awful blows about the face and breast.
Billy made two efforts to rise by main strength, but failed. "Lord
bless you, man, don't try to get up! *Lay* still and take it! You
bleege to have it!"

Billy now turned his face suddenly to the ground, and rose
upon his hands and knees. Bob jerked up both his hands and
threw him on his face. He again recovered his late position, of
which Bob endeavored to deprive him as before; but, missing
one arm, he failed, and Billy rose. But he had scarcely resumed
his feet before they flew up as before, and he came again to the
ground. "No fight, gentlemen!" cried Bob's friends; "the man
can't stand up! Bouncing feet are bad things to fight in." His fall,
however, was this time comparatively light; for, having thrown
his right arm round Bob's neck, he carried his head down with
him. This grasp, which was obstinately maintained, prevented Bob
from getting on him, and they lay head to head, seeming, for a
time, to do nothing. Presently they rose, as if by mutual consent;
and as they rose a shout burst from both battalions. "Oh, my
lark!" cried the east, "has he foxed you? Do you begin to feel
him! He's only beginning to fight; he ain't got warm yet."

"Look yonder!" cried the west. "Didn't I tell you so? He hit
the ground so hard it jarred his nose off. Now ain't he a pretty
man as he stands? He shall have my sister Sal, just for his pretty
looks. I want to get in the breed of them sort o' men, to drive
ugly out of my kinfolks."

I looked, and saw that Bob had entirely lost his left ear and a
large piece from his left cheek. His right eye was a little discolored, and the blood flowed profusely from his wounds.

Bill presented a hideous spectacle. About a third of his nose,
at the lower extremity, was bit off, and his face so swelled and
bruised that it was difficult to discover in it anything of the human

visage, much more the fine features which he carried into the ring.

They were up only long enough for me to make the foregoing discoveries, when down they went again, precisely as before. They no sooner touched the ground than Bill relinquished his hold upon Bob's neck. In this he seemed to all to have forfeited the only advantage which put him upon an equality with his adversary. But the movement was soon explained. Bill wanted this arm for other purposes than defence; and he had made arrangements whereby he knew that he could make it answer these purposes; for when they rose again he had the middle finger of Bob's left hand in his mouth. He was now secure from Bob's annoying trips; and he began to lend his adversary tremendous blows, every one of which was hailed by a shout from his friends: "Bullets!" "*Hoss*-kicking!" "Thunder!" "That'll do for his face; now feel his short ribs, Billy!"

I now considered the contest settled. I deemed it impossible for any human being to withstand for five seconds the loss of blood which issued from Bob's ear, cheek, nose, and finger, accompanied with such blows as he was receiving. Still he maintained the conflict, and gave blow for blow with considerable effect. But the blows of each became slower and weaker after the first three or four; and it became obvious that Bill wanted the room which Bob's finger occupied for breathing. He would, therefore, probably, in a short time, have let it go, had not Bob anticipated his politeness by jerking away his hand and making him a present of the finger. He now seized Bill again, and brought him to his knees, but he recovered. He again brought him to his knees, but he again recovered. A third effort, however, brought him down, and Bob on top of him. These efforts seemed to exhaust the little remaining strength of both; and they lay, Bill undermost and Bob across his breast, motionless and panting for breath. After a short pause Bob gathered his hand full of dirt and sand and was in the act of grinding it in his adversary's eyes when Bill cried, "Enough!" Language cannot describe the scene that followed—the shouts, oaths, frantic gestures, taunts, replies, and little fights—and therefore I shall not attempt it. The champions were borne off by their seconds and washed; when many a bleeding wound and ugly bruise was discovered on each which no eye had seen before.

Many had gathered round Bob, and were in various ways congratulating and applauding him, when a voice from the centre of the circle cried out, "Boys, hush, and listen to me!" It proceeded from Squire Loggins, who had made his way to Bob's side, and gathered his face up into one of its most flattering and intelligible expressions. All were obedient to the squire's command. "Gentlemen," continued he, with a most knowing smile, "is—Sammy Reynolds—in—this—company—of—gentlemen?"

"Yes," said Sam, "here I am."

"Sammy," said the squire, winking to the company and drawing the head of his cane to his mouth with an arch smile as he closed, "I—wish—you—to tell—Cousin—Bobby—and—these—gentlemen here present—what—your—Uncle—Tommy—said—before—the—fight—began?"

"Oh, get away, Uncle Tom," said Sam, smiling (the squire winked), "you don't know nothing about *fighting*." (The squire winked again.) "All you know about it is how it'll begin, how it'll go on, how it'll end; that's all. Cousin Bob, when you going to fight again, just go to the old man, and let him tell you all about it. If he can't, don't ask nobody else nothing about it, I tell you."

The squire's foresight was complimented in many ways by the bystanders; and he retired, advising "the boys to be at peace, as fighting was a bad business."

Durham and Stallings kept their beds for several weeks, and did not meet again for two months. When they met, Billy stepped up to Bob and offered his hand, saying, "Bobby, you've *licked* me a fair fight; but you wouldn't have done it if I hadn't been in the wrong. I oughtn't to have treated your wife as I did; and I felt so through the whole fight; and it sort o' cowed me."

"Well, Billy," said Bob, "let's be friends. Once in the fight, when you had my finger in your mouth, and was pealing me in the face and breast, I was going to halloo; but I thought of Petsy, and knew the house would be too hot for me if I got whipped when fighting for her, after always whipping when I fought for myself."

"Now that's what I always love to see," said a by-stander. "It's true I brought about the fight, but I wouldn't have done it if it hadn't 'a' been on account of *Miss* (Mrs.) Durham. But dod etarnally darn by soul if I ever could stand by and see any woman put upon, much less *Miss* Durham! If Bobby hadn't been there I'd 'a' took it up myself, be darned if I wouldn't, even if I'd 'a' got whipped for it! But we're all friends now." The reader need hardly be told that this was Ransy Sniffle.

A TIGHT RACE CONSIDERIN'

by Madison Tensas

During my medical studies, passed in a small village in Mississippi, I became acquainted with a family named Hibbs (a *nom de plume* of course), residing a few miles in the country. The family consisted of Mr. and Mrs. Hibbs and son. They were plain, unlettered people, honest in intent and deed, but overflowing with that which amply made up for all their deficiencies of education, namely, warm-hearted hospitality, the distinguishing trait of southern character. They were originally from Virginia, from whence they had emigrated in quest of a clime more genial, and a soil more productive than that in which their fathers toiled. Their search had been rewarded, their expectations realized, and now, in their old age, though not wealthy in the "Astorian" sense, still they had sufficient to keep the "wolf from the door," and drop something more substantial than condolence and tears in the hat that poverty hands round for the kind offerings of humanity.

The old man was like the generality of old planters, men whose ambition is embraced by the family or social circle, and whose thoughts turn more on the relative value of "Sea Island" and "Mastodon," and the improvement of their plantations, than the "glorious victories of Whiggery in Kentucky," or the "triumphs of democracy in Arkansas."

The old lady was a shrewd, active dame, kind-hearted and long-tongued, benevolent and impartial, making her coffee as strong for the poor pedestrian, with his all upon his back, as the broadcloth sojourner, with his "up-country pacer." She was a member of the church, as well as the daughter of a man who had once owned a race-horse: and these circumstances gave her an indisputable right, she thought, to "let on all she knew," when religion or horse-flesh was the theme. At one moment she would be heard discussing whether the new "circus rider," (as she always called him,) was as affecting in Timothy as the old one was pathetic in Paul, and anon (not anonymous, for the old lady did everything above board, except rubbing her corns at supper), protecting dad's horse from the invidious comparisons of some visitor, who, having heard, perhaps, that such horses as Fashion and Boston existed, thought himself qualified to doubt the old lady's assertion that her father's horse "Shumach" had run a mile on one particular occasion. "Don't tell *me*," was her never failing reply to their doubts, "Don't tell *me* 'bout Fashun or Bosting, or any other beating 'Shumach' a fair race, for the thing was unfesible; didn't he run a mile a minute by Squire Dim's watch, which always stopt 'zactly at twelve, and didn't he start a minute afore, and git out, jes as the long hand war givin' its last quiver on ketchin' the short leg of the watch? And didn't he beat everything in Virginny 'cept once? Dad and the folks said he'd beat then, if young Mr. Spotswood hadn't give 'old Swage,' Shumach's rider, some of that 'Croton water,' (that them Yorkers is makin' sich a fuss over as bein' so good, when gracious knows, nothin' but what the doctors call interconception could git me to take a dose) and jis 'fore the race Swage or Shumach, I don't 'stinctly 'member which, but one of them had to '*let down*,' and so dad's hoss got beat."

The son I will describe in few words. Imbibing his parents' contempt for letters, he was very illiterate, and as he had not enjoyed the equivalent of travel, was extremely ignorant on all matters not relating to hunting or plantation duties. He was a stout, active fellow, with a merry twinkling of the eye, indicative of humour, and partiality for practical joking. We had become very intimate, he instructing me in "forest lore," and I, in return, giving amusing stories, or, what was as much to his liking, occasional introductions to my hunting-flask.

Now that I have introduced the "Dramatis Personæ," I will proceed with my story. By way of relaxation, and to relieve the tedium incident more or less to a student's life, I would take my gun, walk out to old Hibbs's, spend a day or two, and return refreshed to my books.

One fine afternoon I started upon such an excursion, and as I had upon a previous occasion missed killing a fine buck, owing to my having nothing but squirrel shot, I determined to go this time for the "antlered monarch," by loading one barrel with fifteen "blue whistlers," reserving the other for small game.

At the near end of the plantation was a fine spring, and adjacent, a small cave, the entrance artfully or naturally concealed, save to one acquainted with its locality. The cave was nothing but one of those subterraneous washes so common in the west and south, and called "sink holes." It was known only to young H. and myself, and we, for peculiar reasons, kept secret, having put it in requisition as the depository of a jug of "old Bourbon," which we favoured, and as the old folks abominated drinking, we had found convenient to keep there, whither we would repair to get our drinks, and return to the house to hear them descant on the evils of drinking, and "vow no 'drap,' 'cept in doctor's truck, should ever come on their plantation."

Feeling very thirsty, I took my way by the spring that evening. As I descended the hill o'ertopping it, I beheld the hind parts of a bear slowly being drawn into the cave. My heart bounded at the idea of killing a bear, and my plans were formed in a second. I had no dogs—the house was distant—and the bear becoming "small by degrees, and beautifully less." Every hunter knows, if you shoot a squirrel in the head when it's sticking out of a hole, ten to one he'll jump out; and I reasoned that if this were true regarding squirrels, might not the operation of the same principle extract a bear, applying it low down in the back.

Quick as thought I levelled my gun and fired, intending to give him the buckshot when his body appeared; but what was my surprise and horror, when, instead of a bear rolling out, the parts were jerked nervously in, and the well-known voice of young H. reached my ears.

"Murder! Hingins! h——l and kuckle-burs! Oh! Lordy! 'nuff!—'nuff!—take him off! Jis let me off this wunst, dad, and I'll never run mam's colt again! Oh! Lordy! Lordy! *all my brains blowed clean out!* Snakes! snakes!" yelled he, in a shriller tone, if possible, "H——l on the outside and snakes in the sink-hole! I'll die a Christian, anyhow, and if I die before I wake," and out scrambled poor H., pursued by a large black-snake.

If my life had depended on it, I could not have restrained my laughter. Down fell the gun, and down dropped I shrieking convulsively. The hill was steep, and over and over I went, until my head striking against a stump at the bottom, stopped me, half senseless. On recovering somewhat from the stunning blow, I found Hibbs upon me, taking satisfaction from me for having blowed out his brains. A contest ensued, and H. finally relinquished his hold, but I saw from the knitting of his brows, that the bear-storm, instead of being over, was just brewing. "Mr. Tensas," he said with awful dignity, "I'm sorry I put into you 'fore you cum to, but you're at yourself now, and as you've tuck a shot at me, it's no more than far I should have a chance 'fore the hunt's up."

It was with the greatest difficulty I could get H. to bear with me until I explained the mistake; but as soon as he learned it, he broke out in a huge laugh. "Oh, Dod busted! that's 'nuff; you has my pardon. I ought to know'd you didn't 'tend it; 'sides, you jis scraped the skin. I war wus skeered than hurt, and if you'll go to the house and beg me off from the old folks, I'll never let on you cuddent tell copperas breeches from bar-skin."

Promising that I would use my influence, I proposed taking a drink, and that he should tell me how he had incurred his parent's anger. He assented, and after we had inspected the cave, and seen that it held no other serpent than the one we craved, we entered its cool recess, and H. commenced.

"You see, Doc, I'd heered so much from mam 'bout her dad's Shumach and his nigger Swage, and the mile a minute, and the Croton water what was gin him, and how she bleved that if it warn't for bettin', and the cussin' and fightin', running race-hosses warn't the sin folks said it war; and if they war anything to make her 'gret gettin' religion and jinin' the church, it war cos she couldn't 'tend races, and have a race-colt of her own to comfort her 'clinin' years, sich as her daddy had afore her, till she got me; so I couldn't rest for wantin' to see a hoss-race, and go shares, p'raps, in the colt she war wishin' for. And then I'd think what sort of a hoss I'd want him to be—a quarter nag, a mile critter, or a hoss wot could run (fur all mam says it can't be did) a whole four mile at a stretch. Sometimes I think I'd rather own a quarter nag, for the suspense wouldn't long be hung, and then we could run up the road to old Nick Bamer's cow-pen, and Sally is almost allers out thar in the cool of the evenin'; and in course we wouldn't be so cruel as to run the poor critter in the heat of the day. But then agin, I'd think I'd rather have a miler,—for the 'citement would be greater, and we could run down the road to old Wither's orchard, an' his gal Miry is frightfully fond of sunnin' herself thar, when she 'spects me 'long, and she'd hear of the race, certain; but then thar war the four miler for my thinkin', and I'd knew'd in such case the 'citement would be greatest of all, and you know, too, from dad's stable to the grocery is jist four miles, an' in case of any 'spute, all hands would be willin' to run over, even if it had to be tried a dozen times. So I never could 'cide on which sort of a colt to wish for. It was fust one, then t'others, till I was nearly 'stracted, and when mam, makin' me religious, told me one night to say grace, I jes shut my eyes, looked pious, and yelled out,

'D——n it, go!' and in 'bout five minutes arter, came near kickin' dad's stumak off, under the table, thinkin' I war spurrin' my critter in a tight place. So I found the best way was to get the hoss fust, and then 'termine whether it should be Sally Bamers, and the cow-pen; Miry Withers, and the peach orchard; or Spillman's grocery, with the bald face.

"You've seed my black colt, that one that dad's father gin me in his will when he died, and I 'spect the reason he wrote that will war, that he might have wun then, for it's more then he had when he was alive, for granma war a monstrus overbearin' woman. The colt would cum up in my mind, every time I'd think whar I was to git a hoss. 'Git out!' said I at fust—*he* never could run, and 'sides if he could, mam rides him now, an he's too old for anything, 'cept totin her and bein' called mine; for you see, though he war named Colt, yet for the old lady to call him old, would bin like the bar 'fecting contempt for the rabbit, on account of the shortness of his tail.

"Well, thought I, it does look sorter unpromisin', but its colt or none; so I 'termined to put him in trainin' the fust chance. Last Saturday, who should cum ridin' up but the new cirkut preacher, a long-legged, weakly, sickly, never-contented-onless-the-best-on-the-plantation-war-cooked-fur-him sort of a man; but I didn't look at him twice, his hoss was the critter that took my eye; for the minute I looked at him, I knew him to be the same hoss as Sam Spooner used to win all his splurgin' dimes with, the folks said, and wot he used to ride past our house so fine on. The hoss war a heap the wuss for age and change of masters; for preachers, though they're mity 'ticular 'bout thar own comfort, seldom tends to thar hosses, for one is privit property and t' other generally borried. I seed from the way the preacher rid, that he didn't know the animal he war straddlin'; but I did, and I 'termined I wouldn't lose sich a chance of trainin' Colt by the side of a hoss wot had run real races. So that night, arter prayers and the folks was abed, I and Nigger Bill tuck the hosses and carried them down to the pastur'. It war a forty-aker lot, and consequently jist a quarter across—for I thought it best to promote Colt, by degrees, to a four-miler. When we got thar, the preacher's hoss showed he war willin'; but Colt, dang him! commenced nibblin' a fodder-stack over the fence. I nearly cried for vexment, but an idea struck me; I hitched the critter, and told Bill to get on Colt and stick tight wen I giv' the word. Bill got reddy, and unbeknownst to him I pulled up a bunch of nettles, and, as I clapped them under Colt's tail, yelled, 'Go!' Down shut his graceful like a steeltrap, and away he shot so quick an' fast that he jumpt clean out from under Bill, and got nearly to the end of the quarter 'fore the nigger toch the ground: he lit on his head, and in course warn't hurt—so we cotched Colt, an' I mounted him.

"The next time I said 'go' he showed that age hadn't spiled his legs or memory. Bill an' me 'greed we could run him now, so Bill mounted Preacher and we got ready. Thar war a narrer part of the track 'tween two oaks, but as it war near the end of the quarter, I 'spected to pass Preacher 'fore we got thar, so I warn't afraid of barkin' my shins.

"We tuck a fair start, and off we went like a peeled ingun, an' I soon 'scovered that it warn't such an easy matter to pass Preacher, though Colt dun delightful; we got nigh the trees, and Preacher warn't past yet, an' I 'gan to get skeered, for it warn't more than wide enuf for a horse and a half; so I hollered to Bill to hold up, but the imperdent nigger turned his ugly pictur, and said, 'he'd be cussed if he warn't goin' to play his han' out.' I gin him to understand he'd better fix for a foot-race when we stopt, and tried to hold up Colt, but he wouldn't stop. We reached the oaks, Colt tried to pass Preacher, Preacher tried to pass Colt, and cowollop, crosh, cochunk! we all cum down like 'simmons arter frost. Colt got up and won the race; Preacher tried hard to rise, but one hind leg had got threw the stirrup, an' t' other in the head stall, an' he had to lay still, doubled up like a long nigger in a short bed. I lit on my feet, but Nigger Bill war gone entire. I looked up in the fork of one of the oaks, and thar he war sittin', lookin' very composed on surroundin' nature. I couldn't git him down till I promised not to hurt him for disobeyin' orders, when he slid down. We'd 'nuff racin' for that night, so we put up the hosses and went to bed.

"Next morning the folks got ready for church, when it was diskivered that the hosses had got out. I an' Bill started off to look for them; we found them cleer off in the field, tryin' to git in the pastur' to run the last night's race over, old Blaze, the reverlushunary mule, bein' along to act as judge.

"By the time we got to the house it war nigh on to meetin' hour; and dad had started to the preachin', to tell the folks to sing on, as preacher and mam would be 'long bimeby. As the passun war in a hurry, and had been complainin' that his creetur war dull, I 'suaded him to put on uncle Jim's spurs what he fotch from Mexico. I saddled the passun's hoss, takin' 'ticular pains to let the saddle-blanket come down low in the flank. By the time these fixins war threw, mam war 'head nigh on to a quarter. 'We must ride on, passun,' I said, 'or the folks 'll think we is lost.' So I whipt up the mule I rid, the passun chirrupt and chuct to make his crittur gallop, but the animal didn't mind him a pic. I 'gan to snicker, an' the passun 'gan to git vext; sudden he thought of his spurs, so he ris up, an' drove them *vim* in his hoss's flanx, till they went through his saddle-blanket, and like to bored his nag to the holler. By gosh! but it war a quickener—the hoss kickt till the passun had to hug him round the neck to keep from pitchin' him over his head. He next jumpt up 'bout as high as a rail fence, passun holdin' on and tryin' to git his spurs—but they war lockt— his breeches split plum across with the strain, and the piece of wearin' truck wot's next the skin made a monstrous putty flag as the old hoss, like drunkards to a barbacue, streakt it up the road.

"Mam war ridin' slowly along, thinkin' how sorry she was, cos Chary Dolin, who always led her off, had sich a bad cold, an' wouldn't be able to 'sist her singin' to-day. She war practisin' the hymns, and had got as far as whar it says, 'I have a race to run,' when the passun huv in sight, an' in 'bout the dodgin' of a die-dapper, she found thar war truth in the words, for the colt, hearin' the hoss cumin' up behind, began to show symptoms of runnin'; but when he heard the passun holler 'wo! wo!' to his hoss, he thought it war me shoutin' 'go!' and sure 'nuff off they started jis as the passun got up even; so it war a fair race. Whoop! git out, but it war egsitin'—the dust flew, and the rail-fence ap-peered strate as a rifle. Thar war the passun, his legs fast to the critter's flanx, arms lockt round his neck, face as pale as a rabbit's belly, and the white flag streemin' far behind—and thar war Mam, fust on one side, then on t'other, her new caliker swelled up round her like a bear with the dropsy, the old lady so much surprized she cuddent ride steddy, an' tryin' to stop her colt, but he war too well trained to stop while he heard 'go!' Mam got 'sited at last, and her eyes 'gan to glimmer like she seen her daddy's ghost axin' 'if he ever trained up a child or a race-hoss to be 'fraid of a small brush on a Sunday,' she commenced ridin' beautiful; she braced herself up in the saddle, and began to make calkerlations how she war to win the race, for it war nose and nose, and she saw the passun spurrin' his critter every jump. She tuk off her shoe, and the way a number ten go-to-meetin' brogan commenced givin' a hoss particular Moses, were a caution to hoss-flesh—but still it kept nose and nose. She found she war carryin' too much weight for Colt, so she 'gan to throw off plunder, till nuthin' was left but her saddle and close, and the spurs kept tellin' still. The old woman commenced strippin' to lighten, till it wouldn't bin the clean thing for her to have taken off one dud more; an' then when she found it war no use while the spurs lasted, she got cantankerous. 'Passun,' said she, 'I'll be cust if it's fair or gentlemanly for you, a preacher of the gospel, to take advantage of an old woman this way, usin' spurs when you know *she* can't wear 'em—'taint Christian-like nuther,' and she burst into cryin'. 'Wo! Miss Hibbs! Wo! Stop! Madam! Wo! Your son!'—he attempted to say, when the old woman tuck him on the back of the head, and fillin' his mouth with right smart of a saddle-horn, and stoppin' the talk, as far as his share went for the present.

"By this time they'd got nigh on to the meetin'-house, and the folks were harkin' away on 'Old Hundred,' and wonderin' what could have become of the passun and mam Hibbs. One sister in a long beard axt another brethren in church, if she'd heered anything 'bout that New York preecher runnin' way with a woman old enough to be his muther. The brethrens gin a long sigh an' groaned 'it ain't possible! marciful heavens! you don't 'spicion?' wen the sound of the hosses comin', roused them up like a touch of the agur, an' broke off their sarpent-talk. Dad run out to see what was to pay, but when he seed the hosses so close together, the passun spurrin', and mam ridin' like close war skase whar she cum, he knew her fix in a second, and 'tarmined to help her; so clinchin' a saplin', he hid 'hind a stump 'bout ten steps off, and held on for the hosses. On they went in beautiful style, the passun's spurs tellin' terrible, and mam's shoe operatin' 'no small pile of punkins,' —passun stretched out the length of two hosses, while mam sot as stiff and strate as a bull yearling in his fust fight, hittin' her nag, fust on one side, next on t'other, and the third for the passun, who had chawed the horn till little of the saddle, and less of his teeth war left, and his voice sounded as holler as a jackass-nicker in an old saw-mill.

"The hosses war nose and nose, jam up together so close that mam's last kiverin' and passun's flag had got lockt, an' 'tween bleached domestic and striped linsey made a beautiful banner for the pious racers.

"On they went like a small arthquake, an' it seemed like it war goin' to be a draun race; but dad, when they got to him, let down with all his might on colt, scarin' him so bad that he jumpt clean ahead of passun, beatin' him by a neck, buttin' his own head agin the meetin'-house, an' pitchin' mam, like a lam for the sacryfise, plum through the winder 'mongst the mourners, leavin' her only garment flutterin' on a nail in the sash. The men shot their eyes and scrambled outen the house, an' the women gin mam so much of their close that they like to put themselves in the same fix.

"The passun quit the circuit, and I haven't been home yet."

SIMON SUGGS

by Johnson J. Hooper

(1815–1863)

SIMON BECOMES CAPTAIN

By reference to memoranda, contemporaneously taken, of incidents to be recorded in the memoirs of Captain Suggs, we find that we have reached the most important period in the history of our hero—his assumption of a military command. And we beg the reader to believe, that we approach this portion of our subject with a profound regret at our own incapacity for its proper illumination. Would that thy pen, O! Kendall, were ours! Then would thy hero and ours—the nation's Jackson and the country's Suggs—go down to far posterity, equal in fame and honors, as in deeds! But so the immortal gods have not decreed! Not to Suggs was Amos given! Aye, jealous of his mighty feats, the thundering Jove denied an historian worthy of his puissance! Would that, like Cæsar, he could write himself! Then, indeed, should Harvard yield him honors, and his country—justice!

Early in May of the year of grace—and excessive bank issues —1836, the Creek war was discovered to have broken out. During that month several persons, residing in the county of Tallapoosa, were cruelly murdered by the "inhuman savages"; and an exceedingly large number of the peaceful citizens of the state— men, women and children—excessively frightened. Consternation seized all! "Shrieks inhuman" rent the air! The more remote from the scenes of blood, the greater the noise. The yeomanry of the country—those to whom, as we are annually told, the nation looks with confidence in all her perils—packed up their carts and wagons, and "incontinently" departed for more peaceful regions! We think we see them now, "strung along the road," a day or two after the intelligence of the massacres below had reached the "settlement" of Captain Suggs! There goes old man Simmons, with his wife and three daughters, together with two feather beds, a few chairs, and a small assortment of pots and ovens, in a cart drawn by a bob-tail, gray pony. On the top-most bed, and forming the apex of this pile of animate and inanimate "luggage," sits

308

the old tom-cat, whom the youngest daughter would not suffer to remain lest he might come to harm. "Who knows," she exclaims, "*what* they might do to the poor old fellow?" On they toil! the old man's head, ever and anon, turned back to see if they are pursued by the remorseless foe; while the wife and daughters scream direfully, every ten minutes, as they discover in the distance a cow or a hog—"Oh, they'll kill us! they'll skelp us! they'll tar us all *to* pieces! Oh, Lord! daddy! Oh, Lord!" But the old tom-cat sits there, gravely and quietly, the very incarnation of tom philosophy!

It was on Sunday that the alarm was sounded in the "Suggs settlement," and most of the neighbours were in attendance upon the "preaching of the word" by brother Snufflenosey, at Poplar Spring meeting-house, when the "runner" who brought the woful tidings, disclosed them at old Tom Rollins', by yelling, as he sat on his horse before the door,—"the Injuns is a-killin every body below! I aint got time to stop! tell the neighbours!" Now, old Mr. Rollins and the "gals" were already at meeting, but the old lady, having staid behind "to fix up a leetle," was, at the identical moment of the messenger's arrival, *en chemise* before a very small glass set in a frame of red paper, preparing to adorn her person with divers new articles of apparel, inclusive of a new blue-and-red calico gown. But no sooner did her mind comprehend the purport of the words from without, than she sprang out of the house, "accoutred as she was," shrieking at every bound, "the Injuns! the Injuns!"—nor stopped until with face, neck, and bosom crimson as a strutting gobbler's snout, she burst into the meeting-house, and having once more screamed "the Injuns!" fell exhausted, at full length, upon the floor. "Will any of the brethering lend me a horse?" asked the Reverend Mr. Snufflenosey, wildly, as he bounded out of the pulpit, in very creditable style— "Wont *none* of you lend me one?" he repeated emphatically; and obtaining no answer, dashed off precipitately afoot! Then went up to Heaven the screams of fifty frightened women, in one vast discord, more dreadful than the war-squalls of a hundred cats in fiercest battle. Men, too, looked pale and trembled, while, strange to relate, all of the dozen young babies in attendance silently dilated their astonished eyes—struck utterly dumb at being so signally beaten at their own peculiar game!

At length an understanding was somehow effected, that Taylor's store, five miles thence, should be the place of rendezvous, for that night at least; and then Mr. Snufflenosey's congregation tumbled itself forth as expeditiously as was possible.

Simon was "duly" at the store with his family, when the wagon, cart, and pony loads of "badly-scared" mortality began to arrive in the afternoon. He was there of course, and he was in his element. Not that Suggs is particularly fond of danger—albeit, he is a hero—but because he delighted in the noise and confusion, the fun and the free drinking, incident to such occasions. And he enjoyed these to the uttermost now, because he was well informed as to the state of feeling of the Indians, in all the country for ten miles around, and knew there was no danger. But Simon did not disclose this to the terrified throng at the store. Not he! Suggs was never the man to destroy his own importance in that sort of way. On the contrary, he magnified the danger, and endeavoured to impress upon the minds of the miscellaneous crowd "then and there" assembled, that he, Simon Suggs, was the only man at whose hands they could expect a deliverance from the imminent peril which impended.

"Gentle*men*," said he impressively, "this here is a criterkle time; the wild savage of the forest are beginnin' of a bloody, hostile war, which they're not a-goin' to spar nither age nor sek—not even to the women and children!"

"Gracious Lord above! what *is* a body to do!" exclaimed the portly widow Haycock, who was accounted wealthy, in consideration of the fact that she had a hundred dollars in money, and was the undisputed owner of one entire negro—"we shall all be skelped, and our truck all burnt up and destr'yed! What shall we do!"

"That's the question," remarked Simon, as he stooped to draw a glass of whiskey from a barrel of that article—the only thing on sale in the "store"—"that's the question. Now, as for you women-folks"—here Suggs dropped a lump of brown sugar in his whiskey, and began to stir it with his finger, looking intently in the tumbler, the while—"as for you women-folks, it's plain enough what *you've* got to do"—here Simon tasted the liquor and added a little more sugar—"plain *enough!* You've only got to look to the Lord and hold your jaws; for that's all you *kin* do! But what's the 'sponsible *men*"—taking his finger out of the tumbler, and drawing it through his mouth—"of this crowd to do? The inemy will be down upon us right away, and before mornin'"—Simon drank half the whiskey—"blood will flow like—like"—the Captain was bothered for a simile, and looked around the room for one, but finding none, continued—"like all the world! Yes, like all the world"—an idea suggested itself—"and the Tallapussey river! It'll pour out," he continued, as his fancy got rightly to work, "like a great guljin ocean!—d——d ef it don't!" And then Simon swallowed the rest of the whiskey, threw the tumbler down, and looked around to observe the effect of this brilliant exordium.

The effect was tremendous!

Mrs. Haycock clasped her hands convulsively, and rolled up her eyes until the "whites" only could be seen. Old Mrs. Rollins—who by this time was fully clothed—and her two daughters had what Simon termed the "high-strikes" in one corner of the room, and kicked up their heels at a prodigious rate; while in another, a group of young women hugged one another most affectionately, sobbing hysterically all the time. Old granny Gilbreth sat in the middle of the floor, rocking her body back and forth, striking the palms of her hands on the planks as she bent forward, and clapping them together as she re-attained the perpendicular.

"My apinion," continued Simon, as he stooped to draw another tumbler of whiskey; "my apinion, folks, is this here. We ought to form a company right away, and make some man capting that aint afeard to fight—mind what I say now—*that—aint— afeard—to—fight!*—some sober, stiddy feller"—here he sipped a little from the tumbler—"that's a good hand to manage women and keep 'em from hollerin—which they're a-needin' somethin' of the sort most damdibly, and I eech to git holt o' that one a-making that devilish racket in the corner, thar"—the noise in the corner was suddenly suspended—"and more'n all, a man that's acquainted with the country and the ways of the Injuns!" Having thus spoken, Suggs drank off the rest of the whiskey, threw himself into a military attitude, and awaited a reply.

"Suggs is the man," shouted twenty voices.

"Keep close to *him*, and you'll never git hurt," said a diminutive, yellow-faced, spindle-legged young man.

"D'ye think so now?" exclaimed Simon furiously, as he "planted" a tremendous kick on that part of the joker's person at which the boot's point is most naturally directed. "D'ye think so now? Take *that* along, and next time keep your jaw, you slink, or I'll kick more clay outen you in a minute, than you can eat again in a month, you durned, little, dirt-eatin' deer-face!"

"Keep the children outen the way," said the little fellow, as he lay sprawling in the farthest corner of the room; "ef you don't, *Cap'en* Suggs will whip 'em all. He's a sight on children and people what's got the *yaller janders!*"

Simon heeded not the sarcasm, but turning to the men he asked—

"Now gentle*men*, who'll you have for capting?"

"Suggs! Suggs! Suggs!" shouted a score and a half of masculine voices.

The women said nothing—only frowned.

"Gentle*men*," said Simon, a smile of gratified, but subdued pride playing about his mouth; "Gentle*men*, my respects—ladies, the same to you!"—and the Captain bowed—"I'm more'n proud to sarve my country at the head of sich an independent and patriotic cumpany! Let who will run, gentle*men*, Simon Suggs will allers be found sticking thar, like a tick onder a cow's belly—"

"Whar do you aim to bury your dead Injuns, Cap'en?" sarcastically inquired the little dirt-eater.

"I'll bury *you*, you little whifflin fice," said Captain Suggs in a rage; and he dashed at yellow-legs furiously.

"Not afore a body's dead, I reckon," replied the dirt-eater, running round the room, upsetting the women and trampling the children, in his efforts to escape. At last he gained the door, out of which he bounced and ran off.

"Durn the little cuss," said the Captain, when he saw that pursuit would be useless; "I oughtent to git aggrawated at him, no how. He's a poor signifiken runt, that's got the mark of the huckle-berry ponds on his legs yit, whar the water come to when he was a-getherin' 'em, in his raisin' in Northkurliny. But I must put a stop to sich, and that right away"; and striding to the door, out of which he thrust his head, he made proclamation: "Oh yes! gentle*men*! Oh yes! This here store-house and two acres all round is now onder *martial law!* If any man or woman don't mind my orders, I'll have 'em shot right away; and children to be whipped accordin' to size. By order of me, Simon Suggs, Capting of the"— the Captain paused.

"Tallapoosy Vollantares," suggested Dick Cannifax.

"The Tallapoosy Vollantares," added Suggs, adopting the suggestion; "so let every body look out, and walk the chalk!"

Thus was formed the nucleus of that renowned band of patriot soldiers, afterwards known as the "FORTY THIEVES"—a name in the highest degree inappropriate, inasmuch as the company, from the very best evidence we have been able to procure, never had upon its roll, at any time, a greater number of names than *thirty-nine!*

As became a prudent commander, Captain Suggs, immediately after the proclamation of martial law, set about rendering his position as strong as possible. A rude rail fence near by was removed and made to enclose the log store, and another building of the same sort, which was used as a stable. The company was then paraded, and a big drink dealt out to each man, and five men were detailed to serve as sentinels, one at each corner of the enclosure, and one at the fence in front of the store door. The Captain then announced that he had appointed Andy Snipes, "fust lewtenant," Bird Stinson "sekkunt ditto," and Dave Lyon "sarjunt."

The guard was set, the women summarily quieted, the mass of the company stowed away in the stable for the night; and the Captain and "Lewtenant Snipes" sat down, with a bottle of bald-face between them, to a social game of "six cards, seven up," by a fire in the middle of the enclosure. About this time, the widow Haycock desired to possess herself of a certain "plug" of tobacco, wherewithal to supply her pipe during the watches of the night. The tobacco was in her cart, which, with a dozen others, stood in the road twenty steps or so from the front door. Now, as the widow Haycock was arrayed rather grotesquely—in a red-flannel wrapper, with a cotton handkerchief about her head—she did not wish to be seen as she passed out. She therefore noiselessly slipped out, and, the sentinel having deserted his post for a few moments to witness the playing between his officers, succeeded in reaching her cart unobserved. As she returned, however, with the weed of comfort in her hand, she was challenged by the sentinel, who, hearing a slight noise, had come back to his post.

"Stand!" said he, as the old lady was climbing the fence.

"Blessed Master!" exclaimed Mrs. Haycock; but the soldier was too much frightened to observe that she spoke English, or to recognize her voice.

"Give the counter-sign or I'll shoot," said he, bringing his gun to a "present," but receding towards the fire as he spoke.

Instead of the counter-sign, Mrs. Haycock gave a scream, which the sentinel, in his fright, mistook for the war-whoop, and instantly fired. The widow dropped from the fence to the ground, on the outside, and the sentinel ran to the Captain's fire.

In a moment was heard the thundering voice of Captain Suggs:

"Turn out, men! Kumpny fo-r-m!"

The women in the store screamed, and the company formed immediately in front of the door. The Captain was convinced that the alarm was a humbug of some sort; but keeping up the farce, kept up his own importance.

"Bring your guns to a level with your breasts, and fire through the cracks of the fence!" he ordered.

An irregular volley was fired, which brought down a pony and a yoke of steers, haltered to their owner's carts in the road; and frightened "yellow-legs" (who had slyly taken lodgings in a little wagon) nearly to death.

"Over the fence now. Hooraw! my galyunt voluntares!" shouted the Captain, made enthusiastic by the discharge of the guns.

The company scaled the fence.

"Now charge baggonets! Hooraw! Let 'em have the cold steel, my brave boys!"

This manœuvre was executed admirably, considering the fact, that the company was entirely without bayonets or a foe. The men brought their pieces to the proper position, ran ten steps, and finding nothing else to pierce, drove the long, projecting ram-rods of their rifles deep in the mellow earth!

"Pickle all them skelps, Cap'en Suggs, or they'll *spile!*" said a derisive voice, which was recognized as belonging to Yellow-legs, and a light form flitted from among the wagons and carts, and was lost in the darkness.

"Somebody kill that critter!" said Suggs, much excited. But the "critter" had "evaporated."

A careful examination of the field of battle was now made, and the prostrate bodies of the pony, the oxen, and the widow Haycock discovered, lying as they had fallen. From the last a slight moaning proceeded. A light was soon brought.

"What's the matter, widder—hurt?" inquired Suggs, raising up one of Mrs. Haycock's huge legs upon his foot, by way of ascertaining how much life was left.

"Only dead—that's all," said the widow as her limb fell heavily upon the ground, with commendable resignation.

"Pshaw!" said Suggs, "you aint bad hurt. Whar-abouts did the bullet hit?"

SIMON SUGGS

The frontispiece of *Adventures of Simon Suggs* (1845) was drawn by F. H. Darley, who illustrated many of the humorous books published in the forties and fifties. This is perhaps the best of his illustrations.

"All over! *only* shot to pieces! It makes *no* odds tho'—kleen through and through—I'm a-goin' mighty fast!" replied the widow, as four stout men raised her from the ground and carried her into the house, where her wounds were demonstrated to consist of a contusion on the bump of philo-progenitiveness, and the loss of a half square inch of the corrugated integument of her left knee.

Captain Suggs and Lieutenant Snipes now resumed their game.

"Lewtenant,"—said Suggs, as he dealt the cards—"we must—there's the tray for low—we must *court-martial* that old 'oman in the mornin'."

"'Twon't do, Capting—the tray I mean—to be sure we must! She's vierlated the rules of war!"

"And Yaller-legs, *too!*" said Suggs.

"Yes, yes; and Yaller-legs, too, ef we kin ketch him," replied Lieutenant Snipes.

"Yes, d——d ef I don't!—court-martial 'em both, as sure as the sun rises—*drum-head* court-martial at that!"

Simon Suggs Attends a Camp-Meeting

Captain Suggs found himself as poor at the conclusion of the Creek war, as he had been at its commencement. Although no "arbitrary," "despotic," "corrupt," and "unprincipled" judge had fined him a thousand dollars for his proclamation of martial law at Fort Suggs, or the enforcement of its rules in the case of Mrs. Haycock; yet somehow—the thing is alike inexplicable to him and to us—the money which he had contrived, by various shifts, to obtain, melted away and was gone forever. To a man like the Captain, of intense domestic affections, this state of destitution was most distressing. "He could stand it himself—didn't care a d——n for it, no way," he observed, "but the old woman and the children; *that* bothered him!"

As he sat one day, ruminating upon the unpleasant condition of his "financial concerns," Mrs. Suggs informed him that "the sugar and coffee was nigh about out," and that there were not "a dozen j'ints and middlins, *all put together*, in the smoke-house." Suggs bounced up on the instant, exclaiming, "D——n it! *somebody* must suffer!" But whether this remark was intended to convey the idea that he and his family were about to experience the want of the necessaries of life; or that some other, and as yet unknown, individual should "suffer" to prevent that prospective exigency, must be left to the commentators, if perchance any of that ingenious class of persons should hereafter see proper to write notes for this history. It is enough for us that we give all the facts in this connection, so that ignorance of the subsequent conduct of Captain Suggs may not lead to an erroneous judgment in respect to his words.

Having uttered the exclamation we have repeated—and perhaps, hurriedly walked once or twice across the room—Captain Suggs drew on his famous old green-blanket overcoat, and ordered his horse, and within five minutes was on his way to a camp-meeting, then in full blast on Sandy Creek, twenty miles distant, where he hoped to find amusement, at least. When he arrived there, he found the hollow square of the encampment filled with people, listening to the mid-day sermon, and its dozen accompanying "exhortations." A half-dozen preachers were dispensing the word; the one in the pulpit, a meek-faced old man, of great simplicity and benevolence. His voice was weak and cracked, notwithstanding which, however, he contrived to make himself heard occasionally, above the din of the exhorting, the singing, and the shouting which were going on around him. The rest were walking to and fro, (engaged in the other exercises we have indicated), among the "mourners"—a host of whom occupied the seat set apart for their especial use—or made personal appeals to the mere spectators. The excitement was intense. Men and women rolled about on the ground, or lay sobbing or shouting in promiscuous heaps. More than all, the negroes sang and screamed and prayed. Several, under the influence of what is technically called "the jerks," were plunging and pitching about with convulsive energy. The great object of all seemed to be, to see who could make the greatest noise—

> "And each—for madness ruled the hour—
> Would try his own expressive power."

"Bless my poor old soul!" screamed the preacher in the pulpit; "ef yonder aint a squad in that corner that we aint got one outen yet! It'll never do"—raising his voice—"you must come outen that! Brother Fant, fetch up that youngster in the blue coat! I see the Lord's a-workin' upon him! Fetch him along—glory—yes!—hold to him!"

"Keep the thing warm!" roared a sensual seeming man, of stout mould and florid countenance, who was exhorting among a bevy of young women, upon whom he was lavishing caresses. "Keep the thing warm, breethring!—come to the Lord, honey!" he added, as he vigorously hugged one of the damsels he sought to save.

"Oh, I've got him!" said another in exulting tones, as he led up a gawky youth among the mourners—"I've got him—he tried to git off, but—ha! Lord!"—shaking his head as much as to say, it took a smart fellow to escape him—"ha! Lord!"—and he wiped the perspiration from his face with one hand, and with the other, patted his neophyte on the shoulder—"he couldn't do it! No! Then he tried to argy wi' me—but bless the Lord!—he couldn't do that nother! Ha! Lord! I tuk him, fust in the Old Testament—bless the Lord!—and I argyed him all thro' Kings—then I throwed him into Proverbs,—and from that, here we had it up and down, kleer down to the New Testament, and then I begun to see it work him!—then we got into Matthy, and from Matthy right straight along to Acts; and *thar* I throwed him! Y-e-s—L-o-r-d!"—assuming the nasal twang and high pitch which are, in some parts, considered the perfection of rhetorical art—"Y-e-s L-o-r-d! and h-e-r-e he is! Now g-i-t down thar," addressing the subject, "and s-e-e ef the L-o-r-d won't do somethin' f-o-r you!" Having thus deposited his charge among the mourners, he started out, summarily to convert another soul!

"Gl-o-*ree!*" yelled a huge, greasy negro woman, as in a fit of the jerks, she threw herself convulsively from her feet, and fell "like a thousand of brick," across a diminutive old man in a little round hat, who was speaking consolation to one of the mourners.

"Good Lord, have mercy!" ejaculated the little man earnestly and unaffectedly, as he strove to crawl from under the sable mass which was crushing him.

In another part of the square a dozen old women were singing. They were in a state of absolute ecstasy, as their shrill pipes gave forth.

> "I rode on the sky,
>   Quite ondestified I,
> And the moon it was under my feet!"

Near these last, stood a delicate woman in that hysterical condition in which the nerves are incontrollable, and which is vulgarly—and almost blasphemously—termed the "holy laugh." A hideous grin distorted her mouth, and was accompanied with a maniac's chuckle; while every muscle and nerve of her face twitched and jerked in horrible spasms.[1]

Amid all this confusion and excitement Suggs stood unmoved. He viewed the whole affair as a grand deception—a sort of "opposition line" running against his own, and looked on with a sort of professional jealousy. Sometimes he would mutter running comments upon what passed before him.

"Well now," said he, as he observed the full-faced brother who was "officiating" among the women, "that ere feller takes *my* eye!—thar he's been this half-hour, a-figurin amongst them galls, and's never said the fust word to nobody else. Wonder what's the reason these here preachers never hugs up the old, ugly women? Never seed one do it in my life—the sperrit never moves 'em that way! It's nater tho'; and the women, *they* never flocks round one o' the old dried-up breethring—bet two to one old splinter-legs thar,"—nodding at one of the ministers—"won't git a chance to say turkey to a good-lookin gall today! Well! Who blames 'em? Nater will be nater, all the world over; and I judge ef I was a preacher, I should save the purtiest souls fust, myself!"

While the Captain was in the middle of this conversation with himself, he caught the attention of the preacher in the pulpit, who inferring from an indescribable something about his appearance that he was a person of some consequence, immediately determined to add him at once to the church if it could be done; and to that end began a vigorous, direct personal attack.

"Breethring," he exclaimed, "I see yonder a man that's a sinner; I *know* he's a sinner! Thar he stands," pointing at Simon, "a missubble old crittur, with his head a-blossomin for the grave! A few more short years, and d-o-w-n he'll go to perdition, lessen the Lord have mer-cy on him! Come up here, you old hoary-headed sinner, a-n-d git down upon your knees, a-n-d put up your cry for the Lord to snatch you from the bottomless pit! You're ripe for the devil—you're b-o-u-n-d for hell, and the Lord only knows what'll become on you!"

[1] The reader is requested to bear in mind, that the scenes described in this story are not *now* to be witnessed. Eight or ten years ago, all classes of population of the Creek country were very different from what they now are. Of course no disrespect is intended to any denomination of Christians. We believe that camp-meetings are not peculiar to any church, though most usual in the Methodist—a denomination whose respectability in Alabama is attested by the fact, that *very many* of its worthy clergymen and lay members hold honourable and profitable offices in the gift of the state legislature; of which, indeed, almost a controlling portion are themselves Methodists.

—Author's footnote

"D——n it," thought Suggs, "ef I only had you down in the krick swamp for a minit or so, *I'd* show you who's *old! I'd* alter your tune *mighty* sudden, you sassy, 'saitful old rascal!" But he judiciously held his tongue and gave no utterance to the thought.

The attention of many having been directed to the Captain by the preacher's remarks, he was soon surrounded by numerous well-meaning, and doubtless very pious persons, each one of whom seemed bent on the application of his own particular recipe for the salvation of souls. For a long time the Captain stood silent, or answered the incessant stream of exhortations only with a sneer; but at length, his countenance began to give token of inward emotion. First his eye-lids twitched—then his upper lip quivered—next a transparent drop formed on one of his eye-lashes, and a similar one on the tip of his nose—and, at last, a sudden bursting of air from nose and mouth, told that Captain Suggs was overpowered by his emotions. At the moment of the explosion, he made a feint as if to rush from the crowd, but he was in experienced hands, who well knew that the battle was more than half won.

"Hold to him!" said one—"it's a-workin in him as strong as a Dick horse!"

"Pour it into him," said another, "it'll all come right directly!"

"That's the way I love to see 'em do," observed a third; "when you begin to draw the water from their eyes, taint gwine to be long afore you'll have 'em on their knees!"

And so they clung to the Captain manfully, and half dragged, half led him to the mourner's bench; by which he threw himself down, altogether unmanned, and bathed in tears. Great was the rejoicing of the brethren, as they sang, shouted, and prayed around him—for by this time it had come to be generally known that the "convicted" old man was Captain Simon Suggs, the very "chief of sinners" in all that region.

The Captain remained grovelling in the dust during the usual time, and gave vent to even more than the requisite number of sobs, and groans, and heart-piercing cries. At length, when the proper time had arrived, he bounced up, and with a face radiant with joy, commenced a series of vaultings and tumblings, which "laid in the shade" all previous performances of the sort at that camp-meeting. The brethren were in ecstasies at this demonstrative evidence of completion of the work; and whenever Suggs shouted "Gloree!" at the top of his lungs, every one of them shouted it back, until the woods rang with echoes.

The effervescence having partially subsided, Suggs was put upon his pins to relate his experience, which he did somewhat in this style—first brushing the tear-drops from his eyes, and giving the end of his nose a preparatory wring with his fingers, to free it of the superabundant moisture:

"Friends," he said, "it don't take long to curry a short horse, accordin' to the old sayin', and I'll give you the perticklers of the way I was 'brought to a knowledge'"—here the Captain wiped his eyes, brushed the tip of his nose and snuffled a little—"in less'n no time."

"Praise the Lord!" ejaculated a bystander.

"You see I come here full o' romancin' and devilment, and jist to make game of all the purceedins. Well, sure enough, I done so for some time, and was a-thinkin how I should play some trick—"

"Dear soul alive! *don't* he talk sweet!" cried an old lady in black silk—"Whar's John Dobbs? You Sukey!" screaming at a negro woman on the other side of the square—"ef you don't hunt up your mass John in a minute, and have him here to listen to this 'sperience, I'll tuck you up when I git home and give you a hundred and fifty lashes, madam!—see ef I don't! Blessed Lord!" —referring again to the Captain's relation—"ain't it a *precious* 'scource!"

"I was jist a-thinkin' how I should play some trick to turn it all into redecule, when they began to come round me and talk. Long at fust I didn't mind it, but arter a little that brother"— pointing to the reverend gentleman who had so successfully carried the unbeliever through the Old and New Testaments, and who Simon was convinced was the "big dog of the tanyard" —"that brother spoke a word that struck me kleen to the heart, and run all over me, like fire in dry grass—"

"*I–I–I* can bring 'em!" cried the preacher alluded to, in a tone of exultation—"Lord thou knows ef thy servant can't stir 'em up, nobody else needn't try—but the glory aint mine! I'm a poor worrum of the dust," he added, with ill-managed affectation.

"And so from that I felt somethin' a-pullin' me inside—"

"Grace! grace! nothin' but grace!" exclaimed one; meaning that "grace" had been operating in the Captain's gastric region.

"And then," continued Suggs, "I wanted to git off, but they hilt me, and bimeby I felt so missuble, I had to go yonder"— pointing to the mourner's seat—"and when I lay down thar it got wuss and wuss, and 'peared like somethin' was a-mashin' down on my back—"

"That was his load o' sin," said one of the brethren—"never mind, it'll tumble off presently, see ef it don't!" and he shook his head professionally and knowingly.

"And it kept a-gittin heavier and heavier, ontwell it looked like it might be a four year old steer, or a big pine log, or somethin' of that sort—"

"Glory to my soul," shouted Mrs. Dobbs, "it's the sweetest talk I *ever* hearn! You Sukey! aint you got John yit? never mind, my lady, *I'll* settle wi' you!" Sukey quailed before the finger which her mistress shook at her.

"And arter awhile," Suggs went on, "'peared like I fell into a trance, like, and I seed—"

"Now we'll git the good on it!" cried one of the sanctified.

"And I seed the biggest, longest, rip-roarenest, blackest, scaliest—" Captain Suggs paused, wiped his brow, and ejaculated "Ah, L-o-r-d!" so as to give full time for curiosity to become impatience to know what he saw.

"*Sarpent!* warn't it?" asked one of the preachers.

"No, not a sarpent," replied Suggs, blowing his nose.

"Do tell us *what* it war, soul alive!—whar *is* John?" said Mrs. Dobbs.

"Allegator!" said the Captain.

"Alligator!" repeated every woman present, and screamed for very life.

Mrs. Dobbs' nerves were so shaken by the announcement, that after repeating the horrible word, she screamed to Sukey, "You Sukey, I say, you S-u-u-k-e-ey! ef you let John come a-nigh this way, whar the dreadful alliga—shaw! what am I thinkin' 'bout? 'Twarn't nothin' but a vishin!"

"Well," said the Captain in continuation, "the allegator kept a-comin' and a-comin' to'ards me, with his great long jaws a-gapin' open like a ten foot pair o' tailor's shears—"

"Oh! oh! oh! Lord! gracious above!" cried the women.

"Satan!" was the laconic ejaculation of the oldest preacher present, who thus informed the congregation that it was the devil which had attacked Suggs in the shape of an alligator.

"And then I concluded the jig was up, 'thout I could block his game some way; for I seed his idee was to snap off my head—"

The women screamed again.

"So I fixed myself jist like I was purfectly willin' for him to take my head, and rather he'd do it as not"—here the women shuddered perceptibly—"and so I hilt my head straight out"—the Captain illustrated by elongating his neck—"and when he come up and was a gwine to *shet down* on it, I jist pitched in a big rock which choked him to death, and that minit I felt the weight slide off, and I had the best feelins—sorter like you'll have from *good* sperrits—any body ever had!"

"Didn't I *tell* you so? Didn't I *tell* you so?" asked the brother who had predicted the off-tumbling of the load of sin. "Ha, Lord! fool *who*! I've been *all* along thar!—yes, *all along thar!* and I know every inch of the way jist as good as I do the road home!"—and then he turned round and round, and looked at all, to receive a silent tribute to his superior penetration.

Captain Suggs was now the "lion of the day." Nobody could pray so well, or exhort so movingly, as "brother Suggs." Nor did his natural modesty prevent the proper performance of appropriate exercises. With the reverend Bela Bugg (him to whom, under providence, he ascribed his conversion) he was a most especial favorite. They walked, sang, and prayed together for hours.

"Come, come up; thar's room for all!" cried brother Bugg, in his evening exhortation. "Come to the 'seat,' and ef you won't pray yourselves, let *me* pray for you!"

"Yes!" said Simon, by way of assisting his friend; "it's a game that all can win at! Ante up! ante up, boys—friends I mean—don't back out!"

"Thar aint a sinner here," said Bugg, "no matter ef his soul's black as a nigger, but what thar's room for him!"

"No matter what sort of a hand you've got," added Simon in the fulness of his benevolence; "take stock! Here am *I*, the wickedest and blindest of sinners—has spent my whole life in the sarvice of the devil—has now come in on *narry pair* and won a *pile!*" and the Captain's face beamed with holy pleasure.

"D-o-n-'t be afeard!" cried the preacher; "come along! the meanest won't be turned away! humble yourselves and come!"

"No!" said Simon, still indulging in his favourite style of metaphor; "the bluff game aint played here! No runnin' of a body off! Every body holds four aces, and when you bet, you win!"

And thus the Captain continued, until the services were concluded, to assist in adding to the number at the mourners' seat; and up to the hour of retiring, he exhibited such enthusiasm in the cause, that he was unanimously voted to be the most efficient addition the church had made during that meeting.

The next morning, when the preacher of the day first entered the pulpit, he announced that "brother Simon Suggs," mourning over his past iniquities, and desirous of going to work in the cause as speedily as possible, would take up a collection to found a church in his own neighbourhood, at which he hoped to make himself useful as soon as he could prepare himself for the ministry, which the preacher didn't doubt, would be in a very few weeks, as brother Suggs was "a man of mighty good *judgment*, and of a great discorse." The funds were to be collected by "brother Suggs," and held in trust by brother Bela Bugg, who was the financial officer of the circuit, until some arrangement could be made to build a suitable house.

"Yes, breethring," said the Captain, rising to his feet; "I want to start a little 'sociation close to me, and I want you all to help. I'm mighty poor myself, as poor as any of you—don't leave, breethring"—observing that several of the well-to-do were about to go off—"don't leave; ef you aint able to afford any thing, jist give us your blessin' and it'll be all the same!"

This insinuation did the business, and the sensitive individuals reseated themselves.

"It's mighty little of this world's goods I've got," resumed Suggs, pulling off his hat and holding it before him; "but I'll bury *that* in the cause any how," and he deposited his last five-dollar bill in the hat.

There was a murmur of approbation at the Captain's liberality throughout the assembly.

Suggs now commenced collecting, and very prudently attacked first the gentlemen who had shown a disposition to escape. These, to exculpate themselves from anything like poverty, contributed handsomely.

"Look here, breethring," said the Captain, displaying the bank-notes thus received, "brother Snooks has drapt a five wi' me, and brother Snodgrass a ten! In course 'taint expected that you *that aint as well off as them*, will give *as much;* let every one give *accordin'* to ther means."

This was another chain-shot that raked as it went! "Who so low" as not to be able to contribute as much as Snooks and Snodgrass?

"Here's all the *small* money I've got about me," said a burly old fellow, ostentatiously handing to Suggs, over the heads of a half dozen, a ten dollar bill.

"That's what I call maganimus!" exclaimed the Captain; "that's the way *every* rich man ought to do!"

These examples were followed, more or less closely, by almost all present, for Simon had excited the pride of purse of the congregation, and a very handsome sum was collected in a very short time.

The reverend Mr. Bugg, as soon as he observed that our hero had obtained all that was to be had at that time, went to him and inquired what amount had been collected. The Captain replied that it was still uncounted, but that it couldn't be much under a hundred.

"Well, brother Suggs, you'd better count it and turn it over to me now, I'm goin' to leave presently."

"No!" said Suggs—"can't do it!"

"Why?—what's the matter?" inquired Bugg.

"It's got to be *prayed over*, fust!" said Simon, a heavenly smile illuminating his whole face.

"Well," replied Bugg, "less go one side and do it!"

"No!" said Simon, solemnly.

Mr. Bugg gave a look of inquiry.

"You see that krick swamp?" asked Suggs—"I'm gwine down in *thar*, and I'm gwine to lay this money down *so*"—showing how he would place it on the ground—"and I'm gwine to git on these here knees"—slapping the right one—"and I'm *n-e-v-e-r* gwine to quit the grit ontwell I feel it's got the blessin'! And nobody aint got to be thar but me!"

Mr. Bugg greatly admired the Captain's fervent piety, and bidding him God-speed, turned off.

Captain Suggs "struck for" the swamp sure enough, where his horse was already hitched. "Ef them fellers aint done to a cracklin," he muttered to himself as he mounted, "*I*'ll never bet on two pair agin! They're peart at the snap game, theyselves; but they're badly lewed this hitch! Well! Live and let live is a good old motter, and it's my sentiments adzactly!" And giving the spur to his horse, off he cantered.

GEORGIA COMEDY

by William Tappan Thompson

(1812–1882)

Pineville, *December* 27, 1842.

To Mr. Thompson:—*Dear Sir*—Crismus is over, and the thing is done did! You know I told you in my last letter I was gwine to bring Miss Mary up to the chalk on Crismus. Well, I done it, slick as a whistle, though it come mighty nigh bein a serious bisness. But I'll tell you all about the whole circumstance.

The fact is, I's made my mind up more'n twenty times to jest go and come right out with the whole bisness; but whenever I got whar she was, and whenever she looked at me with her witchin eyes, and kind o' blushed at me, I always felt sort o' skeered and fainty, and all what I made up to tell her was forgot, so I couldn't think of it to save me. But you's a married man, Mr. Thompson, so I couldn't tell you nothin about poppin the question, as they call it. It's a mighty grate favour to ax of a pretty gall, and to people what aint used to it, it goes monstrous hard, don't it? They say widders don't mind it no more'n nothin. But I'm makin a transgression, as the preacher ses.

Crismus eve I put on my new suit, and shaved my face as slick as a smoothin iron, and after tea went over to old Miss Stallinses. As soon as I went into the parler whar they was all settin round the fire, Miss Carline and Miss Kesiah both laughed right out.

"There! there!" ses they, "I told you so! I know'd it would be Joseph."

"What's I done, Miss Carline?" ses I.

"You come under little sister's chicken bone, and I believe she know'd you was comin when she put it over the dore."

"No, I didn't—I didn't no such thing, now," ses Miss Mary, and her face blushed red all over.

"Oh, you needn't deny it," ses Miss Kesiah, "you belong to Joseph now, jest as sure as ther's any charm in chicken bones."

I know'd that was a first rate chance to say something, but

the dear little creeter looked so sorry and kep blushin so, I couldn't say nothin zactly to the pint! so I tuck a chair and reached up and tuck down the bone and put it in my pocket.

"What are you gwine to do with that old chicken bone now, Majer?" ses Miss Mary.

"I'm gwine to keep it as long as I live," ses I, "as a Crismus present from the handsomest gall in Georgia."

When I sed that, she blushed worse and worse.

"Aint you shamed, Majer?" ses she.

"Now you ought to give *her* a Crismus gift, Joseph, to keep all *her* life," sed Miss Carline.

"Ah," ses old Miss Stallins, "when I was a gall we used to hang up our stockins—"

"Why, mother!" ses all of 'em, "to say stockins right before—"

Then I felt a little streaked too, cause they was all blushin as hard as they could.

"Highty-tity!" ses the old lady—"what monstrous 'finement to be shore! I'd like to know what harm ther is in stockins. People now-a-days is gitting so mealy-mouthed they can't call nothing by its right name, and I don't see as they's any better than the old time people was. When I was a gall like you, child, I used to hang up my stockins and git 'em full of presents."

The galls kep laughin and blushin.

"Never mind," ses Miss Mary, "Majer's got to give me a Crismus gift—won't you, Majer?"

"Oh, yes," ses I, "you know I promised you one."

"But I didn't mean *that*," ses she.

"I've got one for you, what I want you to keep all your life, but it would take a two bushel bag to hold it," ses I.

"Oh, that's the kind," ses she.

"But will you promise to keep it as long as you live?" ses I.

"Certainly I will, Majer."

—"Monstrous 'finement now-a-days—old people don't know nothin about perliteness," said old Miss Stallins, jest gwine to sleep with her nittin in her lap.

"Now you hear that, Miss Carline," ses I. "She ses she'll keep it all her life."

"Yes, I will," ses Miss Mary—"but what is it?"

"Never mind," ses I, "you hang up a bag big enough to hold it and you'll find out what it is, when you see it in the mornin."

Miss Carline winked at Miss Kesiah, and then whispered to

her—then they both laughed and looked at me as mischievous as they could. They 'spicioned something.

"You'll be shore to give it to me now, if I hang up a bag," ses Miss Mary.

"And promise to keep it," ses I.

"Well, I will, cause I know that you wouldn't give me nothing that wasn't worth keepin."

They all agreed they would hang up a bag for me to put Miss Mary's Crismus present in, on the back porch, and about ten o'clock I told 'em good evenin and went home.

I sot up till mid-night, and when they was all gone to bed I went softly into the back gate, and went up to the porch, and thar, shore enough, was a great big meal-bag hangin to the jice. It was monstrous unhandy to git to it, and I was termined not to back out. So I sot some chairs on top of a bench and got hold of the rope and let myself down into the bag; but jest as I was gittin in, it swung agin the chairs, and down they went with a terrible racket; but nobody didn't wake up but Miss Stallinses old cur dog, and here he come rippin and tearin through the yard like rath, and round and round he went tryin to find what was the matter. I scrooch'd down in the bag and didn't breathe louder nor a kitten, for fear he'd find me out, and after a while he quit barkin.

The wind begun to blow bominable cold, and the old bag kep turnin round and swingin so it made me sea-sick as the mischief. I was afraid to move for fear the rope would break and let me fall, and thar I sot with my teeth rattlin like I had a ager. It seemed like it would never come daylight, and I do believe if I didn't love Miss Mary so powerful I would froze to death; for my heart was the only spot that felt warm, and it didn't beat more'n two licks a minit, only when I thought how she would be supprised in the mornin, and then it went in a canter. Bimeby the cussed old dog come up on the porch and begun to smell about the bag, and then he barked like he thought he'd treed something. "Bow! wow! wow!" ses he. Then he'd smell agin, and try to git up to the bag. "Git out!" ses I, very low, for fear the galls mought hear me. "Bow! wow!" ses he. "Be gone! you bominable fool," ses I, and I felt all over in spots, for I spected every minit he'd nip me, and what made it worse, I didn't know whar abouts he'd take hold. "Bow! wow! wow!" Then I tried coaxin—"Come here, good fellow," ses I, and whistled a little to him, but it wasn't no use. Thar he stood and kep up his everlastin whinin and barkin, all night. I couldn't tell when daylight was breakin, only by the chickens crowin, and I was monstrous glad to hear 'em, for if I'd had to stay thar one hour more, I don't believe I'd ever got out of that bag alive.

Old Miss Stallins come out fust, and as soon as she seed the bag, ses she,

"What upon yeath has Joseph went and put in that bag for Mary? I'll lay its a yearlin or some live animal, or Bruin wouldn't bark at it so."

She went in to call the galls, and I sot thar, shiverin all over so I couldn't hardly speak if I tried to—but I didn't say nothin. Bimeby they all come runnin out on the porch.

"My goodness! what is it?" ses Miss Mary.

"Oh, it's alive!" ses Miss Kesiah, "I seed it move."

"Call Cato, and make him cut the rope," ses Miss Carline, "and lets see what it is. Come here, Cato, and git this bag down."

"Don't hurt it for the world," ses Miss Mary.

Cato untied the rope that was round the jice, and let the bag down easy on the floor, and I tumbled out all covered with corn meal, from head to foot.

"Goodness gracious!" ses Miss Mary, "if it aint the Majer himself!"

"Yes," ses I, "and you know you promised to keep my Crismus present as long as you lived."

The galls laughed themselves almost to death, and went to brushin off the meal as fast as they could, sayin they was gwine to hang that bag up every Crismus till they got husbands too. Miss Mary—bless her bright eyes—she blushed as beautiful as a morning-glory, and sed she'd stick to her word. She was right out of bed, and her hair wasn't komed, and her dress wasn't fix'd at all, but the way she looked pretty was real distractin. I do believe if I was froze stiff, one look at her sweet face, as she stood thar lookin down to the floor with her roguish eyes, and her bright curls fallin all over her snowy neck, would have fotched me to. I tell you what, it was worth hanging in a meal bag from one Crismus to another to feel as happy as I have ever sense.

I went home after we had the laugh out, and sot by the fire till I got thawed. In the forenoon all the Stallinses come over to our house and we had one of the greatest Crismus dinners that ever was seed in Georgia, and I don't believe a happier company ever sot down to the same table. Old Miss Stallins and mother settled the match, and talked over every thing that ever happened in ther families, and laughed at me and Mary, and cried about ther dead husbands, cause they wasn't alive to see ther children married.

It's all settled now, 'cept we haint sot the weddin day. I'd like to have it all over at once, but young galls always like to be engaged a while, you know, so I spose I must wait a month or so. Mary (she ses I mustn't call her Miss Mary now) has been a good deal of trouble and botheration to me; but if you could see her you wouldn't think I ought to grudge a little sufferin to git sich a sweet little wife.

You must come to the weddin if you possibly kin, I'll let you know when. No more from

Your friend, till death,

JOS. JONES.

N.B. I like to forgot to tell you about cousin Pete. He got snapt on egnog when he heard of my ingagement, and he's been as meller as hoss-apple ever sense.

A Coon Hunt in a Fency Country

It is really astonishin what a monstrous sight of mischief ther is in a bottle of rum. If one of 'em was to be submitted to a analization as the doctors calls it, it would be found to contain all manner of devilment that ever entered the head of man, from cussin and stealin up to murder and whippin his own mother, and nonsense enough to turn all the men in the world out of ther senses. If a man's got any badness in him, let him drink whiskey, and it will bring it out jest as sassafras tea does the measles; and if he's a good-for-nothin sort of a feller, without no bad traits in partickeler, it'll bring out all his foolishness. It affects different people in different ways—it makes some men monstrous brave and full of fight, and some it makes cowards—some it makes rich and happy and some pore and miserable. And it has different effects on different people's eyes—some it makes see double, and some it makes so blind that they can't tell themselves from a side of bacon. One of the worst cases of rum-foolery that I've heard of for a long time tuck place in Pineville last fall.

Bill Sweeney and Tom Culpepper is the two greatest old coveys in our settlement for coon-huntin. The fact is, they don't do much of any thing else, and when *they* can't catch coons, it's a shore sign that coons is scarce. Well, one night they had every thing ready for a reglar hunt, but owin to some extra good fortin, Tom had got a pocket-pistol, as he called it, of genewine old Jimmaky rum. After takin a good startin horn, they went out on ther hunt, with ther lightwood torch a blazin, and the dogs a barkin and yelpin like they was crazy. They struck out into the woods, gwine in the direction of old Starlin Jones's new ground, a great place for coons. Every now and then they would stop to wait for the dogs, and then they would drink one another's health, until they begun to feel first-rate. On they went, chattin away about one thing and another, takin a nip now and then from Tom's bottle, not mindin much whar they was gwine. Bimeby they come to a fence. Well, over they got without much difficulty.

"Who's fence is this?" ses Bill.

"Taint no matter," ses Tom, "let's take a drink."

After takin a pull at the bottle, they went on agin, wonderin what upon yeath had come of the dogs. The next thing they come to was a terrible muddy branch. After gropin ther way through the bushes and briers and gittin on tother side, they tuck another drink. Fixin up ther torch and startin on agin, they didn't go but a little ways before they come to another branch, as bad as the first one, and a little further they come to another fence—a monstrous high one this time.

"Whar upon yeath is we got to, Culpepper?" ses Bill; "I never seed sich a heap of fences and branches in these parts."

"Why," ses Tom, "it's old Starlin's doins; you know he's always bildin fences and makin infernal improvements, as he calls 'em. But never mind; we's through 'em now."

"The devil we is," ses Bill; "why, here's the alfiredest high fence yit."

Shore enough, thar they was right agin another fence. By this time they begun to be considerable tired and limber in ther jints; and it was sich a terrible high fence. Tom drapped the last piece of the torch, and thar they was in the dark.

"Now you *is* done it!" ses Bill.

Tom knowd he had, but he thought it was no use to grieve over what couldn't be helped, so, ses he,

"Never mind, old hoss—come ahead, and I'll take you out," and the next minit, kerslash! he went into the water up to his neck.

Bill heard the splash, and he clung to the fence with both hands like he thought it was slewin round to throw him off.

"Hellow, Tom!" ses he, "whar in creation has you got to?"

"Here I is!" ses Tom, spittin the water out of his mouth, and coughin like he'd swallered something. "Look out, ther's another dratted branch here."

"Name o' sense, whar is we?" ses Bill. "If this isn't a fency country, dad fetch my buttons!"

"Yes, and a branchy one, too!" ses Tom, "and they is the thickest and the highest and the deepest that I ever seed in all my born days."

After a good deal of cussin and gruntin Bill got himself loose from the fence.

"Which way is you?" ses he.

"Here, right over the branch," ses Tom.

The next minit in Bill went, up to his middle in the branch.

"Come ahead," ses Tom, "and let's go home."

"Come thunder!" ses Bill, "in sich a place as this, whar a feller hain't more'n got his coat-tail unhitched from a fence before he's head and ears in a cussed branch."

Bill made a terrible job of gittin across the branch, which he swore was the deepest one yit. They managed to git together agin after feelin about in the dark a while, and, takin another drink, they sot out for home, cussin the fences and the branches, and helpin one another up now and then when they got ther legs tangled in the brush; but they hadn't gone more'n twenty yards before they found themselves in the middle of another branch. After gittin through the branch and gwine about twenty yards they was brung up all standin agin by another everlastin fence.

"Dad blame my picter," ses Bill, "if I don't think we's bewitched. Who upon yeath would go and build fences all over outdoors this way?"

It tuck 'em a long time to climb this fence, but when they got on top of it they found the ground on tother side without much trouble. This time the bottle was broke, and they come monstrous nigh havin a fight about the catastrofy. But it was a very good thing the licker was spilt, for after crossin three or four more branches and climbin as many more fences, it got to be daylight, when to ther great astonishment they found out that they had been climbin the same fence and wadin the same branch all night, not more'n a hundred yards from the place whar they first come to 'em.

Bill Sweeney ses he can't account for it no other way but that the licker sort o' turned ther heads; and he ses he really does believe if it hadn't gin out, they'd been climbin that same fence and wadin that same branch till now.

The Hoosier and the Salt Pile

It is very refreshin in these days of progress, after rattlin over the country for days and nights, at the rate of twenty miles a ower in a railroad car—with your mouth full of dust and smoke, and with sich a everlastin clatter in your ears that you can't hear yourself think—to git into a good, old-fashioned stage-coach. Ther's something sociable and cosey in stage-coach travelin, so different from the bustle and confusion of a railroad, whar people are whirled along "slam bang to eternal smash," like they wer so many bales and boxes of dry-goods and groceries, without so much as a chance of seein whar they're gwine, or of takin any interest in ther feller sufferers. I love to hear the pop of the whip and the interestin conversation between the driver and his horses; and I like the constant variation in the motion of the stage, the rattle of the wheels over the stones, the stillness of the drag through the heavy sand, the lunging and pitching into the ruts and gullies, the slow pull up the steep hills, the rush down agin, and the splashin of the horses' feet and the wheels in the water and mud. And then one has time to see the country he's passin through, to count the rails in the panels of the fences, and the wimen and children in the doors of the houses, to notice the appearance of the craps and the condition of the stock on the farms, and now and then to say a word to the people on the roadside. All these things is pleasant, after a long voyage on the railroad. But what's still more agreeable about stage-coach travelin, is that we have a oppertunity of makin the acquaintance of our feller passengers, of conversin with 'em and studdyin ther traits of character, which from the strikin contrast they often present, never fail to amuse if they don't interest our mind.

Some years ago I had a tolerably fair specimen of a stage-coach ride from Warrenton to Milledgeville. The road wasn't the best in the world, and didn't run through the most interestin part of Georgia, but we had a good team, a good stage, and a first-rate driver, what could sing like a camp-meetin and whistle like a locomotive, and the company was jest about as good a one as could be jumped up for sich a occasion. Ther was nine of us besides the driver, and I don't believe ther ever was a crowd of the same number that presented a greater variety of characters. Ther was a old gentleman in black, with big round spectacles, and a gold headed cane; a dandy gambler, with a big diamond breast-pin and more gold chains hangin round him than would hang him; a old hardshell preacher, as they call 'em in Gergia, with the biggest mouth and the ugliest teeth I ever seed; a circus clown, whose breath smelled strong enough of whiskey to upset the stage; a cross old maid, as ugly as a tar-bucket; a butiful young school-gall, with rosy cheeks and mischievous bright eyes; a cattle-drover from Indiany, who was gwine to New Orleans to git a army contract for beef, and myself.

For a while after we started from Warrenton nobody didn't have much to say. The young lady put her green vail over her face and leaned her head back in the corner; the old maid, after a row with the driver about her band-boxes, sot up straight in her seat and looked as sharp as a steel-trap; the old gentleman with the spectacles drummed his fingers on his cane and looked out of the coach-winder; the circus-man tried to look interestin; the gambler went to sleep; the preacher looked solemn; and the hoosier stuck his head out of the winder on his side to look at the cattle what we passed every now and then.

"This aint no great stock country," ses he to the old gentleman with the specs.

"No, sir," ses the old gentleman. "There's very little grazing here. The range in these parts is pretty much worn out."

Then ther was nothing said for some time. Bimeby the hoosier opened agin.

"It's the d——st place for 'simmon-trees and turkey-buzzards I ever did see."

The old gentleman didn't say nothin, and the preacher fetched a long groan. The young lady smiled through her vail, and the old maid snapped her eyes and looked sideways at the speaker.

"Don't make much beef down here, I reckon," ses the hoosier.

"No," ses the old gentleman.

"Well, I don't see how in the h——l they manage to live in a country whar ther aint no ranges, and they don't make no beef. A man aint considered worth a cuss in Indiany what hasn't got his brand on a hundred head or so of cattle."

"Your's is a great beef country, I believe," ses the old gentleman.

"Well, sir, it aint nothing else. A man that's got sense enough to foller his own cow-bell, with us, aint no danger of starvin. I'm gwine down to Orleans to see if I can't git a contract out of Uncle Sam, to feed the boys what's been lickin them infernal Mexicans so bad. I spose you've seed them cussed lies what's been in the newspapers about the Indiany boys at Bona Vista?"

"I've read some accounts of the battle," ses the old gentleman, "that didn't give a very flattering account of the conduct of some of our troops."

With that, the Indiany man went into a full explanation of the affair, and gittin warmed up as he went along, begun to cuss and swear like he'd been through a dozen campaigns himself.

The old preacher listened to him with evident signs of displeasure, twistin and groanin every time he uttered a big oath, until he couldn't stand it no longer.

"My friend," ses he, "you must excuse me, but your conversation would be a great deal more interestin to me, and I'm sure it would please the company much better, if you wouldn't swear so terribly. It's very wicked to swear so, and I hope you'll have respect for our religious feelins, if you hain't got no respect for your Maker."

If the hoosier had been struck with a clap of thunder and lightning he couldn't been more completely tuck aback. He shut his mouth right in the middle of what he was sayin, and looked at the preacher, while his face got as red as fire.

"Swearin," continued the old hardshell, "is a terrible bad practise, and ther aint no use in it no how. The Bible says 'swear not at all,' and I spose you know the commandments about taking the Lord's name in vain."

The hoosier didn't open his mouth.

"I know," ses the old preacher, "a great many people swear without thinkin, and that some people don't believe in the Bible."

And then he went on to preach a regular sermon agin, and to quote the Scripture like he knowed the whole Bible by heart. In the course of his argyments he undertook to prove the Scriptures to be true, and told us all about the miracles and prophecies and their fulfillment. The old gentleman with the cane tuck a part in the conversation, and the hoosier listened without ever once openin his head.

"I've jest heard of a gentleman," sed the preacher, "what has been to the Holy Land, and went all over the Bible country.

It's astonishin what wonderful things he seed thar. He was at Soddom and Gomorrow, and seed the place whar Lot's wife fell!"

"Ah?" ses the old gentleman with the specs.

"Yes," ses the preacher. "He went to the very spot, and what's the most remarkablest thing of all, he seed the pillar of salt what she was turned into."

"Is it possible?" ses the old gentleman.

The hoosier's countenance all at once brightened up, and he opened his mouth wide.

"Yes, sir; he seed the salt standin thar to this day."

The hoosier's curiosity was raised to a pint beyond endurance.

"What!" ses he, "real genewine good salt?"

"Yes, sir, a pillar of salt jest as it was when that wicked woman was punished for her disobedience."

All but the gambler, who was snoozin in the corner of the coach, looked at the preacher—the hoosier with an expression of countenance that plainly told that his mind was powerfully convicted of a important fact.

"Standin right out in the open air?" he axed.

"Yes, sir,—right out in the open field where she fell."

"Well," ses the hoosier, "all I've got to say is, *if she'd drap'd in Indiany, the cattle would lick'd her up long ago!*"

THE BIG BEAR OF ARKANSAS

by T. B. Thorpe

(1815–1878)

A steamboat on the Mississippi frequently, in making her regular trips, carries between places varying from one to two thousand miles apart; and as these boats advertise to land passengers and freight at "all intermediate landings," the heterogeneous character of the passengers of one of these up-country boats can scarcely be imagined by one who has never seen it with his own eyes. Starting from New Orleans in one of these boats, you will find yourself associated with men from every state in the Union, and from every portion of the globe; and a man of observation need not lack for amusement or instruction in such a crowd, if he will take the trouble to read the great book of character so favourably opened before him. Here may be seen jostling together the wealthy Southern planter, and the pedlar of tin-ware from New England—the Northern merchant, and the Southern jockey—a venerable bishop, and a desperate gambler—the land speculator, and the honest farmer—professional men of all creeds and characters—Wolvereens, Suckers, Hoosiers, Buckeyes, and Corn-crackers, beside a "plentiful sprinkling" of the half-horse and half-alligator species of men, who are peculiar to "old Mississippi," and who appear to gain a livelihood simply by going up and down the river. In the pursuit of pleasure or business, I have frequently found myself in such a crowd.

On one occasion, when in New Orleans, I had occasion to take a trip of a few miles up the Mississippi, and I hurried on board the well-known "high-pressure-and-beat-every-thing" steamboat *Invincible*, just as the last note of the last bell was sounding; and when the confusion and bustle that is natural to a boat's getting under way had subsided, I discovered that I was associated in as heterogeneous a crowd as was ever got together. As my trip was to be of a few hours' duration only, I made no endeavours to become acquainted with my fellow passengers, most of whom would be together many days. Instead of this, I took out of my pocket the "latest paper," and more critically than usual examined its contents; my fellow passengers at the same time

disposed themselves in little groups. While I was thus busily employed in reading, and my companions were more busily employed in discussing such subjects as suited their humours best,
we were startled most unexpectedly by a loud Indian whoop,
uttered in the "social hall," that part of the cabin fitted off for a
bar; then was to be heard a loud crowing, which would not have
continued to have interested us—such sounds being quite common
in that place of spirits—had not the hero of these windy accomplishments stuck his head into the cabin and hallooed out, "Hurra
for the Big Bar of Arkansaw!" and then might be heard a confused
hum of voices, unintelligible, save in such broken sentences as
"horse," "screamer," "lightning is slow," etc. As might have been
expected, this continued interruption attracted the attention of
every one in the cabin; all conversation dropped, and in the midst
of this surprise the "Big Bar" walked into the cabin, took a chair,
put his feet on the stove, and looking back over his shoulder,
passed the general and familiar salute of "Strangers, how are
you?" He then expressed himself as much at home as if he had
been at "the Forks of Cypress," and "perhaps a little more so."
Some of the company at this familiarity looked a little angry,
and some astonished; but in a moment every face was wreathed
in a smile. There was something about the intruder that won the
heart on sight. He appeared to be a man enjoying perfect health
and contentment: his eyes were as sparkling as diamonds, and
good-natured to simplicity. Then his perfect confidence in himself was irresistibly droll. "Perhaps," said he, "gentlemen," running on without a person speaking, "perhaps you have been to
New Orleans often; I never made *the first visit before*, and I don't
intend to make another in a crow's life. I am thrown away in
that ar place, and useless, that ar a fact. Some of the gentlemen
thar called me *green*—well, perhaps I am, said I, *but I arn't so at
home;* and if I ain't off my trail much, the heads of them perlite
chaps themselves wern't much the hardest; for according to my
notion, they were real *know-nothings*, green as a pumpkin-vine—
couldn't, in farming, I'll bet, raise a crop of turnips; and as for
shooting, they'd miss a barn if the door was swinging, and that,
too, with the best rifle in the country. And then they talked to me
'bout hunting, and laughed at my calling the principal game in
Arkansaw poker, and high-low-jack. 'Perhaps,' said I, 'you prefer
chickens and rolette'; at this they laughed harder than ever, and
asked me if I lived in the woods, and didn't know what *game* was?

At this I rather think I laughed. 'Yes,' I roared, and says, 'Strangers, if you'd asked me *how we got our meat* in Arkansaw, I'd a told you at once, and given you a list of varmints that would make a caravan, beginning with the bar, and ending off with the cat; that's *meat* though, not game.' Game, indeed, that's what city folks call it; and with them it means chippen-birds and shite-pokes; maybe such trash live in my diggens, but I arn't noticed them yet; a bird any way is too trifling. I never did shoot at but one, and I'd never forgiven myself for that, had it weighed less than forty pounds. I wouldn't draw a rifle on any thing less than that; and when I meet with another wild turkey of the same weight I will drap him."

"A wild turkey weighing forty pounds?" exclaimed twenty voices in the cabin at once.

"Yes, strangers, and wasn't it a whopper? You see, the thing was so fat that it couldn't fly far; and when he fell out of the tree, after I shot him, on striking the ground he bust open behind, and the way the pound gobs of tallow rolled out of the opening was perfectly beautiful."

"Where did all that happen?" asked a cynical-looking Hoosier.

"Happen! happened in Arkansaw: where else could it have happened, but in the creation state, the finishing-up country—a state where the *sile* runs down to the centre of the 'arth, and government gives you a title to every inch of it? Then its airs—just breathe them, and they will make you snort like a horse. It's a state without a fault, it is."

"Excepting mosquitoes," cried the Hoosier.

"Well, stranger, except them; for it ar a fact that they are rather *enormous*, and do push themselves in somewhat troublesome. But, stranger, they never stick twice in the same place; and give them a fair chance for a few months, and you will get as much above noticing them as an alligator. They can't hurt my feelings, for they lay under the skin; and I never knew but one case of injury resulting from them, and that was to a Yankee; and they take worse to foreigners, any how, than they do to natives. But the way they used that fellow up! first they punched him until he swelled up and busted; then he su-per-a-ted, as the doctor called it, until he was as raw as beef; then he took the ager, owing to the warm weather, and finally he took a steamboat and left the country. He was the only man that ever took mosquitoes to heart that I know of. But mosquitoes is natur, and I never find fault with her.

If they ar large, Arkansaw is large, her varmints ar large, her trees ar large, her rivers ar large, and a small mosquito would be of no more use in Arkansaw than preaching in a cane-brake."

This knock-down argument in favour of big mosquitoes used the Hoosier up, and the logician started on a new track, to explain how numerous bear were in his "diggins," where he represented them to be "about as plenty as blackberries, and a little plentifuler."

Upon the utterance of this assertion, a timid little man near me inquired if the bear in Arkansaw ever attacked the settlers in numbers.

"No," said our hero, warming with the subject, "no, stranger, for you see it ain't the natur of bar to go in droves; but the way they squander about in pairs and single ones is edifying. And then the way I hunt them the old black rascals know the crack of my gun as well as they know a pig's squealing. They grow thin in our parts, it frightens them so, and they do take the noise dreadfully, poor things. That gun of mine is perfect *epidemic among bar;* if not watched closely, it will go off as quick on a warm scent as my dog Bowie-knife will: and then that dog—whew! why the fellow thinks that the world is full of bar, he finds them so easy. It's lucky he don't talk as well as think; for with his natural modesty, if he should suddenly learn how much he is acknowledged to be ahead of all other dogs in the universe, he would be astonished to death in two minutes. Strangers, the dog knows a bar's way as well as a horse-jockey knows a woman's; he always barks at the right time, bites at the exact place, and whips without getting a scratch. I never could tell whether he was made expressly to hunt bar, or whether bar was made expressly for him to hunt; any way, I believe they were ordained to go together as naturally as Squire Jones says a man and woman is, when he moralizes in marrying a couple. In fact, Jones once said, said he, 'Marriage according to law is a civil contract of divine origin; it's common to all countries as well as Arkansaw, and people take to it as naturally as Jim Doggett's Bowie-knife takes to bar.'"

"What season of the year do your hunts take place?" inquired a gentlemanly foreigner, who, from some peculiarities of his baggage, I suspected to be an Englishman, on some hunting expedition, probably at the foot of the Rocky Mountains.

"The season for bar hunting, stranger," said the man of Arkansaw, "is generally all the year round, and the hunts take place about as regular. I read in history that varmints have their fat season, and their lean season. That is not the case in Arkansaw, feeding as they do upon the *spontenacious* productions of the sile, they have one continued fat season the year round; though in winter things in this way is rather more greasy than in summer, I must admit. For that reason bar with us run in warm weather, but in winter, they only waddle. Fat, fat! it's an enemy to speed; it tames everything that has plenty of it. I have seen wild turkeys, from its influence, as gentle as chickens. Run a bar in this fat condition, and the way it improves the critter for eating is amazing; it sort of mixes the ile up with the meat, until you can't tell t'other from which. I've done this often. I recollect one perty morning in particular, of putting an old fellow on the stretch, and considering the weight he carried, he run well. But the dogs soon tired him down, and when I came up with him wasn't he in a beautiful sweat—I might say fever; and then to see his tongue sticking out of his mouth a feet, and his sides sinking and opening like a bellows, and his cheeks so fat he couldn't look cross. In this fix I blazed at him, and pitch me naked into a briar patch if the steam didn't come out of the bullet-hole ten foot in a straight line. The fellow, I reckon, was made on the high-pressure system, and the lead sort of bust his biler."

"That column of steam was rather curious, or else the bear must have been *warm*," observed the foreigner, with a laugh.

"Stranger, as you observe, that bar was WARM, and the blowing off of the steam show'd it, and also how hard the varmint had been run. I have no doubt if he had kept on two miles farther his insides would have been stewed; and I expect to meet with a varmint yet of extra bottom, who will run himself into a skinfull of bar's grease: it is possible, much onlikelier things have happened."

"Whereabouts are these bears so abundant?" inquired the foreigner, with increasing interest.

"Why, stranger, they inhabit the neighbourhood of my settlement, one of the prettiest places on old Mississippi—a perfect location, and no mistake; a place that had some defects until the river made the 'cut-off' at 'Shirt-tail bend,' and that remedied the evil, as it brought my cabin on the edge of the river—a great advantage in wet weather, I assure you, as you can now roll a barrel of whiskey into my yard in high water from a boat, as easy as falling off a log. It's a great improvement, as toting it by land in a jug, as I used to do, *evaporated* it too fast, and it became expensive. Just stop with me, stranger, a month or two, or a year if you like, and you will appreciate my place. I can give you plenty to eat; for beside hog and hominy, you can have bar-ham, and bar-sausages, and a mattrass of bar-skins to sleep on, and a wildcat-skin, pulled off hull, stuffed with corn-shucks, for a pillow. That bed would put you to sleep if you had the rheumatics in every joint in your body. I call that ar bed a *quietus*. Then look at my land—the government ain' got another such a piece to dispose of. Such timber, and such bottom land, why you can't preserve any thing natural you plant in it unless you pick it young, things thar will grow out of shape so quick. I once planted in those diggins a few potatoes and beets; they took a fine start, and after that an ox team couldn't have kept them from growing. About that time I went off to old Kentuck on bisiness, and did not hear from them things in three months, when I accidentally stumbled on a fellow who had stopped at my place, with an idea of buying me out. 'How did you like things?' said I. 'Pretty well,' said he; 'the cabin is convenient, and the timber land is good; but that bottom land ain't worth the first red cent.' 'Why?' said I. ''Cause,' said he. ''Cause what?' said I. ''Cause it's full of cedar stumps and Indian mounds,' said he, *'and it can't be cleared.'* 'Lord,' said I, 'them ar "cedar stumps" is beets, and them ar "Indian mounds" ar tater hills.' As I expected, the crop was overgrown and useless; the sile is too rich, *and planting in Arkansaw is dangerous.* I had a good-sized sow killed in that same bottom land. The old thief stole an ear of corn, and took it down where she slept at night to eat. Well, she left a grain or two on the ground, and lay down on them; before morning the corn shot up, and the percussion killed her dead. I don't plant any more; natur intended Arkansaw for a hunting ground, and I go according to natur."

The questioner who thus elicited the description of our hero's settlement, seemed to be perfectly satisfied and said no more; but the "Big Bar of Arkansaw" rambled on from one thing to another with a volubility perfectly astonishing, occasionally disputing with those around him, particularly with a "live Sucker" from Illinois, who had the daring to say that our Arkansaw friend's stories "smelt rather tall."

In this manner the evening was spent; but conscious that my own association with so singular a personage would probably end before morning, I asked him if he would not give me a description of some particular bear hunt; adding that I took great interest in such things, though I was no sportsman. The desire seemed to please him, and he squared himself round towards me, saying, that he could give me an idea of a bar hunt that was never beat in this world, or in any other. His manner was so singular, that half of his story consisted in his excellent way of telling it, the great peculiarity of which was the happy manner he had of emphasizing the prominent parts of his conversation. As near as I can recollect, I have italicized them, and given the story in his own words.

"Stranger," said he, "in bar hunts *I am numerous*, and which particular one, as you say, I shall tell, puzzles me. There was the old she devil I shot at the Hurricane last fall—then there was the old hog thief I popped over at the Bloody Crossing, and then— Yes, I have it! I will give you an idea of a hunt, in which the greatest bar was killed that ever lived, *none excepted;* about an old fellow that I hunted, more or less, for two or three years; and if that ain't a particular bar hunt, I ain't got one to tell. But in the first place, stranger, let me say, I am pleased with you, be- cause you ain't ashamed to gain information by asking, and listening, and that's what I say to Countess's pups every day when I'm home; and I have got great hopes of them ar pups, because they are continually *nosing* about; and though they stick it sometimes in the wrong place, they gain experience any how, and may learn something useful to boot. Well, as I was saying about this big bar, you see when I and some more first settled in our region, we were drivin to hunting naturally; we soon liked it, and after that we found it an easy matter to make the thing our business. One old chap who had pioneered 'afore us, gave us to understand that we had settled in the right place. He dwelt upon its merits until it was affecting, and showed us, to prove his asser- tions, more marks on the sassafras trees than I ever saw on a tavern door 'lection time. 'Who keeps that ar reckoning?' said I. 'The bar,' said he. 'What for?' said I. 'Can't tell,' said he; 'but so it is; the bar bite the bark and wood too, at the highest point from the ground they can reach, and you can tell, by the marks,' said he, 'the length of the bar to an inch.' 'Enough,' said I; 'I've learned something here a'ready, and I'll put it in practice.'

"Well, stranger, just one month from that time I killed a bar, and told its exact length before I measured it, by those very marks; and when I did that, I swelled up considerable—I've been a prouder man ever since. So I went on, larning something every day, until I was reckoned a buster, and allowed to be decidedly the best bar hunter in my district; and that is a reputation as much harder to earn than to be reckoned first man in Congress, as an iron ramrod is harder than a toadstool. Did the varmints grow over-cunning by being fooled with by green-horn hunters, and by this means get troublesome, they send for me as a matter of course; and thus I do my own hunting, and most of my neighbours'. I walk into the varmints though, and it has become about as much the same to me as drinking. It is told in two sentences— a bar is started, and he is killed. The thing is somewhat monotonous now—I know just how much they will run, where they will tire, how much they will growl, and what a thundering time I will have in getting them home. I could give you this history of the chase with all particulars at the commencement, I know the signs so well—*Stranger, I'm certain.* Once I met with a match though, and I will tell you about it; for a common hunt would not be worth relating.

"On a fine fall day, long time ago, I was trailing about for bar, and what should I see but fresh marks on the sassafras trees, about eight inches above any in the forests that I knew of. Says I, 'them marks is a hoax, or it indicates the d——t bar that was ever grown.' In fact, stranger, I couldn't believe it was real, and I went on. Again I saw the same marks, at the same height, and *I knew the thing lived.* That conviction came home to my soul like an earthquake. Says I, 'here is something a-purpose for me: that bar is mine, or I give up the hunting business.' The very next morning what should I see but a number of buzzards hovering over my cornfield. 'The rascal has been there,' said I, 'for that sign is certain:' and, sure enough, on examining, I found the bones of what had been as beautiful a hog the day before, as was ever raised by a Buckeye. Then I tracked the critter out of the field to the woods, and all the marks he left behind, showed me that he was *the bar*.

"Well, stranger, the first fair chase I ever had with that big critter, I saw him no less than three distinct times at a distance: the dogs run him over eighteen miles and broke down, my horse gave out, and I was as nearly used up as a man can be, made on *my* principle, *which is patent*. Before this adventure, such things were unknown to me as possible; but, strange as it was, that bar got me used to it before I was done with him; for he got so at last, that he would leave me on a long chase *quite easy*. How he did it, I never could understand. That a bar runs at all, is puzzling; but how this one could tire down and bust up a pack of hounds and a horse, that were used to overhauling everything they started after in no time, was past my understanding. Well, stranger, that bar finally got so sassy, that he used to help himself to a hog off my premises whenever he wanted one; the buzzards followed after what he left, and so between *bar and buzzard*, I rather think I was *out of pork*.

"Well, missing that bar so often took hold of my vitals, and I wasted away. The thing had been carried too far, and it reduced me in flesh faster than an ager. I would see that bar in every thing I did; *he hunted me*, and that, too, like a devil, which I began to think he was. While in this fix, I made preparations to give him a last brush, and be done with it. Having completed every thing to my satisfaction, I started at sunrise, and to my great joy, I discovered from the way the dogs run, that they were near him; finding his trail was nothing, for that had become as plain to the pack as a turnpike road. On we went, and coming to an open country, what should I see but the bar very leisurely ascending a hill, and the dogs close at his heels, either a match for him in speed, or else he did not care to get out of their way—I don't know which. But wasn't he a beauty, though? I loved him like a brother.

"On he went, until he came to a tree, the limbs of which formed a crotch about six feet from the ground. Into this crotch he got and seated himself, the dogs yelling all around it; and there he sat eyeing them as quiet as a pond in low water. A green-horn friend of mine, in company, reached shooting distance before me, and blazed away, hitting the critter in the centre of his forehead. The bar shook his head as the ball struck it, and then walked down from that tree as gently as a lady would from a carriage. 'Twas a beautiful sight to see him do that—he was in such a rage that he seemed to be as little afraid of the dogs as if they had been sucking pigs; and the dogs warn't slow in making a ring around him at a respectful distance, I tell you; even Bowie-knife, himself, stood off. Then the way his eyes flashed—why the fire of them would have singed a cat's hair; in fact that bar was in a *wrath all over*. Only one pup came near him, and he was brushed out so totally with the bar's left paw, that he entirely disappeared; and that made the old dogs more cautious still. In the meantime, I came up, and taking deliberate aim as a man should do, at his side, just back of his foreleg, *if my gun did not snap*, call me a coward, and I won't take it personal. Yes, stranger, *it snapped*, and I could not find a cap about my person. While in this predicament, I turned round to my fool friend—says I, 'Bill,' says I, 'you're an ass—you're a fool—you might as well have tried to kill that bar by barking the tree under his belly, as to have done it by hitting him in the head. Your shot has made a tiger of him, and blast me, if a dog gets killed or wounded when they come to blows, I will stick my knife into your liver, I will—' my wrath was up. I had lost my caps, my gun had snapped, the fellow with me had fired at the bar's head, and I expected every moment to see him close in with the dogs, and kill a dozen of them at least. In this thing I was mistaken, for the bar leaped over the ring formed by the dogs, and giving a fierce growl, was off—the pack, of course, in full cry after him. The run this time was short, for coming to the edge of a lake the varmint jumped in, and swam to a little island in the lake, which it reached just a moment before the dogs. 'I'll have him now,' said I, for I had found my caps in the *lining of my coat*—so, rolling a log into the lake, I paddled myself across to the island, just as the dogs had cornered the bar in a thicket. I rushed up and fired—at the same time the critter leaped over the dogs and came within three feet of me, running like mad; he jumped into the lake, and tried to mount the log I had just deserted, but every time he got half his body on it, it would roll over and send him under; the dogs, too, got around him, and pulled him about, and finally Bowie-knife clenched with him, and they sunk into the lake together. Stranger, about this time, I was excited, and I stripped off my coat, drew my knife, and intended to have taken a part with Bowie-knife myself, when the bar rose to the surface. But the varmint staid under—Bowie-knife came up alone, more dead than alive, and with the pack came ashore. 'Thank God,' said I, 'the old villain has got his deserts at last.' Determined to have the body, I cut a grape-vine for a rope, and dove down where I could see the bar in the water, fastened my queer rope to his leg, and fished him, with great difficulty, ashore. Stranger, may I be chawed to death by young alligators, if the thing I looked at wasn't a *she bar, and not the old critter after all*. The way matters got mixed on that island was onaccountably curious, and thinking of it made me more than ever convinced that I was hunting the devil himself. I went home that night and took to my bed—the thing was killing me. The entire team of Arkansaw in bar-hunting, acknowledged himself used up, and the fact sunk into my feelings like a snagged boat will in the Mississippi. I grew as cross as a bar with two cubs and a sore tail. The thing got out 'mong my neighbours, and I was asked how come on that in-dividu-al that never lost a bar when once started? and if that same individ-u-al didn't wear telescopes when he turned a she bar, of ordinary size, into an old he one, a little larger than a horse? 'Perhaps,' said I, 'friends'—getting wrathy—'perhaps you want to call somebody a liar.' 'Oh, no,' said they, 'we only heard such things as being *rather common* of late, but we don't believe one word of it; oh, no,'—and then they would ride off and laugh like so many hyenas over a dead nigger. It was too much, and I de-termined to catch that bar, go to Texas, or die,—and I made my preparations accordin'. I had the pack shut up and rested. I took my rifle to pieces and iled it. I put caps in every pocket about my person, *for fear of the lining.* I then told my neighbours, that on Monday morning—naming the day—I would start THAT BAR, and bring him home with me, or they might divide my settlement among them, the owner having disappeared. Well, stranger, on the morning previous to the great day of my hunting expedition, I went into the woods near my house, taking my gun and Bowie-knife along, just *from habit*, and there sitting down also from habit, what should I see, getting over my fence, but *the bar!* Yes, the old varmint was within a hundred yards of me, and the way he walked *over that fence*—stranger, he loomed up like a *black mist*, he seemed so large, and he walked right towards me. I raised myself, took deliberate aim, and fired. Instantly the varmint wheeled, gave a yell, and *walked through the fence* like a falling tree would through a cobweb. I started after, but was tripped up by my inexpressibles, which either from habit, or the excitement of the moment, were about my heels, and before I had really gathered myself up, I heard the old varmint groaning in a thicket near by, like a thousand sinners, and by the time I reached him he was a corpse. Stranger, it took five niggers and myself to put that carcase on a mule's back, and old long-ears waddled under the load, as if he was foundered in every leg of his body, and with a common whopper of a bar, he would have trotted off, and enjoyed himself. 'Twould astonish you to know how big he was: I made a *bed-spread of his skin*, and the way it used to cover my bar mattress, and leave several feet on each side to tuck up, would have delighted you. It was in fact a creation bar, and if it had lived in Samson's time, and had met him, in a fair fight, it would have licked him in the twinkling of a dice-box. But, strangers, I never like the way I hunted, and *missed him*. There is something curious about it, I could never understand,—and I never was satisfied at his giving in so easy at last. Perhaps, he had heard of my preparations to hunt him the next day, so he jist come in, like Capt. Scott's coon, to save his wind to grunt with in dying; but that ain't likely. My private opinion is, that that bar was an *unhuntable bar, and died when his time come.*"

When the story was ended, our hero sat some minutes with his auditors in a grave silence; I saw there was a mystery to him connected with the bear whose death he had just related, that had evidently made a strong impression on his mind. It was also evident that there was some superstitious awe connected with the affair,—a feeling common with all "children of the wood," when they meet with any thing out of their everyday experience. He was the first one, however, to break the silence, and jumping up, he asked all present to "liquor" before going to bed,—a thing which he did, with a number of companions, evidently to his heart's content.

Long before day, I was put ashore at my place of destination, and I can only follow with the reader, in imagination, our Arkansas friend, in his adventures at the "Forks of Cypress" on the Mississippi.

THE STANDING CANDIDATE

by John S. Robb

His Excuse for Being a Bachelor

At Buffalo Head, Nianga county, state of Missouri, during the canvass of 1844, there was held an extensive political *Barbecue*, and the several candidates for congress, legislature, county offices, &c., were all congregated at this southern point for the purpose of making an *immense* demonstration. Hards, softs, whigs and Tylerites were represented, and to hear their several expositions of state and general policy, a vast gathering of the Missouri sovereigns had also assembled. While the impatient candidates were awaiting the signal to mount the "stump," an odd-looking old man made his appearance at the brow of a small hill bounding the place of meeting.

"Hurrah for old *Sugar!*" shouted an hundred voices, while on, steadily, progressed the object of the cheer.

Sugar, as he was familiarly styled, was an old man, apparently about fifty years of age, and was clad in a coarse suit of brown linsey-woolsey. His pants were patched at each knee, and around the ankles they had worn off into picturesque points—his coat was not of the modern close-fitting cut, but hung in loose and easy folds upon his broad shoulders, while the total absence of buttons upon this garment, exhibited the owner's contempt for the storm and the tempest. A coarse shirt, tied at the neck with a piece of twine, completed his body covering. His head was ornamented with an old woollen cap, of divers colors, below which beamed a broad, humorous countenance, flanked by a pair of short, funny little grey whiskers. A few wrinkles marked his brow, but time could not count them as sure chronicles of his progress, for *Sugar's* hearty, sonorous laugh oft drove them from their hiding place. Across his shoulder was thrown a sack, in each end of which he was bearing to the scene of political action, a keg of *bran new whiskey*, of his own manufacture, and he strode forward on his moccasin covered feet, encumbered as he was, with all the agility of youth. *Sugar* had long been the *standing candidate* of Nianga county, for the legislature, and founded his claim to the office upon the fact of his being the first "squatter" in that county—his having killed the first *bar* there, ever killed by a white man, and, to place his right beyond cavil, he had *'stilled* the first keg of whiskey! These were strong claims, which urged in his comic rhyming manner would have swept the "diggins," but *Sugar*, when the canvass opened, always yielded his claim to some liberal purchaser of his *fluid*, and duly announced himself a candidate for the *next* term.

"Here you air, old fellar!" shouted an acquaintance, "allays on hand 'bout 'lection."

"Well, Nat," said *Sugar*, "you've jest told the truth as easy as ef you'd taken sum of my mixtur—

'Whar politicians congregate,
I'm allays thar, at any rate!'"

"Set him up!—set the old fellar up somewhar, and let us take a univarsal liquor!" was the general shout.

"Hold on, boys,—keep cool and shady," said old *Sugar*, "whar's the candidates?—none of your splurgin round till I git an appropriation fur the sperits. Send em along and we'll negotiate fur the *fluid*, arter which I shall gin 'em my instructions, and they may then *per*cede to

'Talk away like all cre-*a*-tion,
What they knows about the nation.'"

The candidates were accordingly summoned up to pay for *Sugar's* portable grocery, and to please the crowd and gain the good opinion of the owner, they made up a purse and gathered round him. *Sugar* had placed his two kegs upon a broad stump and seated himself astride of them, with a small tin cup in his hand and a paper containing brown sugar lying before him— each of his kegs was furnished with a *spiggot*, and as soon as the money for the whole contents was paid in, *Sugar* commenced addressing the crowd as follows:

"Boys, fellars, and candidates," said he, "I, *Sugar*, am the furst white man ever seed in these yeur diggins—I killed the furst *bar* ever a white skinned in this county, and I kalkilate I hev hurt the feelings of his relations sum sence, as the *bar-skin* linin' of my cabin will testify;—'sides that, I'm the furst manufacturer of whiskey in the range of this district, and powerful mixtur' it is, too, as the hull bilin' of fellars in this crowd will declar';—more'n that, I'm a candidate for the legislatur', and intend to gin up my claim, *this* term, to the fellar who kin talk the *pootyest;*—now, finally at the eend, boys, this mixtur' of mine will make a fellar talk as iley as goose-grease,—as sharp as lightnin', and as *per*-suadin' as a young gal at a quiltin', so don't spar it while it lasts, and the candidates kin drink furst, 'cause they've got to do the talkin'!"

Having finished his charge he filled the tin cup full of whiskey, put in a handful of brown sugar, and with his forefinger stirred up the sweetening, then surveying the candidates he pulled off his cap, remarking, as he did so:

"Old age, allays, afore beauty!—your daddy furst, in course," then holding up the cup he offered a toast, as follows:

"Here is to the string that binds the states; may it never be bit apart by political *rats!*" Then holding up the cup to his head he took a hearty swig, and passed it to the next oldest looking candidate. While they were tasting it, *Sugar* kept up a fire of lingo at them:

"Pass it along lively, gentle*men*, but don't spar the *fluid.* You can't help tellin' truth arter you've swaller'd enough of my mixtur', jest fur this reason, its ben 'stilled in honesty, rectified in truth, and poured out with wisdom! Take a *leetle* drop more," said he to a fastidious candidate, whose stomach turned at thought of the way the "mixtur'" was mixed. "Why, Mister," said *Sugar*, coaxingly.

'Ef you wur a babby, jest new born,
'Twould do you good, this juicy *corn!*' "

"No more, I thank you," said the candidate, drawing back from the proffer.

"*Sugar* winked his eye at some of his cronies, and muttered—"He's got an *a*-ristocracy stomach, and can't go the *native licker.*" Then dismissing the candidates he shouted,—"crowd up, con-stitooents, into a circle, and let's begin fair—your daddy furst, allays; and mind, no changin' places in the circle to git the sugar in the bottom of the cup. I know you're arter it Tom Williams, but none on your yankeein' round to git the sweetnin'—it's all syrup, fellars, cause *Sugar* made and mixed it. The gals at the frolicks allays git me to prepar' the cordials, 'cause they say I make it mity drinkable. Who next? What *you*, old Ben Dent!—Well, hold your hoss for a minit, and I'll strengthen the tin with a speck more, jest because you can kalkilate the valee of the licker, and do it jestiss!"

Thus chatted *Sugar* as he measured out and sweetened up the contents of his kegs, until all who would drink had taken their share, and then the crowd assembled around the speakers. We need not say that the virtues of each political party were duly set forth to the hearers—that follows as a matter of course, candidates dwell upon the strong points of their argument, always. One among them, however, more than his compeers, attracted the attention of our friend *Sugar*, not because he had highly commended the contents of his kegs, but because he painted with truth and feeling the claims of the western *pioneers!* Among these he ranked the veteran Col. Johnson and his compatriots, and as he rehearsed their struggles in defence of their firesides, how they had been trained to war by conflict with the ruthless savage, their homes oft desolated, and their children murdered,—yet still, ever foremost in the fight, and last to retreat, winning the heritage of these broad valleys for their children, against the opposing arm of the red man, though aided by the civilized power of mighty Britain, and her serried cohorts of trained soldiery! We say as he dwelt upon these themes *Sugar's* eye would fire up, and then, at some touching passage of distress dwelt upon by the speaker, tears would course down his rude cheek. When the speaker concluded he wiped his eyes with his hard hand, and said to those around him:—

"That arr true as the yearth!—thar's suthin' like talk in that fellar!—he's the right breed, and his old daddy has told him about them times. So did mine relate 'em to me, how the ony sister I ever had, when a babby had her brains dashed out by one of the red skinned devils! But didn't we pepper them fur it? Didn't I help the old man, afore he grew too weak to hold his shootin' iron, to send a few on 'em off to rub out the account? Well, I *did!—Hey!*" and shutting his teeth together he yelled through them the exultation of full vengeance.

The speaking being done, candidates and hearers gathered around old *Sugar*, to hear his comments upon the speeches, and to many inquiries of how he liked them, the old man answered:—

"They were all pooty good, but that tall fellar they call Tom, from St. Louis; *you*, I mean, *stranger*," pointing at the same time to the candidate, "you jest scart up my feelin's to the right pint— you jest made me feel wolfish as when I and old dad war arter

the red varmints; and now what'll *you* take? I'm goin' to publicly
*de*cline in your favor."

Pouring out a tin full of the liquor, and stirring it as before, he
stood upright upon the stump, with a foot on each side of his kegs,
and drawing off his cap, toasted:—

"The memory of the western *pioneers!*"

A shout responded to his toast, which echoed far away in the
depths of the adjoining forest, and seemed to awaken a response
from the spirits of those departed heroes.

"That's the way to sing it out, boys," responded old *Sugar*,
"sich a yell as that would *scar* an inimy into ager fits, and make
the United States Eagle scream 'Hail Columby.'"

"While you're up, *Sugar*," said one of the crowd, give us a
stump speech, yourself."

"Bravo!" shouted an hundred voices, "a speech from *Sugar*."

"Agreed, boys," said the old man, "I'll jest gin you a few
words to wind up with, so keep quiet while your daddy's talkin'

> 'Sum tell it out jest like a song,
> I'll gin it to you sweet and strong.'

"The ony objection ever made to me in this arr county, as a
legislatur', was made by the *wimin*, 'cause I war a *bachelor*, and I
never told you afore why I *re*-mained in the state of number *one*—
no fellar stays single *pre*-meditated, and, in course, a hansum fellar
like me, who all the gals declar' to be as enticin' as a jay bird,
warn't goin' to stay alone, ef he could help it. I did see a creatur'
once, named *Sofy Mason*, up the Cumberland, nigh onto Nashville,
Tenne*see*, that I tuk an orful hankerin' arter, and I sot in to lookin'
anxious fur matrimony, and gin to go reglar to meetin', and tuk
to dressin' tremengeous finified, jest to see ef I could win her good
opinion. She did git to lookin' at me, and one day, cumin' from
meetin', she was takin' a look at me a kind of shy, jest as a hoss
does at suthin' he's scart at, when arter champin' at a distance fur
awhile, I sidled up to her and blarted out a few words about the
sarmin'—she said yes, but cuss me ef I know whether that wur the
right answer or not, and I'm a thinkin' she didn't know then,
nuther! Well, we larfed and talked a leetle all the way along to
her daddy's, and thar I gin her the best bend I had in me, and
raised my bran new hat as peert and *per*lite as a minister, lookin'
all the time so enticin' that I sot the gal tremblin'. Her old daddy
had a powerful numerous lot of healthy niggers, and lived right

adjinin' my place, while on tother side lived Jake Simons—a sneakin', cute varmint, who war wusser than a miser fur stinginess, and no sooner did this cussed sarpint see me sidlin' up to Sofy, than he went to slickin' up, too, and sot himself to work to cut me out. That arr wur a struggle ekill to the battle of Orleans. Furst sum new fixup of Jake's would take her eye, and then I'd sport suthin' that would outshine him, until Jake at last gin in tryin' to outdress me, and sot to thinkin' of suthin' else. Our farms wur jest the same number of acres, and we both owned three niggers apiece. Jake knew that Sofy and her dad kept a sharp eye out fur the main chance, so he thort he'd clar me out by buyin' another nigger; but I jest follor'd suit, and bought one the day arter he got his, so he had no advantage thar; he then got a *cow,* and so did I, and jest about then both on our *pusses* gin out. This put Jake to his wits' eend, and I war a wunderin' what in the yearth he would try next. We stood so, hip and thigh, fur about two weeks, both on us talkin' sweet to Sofy, whenever we could git her alone. I thort I seed that Jake, the sneakin' cuss, wur gittin' a mite ahead of me, 'cause his tongue wur so iley; howsever, I didn't let on, but kep a top eye on him. One Sunday mornin' I wur a leetle mite late to meetin', and when I got thar the furst thing I seed war Jake Simons, sittin' close bang up agin Sofy, in the same pew with her daddy! I biled a spell with wrath, and then tarned sour; I could taste myself! Thar they wur, singin' *himes* out of the same book. Je-e-eminy, fellars, I war so *enormous* mad that the new silk handkercher round my neck lost its color! Arter meetin' out they walked, linked arms, a smilin' and lookin' as pleased as a young couple at thar furst christenin', and Sofy tarned her 'cold shoulder' at me so orful pinted, that I wilted down, and gin up right straight—Jake had her, thar wur no disputin' it! I headed toward home, with my hands as fur in my trowsers pockets as I could push 'em, swarin' all the way that she wur the last one would ever git a chance to rile up my feelin's. Passin' by Jake's plantation I looked over the fence, and thar stood an explanation of the marter, right facin' the road, whar every one passin' could see it—his consarned *cow* was tied to a stake in the gardin', *with a most promisin' calf alongside of her!* That *calf* jest soured my milk, and made Sofy think, that a fellar who war allays gittin' ahead like Jake, wur a right smart chance for a lively husband!"

A shout of laughter here drowned *Sugar's* voice, and as soon as silence was restored he added, in a solemn tone, with one eye shut, and his forefinger pointing at his auditory:—

"What is a cussed sight wusser than his gittin' Sofy war the fact, that he *borrowed that calf the night before from Dick Harkley!* Arter the varmint got Sofy hitched, he told the joke all over the settle*ment*, and the boys never seed me arterwards that they didn't *b-a-h* at me fur lettin' a *calf* cut me out of a gal's affections. I'd a shot Jake, but I thort it war a free country, and the gal had a right to her choice without bein' made a widder, so I jest sold out and travelled! I've allays thort since then, boys, that *wimin* wur a good deal like *licker,* ef you love 'em too hard thar sure to throw you some way:

> 'Then here's to *wimin,* then to *licker,*
> Thar's nuthin' swimmin' can be slicker!'"

OVID BOLUS, ESQUIRE

by Joseph G. Baldwin

(1815–1864)

And what history of that halcyon period, ranging from the year of Grace, 1835, to 1837; that golden era, when shin-plasters were the sole currency; when bank-bills were "as thick as Autumn leaves in Vallambrosa," and credit was a franchise,—what history of those times would be complete, that left out the name of Ovid Bolus? As well write the biography of Prince Hal, and forbear all mention of Falstaff. In law phrase, the thing would be a "deed without name," and void; a most unpardonable *casus ommissus*.

I cannot trace, for reasons the sequel suggests, the early history, much less the birth-place, pedigree, and juvenile associations of this worthy. Whence he or his forbears got his name or how, I don't know: but for the fact that it is to be inferred he got it in infancy, I should have thought he borrowed it; he borrowed every thing else he ever had, such things as he got under the credit system only excepted: in deference, however, to the axiom, that there is *some* exception to *all* general rules, I am willing to believe that he got this much honestly, by *bona fide* gift or inheritance, and without false pretense.

I have had a hard time of it in endeavoring to assign to Bolus his leading vice; I have given up the task in despair; but I have essayed to designate that one which gave him, in the end, most celebrity. I am aware that it is invidious to make comparisons, and to give pre-eminence to one over other rival qualities and gifts, where all have high claims to distinction: but, then, the stern justice of criticism, in this case, requires a discrimination, which, to be intelligible and definite, must be relative and comparative. I, therefore, take the responsibility of saying, after due reflection, that in my opinion, Bolus's reputation stood higher for lying than for any thing else; and in thus assigning pre-eminence to this poetic property, I do it without any desire to derogate from other brilliant characteristics belonging to the same general category, which have drawn the wondering notice of the world.

Some men are liars from interest; not because they have no regard for truth, but because they have less regard for it than for gain: some are liars from vanity, because they would rather be well thought of by others, than have reason for thinking well of themselves: some are liars from a sort of necessity, which over-bears, by the weight of temptation, the sense of virtue; some are enticed away by the beguilements of pleasure, or seduced by evil example and education. Bolus was none of these; he belonged to a higher department of the fine arts, and to a higher class of pro-fessors of this sort of Belles-Lettres. Bolus was a natural liar, just as some horses are natural pacers, and some dogs natural setters. What he did in that walk, was from the irresistible promptings of instinct, and a disinterested love of art. His genius and his per-formances were free from the vulgar alloy of interest or temp-tation. Accordingly he did not labor a lie: he lied with relish: he lied with a coming appetite, growing with what it fed on: he lied from the delight of invention and the charm of fictitious narra-tive. It is true he applied his art to the practical purposes of life; but in so far did he glory the more in it; just as an ingenious machinist rejoices that his invention, while it has honored science, has also supplied a common want.

Bolus's genius for lying was encyclopediacal: it was what Ger-man criticism calls many-sided. It embraced all subjects without distinction or partiality. It was equally good upon all, "from grave to gay, from lively to severe."

Bolus's lying came from his greatness of soul and his compre-hensiveness of mind. The truth was too small for him. Fact was too dry and common-place for the fervor of his genius. Besides, great as was his memory—for he even remembered the outlines of his chief lies—his invention was still larger. He had a great contempt for history and historians. He thought them tame and timid cobblers; mere tinkers on other people's wares,—simple parrots and magpies of other men's sayings or doings; borrowers of and acknowledged debtors for others' chattels, got without skill; they had no separate estate in their ideas: they were bailees of goods, which they did not pretend to hold by adverse title; buriers of talents in napkins making no usury; barren and un-profitable non-producers in the intellectual vineyard—*nati con-sumere fruges*.

He adopted a fact occasionally to start with, but, like a Shef-field razor and the crude ore, the workmanship, polish and value were all his own: a Thibet shawl could as well be credited to the insensate goat that grew the wool, as the author of a fact Bolus honored with his artistical skill, could claim to be the inventor of the story.

His experiments upon credulity, like charity, began at home. He had long torn down the partition wall between his imagination and his memory. He had long ceased to distinguish between the impressions made upon his mind by what came *from* it, and what came *to* it: all ideas were facts to him.

Bolus's life was not a common man's life. His world was not the hard, work-day world the groundlings live in: he moved in a sphere of poetry; he lived amidst the ideal and romantic. Not that he was not practical enough, when he chose to be: by no means. He bought goods and chattels, lands and tenements, like other men; but he got them under a state of poetic illusion, and paid for them in an imaginary way. Even the titles he gave were not of the *earthy* sort—they were sometimes *clouded*. He gave notes, too—how well I know it!—like other men; he paid them like himself.

How well he asserted the Spiritual over the Material! How he delighted to turn an abstract idea to concrete cash—to make a few blots of ink, representing a little thought, turn out a labor-saving machine, and bring into his pocket money which many days of hard exhausting labor would not procure! What pious joy it gave him to see the days of the Good Samaritan return, and the hard hand of avarice relax its grasp on land and negroes, pork and clothes, beneath the soft speeches and kind promises of future rewards—blending in the act the three cardinal virtues, Faith, Hope, and Charity; while, in the result, the chief of these three was *Charity!*

There was something sublime in the idea—this elevating the spirit of man to its true and primeval dominion over things of sense and grosser matter.

It is true, that in these practical romances, Bolus was charged with a defective taste in repeating himself. The justice of the charge must be, at least, partially acknowledged: this I know from a client, to whom Ovid sold a tract of land after having sold it twice before: I cannot say, though, that his forgetting to mention this circumstance made any difference, for Bolus originally had no title.

There was nothing narrow, sectarian, or sectional in Bolus's lying. It was on the contrary broad and catholic. It had no respect to times or places. It was as wide, illimitable, as elastic and

variable as the air he spent in giving it expression. It was a generous, gentlemanly, whole-souled faculty. It was employed often on,
and in behalf of, objects and occasions of thrift, but no more;
and no more zealously on these than on others of no profit to himself. He was an Egotist, but a magnificent one: he was not a liar
because an egotist, but an egotist because a liar. He usually made
himself the hero of the romantic exploits and adventures he narrated; but this was not so much to exalt himself, as because it was
more convenient to his art. He had nothing malignant or invidious in his nature. If he exalted himself, it was seldom or
never to the disparagement of others, unless, indeed, those others
were merely imaginary persons, or too far off to be hurt. He
would as soon lie for you as for himself. It was all the same, so
there was something doing in his line of business, except in those
cases in which his necessities required to be fed at your expense.

He did not confine himself to mere lingual lying: one tongue
was not enough for all the business he had on hand. He acted
lies as well. Indeed, sometimes his very silence was a lie. He
made nonentity fib for him, and performed wondrous feats by a
"masterly inactivity."

The *personnel* of this distinguished Votary of the Muse, was
happily fitted to his art. He was strikingly handsome. There was
something in his air and bearing almost princely, certainly quite
distinguished. His manners were winning, his address frank, cordial and flowing. He was built after the model and structure of
Bolingbroke in his youth, *Americanized* and *Hoosierized* a little
by a "raising in," and an adaptation to, the Backwoods. He was
fluent but choice of diction, a little sonorous in the structure of his
sentences to give effect to a voice like an organ. His countenance
was open and engaging, usually sedate of expression, but capable
of any modifications at the shortest notice. Add to this his intelligence, shrewdness, tact, humor, and that he was a ready debator
and elegant declaimer, and had the gift of bringing out, to the
fullest extent, his resources, and you may see that Ovid, in a new
country, was a man apt to make no mean impression. He drew
the loose population around him, as the magnet draws iron filings.
He was the man for the "boys,"—then a numerous and influential
class. His generous profusion and free-handed manner impressed
them as the bounty of Caesar the loafing commonalty of Rome:
Bolus was no niggard. He never higgled or chaffered about small
things. He was as free with his own money—if he ever had any of

his own—as with yours. If he never paid borrowed money, he never asked payment of others. If you wished him to loan you any he would hand you a handful without counting it: if you handed him any, you were losing time in counting it, for you never saw any thing of it again: Shallow's funded debt on Falstaff were as safe an investment: this would have been an equal commerce, but, unfortunately for Bolus's friends, the proportion between his disbursements and receipts was something scant. Such a spend-thrift never made a track even in the flush times of 1836. It took as much to support him as a first class steamboat. His bills at the groceries were as long as John Q. Adams' Abolition petition, or, if pasted together, would have matched the great Chartist memorial. He would as soon treat a regiment or charter the gro-cery for the day, as any other way; and after the crowd had heartily drunk—some of them "laying their souls in soak,"—if he did not have the money convenient—as when did he?—he would fumble in his pocket, mutter something about nothing less than a $100 bill, and direct the score, with a lordly familiar-ity, to be charged to his account.

Ovid had early possessed the faculty of ubiquity. He had been born in more places than Homer. In an hour's discourse, *he* would, with more than the speed of Ariel, travel at every point of the compass, from Portland to San Antonio, some famous ad-venture always occurring just as he "rounded to," or while sta-tionary, though he did not remain longer than to see it. He was present at every important debate in the Senate at Washington, and had heard every popular speaker on the hustings, at the bar and in the pulpit, in the United States. He had been concerned in many important causes with Grymes and against Mazereau in New Orleans, and had borne no small share in the fierce forensic battles, which, with singular luck, *he* and Grymes always won in the courts of the Crescent City. And such frolics as they had when they laid aside their heavy armor, after the heat and burden of the day! Such gambling! A negro *ante* and twenty on the call, was moderate playing. What lots of "Ethiopian captives" and other plunder he *raked down* vexed Arithmetic to count and credu-lity to believe; and, had it not been for Bolus's generosity in giving "the boys" a chance to win back by *doubling off on the high hand,* there is no knowing what changes of owners would have not occurred in the Rapides or on the German Coast.

The Florida war and the Texas Revolution, had each furnished a brilliant theatre for Ovid's chivalrous emprise. Jack Hays and he were great chums. Jack and he had many a hearty laugh over the odd trick of Ovid, in lassoing a Camanche Chief, while galloping a stolen horse bare-backed, up the San Saba hills. But he had the rig on Jack again, when he made him charge on a brood of about twenty Camanches, who had got into a mot of timber in the prairies, and were shooting their arrows from the covert, Ovid, with a six-barrelled rifle, taking them on the wing as Jack rode in and flushed them!

It was an affecting story and feelingly told, that of his and Jim Bowie's rescuing an American girl from the Apaches, and returning her to her parents in St. Louis; and it would have been still more tender, had it not been for the unfortunate necessity Bolus was under of shooting a brace of gay lieutenants on the border, one frosty morning, before breakfast, back of the fort, for taking unbecoming liberties with the fair damosel, the spoil of his bow and spear.

But the girls Ovid courted, and the miraculous adventures he had met with in love beggared by comparison, all the fortune of war had done for him. Old Nugent's daughter, Sallie, was his narrowest escape. Sallie was accomplished to the romantic extent of two ocean steamers, and four blocks of buildings in Boston, separated only from immediate "perception and pernancy," by the contingency of Old Nugent's recovering from a confirmed dropsy, for which he had been twice ineffectually tapped. The day was set—the presents made—*enperle* of course—the guests invited; the old Sea Captain insisted on Bolus's setting his negroes free, and taking five thousand dollars apiece for the loss. Bolus's love for the "peculiar institution" wouldn't stand it. Rather than submit to such degradation, Ovid broke off the match, and left Sallie broken-hearted; a disease from which she did not recover until about six months afterwards, when she ran off with the mate of her father's ship, the Sea Serpent, in the Rio trade.

Gossip and personal anecdote were the especial subjects of Ovid's elocution. He was intimate with all the notabilities of the political circles. He was a privileged visitor of the political greenroom. He was admitted back into the laboratory where the political thunder was manufactured, and into the office where the magnetic wires were worked. He knew the origin of every party question and movement, and had a finger in every pie the party cooks of Tammany baked for the body politic.

One thing in Ovid I can never forgive. This was his coming it over poor Ben O. I don't object to it on the score of the swindle. That was to have been expected. But swindling Ben was degrading the dignity of the art. True, it illustrated the universality of his sciences, but it lowered it to a beggarly process of mean deception. There was not skill in it. It was little better than crude larceny. A child could have done it; it had as well been done to a child. It was like catching a cow with a lariat, or setting a steel trap for a pet pig. True, Bolus had nearly practised out of custom. He had worn his art threadbare. Men, who could afford to be cheated, had all been worked up or been scared away. Besides, Ford couldn't be put off. He talked of money in a most ominous connection with blood. The thing could be settled by a bill of exchange. Ben's name was unfortunately good—the amount some $1,600. Ben *had* a fine tract of land in S——r. He has not got it now. Bolus only gave Ben one wrench—that was enough. Ben never breathed easy afterwards. All the V's and X's of ten years' hard practice, went in that penful of ink. Fie! Bolus, Monroe Edwards wouldn't have done that. He would sooner have sunk down to the level of some honest calling for a living, than have put his profession to so mean a shift. I can conceive of but one extenuation; Bolus was on the lift for Texas, and the desire was natural to qualify himself for citizenship.

The genius of Bolus, strong in its unassisted strength, yet gleamed out more brilliantly under the genial influence of "the rosy." With boon companions and "reaming suats," it was worth while to hear him of a winter evening. He could "gild the palpable and the familiar, with golden exhalations of the dawn." The most common-place objects became dignified. There was a history to the commonest articles about him; that book was given him by Mr. Van Buren—the walking stick was a present from Gen. Jackson. A thrice-watered Monongahela, just drawn from the grocery hard by, was the last of a distillation of 1825, smuggled in from Ireland, and presented to him by a friend in New Orleans, on easy terms with the collector; the cigars, not too fragrant, were of a box sent him by a schoolmate from Cuba *before* he visited the Island. And talking of Cuba—he had met with an adventure there, the impression of which never could be effaced from his mind. He had gone, at the instance of Don Carlos y Cubanos, (an intimate classmate in a Kentucky Catholic College,) whose life he had saved from a mob in Louisville, at the imminent risk of his own. The Don had a sister of blooming sixteen, the least of whose charms was two or three plantations, some hundreds of slaves, and a suitable garnish of doubloons, accumulated during her minority, in the hands of her uncle and guardian, the Captain General. All went well with the young lovers—for such, of course, they were—until Bolus, with his usual frank indiscretion, in a conversation with the Priest, avowed himself a Protestant. Then came trouble. Every effort was made to convert him; but Bolus's faith resisted the eloquent tongue of the Priest, and the more eloquent eyes of Donna Isabella. The brother pleaded the old friendship—urged a seeming and formal conformity—the Captain General urged the case like a politician—the Senorita like a warm and devoted woman. All would not do. The Captain General forbade his longer sojourn on the Island. Bolus took leave of the fair Senorita: the parting interview held in the orange bower, was affecting: Donna Isabella, with dishevelled hair, threw herself at his feet: the tears streamed from her eyes; in liquid tones, broken by grief, she implored him to relent—reminded him of her love, of her trust in him, and of the consequences—now not much longer to be concealed—of that love and trust; ("though I protest," Bolus would say, "I don't know what she meant exactly by *that*.") "Gentlemen," Bolus continued, "I confess to the weakness—I wavered—but then my eyes happened to fall on the breast-pin with a lock of my mother's hair—I recovered my courage: I shook her gently from me. I felt my last hold on earth was loosened—my last hope of peace destroyed. Since that hour, my life has been a burden. Yes, gentlemen, you see before you a broken man—a martyr to his Religion. But, away with these melancholy thoughts: boys, pass around the jorum." And wiping his eyes, he drowned the wasting sorrow in a long draught of the poteen; and, being much refreshed, was able to carry the burden on a little further—*videlicet*, to the next lie.

It must not be supposed that Bolus was destitute of the tame virtue of prudence—or that this was confined to the avoidance of the improvident habit of squandering his money in paying old debts. He took reasonably good care of his person. He avoided all unnecessary exposures, chiefly from a patriotic sense, probably, of continuing his good offices to his country. His recklessness was, for the most part, lingual. To hear him talk, one might suppose he held his carcass merely for a target to try guns and knives upon; or, that the business of his life was to draw men up to ten paces or less, for sheer improvement in marksmanship. Such exploits as he had gone through with, dwarfed the heroes of romance to very pigmy and sneaking proportions. Pistol at the Bridge when he bluffed at honest Fluellen, might have envied the swash-buckler airs, Ovid would sometimes put on. But I never could exactly identify the place he had laid out for his burying-ground. Indeed, I had occasion to know that he declined to understand several not very ambiguous hints, upon which he might, with as good a grace as Othello, have spoken, not to mention one or two pressing invitations which his modesty led him to refuse. I do not know that the base sense of fear had any thing to do with these declinations: possibly he might have thought he had done his share of fighting, and did not wish to monopolize: or his principles forbade it—I mean those which opposed his paying a debt: knowing he could not cheat that inexorable creditor, Death, of his claim, he did the next thing to it; which was to delay and shirk payment as long as possible.

It remains to add a word of criticism on this great *Lyric* artist.

In lying, Bolus was not only a successful, but he was a very able practitioneer. Like every other eminent artist, he brought all his faculties to bear upon his art. Though quick of perception and prompt of invention, he did not trust himself to the inspirations of his genius for *improvising* a lie, when he could well premeditate one. He deliberately built up the substantial masonry, relying upon the occasion and its accessories, chiefly for embellishment and collateral supports: as Burke excogitated the more solid parts of his great speeches, and left unprepared only the illustrations and fancy-work.

Bolus's manner was, like every truly great man's, his own. It was excellent. He did not come blushing up to a lie, as some otherwise very passable liars do, as if he were making a mean compromise between his guilty passion or morbid vanity, and a struggling conscience. Bolus had long since settled all disputes with *his* conscience. He and it were on very good terms—at least, if there was no affection between the couple, there was no fuss in the family; or, if there were any scenes or angry passages, they were reserved for strict privacy and never got out. My own opinion is, that he was as destitute of the article as an ostrich. Thus he came to his work bravely, cheerfully and composedly. The delights of composition, invention and narration, did not fluster his style or agitate his delivery. He knew how, in the tumult of passion, to assume the "temperance to give it smoothness." A lie never ran away with him, as it is apt to do with young performers; he could always manage and guide it; and to have seen him fairly mounted, would have given you some idea of the polished elegance of D'Orsay, and the superb *ménage* of Murat. There is a tone and manner of narration different from those used in delivering ideas just conceived; just as there is a difference between the sound of the voice in reading and in speaking. Bolus knew this, and practised on it. When he was narrating, he put the facts in order, and seemed to speak them out of his memory; but not formally, or as if by rote. He would stop himself to correct a date; recollect he was wrong—he was *that* year at the White Sulphur or Saratoga, &c.: having got the date right, the names of persons present would be incorrect, &c.: and these he corrected in turn. A stranger hearing him, would have feared the marring of a good story by too fastidious a conscientiousness in the narrator.

His zeal in pursuit of a lie under difficulties, was remarkable. The society around him—if such it could be called—was hardly fitted, without some previous preparation, for an immediate introduction to Almack's or the classic precincts of Gore House. The manners of the nation were rather plain than ornate, and candor rather than polish predominated in their conversation. Bolus had need of some forbearance to withstand the interruptions and cross-examinations, with which his revelations were sometimes received. But he possessed this in a remarkable degree. I recollect, on one occasion, when he was giving an account of a providential escape he was signally favored with, (when boarded by a pirate off the Isle of Pines, and he pleaded masonry, and gave a sign he had got out of the Disclosures of Morgan,) Tom Johnson interrupted him to say that he had heard *that* before, (which was more than Bolus had ever done). B. immediately rejoined, that he had, he believed, given him, Tom, a *running* sketch of the incident. "Rather," said Tom, "I think, a *lying* sketch." Bolus scarcely smiled, as he replied, that Tom was a wag, and couldn't help turning the most serious things into jests; and went on with his usual brilliancy, to finish the narrative. Bolus did not overcrowd his canvas. His figures were never confused, and the subordinates and accessories did not withdraw attention from the main and substantive lie. He never squandered his lies profusely: thinking, with the poet, that "bounteous, not prodigal, is kind Nature's hand," he kept the golden mean between penuriousness and prodigality; never stingy of his lies, he was not wasteful of them, but was rather forehanded than pushed, or embarrassed, having, usually, fictitious stock to be freshly put on 'change, when he wished to "make a raise." In most of his fables, he inculcated but a single leading idea; but contrived to make the several facts of the narrative fall in very gracefully with the principal scheme.

The rock on which many promising young liars, who might otherwise have risen to merited distinction, have split, is vanity: this marplot vice betrays itself in the exultation manifested on the occasion of a decided hit, an exultation too inordinate for mere recital, and which betrays authorship; and to betray authorship, in the present barbaric, moral and intellectual condition of the world is fatal. True, there seems to be some inconsistency here. Dickens and Bulwer can do as much lying, for money too, as they choose, and no one blames them, any more than they would blame a lawyer regularly *fee'd* to do it; but let any man, gifted with the same genius, try his hand at it, not deliberately and in writing, but merely orally, and ugly names are given him, and he is proscribed! Bolus heroically suppressed exultation over the victories his lies achieved.

Alas! for the beautiful things of Earth, its flowers, its sunsets— its lovely girls—its lies—brief and fleeting are their date. Lying is a very delicate accomplishment. It must be tenderly cared for, and jealously guarded. It must not be overworked. Bolus forgot this salutary caution. The people found out his art. However dull the commons are as to other matters, they get sharp enough after a while, to whatever concerns their bread and butter. Bolus not having confined his art to political matters, sounded, at last, the depths, and explored the limits of popular credulity. The denizens of this degenerate age, had not the disinterestedness of Prince Hal, who "cared not how many fed at his cost"; they got tired, at last, of promises to pay. The credit system, common before as pump-water, adhering like the elective franchise to every voter, began to take the worldly wisdom of Falstaff's mercer, and ask security; and security liked something more substantial than plausible promises. In this forlorn condition of the country, returning to its savage state, and abandoning the refinements of a ripe Anglo-Saxon civilization for the sordid safety of Mexican or Chinese modes of traffic; deserting the sweet simplicity of its ancient truthfulness and the poetic illusions of Augustus Tomlinson, for the vulgar saws of poor Richard—Bolus, with a sigh like that breathed out by his great prototype after his apostrophe to London, gathered up, one bright moonlight night, his articles of value, shook the dust from his feet, and departed from a land unworthy of his longer sojourn. With that delicate consideration for the feelings of his friends, which, like the politeness of Charles II., never forsook him, he spared them the pain of a parting interview. He left no greetings of kindness; no messages of love; nor did he ask assurances of their lively remembrance. It was quite unnecessary. In every house he had left an autograph, in every ledger a souvenir. They will never forget him. Their connection with him will be ever regarded as

> —"The *greenest* spot
> In memory's waste."

Poor Ben, whom he had honored with the last marks of his confidence, can scarcely speak of him to this day, without tears in his eyes. Far away toward the setting sun he hied him, until, at last, with a hermit's disgust at the degradation of the world, like Ignatius turned monk, he pitched his tabernacle amidst the smiling prairies that sleep in vernal beauty, in the shadow of the San Saba mountains. There let his mighty genius rest. It has earned repose. We leave Themistocles to his voluntary exile.

COMIC HAPPENINGS IN TENNESSEE

by George W. Harris

(1814–1869)

THE KNOB DANCE

Knoxville, July 16, 1845.

You may talk of your bar hunts, Mister Porter, and your deer hunts, and knottin tigers' tails through the bung-holes of barrels, an cock fitin, and all that but if a regular bilt frolick in the Nobs of "Old Knox," don't beat 'em all blind for fun, then I'm no judge of fun, that's all! I said *fun*, and I say it agin, from a *kiss* that cracks like a wagin-whip up to a *fite* that rouses up all out-doors—and as to laffin, why they *invented* laffin, and the *last* laff will be hearn at a Nob dance about three in the morning! I'm jest gettin so I can ride arter the motions I made at one at Jo Spraggins's a few days ago.

I'll try and tell you who Jo Spraggins is. He's a squire, a school comishner, overlooker of a mile of Nob road *that leads towards Roody's still-house*—a fiddler, a judge of a hoss, and a hoss himself! He can belt six shillins worth of corn-juice at still-house rates and travel—can out shute and out lie any feller from the Smoky Mounting to Noxville, and, if they'll bar one feller in Nox, I'll say to the old Kaintuck Line! (I'm sorter feared of him for they say that he lied a jassack to death in two hours!)—can make more spinin-wheels, kiss more spinners, thrash more wheat an more men than any one-eyed man I know on. He hates a circuit rider, a nigger, and a shot gun—loves a woman, old sledge, and sin in eny shape. He lives in a log hous about ten yards squar; it has two rooms one at the bottom an one at the top of the ladder—has all out ove doors fur a yard, and all the South fur its ocupants at times. He gives a frolick onst in three weeks in plowin time and one every Saturday-nite the ballance of the year, and only axes a "fip" for a reel, and two "bits" fur what corn-juice you suck; he throws the galls in, and a bed too in the hay, if you git too hot to locomote. The supper is made up by the fellers; every one fetches sumthin; sum a lick of meal, sum a middlin of bacon, sum a hen, sum a possum, sum a punkin, sum a grab of taters, or a pocket full of peas, or dried apples, an sum only fetches a good appetite and a skin chock full of perticular deviltry, and if thars been a shutin match for beef the day before, why a *leg* finds its way to Jo's, sure, without eny help from the ballance of the critter. He gives Jim Smith, (the store-keeper over Bay's Mounting), *warnin* to fetch a skane of silk fur fiddle-strings, and sum "Orleans" for sweetnin, or not to fetch himself; the silk and sugar has never failed to be thar yet. Jo then mounts Punkinslinger bar backed, about three hours afore sun down and gives all the galls *item*. He does this a leetle of the slickest—jist rides past in a peart rack, singin,

> "Oh, I met a frog, with a fiddle on his back,
> A axin his way to the fro-l-i-c-k!
> Wha-a he! wha he! wha he! wha he! he-ke-he!"

That's enuf! The galls nows *that* aint a jackass, so by sun down they come pourin out of the woods like pissants out of an old log when tother end's afire, jest "as fine as silk" and full of fun, fixed out in all sorts of fancy doins, from the broad-striped homespun to the sunflower callico, with the thunder-and-lightnin ground. As for silk, if one had a silk gown she's be too smart to wear it to Jo Spraggins's, fur if she did she'd go home in hir petticote-tale *sartin*, for the homespun wud tare it off of hir quicker nor winkin, and if the sunflowers dident help the homespuns, they woudn't do the silk eny good, so you see that silk is never ratlin about your ears at a Nob dance.

The sun had about sot afore I got the things fed an had Barkmill saddled (you'll larn directly why I call my poney Barkmill), but an owl couldent have cotch a rat afore I was in site of Jo's with my gall, Jule Sawyers, up behind me. She hugged me mity tite she was *"so feerd of fallin off that drated poney."* She said she didn't mind a fall but it mought break hir leg an then good bye frolicks—she'd be fit fur nuthin but to nuss brats ollers arterwards. I now hearn the fiddle ting-tong-ding-domb. The yard was full of fellers and two tall fine lookin galls was standin in the door, face to face holdin up the door posts with their backs, laffin, an castin sly looks into the house, an now an then kickin each other with their knees, an then the one kicked wud bow so perlite, and quick at that, and then they'd laff agin an turn red. Jo was a standin in the hous helpin the galls to hold the facins up, an when they'd kick each other he'd wink at the fellers in the yard an grin. Jule, she bounced off just like a bag of wool-rolls, and I hitched my bark-machine up to a saplin that warnt skinned, so he'd git a craw-full of good fresh bark afore mornin. I giv Jule a kiss to sorter molify my natur an put hir in heart like, and in we walked. "Hey! hurray!" said the boys, "my gracious!" said the galls, "if here aint Dick an Jule!" jist like we hadent been *rite thar* only last Saturday nite. "Well, I know we'll have reel now!" "Hurraw!—Go it while you're young!" "Hurraw for the brimstone kiln—every man praise his country!" "Clar the ring!" "Misses Spraggins drive out these dratted tow-headed brats of your'n—give room!" "Who-oo-whoop! whar's that crock of baldface, and that gourd of honey? Jim Smith, hand over that spoon, an quit a lickin it like "sank in a bean-pot." "You, Jake Snyder, don't holler so!" says the old oman—"why you are worse nor a painter." "Holler! why I was jist *whispering* to that gall on the bed—*who-a-whoopee!* now I'm beginning to *holler!* Did you hear *that*, Misses Spraggins, and be darned to your bar legs? You'd make a nice hemp-brake, you would." "Come here, Suse Thompson, and let me pin your dress behind? Your back looks adzactly like a blaze on a white oak!" "My *back* aint nuffin to you, Mister Smarty!" "Bill Jones, quit a smashin that ar cat's tail!" "Well, let hir keep hir tail clar of my ant killers!" "Het Goins, stop tumblin that bed an tie your *sock!*" "Thankee marm, its a longer stockin than you've got—look at it!" "Jim Clark has gone to the woods for fat pine, and Peggy Willet is along to take a lite for him—they've been gone a coon's age. Oh, here comes the lost 'babes in the wood,' and no *lite!*" "Whar's that lite! whar's that torch! I say, Peggy, whar *is* that bundle of lite wood?" "Why, I fell over a log and lost it, and we hunted clar to the foot of the holler for it, and never found it. It's no account, no how—nuthin but a little pine—who cares?" "Hello, thar, gin us 'Forked Deer,' old fiddle-teazer, or I'll give you forked litnin! *Ar* you a goin to tum-tum all nite on that pot-gutted old pine box of a fiddle, *say?*" "Give him a sock at the crock and a lick at the patent beehive—it'll *ile* his elbows." "Misses Spraggins you're a hoss! cook on, don't mind me—I dident aim to slap *you;* it was Suze Winters I *wanted* to hit; but you stooped so fair—" "Yes, and it's well for your good looks that you didn't hit to hurt me, old feller!" "Turn over them rashers of bacon, they're a burnin!" "Mind your own business, Bob Proffit, I've cooked for frolicks afore you shed your petticotes—so jist hush an talk to Marth Giffin! See! she is beckonin to you!" "That's a lie, marm! If he comes a near me I'll unjint his dratted neck! No sech fool that when a gall puts hir arm round his neck will break and run, shall look at *me*, that's flat! Go an try Bet Holden!" "Thankee, marm, I don't take your leavins," says Bet, hir face lookin like a full cross between a grid-iron and a steel-trap.

Whoop! hurraw! Gether your galls for a break down! Give us "Forked Deer!" "No, give us 'Natchez-under-the-hill!'" "Oh, Shucks! give us 'Rocky Mounting', or 'Misses McCloud!'" "'Misses McCloud' be darned, and 'Rocky Mounting' too! jist give us

"She woudent, and she coudent, and she dident come at all!"

"Thar! that's it! Now make a brake! *Tang!* Thar is a brake—a string's gone!" "Thar'll be a head broke afore long!" "Give him goss—no giv him a horn and every time he stops repeat the dose, and nar another string'll brake to nite. Tink-tong! Ting-tong! all rite! Now go it!" and if I know what *goin it* is, we *did* go it.

About midnite, Misses Spraggins sung out "stop that ar dancin and come and get your supper!" It was sot in the yard on a table made of forks stuck in the ground and plank of the stable loft, with sheets for table cloths. We had danced, kissed and drank ourselves into a perfect thrashin-machine apetite, and the vittals *hid* themselves in a way quite alarmin to tavern-keepers. Jo sung out "nives is scase, so give what thar is to the galls and let the ballance use thar paws—they was invented afore nives, eney how. Now, Gents, jist walk into the fat of this land. I'm sorter feerd the honey wont last till day break, but the liquor will, I *think*, so you men when you drink your'n, run an kiss the galls fur sweetnin —let them have the honey—it belongs to them, naturaly!"— "Hurraw, my Jo! You know how to do things rite." "Well, I rayther think I do; I never was rong but onst in my life and then I mistook a camp meetin for a political speechifyin so I rid up an axed the speaker 'how much Tarrif there was on rot-gut?' and he said 'about here there *appeared* to be none!' That rayther sot me, as I was right smartly smoked, myself, jist at that time. I had enough liquor plumb in me to swim a skunk, so I come agin at him. I axed him 'who was the bigest fool the Bible told of?' an he said 'Noah for he'd get tite!' I *thought*, mind, I only thought he might be a pokin his dead cat at somebody what lives in this holler; I felt my bristles a raisin my jacket-back up like a tent cloth, so I axed him if he'd '*ever seed the Elephant?*' He said no, but he had seen *a grocery walk*, and he expected to see one *rot down* from its *totterin* looks, purty soon!' Thinks I, Jo you're beat at your own game; I sorter felt mean, so I spurr'd and sot old Punkinslinger to cavortin like he was skeered, and I wheeled and twisted out of *that* crowd, an when I *did* git out of site the way I did sail was a caution to turkles and all the other slow varmints."

Well, we danced, and hurrawed without eny thing of *very* particular interest to happen, till about three o'clock, when the darndest muss was kicked up you ever did see. Jim Smith sot down on the bed alongside of Bet Holden (the steel-trap gall), and jist fell to huggin of hir bar fashion. She tuck it very kind till she seed Sam Henry a looking on from behind about a dozen galls, *then* she fell to kickin *an* a hollerin, *an* a screechin like all rath. Sam he come up an told Jim to let Bet go! Jim told him to go to a far off countrie whar they give away brimestone and throw in the fire to burn it. Sam hit him strate atween the eyes an after a few licks the fitin *started*. Oh hush! It makes my mouth water now to think what a beautiful row we had. One feller from Cady's Grove, nocked a hole in the bottom of a fryin-pan over Dan Turner's head, and left it a hangin round his neck, the handle flyin about like a long que, and thar it hung till Jabe Thurman cut it off with a cold chissel next day! That was *his share*, fur that nite, sure. Another feller got nocked into a meal-barrel; he was as mealy as an Irish tater, and as *hot* as hoss-radish; when he bursted the hoops and cum out he rared a few. Two fellers fit out of the door, down the hill, and into the creek, and thar ended it, in a quiet way, all alone. A perfect mule from Stock Creek hit *me* a wipe with a pair of windin blades; he made kindlin-wood of them, an I lit on him. We had it head-and-tails fur a very long time, all over the house, but the truth must come and shame my kin, he warped me *nice*, so, jist to save his time I *hollered!* The lickin he give me made me sorter oneasy and hostile like; it weakened my wolf wide awake, so I begin to look about for a man I *could* lick and *no mistake!* The little fiddler cum a scrougin past, holdin his fiddle up over his head to keep it *in tune*, for the fitin was gettin tolerable brisk. You're the one, thinks I, and jist I grabbed the dough-tray and split it plumb open over his head! *He* rotted down, right thar, and I paddled his 'tother end with one of the pieces!— while I was a molifyin my feelins in that way his gall slip'd up behind me and fecht'd me a rake with the pot-hooks. Jule Sawyer was *thar,* and jist *anexed to her rite* off, and a mity nice fite it was, Jule carried enuf har from hir hed to make a sifter, and striped and checked her face nice, like a partridge-net hung on a white fence. She hollered fur hir fiddler, but oh, shaw! he coudent do hir a bit of good; he was too buisy a rubbin first his broken head and then his blistered extremities, so when I thought Jule had given her a plenty I pulled hir off and put hir in a good humor by given hir about as many kisses as would cover a barn door.

Well, I thought at last, if I had a drink I'd be *about done,* so I started for the creek; *and* the first thing I saw was more stars with my eyes shut than I ever did with them open. I looked round, and it was the little fiddler's *big brother! I know'd what it meant,* so we locked horns without a word, thar all alone, and I do think we fit an hour. At last some fellers hearn the jolts at the house, and they cum and *dug us out,* for we had fit into a hole whar a big pine stump had burnt out, and thar we was, up to our girths a peggin away, face to face, and *no dodgin!*

Well, it is now sixteen days since that fite, and last night Jule picked gravels out of my knees as big as squirell shot. Luck rayther run agin me that nite, fur I dident lick eny body but the fiddler, and had three fites—but Jule licked her gall, that's some comfort, and I suppose a feller cant *always* win! Arter my fite in the ground we made friends all round (except the fiddler—he's hot yet,) and danced and liquored at the tail of every Reel till sun up, when them that was sober enuff went home, and them that was *wounded* staid whar they fell. *I* was in the list of wounded, but could have got away if my bark-mill hadn't *ground* off the saplin and gone home without a parting word; so Dick and Jule had to ride "Shanks' mar," and a rite peart *four-legged* nag she is. She was *weak* in *two* of hir legs, but 'tother two—oh, my stars and possum dogs! they make a man swaller tobacker jist to look at 'em, and feel sorter like a June bug was crawlin up his trowses and the waistband too tite for it to git out. I'm agoin to marry Jule, I swar I am, and *sich* a cross! Think of a locomotive and a cotton gin! Who! Whoopee!

That's Dick Harlan's story, Mr. Editor, and if the man "In the Swamp" could see Dick at a *Knob Dance* he would think that something besides politicks and religion occupied the mind of *some* of the inhabitants of the "peaceful valley."

Is Mr. Free dead? I have a yarn to spin on him, also, one about "Sleep Walking," and I will do it some day if I can over come my laziness. You see I am a *hot* hand at the *location* of capital letters and punctuation, (the spelling is Dick's). If you think I have made one "capital" letter I shall be agreeably disappointed.

Your Friend,

SUGARTAIL.

SICILY BURNS'S WEDDING

"Hey Ge-orge!" rang among the mountain slopes; and looking up to my left, I saw "Sut," tearing along down a steep point, heading me off, in a long kangaroo lope, holding his flask high above his head, and hat in hand. He brought up near me, banteringly shaking the half-full "tickler," within an inch of my face.

"Whar am yu gwine? take a suck, hoss? This yere truck's *ole*. I kotch hit myse'f, hot this morning frum the still wum. Nara durn'd bit ove strike-nine in hit—I put that ar piece ove burnt dried peach in myse'f tu gin hit color—better nur ole Bullen's plan: he puts in tan ooze, in what he sells, an' when that haint handy, he uses the red warter outen a pon' jis' below his barn;—makes a pow'ful natral color, but don't help the taste much. Then he correcks that wif red pepper; hits an orful mixtry, that whisky ole Bullen makes; no wonder he seed 'Hell-sarpints.' He's pisent ni ontu three quarters ove the b'levin parts ove his congregashun wif hit, an' tuther quarter he's sot intu ruff stealin an' cussin. Ef his still-'ouse don't burn down, ur he peg out hisse'f, the neighborhood am ruinated a-pas' salvashum. Haint he the durndes sampil ove a passun yu ever seed enyhow?

"Say George, du yu see these yere well-poles what I uses fur laigs? Yu sez yu sees 'em, dus yu?"

"Yes."

"Very well; I passed 'em a-pas' each uther tuther day, right peart. I put one out a-head jis' so, an' then tuther 'bout nine feet a-head ove hit agin jis' so, an' then kep on a-duin hit. I'll jis' gin yu leave tu go tu the devil ha'f hamon, ef I didn't make fewer tracks tu the mile, an' more tu the minit, than wer ever made by eny human man body, since Bark Wilson beat the sawlog frum the top ove the Frog Mountin intu the Oconee River, an' dove, an' dodged hit at las'. I hes allers look'd ontu that performince ove Bark's as onekel'd in histery, allers givin way tu dad's ho'net race, however.

"George, every livin thing hes hits pint, a pint ove sum sort. Ole Bullen's pint is a durn'ed fust rate, three bladed, dubbil barril'd, warter-proof, hypockracy, an' a never-tirein appertite fur bal'-face. Sicily Burns's pint am tu drive men folks plum crazy, an' then bring em too agin. Gin em a rale Orleans fever in five minits, an' then in five minits more, gin them a Floridy ager. Durn her, she's down on her heels flat-footed now. Dad's pint is tu be king ove all durn'd fools, ever since the day ove that feller what cribb'd up so much co'n down in Yegipt, long time ago, (he run outen his coat yu minds). The Bibil tells us hu wer the stronges' man—hu wer the bes' man—hu wer the meekis' man, an' hu the wises' man, but leaves yu tu guess hu wer the bigges' fool.

"Well, eny man what cudent guess arter readin that ar scrim-mage wif an 'oman 'bout the coat, haint sense enuf tu run intu the hous', ef hit wer rainin ded cats, that's all. Mam's pint am in kitchen insex, bakin hoecake, bilin greens, an' runnin bar laiged. My pint am in takin abroad big skeers, an' then beatin enybody's hoss, ur skared dorg, a-runnin frum onder em agin. I used tu think my pint an' dad's wer jis' the same, sulky, unmix'd king durn'd fool; but when he acted hoss, an' mistook hossflies fur ho'nets, I los' heart. Never mine, when I gits his 'sperence, I may be king fool, but yet great golly, he gets frum bad tu wus, mon-strus fas'.

"Now ef a feller happens tu known what his pint am, he kin allers git along, sumhow, purvided he don't swar away his liberty tu a temprins s'ciety, live tu fur frum a still-'ous, an' too ni a chu'ch ur a jail. Them's my sentimints on 'pints,'—an' yere's my sentimints ontu folks: Men wer made a-purpus jis' tu eat, drink, an' fur stayin awake in the yearly part ove the nites: an' wimen wer made tu cook the vittils, mix the sperits, an' help the men du the stayin awake. That's all, an' nuthin more, onless hits fur the wimen tu raise the devil atwix meals, an' knit socks atwix drams, an' the men tu play short kerds, swap hosses wif fools, an' fite fur exersise, at odd spells.

"George, yu don't onderstan life yet scarcely at all, got a heap tu larn, a heap. But 'bout my swappin my laigs so fas'—these yere very par ove laigs. I hed got about a fox squirril skin full ove biled co'n juice packed onder my shut, an' onder my hide too, I mout es well add, an' wer aimin fur Bill Carr's on foot. When I got in sight ove ole man Burns's, I seed ni ontu fifty hosses an' muels hitch'd tu the fence. Durnashun! I jis' then tho't ove hit, 'twer Sicily's wedding day. She married ole Clapshaw, the suckit rider. The very feller hu's faith gin out when he met me sendin sody all over creashun. Suckit-riders am surjestif things tu me. They preaches agin me, an' I hes no chance tu preach back at them. Ef I cud I'd make the institushun behave hitself better nur hit dus. They hes sum wunderful pints, George. Thar am two things nobody never seed; wun am a dead muel, an' tuther is a suckit-rider's grave. Kaze why, the he muels all turn intu old field school-masters, an' the she ones intu strong minded wimen, an' then when thar time cums, they dies sorter like uther folks. An' the suckit-riders ride ontil they marry; ef they marrys money, they turns intu store-keepers, swaps hosses, an' stays away ove colleckshun Sundays. Them what marrys an' by sum orful mistake *misses the money*, jis' turns intu polertishuns, sells 'ile well stock,' an' dies sorter in the human way too.

"But 'bout the wedding. Ole Burns hed a big black an' white bull, wif a ring in his snout, an' the rope tied up roun his ho'ns. They rid 'im tu mill, an' sich like wif a saddil made outen two dorgwood forks, an' two clapboards, kivered wif a ole piece ove carpet, rope girth, an' rope stirrups wif a loop in hit fur the foot. Ole 'Sock,' es they call'd the bull, hed jis' got back frum mill, an' wer turn'd intu the yard, saddil an' all, tu solace hissef a-pickin grass. I wer slungin roun the outside ove the hous', fur they hedn't hed the manners tu ax me in, when they sot down tu dinner. I wer pow'fully hurt 'bout hit, an' happen'd tu think—SODY. So I sot in a-watchin fur a chance tu du sumthin. I fus' tho't I'd shave ole Clapshaw's hoss's tal, go tu the stabil an' shave Sicily's mare's tal, an' ketch ole Burns out, an' shave his tail too. While I wer a-studyin 'bout this, ole Sock wer a-nosin 'roun, an' cum up ontu a big baskit what hilt a littil shattered co'n; he dipp'd in his head tu git hit, an' I slipp'd up an' jerked the handil over his ho'ns.

"Now, George, ef yu knows the nater ove a cow brute, they is the durndes' fools amung all the beastes, ('cept the Lovingoods;) when they gits intu tribulashun, they knows nuffin but tu shot thar eyes, beller, an' back, an' keep a-backin. Well, when ole Sock raised his head an' foun hissef in darkness, he jis' twisted up his tail, snorted the shatter'd co'n outen the baskit, an' made a tremenjus lunge agin the hous'. I hearn the picters a-hangin agin the wall on the inside a-fallin. He fotch a deep loud rusty beller, mout been hearn a mile, an' then sot intu a onendin sistem ove backin. A big craw-fish wif a hungry coon a-reachin fur him, wer jis' nowhar. Fust agin one thing, then over anuther, an' at las' agin the bee-bainch, knockin hit an' a dozen stan ove bees heads over heels, an' then stompin back'ards thru the mess. Hit haint much wuf while tu tell what the bees did, ur how soon they sot into duin hit. They am pow'ful quick-tempered littil critters, enyhow. The air wer dark wif 'em, an' Sock wer kivered all over, frum snout tu tail, so clost yu cudent a-sot down a grain ove wheat fur bees, an' they wer a-fitin one anuther in the air, fur a place on the bull. The hous' stood on sidelin groun, an' the back door wer even wif hit. So Sock happen tu hit hit plum, jis' backed intu the hous' onder 'bout two hundred an' fifty pouns ove steam, bawlin orful, an' every snort he fotch he snorted away a quart ove bees ofen his sweaty snout. He wer the leader ove the bigges' an' the madest army ove bees in the worild. Thar wer at leas' five solid bushels ove 'em. They hed filled the baskit, an' hed loged ontu his tail, ten deep, ontil hit were es thick es a waggin tung. He hed hit stuck strait up in the air, an' hit looked adzactly like a dead pine kivered wif ivey. I think he wer the hottes' and wuz hurtin bull then livin; his temper, too, seemed tu be pow'fully flustrated. Ove *all* the durn'd times an' kerryins on yu *ever* hearn tell on wer thar an' thar abouts. He cum tail fust agin the ole two story Dutch clock, an' fotch hit, bustin hits runnin geer outen hit, the littil wheels a-trundlin over the floor, an' the bees even chasin them. Nex pass, he fotch up agin the foot ove a big dubbil injine bedstead, rarin hit on aind, an' punchin one ove the posts thru a glass winder. The nex tail fus' experdishun wer made aginst the caticorner'd cupboard, outen which he made a perfeck momox. Fus' he upsot hit, smashin in the glass doors, an' then jis' sot in an' stomp'd everything on the shelves intu giblits, a-tryin tu bak furder in that direckshun, an' tu git the bees ofen his laigs.

"Pickil crocks, perserves jars, vinegar jugs, seed bags, yarb bunches, paragorick bottils, aig baskits, an' delf war—all mix'd dam permiskusly, an' not worth the sortin, by a duller an' a 'alf. Nex he got a far back acrost the room agin the board pertishun; he went thru hit like hit hed been paper, takin wif him 'bout six foot squar ove hit in splinters, an' broken boards, intu the nex room, whar they wer eatin dinner, an' rite yere the fitin becum gineral, an' the dancin, squawkin, cussin, an' dodgin begun.

"Clapshaw's ole mam wer es deaf es a dogiron, an sot at the

aind ove the tabil, nex tu whar old Sock busted thru the wall; til fus' he cum agin her cheer, a-histin her an' hit ontu the tabil. Now, the smashin ove delf, an' the mixin ove vittils begun. They hed sot severil tabils tugether tu make hit long enuf. So he jis' rolled 'em up a-top ove one anuther, an' thar sot ole Misses Clap-shaw, a-straddil ove the top ove the pile, a-fitin bees like a wind-mill, wif her calliker cap in one han, fur a wepun, an' a cract frame in tuther, an' a-kickin, an' a-spurrin like she wer ridin a lazy hoss arter the doctor, an' a-screamin rape, fire, an' murder, es fas' es she cud name 'em over.

"Taters, cabbige, meat, soup, beans, sop, dumplins, an' the truck what yu wallers 'em in; milk, plates, pies, puddins, an' every durn fixin yu cud think ove in a week, wer thar, mix'd an' mashed, like hit had been thru a thrashin-meesheen. Old Sock still kep a-backin, an' backed the hole pile, old 'oman an' all, also sum cheers, outen the frunt door, an' down seven steps intu the lane, an' then by golly, turn'd a fifteen hundred poun summerset hissef arter 'em, lit a-top ove the mix'd up mess, flat ove his back, an' then kicked hissef ontu his feet agin. About the time he ris, ole man Burns—you know how fat, an' stumpy, an' cross-grained he is, enyhow—made a vigrus mad snatch at the baskit an' got a savin holt ontu hit, but cudent *let go quick enuf;* fur ole Sock jis' snorted, bawled, an' histed the ole cuss heels fust up intu the air, an' he lit on the bull's back, an' hed the baskit in his han.

"Jis' es soon es ole Blackey got the use ove his eyes, he tore off down the lane tu out-run the bees, so durn'd fas' that ole Burns was feard tu try tu git off. So he jis' socked his feet intu the rope loops, an' then cummenc'd the durndes' bull-ride ever mortal man ondertuck. Sock run atwix the hitched critters an' the rail-fence, ole Burns fust fitin him over the head wif the baskit tu stop him, an' then fitin the bees wif hit. I'll jis' be durn'd ef I didn't think he hed four ur five baskits, hit wer in so menny places at onst. Well, Burns, baskit, an' bull, an' bees, skared every durn'd hoss an' muel loose frum that fence—bees ontu all ove 'em, bees, by golly, everywhar. Mos' on 'em, too, tuck a fence rail along, fas' tu the bridil reins. Now I'll jis' gin yu leave tu kiss my sister Sall till she squalls, ef ever sich a sight wer seed ur sich nises hearn, es filled up that long lane. A heavy cloud ove dus', like a harycane hed been blowin, hid all the hosses, an' away abuv hit yu cud see tails, an' ainds ove fence-rails a-flyin about; now an' then a par ove bright hine shoes wud flash in the sun like two sparks, an' away ahead wer the baskit a-sirklin roun an' about at random. Brayin, nickerin, the bellerin ove the bull, clatterin ove runnin hoofs, an' a mons'ous rushin soun, made up the noise. Lively times in that lane jis' then, warnt thar?

"I swar ole Burns kin beat eny man on top ove the yeath a-fitin bees wif a baskit. Jis' set 'im a-straddil ove a mad bull, an' let thar be bees enuf tu exhite the ole man, an' the man what beats him kin break me. Hosses an' muels wer tuck up all over the county, an' sum wer forever los'. Yu cudent go eny course, in a cirkil ove a mile, an' not find buckils, stirrups, straps, saddil blankits, ur somethin belongin tu a saddil hoss. Now don't forgit that about that hous' thar were a good time bein had ginerally. Fellers an' gals loped outen windows, they rolled outen the doors in bunches, they clomb the chimleys, they darted onder the house jis' tu dart out agin, they tuck tu the thicket, they rolled in the wheat field, lay down in the krick, did everything but stan still. Sum made a strait run *fur* home, an' sum es strait a run *frum* home; livelyest folks I ever did see. Clapshaw crawled onder a straw pile in the barn, an' sot intu prayin—you cud a-hearn him a mile— sumthin 'bout the plagues ove Yegipt, an' the pains ove the secon death. I tell yu now he lumbered.

"Sicily, she squatted in the cold spring, up tu her years, an' turn'd a milk crock over her head, while she wer a drownin a mess ove bees onder her coats. I went tu her, an' sez I, 'Yu hes got anuther new sensashun haint you?' Sez she—

"'Shet yer mouth, yu cussed fool!'

"Sez I, 'Power'ful sarchin feelin bees gins a body, don't they?'

"'Oh, lordy, lordy, Sut, these yere 'bominabil insex is jis' burnin me up!'

"'Gin 'em a mess ove sody,' sez I, 'that'll cool 'em off, an' skeer the las' durn'd one ofen the place.'

"She lifted the crock, so she cud flash her eyes at me, an' sed, 'Yu go tu hell!' *jis es plain.* I thought, takin all things tugether, that p'raps I mout as well put the mountain atwix me an' that plantashun; an' I did hit.

"Thar warnt an' 'oman, ur a gal at that weddin, but what thar frocks, an' stockins were too tite fur a week. Bees am wus on wimen than men, enyhow. They hev a farer chance at 'em. Nex day I passed old Hawley's, an' his gal Betts wer sittin in the porch, wif a white hankerchef tied roun her jaws; her face wer es red es a beet, an' her eyebrows hung 'way over heavy. Sez I, 'Hed a fine time at the weddin, didn't yu?' 'You mus' be a durn'd fool,' wer every word she sed. I hadent gone a hundred yards, ontil I met Missis Brady, her hans fat, an' her ankils swelled ontil they shined. Sez she—

"'Whar you gwine, Sut?'

"'Bee huntin,' sez I.

"'Yu jis' say bees agin, yu infunel gallinipper, an' I'll scab yer head wif a rock.'

"Now haint hit strange how tetchus they am, on the subjick ove bees?

"Ove all the durn'd misfortinit weddins ever since ole Adam married that heifer, what wer so fon' ove talkin tu snaix, an' eatin appils, down ontil now, that one ove Sicily's an' Clapshaw's wer the worst one fur noise, disappintment, skeer, breakin things, hurtin, trubbil, vexashun ove spirrit, an' gineral swellen. Why, George, her an' him cudent sleep tugether fur ni ontu a week, on account ove the doins ove them are hot-footed, 'vengeful, 'bomina-bil littil insex. They never will gee tugether, got tu bad a start, mine what I tell yu. Yu haint time now tu hear how ole Burns finished his bull-ride, an' how I cum tu du that lofty, topliftical speciment ove fas' runnin. I'll tell yu all that, sum uther time. Ef eny ove 'em axes after me, tell 'em that I'm over in Fannin, on my way tu Dahlonega. They is huntin me tu kill me, I is fear'd.

"Hit am an orful thing, George, tu be a natral born durn'd fool. Yu'se never 'sperienced hit pussonally, hev yu? Hits made pow'fully again our famerly, and all owin tu dad. I orter bust my head open agin a bluff ove rocks, an' jis' wud du hit, ef I warnt a cussed coward. All my yeathly 'pendence is in these yere laigs—d'ye see 'em? Ef they don't fail, I may turn human sum day, that is sorter human, enuf tu be a Squire or school cummisiner. Ef I wer jis' es smart es I am mean, an' ornary, I'd be President ove a Wild Cat Bank in less nor a week. Is sperrits plenty over wif yu?"

RARE RIPE GARDEN SEED

I tell yu now, I minds my fust big skeer jis' as well as rich boys minds thar fust boots, ur seeing the fust spotted hoss sirkis. The red top ove them boots am still a rich red stripe in thar minds, an' the burnin red ove my fust skeer hes lef es deep a scar ontu my thinkin works. Mam hed me a standin atwixt her knees. I kin feel the knobs ove her jints a-rattlin a-pas' my ribs yet. She didn't hev much petticoats tu speak ove, an' I hed but one, an' hit wer calliker slit frum the nap ove my naik tu the tail, hilt tugether at the top wif a draw-string, an' at the bottom by the hem; hit wer the handiest close I ever seed, an' wud be pow'ful comfurtin in summer if hit warn't fur the flies. Ef they was good tu run in, I'd war one yet. They beats pasted shuts, an' britches, es bad es a feather bed beats a bag ove warnut shells fur sleepin on.

"Say, George, wudn't yu like tu see me intu one 'bout haf fadid, slit, an' a-walkin jis' so, up the middil street ove yure city chuch, a-aimin fur yure pew pen, an' hit chock full ove yure fine city gal friends, jis' arter the peopil hed sot down frum the fust prayer, an' the orgin beginin tu groan; what wud yu du in sich a margincy? say hoss?"

"Why, I'd shoot you dead, Monday morning before eight o'clock," was my reply.

"Well, I speck yu wud; but yu'd take a rale ole maid faint fus, rite amung them ar gals. Lordy! wudn't yu be shamed ove me! Yit why not teu chuch in sich a suit, when yu hesn't got no store clothes?

"Well, es I wer sayin, mam wer feedin us brats ontu mush an' milk, wifout the milk, an' es I wer the baby then, she hilt me so es tu see that I got my sheer. Whar thar ain't enuf feed, big childer roots littil childer outen the troff, an' gobbils up thar part. Jis' so the yeath over: bishops eats elders, elders eats common peopil; they eats sich cattil es me, I eats possums, possums eats chickins, chickins swallers wums, an' wums am content tu eat dus, an' the dus am the aind ove hit all. Hit am all es regilur es the souns frum the tribil down tu the bull base ove a fiddil in good tchune, an' I speck hit am right, ur hit wudn't be 'lowed.

"'*The sheriff!*' his'd mam in a keen trimblin whisper; hit sounded tu me like the skreech ove a hen when she sez 'hawk', tu her little roun-sturn'd, fuzzy, bead-eyed, stripid-backs.

"I actid jis' adzacly as they dus; I darted on all fours onder mam's petticoatails, an' thar I met, face tu face, the wooden bowl, an' the mush, an' the spoon what she slid onder frum tuther side. I'se mad at mysef yet, fur rite thar I show'd the fust flash ove the nat'ral born durn fool what I now is. I orter et hit all up, in jestis tu my stumick an' my growin, while the sheriff wer levyin ontu the bed an' the cheers. Tu this day, ef enybody sez 'sheriff', I feels skeer, an' ef I hears constabil menshun'd, my laigs goes thru runnin moshuns, even ef I is asleep. Did yu ever watch a dorg dreamin ove rabbit huntin? Thems the moshuns, an' the feelin am the rabbit's.

"Sheriffs am orful 'spectabil peopil; everybody looks up tu em. I never adzacly seed the 'spectabil part mysef. I'se too fear'd ove em, I reckon, tu 'zamin fur hit much. One thing I know, no country atwix yere an' Tophit kin ever 'lect me tu sell out widders' plunder, ur poor men's co'n, an' the tho'ts ove hit gins me a good feelin; hit sorter flashes thru my heart when I thinks ove hit. I axed a passun onst, what hit cud be, an' he pernounced hit tu be *onregenerit pride*, what I orter squelch in prayer, an' in tendin chuch on colleckshun days. I wer in hopes it mout be 'ligion, ur sence, a-soakin intu me; hit feels good, enyhow, an' I don't keer ef every suckit rider outen jail knows hit. Sheriffs' shuts allers hes nettil dus ur fleas inside ove em when they lies down tu sleep, an' I'se glad ove hit, fur they'se allers discumfortin me, durn em. I scarcely ever git tu drink a ho'n, ur eat a mess in peace. I'll hurt one sum day, see ef I don't. Show me a sheriff a-steppin softly roun, an' a-sorter sightin at me, an' I'll show yu a far sampil ove the speed ove a express ingine, fired up wif rich, dry, rosiny skeers. They don't ketch me *much*, usin only human laigs es wepuns.

"Ole John Doltin wer a 'spectabil sheriff, monsusly so, an' hed the bes' scent fur poor fugatif devils, an' wimen, I ever seed; he wer sure fire. Well, he toted a warrun fur this yere skinful ove durn'd fool, 'bout that ar misfortnit nigger meetin bisness, ontil he wore hit intu six seperit squar bits, an' hed wore out much shoe leather a-chasin ove me. I'd foun a doggery in full milk, an' hated pow'ful bad tu leave that settilment while hit suck'd free; so I sot intu sorter try an' wean him off frum botherin me so much. I suckseedid so well that he not only quit racin ove me, an' wimen, but he wer tetotaly spiled es a sheriff, an' los' the 'spectabil seckshun ove his karacter. Tu make yu fool fellers onderstan how hit wer done, I mus' interjuice yure minds tu one Wat Mastin, a bullitheaded yung black-smith.

"Well, las' year—no hit wer the year afore las'—in struttin an' gobblin time, Wat felt his keepin right warm, so he sot intu bellerin an' pawin up dus in the neighborhood roun the ole widder McKildrin's. The more dus he flung up, the wus he got, ontil at las' he jis cudn't stan the ticklin sensashuns anuther minnit; so he put fur the county court clark's offis, wif his hans sock'd down deep intu his britchis pockets, like he wer fear'd ove pick-pockets, his back roach'd roun, an' a-chompin his teef ontil he splotch'd his whiskers wif foam. Oh! he wer yearnis' hot, an' es restless es a cockroach in a hot skillit."

"What was the matter with this Mr. Mastin? I cannot understand you, Mr. Lovingood; had he hydrophobia?" remarked a man in a square-tail coat, and cloth gaiters, who was obtaining subscribers for some forthcoming Encyclopedia of Useful Knowledge, who had quartered at our camp, uninvited, and really unwanted.

"What du yu mean by high-dry-foby?" and Sut looked puzzled.

"A madness produced by being bit by some rabid animal," explained Square-tail, in a pompous manner.

"Yas, hoss, he hed high-dry-foby *orful*, an' Mary McKildrin, the widder McKildrin's only darter, hed gin him the complaint; I don't know whether she bit 'im ur not; he mout a-cotch hit frum her bref, an' he wer now in the roach back, chompin stage ove the sickness, so he wer arter the clark fur a tickit tu the hospital. Well, the clark sole 'im a piece ove paper, part printin an' part ritin, wif a picter ove two pigs' hearts, what sum boy hed shot a arrer thru, an' lef hit stickin, printed at the top. That paper wer a splicin pass—sum calls hit a par ove licins—an' that very nite he tuck Mary, fur better, fur wus, tu hev an' tu hole tu him his heirs, an'—"

"Allow me to interrupt you," said our guest; "you do not quote the marriage ceremony correctly."

"Yu go tu *hell*, mistofer; yu bothers me."

This outrageous rebuff took the stranger all aback, and he sat down.

"Whar wer I? Oh yas, he married Mary tight an' fas', an' nex day he wer abil tu be about. His coat tho', an' his trousis look'd jis' a skrimshun too big, loose like, an' heavy tu tote. I axed him ef he felt soun. He sed yas, but he'd welded a steamboat shaftez the day afore, an' wer sorter tired like. Thar he tole a durn lie, fur he'd been a-ho'nin up dirt mos' ove the day, roun the widder's garden an' bellerin in the orchard. Mary an' him sot squar intu hous'-keepin, an' 'mung uther things he bot a lot ove *rar ripe garden-seed*, frum a Yankee peddler. Rar ripe co'n, rar ripe peas, rar ripe taters, rar ripe everything, an' the two yung durn'd fools wer dreadfully exercis'd 'bout hit. Wat sed he ment tu git him a rar ripe hammer an' anvil, an' Mary vow'd tu grashus, that she'd hev a rar ripe wheel an' loom, ef money wud git em. Purty soon arter he hed made the garden, he tuck a noshun tu work a spell down tu Ataylanty, in the railroad shop, es he sed he hed a sorter ailin in his back, an' he tho't weldin rail car-tire an' ingine axiltrees, wer lighter work nur sharpinin plows, an' puttin lap-links in trace-chains. So down he went, an' foun hit agreed wif him, fur he didn't cum back ontil the middil ove August. The fust thing he seed when he landid intu his cabin-door, wer a shoe-box wif rockers onder hit, an' the nex thing he seed, wer Mary herself, propped up in bed, an' the nex thing he seed arter that, wer a par ove littil rat-eyes a-shinin' abuv the aind ove the quilt, ontu Mary's arm, an' the nex an' las' thing he seed wer the two littil rat-eyes aforesed, a-turnin intu two hundred thousand big green stars, an' a-swingin roun an' roun the room, faster an' faster, ontil they mix'd intu one orful green flash. He drap't intu a limber pile on the floor. The durn'd fool what hed weldid the steamboat shaftez hed fainted safe an' soun es a gal skeered at a mad bull. Mary fotch a weak cat-scream, an' kivered her head, an' sot intu work ontu a whifflin dry cry, while littil Rat-eyes gin hitssef up tu suckin. Cryin an' suckin bof at onst ain't far; mus' cum pow'ful strainin on the wet secksun ove an' 'oman's constitushun; yet hit am ofen dun, an' more too. Ole Missis McKildrin, what wer a-nussin Mary, jis' got up frum knittin, an' flung a big gourd ove warter squar intu Wat's face, then she fotch a glass bottil ove swell-skull whisky outen the three-cornered cup-board, an' stood furnint Wat, a-holdin hit in wun han, an' the tin cup in tuther, waitin fur Wat tu cum to. She wer the piusses lookin ole 'oman jis' then, yu ever seed outside ove a prayer-meetin. Arter a spell, Wat begun tu move, twitchin his fingers, an' battin his eyes, sorter 'stonished like. That pius lookin statue sed tu him:

"'My son, jis' take a drap ove sperrits, honey. Yu'se very sick, dumplin, don't take on darlin, ef yu kin help hit, ducky, fur poor Margarit Jane am mons'ous ailin, an' the leas' nise ur takin on will kill the poor sufferin dear, an' yu'll loose yure tuckil ducky duv ove a sweet wifey, arter all she's dun gone thru fur yu. My dear son Watty, yu mus' consider her feelins a littil.' Sez Wat, a-turnin up his eyes at that vartus ole relick, sorter sick like—

"'I is a-considerin em a heap, rite now.'

"'Oh that's right, my good kine child.'

"Oh dam ef ole muther-in-lors can't plaster humbug over a feller, jis' es saft an' easy es they spreads a camrick hanketcher over a three hour ole baby's face; yu don't feel hit at all, but hit am thar, a plum inch thick, an' stickin fas es court-plaster. She raised Wat's head, an' sot the aidge ove the tin cup agin his lower teef, an' turned up the bottim slow an' keerful, a-winkin at Mary, hu wer a-peepin over the aidge ove the coverlid, tu see ef Wat *tuck the perskripshun*, fur a heap ove famerly cumfort 'pended on that ar ho'n ove sperrits. *Wun* ho'n allers saftens a man, the yeath over. Wat keep a-battin his eyes, wus nur a owl in daylight; at las' he raised hissef ontu wun elbow, an' rested his head in that han, sorter weak like. Sez he, mons'ous trimblin an' slow: 'Aprile—May—June—July—an' mos'—haf—ove—August,' a-countin the munths ontu the fingers ove tuther han, wif the thumb, a-shakin ove his head an' lookin at his spread fingers like they warn't his'n, ur they wer nastied wif sumfin. Then he counted em agin, slower, Aprile—May—June—July—an', mos' haf ove August, an' he run his thumb atwixt his fingers, es meanin mos' haf ove August, an' look'd at the pint ove hit, like hit mout be a snake's head. He raised his eyes tu the widder's face, who wer standin jis' es steady es a hitchin pos', an' still a-warin that pius 'spression ontu her pussonal feturs, an' a flood ove saft luv fur Wat, a-shinin strait frum her eyes intu his'n. Sez he, 'That jis' makes four munths, an' mos' a half, don't hit, Missis McKildrin?' She never sed one word. Wat reached fur the hath, an' got a dead fire-coal; then he made a mark clean acrost a floor-plank. Sez he, 'Aprile,' a-holdin down the coal ontu the aind ove the mark, like he wer fear'd hit mout blow away afore he got hit christened Aprile. Sez he, 'May'—an' he marked across the board agin; then he counted the marks, one, two, a-dottin at em wif the coal. 'June', an' he marked agin, one, two, three; counted wif the pint ove the coal. He scratched his head wif the littil finger ove the han holdin the charcoal, an' he drawed hit slowly acrost the board agin, peepin onder his wrist tu see when hit reached the crack, an' sez he, 'July,' es he lifted the coal; 'one, two, three, four,' countin frum lef tu right, an' then frum right tu lef. 'That haint but four, no way I kin fix hit. Ole Pike hissef cudn't make hit five, ef he wer tu sifer ontu hit ontil his laigs turned intu figger eights.' Then he made a mark, haf acrost a plank, spit on his finger, an' rubbed off a haf inch ove the aind, an' sez he, 'Mos haf ove August.' He looked up at the widder, an' thar she wer, same es ever, still a-holdin the flask agin her bussum, an' sez he 'Four months, an' mos' a haf. *Haint enuf, is hit, mammy?* hits jis' 'bout (lackin a littil) *haf enuf*, haint hit, mammy?'

"Missis McKildrin shuck her head sorter onsartin like, an' sez she, 'Take a drap more sperrits, Watty, my dear pet; dus yu mine buyin that ar rar ripe seed, frum the peddler?' Wat nodded his head, an' looked 'what ove hit,' but didn't say hit.

"'This is what cums ove hit, an' four months an' a half am rar ripe time fur babys, adzackly. Tu be sure, hit lacks a day ur two, but Margarit Jane wer allers a pow'ful interprizin gal, an' a yearly rizer.' Sez Wat,

"'How about the 'taters?'

"'Oh, *we* et 'taters es big es goose aigs, afore ole Missis Collinze's blossomed.'

"'How 'bout co'n?'

"'Oh, we shaved down roasin years afore hern tassel'd—'

"'An' peas?'

"'Yes son, we hed gobs an' lots in three weeks. Everything cums in adzackly half the time that hit takes the ole sort, an' yu *knows*, my darlin son, yu planted hit waseful. I tho't then you'd rar ripe everything on the place. Yu planted *often*, too, didn't yu luv? fur fear hit wudn't cum up.'

"'Ye-ye-s-s he—he did,' sed Mary a-cryin. Wat studied pow'ful deep a spell, an' the widder jis' waited. Widders allers wait, an' allers win. At las, sez he, 'Mammy.' She looked at Mary, an' winked these yere words at her, es plain es she cud a-talked em. 'Yu hearn him call me *mammy twiste*. I'se *got him* now. His backbone's a-limberin fas', he'll own the baby yet, see ef he don't. Jis' hole still, my darter, an' let yer mammy knead this dough, then yu may bake hit es brown es yu please.'

"'Mammy, when I married on the fust day ove Aprile'—The widder look'd oneasy; she tho't he mout be a-cupplin that day, his weddin, an' the idear, dam fool, tugether. But he warn't, fur he sed 'That day I gin ole man Collins my note ove han fur a hundred dullars, jew in one year arter date, the balluns on this lan. Dus yu think that ar seed will change the *time* eny, ur will hit alter the *amount?*' An' Wat looked at her powerful ankshus. She raised the whisky bottil way abuv her head, wif her thumb on the mouf, an' fotch the bottim down ontu her han, spat. Sez she, 'Watty, my dear b'lovid son, pripar tu pay *two* hundred dullars 'bout the fust ove October, fur hit'll be jew jis' then, *es* sure es that littil black-eyed angel in the bed thar, am yer darter.'

"Wat drap't his head, an' sed, '*Then hits a dam sure thing.*' Rite yere, the baby fotch a rattlin loud squall, (I speck Mary wer sorter figetty jis' then, an' hurt hit). 'Yas' (sez Wat, a-wallin a red eye to'ards the bed); 'my littil she—what wer hit yu called her name, mammy?' 'I called her a sweet littil angel, an' she is wun, es sure es yu're her daddy, my b'loved son.' 'Well,' sez Wat, 'my littil sweet, patent rar ripe she angel, ef yu lives tu marryin time, yu'll 'stonish sum man body outen his shut, ef yu don't rar ripe lose hits vartu arter the fust plantin, that's all.' He rared up on aind, wif his mouf pouch'd out. He had a pow'ful forrid, fur-reachin, bread funnel, enyhow—cud a-bit the aigs outen a cat-fish, in two-foot warter, wifout wettin his eyebrows. 'Dod durn rar ripe seed, an' rare ripe peddlers, an' rare ripe notes tu the hottes' corner ove—'

"'Stop Watty, *darlin*, don't swar; 'member yu belongs tu meetin.'

"'My blacksmith's fire,' ainded Wat, an' he studies a long spell; sez he,

"'Did you save eny ove that infunnel doubil-trigger seed?' 'Yas,' sez the widder, 'thar in that bag by the cupboard.' Wat got up ofen the floor, tuck a countin sorter look at the charcoal marks, an' reached down the bag; he went tu the door an' called 'Suke, muley! Suke, Suke, cow, chick, chick, chicky chick.' 'Wat's yu gwine tu du now, my dear son?' sed Missis McKildrin. 'I'se jis' gwine tu feed this actif *smart* trick tu the cow, an' the hens, that's what I'se gwine tu du. Ole muley haint hed a calf in two years, an' I'll eat sum rar ripe aigs.' Mary now venter'd tu speak: 'Husban, I ain't sure hit'll work on hens; cum an' kiss me my luv.' I hain't sure hit'll work on hens, either,' sed Wat. 'They's powerful onsartin in thar ways, well es wimen,' an' he flung out a hanful spiteful like. 'Takin the rar ripe invenshun all tugether, frum 'taters an' peas tu notes ove han, an' childer, I can't say I likes hit much,' an' he flung out anuther hanful. 'Yer mam hed thuteen the ole way, an' ef this truck stays 'bout the hous', yu'se good fur twenty-six, maybe thuty, fur yu'se a pow'ful interprizin gal, yer mam sez,' an' he flung out anuther hanful, overhandid, es hard es ef he wer flingin rocks at a stealin sow. 'Make yere mine easy,' sed the widder 'hit never works on married folks only the fust time.' 'Say them words agin,' sed Wat, 'I'se glad tu hear em. Is hit the same way wif notes ove han?' 'I speck hit am,' answer'd the widder, wif jis' a taste ove strong vinegar in the words, es she sot the flask in the cupboard wif a push.

* * *

THE HARP OF A THOUSAND STRINGS

by Henry Taliaferro Lewis

(1823–1870)

"I may say to yo, my brethering, that I am not an edecated man, an' I am not one o' them that beleeves edecation is necessary for a gospel minister, fur I beleeve the Lord edecates his preachers jest as he wants 'em to be edecated; and although I say it that ought n't to say it, yet in the State of Indianny, whar I live, thar's no man as gits a bigger congregation nor what I gits.

"Thar may be some here today, my brethering, as don't know what persuasion I am uv. Well, I may say to you, my brethering, that I am a Hard-Shell Baptist. Thar's some folks as don't like the Hard-Shell Baptists, but I'd rather hev a hard shell as no shell at all. You see me here today, my brethering, dressed up in fine close; you mout think I was proud, but I am not proud, my brethering; and although I've been a preacher uv the gospel for twenty years, and although I'm capting uv that flat-boat that lies at your landing, I'm not proud, my brethering.

"I'm not gwine ter tell you *edzackly* whar my tex may be found; suffice it tu say, it's in the leds of the Bible, and you'll find it somewhar 'tween the fust chapter of the book of Generation, and the last chapter of the book of Revolutions, and ef you'll go and sarch the Scripturs, you'll not only find *my* tex thar, but a great many other *texes* as will do you good to read; and my tex, when you shill find it, you shill find it to read thus:

"'And he played on a harp uv a thousand strings—sperits of just men made perfeck.'

"My tex, brethren, leads me to speak uv sperits. Now thar's a great many kind of sperits in the world—in the fust place, thar's the sperits as som folks call ghosts; then thar's the sperits uv tur-pen*time;* and then thar's the sperits as some folks call liquor, and I've got as good artikel uv them kind uv sperits on my flat-boat as ever was fotched down the Mississippi River; but thar's a great many other kind of sperits, for the tex says: 'He played on a harp uv a *thou*-sand strings—sperits of just men made perfeck.'

"But I'll tell you the kind of sperits as is ment in the tex: it's *fire.* That is the kind of sperits as is ment in the tex, my brethering. Now thar's a great many kinds of fire in the world. In the fust place, thar's the common sort uv fire you light a segar or pipe with, and then thar's camfire, fire before you're ready to fall back, and many other kinds uv fire, for the tex ses: 'He played on a harp uv a *thou*-sand strings—sperits uv just men made perfeck.'

"But I'll tell you the kind of fire as is ment in the tex, my brethering—it's *hell-fire!* an' that's the kind of fire as a great many of you'll come to, ef you don't do better nor what you have bin doin'—for 'He played on a harp uv a *thou*-sand strings—sperits of just men made perfeck.'

"Now, the different sorts uv fire in the world may be likened unto the different persuasions in the world. In the first place, we have the 'Piscapalions, and they are a high salin' and a highfalutin' set, and they may be likened unto a turkey-buzzard, that flies up into the air, and he goes up and up till he looks no bigger than your finger-nail, and the fust thing you know, he cums down and down, and is a fillin' himself on the karkiss of a dead hoss by the side uv the road—and 'He played on a harp uv a *thou*-sand strings—sperits of just men made perfeck.'

"And then, thar's the Methodis, and they may be likened unto the squirrel, runnin' up into a tree, for the Methodis believes in gwine on from one degree uv grace to another, and finally on to perfecshun; and the squirrel goes up and up, and he jumps from lim' to lim', and branch to branch, and the fust thing you know, he falls, and down he comes kerflummux; and that's like the Methodis, for they is allers fallin' from Grace, ah! And 'He played on a harp uv a *thou*-sand strings—sperits of just men made perfeck.'

"And then, my brethering, thar's the Baptist, ah! and they hev bin likened unto a possum on a 'simmon tree, and the thunders may roll, and then the earth may quake, but that possum clings there still, ah! And you may shake one foot loose, and the other's thar; and you may shake all feet loose, and he laps his tail around the lim', and he clings fur ever—for 'He played on a harp of a *thou*-sand strings—sperits of just men made perfeck.'"

LITERARY COMEDIANS

∞

(1855–1900)

PHOENIXIANA

by George Horatio Derby

(1823–1861)

Musical Review Extraordinary

San Diego, July 10th, 1854.

As your valuable work is not supposed to be so entirely identified with San Franciscan interests, as to be careless what takes place in other portions of this great *kedntry*, and as it is received and read in San Diego with great interest (I have loaned my copy to over four different literary gentlemen, most of whom have read some of it), I have thought it not improbable that a few critical notices of the musical performances and the drama of this place might be acceptable to you, and interest your readers. I have been, moreover, encouraged to this task by the perusal of your interesting musical and theatrical critiques on San Francisco performers and performances; as I feel convinced that, if you devote so much space to them, you will not allow any little feeling of rivalry between the two great cities to prevent your noticing ours, which, without the slightest feeling of prejudice, I must consider as infinitely superior. I propose this month to call your attention to the two great events in our theatrical and musical world—the appearance of the talented Miss Pelican, and the production of Tarbox's celebrated "Ode Symphonie" of "The Plains."

The critiques on the former are from the columns of *The Vallecetos Sentinel*, to which they were originally contributed by me, appearing on the respective dates of June 1st and June 31st.

From the Vallecetos Sentinel, June 1st.

Miss Pelican.—Never during our dramatic experience, has a more exciting event occurred than the sudden bursting upon our theatrical firmament, full, blazing, unparalleled, of the bright, resplendent and particular star, whose honored name shines refulgent at the head of this article. Coming among us unheralded, almost unknown, without claptrap, in a wagon drawn by oxen across the plains, with no agent to get up a counterfeit enthusiasm in her favor, she appeared before us for the first time at the San Diego Lyceum, last evening, in the trying and difficult character of Ingomar, or the Tame Savage. We are at a loss to describe our sensations, our admiration, at her magnificent, her superhuman efforts. We do not hesitate to say that she is by far the superior of any living actress; and, as we believe hers to be the perfection of acting, we cannot be wrong in the belief that no one hereafter will ever be found to approach her. Her conception of the character of Ingomar was perfection itself; her playful and ingenuous manner, her light girlish laughter, in the scene with Sir Peter, showed an appreciation of the savage character, which nothing but the most arduous study, the most elaborate training could produce; while her awful change to the stern, unyielding, uncompromising father in the tragic scene of Duncan's murder, was indeed nature itself. Miss Pelican is about seventeen years of age, of miraculous beauty, and most thrilling voice. It is needless to say she dresses admirably, as in fact we have said all we can say when we called her most truthfully, perfection. Mr. John Boots took the part of Parthenia very creditably, etc., etc.

From the Vallecetos Sentinel, June 31st.

MISS PELICAN.—As this lady is about to leave us to commence an engagement on the San Francisco stage, we should regret exceedingly if any thing we have said about her, should send with her a *prestige* which might be found undeserved on trial. The fact is, Miss Pelican is a very ordinary actress; indeed, one of the most indifferent ones we ever happened to see. She came here from the Museum at Fort Laramie, and we praised her so injudiciously that she became completely spoiled. She has performed a round of characters during the last week, very miserably, though we are bound to confess that her performance of King Lear last evening, was superior to any thing of the kind we ever saw. Miss Pelican is about forty-three years of age, singularly plain in her personal appearance, awkward and embarrassed, with a cracked and squeaking voice, and really dresses quite outrageously. *She has much to learn—poor thing!*

I take it the above notices are rather ingenious. The fact is, I'm no judge of acting, and don't know how Miss Pelican will turn out. If well, why there's my notice of June the 1st; if ill, then

June 31st comes in play, and, as there is but one copy of the *Sentinel* printed, it's an easy matter to destroy the incorrect one; *both can't be wrong;* so I've made a sure thing of it in any event. Here follows my musical critique, which I flatter myself is of rather superior order:

THE PLAINS. ODE SYMPHONIE PAR JABEZ TARBOX.—This glorious composition was produced at the San Diego Odeon, on the 31st of June, ult., for the first time in this or any other country, by a very full orchestra (the performance taking place immediately after supper), and a chorus composed of the entire "Sauer Kraut-Verein," the "Wee Gates Association," and choice selections from the "Gyascutus" and "Pikeharmonic" societies. The solos were rendered by Herr Tuden Links, the recitations by Herr Von Hyden Schnapps, both performers being assisted by Messrs. John Smith and Joseph Brown, who held their coats, fanned them, and furnished water during the more overpowering passages.

"The Plains" we consider the greatest musical achievement that has been presented to an enraptured public. Like Waterloo among battles; Napoleon among warriors; Niagara among falls, and Peck among senators, this magnificent composition stands among Oratorios, Operas, Musical Melodramas and performances of Ethiopian Serenaders, peerless and unrivalled. *Il frappe toute chose parfaitement froid.*

"It does not depend for its success" upon its plot, its theme, its school or its master, for it has very little if any of them, but upon its soul-subduing, all-absorbing, high-faluting effect upon the audience, every member of which it causes to experience the most singular and exquisite sensations. Its strains at times remind us of those of the old master of the steamer McKim, who never went to sea without being unpleasantly affected;—a straining after effect he used to term it. Blair in his lecture on beauty, and Mills in his treatise on logic (p. 31) have alluded to the feeling which might be produced in the human mind, by something of this transcendentally sublime description, but it has remained for M. Tarbox, in the production of The Plains, to call this feeling forth.

The symphonie opens upon the wide and boundless plains, in longitude 115° W., latitude 35° 21′ 03″ N., and about sixty miles from the west bank of Pitt River. These data are beautifully and clearly expressed by a long (topographically) drawn note from an E flat clarinet. The sandy nature of the soil, sparsely dotted with bunches of cactus and artemisia, the extended view, flat and unbroken to the horizon, save by the rising smoke in the extreme verge, denoting the vicinity of a Pi Utah village, are represented by the bass drum. A few notes on the piccolo, calls the attention to a solitary antelope, picking up mescal beans in the foreground. The sun having an altitude of 36° 27', blazes down upon the scene in indescribable majesty. "Gradually the sounds roll forth in a song" of rejoicing to the God of Day.

> "Of thy intensity
> And great immensity
> Now then we sing;
> Beholding in gratitude
> Thee in this latitude,
> Curious thing."

Which swells out into "Hey Jim along, Jim along Josey," then *decrescendo, mas o menos, poco pocita,* dies away and dries up.

Suddenly we hear approaching a train from Pike County, consisting of seven families, with forty-six wagons, each drawn by thirteen oxen; each family consists of a man in butternut-colored clothing driving the oxen; a wife in butternut-colored clothing riding in the wagon, holding a butternut baby, and seventeen butternut children running promiscuously about the establishment; all are barefooted, dusty, and smell unpleasantly. (All these circumstances are expressed by pretty rapid fiddling for some minutes, winding up with a puff from the orpheclide played by an intoxicated Teuton with an atrocious breath—it is impossible to misunderstand the description.) Now rises o'er the plains in mellifluous accents, the grand Pike County Chorus.

> "Oh we'll soon be thar
> In the land of gold,
> Through the forest old,
> O'er the mounting cold,
> With spirits bold—
> Oh, we come, we come,
> And we'll soon be thar.
> Gee up Bolly! whoo, up, whoo haw!"

The train now encamp. The unpacking of the kettles and mess-pans, the unyoking of the oxen, the gathering about the various camp-fires, the frizzling of the pork, are so clearly expressed by the music, that the most untutored savage could readily comprehend it. Indeed, so vivid and lifelike was the representation, that a lady sitting near us, involuntarily exclaimed aloud, at a certain passage, "*Thar, that pork's burning!*" and it was truly interesting to watch the gratified expression of her face, when, by a few notes of the guitar, the pan was removed from the fire, and the blazing pork extinguished.

This is followed by the beautiful aria:—

> "O! marm, I want a pancake!"

Followed by that touching recitative:—

> "Shet up, or I will spank you!"

To which succeeds a grand *crescendo* movement, representing the flight of the child, with the pancake, the pursuit of the mother, and the final arrest and summary punishment of the former, represented by the rapid and successive strokes of the castanet.

The turning in for the night follows; and the deep and stertorous breathing of the encampment, is well given by the bassoon, while the sufferings and trials of an unhappy father with an unpleasant infant, are touchingly set forth by the *cornet à piston.*

Part Second—the Night attack of the Pi Utahs; the fearful cries of the demoniac Indians; the shrieks of the females and children; the rapid and effective fire of the rifles; the stampede of the oxen; their recovery and the final repulse; the Pi Utahs being routed after a loss of thirty-six killed and wounded, while the Pikes lose but one scalp (from an old fellow who wore a wig, and lost it in the scuffle), are faithfully given, and excite the most intense interest in the minds of the hearers; the emotions of fear, admiration and delight, succeeding each other in their minds, with almost painful rapidity. Then follows the grand chorus:

> "Oh! we gin them fits,
> The Ingen Utahs.
> With our six-shooters—
> We gin 'em pertickuler fits."

After which, we have the charming recitative of Herr Tuden Links, to the infant, which is really one of the most charming gems in the performance:

> "Now, dern your skin, *can't* you be easy?"

Morning succeeds. The sun rises magnificently (octavo flute)—breakfast is eaten—in a rapid movement on three sharps; the oxen are caught and yoked up—with a small drum and triangle; the watches, purses, and other valuables of the conquered Pi Utahs, are stored away in a camp-kettle, to a small movement on the piccolo, and the train moves on, with the grand chorus:—

> "We'll soon be thar,
> Gee up Bolly! Whoo hup! whoo haw!"

The whole concludes with the grand hymn and chorus:—

> "When we die we'll go to Benton,
> Whup! Whoo, haw!
> The greatest man that e'er land saw,
> Gee!
> Who this little airth was sent on
> Whup! whoo, haw!
> To tell a 'hawk from a hand-saw!'
> Gee!"

The immense expense attending the production of this magnificent work; the length of time required to prepare the chorus; the incredible number of instruments destroyed at each rehearsal, have hitherto prevented M. Tarbox from placing it before the American public, and it has remained for San Diego to show herself superior to her sister cities of the Union, in musical taste and appreciation, and in high-souled liberality, by patronizing this immortal prodigy, and enabling its author to bring it forth in accordance with his wishes and its capabilities. We trust every citizen of San Diego and Vallecetos will listen to it ere it is withdrawn; and if there yet lingers in San Francisco one spark of musical fervor, or a remnant of taste for pure harmony, we can only say that the Southerner sails from that place once a fortnight and that the passage money is but forty-five dollars.

INTERVIEW BETWEEN THE EDITOR AND PHOENIX

The Thomas Hunt had arrived, she lay at the wharf at New Town, and a rumor had reached our ears that "the Judge" was on board. Public anxiety had been excited to the highest pitch to witness the result of the meeting between us. It had been stated publicly that "the Judge" would whip us the moment he arrived; but though we thought a conflict probable, we had never been very sanguine as to its terminating in this manner. Coolly we gazed from the window of the Office upon the New Town road; we descried a cloud of dust in the distance; high above it waved a whip lash, and we said, "the Judge" cometh, and "his driving is like that of Jehu the son of Nimshi, for he driveth furiously."

Calmly we seated ourselves in the "arm chair," and continued our labors upon our magnificent Pictorial. Anon, a step, a heavy step, was heard upon the stairs, and "the Judge" stood before us.

"In shape and gesture proudly eminent, stood like a tower: . . . but his face deep scars of thunder had entrenched, and care sat on his faded cheek; but under brows of dauntless courage and considerate pride, waiting revenge."

We rose, and with an unfaltering voice said: "Well, Judge, how do you do?" He made no reply, but commenced taking off his coat.

We removed ours, also our cravat.

$$* \quad * \quad * \quad * \quad * \quad * \quad * \quad *$$
$$* \quad * \quad * \quad * \quad * \quad * \quad * \quad *$$

The sixth and last round, is described by the pressman and compositors, as having been fearfully scientific. We held "the Judge" down over the Press by our nose (which we had inserted between his teeth for that purpose), and while our hair was employed in holding one of his hands, we held the other in our left, and with the "sheep's foot" brandished above our head, shouted to him, "say Waldo," Never! he gasped—

> Oh! my Bigler he would have muttered,
> But that he 'dried up,' ere the word was uttered.

At this moment, we discovered that we had been laboring under a "misunderstanding," and through the amicable intervention of the pressman, who thrust a roller between our faces (which gave the whole affair a very different complexion), the *matter* was finally settled in the most friendly terms—"and without prejudice to the honor of either party." We write this while sitting without any clothing, except our left stocking, and the rim of our hat encircling our neck like the 'ruff' of the Elizabethan era. . . .

THE WRITINGS OF ARTEMUS WARD

by Charles Farrar Browne

(1834–1867)

ONE OF MR. WARD'S BUSINESS LETTERS

To the Editor of the ——

SIR—I'm movin along—slowly along—down tords your place. I want you should rite me a letter, sayin how is the show bizniss in your place. My show at present consists of three moral Bares, a Kangaroo (a amoozin little Raskal—t'would make you larf yerself to deth to see the little cuss jump up and squeal) wax figgers of G. Washington Gen. Taylor John Bunyan Capt. Kidd and Dr. Webster in the act of killin Dr. Parkman, besides several miscellanyus moral wax statoots of celebrated piruts & murderers, &c., ekalled by few & exceld by none. Now Mr. Editor, scratch orf a few lines sayin how is the show bizniss down to your place. I shall hav my hanbills dun at your offiss. Depend upon it. I want you should git my hanbills up in flamin stile. Also git up a tremenjus excitemunt in yr. paper 'bowt my onparaleld Show. We must fetch the public sumhow. We must wurk on their feelins. Cum the moral on 'em strong. If it's a temprance community tell 'em I sined the pledge fifteen minits arter Ise born, but on the contery ef your peple take their tods, say Mister Ward is as Jenial a feller as we ever met, full of conwiviality, & the life an sole of the Soshul Bored. Take, don't you? If you say anythin abowt my show say my snaiks is as harmliss as the new born Babe. What a interestin study it is to see a zewological animil like a snaik under perfeck subjecshun! My kangaroo is the most larfable little cuss I ever saw. All for 15 cents. I am anxyus to skewer your infloounce. I repeet in regard to them hanbills that I shall git 'em struck orf up to your printin office. My perlitercal sentiments agree with yourn exackly. I know thay do, becawz I never saw a man whoos didn't.

Respectively yures,

A. Ward.

P.S.—You scratch my back & Ile scratch your back.

INTERVIEW WITH PRESIDENT LINCOLN

I hav no politics. Nary a one. I'm not in the bisiness. If I was I spose I should holler versiffrusly in the streets at nite and go home to Betsy Jane smellen of coal ile and gin, in the mornin. I should go to the Poles arly. I should stay there all day. I should see to it that my nabers was thar. I should git carriges to take the kripples, the infirm and the indignant thar. I should be on guard agin frauds and sich. I should be on the look out for the infamus lise of the enemy, got up just be4 elecshun for perlitical effeck. When all was over and my candydate was elected, I should move heving & arth—so to speak—until I got orfice, which if I didn't git a orfice I should turn round and abooze the Administration with all my mite and maine. But I'm not in the bisniss. I'm in a far more respectful bisniss nor what pollertics is. I wouldn't giv two cents to be a Congresser. The wuss insult I ever received was when sertin citizens of Baldinsville axed me to run fur the Legislater. Sez I, My frends, dostest think I'd stoop to that there?" They turned as white as a sheet. I spoke in my most orfullest tones, & they knowd I wasn't to be trifled with. They slunked out of site to onct.

There4, havin no politics, I made bold to visit Old Abe at his humstid in Springfield. I found the old feller in his parler, surrounded by a perfeck swarm of orfice seekers. Knowin he had been capting of a flat boat on the roarin Mississippy I thought I'd address him in sailor lingo, so sez I "Old Abe, ahoy! Let out yer main-suls, reef hum the fore-castle & throw yer jib-poop overboard! Shiver my timbers, my harty!" (N.B. This is ginuine mariner langwidge. I know, becawz I've seen sailor plays acted out by them New York theater fellers.) Old Abe lookt up quite cross & sez, "Send in yer petition by & by. I can't possibly look at it now. Indeed, I can't. It's onpossible sir!"

"Mr. Linkin, who do you spect I air?" sed I.

"A orfice-seeker, to be sure?" sed he.

"Wall, sir," sed I, "you s never more mistaken in your life. You hain't gut a orfiss I'd take under no circumstances. I'm A. Ward. Wax figgers is my perfeshun. I'm the father of Twins, and they look like me—*both of them*. I cum to pay a frendly visit to the President eleck of the United States. If so be you wants to see me say so—if not, say so, & I'm orf like a jug handle."

"Mr. Ward, sit down. I am glad to see you, Sir."

"Repose in Abraham's Buzzum!" sed one of the orfice seekers, his idee bein to git orf a goak at my expense.

"Wall," sez I, "ef all you fellers repose in that there Buzzum thare'll be mity poor nussin for sum of you!" whereupon Old Abe buttoned his weskit clear up and blusht like a maidin of sweet 16. Jest at this pint of the conversation another swarm of orfice-seekers arrove & cum pilin into the parler. Sum wanted post orfices, sum wanted collectorships, sum wantid furrin missions, and all wanted sumthin. I thought Old Abe would go crazy. He hadn't more than had time to shake hands with 'em, before another tremenjis crowd cum porein onto his premises. His house and dooryard was now perfeckly overflowed with orfice seekers, all clameruss for a immejit interview with Old Abe. One man from Ohio, who had about seven inches of corn whisky into him, mistook me for Old Abe and addrest me as "The Pra-hayrie Flower of the West!" Thinks I *you* want a offiss putty bad. Another man with a gold heded cane and a red nose told Old Abe he was "a seckind Washington & the Pride of the Boundliss West."

Sez I, "Squire, you wouldn't take a small post-offis if you could git it, would you?"

Sez he, "a patrit is abuv them things, sir!"

"There's a putty big crop of patrits this season, aint there Squire?" sez I, when *another* crowd of offiss seekers pored in. The house, door-yard, barn & woodshed was now all full, and when *another* crowd cum I told 'em not to go away for want of room as the hog-pen was still empty. One patrit from a small town in Michygan went up on top the house, got into the chimney and slid down into the parler where Old Abe was endeverin to keep the hungry pack of orfice-seekers from chawin him up alive without benefit of clergy. The minit he reached the fire-place he jumpt up, brusht the soot out of his eyes, and yelled: "Don't make eny pint-ment at the Spunkville postoffiss till you've read my papers. All the respectful men in our town is signers to that there dockyment!"

"Good God!" cride Old Abe, "they cum upon me from the skize—down the chimneys, and from the bowels of the yearth!" He hadn't more'n got them words out of his delikit mouth before two fat offiss-seekers from Wisconsin, in endeverin to crawl atween his legs for the purpuss of applyin for the tollgateship at Mil-wawky, upsot the President eleck & he would hev gone sprawlin into the fire-place if I hadn't caught him in these arms. But I hadn't morn'n stood him up strate before another man cum crashin down the chimney, his head strikin me vilently agin the inards and prostratin my voluptoous form onto the floor. "Mr. Linkin," shoutid the infatooated being, "my papers is signed by every clergyman in our town, and likewise the skoolmaster!"

Sez I, "you egrejis ass," gittin up & brushin the dust from my eyes, "I'll sign your papers with this bunch of bones, if you don't be a little more keerful how you make my bread basket a depot in the futer. How do you like that air perfumery?" sez I, shuving my fist under his nose. "Them's the kind of papers I'll giv you! Them's the paper's *you* want!"

"But I workt hard for the ticket; I toiled night and day! The patrit should be rewarded!"

"Virtoo," sed I, holdin' the infatooated man by the coat-collar, "virtoo, sir, is its own reward. Look at me!" He did look at me, and qualed be4 my gase. "The fact is," I continued, lookin' round on the hungry crowd, "there is scacely a offiss for every ile lamp carrid round durin' this campane. I wish thare was. I wish thare was furrin missions to be filled on varis lonely Islands where eppydemics rage incessantly, and if I was in Old Abe's place I'd send every mother's son of you to them. What air you here for?" I continnered, warmin up considerable, "can't you giv Abe a minit's peace? Don't you see he's worrid most to death! Go home, you miserable men, go home & till the sile! Go to peddlin tin-ware—go to choppin wood—go to bilin' sope—stuff sassengers—black boots—git a clerkship on sum respectable manure cart—go round as original Swiss Bell Ringers—becum 'origenal and only' Campbell Minstrels—go to lecturin at 50 dollars a nite—imbark in the peanut bizniss—*write for the Ledger*—saw off your legs and go round givin concerts, with techin appeals to a charitable public, printed on your handbills—anything for a honest living, but don't come round here drivin Old Abe crazy by your outrajis cuttings up! Go home. Stand not upon the order of your goin', but go to onct! If in five minits from this time," sez I pullin' out my new sixteen dollar huntin cased watch, and brandishin' it before their eyes, "Ef in five minits from this time a single sole of you remains on these here premises, I'll go out to my cage near by, and let my Boy Constructor loose! & ef he gits amung you, you'll think old Solferino has cum again and no mistake!" You ought to hev seen them scamper, Mr. Fair. They run orf as tho Satun his self was arter them with a red hot ten pronged pitchfork. In five minits the premises was clear.

"How kin I ever repay you, Mr. Ward, for your kindness?" sed Old Abe, advancin and shakin me warmly by the hand. "How kin I ever repay you, sir?"

"By givin the whole country a good, sound administration. By poerin' ile upon the troubled waturs, North and South. By pursooin' a patriotic, firm, and just course, and then if any State wants to secede, let 'em Sesesh!"

"How 'bout my Cabinit, Mister Ward?" sed Abe.

"Fill it up with Showmen sir! Showmen is devoid of politics. They hain't got any principles! They know how to cater for the public. They know what the public wants, North & South. Showmen, sir, is honest men. Ef you doubt their literary ability, look at their posters, and see small bills! Ef you want a Cabinit as is a Cabinit fill it up with showmen, but don't call on me. The moral wax figger perfeshun musn't be permitted to go down while there's a drop of blood in these vains! A. Linkin, I wish you well! Ef Powers or Walcutt wus to pick out a model for a beautiful man, I scarcely think they'd sculp you; but ef you do the fair thing by your country you'll make as putty a angel as any of us! A. Linkin, use the talents which Nature has put into you judishusly and firmly, and all will be well! A. Linkin, adoo!"

He shook me cordyully by the hand—we exchanged picters, so we could gaze upon each others' liniments when far away from one another—he at the hellum of the ship of State, and I at the hellum of the show bizniss—admittance only 15 cents.

The Tower of London

Mr. Punch, My dear Sir,—I skurcely need inform you that your excellent Tower is very pop'lar with peple from the agricultooral districks, and it was chiefly them class which I found waitin at the gates the other mornin.

I saw at once that the Tower was established on a firm basis. In the entire history of firm basisis I don't find a basis more firmer than this one.

"You have no Tower in America?" said a man in the crowd, who had somehow detected my denomination.

"Alars! no," I ansered; "we boste of our enterprise and improovements, and yit we are devoid of a Tower. America, oh my onhappy country! thou hast not got no Tower! It's a sweet Boon."

The gates was opened after awhile, and we all purchist tickets and went into a waitin-room.

"My frens," said a pale-faced little man, in black close, "this is a sad day."

"Inasmuch as to how?" I say.

"I mean it is sad to think that so many people have been killed within these gloomy walls. My frens, let us drop a tear!"

"No," I said, "you must excuse me. Others may drop one if they feel like it; but as for me, I decline. The early managers of this institootion were a bad lot, and their crimes were trooly orful; but I can't sob for those who died four or five hundred years ago. If they was my own relations I couldn't. It's absurb to shed sobs over things which occurd durin the rain of Henry the Three. Let us be cheerful," I continnerd. "Look at the festiv Warders, in their red flannil jackets. They are cheerful, and why should it not be thusly with us?"

A Warder now took us in charge, and showed us the Trater's Gate, the armers and things. The Trater's Gate is wide enuff to admit about twenty trater's abrest, I should jedge; but beyond this, I couldn't see that it was superior to gates in gen'ral.

Traters, I will here remark, are a onfortnit class of people. If they wasn't they wouldn't be traters. They conspire to bust up a country—they fail, and they're traters. They bust her, and they become statesmen and heroes.

Take the case of Gloster, afterwards Old Dick the Three, who may be seen at the Tower on horseback, in a heavy tin overcoat—take Mr. Gloster's case. Mr. G. was a conspirator of the basist dye, and if he'd failed, he would have been hung on a sour apple tree. But Mr. G. succeeded, and became great. He was slewed by Col. Richmond, but he lives in histry, and his equestrian figger may be seen daily for a sixpence, in conjunction with other em'nent persons, and no extra charge for the Warder's able and bootiful lectur.

There's one king in the room who is mounted onto a foamin steed, his right hand graspin a barber's pole. I didn't learn his name.

The room where the daggers and pistils and other weppins is kept is interestin. Among this collection of choice cuttlery I notist the bow and arrer used at this day by certin tribes of American Injuns, and they shoot 'em off with such a excellent precision that I almost sigh'd to be a Injun, when I was in the Rocky

Mountin regin. They are a pleasant lot them Injuns. Mr. Cooper and Dr. Catlin have told us of the red man's wonerful eloquence, and I found it so. Our party was stopt on the plains of Utah by a band of Shoshones, whose chief said:

"Brothers! the pale face is welcome. Brothers! the sun is sinking in the west, and Wa-na-bucky-she will soon cease speakin. Brothers! the poor red man belongs to a race which is fast becomin extink."

He then whooped in a shrill manner, stole all our blankets and whisky, and fled to the primeval forest to conceal his emotions.

I will remark here, while on the subjeck of Injuns, that they are in the main a very shaky set, with even less sense than the Fenians, and when I hear philanthropists bewailin the fack that every year "carries the noble red man nearer the settin sun," I simply have to say I'm glad of it, tho' it is rough on the settin sun. They call you by the sweet name of Brother one minit, and the next they scalp you with their Thomas-hawks. But I wander. Let us return to the Tower.

At one end of the room where the weppins is kept, is a wax figger of Queen Elizabeth, mounted on a fiery stuffed hoss, whose glass eye flashes with pride, and whose red morocker nostril dilates hawtily, as if conscious of the royal burden he bears. I have associated Elizabeth with the Spanish Armady. She's mixed up with it at the Surrey Theatre, where Troo to the Core is bein' acted, and in which a full bally core is introjooced on board the Spanish Admiral's ship, givin the audiens the idee that he intends openin a moosic-hall in Plymouth the moment he conkers that town. But a very interesting drammer is Troo to the Core, notwithstandin the eccentric conduck of the Spanish Admiral; and very nice it is in Queen Elizabeth to make Martin Truegold a baronet.

The Warder shows us some instrooments of tortur, such as thumbscrews, throat-collars, etc., statin that these was conkerd from the Spanish Armady, and addin what a crooil peple the Spaniards was in them days—which elissited from a bright eyed little girl of about twelve summers the remark that she tho't it *was* rich to talk about the croolity of the Spaniards usin thumbscrews, when we was in a Tower where so many poor peple's heads had been cut off. This made the Warder stammer and turn red.

I was so blessed with the little girl's brightness that I could have kissed the dear child, and I would if she'd been six years older.

I think my companions intended makin a day of it, for they

all had sandwiches, sassiges, etc. The sad-lookin man, who had wanted us to drop a tear afore we started to go round, fling'd such quantities of sassige into his mouth, that I expected to see him choke hisself to death; he said to me, in the Beauchamp Tower, where the poor prisoners writ their onhappy names on the cold walls, "This is a sad sight."

"It is, indeed," I anserd. "You're black in the face. You shouldn't eat sassige in public without some rehearsals before-hand. You manage it orkwardly."

"No," he said, "I mean this sad room."

Indeed, he was quite right. Tho' so long ago all these drefful things happened I was very glad to git away from this gloomy room, and go where the rich and sparklin Crown Jewils is kept. I was so pleased with the Queen's Crown, that it occurd to me what a agree'ble surprise it would be to send a sim'lar one home to my wife; and I asked the Warder what was the vally of a good, well-constructed Crown like that. He told me, but on cypherin up with a pencil the amount of funs I have in the Jint Stock Bank, I conclooded I'd send her a genteel silver watch instid.

And so I left the Tower. It is a solid and commandin edifis, but I deny that it is cheerful. I bid it adoo without a pang.

I was droven to my hotel by the most melancholly driver of a four-wheeler that I ever saw. He heaved a deep sigh as I gave him two shillings. "I'll give you six d's more," I said, "if it hurts you so."

"It isn't that," he said, with a hart-rendin groan, "it's only a way I have. My mind's upset to-day. I at one time thot I'd drive you into the Thames. I've been reading all the daily papers to try and understand about Governor Ayre, and my mind is totterin. It's really wonderful I didn't drive you into the Thames."

I asked the onhappy man what his number was, so I could readily find him in case I should want him agin, and bad him good-bye. And then I tho't what a frollicsome day I'd made of it. Respectably, etc.,

ARTEMUS WARD

"I AM HERE"

There is no mistake about that, and there is a good prospect of my staying here for some time to come. The snow is deep on the ground, and more is falling.

The Doctor looks glum, and speaks of his ill-starred country-man Sir J. Franklin, who went to the Arctic once too much.

"A good thing happened down here the other day," said a miner from New Hampshire to me. "A man of Boston dressin' went through there, and at one of the stations there wasn't any mules. Says the man who was fixed out to kill in his Boston dressin', 'Where's them mules?' Says the driver, 'Them mules is into the sage-brush. You go catch 'em—that's wot *you* do.' Says the man of Boston dressin', 'Oh no!' Says the driver, 'Oh yes!' and he took his long coach-whip and licked the man of Boston dressin' till he went and caught them mules. How does that strike you as a joke?"

It didn't strike me as much of a joke to pay a hundred and seventy-five dollars in gold fare, and then be horse-whipped by stage-drivers, for declining to chase mules. But people's ideas of humor differ, just as people's ideas differ in regard to shrewdness—which "reminds me of a little story." Sitting in a New England country store one day I over-heard the following dialogue between two brothers:

"Say, Bill, wot you done with that air sorrel mare of yourn?"

"Sold her," said William, with a smile of satisfaction.

"Wot'd you git?"

"Hund'd an' fifty dollars, cash deown!"

"Show! Hund'd an' fifty for that kickin' spavin'd critter? Who'd you sell her to?"

"Sold her to mother!"

"Wot!" exclaimed brother No. 1, "did you railly sell that kickin' spavin'd critter to mother? Wall, you *air* a shrewd one!"

A Sensation-Arrival by the Overland Stage of two Missouri girls, who have come unescorted all the way through. They are going to Nevada territory to join their father. They are pretty, but, merciful heavens! how they throw the meat and potatoes down their throats. "This is the first Squar' meal we've had since we left Rocky Thompson's," said the eldest. Then addressing herself to me, she said:

"Air you the literary man?"

I politely replied that I was one of "them fellers."

"Wall, don't make fun of our clothes in the papers. We air goin' right straight through in these here clothes, *we* air! We ain't goin' to *rag out* till we git to Nevady! Pass them sassiges!"

A Romance—William Barker, the Young Patriot

I

"No, William Barker, you cannot have my daughter's hand in marriage until you are her equal in wealth and social position."

The speaker was a haughty old man of some sixty years, and the person whom he addressed was a fine-looking young man of twenty-five.

With a sad aspect the young man withdrew from the stately mansion.

II

Six months later the young man stood in the presence of the haughty old man.

"What! *you* here again?" angrily cried the old man.

"Ay, old man," proudly exclaimed William Barker. "I am here, your daughter's equal and yours."

The old man's lips curled with scorn. A derisive smile lit up his cold features; when, casting violently upon the marble centre table an enormous roll of greenbacks, William Barker cried—

"See! Look on this wealth. And I've tenfold more! Listen, old man! You spurned me from your door. But I did not despair. I secured a contract for furnishing the Army of the —— with beef—"

"Yes, yes!" eagerly exclaimed the old man.

"—and I bought up all the disabled cavalry horses I còuld find—"

"I see! I see!" cried the old man. "And good beef they make, too."

"They do! they do! and the profits are immense."

"I should say so!"

"And now, sir, I claim your daughter's fair hand!"

"Boy, she is yours. But hold! Look me in the eye. Throughout all this have you been loyal?"

"To the core!" cried William Barker.

"And," continued the old man, in a voice husky with emotion, "are you in favor of a vigorous prosecution of the war?"

"I am, I am!"

"Then, boy, take her! Maria, child, come hither. Your William claims thee. Be happy, my children! and whatever our lot in life may be, *let us all support the Government!*"

LETTERS OF PETROLEUM V. NASBY

by David Ross Locke

(1833–1888)

Shows Why He Should Not Be Drafted [1]

August the 6th, 1862.

I see in the papers last nite that the Government hez insti-tooted a draft, and that in a few weeks sum hundreds uv thousands uv peeceable citizens will be dragged to the tented field. I know not wat uthers may do, but ez for me, I cant go. Upon a rigid eggsaminashun uv my fizzleckle man, I find it wood be wus nor madnis for me to undertake a campane, to-wit:—

1. I'm bald-headid, and hev bin obliged to wear a wig these 22 years.

2. I hev dandruff in wat scanty hair still hangs around my venerable temples.

3. I hev a kronic katarr.

4. I hev lost, sence Stanton's order to draft, the use uv wun eye entirely, and hev kronic inflammashen in the other.

5. My teeth is all unsound, my palit aint eggsactly rite, and I hev hed bronkeetis 31 yeres last Joon. At present I hev a koff, the paroxisms uv wich is friteful to behold.

6. I'm holler-chestid, am short-winded, and hev alluz hed pains in my back and side.

7. I am afflictid with kronic diarrear and kostivniss. The money I hev paid (or promist to pay), for Jayneses karminnytiv balsam and pills wood astonish almost enny body.

8. I am rupchered in nine places, and am entirely enveloped with trusses.

9. I hev verrykose vanes, hev a white-swellin on wun leg and a fever sore on the uther; also wun leg is shorter than tother, though I handle it so expert that nobody never noticed it.

10. I hev korns and bunyons on both feet, wich wood prevent me from marchin.

---

[1] One of the most surprising results of the conscription was the amount of disease disclosed among men between "eighteen and forty-five," in districts where quotas could not be raised by volunteering.—Locke's note.

I dont suppose that my political opinions, wich are aginst the prossekooshn uv this unconstooshnel war, wood hev any wate, with a draftin orfiser; but the above reesons why I cant go, will, I make no doubt, be suffishent.

PETROLEUM V. NASBY

THE ASSASSINATION [1]

Saint's Rest
(wich is in the Stait of Noo Jersey),
April the 20th, 1865.

The nashen mourns! The hand uv the vile assassin hez bin raised agin the Goril—the head uv the nashen, and the people's Father hez fallen beneath the hand uv a patr—vile assassin.

While Aberham Linkin wuz a livin, I need not say that I did not love him. Blessed with a mind uv no ordinary dimensions, endowed with all the goodness uv Washinton, I alluz bleeved him to hev bin guilty uv all the crimes uv a Nero.

No man in Noo Jersey laments his untimely death more than the undersined. I commenst weepin perfoosely the minit I diskivered a squad uv returned soljers comin round the corner, who wuz a forcin constooshnel Dimekrats to hang out mournin.

Troo, he didn't agree with me, but I kin overlook that—it wuz his misforchoon. Troo, he hung unoffendin men, in Kentucky, whose only crime wuz in bein loyal to wat *they* deemed *their* guverment, ez tho a man in this free country coodent choose wich guverment he'd live under. Troo, he made cold-blooded war, in the most fiendish manner, on the brave men uv the South, who wuz only assertin the heaven-born rite uv roolin theirselves. Troo, he levied armies, made up uv pimps, whose chiefest delite wuz in ravishin the wives and daughters uv the South, and a miscellaneous burnin their houses. Troo, he kept into offis jist sich men ez wood sekund him in his hell-begotten skeems, and dismist every man who refused to becum ez depraved ez he wuz. Troo, he wood read uv these scenes uv blood and carnage, and in high glee tell filthy anecdotes; likewise wood he ride over the field of battle, and ez the wheels uv his gorjus carriage crushed into the

[1] The northern secessionists had, from the beginning, represented President Lincoln as worse than a brute. The leading men of the party were in a peculiar situation at his death. The loyal people compelled them to conceal the satisfaction they felt at his tragical taking off. Like the Parson, they "wept profusely the moment they saw a squad of returned soldiers coming round the corner."—Locke's note.

shuddrin earth the bodies uv the fallen braves, sing Afrikin melodies. Yet I, in common with all troo Dimekrats, weep! We weep! We wish it to be distinkly understood, we weep! Ther wuz that in him that instinktively forces us to weep over his death, and to loathe the foul assassin who so suddenly removed so much loveliness uv character. He hed ended the war uv oppression—he hed subjoogatid a free and brave people, who were strugglin for their rites, and hed em under his feet; but I, in common with all Dimekrats, mourn his death!

Hed it happened in 1862, when it wood hev been uv sum use to us, we wood not be so bowed down with woe and anguish. It wood hev throwd the guverment into confusion, and probably hev sekoored the independence uv the South.

But alas! the tragedy cum at the wrong time!

Now, we are saddled with the damnin crime, when it will prodoose no results. The war wuz over. The game wuz up when Richmond wuz evacuated. Why kill Linkin then? For revenge? Revenge is a costly luxury—a party so near bankrupt ez the Dimokrasy cannot afford to indulge in it. The wise man hez no sich word ez revenge in his dictionary—the fool barters his hope for it.

Didst think that Linkin's death wood help the South? Linkin's hand wuz velvet—Johnson's may be, to the eye, but to the feel it will be found iron. Where Linkin switched, Johnson will flay. Where Linkin banished, Johnson will hang.

Davis wuz shocked when he heard it—so wuz I, and, in common with all troo Dimekrats, I weep.

PETROLEUM V. NASBY.

Lait Paster uv the Church uv the Noo Dispensashun.

The Reward of Virtue

Confedrit X Roads
(wich is in the Stait uv Kentucky),
August 12, 1866.

At last I hev it! Finally it come! After five weary trips to Washington, after much weary waitin and much travail, I hev got it. I am now Post Master at Confedrit X Roads, and am dooly installed in my new position. Ef I ever hed any doubts ez to A. Johnson bein a better man than Paul the Apossle, a look at my commission removes it. Ef I ketch myself a feelin that he deserted us onnecessarily five years ago, another look, and my resentment softens into pity. Ef I doubt his Democrisy, I look at that blessed commission, and am reassured, for a President who cood turn out a wounded Federal soldier, and apoint sich a man ez ME, must be above suspicion.

I felt it wuz coming two weeks ago. I received a cirkler from Randall, now my sooperior in offis, propoundin these questions:—

1. Do yoo hev the most implicit faith in Androo Johnson, in all that he hez done, all that he is doin, and all he may hereafter do?

2. Do yoo bleeve that the Philadelphia Convenshun will be a convocashen uv saints, all actuated by pure motives, and devoted to the salvation uv our wunst happy, but now distractid country?

3. Do yoo bleeve that, next to A. Johnson, Seward, Doolittle, Cowan, and Randall are the four greatest, and purest, and bestest, and self-sacrificinest, and honestest, and righteousist men that this country hez ever prodost?

4. Do yoo bleeve that there is a partikelerly hot place reserved in the next world for Trumbull, a hotter for Wade, and the hottest for Sumner and Thad Stevens?

5. Do yoo approve uv the canin uv Grinnell by Rosso?

6. Do yoo consider the keepin out uv Congris eleven sovrin states a unconstooshnel and unwarrantid assumption uv power by a secshnal Congris?

7. Do yoo bleeve the present Congris a rump, and that (eleven states bein unrepresented) all their acts are unconstooshnel and illegal, ceptin them wich provides for payin salaries?

8. Do yoo bleeve that the Memphis and Noo Orleans unpleasantnesses wuz brot about by the unholy machinashens uv them Radical agitators, actin in conjunction with ignorant and besotted niggers, to wreak their spite on the now loyal citizens uv those properly reconstructed cities?

9. Are yoo not satisfied that the Afrikin citizens uv Amerikin descent kin be safely trusted to the operations uv the universal law wich governs labor and capital?

10. Are yoo willin to contribute a reasonable per cent. uv yoor salary to a fund to be used for the defeat uv objectionable Congrismen in the disloyal states North?

To all uv these inquiries I not only answered yes, but went afore a Justis uv the Peace and took an affidavit to em, forwarded it back, and my commission wuz forthwith sent to me.

There wuz a jubilee the nite it arriv. The news spread rapidly through the four groceries uv the town, and sich anuther spontaneous outbust uv joy I never witnessed.

The bells rung, and for an hour or two the Corners wuz in the wildest stait uv eggsitement. The citizens congratoolated each other on the certainty uv the acceshun uv the President to the Dimocrisy, and in their enthoosiasm five nigger families were cleaned out, two uv em, one a male and the tother a female, wuz killed. Then a perceshun wuz organized as follers:—

Two grocery keepers with bottles.

Deekin Pogram.

ME, with my commishun pinned onto a banner, and under it written, "In this Sign we Conker."

Wagon with tabloo onto it: A nigger on the bottom boards, Bascom, the grocery keeper, with one foot onto him, holdin a banner inscribed, "The Nigger where he oughter be."

Citizen with bottle.

Deekin Pogram's daughter Mirandy in a attitood uv wallopin a wench. Banner: "We've Regained our Rites."

Two citizens with bottles tryin to keep in perceshun.

Two more citizens, wich hed emptyd their bottles, fallin out by the way side.

Citizens, two and two, with bottles.

Wagon, loaded with the books and furnitur uv a nigger skool, in a stait uv wreck, with a ded nigger layin on top uv it, wich hed bin captoored within the hour. Banner: "My Policy."

The perceshun mooved to the meetin hous, and Deekin Pogram takin the Chair, a meetin wuz to wunst organized.

The Deekin remarked that this wuz the proudest moment uv his life. He wuz gratified at the appointment uv his esteemed friend, becoz he appreciated the noble qualities wich wuz so conspikuous into him, and becoz his arduous services in the coz uv Dimokrisy entitled him to the posishun. All these wuz aside uv and entirely disconnected from the fact that thare wood now be a probability uv his gittin back a little matter uv nine dollars and sixty-two cents ("Hear! hear!") wich he hed loaned him about eighteen months ago, afore he had knowed him well, or larned to luv him. But thare wuz anuther reason why he met to rejoyce to-nite. It showed that A. Johnson meant biznis; that A. Johnson wuz troo to the Dimokrasy, and that he hed fully made up his mind to hurl the bolts uv offishl thunder wich he held in his Presidenshal hands at his enemies, and to make fight in earnest; that he wuz goin to reward his friends—them ez he cood trust. Our venerable friend's bein put in condishun to pay the confidin residents uv the Corners the little sums he owes them is a good thing ("Hear!" "Hear!" "Troo!" "Troo!" with singular unanimity from every man in the bildin), but wat wuz sich considerashuns when compared to the grate moral effect uv the decisive movement? ("A d——d site!" shouted one grocery keeper, and "We don't want no moral effect!" cried another.) My friends, when the news uv this bold step uv the President goes forth to the South, the price uv Confedrit skript will go up, and the shootin uv niggers will cease; for the redempshun uv the first I consider ashoored, and the redoosin uv the latter to their normal condishun I count ez good ez done.

Squire Gavitt remarked that he wuz too much overpowered with emoshun to speak. For four years, nearly five, the only newspaper wich come to that offis hed passed thro' the polluted hands uv a Ablishnist. He hed no partikler objecshun to the misguided man, but he wuz a symbol uv tyranny, and so long ez he sot there, he reminded em that they were wearin chains. Thank the Lord, that day is over! The Corners is redeemed, the second Jaxson hez risin, and struck off the shackles. He wood not allood to the trifle uv twelve dollars and a half that he loaned the appintee some months ago, knowin that it wood be paid out uv the first money—

Bascom, the principal grocery keeper, rose, and called the Squire to order. He wanted to know ef it wuz fair play to talk sich talk. No man cood feel a more hart-felt satisfaction at the appointment uv our honored friend than him, showin, ez it did, that the President hed cut loose from Ablishnism, wich he dispised, but he protestid agin the Squire undertakin to git in his bill afore the rest hed a chance. Who furnisht him his licker for eight months, and who hez the best rite for the first dig at the proceeds uv the position? He wood never—

The other three grocery keepers rose, when Deekin Pogram rooled em all out uv order, and offered the followin resolutions:—

Whereas, the President hez, in a strictly constooshnel manner, relieved this commoonity uv an offensive Ablishunist, appinted

PETROLEUM VESUVIUS NASBY

The famous cartoonist, Thomas Nast, drew this portrait as a frontispiece for *Swingin Round the Cirkle* (1867).

by that abhorred tyrant Linkin, and appinted in his place a sound constooshnel Demokrat—one whom to know is to lend; therefore, be it

Resolved, That we greet the President, and ashoor him uv our continyood support and confidence.

Resolved, That we now consider the work uv Reconstruction, so far ez this community is concerned, completed, and that we feel that we are wunst more restored to our proper relations with the federal government.

Resolved, That the glorious defence made by the loyal Democracy uv Noo Orleans agin the combined conventioners and niggers, shows that freemen kin not be conkered, and that white men shel rule America.

Resolved, That, on this happy occasion, we forgive the Government for what we did, and cherish nary resentment agin anybody.

The resolutions wuz adopted, and the meetin adjourned with three cheers for Johnson and his policy.

Then came a scene. Every last one uv em hed come there with a note made out for the amount I owed him at three months. Kindness of heart is a weakness of mine, and I signed em all, feelin that ef the mere fact of writin my name wood do em any good, it wood be crooel in me to object to the little laber required. Bless their innocent soles! they went away happy.

The next mornin I took possesshun uv the offis.

Am I awake, or am I dreamin? thought I. No, no! It is no dream. Here is the stamps, here is the blanks, and here is the commisshun! It is troo! it is troo!

I heerd a child, across the way, singin,—

> "I'd like to be a angel,
> And with the angels stand."

I woodn't, thought I. I woodn't trade place with an angel, even up. A Offis with but little to do, with four grocerys within a stone's throw, is ez much happiness ez my bilers will stand without bustin. A angel 4sooth!

PETROLEUM V. NASBY, P.M.

(wich is Postmaster.)

ORPHEUS C. KERR'S CHILDHOOD

by Robert Henry Newell

(1836–1901)

Washington, D.C., March 20th, 1861

Judge not by appearances, my boy; for appearances are very deceptive, as the old lady cholerically remarked when one, who was really a virgin on to forty, blushingly informed her that she was "just twenty-five this month."

Though you find me in Washington now, I was born of respectable parents, and gave every indication, in my satchel and apron days, of coming to something better than this—much better, my boy.

Slightly northward of the Connecticut river, where a pleasant little conservative village mediates between two opposition hills, you may behold the landscape on which my infantile New England eyes first traced the courses of future railroads.

Near the centre of this village in the valley, my boy, and a little back from its principal road, stood the residence of my worthy sire—and a very pretty residence it was. From the frequent addition of a new upper-room here, a new dormer window there, and an innovating skylight elsewhere, the roof of the mansion had gradually assumed an Alpine variety of juts and peaks somewhat confusing to behold. Local tradition related that, on a certain showery occasion, a streak of lightning was seen to descend upon that roof, skip vaguely about from one peak to another, and finally slink ignominiously down the water-pipe, as though utterly disgusted with its own inability to determine, where there are so many, which peak it should particularly perforate.

Years afterwards, my boy, this strange tale was told me by a venerable chap of the village; and I might have believed it, had he not outraged the probability of the meteorological narrative with a sequel.

'And when that streak came down the pipe,' says the aged chap thoughtfully, 'it struck a man who was leaning against the house, ran down to his feet, and went into the ground without hurting him a mite!'

With the natural ingeniousness of childhood I closed one eye, my boy, and says I:

'Do you mean to tell me, old man, that he was struck by lightning, and yet wasn't hurt?'

'Yes,' says the venerable chap, abstractedly cutting a small log from the door-frame of the grocery store with his jack-knife; 'the streak passed off from him, because he was a conductor.'

'A conductor?' says I, picking up another stone to throw at the same dog.

'Yes,' says the chap confidentially, 'he was a conductor—on a railroad.'

The human mind, my boy, when long affected by country air, tends naturally to the marvellous, and affiliates with the German in normal transcendentalism.

Such has the house in which I came to life a certain number of years ago, entering the world, like a human exclamation point, between two of the angriest sentences of a September storm, and adding materially to the uproar prevailing at the time.

Next to my parents, of whom I shall say little at present, the person I can best remember, as I look back, was our family physician. A very obese man was he, my boy, with a certain sweet-oiliness of manner, and never out of patients. I think I can see him still, as he arose from his chair after a profound study of the case before him, and wrote a prescription so circumlocutory in its effect, that it sent a servant half a mile to his friend the druggist, for articles she might have found in her own kitchen, *aqua pumpaginis* and sugar being the sole ingredients required.

The doctor had started business in our village as a veterinary surgeon, my boy; but, as the entire extent of his practice for six months in that line was a call to mend one of Colt's revolvers, he finally turned his attention to the ailings of his fellows, and wrought many cures with sugar and water Latinised.

At first, my father did not patronise the new doctor, having very little faith in the efficacy of sugar and water without the addition of a certain other composite often seen in bottles; but the doctor's neat speech at a Sunday-school festival won his heart at last.

The festival was held near a series of small waterfalls just out of the village, my boy; and the doctor, who was an invited guest, was called upon for a few appropriate remarks. In compliance with the demand, he made a speech of some compass, ending with a peroration that is still quoted in my native place. He pointed impressively to the waterfalls, and says he:

'All the works of nature is somewhat beautiful, with a good moral. Even them cataracts,' says he sagely, 'have a moral, and seem eternally whispering to the young, that "Those what err falls." '

The effect of this happy illustration was very pleasing, my boy, especially with those who prefer morality to grammar; and after that the physician had the run of all the pious families—our own included.

It was a handsome compliment this worthy man paid me when I was about six months old.

Having just received from my father the amount of the last bill, he was complacent to the last degree, and felt inclined to do the handsome thing. He patted my head as I sat upon my mother's lap, and says he:

'How beautiful is babes! So small, and yet so much like human beings, only not so large. This boy,' says he, fatly, looking down at me, 'will make a noise in the world yet. He has a long head—a very long head.'

'Do you think so?' says my father.

'Indeed I do,' says the doctor. 'The little fellow,' says he, in a sudden fit of abstraction, 'has a long head—a very long head; and it's as thick as it is long.'

There was some coolness between the doctor and my father after that, my boy; and on the following Sunday my mother refused to look at his wife's new bonnet in church.

I might cover many pages with further account of childhood's sunny hours; but enough has been given already to establish the respectability of my birth, despite my present location; and there I let the matter rest, my boy, for the time being.

Yours, retrospectively,

ORPHEUS C. KERR

BILL ARP'S CORRESPONDENCE

by Charles Henry Smith

(1826–1903)

BILL ARP TO ABE LINKHORN

Rome, Ga., Aprile 1861.

Mr. Linkhorn—Sur: These are to inform you that we are all well, and hope these lines may find you in statue ko. We received your proklamation, and as you have put us on very short notis, a few of us boys have konkluded to write you, and ax for a little more time. The fact is, we are most obleeged to have a few more days, for the way things are happening, it is utterly onpossible for us to disperse in twenty days. Old Virginy, and Tennessee, and North Callina, are continually aggravatin us into tumults and carousements, and a body can't disperse until you put a stop to sich onruly condukt on their part. I tried my darndest yisterday to disperse and retire, but it was no go; and besides, your marshal here ain't doing a darned thing—he don't read the riot act, nor remonstrate, nor nothing, and ought to be turned out. If you konklude to do so, I am orthorized to rekummend to you Col. Gibbons or Mr. McLung, who would attend to the bizniss as well as most anybody.

The fact is, the boys round here want watchin, or they'll take sumthin. A few days ago I heard they surrounded two of our best citizens, because they was named Fort and Sumter. Most of em are so hot that they fairly siz when you pour water on em, and that's the way they make up their military companies here now—when a man applies to jine the volunteers, they sprinkle him, and if he sizzes they take him, and if he don't they don't.

Mr. Linkhorn, sur, privately speakin, I'm afeerd I'll git in a tite place here among these bloods, and have to slope out of it, and I would like to have your Skotch cap and kloak that you travelled in to Washington. I suppose you wouldn't be likely to use the same disgize agin, when you left, and therefore I would propose to swap. I am five feet five, and could git my plow breeches and coat to you in eight or ten days if you can wait that long. I want you to write to me immegitly about things generally, and

let us know whereabouts you intend to do your fitin. Your proklamation says somethin about takin possession of all the private
property at "All Hazards." We can't find no such place on the
map. I thot it must be about Charleston, or Savannah, or Harper's
Ferry, but they say it ain't anywhere down South. One man said
it was a little Faktory on an iland in Lake Champlain, where they
make sand bags. My opinion is, that sand bag bisniss won't pay,
and it is a great waste of money. Our boys here carry there sand
in there gizzards, where it keeps better, and is always handy.
I'm afeered your Government is givin you and your kangaroo a
great deal of onnecessary trubbul, and my humble advice is, if
things don't work better soon, you'd better grease it, or trade the
darned old thing off. I'd show you a slite-of-hand trick that would
change the whole concern into buttons quick. If you don't trade
or do sumthin else with it soon, it will spile or die on your hands,
sertain.

Give my respekts to Bill Seward and the other members of the
kangaroo. What's Hannibal doin? I don't hear anything from him
nowadays.

Yours, with care,

BILL ARP.

P.S.—If you can possibly extend that order to thirty days, do
so. We have sent you a CHECK at Harper's Ferry (who keeps that
darnd old ferry now? its giving us a heap of trubble), but if you
positively won't extend, we'll send you a check drawn by Jeff Davis,
Borygard endorser, payable on sight anywhere.

Yours,

B. A.

BILL ARP ADDRESSES ARTEMUS WARD

Rome, Ga., September 1, 1865

Mr. Artemus Ward, *Showman*,

Sur: The reesun I write to you in pertikler, is bekaus you are
about the only man I know in all "God's kountry," *so called*. For
sum sevrul years we Rebs, *so called*, but now late of said kountry
deceased, hav been a tryin mity hard to do sumthin. We didn't
quite do it, and now it is very paneful, I ashoor you, to dry up all
of a sudden, and make out like we wasn't there.

My frend, I want to say sumthin. I spose there is no law agin thinkin, but thinkin don't help me. It don't let down my thermomyter. I must explode myself genrully so as to feel better. You see I am tryin to harmonise. I'm tryin to soften down my feelins. I'm endeverin to subjergate myself to the level of surroundin sirkumstances, *so called*. But I can't do it till I am allowed to say sumthin. I want to quarrel with sumboddy and then make frends. I ain't no giant killer. I ain't no Norwegun bar. I ain't no Bo Konstrikter, but I'll be hornswoggled if the talkin, and the writin, and the slanderin hav got to be all done on one side eny longer. Sum of your foaks hav got to dry up or turn our foaks loose. It's a blamed outrage, *so called*. Ain't your editers got nuthin else to do but to peck at us, skwib at us, and krow over us? Is evry man what can write a paragraf to konsider us as bars in a kage, and be always a jobbin at us to hear us growl? Now you see, my frend, that's what's disharmonyus, and do you jest tell em, one and all, E Pluribus Unum, *so called*, that if they don't stop it at onst, or turn us loose to say what we please, why we Rebs, *so called*, hav unanimously, and jintly, and sevrully resolved to—to—to—think very hard of it—if not harder.

That's the way to talk it. I ain't a gwine to kommit myself. I know when to put on the brakes. I ain't a gwine to say *all* I think. Nary time. No, sur. But I'll jest tell you, Artemus, and you may tell it to your show! If we ain't allowed to xpress our sentiments, we can take it out in *hatin;* and hatin runs hevy in my family, shore. I hated a man so bad onst that all the har cum off my hed, and the man drowned himself in a hog waller that nite. I could do it agin, but you see I am tryin to harmonise, to acquiess, to becum cam and sereen.

> "In Dixie's fall,
> We sinned all."

But talkin the way I see it, a big feller and a little feller, *so called*, got into a fite, and they fout, and fout, and fout a long time, and evry boddy all around a hollerin hands off, but kep a helping the big feller, till finally the little feller caved in and hollered enuf. He made a bully fite, I tell you, selah. Well, what did the big feller do? Take him by the han and help him up, and bresh the dirt offen his close? Nary time! No, sur! But he kiked him atter he was down and throwd mud on him and drug him about and rubbed sand in his eyes and now hes a gwine about a huntin up his poor little property. Wants to konfiskate it *so called*. Blame my jacket if it ain't enuf to make your hed swim.

But *I'm* a good Union man *so called*. *I* ain't a gwine to fite any more. *I* shan't vote for the next war. *I* ain't no gurilla. I've dun tuk the oath, and I'm gwine to keep it, but as for my bein subjergated, and humilyated, and amalgamated, and enervated, as Mr. Chase says, it ain't so—nary time. I ain't ashamed of nuthin, neather—ain't repentin—ain't axin for no one hoss, short-winded pardin. Nobody needn't be a playin preest about me. I ain't got no twenty thousan dollars. Wish I had; I'd give it to these poor widders and orfins. I'd fatten my own numerus and interestin offspring in about two minits and a half. They shouldn't eat roots and drink branch water no longer. Poor unfortinate things! To cum into this subloonery world at sich a time. There's Bull Run Arp, and Harper's Ferry Arp, and Chickahominy Arp, that never seed the pikturs in a spellin book. I tell you, my frend, we are the poorest peepul on the face of the yearth—but we are poor and proud. We made a bully fite, selah, and the whole Amerikan nation ought to feel proud of it. It shows what Amerikans can do when they think they are imposed on—"*so called*." Didn't our four fathers fite, bleed, and die about a little tax on tea, when not one in a thousan drunk it? Becaus they sukseeded, wasn't it glory? But if they hadn't, I spose it would hav been treeson, and they would have been a bowin and scrapin around King George for pardin. So it goes, Artemus, and to my mind, if the whole thing was stewed down it would make about a haf pint of humbug. We had good men, grate men, kristyun men, who thot we was right, and many of them hav gone to the undiskivered kountry, and hav got a pardin as is a pardin. When I die I am mighty willin to risk myself under the shadder of their wings, whether the klimate is hot or cold. So mote it be. Selah!

Well, maybe I've sed enuf. But I don't feel esy yet. I'm a good Union man, sertin and shore. I've had my britches dide *blue*, and I've bot a *blue* blanket, and I very often feel *blue*, and about twist in a while I go to the doggery and get *blue*, and then I look up at the *blue* serulyun hevins and sing the melonkolly korus of the *Blue*-taled fly. I'm doin my durndest to harmonise, and I think I could sukseed if it wasn't for sum things. When I see a blakgard a goin roun the streets with a gun on his shoulder, why rite then, for a few minits, I hate the whole Yanky nashun. Jerusalem! how my blood biles! The institushun which wer handed down to us by the hevinly kingdum of Massychusetts, now put over us with powder and ball! Harmonise the devil! Ain't we human beins? Ain't we got eyes and ears and feelin and thinkin? Why the whole of Afriky have cum to town, wimmin and children, and boys and baboons, and all. A man can tell how far it ar to the sitty better by the smell than the mile-post. They won't work for us, and they won't work for themselves, and they'll perish to deth this winter, as shore as the devil is a hog, *so called*. They are now baskin in the summer's sun, a livin on roastin ears and freedum, with nary idee that winter will cum agin, or that Caster Ile and Salts cost munny. Sum of em, a hundred years old, are a whinin aroun about going to kawllidge. The truth is, my frend, sumboddy's badly fooled about this bizniss. Sumboddy have drawd the elefant in the lottery, and don't know what to do with him. He's jest a throwin his snout aroun loose, and by and by he'll hurt sumboddy. These niggers will have to go back to the plantashuns and wurk. I ain't a goin to support nary one of em, and when you heer anybody say so, you tell em its a lie, *so called*. By golly, I ain't got nuthin to support myself on. We fout ourselves out of evrything, xceptin children and land, and I spose the land are to be turned over to the niggers for graveyards.

Well, my frend, I don't want mutch. I ain't ambishus, as I used to was. You all have got your shose, and monkys, and sirkusses, and brass bans, and orgins, and can play on the petrolyum and the harp of a thousan strings, and so on, but I've only got one favor to ax of you. I want enuf powder to kill a big yaller stumptail dog that prowls aroun my premmyses at nite. Pon honer I won't shoot at enything blue, black, or mullatter. Will you send it? Are you, and your foaks so skeered of me, and my foaks, that you won't let us hav any amunishun? Are the squirrells and krows, and blak rakkoons to eat up our poor littel korn paches? Are the wild turkys to gobbel all aroun us with impunity? If a mad dog takes the hyderfoby, is the hole kommunity to run itself to deth to git out of the way? I golly! It looks like foaks had all took the rebelfoby for good, and was never a gwine to git over it. See here, my frend, you must send me a little powder and a ticket to your show, and me and you will harmonise sertin.

With these few remarks I think I feel better, and hope I hain't made nobody fitin mad, for I am not on that line at this time.

I am truly your frend, all present, or akkounted for,

BILL ARP, *so called*.

P.S.—Old man Harris wanted to buy my fiddle the other day with Konfedrit munny. He said it would be good agin. *He* says that Jim Funderburk told him that Warren's Jack seed a man what had jest cum from Virginny, and *he* sed a man had told his cousin Mandy that Lee had whipped me *agin*. Old Harris says that a man by the name of Mack C. Millin is a comin over with a million o' men. But nevertheless, notwithstandin, sumhow else, I'm dubus about the munny. If you was me, Artemus, would you make the fiddle trade?   B. A.

JOSH BILLINGS' MEDITATIONS

by Henry W. Shaw

(1818–1885)

AMERIKANS

Amerikans love caustick things; they would prefer turpentine tew colone-water, if they had tew drink either.

So with their relish of humor; they must hav it on the half-shell with cayenne.

An Englishman wants hiz fun smothered deep in mint sauce, and he iz willin tew wait till next day before he tastes it.

If you tickle or convince an Amerikan yu hav got tew do it quick.

An Amerikan luvs tew laff, but he don't luv tew make a bizzness ov it; he works, eats, and haw-haws on a canter.

I guess the English hav more wit, and the Amerikans more humor.

We havn't had time, yet, tew bile down our humor and git the wit out ov it.

The English are better punsters, but i konsider punning a sort ov literary prostitushun in which future happynesz iz swopped oph for the plezzure ov the moment.

Thare iz one thing i hav noticed: evryboddy that writes expeckts tew be wize or witty—so duz evrybody expect tew be saved when they die; but thare iz good reason tew beleave that the goats hereafter will be in the majority, just az the sheep are here.

Don't forget *one* thing, yu hav got tew be wize before yu kan be witty; and don't forget *two* things, a single paragraff haz made sum men immortal, while a volume haz bin wuss than a pile-driver tew others—but what would Amerikans dew if it want for their sensashuns?

Sumthing new, sumthing startling iz necessary for us az a people, and it don't make mutch matter what it iz—a huge defalkashun—a red elephant—or Jersee clams with pearls in them will answer if nothing better offers.

Englishmen all laff at us for our sensashuns, and sum ov them fret about it, and spred their feathers in distress for us, az a fond and foolish old hen, who haz hatched out a setting ov ducks' eggs, will stand on the banks ov a mill pond, wringing her hands in agony to see her brood pitch in and take a sail. *She* kant understand it, but the *Ducks* know awl about it.

N.B.—Yu kan bet 50 dollars the Ducks know all about it.

N.B.—Yu kan bet 50 dollars more that it makes no difference who hatches out an Amerikan, the fust thing he will do, iz to pitch into sumthin.

N.B.—No more bets at present.

Live Yankees

Live Yankees are chuck full of karakter and sissing hot with enterprize and curiosty.

In bild we find them az lean az a hunter's dorg, with a parched countenance, reddy for a grin, or for a sorrow; ov elaastick step: thortful, but not abstrakted; pashunt, bekauze cunnin; ever watchful; slo to anger; avoiding a fight; but rezolute at bay.

In dress alwuz slik, but not stuck up; their harness alwuz betrays them wherever they go.

The oil ov their langwidge iz their dezire tew pleze, and their greezy words foreshadder a proffit.

They are natral mechanicks; the histry ov man's necessitys iz the histry ov their invenshuns.

The Live Yankee haz no hum; hiz luv ov invenshun breeds a luv ov change, and wharever a human trail shows itself we find him pantin on the trak.

He never gits sick at the stummuk in a furrin land, or grows sentermental; the buty ov a river tew him iz its capacity for a steambote; its sloping banks checker into bildin lots, and its poetry waters might do the drudgery ov a cottin mill.

He looks at a marble pyramid, guesses at its height, calkulates the stone by the perch, and sells the mangifisent relick in Boston at a proffit.

He climbs the Alpin hights, crossed by conkerin heroes, and iz struk with the proprierty ov tunneling it.

He sits, cross-legged, beneath the sheltring vine and listens to the oneazy sea, sees the warm promise ov the grape, and forgettin the holy memrys ov the land ov song, grinds the smilin vintage into wine and maiks a happy bargin.

You can meet him in Constanternopel, makin up in grimace

what he lacks in langwidge, spreadin a plaster with hiz tounge, for the man ov Mahomet.

Go where you will, from the numb palsied North tew the swetting limberness ov the South, from the top ov earth's mornin tew half past eleven at night, and the everlastin Yankee you will find, either vehement in an argue, or purswazive in a swop.

Hiz religion iz praktikal; he mourns over the heathen, and iz reddy tew save them by the job.

He luvs liberty with a red pepper enthuziasm, and fully beleafs Nu England kan whip the universe.

If the phlegmatick Englishman brags about roast beef and hiz ansesters, Jonathan haz a pumkin pie and a grandpop tew match them.

If the Frenchman grows crazy over a frigazee ov frog's hind legs, Jonathan pulls out a donut and a Rhode Island greening.

If the dusky Italian talks about the mad vomits ov vesuvius, Jonathan turns in the water power ov Niagara.

In argument alwuz ernest, and in reazoning alwuz specius, this progressive phenomena tramps the world with the skeleton ov a pattent right in hiz carpet bag, and, in his ever open hand and face a pleasant "Heow air yer?"

If you would save your pride from bein sand-papered, risk it not in a dicker with Jonathan.

Hiz razor is the true Damascus, strapped on the wand ov Midas for a golden harvest; hiz sanctity iz often shrewdness, and hiz sweet savor iz often the reflekted halo ov the comin shillin.

Constitushunaly and by edukashun honest, he iz alwuz reddy tew cry for the deeds dun in the boddy; hiz hospitalitys and charities are cerimonial dutys, and if hiz religion iz sometimes only the severitys ov a sabbath, it iz bekauze hiz bias iz the thursting impulse ov a creatin genius chained tew the more sordid pashun for lucre.

THE HAUNTED MAN

by Bret Harte

(1839–1902)

A CHRISTMAS STORY

BY CH—R—S D—CK—N—S

PART I

THE FIRST PHANTOM

Don't tell me that it wasn't a knocker. I had seen it often enough, and I ought to know. So ought the three o'clock beer, in dirty high-lows, swinging himself over the railing, or executing a demoniacal jig upon the doorstep; so ought the butcher, although butchers as a general thing are scornful of such trifles; so ought the postman, to whom knockers of the most extravagant description were merely human weaknesses, that were to be pitied and used. And so ought, for the matter of that, etc., etc., etc.

But then it was *such* a knocker. A wild, extravagant, and utterly incomprehensible knocker. A knocker so mysterious and suspicious that Policeman X 37, first coming upon it, felt inclined to take it instantly in custody, but compromised with his professional instincts by sharply and sternly noting it with an eye that admitted of no nonsense, but confidently expected to detect its secret yet. An ugly knocker; a knocker with a hard, human face, that was a type of the harder human face within. A human face that held between its teeth a brazen rod. So hereafter, in the mysterious future should be held, etc., etc.

But if the knocker had a fierce human aspect in the glare of day, you should have seen it at night, when it peered out of the gathering shadows and suggested an ambushed figure; when the light of the street lamps fell upon it, and wrought a play of sinister expression in its hard outlines; when it seemed to wink meaningly at a shrouded figure who, as the night fell darkly, crept up the steps and passed into the mysterious house; when the swinging door disclosed a black passage into which the figure seemed to lose itself and become a part of the mysterious gloom; when the night grew boisterous and the fierce wind made furious charges at the knocker, as if to wrench it off and carry it away in triumph. Such a night as this.

It was a wild and pitiless wind. A wind that had commenced life as a gentle country zephyr, but wandering through manufacturing towns had become demoralised, and reaching the city had plunged into extravagant dissipation and wild excesses. A roistering wind that indulged in Bacchanalian shouts on the street corners, that knocked off the hats from the heads of helpless passengers, and then fulfilled its duties by speeding away, like all young prodigals,—to sea.

He sat alone in a gloomy library listening to the wind that roared in the chimney. Around him novels and story-books were strewn thickly; in his lap he held one with its pages freshly cut, and turned the leaves wearily until his eyes rested upon a portrait in its frontispiece. And as the wind howled the more fiercely, and the darkness without fell blacker, a strange and fateful likeness to that portrait appeared above his chair and leaned upon his shoulder. The Haunted Man gazed at the portrait and sighed. The figure gazed at the portrait and sighed too.

"Here again?" said the Haunted Man.

"Here again," it repeated in a low voice.

"Another novel?"

"Another novel."

"The old story?"

"The old story."

"I see a child," said the Haunted Man, gazing from the pages of the book into the fire,—"a most unnatural child, a model infant. It is prematurely old and philosophic. It dies in poverty to slow music. It dies surrounded by luxury to slow music. It dies with an accompaniment of golden water and rattling carts to slow music. Previous to its decease it makes a will; it repeats the Lord's Prayer, it kisses the 'boofer lady.' That child"——

"Is mine," said the phantom.

"I see a good woman, undersized. I see several charming women, but they are all undersized. They are more or less imbecile and idiotic, but always fascinating and undersized. They wear coquettish caps and aprons. I observe that feminine virtue is invariably below the medium height, and that it is always babyish and infantine. These women"——

"Are mine."

"I see a haughty, proud, and wicked lady. She is tall and queenly. I remark that all proud and wicked women are tall and queenly. That woman"——

"Is mine," said the phantom, wringing his hands.

"I see several things continually impending. I observe that whenever an accident, a murder, or death is about to happen, there is something in the furniture, in the locality, in the atmosphere, that foreshadows and suggests it years in advance. I cannot say that in real life I have noticed it,—the perception of this surprising fact belongs"——

"To me!" said the phantom. The Haunted Man continued, in a despairing tone—

"I see the influence of this in the magazines and daily papers; I see weak imitators rise up and enfeeble the world with senseless formula. I am getting tired of it. It won't do, Charles! it won't do!" and the Haunted Man buried his head in his hands and groaned. The figure looked down upon him sternly: the portrait in the frontispiece frowned as he gazed.

"Wretched man," said the phantom, "and how have these things affected you?"

"Once I laughed and cried, but then I was younger. Now, I would forget them if I could."

"Have then your wish. And take this with you, man whom I renounce. From this day henceforth you shall live with those whom I displace. Without forgetting me, 'twill be your lot to walk through life as if we had not met. But first, you shall survey these scenes that henceforth must be yours. At one to-night, prepare to meet the phantom I have raised. Farewell!"

The sound of its voice seemed to fade away with the dying wind, and the Haunted Man was alone. But the firelight flickered gaily, and the light danced on the walls, making grotesque figures of the furniture.

"Ha, ha!" said the Haunted Man, rubbing his hands gleefully; "now for a whiskey punch and a cigar."

NEW YEAR'S CALLS

by Melville D. Landon

(1839–1910)

Fifth Avenue Hotel, 1 A.M., Jan. 2.

I don't feel like writing to-day, my head aches. I made calls yesterday—made 125 calls. I finished them about twelve o'clock —an hour ago.

I had my call list written off, and commenced at Sixtieth street, and came down. My idea was to make 125 calls of five minutes each. This would take 625 minutes, or ten hours. I think I did it. I worked hard. I was an intermittent perpetual motion. I did all that anybody *could* do. If any fellow says he made 126 calls, he— well, he is guilty of li-bel. I tried it. I made my 125th call with my eyes closed, and at my 126th I swooned on the hall stairs. Nature was exhausted. Oh! but wasn't it fun! It is nothing to make calls after you have been at it a spell. The last twenty calls were made with one eye closed. I was actually taking a mental nap all the time. My tongue talked right straight ahead, from force of habit. Talking came as easy as ordinary respiration. All I had to do was to open my mouth, and the same words tumbled out:

"Hap—new year, Miss Smitte!"

"Ah, Mr. Perkins! I'm delighted—"

"May you have man' hap' returns—bye—by!"

"But ar'n't you going to drink to—"

"Thank—pleasure (drank). May you live thousand years. By— by" (sliding into the hall and down the front steps).

I started at noon. Made first call on young lady.

She said, "You have many calls to make. Won't you fortify yourself with a little sherry?"

I said I would, and drank small glass.

Called next on married lady on Fifth Avenue.

She said, "Let's drink to William."—(You know Will is off making calls on the girls.)

"All right, Mrs. Mason"—then we drank some nice old port to absent William.

On Forty-ninth street met a sainted Virginia mother, who had some real old Virginia egg-nog.

Very nice Southern egg-nog. Abused the Yankees, and drank two glasses with Virginia mother.

On Forty-sixth street met lady who had some nice California wine. Tried it. Then went across the street with Democratic friend to say New Years and get some of old Skinner's 1836 brandy. Got it. Mrs. Skinner wanted us to drink to Skinner. Drank to Skinner, and ate lobster salad.

Met a friend, who said:

"Let's run in and see Coe, the temperance man."

Coe said:

"Ah! happy time! Let's drink to my wife."

Drank bottle of champagne to Mrs. Coe—then drank to children.

Drove round to Miss Thompson's, on Fifth Avenue. The Thompsons are famous for rum punch. Tried two glasses with Miss Thompson. Very happy. House looked lovely. Ate brandy peaches. Good many lights. Pretty girls, quite numerous. Drank their health. Drank claret. Then drank Roman punch. Went out, leaving hat and a twelve-dollar umbrella in the hat-rack.

Happy thought!—Took Charley Brown in the carriage. Charley said, "Let's drop in on the Madison Avenue Masons." "All right." Dropped in. Miss Mason says, "Have some nice old Madeira?" Said, "Yes, Miss Mas'n, will have some, my dearie." Drank to Mrs. Mason, and ate boned turkey to young ladies. Young ladies dressed beautifully—hair, court train, and shoes *à la Pompadour*. Left overcoat and changed high hat for fur cap. Saw a span of horses in a carriage drawn by Charley King. Charley was tight-ually slight. Said he had been in to Lees, eating boned sherry and drinking pale turkey.

Now all called on the Lambs on Thirty-fourth Avenue. Old Lamb was round. "Lam's chops very good," says Charley.

Also drank brandy peaches here, and ate more pony brandy. Young ladies beau'ful—high heeled dress and shoes cut *décolleté*. Great many of them. Nice Roman punch with monogram on it. Had fried sandwich with brandy on it. Presented large bouquet in corner to Mrs. Lamb. Exchanged hat for hall card basket, and slid down front banisters.

Called on Vanderbilt. Hang Vanderbilt! Vanderbilt did't rec'v calls. Carried off card basket and hung Charley's hat on bell knob. Used Van's cards to make other calls with. Kept calling. Called steady. Called between calls. Drank more. Drank everywhere. Young ladies more beau'ful. Wanted us to come back to party in the evening. Came back. Grand party. Bernstein furnished by music. Drank more lobster salad. Drank half a glass of silk dress and poured rest on skirt of Miss Smith's champagne in corner. Slumped plate gas-light green silk down on to nice ice cream. Dresses wore white tarletan—young ladies cut swallow tail. Sat on young lady's hand and held stairs. Very happy. Fellows had been drinking.

11 P.M. Left party. Carriage outside wanted me to get into Fred Young and promenade over to the Stewarts. Roman punch had been drinking Fred. He invited eight other horses to get into the fellows and ride around to the Stewarts. Stewart tight and house closed up. Left pocketbook in card-basket outside, and hung watch and chain over bell knob.

Called on the Furgisons. All up. Had old Burgundy. Furgison's a brick. Took sherry. Beau'ful young lady dressed in blue Roman punch. Opened bottle of white *gross grain* trimmed with Westchester County lace. Drank it up. Got on (hic) outside and drove driver home. Fellows getting more tete-uly slight. Drank *Pompadour* rum with young lady dressed *à la Jamaica*. Hadn't strength to refuse. Drank hap' (hic) new year fifteen times—then got into Fif Thavenue Hotel, and told driver to drive round to the carriage. Came up to letter, and wrote this room for the *Com-vertiser*. Pulled coat off with the boot-jack, and stood self up by the regster to dry. Then wrote——(hic)——wrote more—— (hic).

U – LI PERKINGS.

LIFE IN DANBURY

by J. M. Bailey

(1841–1894)

[MOVING TROUBLES]

It is singular the influence a stove-pipe has upon a married man. There is nothing in this world he respects so much. A passing load of furniture may, in its general appearance, be so grotesque as to call forth the merriment of the thoughtless young; but, if there is a piece of stove-pipe in it no larger than a hat, he will not laugh. We don't care who the man is, how he has been brought up, what is his position, wealth, or influence: there is that about a length of stove-pipe which takes hold upon his very soul with a force that he is helpless to resist; and the married man who can stand within reaching-distance of a stove-pipe, without feeling his heart throb, his hands clinch, his hair raise, and his throat grow dry and husky, is an anomaly which does not exist. Stove-pipe has only one ingredient, and that is contrariness. It is the most perverse article in existence. It has done more to create heart-aches, imbitter lives, break up homes, and scrape off skin, than all other domestic articles together. The domestic screw-driver pales its ineffectual fires in the presence of a stove-pipe; and the family hammer just paws in the dust, and weeps. We don't care how much pains are taken to remember and keep in order the links: they will not come together as they came apart. This is not a joke; this is not an exaggeration: it is simply the solemn, heaven-born truth. If we appear unduly excited in this matter, we are sorry for it; but we cannot help it. We cannot write upon the subject at all without feeling the blood tingle at our very fingers' ends.

One of the most disastrous elements in a moving is a small boy with an aspiring disposition. If he carries any thing, it must be a chair, which he takes on his head, with the back at the front, so as to prevent him from seeing where he is going, and with the erect legs in range of the chandelier and upper door-casings. Thus equipped, he strikes a military step, improvising his mouth into a trumpet, and starts out. In less than a quarter of an hour he has that chair safely on the cart, where it is not wanted, and is hurrying back after another. Before the carman has returned for the second load, the one boy has developed into eight; each boy with a chair, each boy under feet, and each boy making as much noise as a planing-mill on a damp day. If a boy cannot get a chair to carry, he wants two bed-posts. He wants two, so he can carry one under each arm. Then he starts down stairs. First the posts cross each other at the front, and nearly throw him down; then they cross at the back, and the front ends fly off at a tangent, one of them digging into the kalsomined wall, and the other entangling in the banisters. But he won't let one of them go, but hangs on to both with exasperating obstinacy. In the mean time, the carman, who is working by the load, and not by the day, is waiting at the foot of the stairs, and wishing that he had that boy back of the Rocky Mountains for about fifteen minutes; and the anxious father, with a straw bed in his arms, and his eyes full of dust, is at the head of the stairs, waiting to come down, and vociferating at the top of his voice, until the dust from the tick gets into his throat, and precipitates him into a violent fit of coughing. By the time the third load is on the way, the novelty of helping carry furniture is worn off to the boy; and he and his companions are firing rubbish from the garret at each other, or fooling with the horse just as some heavy object is being lifted on to the cart. The best plan for a moving family that has a boy is to get him a half-bushel of frozen potatoes to throw, and set him out in the suburbs until the affair is over.

A Peculiar Torture

Having a photograph taken is one of the great events in a man's life. The chief desire is to look the very best; and on the success of the picture hinges, in many cases, the most important epoch in life. To work up a proper appearance time enough is used, which, if devoted to catching fleas for their phosphorus, would cancel the entire national debt, and establish a New-York daily paper. When you have completed your toilet, you go to the gallery, and force yourself into a nonchalance of expression that is too absurd for any thing. Then you take the chair, spread your legs gracefully, appropriate a calm and indifferent look, and commence to perspire. An attenuated man with a pale face, long hair, and a soiled nose, now comes out of a cavern and adjusts the camera. Then he gets back of you, and tells you to sit back as far as you can in the chair, and that it has been a remarkably backward spring. After getting you back till your spine interferes with the chair itself, he shoves your head into a pair of ice-tongs, and dashes at the camera again. Here, with a piece of discolored velvet over his head, he bombards you in this manner: "Your chin out a little, please." The chin is protruded. "That's nicely: now a little more." The chin advances again; and the pomade commences to melt, and start for freedom. Then he comes back to you, and slaps one of your hands on your leg in such a position as to give you the appearance of trying to lift it over your head. The other is turned under itself, and has become so sweaty, that you begin to fear that it will stick there permanently. A new stream of pomade finds its way out, and starts downward. Then he shakes your head in the tongs till it settles right, and says it looks like rain, and puts your chin out again, and punches out your chest, and says he doesn't know what the poor are to do next winter, unless there is a radical change in affairs; and then takes the top of your head in one hand, and your chin in the other, and gives your neck a wrench that would earn any other man a prominent position in a new hospital. Then he runs his hands through your hair, and scratches your scalp, and steps back to the camera and the injured velvet for another look. By this time, new sweat and pomade have started out. The whites of your eyes show unpleasantly; and your whole body feels as if it had been visited by an enormous cramp, and another and much bigger one was momentarily expected. Then he points at something for you to look at; tells you to look cheerful and composed; and snatches away the velvet, and pulls out his watch. When he gets tired, and you feel as if there was but very little left in this world to live for, he restores the velvet, says it is an unfavorable day for a picture, but he hopes for the best, and immediately disappears in his den. Then you get up and stretch yourself, slap on your hat, and immediately sneak home, feeling mean, humbled, and altogether too wretched for description. The first friend who sees the picture says he can see enough resemblance to make certain that it is you; but you have *tried* to look too formal to be natural and graceful.

LIFE IN AN ODD CORNER

by Charles Heber Clark

(1841–1915)

THE MORNING ARGUS CREATES A SENSATION

A rather unusual sensation has been excited in the village by the *Morning Argus* within a day or two; and while most of the readers of that wonderful sheet have thus been supplied with amusement, the soul of the editor has been filled with gloom and wrath and despair. Colonel Bangs recently determined to engage an assistant to take the place made vacant by the retirement of the eminent art-critic, Mr. Murphy, and he found in one of the lower counties of the State a person who appeared to him to be suitable. The name of the new man is Slimmer. He has often contributed to the *Argus* verses of a distressing character, and I suppose Bangs must have become acquainted with him through the medium of the correspondence thus begun. No one in the world but Bangs would ever have selected such a poet for an editorial position. But Bangs is singular—he is exceptional. He never operates in accordance with any known laws, and he is more than likely to do any given thing in such a fashion as no other person could possibly have adopted for the purpose. As the *Argus* is also *sui generis*, perhaps Bangs does right to conduct it in a peculiar manner. But he made a mistake when he employed Mr. Slimmer.

The colonel, in his own small way, is tolerably shrewd. He had observed the disposition of persons who have been bereaved of their relatives to give expression to their feelings in verse, and it occurred to him that it might be profitable to use Slimmer's poetical talent in such a way as to make the *Argus* a very popular vehicle for the conveyance to the public of notices of deaths. That kind of intelligence, he well knew, is especially interesting to a very large class of readers, and he believed that if he could offer to each advertiser a gratuitous verse to accompany the obituary paragraph, the *Argus* would not only attract advertisements of that description from the country round about the village, but it would secure a much larger circulation.

When Mr. Slimmer arrived, therefore, and entered upon the

439

performance of his duties, Colonel Bangs explained his theory to the poet, and suggested that whenever a death-notice reached the office, he should immediately write a rhyme or two which should express the sentiments most suitable to the occasion.

"You understand, Mr. Slimmer," said the colonel, "that when the death of an individual is announced I want you, as it were, to cheer the members of the afflicted family with the resources of your noble art. I wish you to throw yourself, you may say, into their situation, and to give them, f'r instance, a few lines about the deceased which will seem to be the expression of the emotion which agitates the breasts of the bereaved."

"To lighten the gloom in a certain sense," said Mr. Slimmer, "and to—"

"Precisely," exclaimed Colonel Bangs. "Lighten the gloom. Do not mourn over the departed, but rather take a joyous view of death, which, after all, Mr. Slimmer, is, as it were, but the entrance to a better life. Therefore, I wish you to touch the heart-strings of the afflicted with a tender hand, and to endeavor, f'r instance, to divert their minds from contemplation of the horrors of the tomb."

"Refrain from despondency, I suppose, and lift their thoughts to—"

"Just so! And at the same time combine elevating sentiment with such practical information as you can obtain from the advertisement. Throw a glamour of poesy, f'r instance, over the commonplace details of the every-day life of the deceased. People are fond of minute descriptions. Some facts useful for this purpose may be obtained from the man who brings the notice to the office; others you may perhaps be able to supply from your imagination."

"I think I can do it first rate," said Mr. Slimmer.

"But, above all," continued the colonel, "try always to take a bright view of the matter. Cause the sunshine of smiles, as it were, to burst through the tempest of tears; and if we don't make the *Morning Argus* hum around this town, it will be queer."

Mr. Slimmer had charge of the editorial department the next day during the absence of Colonel Bangs in Wilmington. Throughout the afternoon and evening death-notices arrived; and when one would reach Mr. Slimmer's desk, he would lock the door, place the fingers of his left hand among his hair and agonize until he succeeded in completing a verse that seemed to him to accord with his instructions.

The next morning Mr. Slimmer proceeded calmly to the office for the purpose of embalming in sympathetic verse the memories of other departed ones. As he came near to the establishment he observed a crowd of people in front of it, struggling to get into the door. Ascending some steps upon the other side of the street, he overlooked the crowd, and could see within the office the clerks selling papers as fast as they could handle them, while the mob pushed and yelled in frantic efforts to obtain copies, the presses in the cellar meanwhile clanging furiously. Standing upon the curbstone in front of the office there was a long row of men, each of whom was engaged in reading *The Morning Argus* with an earnestness that Mr. Slimmer had never before seen displayed by the patrons of that sheet. The bard concluded that either his poetry had touched a sympathetic chord in the popular heart, or that an appalling disaster had occurred in some quarter of the globe.

He went around to the back of the office and ascended to the editorial rooms. As he approached the sanctum, loud voices were heard within. Mr. Slimmer determined to ascertain the cause before entering. He obtained a chair, and placing it by the side door, he mounted and peeped over the door through the transom. There sat Colonel Bangs, holding *The Morning Argus* in both hands, while the fringe which grew in a semicircle around the edge of his bald head stood straight out, until he seemed to resemble a gigantic gun-swab. Two or three persons stood in front of him in threatening attitudes. Slimmer heard one of them say:

"My name is McGlue, sir!—William McGlue! I am a brother of the late Alexander McGlue. I picked up your paper this morning, and perceived in it an outrageous insult to my deceased relative, and I have come around to demand, sir, WHAT YOU MEAN by the following infamous language:

"'The death-angel smote Alexander McGlue,
    And gave him protracted repose;
He wore a checked shirt and a Number Nine shoe,
    And he had a pink wart on his nose.
No doubt he is happier dwelling in space
    Over there on the evergreen shore.
His friends are informed that his funeral takes place
    Precisely at quarter-past four.'

"This is simply diabolical! My late brother had no wart on his nose, sir. He had upon his nose neither a pink wart nor a green wart, nor a cream-colored wart, nor a wart of any other color.

It is a slander! It is a gratuitous insult to my family, and I distinctly want you to say *what do you mean* by such conduct?"

"Really, sir," said Bangs, "it is a mistake. This is the horrible work of a miscreant in whom I reposed perfect confidence. He shall be punished by my own hand for this outrage. A pink wart! Awful! sir—awful! The miserable scoundrel shall suffer for this—he shall, indeed!"

"How could I know," murmured Mr. Slimmer to the foreman, who with him was listening, "that the corpse hadn't a pink wart? I used to know a man named McGlue, and *he* had one, and I thought *all* the McGlues had. This comes of irregularities in families."

"And who," said another man, addressing the editor, "authorized you to print this hideous stuff about my deceased son? Do you mean to say, Bangs, that it was not with your authority that your low comedian inserted with my advertisement the following scandalous burlesque? Listen to this:

" 'Willie had a purple monkey climbing on a yellow stick,
    And when he sucked the paint all off it made him deathly sick;
    And in his latest hours he clasped that monkey in his hand,
    And bade good-bye to earth and went into a better land.

" 'Oh! no more he'll shoot his sister with his little wooden gun;
    And no more he'll twist the pussy's tail and make her yowl, for fun.
    The pussy's tail now stands out straight; the gun is laid aside;
    The monkey doesn't jump around since little Willie died.'

"The atrocious character of this libel will appear when I say that my son was twenty years old, and that he died of liver complaint."

"Infamous!—utterly infamous!" groaned the editor as he cast his eyes over the lines. "And the wretch who did this still remains unpunished! It is too much!"

"And yet," whispered Slimmer to the foreman, "he told me to lighten the gloom and to cheer the afflicted family with the resources of my art; and I certainly thought that idea about the monkey would have that effect, somehow. Bangs is ungrateful!"

* * *

At this juncture the sheriff entered, his brow clothed with thunder. He had a copy of *The Morning Argus* in his hand. He approached the editor, and pointing to a death-notice, said,

"Read that outrageous burlesque, and tell me the name of the writer, so that I can chastise him."

The editor read as follows:

"We have lost our little Hanner in a very painful manner,
  And we often asked, How can her harsh sufferings be borne?
When her death was first reported, her aunt got up and snorted
  With the grief that she supported, for it made her feel forlorn.

"She was such a little seraph that her father, who is sheriff,
  Really doesn't seem to care if he ne'er smiles in life again.
She has gone, we hope, to heaven, at the early age of seven
  (Funeral starts off at eleven), where she'll nevermore have pain."

"As a consequence of this, I withdraw all the county advertising from your paper. A man who could trifle in this manner with the feelings of a parent is a savage and a scoundrel!"

As the sheriff went out, Colonel Bangs placed his head upon the table and groaned.

"Really," Mr. Slimmer said, "that person must be deranged. I tried, in his case, to put myself in his place, and to write as if I was one of the family, according to instructions. The verses are beautiful. That allusion to the grief of the aunt, particularly, seemed to me to be very happy. It expresses violent emotion with a felicitous combination of sweetness and force. These people have no soul—no appreciation of the beautiful in art."

While the poet mused, hurried steps were heard upon the stairs, and in a moment a middle-aged man dashed in abruptly, and seizing the colonel's scattered hair, bumped his prostrate head against the table three or four times with considerable force. Having expended the violence of his emotion in this manner, he held the editor's head down with one hand, shaking it occasionally by way of emphasis, and with the other hand seized the paper and said,

"You disgraceful old reprobate! You disgusting vampire! You hoary-headed old ghoul! What d'you mean by putting such stuff as this in your paper about my deceased son? What d'you mean by printing such awful doggerel as this, you depraved and dissolute ink-slinger—you imbecile quill-driver, you!

"'Oh! bury Bartholomew out in the woods,
  In a beautiful hole in the ground,
Where the bumble-bees buzz and the woodpeckers sing,
  And the straddle-bugs tumble around;

> So that, in winter, when the snow and the slush
> Have covered his last little bed,
> His brother Artemas can go out with Jane
> And visit the place with his sled.'

"I'll teach you to talk about straddle-bugs! I'll instruct you about slush! I'll enlighten your insane old intellect on the subject of singing woodpeckers! What do *you* know about Jane and Artemas, you wretched buccaneer, you despicable butcher of the English language? Go out with a sled! I'll carry you out in a hearse before I'm done with you, you deplorable lunatic!"

At the end of every phrase the visitor gave the editor's head a fresh knock against the table. When the exercise was ended, Colonel Bangs explained and apologized in the humblest manner, promising at the same time to give his assailant a chance to flog Mr. Slimmer, who was expected to arrive in a few moments.

"The treachery of this man," murmured the poet to the foreman, "is dreadful. Didn't he desire me to throw a glamour of poesy over commonplace details? But for that I should never have thought of alluding to woodpeckers and bugs, and other children of Nature. The man objects to the remarks about the sled. Can the idiot know that it was necessary to have a rhyme for 'bed'? Can he suppose that I could write poetry without rhymes? The man is a lunatic! He ought not to be at large!"

Hardly had the indignant and energetic parent of Bartholomew departed when a man with red hair and a ferocious glare in his eyes entered, carrying a club and accompanied by a savage-looking dog.

"I want to see the editor," he shouted.

A ghastly pallor overspread the colonel's face, and he said, "The editor is not in."

"Well, when *will* he be in, then?"

"Not for a week—for a month—for a year—forever! He will never come in any more!" screamed Bangs. "He has gone to South America, with the intention to remain there during the rest of his life. He has departed. He has fled. If you want to see him, you had better follow him to the equator. He will be glad to see you. I would advise you, as a friend, to take the next boat—to start at once."

"That is unfortunate," said the man; "I came all the way from Delaware City for the purpose of battering him up a lot with this club."

"He will be sorry," said Bangs, sarcastically. "He will regret missing you. I will write to him, and mention that you dropped in."

[My First Political Speech]

The chairman began with a short speech in which he went over almost precisely the ground covered by my introduction; and as that portion of my oration was . . . reduced to a fragment . . ., I quietly resolved to begin, when my turn came, with point number two.

The chairman introduced to the crowd Mr. Keyser, who was received with cheers. He was a ready speaker, and he began, to my deep regret, by telling in capital style my story number three, after which he used up some of my number six arguments, and concluded with the remark that it was not his purpose to occupy the attention of the meeting for any length of time, because the executive committee in Wilmington had sent an eloquent orator who was now upon the platform and would present the cause of the party in a manner which he could not hope to approach.

Mr. Keyser then sat down, and Mr. Schwartz was introduced. Mr. Schwartz observed that it was hardly worth while for him to attempt to make anything like a speech, because the gentleman from New Castle had come down on purpose to discuss the issues of the campaign, and the audience, of course, was anxious to hear him. Mr. Schwartz would only tell a little story which seemed to illustrate a point he wished to make, and he thereupon related my anecdote number seven. . . . The point illustrated I was shocked to find was almost precisely that which I had attached to my story number seven. The situation began to have a serious appearance. Here, at one fell swoop, two of my best stories and three of my sets of arguments were swept off into utter uselessness.

When Schwartz withdrew, a man named Krumbauer was brought forward. Krumbauer was a German, and the chairman announced that he would speak in that language for the benefit of those persons in the audience to whom the tongue was pleasantly familiar. Krumbauer went ahead, and the crowd received his remarks with roars of laughter. After one particularly exuberant outburst of merriment, I asked the man who sat next to me, and who seemed deeply interested in the story,

"What was that little joke of Krumbauer's? It must have been first rate."

"So it was," he said. "It was about a Dutchman up in Berks county, Penna., who got mixed up in his dates."

"What dates?" I gasped, in awful apprehension.

"Why, his Fourths of July, you know. Got seven or eight years in arrears and tried to make them all up at once. Good, wasn't it?"

"Good? I should think so; ha! ha! My very best story, as I'm a sinner!"

It was awfully bad. I could have strangled Krumbauer and then chopped him into bits. The ground seemed slipping away beneath me; there was the merest skeleton of a speech left. But I determined to take that and do my best, trusting to luck for a happy result.

But my turn had not yet come. Mr. Wilson was dragged out next, and I thought I perceived a demoniac smile steal over the countenance of the cymbal player as Wilson said he was too hoarse to say much; he would leave the heavy work for the brilliant young orator who was here from New Castle. He would skim rapidly over the ground and then retire. He did. Wilson rapidly skimmed all the cream off of my arguments numbers two, five and six, and wound up by offering the whole of my number four argument. My hair fairly stood on end when Wilson bowed and left the stand. What on earth was I to do now? Not an argument left to stand upon; all my anecdotes gone but two, and my mind in such a condition of frenzied bewilderment that it seemed as if there was not another available argument or suggestion or hint or anecdote remaining in the entire universe. In an agony of despair, I turned to the man next to me and asked him if I would have to follow Wilson.

He said it was his turn now.

"And what are you going to say?" I demanded, suspiciously.

"Oh, nothing," he replied—"nothing at all. I want to leave room for you. I'll just tell a little story or so, to amuse them, and then sit down."

"What story, for instance?" I asked.

"Oh, nothing, nothing; only a little yarn I happen to remember about a farmer who married a woman who said she could cut four cords of wood, when she couldn't."

My worst fears were realized. I turned to the man next to me, and said, with suppressed emotion.

"May I ask your name, my friend?"

He said his name was Gumbs.

"May I inquire what your Christian name is?"

He said it was William Henry.

"Well, William Henry Gumbs," I exclaimed, "gaze at me! Do I look like a man who would slay a human being in cold blood?"

"Hm-m-m, n-no; you don't," he replied, with an air of critical consideration.

"But I AM!" said I, fiercely—"I AM; and I tell you now that if you undertake to relate that anecdote about the farmer's wife I will blow you into eternity without a moment's warning; I will, by George!"

Mr. Gumbs instantly jumped up, placed his hand on the railing of the porch, and got over suddenly into the crowd. He stood there pointing me out to the bystanders, and doubtless advancing the theory that I was an original kind of a lunatic, who might be expected to have at any moment a fit which would be interesting when studied from a distance.

The chairman looked around, intending to call upon my friend Mr. Gumbs; but not perceiving him, he came to me and said:

"Now is your chance, sir; splendid opportunity; crowd worked up to just the proper pitch. We have paved the way for you; go in and do your best."

"Oh yes; but hold on for a few moments, will you? I can't speak now; the fact is I am not quite ready. Run out some other man."

"Haven't got another man. Kept you for the last purposely, and the crowd is waiting. Come ahead and pitch in, and give it to 'em hot and heavy."

It was very easy for him to say "give it to them," but I had nothing to give. Beautifully they paved the way for me! Nicely they had worked up the crowd to the proper pitch! Here I was in a condition of frantic despair, with a crowd of one thousand people expecting a brilliant oration from me who had not a thing in my mind but a beggarly story about a fire-extinguisher and a worse one about a farmer's wife. I groaned in spirit and wished I had been born far away in some distant clime among savages who knew not of mass meetings, and whose language contained such a small number of words that speech-making was impossible.

But the chairman was determined. He seized me by the arm and fairly dragged me to the front. He introduced me to the crowd in flattering, and I may say outrageously ridiculous, terms, and then whispering in my ear, "Hit 'em hard, old fellow, hit 'em hard," he sat down.

The crowd received me with three hearty cheers. As I heard them I began to feel dizzy. The audience seemed to swim around and to increase tenfold in size. By a resolute effort I recovered my self-possession partially, and determined to begin. I could not think of anything but the two stories, and I resolved to tell them as well as I could. I said,

"Fellow-citizens: It is so late now that I will not attempt to make a speech to you." (Cries of "Yes!" "Go ahead!" "Never mind the time!" etc., etc.) Elevating my voice, I repeated: "I say it is so late now that I can't make a speech as I intended on account of its being so late that the speech which I intended to make would keep you here too late if I made it as I intended to. So I will tell you a story about a man who bought a patent fire-extinguisher which was warranted to split four cords of wood a day; so he set fire to his house to try her, and—No, it was his wife who was warranted to split four cords of wood—I got it wrong; and when the flames obtained full headway, he found she could only split two cords and a half, and it made him—What I mean is that the farmer, when he bought the exting—courted her, that is, she said she could set fire to the house, and when he tried her, she collapsed the first time—the extinguisher did, and he wanted a divorce because his house—Oh, hang it, fellow-citizens, you understand that this man, or farmer, rather, bought a—I should say courted a— that is, a fire-ex—" (Desperately.) "Fellow-citizens! IF ANY MAN SHOOTS THE AMERICAN FLAG, PULL HIM DOWN UPON THE SPOT; BUT AS FOR ME, GIVE ME LIBERTY OR GIVE ME DEATH!"

As I shouted this out at the top of my voice, in an ecstasy of confusion, a wild, tumultuous yell of laughter came up from the crowd. I paused for a second beneath the spell of that cold eye in the band, and then, dashing through the throng at the back of the porch, I rushed down the street to the dépôt, with the shouts of the crowd and the uproarious music of the band ringing in my ears. I got upon a freight train, gave the engineer five dollars to take me along on the locomotive, and spent the night riding to New Castle.

THE BRAKEMAN AT CHURCH

by Robert J. Burdette

(1844–1914)

On the road once more, with Lebanon fading away in the distance, the fat passenger drumming idly on the window pane, the cross passenger sound asleep, and the tall, thin passenger reading "Gen. Grant's Tour Around the World," and wondering why Green's August Flower should be printed above the doors of a "Buddhist Temple at Benares." To me comes the brakeman, and seating himself on the arm of the seat, says:

"I went to church yesterday."

"Yes!" I said, with that interested inflection that asks for more. "And what church did you attend?"

"Which do you guess?" he asked.

"Some union mission church?" I hazarded.

"Naw," he said, "I don't like to run on those branch roads very much. I don't often go to church, and when I do, I want to run on the main line, where your run is regular and you go on schedule time and don't have to wait on connections. I don't like to run on a branch. Good enough, but I don't like it."

"Episcopal?" I guessed.

"Limited express," he said, "all palace cars and $2 extra for a seat; fast time and stop at the big stations. Nice line, but too exhaustive for a brakeman. All train-men in uniform; conductor's punch and lantern silver-plated, and no train-boys allowed. Then the passengers are allowed to talk back at the conductor, and it makes them too free and easy. No, I couldn't stand the palace car. Rich road, though. Don't often hear of a receiver being appointed for that line. Some mighty nice people travel on it too."

"Universalist?" I guessed.

"Broad gauge," said the brakeman; "does too much complimentary business. Everybody travels on a pass. Conductor doesn't get a fare once in fifty miles. Stops at all flag stations and won't run into anything but a union depot. No smoking car on the train. Train orders are rather vague, though, and the train-men don't get along well with the passengers. No, I didn't go to the Universalist, though I know some awfully good men who run on that road."

"Presbyterian?" I asked.

"Narrow gauge, eh?" said the brakeman: "pretty track, straight as a rule; tunnel right through the mountain rather than go around it, spirit-level grade, passengers have to show their tickets before they get on the train. Mighty strict road, but the cars are a little narrow, have to sit one in a seat and no room in the aisle to dance. Then there's no stop-over tickets allowed, got to go straight through to the station you're ticketed for, or you can't get on at all. When the car's full, no extra coaches, cars built at the shops to hold just so many, and nobody else allowed on. But you don't hear of an accident on that road, it's run right up to the rules."

"Maybe you joined the Free Thinkers?" I said.

"Scrub road," said the brakeman: "dirt road bed, and no ballast, no time card and no train dispatcher. All trains run wild, and every engineer makes his own time just as he pleases. Smoke if you want to; kind of go-as-you-please road. Too many side tracks, and every switch wide open all the time, with the switch-man sound asleep, and the target-lamp dead out. Get on as you please, and get off when you want to. Don't have to show your tickets, and the conductor isn't expected to do anything but amuse the passengers. No, sir; I was offered a pass, but I don't like the line. I don't like to travel on a road that has no terminus. Don't you know sir, I asked a Division Superintendent where that road run to, and said he hoped to die if he knew. I asked him if the General Superintendent could tell me, and he said he didn't believe they had a General Superintendent, and if they had, he didn't know anything more about the road than the passengers. I asked him who he reported to, and he said, 'nobody.' I asked a conductor who he got his orders from, and he said he didn't take orders from any living man or dead ghost. And when I asked the engineer who he got his orders from, he said he'd like to see anybody give him orders; he'd run that train to suit himself, or he'd run it into the ditch. Now, you see, sir, I'm a railroad man, and I don't care to run on a road that has no time, makes no connections, runs nowhere, and has no Superintendent. It may be all right, but I've railroaded too long to understand it."

"Did you try the Methodist?" I said.

"Now you are shouting," he said, with some enthusiasm. "Nice road, eh? Fast time and plenty of passengers. Engineers carry a power of steam, and don't you forget it; steam gauge shows 100, and enough all the time. Lively road; when the conductor shouts 'all aboard!' you can hear him to the next station. Every train-lamp shines like a headlight. Stop-over checks given on all through tickets; passengers can drop off the train as often as they like, do the stations two or three days, and hop on the revival train that comes thundering along. Good, whole-souled, companionable conductors; ain't any road in the country where the passengers feel more at home. No passes; every passenger pays full traffic rates for his ticket. Wesleyanhouse air-brakes on all trains, too; pretty safe road, but I didn't ride over it yesterday."

"Maybe you went to the Congregational church," I said.

"Popular road," said the brakeman; "an old road, too, one of the very oldest in the country. Good road bed and comfortable cars. Well managed road, too; Directors don't interfere with Division Superintendents and train orders. Road's mighty popular, but it's pretty independent, too. See, didn't one of the Division Superintendents down East discontinue one of the oldest stations on the line two or three years ago? But it is a mighty pleasant road to travel on. Always has such a splendid class of passengers."

"Perhaps you tried the Baptist?" I guessed once more.

"Ah, ha!" said the brakeman, "she's a daisy, isn't she? River road; beautiful curves; sweep around anything to keep close to the river, but it's all steel rail and rock ballast, single track all the way and not a side track from the round-house to the terminus. Takes a heap of water to run it, though; double tanks at every station, and there isn't an engine in the shops that can pull a pound or run a mile with less than two gauges. But it runs through a lovely country; these river roads always do; river on one side and hills on the other, and it's a steady climb up the grade all the way till the run ends where the fountain-head of the river begins. Yes, sir, I'll take the river road every time for a lovely trip, sure connections and good time and no prairie dust blowing in at the windows. And yesterday, when the conductor came around for the tickets with a little basket punch, I didn't ask him to pass me, but paid my fare like a little man—25 cents for an hour's run, and a little concert by the passengers throwed in. I tell you, Pilgrim, you take the river road when you want—"

But just here the long whistle from the engine announced a station, and a brakeman hurried to the door, shouting:

"Zionsville! This train makes no stop between here and Indianapolis."

BILL NYE'S ADVENTURES IN POLITICS
by Edgar Wilson Nye
(1850–1896)

ACCEPTING THE LARAMIE POSTOFFICE

Office of Daily Boomerang, Laramie City, Wy.
August 9, 1882.

My dear General:

I have received by telegraph the news of my nomination by the President and my confirmation by the Senate, as postmaster at Laramie, and wish to extend my thanks for the same.

I have ordered an entirely new set of boxes and post-office outfit, including new corrugated cuspidors for the lady clerks.

I look upon the appointment as a great triumph of eternal truth over error and wrong. It is one of the epochs, I may say, in the Nation's onward march toward political purity and perfection. I do not know when I have noticed any stride in the affairs of state, which so thoroughly impressed me with its wisdom.

Now that we are co-workers in the same department, I trust that you will not feel shy or backward in consulting me at any time relative to matters concerning postoffice affairs. Be perfectly frank with me, and feel free to bring anything of that kind right to me. Do not feel reluctant because I may at times appear haughty and indifferent, cold or reserved. Perhaps you do not think I know the difference between a general delivery window and a three-em quad, but that is a mistake.

My general information is far beyond my years.

With profoundest regard, and a hearty endorsement of the policy of the President and the Senate, whatever it may be,

I remain, sincerely yours,

BILL NYE, P.M.

A Resign

Postoffice Divan, Laramie City, W.T.,
Ct. 1, 1883

To the President of the United States:

Sir: I beg leave at this time officially to tender my resignation as postmaster at this place, and in due form to deliver the great seal and the key to the front door of the office. The safe combination is set on the numbers 33, 66 and 99, though I do not remember at this moment which comes first, or how many times you revolve the knob, or in which direction you should turn it first to make it operate.

There is some mining stock in my private drawer in the safe, which I have not yet removed. It is a luxury, but you may have it. I have decided to keep a horse instead of this mining stock. The horse may not be so pretty, but it will cost less to keep him.

You will find the postal cards that have not been used under the distributing table, and the coal down in the cellar. If the stove draws too hard, close the damper in the pipe and shut the general delivery window.

Looking over my stormy and eventful administration as postmaster here, I find abundant cause for thanksgiving. At the time I entered upon the duties of my office the department was not yet on a paying basis. It was not even self-sustaining. Since that time, with the active coöperation of the chief executive and the heads of the department, I have been able to make our postal system a paying one, and on top of that I am now able to reduce the tariff on average-sized letters from three cents to two. I might add that this is rather too too, but I will not say anything that might seem undignified in an official resignation which is to become a matter of history.

Acting under the advice of Gen. Hatton, a year ago, I removed the feather bed with which my predecessor, Deacon Hayford, had bolstered up his administration by stuffing the window, and substituted glass. Finding nothing in the book of instructions to postmasters which made the feather bed a part of my official duties, I filed it away in an obscure place and burned it in effigy, also in the gloaming.

It was not long after I had taken my official oath before an era of unexampled prosperity opened for the American people.

The price of beef rose to a remarkable altitude, and other vegetables commanded a good figure and a ready market. We then began to make active preparations for the introduction of the strawberry-roan two-cent stamps and the black-and-tan postal note. One reform has crowded upon the heels of another, until the country is to-day upon the foam-crested wave of permanent prosperity.

Mr. President, I cannot close this letter without thanking yourself and the heads of departments at Washington for your active, cheery and prompt coöperation in these matters. You may do as you see fit, of course, about incorporating this idea into your Thanksgiving proclamation, but rest assured it would not be ill-timed or inopportune. It is not alone a credit to myself. It reflects credit upon the administration also.

I need not say that I herewith transmit my resignation with great sorrow and genuine regret. We have toiled on together month after month, asking for no reward except the innate consciousness of rectitude and the salary as fixed by law. Now we are to separate. Here the roads seem to fork, as it were, and you and I, and the cabinet, must leave each other at this point.

You will find the key under the door-mat, and you had better turn the cat out at night when you close the office. If she does not go readily, you can make it clearer to her mind by throwing the cancelling stamp at her.

If Deacon Hayford does not pay up his box-rent, you might as well put his mail in the general delivery, and when Bob Head gets drunk and insists on a letter from one of his wives every day in the week, you can salute him through the box delivery with an old Queen Anne tomahawk, which you will find near the Etruscan water-pail. This will not in any manner surprise either of these parties.

Tears are unavailing! I once more become a private citizen, clothed only with the right to read such postal cards as may be addressed to me, and to curse the inefficiency of the postoffice department. I believe the voting class to be divided into two parties; viz., those who are in the postal service, and those who are mad because they cannot receive a registered letter every fifteen minutes of each day, including Sunday.

Mr. President, as an official of this Government I now retire. My term of office would not expire until 1886. I must, therefore, beg pardon for my eccentricity in resigning. It will be best, perhaps, to keep the heart-breaking news from the ears of European powers until the dangers of a financial panic are fully past. Then hurl it broadcast with a sickening thud.

HE SEES THE NAVY

It has become such a general practice to speak disrespectfully of the United States Navy that a few days ago I decided to visit the Brooklyn Navy Yard for the purpose of ascertaining, if possible, how much cause there might be for this light and airy manner of treating the navy, and, if necessary, to take immediate steps towards purifying the system.

I found that the matter had been grossly misrepresented, and that our navy, so far as I was able to discover, is self-sustaining. It has been thoroughly refitted and refurnished throughout, and is as pleasant a navy as one would see in a day's journey.

I had the pleasure of boarding the man-of-war Richmond under a flag of truce and the Atlantic under a suspension of the rules. I remained some time on board each of these war ships, and any man who speaks lightly of the United States Navy in my presence hereafter will receive a stinging rebuke.

The Brooklyn Navy Yard was inaugurated by the purchase of forty acres of ground in 1801. It has a pleasant water-front, which is at all times dotted here and there with new war vessels undergoing repairs. Since the original purchase others have been made and the land side of the yard inclosed by means of a large brick wall, so that in case there should be a local disturbance in Brooklyn the rioters could not break through and bite the navy. In this way a man on board the Atlanta while at anchor in Brooklyn is just as safe as he would be at home.

In order to enter and explore the Navy Yard it is necessary that one should have a pass. This is a safeguard, wisely adopted by the Commandant, in order to keep out strangers who might get in under the pretext of wishing to view the yard and afterwards attack one of the new vessels.

On the day I visited the Navy Yard just ahead of me a plain but dignified person in citizen's dress passed through the gate. He had the bearing of an officer, I thought, and kept his eye on some object about nine and one-fourth miles ahead as he walked past the guard. He was told to halt, but, of course, he did not do so. He was above it. Then the guard overhauled him, and even felt in his pockets for his pass, as I supposed. Concealed on his person the guard found four pint bottles filled with the essence of crime. They poured the poor man's rum on the grass and then fired him out, accompanied by a rebuke which will make him more deliberate about sitting down for a week or two.

The feeling against arduous spirits in the United States Navy is certainly on the increase, and the day is not far distant when alcohol in a free state will only be used in the arts, sciences, music, literature, and the drama.

The Richmond is a large but buoyant vessel painted black. It has a front stairway hanging over the balcony, and the latch-string to the front door was hanging cheerily out as we drew alongside. During an engagement, however, on the approach of the enemy, the front stairs are hauled up and the latch-string is pulled in, while the commanding officer makes the statement, "April Fool" through a speaking-trumpet to the chagrined and infuriated foe.

The Richmond is a veteran of the late war, a war which no one ever regretted more than I did; not so much because of the blood-shed and desolation it caused at the time, but on account of the rude remarks since made to those who did not believe in the war and whose feelings have been repeatedly hurt by reference to it since the war closed.

The guns of the Richmond are muzzle-loaders, *i.e.*, the load or charge of ammunition is put into the other or outer end of the gun instead of the inner extremity or base of the gun, as is the case with the breech-loader. The breech-loader is a great improvement on the old style gun, making warfare a constant source of delirious joy now, whereas in former times in case of a naval combat during a severe storm, the man who went outside the ship to load the gun, while it was raining, frequently contracted pneumonia.

Modern guns are made with breeches, which may be easily removed during a fight and replaced when visitors come on board. A sort of grim humor pervades the above remark.

The Richmond is about to sail away to China. I do not know why she is going to China but presume she does not care to be here during the amenities, antipathies and aspersions of a Presidential campaign. A man-of-war would rather make some sacrifices generally than to get into trouble.

I must here say that I would rather be captured by our naval officers than by any other naval officers I have ever seen. The older officers were calm and self-possessed during my visit on board both the Richmond and Atlanta, and the young fellows are as handsome as a steel engraving. While gazing on them as they proudly trod the quarter deck or any other deck that needed it, I was proud of my sex, and I could not help thinking that had I been an unprotected but beautiful girl, hostile to the United States, I could have picked out five or six young men there to either of whom I would be glad to talk over the details of an armistice. I could not help enjoying fully my hospitable treatment by the officers above referred to after having been only a little while before rudely repulsed and most cruelly snubbed by a haughty young cotton-sock broker in a New York store.

When will people ever learn that the way to have fun with me is to treat me for the time being as an equal?

It was wash-day on board ship, and I could not help noticing how the tyrant man asserts himself when he becomes sole boss of the household. The rule on board a man-of-war is that the first man who on wash-day shall suggest a "picked-up dinner" shall be loaded into the double-barrelled howitzer and shot into the bosom of Venus.

On the clothes-line I noticed very few frills. The lingerie on board a war vessel is severe in outline and almost harsh in detail. Here the salt breezes search in vain for the singularly sawed-off and fluently trimmed toga of our home life. Here all is changed. From the basement to the top of the lightning rod, from pit to dome, as I was about to say, a belligerent ship on wash-day is not gayly caparisoned.

The Atlanta is a fair representative of the modern war vessel and would be the most effective craft in the world if she could use her guns. She has all the modern improvements, hot and cold water, electric lights, handy to depots and a good view of the ocean, but when she shoots off her guns they pull out her circles, abrade her deck, concuss her rotunda, contuse the main brace and injure people who have always been friendly to the Government. Her guns are now being removed and new circles put in, so that in future she would be enabled to give less pain to her friends and squirt more gloom into the ranks of the enemy. She is at present as useful for purposes of defense as a revolver in the bottom of a locked-up bureau drawer, the key of which is in the pocket of your wife's dress in a dark closet, wherein also the burglar is, for the nonce, concealed.

Politics has very little to do with the conduct of a navy-yard. No one would talk politics with me. I could not arouse any interest there at all in the election. Every one seemed delighted with the present Administration, however. The navy-yard always feels that way.

In the choky or brig at the guard-house I saw a sailor locked up who was extremely drunk.

"How did you get it here, my man?" I asked.

"Through thinfloonce of prominent Democrat, you damphool. Howje spose?" he unto me straightway did reply.

The sailor is sometimes infested with a style of arid humor which asserts itself in the most unlooked-for fashion. I laughed heartily at his odd yet coarse repartee, and went away.

The guard-house contains a choice collection of manacles, handcuffs, lily irons and other rare gems. The lily irons are not now in use. They consist of two iron bands for the wrists, connected by means of a flat iron, which can be opened up to let the wrists into place; then they are both locked at one time by means of a wrench like the one used by a piano-tuner. With a pair of lily irons on the wrists and another pair on the ankles a man locked in the brig and caught out 2,000 miles at sea in a big gale, with the rudder knocked off the ship and a large litter of kittens in the steam cylinder, would feel almost helpless.

I had almost forgotten to mention the drug store on board ship. Each man-of-war has a small pharmacy on the second floor. It is open all night, and prescriptions are carefully compounded. Pure drugs, paints, oils, varnishes and putty are to be had there at all times. The ship's dispensary is not a large room, but two ordinary men and a truss would not feel crowded there. The druggists treated me well on board both ships, and offered me my choice of antiseptics and anodynes, or anything else I might take a fancy to. I shall do my trading in that line hereafter on board ship.

The Atlanta has many very modern improvements, and is said to be a wonderful sailor. She also has a log. I saw it. It does not look exactly like what I had, as an old lumberman, imagined that it would.

It is a book, with writing in it, about the size of the tax-roll for 1888. In the cupola of the ship, where the wheel is located, there is also a big brass compass about as large as the third stomach of a cow. In this there is a little index or dingus, which always points towards the north. That is all it has to do. On each side of the compass is a large cannon ball so magnetized or polarized or influenced as to overcome the attraction of the needle for some desirable portion of the ship. There is also an index connected with the shaft whereby the man at the wheel can ascertain the position of the shaft and also ascertain at night whether the ship is advancing or retreating—a thing that he should inform himself about at the earliest possible moment.

The culinary arrangements on board these ships would make many a hotel blush, and I have paid $4 a day for a worse room than the choky at the guard-house.

In the Navy-Yard at Brooklyn is the big iron hull or running gears of an old ship of some kind which the Republicans were in the habit of hammering on for a few weeks prior to election every four years. Four years ago, through an oversight, the workmen were not called off nor informed of Blaine's defeat for several days after the election.

The Democrats have an entirely different hull in another part of the yard on which they are hammering.

The keel blocks of a new cruiser, 375 feet long, are just laid in the big ship-house at the Brooklyn Navy-Yard. She will be a very airy and cheerful boat, I judge, if the keel blocks are anything to go by.

In closing this account I desire to state that I hope I have avoided the inordinate use of marine terms, as I desire to make myself perfectly clear to the ordinary landsman, even at the expense of beauty and style of description. I would rather be thoroughly understood than confuse the reader while exerting myself to show my knowledge of terms. I also desire to express my thanks to the United States Navy for its kindness and consideration during my visit. I could have been easily blown into space half a dozen times without any opportunity to blow back through the papers, had the navy so desired, and yet nothing but terms of endearment passed between the navy and myself.

Lieut. Arthur P. Nazro, Chief Engineer Henry B. Nones, Passed Assistant Engineer E. A. Magee, Capt. F. H. Harrington, of the United States Marine Corps; Mr. Gus C. Roeder, Apothecary Henry Wimmer and the dog Zib, of the Richmond; Master Shipwright McGee, Capt. Miller, captain of the yard, and Mr. Milligan, apothecary of the Atlanta, deserve honorable mention for coolness and heroic endurance while I was there.

MR. DOOLEY TO MR. HENNESSY

by Finley Peter Dunne

(1867–1936)

ON THE VICTORIAN ERA

"Ar-re ye goin' to cillybrate th' queen's jubilee?" asked Mr. Dooley.

"What's that?" demanded Mr. Hennessy, with a violent start.

"To-day," said Mr. Dooley, "her gracious Majesty Victorya, Queen iv Great Britain an' that part iv Ireland north iv Sligo, has reigned f'r sixty long and tiresome years."

"I don't care if she has snowed f'r sixty years," said Mr. Hennessy. "I'll not cillybrate it. She may be a good woman f'r all I know, but dam her pollytics."

"Ye needn't be pro-fane about it," said Mr. Dooley. "I on'y ast ye a civil question. F'r mesilf, I have no feelin' on th' subject. I am not with th' queen an' I'm not again her. At th' same time I corjally agree with me frind Captain Finerty, who's put his newspaper in mournin' f'r th' ivint. I won't march in th' parade, an' I won't put anny dinnymite undher thim that does. I don't say th' marchers an' dinnymiters ar-re not both r-right. 'Tis purely a question iv taste, an', as the ixicutive says whin both candydates are mimbers iv th' camp, 'Pathrites will use their own discreetion.'

"Th' good woman niver done me no har-rm; an', beyond throwin' a rock or two into an orangey's procission an' subscribin' to tin dollars' worth iv Fenian bonds, I've threated her like a lady. Anny gredge I iver had again her I burrid long ago. We're both well on in years, an' 'tis no use carrying har-rd feelin's to th' grave. About th' time th' lord chamberlain wint over to tell her she was queen, an' she came out in her nitey to hear th' good news, I was announced into this wurruld iv sin an' sorrow. So ye see we've reigned about th' same lenth iv time, an' I ought to be cillybratin' me di'mon' jubilee. I wud, too, if I had anny di'mon's. Do ye r-run down to Aldherman O'Brien's an' borrow twinty or thirty f'r me.

"Great happenin's have me an' Queen Victorya seen in these sixty years. Durin' our binificent prisince on earth th' nations have

460

grown r-rich an' prosperous. Great Britain has ixtinded her domain until th' sun niver sets on it. No more do th' original owners iv th' sile, they bein' kept movin' be th' polis. While she was lookin' on in England, I was lookin' on in this counthry. I have seen America spread out fr'm th' Atlantic to th' Pacific, with a branch office iv the Standard Ile Comp'ny in ivry hamlet. I've seen th' shackles dropped fr'm th' slave, so's he cud be lynched in Ohio. I've seen this gr-reat city desthroyed be fire fr'm De Koven Sthreet to th' Lake View pumpin' station, and thin rise felix-like fr'm its ashes, all but th' West Side, which was not burned. I've seen Jim Mace beat Mike McCool, an' Tom Allen beat Jim Mace, an' somebody beat Tom Allen, an' Jawn Sullivan beat him an' Corbett beat Sullivan, an' Fitz beat Corbett; an', if I live to cillybrate me goold-watch-an'-chain jubilee, I may see some wan put it all over Fitz.

"Oh, what things I've seen in me day an' Victorya's! Think iv that gran' procission iv lithry men,—Tinnyson an' Longfellow an' Bill Nye an' Ella Wheeler Wilcox an' Tim Scanlan an'—an' I can't name thim all: they're too manny. An' th' brave gin'rals,— Von Molkey an' Bismarck an' U. S. Grant an' gallant Phil Shurdan an' Coxey. Think iv thim durin' me reign. An' th' invintions,—th' steam-injine an' th' printin'-press an' th' cotton-gin an' the gin sour an' th' bicycle an' th' flyin'-machine an' th' nickel-in-th'-slot machine an' th' Croker machine an' th' sody fountain an'—crownin' wur-ruk iv our civilization—th' cash raygisther. What gr-reat advances has science made in my time an' Victorya's! f'r, whin we entered public life, it took three men to watch th' bar-keep, while to-day ye can tell within eight dollars an hour what he's took in.

"Glory be, whin I look back fr'm this day iv gin'ral rejoicin' in me rhinestone jubilee, an' see what changes has taken place an' how manny people have died an' how much betther off th' wurruld is, I'm proud iv mesilf. War an' pest'lence an' famine have occurred in me time, but I count thim light compared with th' binifits that have fallen to th' race since I come on th' earth."

"What ar-re ye talkin' about?" cried Mr. Hennessy, in deep disgust. "All this time ye've been standin' behind this bar ladlin' out disturbance to th' Sixth Wa-ard, an' ye haven't been as far east as Mitchigan Avnoo in twinty years. What have ye had to do with all these things?"

"Well," said Mr. Dooley, "I had as much to do with thim as th' queen."

On Books

"Ivry time I pick up me mornin' paper to see how th' scrap come out at Batthry D," said Mr. Dooley, "th' first thing I r-run acrost is somethin' like this: 'A hot an' handsome gift f'r Christmas is Lucy Ann Patzooni's "Jims iv Englewood Thought"'; or 'If ye wud delight th' hear-rt iv yer child, ye'll give him Dr. Harper's monymental histhry iv th' Jewish thribes fr'm Moses to Dhryfuss' or 'Ivrybody is r-readin' Roodyard Kiplin's "Busy Pomes f'r Busy People."' Th' idee iv givin' books f'r Christmas prisints whin th' stores are full iv tin hor-rns an' dhrums an' boxin' gloves an choo-choo ca-ars! People must be crazy."

"They ar-re," said Mr. Hennessy. "My house is so full iv books ye cudden't tur-rn around without stumblin' over thim. I found th' life iv an ex-convict, the 'Prisoner iv Zinders,' in me high hat th' other day, where Mary Ann was hidin' it fr'm her sister. In-stead iv th' childher fightin' an' skylarkin' in th' evenin', they're settin' around th' table with their noses glued into books. Th' ol' woman doesn't read, but she picks up what's goin' on. 'Tis 'Honoria, did Lor-rd What's-his-name marry th' fair Aminta?' or 'But that Lady Jane was a case.' An' so it goes. There's no injymint in th' house, an' they're usin' me cravats f'r bookmarks."

"'Tis all wrong," said Mr. Dooley. "They're on'y three books in th' wurruld worth readin',—Shakespeare, th' Bible, an' Mike Ahearn's histhry iv Chicago. I have Shakespeare on thrust, Father Kelly r-reads th' Bible f'r me, an' I didn't buy Mike Ahearn's histhry because I seen more thin he cud put into it. Books is th' roon iv people, specially novels. Whin I was a young man, th' parish priest used to preach again thim; but nobody knowed what he meant. At that time Willum Joyce had th' on'y library in th' Sixth Wa-ard. Th' mayor give him th' bound volumes iv th' coun-cil proceedings, an' they was a very handsome set. Th' on'y books I seen was th' kind that has th' life iv th' pope on th' outside an' a set iv dominos on th' inside. They're good readin'. Nawthin' cud be better f'r a man whin he's tired out afther a day's wurruk thin to go to his library an' take down wan iv th' gr-reat wurruks iv lithratchoor an' play a game iv dominos f'r th' dhrinks out iv it. Anny other kind iv r-readin', barrin' th' newspapers, which will niver hurt anny onedycated man, is desthructive iv morals.

"I had it out with Father Kelly th' other day in this very matther. He was comin' up fr'm down town with an ar-rmful iv books f'r prizes at th' school. 'Have ye th' Key to Heaven there?' says I. 'No,' says he, 'th' childher that'll get these books don't need no key. They go in under th' turn-stile,' he says, laughin'. 'Have ye th' Lives iv th' Saints, or the Christyan Dooty, or th' Story iv Saint Rose iv Lima?' I says. 'I have not,' says he, 'I have some good story books. I'd rather th' kids'd r-read Char-les Dickens than anny iv th' tales iv thim holy men that was burned in ile or et up be lines,' he says. 'It does no good in these degin'rate days to prove that th' best that can come to a man f'r behavin' himsilf is to be cooked in a pot or di-gisted be a line,' he says. 'Ye're wrong,' says I. 'Beggin' ye'er riv'rince's pardon, ye're wrong,' I says. 'What ar-re ye goin' to do with thim young wans? Ye're goin' to make thim near-sighted an' round-shouldered,' I says. 'Ye're goin' to have thim believe that, if they behave thimsilves an' lead a virchous life, they'll marry rich an' go to Congress. They'll wake up some day, an' find out that gettin' money an behavin' ye'ersilf don't always go together,' I says. 'Some iv th' wickedest men in th' wur-ruld have marrid rich,' I says. 'Ye're goin' to teach thim that a man doesn't have to use an ax to get along in th' wur-ruld. Ye're goin' to teach thim that a la-ad with a curlin' black mustache an' smokin' a cigareet is always a villyan, whin he's more often a barber with a lar-rge family. Life, says ye! There's no life in a book. If ye want to show thim what life is, tell thim to look around thim. There's more life on a Saturdah night in th' Ar-rchy Road thin in all th' books fr'm Shakespeare to th' rayport iv th' drainage thrustees. No man,' I says, 'iver wrote a book if he had annything to write about, except Shakespeare an' Mike Ahearn. Shakespeare was all r-right. I niver read anny of his pieces, but they sound good; an' I know Mike Ahearn is all r-right.'"

"What did he say?" asked Mr. Hennessy.

"He took it all r-right," said Mr. Dooley. "He kind o' grinned, an' says he: 'What ye say is thrue, an' it's not thrue,' he says. 'Books is f'r thim that can't injye thimsilves in anny other way,' he says. 'If ye're in good health, an' ar-re eatin' three squares a day, an' not ayether sad or very much in love with ye'er lot, but just lookin' on an' not carin' a'—he said rush—'not carin' a rush, ye don't need books,' he says. 'But if ye're a down-spirited thing an' want to get away an' can't, ye need books. 'Tis betther to be comfortable at home thin to go to th' circus, an' 'tis betther to go to th' circus thin to r-read anny book. But 'tis betther to r-read a book thin to want to go to th' circus an' not be able to,' he says. 'Well,' says I, 'whin I was growin' up, half th' congregation heard mass with their prayer books tur-rned upside down, an' they were as pious as anny. Th' Apostles' Creed niver was as con-vincin' to me afther I larned to r-read it as it was whin I cudden't read it, but believed it.'"

LOCAL COLORISTS

(1868–1900)

IN CALIFORNIA

by Bret Harte

(1839–1902)

The Society Upon the Stanislaus

I reside at Table Mountain, and my name is Truthful James;
I am not up to small deceit or any sinful games;
And I'll tell in simple language what I know about the row
That broke up our Society upon the Stanislow.

But first I would remark, that it is not a proper plan
For any scientific gent to whale his fellow-man,
And, if a member don't agree with his peculiar whim,
To lay for that same member for to "put a head" on him.

Now nothing could be finer or more beautiful to see
Than the first six months' proceedings of that same Society,
Till Brown of Calaveras brought a lot of fossil bones
That he found within a tunnel near the tenement of Jones.

Then Brown he read a paper, and he reconstructed there,
From those same bones, an animal that was extremely rare;
And Jones then asked the Chair for a suspension of the rules,
Till he could prove that those same bones was one of his lost mules.

Then Brown he smiled a bitter smile, and said he was at fault.
It seemed he had been trespassing on Jones's family vault;
He was a most sarcastic man, this quiet Mr. Brown,
And on several occasions he had cleaned out the town.

Now I hold it is not decent for a scientific gent
To say another is an ass,—at least, to all intent;
Nor should the individual who happens to be meant
Reply by heaving rocks at him, to any great extent.

Then Abner Dean of Angel's raised a point of order, when
A chunk of old red sandstone took him in the abdomen,
And he smiled a kind of sickly smile, and curled up on the floor,
And the subsequent proceedings interested him no more.

For, in less time than I write it, every member did engage
In a warfare with the remnants of a palæozoic age;

And the way they heaved those fossils in their anger was a sin,
Till the skull of an old mammoth caved the head of Thompson in.

And this is all I have to say of these improper games,
For I live at Table Mountain, and my name is Truthful James;
And I've told in simple language what I know about the row
That broke up our Society upon the Stanislow.

The Luck of Roaring Camp

There was commotion in Roaring Camp. It could not have
been a fight, for in 1850 that was not novel enough to have called
together the entire settlement. The ditches and claims were not
only deserted, but "Tuttle's grocery" had contributed its gamblers,
who, it will be remembered, calmly continued their game the day
that French Pete and Kanaka Joe shot each other to death over
the bar in the front room. The whole camp was collected before a
rude cabin on the outer edge of the clearing. Conversation was
carried on in a low tone, but the name of a woman was frequently
repeated. It was a name familiar enough in the camp,—"Cherokee
Sal."

Perhaps the less said of her the better. She was a coarse, and,
it is to be feared, a very sinful woman. But at that time she was
the only woman in Roaring Camp, and was just then lying in sore
extremity, when she most needed the ministration of her own sex.
Dissolute, abandoned, and irreclaimable, she was yet suffering a
martyrdom hard enough to bear even when veiled by sympathizing
womanhood, but now terrible in her loneliness. The primal curse
had come to her in that original isolation which must have made
the punishment of the first transgression so dreadful. It was, perhaps, part of the expiation of her sin, that, at a moment when she
most lacked her sex's intuitive tenderness and care, she met only
the half-contemptuous faces of her masculine associates. Yet a few
of the spectators were, I think, touched by her sufferings. Sandy
Tipton thought it was "rough on Sal," and, in the contemplation
of her condition, for a moment rose superior to the fact that he
had an ace and two bowers in his sleeve.

It will be seen, also, that the situation was novel. Deaths were
by no means uncommon in Roaring Camp, but a birth was a new
thing. People had been dismissed from the camp effectively, finally,
and with no possibility of return; but this was the first time that
anybody had been introduced *ab initio*. Hence the excitement.

"You go in there, Stumpy," said a prominent citizen known as "Kentuck," addressing one of the loungers. "Go in there, and see what you kin do. You've had experience in them things."

Perhaps there was a fitness in the selection. Stumpy, in other climes, had been the putative head of two families; in fact, it was owing to some legal informality in these proceedings that Roaring Camp—a city of refuge—was indebted to his company. The crowd approved the choice, and Stumpy was wise enough to bow to the majority. The door closed on the extempore surgeon and midwife, and Roaring Camp sat down outside, smoked its pipe, and awaited the issue.

The assemblage numbered about a hundred men. One or two of these were actual fugitives from justice, some were criminal, and all were reckless. Physically, they exhibited no indication of their past lives and character. The greatest scamp had a Raphael face, with a profusion of blond hair; Oakhurst, a gambler, had the melancholy air and intellectual abstraction of a Hamlet; the coolest and most courageous man was scarcely over five feet in height, with a soft voice and an embarrassed, timid manner. The term "roughs" applied to them was a distinction rather than a definition. Perhaps in the minor details of fingers, toes, ears, etc., the camp may have been deficient, but these slight omissions did not detract from their aggregate force. The strongest man had but three fingers on his right hand; the best shot had but one eye.

Such was the physical aspect of the men that were dispersed around the cabin. The camp lay in a triangular valley between two hills and a river. The only outlet was a steep trail over the summit of a hill that faced the cabin, now illuminated by the rising moon. The suffering woman might have seen it from the rude bunk whereon she lay,—seen it winding like a silver thread until it was lost in the stars above.

A fire of withered pine-boughs added sociability to the gathering. By degrees the natural levity of Roaring Camp returned. Bets were freely offered and taken regarding the result. Three to five that "Sal would get through with it"; even that the child would survive; side bets as to the sex and complexion of the coming stranger. In the midst of an excited discussion an exclamation came from those nearest the door, and the camp stopped to listen. Above the swaying and moaning of the pines, the swift rush of the river, and the crackling of the fire rose a sharp, querulous cry,—a cry unlike anything heard before in the camp. The pines stopped moaning, the river ceased to rush, and the fire to crackle. It seemed as if Nature had stopped to listen too.

The camp rose to its feet as one man! It was proposed to explode a barrel òf gunpowder, but, in consideration of the situation of the mother, better counsels prevailed, and only a few revolvers were discharged; for, whether owing to the rude surgery of the camp, or some other reason, Cherokee Sal was sinking fast. Within an hour she had climbed, as it were, that rugged road that led to the stars, and so passed out of Roaring Camp, its sin and shame, forever. I do not think that the announcement disturbed them much, except in speculation as to the fate of the child. "Can he live now?" was asked of Stumpy. The answer was doubtful. The only other being of Cherokee Sal's sex and maternal condition in the settlement was an ass. There was some conjecture as to fitness, but the experiment was tried. It was less problematical than the ancient treatment of Romulus and Remus, and apparently as successful.

When these details were completed, which exhausted another hour, the door was opened, and the anxious crowd of men who had already formed themselves into a queue, entered in single file. Beside the low bunk or shelf, on which the figure of the mother was starkly outlined below the blankets, stood a pine table. On this a candle-box was placed, and within it, swathed in staring red flannel, lay the last arrival at Roaring Camp. Beside the candle-box was placed a hat. Its use was soon indicated. "Gentlemen," said Stumpy, with a singular mixture of authority and *ex officio* complacency,—"Gentlemen will please pass in at the front door, round the table, and out at the back door. Them as wishes to contribute anything toward the orphan will find a hat handy." The first man entered with his hat on; he uncovered, however, as he looked about him, and so unconsciously set an example to the next. In such communities good and bad actions are catching. As the procession filed in comments were audible,—criticisms addressed perhaps rather to Stumpy in the character of show-man:—"Is that him?" "mighty small specimen"; "hasn't mor'n got the color"; "ain't bigger nor a derringer." The contributions were as characteristic:—A silver tobacco box; a doubloon; a navy revolver, silver mounted; a gold specimen; a very beautifully embroidered lady's handkerchief (from Oakhurst the gambler); a diamond breastpin; a diamond ring (suggested by the pin, with the remark from the giver that he "saw that pin and went two

diamonds better"); a slung shot; a Bible (contributor not detected); a golden spur; a silver teaspoon (the initials, I regret to
say, were not the giver's); a pair of surgeon's shears; a lancet; a
Bank of England note for £5; and about $200 in loose gold and
silver coin. During these proceedings Stumpy maintained a silence
as impassive as the dead on his left, a gravity as inscrutable as that
of the newly-born on his right. Only one incident occurred to
break the monotony of the curious procession. As Kentuck bent
over the candle-box half curiously, the child turned, and, in a
spasm of pain, caught at his groping finger, and held it fast for
a moment. Kentuck looked foolish and embarrassed. Something
like a blush tried to assert itself in his weather-beaten cheek.
"The d——d little cuss!" he said, as he extricated his finger, with
perhaps more tenderness and care than he might have been
deemed capable of showing. He held that finger a little apart
from its fellows as he went out, and examined it curiously. The
examination provoked the same original remark in regard to the
child. In fact, he seemed to enjoy repeating it. "He rastled with my
finger," he remarked to Tipton, holding up the member, "the
d——d little cuss!"

It was four o'clock before the camp sought repose. A light
burnt in the cabin where the watchers sat, for Stumpy did not go
to bed that night. Nor did Kentuck. He drank quite freely, and
related with great gusto his experience, invariably ending with his
characteristic condemnation of the newcomer. It seemed to relieve
him of any unjust implication of sentiment, and Kentuck had the
weaknesses of the nobler sex. When everybody else had gone to
bed, he walked down to the river and whistled reflectingly. Then
he walked up the gulch, past the cabin, still whistling with demonstrative unconcern. At a large redwood tree he paused and re-
traced his steps, and again passed the cabin. Half-way down to the
river's bank he again paused, and then returned and knocked at
the door. It was opened by Stumpy. "How goes it?" said Kentuck,
looking past Stumpy toward the candle-box. "All serene!" replied
Stumpy. "Anything up?" "Nothing." There was a pause—an
embarrassing one—Stumpy still holding the door. Then Kentuck
had recourse to his finger, which he held up to Stumpy. "Rastled
with it,—the d——d little cuss," he said, and retired.

The next day Cherokee Sal had such rude sepulture as Roaring Camp afforded. After her body had been committed to the
hillside, there was a formal meeting of the camp to discuss what

should be done with her infant. A resolution to adopt it was unanimous and enthusiastic. But an animated discussion in regard to the manner and feasibility of providing for its wants at once sprung up. It was remarkable that the argument partook of none of those fierce personalities with which discussions were usually conducted at Roaring Camp. Tipton proposed that they should send the child to Red Dog,—a distance of forty miles,—where female attention could be procured. But the unlucky suggestion met with fierce and unanimous opposition. It was evident that no plan which entailed parting from their new acquisition would for a moment be entertained. "Besides," said Tom Ryder, "them fellows at Red Dog would swap it, and ring in somebody else on us." A disbelief in the honesty of other camps prevailed at Roaring Camp, as in other places.

The introduction of a female nurse in the camp also met with objection. It was argued that no decent woman could be prevailed to accept Roaring Camp as her home, and the speaker urged that "they didn't want any more of the other kind." This unkind allusion to the defunct mother, harsh as it may seem, was the first spasm of propriety,—the first symptom of the camp's regeneration. Stumpy advanced nothing. Perhaps he felt a certain delicacy in interfering with the selection of a possible successor in office. But, when questioned, he averred stoutly that he and "Jinny"—the mammal before alluded to—could manage to rear the child. There was something original, independent, and heroic about the plan that pleased the camp. Stumpy was retained. Certain articles were sent for to Sacramento. "Mind," said the treasurer, as he pressed a bag of gold-dust into the expressman's hand, "the best that can be got,—lace, you know, and filigree-work and frills,—d——n the cost!"

Strange to say, the child thrived. Perhaps the invigorating climate of the mountain camp was compensation for material deficiencies. Nature took the foundling to her broader breast. In that rare atmosphere of the Sierra foot-hills,—that air pungent with balsamic odor, that ethereal cordial at once bracing and exhilarating,—he may have found food and nourishment, or a subtle chemistry that transmuted ass's milk to lime and phosphorus. Stumpy inclined to the belief that it was the latter and good nursing. "Me and that ass," he would say, "has been father and mother to him! Don't you," he would add, apostrophising the helpless bundle before him, "never go back on us."

By the time he was a month old, the necessity of giving him a name became apparent. He had generally been known as "The Kid," "Stumpy's Boy," "The Cayote" (an allusion to his vocal powers), and even by Kentuck's endearing diminutive of "The d——d little cuss." But these were felt to be vague and unsatisfactory and were at last dismissed under another influence. Gamblers and adventurers are generally superstitious, and Oakhurst one day declared that the baby had brought "the luck" to Roaring Camp. It was certain that of late they had been successful. "Luck" was the name agreed upon, with the prefix of Tommy for greater convenience. No allusion was made to the mother, and the father was unknown. "It's better," said the philosophical Oakhurst, "to take a fresh deal all round. Call him Luck, and start him fair." A day was accordingly set apart for the christening. What was meant by this ceremony the reader may imagine, who has already gathered some idea of the reckless irreverence of Roaring Camp. The master of ceremonies was one "Boston," a noted wag, and the occasion seemed to promise the greatest facetiousness. This ingenious satirist had spent two days in preparing a burlesque of the church service, with pointed local allusions. The choir was properly trained, and Sandy Tipton was to stand godfather. But after the procession had marched to the grove with music and banners, and the child had been deposited before a mock altar, Stumpy stepped before the expectant crowd. "It ain't my style to spoil fun, boys," said the little man, stoutly eyeing the faces around him, "but it strikes me that this thing ain't exactly on the squar. It's playing it pretty low down on this yer baby to ring in fun on him that he ain't goin' to understand. And ef there's goin' to be any godfathers round, I'd like to see who's got any better rights than me." A silence followed Stumpy's speech. To the credit of all humorists be it said, that the first man to acknowledge its justice was the satirist thus stopped of his fun. "But," said Stumpy, quickly following up his advantage, "we're here for a christening, and we'll have it. I proclaim you Thomas Luck, according to the laws of the United States and the State of California, so help me God." It was the first time that the name of the Deity had been uttered otherwise than profanely in the camp. The form of christening was perhaps even more ludicrous than the satirist had conceived; but nobody saw it and nobody laughed. "Tommy" was christened as seriously as he would have been under a Christian roof, and cried and was comforted in as orthodox fashion.

And so the work of regeneration began in Roaring Camp. Almost imperceptibly a change came over the settlement. The cabin assigned to "Tommy Luck"—or "The Luck," as he was more frequently called—first showed signs of improvement. It was kept scrupulously clean and whitewashed. Then it was boarded, clothed, and papered. The rosewood cradle—packed eighty miles by mule—had, in Stumpy's way of putting it, "sorter killed the rest of the furniture." So the rehabilitation of the cabin became a necessity. The men who were in the habit of lounging in at Stumpy's to see "how 'The Luck' got on" seemed to appreciate the change, and, in self-defence, the rival establishment of "Tuttle's grocery" bestirred itself and imported a carpet and mirrors. The reflections of the latter on the appearance of Roaring Camp tended to produce stricter habits of personal cleanliness. Again, Stumpy imposed a kind of quarantine upon those who aspired to the honor and privilege of holding "The Luck." It was a cruel mortification to Kentuck—who, in the carelessness of a large nature and the habits of frontier life, had begun to regard all garments as a second cuticle, which, like a snake's, only sloughed off through decay—to be debarred this privilege from certain prudential reasons. Yet such was the subtle influence of innovation that he thereafter appeared regularly every afternoon in a clean shirt and face still shining from his ablutions. Nor were moral and social sanitary laws neglected. "Tommy," who was supposed to spend his whole existence in a persistent attempt to repose, must not be disturbed by noise. The shouting and yelling which had gained the camp its infelicitous title were not permitted within hearing distance of Stumpy's. The men conversed in whispers or smoked with Indian gravity. Profanity was tacitly given up in these sacred precincts, and throughout the camp a popular form of expletive, known as "D——n the luck!" and "Curse the luck!" was abandoned, as having a new personal bearing. Vocal music was not interdicted, being supposed to have a soothing, tranquillizing quality, and one song, sung by "Man-o'-War Jack," an English sailor from her Majesty's Australian colonies, was quite popular as a lullaby. It was a lugubrious recital of the exploits of "the Arethusa, Seventy-four," in a muffled minor, ending with a prolonged dying fall at the burden of each verse, "On b-oo-o-ard of the Arethusa." It was a fine sight to see Jack holding The Luck, rocking from side to side as if with the motion of a ship, and crooning forth this naval ditty. Either through the peculiar rocking of Jack or the length of his song,—it contained ninety stanzas, and was continued with conscientious deliberation to the bitter end,—the lullaby generally had the desired effect. At such times the men would lie at full length under the trees in the soft summer twilight, smoking their pipes and drinking in the melodious utterances. An indistinct idea that this was pastoral happiness pervaded the camp. "This 'ere kind o' think," said the Cockney Simmons, meditatively reclining on his elbow, "is 'evingly." It reminded him of Greenwich.

On the long summer days The Luck was usually carried to the gulch from whence the golden store of Roaring Camp was taken. There, on a blanket spread over pine-boughs, he would lie while the men were working in the ditches below. Latterly, there was a rude attempt to decorate this bower with flowers and sweet-smelling shrubs, and generally some one would bring him a cluster of wild honeysuckles, azaleas, or the painted blossoms of Las Mariposas. The men had suddenly awakened to the fact that there were beauty and significance in these trifles, which they had so long trodden carelessly beneath their feet. A flake of glittering mica, a fragment of variegated quartz, a bright pebble from the bed of the creek, became beautiful to eyes thus cleared and strengthened, and were invariably put aside for "The Luck." It was wonderful how many treasures the woods and hillsides yielded that "would do for Tommy." Surrounded by playthings such as never child out of fairyland had before, it is to be hoped that Tommy was content. He appeared to be securely happy, albeit there was an infantine gravity about him, a contemplative light in his round grey eyes, that sometimes worried Stumpy. He was always tractable and quiet, and it is recorded that once, having crept beyond his "corral,"—a hedge of tessellated pine-boughs, which surrounded his bed,—he dropped over the bank on his head in the soft earth, and remained with his mottled legs in the air in that position for at least five minutes with unflinching gravity. He was extricated without a murmur. I hesitate to record the many other instances of his sagacity, which rest, unfortunately, upon the statements of prejudiced friends. Some of them were not without a tinge of superstition. "I crep' up the bank just now," said Kentuck one day, in a breathless state of excitement, "and dern my skin if he wasn't a talking to a jaybird as was a sittin' on his lap. There they was, just as free and sociable as anything you please, a jawin' at each other just like two cherry-bums." Howbeit, whether creeping over the pine-boughs or lying lazily on his back blinking at the leaves above him, to him the birds sang, the squirrels chattered, and the flowers bloomed. Nature was his nurse and playfellow. For him she would let slip between the leaves golden shafts of sunlight that fell just within his grasp; she would send wandering breezes to visit him with the balm of bay and resinous gums; to him the tall redwoods nodded familiarly and sleepily, the bumble-bees buzzed, and the rooks cawed a slumbrous accompaniment.

Such was the golden summer of Roaring Camp. They were "flush times," and the Luck was with them. The claims had yielded enormously. The camp was jealous of its privileges and looked suspiciously on strangers. No encouragement was given to immigration, and, to make their seclusion more perfect, the land on either side of the mountain wall that surrounded the camp they duly pre-empted. This, and a reputation for singular proficiency with the revolver, kept the reserve of Roaring Camp inviolate. The expressman—their only connecting link with the surrounding world—sometimes told wonderful stories of the camp. He would say, "They've a street up there in 'Roaring' that would lay over any street in Red Dog. They've got vines and flowers round their houses, and they wash themselves twice a day. But they're mighty rough on strangers, and they worship an Ingin baby."

With the prosperity of the camp came a desire for further improvement. It was proposed to build a hotel in the following spring, and to invite one or two decent families to reside there for the sake of "The Luck," who might perhaps profit by female companionship. The sacrifice that this concession to the sex cost these men, who were fiercely sceptical in regard to its general virtue and usefulness, can only be accounted for by their affection for Tommy. A few still held out. But the resolve could not be carried into effect for three months, and the minority meekly yielded in the hope that something might turn up to prevent it. And it did.

The winter of 1851 will long be remembered in the foot-hills. The snow lay deep on the Sierras, and every mountain creek became a river, and every river a lake. Each gorge and gulch was transformed into a tumultuous watercourse that descended the hillsides, tearing down giant trees and scattering its drift and débris along the plain. Red Dog had been twice under water, and Roaring Camp had been forewarned. "Water put the gold into them gulches," said Stumpy. "It's been here once and will be here again!" And that night the North Fork suddenly leaped over its banks and swept up the triangular valley of Roaring Camp.

In the confusion of rushing water, crushing trees, and crackling timber, and the darkness which seemed to flow with the water and blot out the fair valley, but little could be done to collect the scattered camp. When the morning broke, the cabin of Stumpy nearest the river-bank was gone. Higher up the gulch they found the body of its unlucky owner; but the pride, the hope, the joy, The Luck, of Roaring Camp had disappeared. They were returning with sad hearts when a shout from the bank recalled them.

It was a relief-boat from down the river. They had picked up, they said, a man and an infant, nearly exhausted, about two miles below. Did anybody know them, and did they belong here?

It needed but a glance to show them Kentuck lying there, cruelly crushed and bruised, but still holding The Luck of Roaring Camp in his arms. As they bent over the strangely assorted pair, they saw that the child was cold and pulseless. "He is dead," said one. Kentuck opened his eyes. "Dead?" he repeated feebly. "Yes, my man, and you are dying too." A smile lit the eyes of the expiring Kentuck. "Dying!" he repeated: "he's a taking me with him. Tell the boys I've got The Luck with me now"; and the strong man, clinging to the frail babe as a drowning man is said to cling to a straw, drifted away into the shadowy river that flows forever to the unknown sea.

IN THE MIDDLE WEST

by Edward Eggleston

(1837–1902)

TREEING A PREACHER

Had I but bethought myself in time to call this history by one of those gentle titles now in vogue, as "The Wild Hunters of the Far West," or even by one of the labels with which juvenile and Sunday-school literature—milk for babes—is now made attractive, as, for instance, "Kike, the Young Bear Hunter," I might here have entertained the reader with a vigorous description of the death of Bruin, fierce and fat, at the hands of the triumphant Kike, and of the exciting chase after deer under the direction of Morton.

After two weeks of such varying success as hunters have, they found that it would be necessary to forego the discomforts of camp-life for a day, and visit the nearest settlement in order to replenish their stock of ammunition. Wilkins' store, which was the center of a settlement, was a double log-building. In one end the proprietor kept for sale powder and lead, a few bonnets, cheap ribbons, and artificial flowers, a small stock of earthenware, and cheap crockery, a little homespun cotton cloth, some bolts of jeans and linsey, hanks of yarn and skeins of thread, tobacco for smoking and tobacco for "chawing," a little "store-tea"—so called in contradistinction to the sage, sassafras and crop-vine teas in general use—with a plentiful stock of whisky, and some apple-brandy. The other end of this building was a large room, festooned with strings of drying pumpkin, cheered by an enormous fire-place, and lighted by one small window with four lights of glass. In this room, which contained three beds, and in the loft above, Wilkins and his family lived and kept a first-class hotel.

In the early West, Sunday was a day sacred to Diana and Bacchus. Our young friends visited the settlement at Wilkins' on that day, not because they wished to rest, but because they had begun to get lonely, and they knew that Sunday would not fail to find some frolic in progress, and in making new acquaintances, fifty miles from home, they would be able to relieve the

tedium of the wilderness with games at cards, and other social
enjoyments.

Morton and Kike arrived at Wilkins' combined store and
tavern at ten o'clock in the morning, and found the expected
crowd of loafers. The new-comers "took a hand" in all the sports,
the jumping, the foot-racing, the quoit-pitching, the "wras'lin',"
the target-shooting, the poker-playing, and the rest, and were
soon accepted as clever fellows. A frontierman could bestow no
higher praise—to be a clever fellow in his sense was to know how
to lose at cards, without grumbling, the peltries hard-earned in
hunting, to be always ready to change your coon-skins into "drinks
for the crowd," and to be able to hit a three-inch "mark" at two
hundred paces without bragging.

Just as the sports had begun to lose their zest a little, there
walked up to the tavern door a man in homespun dress, carrying
one of his shoes in his hand, and yet not seeming to be a plain
backwoodsman. He looked a trifle over thirty years of age, and
an acute observer might have guessed from his face that his life
had been one of daring adventure, and many vicissitudes. There
were traces also of conflicting purposes, of a certain strength, and
a certain weakness of character; the melancholy history of good
intentions overslaughed by bad passions and evil associations was
written in his countenance.

"Some feller 'lectioneerin', I'll bet," said one of Morton's
companions.

The crowd gathered about the stranger, who spoke to each
one as though he had known him always. He proposed "the
drinks" as the surest road to an acquaintance, and when all had
drunk, the stranger paid the score, not in skins but in silver coin.

"See here, stranger," said Morton, mischievously, "you're
mighty clever, by hokey. What are you running fer?"

"Well, gentlemen, you guessed me out that time. I 'low to
run for sheriff next heat," said the stranger, who affected dialect
for the sake of popularity.

"What mout your name be?" asked one of the company.

"Marcus Burchard's my name when I'm at home. I live at Jen-
kinsville. I sot out in life a poor boy. I'm so used to bein' bar'
footed that my shoes hurts my feet an' I have to pack one of 'em
in my hand most of the time."

Morton here set down his glass, and looking at the stranger
with perfect seriousness said, dryly: "Well, Mr. Burchard, I never

heard that speech so well done before. We're all goin' to vote for you, without t'other man happens to do it up slicker'n you do. I don't believe he can, though. That was got off very nice."

Burchard was acute enough to join in the laugh which this sally produced, and to make friends with Morton, who was clearly the leader of the party, and whose influence was worth securing.

Nothing grows wearisome so soon as idleness and play, and as evening drew on, the crowd tired even of Mr. Burchard's choice collection of funny anecdotes—little stories that had been aired in the same order at every other tavern and store in the county. From sheer *ennui* it was proposed that they should attend Methodist preaching at a house two miles away. They could at least get some fun out of it. Burchard, foreseeing a disturbance, excused himself. He wished he might enjoy the sport, but he must push on. And "push on" he did. In a closely contested election even Methodist votes were not to be thrown away.

Morton and Kike relished the expedition. They had heard that the Methodists were a rude, canting, illiterate race, cloaking the worst practices under an appearance of piety. Mr. Donaldson had often fulminated against them from the pulpit, and they felt almost sure that they could count on his apostolic approval in their laudable enterprise of disturbing a Methodist meeting.

The preacher whom they heard was of the roughest type. His speech was full of dialectic forms and ungrammatical phrases. His illustrations were exceedingly uncouth. It by no means followed that he was not an effective preacher. All these defects were rather to his advantage,—the backwoods rhetoric was suited to move the backwoods audience. But the party from the tavern were in no mood to be moved by anything. They came for amusement, and set themselves diligently to seek it. Morton was ambitious to lead among his new friends, as he did at home, and on this occasion he made use of his rarest gift. The preacher, Mr. Mellen, was just getting "warmed up" with his theme; he was beginning to sling his rude metaphors to the right and left, and the audience was fast coming under his influence, when Morton Goodwin, who had cultivated a ventriloquial gift for the diversion of country parties, and the disturbance of Mr. Brady's school, now began to squeak like a rat in a trap, looking all the while straight at the preacher, as if profoundly interested in the discourse. The women were startled and the grave brethren turned their austere faces round to look stern reproofs at the young men. In a moment the squeaking ceased, and there began the shrill yelping of a little dog, which seemed to be on the women's side of the room. Brother Mellen, the preacher, paused, and was about to request that the dog should be removed, when he began to suspect from the sensation among the young men that the disturbance was from them.

"You needn't be afeard, sisters," he said, "puppies will bark, even when they walk on two legs instid of four."

This rude joke produced a laugh, but gained no permanent advantage to the preacher, for Morton, being a stranger, did not care for the good opinion of the audience, but for the applause of the young revelers with whom he had come. He kept silence now, until the preacher again approached a climax, swinging his stalwart arms and raising his voice to a tremendous pitch in the endeavor to make the day of doom seem sufficiently terrible to his hearers. At last, when he got to the terror of the wicked, he cried out dramatically, "What are these awful sounds I hear?" At this point he made a pause, which would have been very effective, had it not been for young Goodwin.

"Caw! caw! caw-aw! cah!" he said, mimicking a crow.

"Young man," roared the preacher, "you are hair-hung and breeze-shaken over that pit that has no bottom."

"Oh, golly!" piped the voice of Morton, seeming to come from nowhere in particular. Mr. Mellen now ceased preaching, and started toward the part of the room in which the young men sat, evidently intending to deal out summary justice to some one. He was a man of immense strength, and his face indicated that he meant to eject the whole party. But they all left in haste except Morton, who staid and met the preacher's gaze with a look of offended innocence. Mr. Mellen was perplexed. A disembodied voice wandering about the room would have been too much for Hercules himself. When the baffled orator turned back to begin to preach again, Morton squeaked in an aggravating falsetto, but with a good imitation of Mr. Mellen's inflections, "Hair-hung and breeze-shaken!"

And when the angry preacher turned fiercely upon him, the scoffer was already fleeing through the door.

SAM LAWSON'S NEW ENGLAND STORIES

by Harriet Beecher Stowe

(1811–1896)

CAPTAIN KIDD'S MONEY

One of our most favorite legendary resorts was the old barn. Sam Lawson preferred it on many accounts. It was quiet and retired, that is to say, at such a distance from his own house, that he could not hear if Hepsy called ever so loudly, and farther off than it would be convenient for that industrious and painstaking woman to follow him. Then there was the soft fragrant cushion of hay, on which his length of limb could be easily bestowed.

Our barn had an upper loft with a swinging outer door that commanded a view of the old mill, the waterfall, and the distant windings of the river, with its grassy green banks, its graceful elm draperies, and its white flocks of water-lilies; and then on this Saturday afternoon we had Sam all to ourselves. It was a drowsy, dreamy October day, when the hens were lazily "craw, crawing," in a soft, conversational undertone with each other, as they scratched and picked the hay-seed under the barn windows. Below in the barn black Cæsar sat quietly hatchelling flax, sometimes gurgling and giggling to himself with an overflow of that interior jollity with which he seemed to be always full. The African in New England was a curious contrast to everybody around him in the joy and satisfaction that he seemed to feel in the mere fact of being alive. Every white person was glad or sorry for some appreciable cause in the past, present, or future, which was capable of being definitely stated; but black Cæsar was in an eternal giggle and frizzle and simmer of enjoyment for which he could give no earthly reason: he was an "embodied joy," like Shelley's skylark.

"Jest hear him," said Sam Lawson, looking pensively over the hay-mow, and strewing hayseed down on his wool. "How that 'ere critter seems to tickle and laugh all the while 'bout nothin'. Lordy massy, he don't seem never to consider that 'this life's a dream, an empty show.'"

"Look here, Sam," we broke in, anxious to cut short a threat-

ened stream of morality, "you promised to tell us about Captain
Kidd, and how you dug for his money."

"Did I, now? Wal, boys, that 'are history o' Kidd's is a warnin'
to fellers. Why, Kidd had pious parents and Bible and sanctuary
privileges when he was a boy, and yet come to be hanged. It's all
in this 'ere song I'm a-goin' to sing ye. Lordy massy! I wish I had
my bass-viol now. Cæsar," he said, calling down from his perch,
"can't you strike the pitch o' 'Cap'n Kidd' on your fiddle?"

Cæsar's fiddle was never far from him. It was, in fact, tucked
away in a nice little nook just over the manger; and he often
caught an interval from his work to scrape a dancing-tune on it,
keeping time with his heels, to our great delight.

A most wailing minor-keyed tune was doled forth, which
seemed quite refreshing to Sam's pathetic vein, as he sang in his
most lugubrious tones:—

> " 'My name was Robert Kidd
>   As I sailed, as I sailed,
>   My name was Robert Kidd;
>   God's laws I did forbid,
>   And so wickedly I did,
>   As I sailed, as I sailed.' "

"Now ye see, boys, he's a-goin' to tell how he abused his
religious privileges; just hear now:—

> 'My father taught me well,
>   As I sailed, as I sailed;
>   My father taught me well
>   To shun the gates of hell,
>   But yet I did rebel,
>   As I sailed, as I sailed.
>
> 'He put a Bible in my hand,
>   As I sailed, as I sailed;
>   He put a Bible in my hand,
>   And I sunk it in the sand
>   Before I left the strand,
>   As I sailed, as I sailed.'

"Did ye ever hear o' such a hardened, contrary critter, boys?
It's awful to think on. Wal, ye see that 'are's the way fellers allers
begin the ways o' sin, by turnin' their backs on the Bible and the
advice o' pious parents. Now hear what he come to:—

'Then I murdered William More,
  As I sailed, as I sailed;
I murdered William More,
And left him in his gore,
Not many leagues from shore,
  As I sailed, as I sailed.

'To execution dock
  I must go, I must go.
To execution dock,
While thousands round me flock,
To see me on the block,
  I must go, I must go.'

"There was a good deal more on 't," said Sam, pausing, "but I don't seem to remember it; but it's real solemn and affectin'."

"Who was Capt. Kidd, Sam?" said I.

"Wal, he was an officer in the British navy, and he got to bein' a pirate: used to take ships and sink 'em, and murder the folks; and so they say he got no end o' money,—gold and silver and precious stones, as many as the wise men in the East. But ye see, what good did it all do him? He could n't use it, and dar'sn't keep it; so he used to bury it in spots round here and there in the awfullest heathen way ye ever heard of. Why, they say he allers used to kill one or two men or women or children of his prisoners, and bury with it, so that their sperits might keep watch on it ef anybody was to dig arter it. That 'are thing has been tried and tried, but no man nor mother's son on 'em ever got a cent that dug. 'T was tried here 'n Oldtown; and they come pretty nigh gettin' on 't, but it gin 'em the slip. Ye see, boys, *it's the Devil's money*, and he holds a pretty tight grip on 't."

"Well, how was it about digging for it? Tell us, did you do it? Were you there? Did you see it? And why could n't they get it?" we both asked eagerly and in one breath.

"Why, Lordy massy! boys, your questions tumbles over each other thick as martins out o' a martin-box. Now, you jest be moderate and let alone, and I'll tell you all about it from the beginnin' to the end. I did n't railly have no hand in 't, though I was knowin' to 't, as I be to most things that goes on round here; but my conscience would n't railly a let me start on no sich undertakin'.

"Wal, the one that fust sot the thing a-goin' was old Mother Hokum, that used to live up in that little tumble-down shed by the cranberry-pond up beyond the spring pastur'. They had a putty bad name, them Hokums. How they got a livin' nobody knew; for they did n't seem to pay no attention to raisin' nothin' but childun, but the deuce knows, there was plenty o' them. Their old hut was like a rabbit-pen: there was a tow-head to every crack and cranny. 'Member what old Cæsar said once when the word come to the store that old Hokum had got twins. 'S'pose de Lord knows best,' says Cæsar, 'but *I* thought dere was Hokums enough afore.' Wal, even poor workin' industrious folks like me finds it's hard gettin' along when there's so many mouths to feed. Lordy massy! there don't never seem to be no end on 't, and so it ain't wonderful, come to think on 't, ef folks like them Hokums gets tempted to help along in ways that ain't quite right. Anyhow, folks did use to think that old Hokum was too sort o' familiar with their wood-piles 'long in the night, though they could n't never prove it on him; and when Mother Hokum come to houses round to wash, folks use sometimes to miss pieces, here and there, though they never could find 'em on her; then they was allers a gettin' in debt here and a gettin' in debt there. Why, they got to owin' two dollars to Joe Gidger for butcher's meat. Joe was sort o' good-natured and let 'em have meat, 'cause Hokum he promised so fair to pay; but he could n't never get it out o' him. 'Member once Joe walked clear up to the cranberry-pond arter that 'are two dollars; but Mother Hokum she see him a-comin' jest as he come past the juniper-bush on the corner. She says to Hokum, 'Get into bed, old man, quick, and let me tell the story,' says she. So she covered him up; and when Gidger come in she come up to him, and says she, 'Why, Mr. Gidger, I'm jest ashamed to see ye: why, Mr. Hokum was jest a-comin' down to pay ye that 'are money last week, but ye see he was took down with the small-pox'—Joe did n't hear no more: he just turned round, and streaked it out that 'are door with his coat-tails flyin' out straight ahind him; and old Mother Hokum she jest stood at the window holdin' her sides and laughin' fit to split, to see him run. That 'are's jest a sample o' the ways them Hokums cut up.

"Wal, you see, boys, there's a queer kind o' rock down on the bank o' the river, that looks sort o' like a grave-stone. The biggest part on 't is sunk down under ground, and it's pretty well growed over with blackberry-vines; but, when you scratch the bushes away, they used to make out some queer marks on that 'are rock. They was sort o' lines and crosses; and folks would have it that them was Kidd's private marks, and that there was one o' the places where he hid his money.

"Wal, there's no sayin' fairly how it come to be thought so; but fellers used to say so, and they used sometimes to talk it over to the tahvern, and kind o' wonder whether or no, if they should dig, they would n't come to suthin'.

"Wal, old Mother Hokum she heard on 't, and she was sort o' enterprisin' old crittur: fact was, she had to be, 'cause the young Hokums was jest like bag-worms, the more they growed the more they eat, and I expect she found it pretty hard to fill their mouths; and so she said ef there *was* anything under that 'are rock, they'd as good's have it as the Devil; and so she did n't give old Hokum no peace o' his life, but he must see what there was there.

"Wal, I was with 'em the night they was a-talkin' on 't up. Ye see, Hokum he got thirty-seven cents' worth o' lemons and sperit. I see him goin' by as I was out a splittin' kindlin's; and says he: 'Toddy Whitney and Harry Wiggin's comin' up, and we're goin' to have a little suthin' hot,' says he; and he kind o' showed me the lemons and sperit. And I told him I guessed I would go 'long. Wal, I kind o' wanted to see what they'd be up to, ye know.

"Wal, come to find out, they was a talkin' about Cap'n Kidd's treasures, and layin' out how they should get it, and a settin' one another on with gret stories about it.

"'I've heard that there was whole chists full o' gold guineas,' says one.

"'And I've heard o' gold bracelets and ear-rings and finger-rings all sparklin' with diamonds,' says another.

"'Maybe it's old silver plate from some o' them old West Indian grandees,' says another.

"'Wal, whatever it is,' says Mother Hokum, 'I want to be into it,' says she.

"'Wal, Sam, won't you jine?' says they.

"'Wal, boys,' says I, 'I kind o' don't feel jest like j'inin'. I sort o' ain't clear about the rights on 't: seems to me it's mighty like goin' to the Devil for money.'

"'Wal,' says Mother Hokum, 'what if 'tis? Money's money, get it how ye will; and the Devil's money 'll buy as much meat as any. I'd go to the Devil if he gave good money.'

"'Wal, I guess I wouldn't,' says I. 'Don't you 'member the

sermon Parson Lothrop preached about hastin' to be rich, last sabba' day?'

"'Parson Lothrop be hanged!' says she. 'Wal, now,' says she, 'I like to see a parson with his silk stockin's and great gold-headed cane, a lollopin' on his carriage behind his fat, prancin' hosses, comin' to meetin' to preach to us poor folks not to want to be rich! How'd he like it to have forty-'leven children, and nothin' to put onto 'em or into 'em, I wonder? Guess if Lady Lothrop had to rub and scrub, and wear her fingers to the bone as I do, she'd want to be rich; and I guess the parson, if he could n't get a bellyful for a week, would be for diggin' up Kidd's money, or doing 'most anything else to make the pot bile.'

"'Wal,' says I, 'I'll kind o' go with ye, boys, and sort o' see how things turn out; but I guess I won't take no shere in 't,' says I.

"Wal, they got it all planned out. They was to wait till the full moon, and then they was to get Primus King to go with 'em and help do the diggin'. Ye see, Hokum and Toddy Whitney and Wiggin are all putty softly fellers, and hate dreffully to work; and I tell you the Kidd money ain't to be got without a pretty tough piece o' diggin'. Why, it's jest like diggin' a well to get at it. Now, Primus King was the master hand for diggin' wells, and so they said they'd get him by givin' on him a shere.

"Harry Wiggin he did n't want no nigger a sherin' in it, he said; but Toddy and Hokum they said that when there was such stiff diggin' to be done, they did n't care if they did go in with a nigger.

"Wal, Wiggin he said he hadn't no objection to havin' the nigger do the diggin', it was *sherin' the profits* he objected to.

"'Wal,' said Hokum, 'you can't get him without,' says he. 'Primus knows too much,' says he: 'you can't fool him.' Finally they 'greed that they was to give Primus twenty dollars, and shere the treasure 'mong themselves.

"Come to talk to Primus, he wouldn't stick in a spade, unless they'd pay him aforehand. Ye see, Primus was up to 'em; he knowed about Gidger, and there wa'n't none on 'em that was particular good pay; and so they all jest hed to rake and scrape, and pay him down the twenty dollars among 'em; and they 'greed for the fust full moon, at twelve o'clock at night, the 9th of October.

"Wal, ye see, I had to tell Hepsy I was goin' out to watch. Wal, so I was; but not jest in the way she took it: but Lordy massy!

a feller has to tell his wife suthin' to keep her quiet, ye know, 'specially Hepsy.

"Wal, wal, of all the moonlight nights that ever I did see, I never did see one equal to that. Why, you could see the color o' everything. I 'member I could see how the huckleberry-bushes on the rock was red as blood when the moonlight shone through 'em; 'cause the leaves, you see, had begun to turn.

"Goin' on our way we got to talkin' about the sperits.

"'I ain't afraid on 'em,' says Hokum. 'What harm can a sperit do me?' says he. 'I don't care ef there's a dozen on 'em;' and he took a swig at his bottle.

"'Oh! there ain't no sperits,' says Harry Wiggin. 'That 'are talk's all nonsense;' and he took a swig at *his* bottle.

"'Wal,' says Toddy, 'I don't know 'bout that 'ere. Me and Ike Sanders has seen the sperits in the Cap'n Brown house. We thought we'd jest have a peek into the window one night; and there was a whole flock o' black colts without no heads on come rushin' on us and knocked us flat.'

"'I expect you'd been at the tahvern,' said Hokum.

"'Wal, yes, we had; but them was sperits: we wa'n't drunk, now; we was jest as sober as ever we was.'

"'Wal, they won't get away my money,' says Primus, 'for I put it safe away in Dinah's teapot afore I come out;' and then he showed all his ivories from ear to ear. 'I think all this 'are's sort o' foolishness,' says Primus.

"'Wal,' says I, 'boys, I ain't a-goin' to have no part or lot in this 'ere matter, but I'll jest lay it off to you how it's to be done. Ef Kidd's money is under this rock, there's *sperits* that watch it, and you mustn't give 'em no advantage. There mustn't be a word spoke from the time ye get sight o' the treasure till ye get it safe up on to firm ground,' says I. 'Ef ye do, it'll vanish right out o' sight. I've talked with them that has dug down to it and seen it; but they allers lost it, 'cause they'd call out and say suthin'; and the minute they spoke, away it went.'

"Wal, so they marked off the ground; and Primus he begun to dig, and the rest kind o' sot round. It was so still it was kind o' solemn. Ye see, it was past twelve o'clock, and every critter in Oldtown was asleep; and there was two whippoorwills on the great Cap'n Brown elm-trees, that kep' a answerin' each other back and forward sort o' solitary like; and then every once in a while there'd come a sort o' strange whisper up among the elm-tree leaves, jest as if there was talkin' goin' on; and every time Primus struck his spade into the ground it sounded sort o' holler, jest as if he'd been a-diggin' a grave. 'It's kind o' melancholy,' says I, 'to think o' them poor critters that had to be killed and buried jest to keep this 'ere treasure. What awful things'll be brought to light in the judgment day! Them poor critters they loved to live and hated to die as much as any on us; but no, they hed to die jest to satisfy that critter's wicked will. I've heard them as thought they could tell the Cap'n Kidd places by layin' their ear to the ground at midnight, and they'd hear groans and wail-in's.'"

"Why, Sam! were there really people who could tell where Kidd's money was?" I here interposed.

"Oh, sartin! why, yis. There was Shebna Bascom, he was one. Shebna could always tell what was under the earth. He'd cut a hazel-stick, and hold it in hish and when folks was wantin' to know where to dig wells; and that 'are stick would jest turn in his hand, and p'int down till it would fairly grind the bark off; and ef you dug in that place you was sure to find a spring. Oh, yis! Shebna he's told many where the Kidd money was, and been with 'em when they dug for it; but the pester on 't was they allers lost it, 'cause they would some on 'em speak afore they thought."

"But, Sam, what about this digging? Let's know what came of it," said we, as Sam appeared to lose his way in his story.

"Wal, ye see, they dug down about five feet, when Primus he struck his spade smack on something that chinked like iron.

"Wal, then Hokum and Toddy Whitney was into the hole in a minute; they made Primus get out, and they took the spade, 'cause they wanted to be sure to come on it themselves.

"Wal, they begun, and they dug and he scraped, and sure enough they come to a gret iron pot as big as your granny's dinner-pot, with an iron bale to it.

"Wal, then they put down a rope, and he put the rope through the handle; then Hokum and Toddy they clambered upon the bank, and all on 'em began to draw up jest as still and silent as could be. They drawed and they drawed, till they jest got it even with the ground, when Toddy spoke out all in a tremble, 'There,' says he, *'we've got it!'* And the minit he spoke they was both struck by *suthin'* that knocked 'em clean over; and the rope give a crack like a pistol-shot, and broke short off; and the pot went down, down, down, and they heard it goin', jink, jink, jink; and it went way down into the earth, and the ground closed over it; and then they heard the screechin'est laugh ye ever did hear."

"I want to know, Sam, did you see that pot?" I exclaimed at this part of the story.

"Wal, no, I didn't. Ye see, I jest happened to drop asleep while they was diggin', I was so kind o' tired, and I did n't wake up till it was all over.

"I was waked up, 'cause there was consid'able of a scuffle; for Hokum was so mad at Toddy for speakin', that he was a-fistin' on him; and old Primus he jest haw-hawed and laughed. 'Wal, I got *my* money safe, anyhow,' says he.

"'Wal, come to,' says I. ''Tain't no use cryin' for spilt milk: you've jest got to turn in now and fill up this 'ere hole, else the selectmen'll be down on ye.'

"'Wal,' says Primus, 'I did n't engage to fill up no holes;' and he put his spade on his shoulder and trudged off.

"Wal, it was putty hard work, fillin' in that hole; but Hokum and Toddy and Wiggin had to do it, 'cause they did n't want to have everybody a-laughin' at 'em; and I kind o' tried to set it home to 'em, showin' on 'em that 'twas all for the best.

"'Ef you'd 'a' been left to get that 'ere money, there'd 'a' come a cuss with it,' says I. 'It shows the vanity o' hastin' to be rich.'

"'Oh, you shet up!' says Hokum, says he. 'You never hasted to anything,' says he. Ye see, he was riled, that's why he spoke so."

"Sam," said we, after maturely reflecting over the story, "what do you suppose was in that pot?"

"Lordy massy, boys! ye never will be done askin' questions. Why, how should I know?"

THE MINISTER'S HOUSEKEEPER

scene.—The shady side of a blueberry-pasture.—Sam Lawson with the boys, picking blueberries.—Sam, *loq.*

"Wal, you see, boys, 't was just here,—Parson Carryl's wife she died along in the forepart o' March: my cousin Huldy, she undertook to keep house for him. The way on 't was, that Huldy she went to take care o' Mis' Carryl in the fust on 't, when she fust took sick. Huldy was a tailoress by trade; but then she was one o' these 'ere facultised persons that has a gift for most any thing, and that was how Mis' Carryl come to set sech store by her, that, when she was sick, nothin' would do for her but she must have Huldy round all the time: and the minister, he said he'd make it good to her all the same, and she should n't lose nothin' by it. And so Huldy, she staid with Mis' Carryl full three months afore she died, and got to seein' to every thing pretty much round the place.

"Wal, arter Mis' Carryl died, Parson Carryl he'd got so kind o' used to hevin' on her 'round, takin' care o' things, that he wanted her to stay along a spell; and so Huldy she staid along a spell, and poured out his tea, and mended his close, and made pies and cakes, and cooked and washed and ironed, and kep' everything as neat as a pin. Huldy was a drefful chipper sort o' gal; and work sort o' rolled off from her like water off a duck's back. There warn't no gal in Sherburne that could put sich a sight o' work through as Huldy; and yet, Sunday mornin', she always come out in the singers' seat like one o' these 'ere June roses, lookin' so fresh and smilin', and her voice was jest as clear and sweet as a meadow lark's—Lordy massy! I 'member how she used to sing some o' them 'are places where the treble and counter used to go together: her voice kind o' trembled a little, and it sort o' went thro' and thro' a feller! tuck him right where he lived!"

Here Sam leaned contemplatively back with his head in a clump of sweet fern, and refreshed himself with a chew of young wintergreen. "This 'ere young wintergreen, boys, is jest like a feller's thoughts o' things that happened when he was young: it comes up jest so fresh and tender every year, the longest time you hev to live; and you can't help chawin' on 't though 'tis sort o' stingin'. I don't never get over likin' young wintergreen."

"But about Huldah, Sam?"

"Oh yes! about Huldy. Lordy massy! when a feller is Indianin' round, these 'ere pleasant summer days, a feller's thoughts gits like a flock o' young partridges: they's up and down and everywhere; 'cause one place is jest about as good as another, when they's all so kind o' comfortable and nice. Wal, about Huldy,—as I was a-sayin'. She was jest as handsome a gal to look at as a feller could have; and I think a nice, well-behaved young gal in the singers' seat of a Sunday is a means o' grace: it's sort o' drawin' to the unregenerate, you know. Why, boys, in them days, I've walked ten miles over to Sherburne of a Sunday mornin', jest to play the bass-viol in the same singers' seat with Huldy.

She was very much respected, Huldy was; and, when she went out to tailorin', she was allers bespoke six months ahead, and sent for in waggins up and down for ten miles round; for the young fellers was allers 'mazin' anxious to be sent after Huldy, and was quite free to offer to go for her. Wal, after Mis' Carryl died, Huldy got to be sort o' housekeeper at the minister's, and saw to every thing, and did everything: so that there wa'n't a pin out o' the way.

"But you know how 'tis in parishes: there allers is women that thinks the minister's affairs belongs to them, and they ought to have the rulin' and guidin' of 'em; and, if a minister's wife dies, there's folks that allers has their eyes open on providences,— lookin' out who's to be the next one.

"Now, there was Mis' Amaziah Pipperidge, a widder with snappin' black eyes, and a hook nose,—kind o' like a hawk; and she was one o' them up-and-down commandin' sort o' women, that feel that they have a call to be seein' to every thing that goes on in the parish, and 'specially to the minister.

"Folks did say that Mis' Pipperidge sort o' sot her eye on the Parson for herself: wal, now that 'are might a been, or it might not. Some folks thought it was a very suitable connection. You see she hed a good property of her own, right nigh to the minister's lot, and was allers kind o' active and busy; so, takin' one thing with another, I should n't wonder if Mis' Pipperidge should a thought that Providence p'inted that way. At any rate, she went up to Deakin Blodgett's wife, and they two sort o' put their heads together a mournin' and condolin' about the way things was likely to go on at the minister's now Mis' Carryl was dead. Ye see, the parson's wife, she was one of them women who hed their eyes everywhere and on every thing. She was a little thin woman, but tough as Inger rubber, ans smart as a steel trap; and there warn't a hen laid an egg, or cackled, but Mis' Carryl was right there to see about it; and she hed the garden made in the spring, and the medders mowed in summer, and the cider made, and the corn husked, and the apples got in the fall; and the doctor, he hed n't nothin' to do but jest sit stock still a meditatin' on Jerusalem and Jericho and them things that ministers think about. But Lordy massy! he did n't know nothin' about where anything he eat or drunk or wore come from or went to: his wife jest led him round in temporal things and took care on him like a baby.

"Wal, to be sure, Mis' Carryl looked up to him in spirituals, and thought all the world on him; for there wa'n't a smarter minister no where 'round. Why, when he preached on decrees and election, they used to come clear over from South Parish, and West Sherburne, and Old Town to hear him; and there was sich a row o' waggins tied along by the meetin'-house that the stables was all full, and all the hitchin'-posts was full clean up to the tavern, so that folks said the doctor made the town look like a gineral train'-day a Sunday.

"He was gret on texts, the doctor was. When he hed a p'int to prove, he'd jest go thro' the Bible, and drive all the texts ahead o' him like a flock o' sheep; and then, if there was a text that seemed agin him, why, he'd come out with his Greek and Hebrew, and kind o' chase it round a spell, jest as ye see a feller chase a contrary bell-wether, and make him jump the fence arter the rest. I tell you, there wa'n't no text in the Bible that could stand agin the doctor when his blood was up. The year arter the doctor was app'inted to preach the 'lection sermon in Boston, he made such a figger that the Brattle Street Church sent a committee right down to see if they could n't get him to Boston; and then the Sherburne folks, they up and raised his salary; ye see, there ain't nothin' wakes folks up like somebody else's wantin' what you've got. Wal, that fall they made him a Doctor o' Divinity at Cambridge College, and so they sot more by him than ever. Wal, you see, the doctor, of course he felt kind o' lonesome and afflicted when Mis' Carryl was gone; but railly and truly, Huldy was so up to every thing about house, that the doctor did n't miss nothin' in a temporal way. His shirt-bosoms was pleated finer than they ever was, and them ruffles round his wrists was kep' like the driven snow; and there warn't a brack in his silk stockin's, and his shoe-buckles was kep' polished up, and his coats brushed; and then there warn't no bread and biscuit like Huldy's; and her butter was like solid lumps o' gold; and there wern't no pies to equal hers; and so the doctor never felt the loss o' Mis' Carryl at table. Then there was Huldy allers oppisite to him, with her blue eyes and her cheeks like two fresh peaches. She was kind o' pleasant to look at; and the more the doctor looked at her the better he liked her; and so things seemed to be goin' on quite quiet and comfortable ef it had n't been that Mis' Pipperidge and Mis' Deakin Blodgett and Mis' Sawin got their heads together a talkin' about things.

"'Poor man,' says Mis' Pipperidge, 'what can that child that he's got there do towards takin' the care of all that place? It takes a mature woman,' she says, 'to tread in Mis' Carryl's shoes.'

"'That it does,' said Mis' Blodgett; 'and, when things once get to runnin' down hill, there ain't no stoppin' on 'em,' says she.

"Then Mis' Sawin she took it up. (Ye see, Mis' Sawin used to go out to dress-makin', and was sort o' jealous, 'cause folks sot more by Huldy than they did by her.) 'Well,' says she, 'Huldy Peters is well enough at her trade. I never denied that, though I do say I never did believe in her way o' makin' button-holes; and I must say, if 'twas the dearest friend I hed, that I thought Huldy tryin' to fit Mis' Kittridge's plumb-colored silk was a clear piece o' presumption; the silk was jist spiled, so 'twarn't fit to come into the meetin'-house. I must say, Huldy's a gal that's always too ventersome about takin' 'sponsibilities she don't know nothin' about.'

"'Of course she don't,' said Mis' Deakin Blodgett. 'What does she know about all the lookin' and seein' to that there ought to be in guidin' the minister's house. Huldy's well meanin', and she's good at her work, and good in the singers' seat; but Lordy massy! she hain't got no experience. Parson Carryl ought to have an experienced woman to keep house for him. There's the spring house-cleanin' and the fall house-cleanin' to be seen to, and the things to be put away from the moths; and then the gettin' ready for the Association and all the ministers' meetin's; and the makin' the soap and the candles, and settin' the hens and turkeys, watchin' the calves, and seein' after the hired men and the garden; and there that 'are blessed man jist sets there at home as serene, and has nobody round but that 'are gal, and don't even know how things must be a runnin' to waste!'

"Wal, the upshot on 't was, they fussed and fuzzled and wuzzled till they'd drinked up all the tea in the teapot; and then they went down and called on the parson, and wuzzled him all up talkin' about this, that, and t'other that wanted lookin' to, and that it was no way to leave everything to a young chit like Huldy, and that he ought to be lookin' about for an experienced woman. The parson he thanked 'em kindly, and said he believed their motives was good, but he didn't go no further. He didn't ask Mis' Pipperidge to come and stay there and help him, nor nothin' o' that kind; but he said he'd attend to matters himself. The fact was, the parson had got such a likin' for havin' Huldy round, that he could n't think o' such a thing as swappin' her off for the Widder Pipperidge.

"But he thought to himself, 'Huldy is a good girl; but I ought n't to be a-leavin' everything to her,—it's too hard on her. I ought to be instructin' and guidin' and helpin' of her; 'cause 't ain't everybody could be expected to know and do what Mis' Carryl did;' and so at it he went; and Lordy massy! did n't Huldy hev a time on 't when the minister began to come out of his study, and want to tew round and see to things? Huldy, you see, thought all the world of the minister, and she was 'most afraid to laugh; but she told me she could n't for the life of her, help it when his back was turned, for he wuzzled things up in the most singular way. But Huldy she'd jest say, 'Yes, sir,' and get him off into his study, and go on her own way.

"'Huldy,' says the minister one day, 'you ain't experienced outdoors; and, when you want to know anything, you must come to me.'

"'Yes, sir,' says Huldy.

"'Now, Huldy,' says the parson, 'you must be sure to save the turkey-eggs, so that we can have a lot of turkeys for Thanksgiving.'

"'Yes, sir,' says Huldy; and she opened the pantry-door, and showed him a nice dishful she'd been a-savin' up. Wal, the very next day the parson's hen-turkey was found killed up to old Jim Scroggs's barn. Folks said Scroggs killed it; though Scroggs, he stood to it he did n't: at any rate, the Scroggses, they made a meal on 't; and Huldy she felt bad about it, 'cause she 'd set her heart on raisin' the turkeys; and says she, 'Oh, dear! I don't know what I shall do. I was just ready to set her.'

"'Do, Huldy?' says the parson. 'Why, there's the other turkey, out there by the door; and a fine bird, too, he is.'

"Sure enough, there was the old tom-turkey a struttin' and a sidlin' and a quitterin', and a floutin' his tail-feathers in the sun, like a lively young widower, all ready to begin life over ag'in.

"'But,' says Huldy, 'you know *he* can't set on eggs.'

"'He can't? I'd like to know why,' says the parson. 'He shall set on eggs, and hatch 'em too.'

"'O doctor!' says Huldy, all in a tremble; 'cause, you know, she did n't want to contradict the minister, and she was afraid she should laugh,—'I never heard that a tom-turkey would set on eggs.'

" 'Why, they ought to,' said the parson, getting quite 'arnest; 'what else be they good for? you just bring out the eggs, now, and put 'em in the nest, and I'll make him set on 'em.'

"So Huldy she thought there weren't no way to convince him but to let him try: so she took the eggs out, and fixed 'em all nice in the nest; and then she come back and found old Tom a skirmishin' with the parson pretty lively, I tell ye. Ye see, old Tom he did n't take the idee at all; and he flopped and gobbled, and fit the parson; and the parson's wig got round so that his cue stuck straight out over his ear, but he'd got his blood up. Ye see, the old doctor was used to carryin' his p'ints o' doctrine; and he hadn't fit the Arminians and Socinians to be beat by a tom-turkey; so finally he made a dive, and ketched him by the neck in spite o' his floppin', and stroked him down, and put Huldy's apron round him.

" 'There, Huldy,' he says, quite red in the face, 'we've got him now;' and he travelled off to the barn with him as lively as a cricket.

"Huldy came behind jist chokin' with laugh, and afraid the minister would look 'round and see her.

" 'Now, Huldy, we'll crook his legs, and set him down,' says the parson, when they got him to the nest; 'you see he is getting quiet, and he'll set there all right.'

"And the parson he sot him down; and old Tom he sot there solemn enough, and held his head down all droopin', lookin' like a rail pious old cock, as long as the parson sot by him.

" 'There! you see how still he sets,' says the parson to Huldy.

"Huldy was 'most dyin' for fear she should laugh. 'I'm afraid he'll get up,' says she, 'when you do.'

" 'Oh no, he won't!' says the parson, quite confident. 'There, there,' says he, layin' his hands on him, as if pronouncin' a blessin'. But when the parson riz up, old Tom he riz up too, and began to march over the eggs.

" 'Stop, now!' says the parson. 'I'll make him get down ag'in: hand me that corn-basket; we'll put that over him.'

"So he crooked old Tom's legs, and got him down ag'in; and they put the corn-basket over him, and then they both stood and waited.

" 'That'll do the thing, Huldy,' said the parson.

" 'I don't know about it,' says Huldy.

" 'Oh yes, it will, child! I understand,' says he.

"Just as he spoke, the basket riz right up and stood, and they could see old Tom's legs.

"'I'll make him stay down, confound him,' says the parson; for, ye see, parsons is men, like the rest on us, and the doctor had got his spunk up.

"'You jist hold him a minute, and I'll get something that'll make him stay, I guess;' and out he went to the fence, and brought in a long, thin, flat stone, and laid it on old Tom's back.

"Old Tom he wilted down considerable under this, and looked railly as if he was goin' to give in. He staid still there a good long spell, and the minister and Huldy left him there and come up to the house; but they hadn't more than got in the door before they see old Tom a hippin' along, as high-steppin' as ever, sayin', 'Talk! talk! and quitter! quitter!' and struttin' and gob-blin' as if he'd come through the Red Sea, and got the victory.

"'Oh, my eggs!' says Huldy. 'I'm afraid he's smashed 'em!'

"And sure enough, there they was, smashed flat enough under the stone.

"'I'll have him killed,' said the parson: 'we won't have such a critter round.'

"But the parson he slep' on 't, and then did n't do it; he only come out next Sunday with a tip-top sermon on the 'Riginal Cuss' that was pronounced on things in gineral, when Adam fell, and showed how everything was allowed to go contrary ever since. There was pigweed, and pusley, and Canady thistles, cut-worms, and bag-worms, and canker-worms, to say nothin' of rattlesnakes. The doctor made it very impressive and sort o' improvin'; but Huldy she told me, goin' home, that she hardly could keep from laughin' two or three times in the sermon when she thought of old Tom a standin' up with the corn-basket on his back.

"Wal, next week Huldy she jist borrowed the minister's horse and side-saddle, and rode over to South Parish to her Aunt Bas-come's,—Widder Bascome's, you know, that lives there by the trout-brook,—and got a lot o' turkey-eggs o' her, and come back and set a hen on 'em, and said nothin'; and in good time there was as nice a lot o' turkey-chicks as ever ye see.

"Huldy never said a word to the minister about his experi-ment, and he never said a word to her; but he sort o' kep' more to his books, and did n't take it on him to advise so much.

"But not long arter he took it into his head that Huldy ought to have a pig to be a fattin' with the buttermilk. Mis' Pipperidge set him up to it; and jist then old Tim Bigelow, out to Juniper Hill, told him if he'd call over he'd give him a little pig.

"So he sent for a man, and told him to build a pig-pen right out by the well, and have it all ready when he came home with his pig.

"Huldy she said she wished he might put a curb round the well out there, because in the dark, sometimes, a body might stumble into it; and the parson, he told him he might do that.

"Wal, old Aikin, the carpenter, he didn't come till most the middle of the arternoon; and then he sort o' idled, so that he didn't get up the well-curb till sundown; and then he went off and said he'd come and do the pig-pen next day.

"Wal, arter dark, Parson Carryl he driv into the yard, full chizel, with his pig. He'd tied up his mouth to keep him from squeelin'; and he see what he thought was the pig-pen,—he was rather near-sighted,—and so he ran and threw piggy over; and down he dropped into the water, and the minister put out his horse and pranced off into the house quite delighted.

"'There, Huldy, I've got you a nice little pig.'

"'Dear me!' says Huldy: 'where have you put him?'

"'Why, out there in the pig-pen, to be sure.'

"'Oh dear me!' says Huldy: 'that's the well-curb. There ain't no pig-pen built,' says she.

"'Lordy massy!' says the parson: 'then I've thrown the pig in the well!'

"Wal, Huldy she worked and worked, and finally she fished piggy out in the bucket, but he was dead as a door-nail; and she got him out o' the way quietly, and did n't say much; and the parson, he took to a great Hebrew book in his study; and says he, 'Huldy, I ain't much in temporals,' says he. Huldy says she kind o' felt her heart go out to him, he was so sort o' meek and helpless and larned; and says she, 'Wal, Parson Carryl, don't trouble your head no more about it; I'll see to things;' and sure enough, a week arter there was a nice pen, all ship-shape, and two little white pigs that Huldy bought with the money for the butter she sold at the store.

"'Wal, Huldy,' said the parson, 'you are a most amazin' child: you don't say nothin', but you do more than most folks.'

"Arter that the parson set sich store by Huldy that he come to her and asked her about everything, and it was amazin' how everything she put her hand to prospered. Huldy planted marigolds and larkspurs, pinks and carnations, all up and down the path to the front door, and trained up mornin'-glories and scarlet-runners round the windows. And she was always a gettin' a root here, and a sprig there, and a seed from somebody else: for Huldy was one o' them that has the gift, so that ef you jist give 'em the leastest sprig of anything they make a great bush out of it right away; so that in six months Huldy had roses and geraniums and lilies, sich as it would a took a gardener to raise. The parson he took no notice at fust; but when the yard was all ablaze with flowers he used to come and stand in a kind o' maze at the front door, and say, 'Beautiful, beautiful! Why, Huldy, I never see anything like it.' And then when her work was done arternoons, Huldy would sit with her sewin' in the porch, and sing and trill away till she'd draw the meadow-larks and the bobolinks and the orioles to answer her, and the great big elm-tree overhead would get perfectly rackety with the birds; and the parson, settin' there in his study, would git to kind o' dreamin' about the angels, and golden harps, and the New Jerusalem; but he would n't speak a word, 'cause Huldy she was jist like them wood-thrushes, she never could sing so well when she thought folks was hearin'. Folks noticed, about this time, that the parson's sermons got to be like Aaron's rod, that budded and blossomed; there was things in 'em about flowers and birds, and more 'special about the music o' heaven. And Huldy she noticed, that ef there was a hymn run in her head while she was 'round a workin' the minister was sure to give it out next Sunday. You see, Huldy was jist like a bee: she always sung when she was workin', and you could hear her trillin', now down in the corn-patch, while she was pickin' the corn; and now in the buttery, while she was workin' the butter; and now she'd go singin' down cellar, and then she'd be singin' up over head, so that she seemed to fill a house chock full o' music.

"Huldy was so sort o' chipper and fair spoken that she got the hired men all under her thumb: they come to her and took her orders jist as meek as so many calves; and she traded at the store, and kep' the accounts, and she hed her eyes everywhere, and tied up all the ends so tight that there wa'n't no gettin' round her. She would n't let nobody put nothin' off on Parson Carryl, 'cause he was a minister. Huldy was allers up to anybody that wanted to make a hard bargain; and, afore he knew jist what he was about, she'd got the best end of it, and everybody said that Huldy was the most capable gal that they'd ever traded with.

"Wal, come to the meetin' of the Association, Mis' Deakin Blodgett and Mis' Pipperidge come callin' up to the parson's, all in a stew, and offerin' their services to get the house ready; but the doctor he jist thanked 'em quite quiet, and turned 'em over to Huldy; and Huldy she told 'em that she'd got everything ready, and showed 'em her pantries, and her cakes and her pies and her puddin's, and took 'em all over the house; and they went peekin' and pokin', openin' cupboard-doors, and lookin' into drawers; and they could n't find so much as a thread out o' the way, from garret to cellar, and so they went off quite discontented. Arter that the women set new trouble a brewin'. Then they begun to talk that it was a year now since Mis' Carryl died; and it railly wasn't proper such a young gal to be stayin' there, who everybody could see was a settin' her cap for the minister.

"Mis' Pipperidge said, that, so long as she looked on Huldy as the hired gal, she hadn't thought much about it; but Huldy was railly takin' on airs as an equal, and appearin' as mistress o' the house in a way that would make talk if it went on. And Mis' Pipperidge she driv round up to Deakin Abner Snow's, and down to Mis' 'Lijah Perry's, and asked them if they wasn't afraid that the way the parson and Huldy was a goin' on might make talk. And they said they hadn't thought on't before, but now, come to think on't, they was sure it would; and they all went and talked with somebody else, and asked them if they didn't think it would make talk. So come Sunday, between meetin's there warn't nothin' else talked about; and Huldy saw folks a noddin' and a winkin', and a lookin' arter her, and she begun to feel drefful sort o' disagreeable. Finally Mis' Sawin she says to her, 'My dear, didn't you never think folks would talk about you and the minister?'

"'No: why should they?' says Huldy, quite innocent.

"'Wal, dear,' says she, 'I think it's a shame; but they say you're tryin' to catch him, and that it's so bold and improper for you to be courtin' of him right in his own house,—you know folks will talk,—I thought I'd tell you 'cause I think so much of you,' says she.

"Huldy was a gal of spirit, and she despised the talk, but it made her drefful uncomfortable; and when she got home at night she sat down in the mornin'-glory porch, quite quiet, and did n't sing a word.

"The minister he had heard the same thing from one of his deakins that day; and when he saw Huldy so kind o' silent, he says to her, 'Why don't you sing, my child?'

"He hed a pleasant sort o' way with him, the minister had, and Huldy had got to likin' to be with him, and it all come over her that perhaps she ought to go away; and her throat kind o' filled up so she could n't hardly speak; and, says she, 'I can't sing to-night.'

"Says he, 'You don't know how much good your singin' has done me, nor how much good *you* have done me in all ways, Huldy. I wish I knew how to show my gratitude.'

"'O sir!' says Huldy, '*is* it improper for me to be here?'

"'No, dear,' says the minister, 'but ill-natured folks will talk; but there is one way we can stop it, Huldy—if you will marry me. You'll make me very happy, and I'll do all I can to make you happy. Will you?'

"Wal, Huldy never told me jist what she said to the minister, —gals never does give you the particulars of them 'ere things jist as you'd like 'em,—only I know the upshot and the hull on 't was, that Huldy she did a consid'able lot o' clear starchin' and ironin' the next two days; and the Friday o' next week the minister and she rode over together to Dr. Lothrop's in Old Town; and the doctor, he jist made 'em man and wife, 'spite of envy of the Jews,' as the hymn says. Wal, you'd better believe there was a starin' and a wonderin' next Sunday mornin' when the second bell was a tollin', and the minister walked up the broad aisle with Huldy, all in white, arm in arm with him, and he opened the minister's pew, and handed her in as if she was a princess; for, you see, Parson Carryl come of a good family, and was a born gentleman, and had a sort o' grand way o' bein' polite to women-folks. Wal, I guess there was a rus'lin' among the bunnets. Mis' Pipperidge gin a great bounce, like corn poppin' on a shovel, and her eyes glared through her glasses at Huldy as if they'd a sot her afire; and everybody in the meetin' house was a starin', I tell *yew*. But they could n't none of 'em say nothin' agin Huldy's looks; for there wa'n't a crimp nor a frill about her that wa'n't jis' *so*; and her frock was white as the driven snow, and she had her bunnet all trimmed up with white ribbins; and all the fellows said the old doctor had stole a march, and got the handsomest gal in the parish.

"Wal, arter meetin' they all come round the parson and

Huldy at the door, shakin' hands and laughin'; for by that time they was about agreed that they'd got to let putty well alone.

"'Why, Parson Carryl,' says Mis' Deakin Blodgett, 'how you've come it over us.'

"'Yes,' says the parson, with a kind o' twinkle in his eye. 'I thought,' says he, 'as folks wanted to talk about Huldy and me, I'd give 'em somethin' wuth talkin' about.'"

UNCLE REMUS'S SOUTHERN NEGRO STORIES

by Joel Chandler Harris

(1848–1908)

UNCLE REMUS INITIATES THE LITTLE BOY

One evening recently, the lady whom Uncle Remus calls "Miss Sally" missed her little seven-year-old. Making search for him through the house and through the yard, she heard the sound of voices in the old man's cabin, and, looking through the window, saw the child sitting by Uncle Remus. His head rested against the old man's arm, and he was gazing with an expression of the most intense interest into the rough, weather-beaten face, that beamed so kindly upon him. This is what "Miss Sally" heard:

"Bimeby, one day, arter Brer Fox bin doin' all dat he could fer ter ketch Brer Rabbit, en Brer Rabbit bin doin' all he could fer ter keep 'im fum it, Brer Fox say to hisse'f dat he'd put up a game on Brer Rabbit, en he ain't mo'n got de wuds out'n his mouf twel Brer Rabbit come a lopin' up de big road, lookin' des ez plump, en ez fat, en ez sassy ez a Moggin hoss in a barley-patch.

"'Hol' on dar, Brer Rabbit,' sez Brer Fox, sezee.

"'I ain't got time, Brer Fox,' sez Brer Rabbit, sezee, sorter mendin' his licks.

"'I wanter have some confab wid you, Brer Rabbit,' sez Brer Fox, sezee.

"'All right, Brer Fox, but you better holler fum whar you stan'. I'm monstus full er fleas dis mawnin',' sez Brer Rabbit, sezee.

"'I seed Brer B'ar yistiddy,' sez Brer Fox, sezee, 'en he sorter rake me over de coals kaze you en me ain't make frens en live naberly, en I tole 'im dat I'd see you.'

"Den Brer Rabbit scratch one year wid his off hine-foot sorter jub'usly, en den he ups en sez, sezee:

"'All a settin', Brer Fox. Spose'n you drap roun' ter-morrer en take dinner wid me. We ain't got no great doin's at our house, but I speck de ole 'oman en de chilluns kin sorter scramble roun' en git up sump'n fer ter stay yo' stummuck.'

"'I'm 'gree'ble, Brer Rabbit,' sez Brer Fox, sezee.

"'Den I'll 'pen' on you,' sez Brer Rabbit, sezee.

"Nex' day, Mr. Rabbit an' Miss Rabbit got up soon, 'fo' day, en raided on a gyarden like Miss Sally's out dar, en got some cabbiges, en some roas'n years, en some sparrer-grass, en dey fix up a smashin' dinner. Bimeby one er de little Rabbits, playin' out in de back-yard, come runnin' in hollerin', 'Oh, ma! oh, ma! I seed Mr. Fox a comin'!' En den Brer Rabbit he tuck de chilluns by der years en make um set down, en den him en Miss Rabbit sorter dally roun' waitin' for Brer Fox. En dey keep on waitin', but no Brer Fox ain't come. Atter 'while Brer Rabbit goes to de do', easy like, en peep out, en dar, stickin' out fum behime de cornder, wuz de tip-een' er Brer Fox tail. Den Brer Rabbit shot de do' en sot down, en put his paws behime his years en begin' fer ter sing:—

> "'De place wharbouts you spill de grease,
>   Right dar youer boun' ter slide,
>   An' whar you fine a bunch er ha'r,
>   You 'll sholy fine de hide.'

"Nex' day, Brer Fox sont word by Mr. Mink, en skuze hisse'f kaze he wuz too sick fer ter come, en he ax Brer Rabbit fer ter come en take dinner wid him, en Brer Rabbit say he wuz 'gree'ble.

"Bimeby, w'en de shadders wuz at der shortes', Brer Rabbit he sorter brush up en santer down ter Brer Fox's house, en w'en he got dar, he yer somebody groanin', en he look in de do' en dar he see Brer Fox settin' up in a rockin' cheer all wrop up wid flannil, en he look mighty weak. Brer Rabbit look all 'roun', he did, but he ain't see no dinner. De dish-pan wuz settin' on de table, en close by wuz a kyarvin' knife.

"'Look like you gwineter have chicken fer dinner, Brer Fox,' sez Brer Rabbit, sezee.

"'Yes, Brer Rabbit, deyer nice, en fresh, en tender,' sez Brer Fox, sezee.

"Den Brer Rabbit sorter pull his mustarsh, en say: 'You ain' got no calamus root, is you, Brer Fox? I done got so now dat I can't eat no chicken 'ceppin she's seasoned up wid calamus root.' En wid dat Brer Rabbit lipt out er de do' and dodge 'mong de bushes, en sot dar watchin' fer Brer Fox; en he ain't watch long, nudder, kaze Brer Fox flung off de flannil en crope out er de house en got whar he could cloze in on Brer Rabbit, en bimeby

Brer Rabbit holler out: 'Oh, Brer Fox! I'll des put yo' calamus root out yer on dish yer stump. Better come git it while hit's fresh,' and wid dat Brer Rabbit gallop off home. En Brer Fox ain't never kotch 'im yet, en w'at's mo', honey, he ain't gwineter."

The Wonderful Tar-Baby Story

"Didn't the fox *never* catch the rabbit, Uncle Remus?" asked the little boy the next evening.

"He come mighty nigh it, honey, sho's you bawn—Brer Fox did. One day atter Brer Rabbit fool 'im wid dat calamus root, Brer Fox went ter wuk en got 'im some tar, en mix it wid some turkentime, en fix up a contrapshun wat he call a Tar-Baby, en he tuck dish yer Tar-Baby en he sot 'er in de big road, en den he lay off in de bushes fer ter see wat de news wuz gwineter be. En he didn't hatter wait long, nudder, kaze bimeby here come Brer Rabbit pacin' down de road—lippity-clippity, clippity-lippity—dez ez sassy ez a jay-bird. Brer Fox, he lay low. Brer Rabbit come prancin' 'long twel he spy de Tar-Baby; en den he fotch up on his behime legs like he wuz 'stonished. De Tar-Baby, she sot dar, she did, en Brer Fox, he lay low.

"'Mawnin'!' sez Brer Rabbit, sezee—'nice wedder dis mawnin',' sezee.

"Tar-Baby ain't sayin' nuthin', en Brer Fox, he lay low.

"'How duz yo' sym'tums seem ter segashuate?' sez Brer Rabbit, sezee.

"Brer Fox, he wink his eye slow, en lay low, en de Tar-Baby, she ain't sayin' nuthin'.

"'How you come on, den? Is you deaf?' sez Brer Rabbit, sezee. 'Kaze if you is, I kin holler louder,' sezee.

"Tar-Baby stay still, en Brer Fox, he lay low.

"'Youer stuck up, dat's w'at you is,' says Brer Rabbit, sezee, 'en I'm gwineter kyore you, dat's w'at I'm a gwineter do,' sezee.

"Brer Fox, he sorter chuckle in his stummuck, he did, but Tar-Baby ain't sayin' nuthin'.

"'I'm gwineter larn you howter talk ter 'specttubble fokes ef hit's de las' ack,' sez Brer Rabbit, sezee. 'Ef you don't take off dat hat en tell me howdy, I'm gwineter bus' you wide open,' sezee.

"Tar-Baby stay still, en Brer Fox, he lay low.

"Brer Rabbit keep on axin' 'im, en de Tar-Baby, she keep on sayin' nuthin', twel present'y Brer Rabbit draw back wid his fis', he did, en blip he tuck 'er side er de head. Right dar's whar he broke his merlasses jug. His fis' stuck, en he can't pull loose. De tar hilt 'im. But Tar-Baby, she stay still, en Brer Fox, he lay low.

"'Ef you don't lemme loose, I'll knock you agin,' sez Brer Rabbit, sezee, en wid dat he fotch 'er a wipe wid de udder han', en dat stuck. Tar-Baby, she ain't sayin' nuthin', en Brer Fox, he lay low.

"'Tu'n me loose, fo' I kick de natal stuffin' outen you,' sez Brer Rabbit, sezee, but de Tar-Baby, she ain't sayin' nuthin'. She des hilt on, en den Brer Rabbit lose de use er his feet in de same way. Brer Fox, he lay low. Den Brer Rabbit squall out dat ef de Tar-Baby don't tu'n 'im loose he butt 'er cranksided. En den he butted, en his head got stuck. Den Brer Fox, he sa'ntered fort', lookin' des ez innercent ez wunner yo' mammy's mockin'-birds.

"'Howdy, Brer Rabbit,' sez Brer Fox, sezee. 'You look sorter stuck up dis mawnin',' sezee, en den he rolled on de groun', en laft en laft twel he couldn't laff no mo'. 'I speck you'll take dinner wid me dis time, Brer Rabbit. I done laid in some calamus root, en I ain't gwineter take no skuse,' sez Brer Fox, sezee."

Here Uncle Remus paused, and drew a two-pound yam out of the ashes.

"Did the fox eat the rabbit?" asked the little boy to whom the story had been told.

"Dat's all de fur de tale goes," replied the old man. "He mout, en den agin he moutent. Some say Jedge B'ar come 'long en loosed 'im—some say he didn't. I hear Miss Sally callin'. You better run 'long."

How Mr. Rabbit Was Too Sharp for Mr. Fox

"Uncle Remus," said the little boy one evening, when he had found the old man with little or nothing to do, "did the fox kill and eat the rabbit when he caught him with the Tar-Baby?"

"Law, honey, ain't I tell you 'bout dat?" replied the old darkey, chuckling slyly. "I 'clar ter grashus I ought er tole you dat, but ole man Nod wuz ridin' on my eyeleds 'twel a little mo'n I'd a dis'member'd my own name, en den on to dat here come yo' mammy hollerin' atter you.

"W'at I tell you w'en I fus' begin? I tole you Brer Rabbit wuz a monstus soon beas'; leas'ways dat's w'at I laid out fer ter tell you. Well, den, honey, don't you go en make no udder kalkala-shuns, kaze in dem days Brer Rabbit en his fambly wuz at de head er de gang w'en enny racket wuz on han', en dar dey stayed. 'Fo' you begins fer ter wipe yo' eyes 'bout Brer Rabbit, you wait and see whar'bouts Brer Rabbit gwineter fetch up at. But dat's needer yer ner dar.

"W'en Brer Fox fine Brer Rabbit mixt up wid de Tar-Baby, he feel mighty good, en he roll on de groun' en laff. Bimeby he up'n say, sezee:—

"'Well, I speck I got you dis time, Brer Rabbit,' sezee: 'maybe I ain't, but I speck I is. You been runnin' roun' here sassin' atter me a mighty long time, but I speck you done come ter de een' er de row. You bin cuttin' up yo' capers en bouncin' 'roun' in dis naberhood ontwel you come ter b'leeve yo'se'f de boss er de whole gang. En den youer allers some'rs whar you got no bizness,' sez Brer Fox, sezee. 'Who ax you fer ter come en strike up a 'quaintence wid dish yer Tar-Baby? En who stuck you up dar whar you iz? Nobody in de roun' worril. You des tuck en jam yo'se'f on dat Tar-Baby widout waitin' fer enny invite,' sez Brer Fox, sezee, 'en dar you is, en dar you'll stay twel I fixes up a bresh-pile and fires her up, kaze I'm gwineter bobbycue you dis day, sho,' sez Brer Fox, sezee.

"Den Brer Rabbit talk mighty 'umble.

"'I don't keer w'at you do wid me, Brer Fox,' sezee, 'so you don't fling me in dat brier-patch. Roas' me, Brer Fox,' sezee, 'but don't fling me in dat brier-patch,' sezee.

"'Hit's so much trouble fer ter kindle a fier,' sez Brer Fox, sezee, 'dat I speck I'll hatter hang you,' sezee.

"'Hang me des ez high as you please, Brer Fox,' sez Brer Rabbit, sezee, 'but do fer de Lord's sake don't fling me in dat brier-patch,' sezee.

"'I ain't got no string,' sez Brer Fox, sezee, 'en now I speck I'll hatter drown you,' sezee.

"'Drown me des ez deep ez you please, Brer Fox,' sez Brer Rabbit, sezee, 'but don't fling me in dat brier-patch,' sezee.

"'Dey ain't no water nigh,' sez Brer Fox, sezee, 'en now I speck I'll hatter skin you,' sezee.

"'Skin me, Brer Fox,' sez Brer Rabbit, sezee, 'snatch out my eyeballs, t'ar out my years by de roots, en cut off my legs,' sezee, 'but do please, Brer Fox, don't fling me in dat brier-patch,' sezee.

"Co'se Brer Fox wanter hurt Brer Rabbit bad ez he kin, so he cotch 'im by de behime legs en slung 'im right in de middle er de brier-patch. Dar wuz a considerbul flutter whar Brer Rabbit struck de bushes, en Brer Fox sorter hang 'roun' fer ter see w'at wuz gwineter happen. Bimeby he hear somebody call 'im, en way up de hill he see Brer Rabbit settin' cross-legged on a chink-apin log koamin' de pitch outen his har wid a chip. Den Brer Fox know dat he bin swop off mighty bad. Brer Rabbit wuz bleedzed fer ter fling back some er his sass, en he holler out:

"'Bred en bawn in a brier-patch, Brer Fox—bred en bawn in a brier-patch!' en wid dat he skip out des ez lively ez a cricket in de embers."

Mr. Rabbit Grossly Deceives Mr. Fox

One evening, when the little boy, whose nights with Uncle Remus are as entertaining as those Arabian ones of blessed memory, had finished supper and hurried out to sit with his venerable patron, he found the old man in great glee. Indeed, Uncle Remus was talking and laughing to himself at such a rate that the little boy was afraid he had company. The truth is, Uncle Remus had heard the child coming, and, when the rosy-cheeked chap put his head in at the door, was engaged in a monologue, the burden of which seemed to be—

> "Ole Molly Har',
> W'at you doin' dar,
> Settin' in de cornder
> Smokin' yo' seegyar?"

As a matter of course this vague allusion reminded the little boy of the fact that the wicked Fox was still in pursuit of the Rabbit, and he immediately put his curiosity in the shape of a question.

"Uncle Remus, did the Rabbit have to go clean away when he got loose from the Tar-Baby?"

"Bless grashus, honey, dat he did n't. Who? Him? You dunno nuthin' 'tall 'bout Brer Rabbit ef dat's de way you puttin' 'im down. W'at he gwine 'way fer? He mouter stayed sorter close twel de pitch rub off 'n his ha'r, but twern't menny days 'fo' he wuz lopin' up en down de naberhood same ez ever, en I dunno ef he wern't mo' sassier dan befo'.

"Seem like dat de tale 'bout how he got mixt up wid de Tar-

Baby got 'roun' 'mongst de nabers. Leas'ways, Miss Meadows en de gals got win' un' it, en de nex' time Brer Rabbit paid um a visit Miss Meadows tackled 'im 'bout it, en de gals sot up a monstus gigglement. Brer Rabbit, he sot up des ez cool ez a cowcumber, he did, en let 'em run on."

"Who was Miss Meadows, Uncle Remus?" inquired the little boy.

"Don't ax me, honey. She wuz in de tale, Miss Meadows en de gals wuz, en de tale I give you like hi't wer' gun ter me. Brer Rabbit, he sot dar, he did, sorter lam' like, en den bimeby he cross his legs, he did, and wink his eye slow, en up en say, sezee:

"'Ladies, Brer Fox wuz my daddy's ridin'-hoss fer thirty year; maybe mo', but thirty year dat I knows un,' sezee; en den he paid um his 'specks, en tip his beaver, en march off, he did, des ez stiff en ez stuck up ez a fire-stick.

"Nex' day, Brer Fox cum a callin', and w'en he gun fer ter laff 'bout Brer Rabbit, Miss Meadows en de gals, dey ups en tells 'im 'bout w'at Brer Rabbit say. Den Brer Fox grit his toof sho' nuff, he did, en he look mighty dumpy, but w'en he riz fer ter go he up en say, sezee:

"'Ladies, I ain't 'sputin' w'at you say, but I'll make Brer Rabbit chaw up his words en spit um out right yer whar you kin see 'im,' sezee, en wid dat off Brer Fox marcht.

"En w'en he got in de big road, he shuck de dew off 'n his tail, en made a straight shoot fer Brer Rabbit's house. W'en he got dar, Brer Rabbit wuz spectin' un 'im, en de do' wuz shet fas'. Brer Fox knock. Nobody ain't ans'er. Brer Fox knock. Nobody ans'er. Den he knock agin— blam! blam! Den Brer Rabbit holler out mighty weak:

"'Is dat you, Brer Fox? I want you ter run en fetch de doctor. Dat bait er pusly w'at I e't dis mawnin' is gittin' 'way wid me. Do, please, Brer Fox, run quick,' sez Brer Rabbit, sezee.

"'I come atter you, Brer Rabbit,' sez Brer Fox, sezee. 'Dere's gwineter be a party up at Miss Meadows's,' sezee. 'All de gals 'll be dere, en I promus' dat I'd fetch you. De gals, dey 'lowed dat hit wouldn't be no party 'ceppin' I fotch you,' sez Brer Fox, sezee.

"Den Brer Rabbit say he wuz too sick, en Brer Fox say he wuzzent, en dar dey had it up and down, 'sputin' en contendin'. Brer Rabbit say he can't walk. Brer Fox say he tote 'im. Brer Rabbit say how? Brer Fox say in his arms. Brer Rabbit say he drap 'im. Brer Fox 'low he won't. Bimeby Brer Rabbit say he go ef Brer Fox tote 'im on his back. Brer Fox say he would. Brer Rabbit say he can't ride widout a saddle. Brer Fox say he git de saddle. Brer Rabbit say he can't set in saddle less he have bridle fer ter hol' by. Brer Fox say he git de bridle. Brer Rabbit say he can't ride widout bline bridle, kaze Brer Fox be shyin' at stumps 'long de road, en fling 'im off. Brer Fox say he git bline bridle. Den Brer Rabbit say he go. Den Brer Fox say he ride Brer Rabbit mos' up ter Miss Meadows's, en den he could git down en walk de balance er de way. Brer Rabbit 'greed, en den Brer Fox lipt out atter de saddle en de bridle.

"Co'se Brer Rabbit know de game dat Brer Fox wuz fixin' fer ter play, en he 'termin' fer ter outdo 'im, en by de time he koam his ha'r en twis' his mustarsh, en sorter rig up, yer come Brer Fox, saddle en bridle on, en lookin' ez peart ez a circus pony. He trot up ter de do' en stan' dar pawin' de ground en chompin' de bit same like sho 'nuff hoss, en Brer Rabbit he mount, he did, en dey amble off. Brer Fox can't see behime wid de bline bridle on, but bimeby he feel Brer Rabbit raise one er his foots.

" 'W'at you doin' now, Brer Rabbit?' sezee.

" 'Short'nin' de lef stir'p, Brer Fox,' sezee.

"Bimeby Brer Rabbit raise up the udder foot.

" 'W'at you doin' now, Brer Rabbit?' sezee.

" 'Pullin' down my pants, Brer Fox,' sezee.

"All de time, bless grashus, honey, Brer Rabbit wer puttin' on his spurrers, en w'en dey got close to Miss Meadows's, whar Brer Rabbit wuz to git off, en Brer Fox made a motion fer ter stan' still, Brer Rabbit slap de spurrers into Brer Fox flanks, en you better b'leeve he got over groun'. W'en dey got ter de house, Miss Meadows en all de gals wuz settin' on de peazzer, en stidder stoppin' at de gate, Brer Rabbit rid on by, he did, en den come gallopin' down de road en up ter de hoss-rack, w'ich he hitch Brer Fox at, en den he santer inter de house, he did, en shake han's wid de gals, en set dar, smokin' his seegyar same ez a town man. Bimeby he draw in long puff, en den let hit out in a cloud, en squar hisse'f back en holler out, he did:

" 'Ladies, ain't I done tell you Brer Fox wuz de ridin'-hoss fer our fambly? He sorter losin' his gait' now, but I speck I kin fetch 'im all right in a mont' er so,' sezee.

"En den Brer Rabbit sorter grin, he did, en de gals giggle, en

Miss Meadows, she praise up de pony, en dar wuz Brer Fox hitch fas' ter de rack, en could n't he'p hisse'f."

"Is that all, Uncle Remus?" asked the little boy as the old man paused.

"Dat ain't all, honey, but 'twon't do fer ter give out too much cloff fer ter cut one pa'r pants," replied the old man sententiously.

MARK TWAIN

(1835–1910)

THE NOTORIOUS JUMPING FROG OF
CALAVERAS COUNTY

In compliance with the request of a friend of mine, who wrote me from the East, I called on good-natured, garrulous old Simon Wheeler, and inquired after my friend's friend, Leonidas W. Smiley, as requested to do, and I hereunto append the result. I have a lurking suspicion that *Leonidas W.* Smiley is a myth; that my friend never knew such a personage; and that he only conjectured that if I asked old Wheeler about him, it would remind me of his infamous *Jim* Smiley, and he would go to work and bore me to death with some exasperating reminiscence of him as long and as tedious as it should be useless to me. If that was the design, it succeeded.

I found Simon Wheeler dozing comfortably by the bar-room stove of the dilapidated tavern in the decayed mining camp of Angel's, and I noticed that he was fat and bald-headed, and had an expression of winning gentleness and simplicity upon his tranquil countenance. He roused up, and gave me good-day. I told him a friend of mine had commissioned me to make some inquiries about a cherished companion of his boyhood named *Leonidas W.* Smiley—*Rev. Leonidas W.* Smiley, a young minister of the Gospel, who he had heard was at one time a resident of Angel's Camp. I added that if Mr. Wheeler could tell me anything about this Rev. Leonidas W. Smiley, I would feel under many obligations to him.

Simon Wheeler backed me into a corner and blockaded me there with his chair, and then sat down and reeled off the monotonous narrative which follows this paragraph. He never smiled, he never frowned, he never changed his voice from the gentle-flowing key to which he tuned his initial sentence, he never betrayed the slightest suspicion of enthusiasm; but all through the interminable narrative there ran a vein of impressive earnestness and sincerity, which showed me plainly that, so far from his imagining that there was anything ridiculous or funny about his story, he regarded it as a really important matter, and admired its two heroes as men of transcendent genius in *finesse*. I let him go on in his own way, and never interrupted him once.

"Rev. Leonidas W. H'm, Reverend Le—well, there was a

feller here once by the name of *Jim* Smiley, in the winter of '49 —or may be it was the spring of '50—I don't recollect exactly, somehow, though what makes me think it was one or the other is because I remember the big flume warn't finished when he first come to the camp; but any way, he was the curiosest man about always betting on anything that turned up you ever see, if he could get anybody to bet on the other side; and if he couldn't he'd change sides. Any way that suited the other man would suit *him*—any way just so's he got a bet, *he* was satisfied. But still he was lucky, uncommon lucky; he most always come out winner. He was always ready and laying for a chance; there couldn't be no solit'ry thing mentioned but that feller'd offer to bet on it, and take ary side you please, as I was just telling you. If there was a horse-race, you'd find him flush or you'd find him busted at the end of it; if there was a dog-fight, he'd bet on it; if there was a cat-fight, he'd bet on it; if there was a chicken-fight, he'd bet on it; why, if there was two birds setting on a fence, he would bet you which one would fly first; or if there was a camp-meeting, he would be there reg'lar to bet on Parson Walker, which he judged to be the best exhorter about here, and so he was too, and a good man. If he even see a straddle-bug start to go anywheres, he would bet you how long it would take him to get to—to wherever he was going to, and if you took him up, he would foller that straddle-bug to Mexico but what he would find out where he was bound for and how long he was on the road. Lots of the boys here has seen that Smiley, and can tell you about him. Why, it never made no difference to *him*—he'd bet on *any* thing—the dangdest feller. Parson Walker's wife laid very sick once, for a good while, and it seemed as if they warn't going to save her; but one morning he come in, and Smiley up and asked him how she was, and he said she was considable better—thank the Lord for his inf'nit mercy —and coming on so smart that with the blessing of Prov'dence she'd get well yet; and Smiley, before he thought says, "Well, I'll resk two-and-a-half she don't anyway."

Thish-yer Smiley had a mare—the boys called her the fifteen-minute nag, but that was only in fun, you know, because of course she was faster than that—and he used to win money on that horse, for all she was so slow and always had the asthma, or the distemper, or the consumption, or something of that kind. They used to give her two or three hundred yards' start, and then pass her under way; but always at the fag-end of the race she'd get

MRS. PARTINGTON (1854)—AUNT POLLY (1876)

This frontispiece for *Life and Sayings of Mrs. Partington* (1854) was labeled "Ruth Partington" when it first appeared. Later, captioned "Contentment," it was used as an illustration for *The Adventures of Tom Sawyer* (1876), and presumably it represented Tom's Aunt Polly. See p. 151.

excited and desperate-like, and come cavorting and straddling up, and scattering her legs around limber, sometimes in the air, and sometimes out to one side amongst the fences, and kicking up m-o-r-e dust and raising m-o-r-e racket with her coughing and sneezing and blowing her nose—and *always* fetch up at the stand just about a neck ahead, as near as you could cipher it down.

And he had a little small bull-pup, that to look at him you'd think he warn't worth a cent but to set around and look ornery and lay for a chance to steal something. But as soon as money was up on him he was a different dog; his under-jaw'd begin to stick out like the fo'castle of a steamboat, and his teeth would uncover and shine like the furnaces. And a dog might tackle him and bully-rag him, and bite him, and throw him over his shoulder two or three times, and Andrew Jackson—which was the name of the pup—Andrew Jackson would never let on but what *he* was satisfied, and hadn't expected nothing else—and the bets being doubled and doubled on the other side all the time, till the money was all up; and then all of a sudden he would grab that other dog jest by the j'int of his hind leg and freeze to it—not chaw, you understand, but only just grip and hang on till they throwed up the sponge, if it was a year. Smiley always come out winner on that pup, till he harnessed a dog once that didn't have no hind legs, because they'd been sawed off in a circular saw, and when the thing had gone along far enough, and the money was all up, and he come to make a snatch for his pet holt, he see in a minute how he'd been imposed on, and how the other dog had him in the door, so to speak, and he 'peared surprised, and then he looked sorter discouraged-like, and didn't try no more to win the fight, and so he got shucked out bad. He give Smiley a look, as much as to say his heart was broke, and it was *his* fault, for putting up a dog that hadn't no hind legs for him to take holt of, which was his main dependence in a fight, and then he limped off a piece and laid down and died. It was a good pup, was that Andrew Jackson, and would have made a name for hisself if he'd lived, for the stuff was in him and he had genius—I know it, because he hadn't no opportunities to speak of, and it don't stand to reason that a dog could make such a fight as he could under them circumstances if he hadn't no talent. It always makes me feel sorry when I think of that last fight of his'n, and the way it turned out.

Well, thish-yer Smiley had rat-tarriers, and chicken cocks, and tom-cats and all them kind of things, till you couldn't rest, and you couldn't fetch nothing for him to bet on but he'd match you. He ketched a frog one day, and took him home, and said he cal'lated to educate him; and so he never done nothing for three months but set in his back yard and learn that frog to jump. And you bet you he *did* learn him, too. He'd give him a little punch behind, and the next minute you'd see that frog whirling in the air like a doughnut—see him turn one summerset, or may be a couple, if he got a good start, and come down flat-footed and all right, like a cat. He got him up so in the matter of ketching flies, and kep' him in practice so constant, that he'd nail a fly every time as fur as he could see him. Smiley said all a frog wanted was education, and he could do 'most anything—and I believe him. Why, I've seen him set Dan'l Webster down here on this floor— Dan'l Webster was the name of the frog—and sing out, "Flies, Dan'l, flies!" and quicker'n you could wink he'd spring straight up and snake a fly off'n the counter there, and flop down on the floor ag'in as solid as a gob of mud, and fall to scratching the side of his head with his hind foot as indifferent as if he hadn't no idea he'd been doin' any more'n any frog might do. You never see a frog so modest and straightfor'ard as he was, for all he was so gifted. And when it come to fair and square jumping on a dead level, he could get over more ground at one straddle than any animal of his breed you ever see. Jumping on a dead level was his strong suit, you understand; and when it come to that, Smiley would ante up money on him as long as he had a red. Smiley was monstrous proud of his frog, and well he might be, for fellers that had traveled and been everywhere, all said he laid over any frog that ever *they* see.

Well, Smiley kep' the beast in a little lattice box, and he used to fetch him down town sometimes and lay for a bet. One day a feller—a stranger in the camp, he was—come acrost him with his box, and says:

"What might it be that you've got in the box?"

And Smiley says, sorter indifferent-like, "It might be a parrot, or it might be a canary, maybe, but it ain't—it's only just a frog."

And the feller took it, and looked at it careful, and turned it round this way and that, and says, "H'm—so 'tis. Well, what's *he* good for?"

"Well," Smiley says, easy and careless, "he's good enough for *one* thing, I should judge—he can outjump any frog in Calaveras county."

The feller took the box again, and took another long, particular look, and give it back to Smiley, and says, very deliberate, "Well," he says, "I don't see no p'ints about that frog that's any better'n any other frog."

"Maybe you don't," Smiley says. "Maybe you understand frogs and maybe you don't understand 'em; maybe you've had experience, and maybe you ain't only a amature, as it were. Anyways, I've got *my* opinion and I'll resk forty dollars that he can outjump any frog in Calaveras county."

And the feller studied a minute, and then says, kinder sad like, "Well, I'm only a stranger here, and I ain't got no frog; but if I had a frog, I'd bet you."

And then Smiley says, "That's all right—that's all right—if you'll hold my box a minute, I'll go and get you a frog." And so the feller took the box, and put up his forty dollars along with Smiley's and set down to wait.

So he set there a good while thinking and thinking to hisself, and then he got the frog out and prized his mouth open and took a teaspoon and filled him full of quail shot—filled him pretty near up to his chin—and set him on the floor. Smiley he went to the swamp and slopped around in the mud for a long time, and finally he ketched a frog, and fetched him in, and give him to this feller, and says:

"Now, if you're ready, set him alongside of Dan'l, with his fore-paws just even with Dan'l's, and I'll give the word." Then he says, "One—two—three—*git!*" and him and the feller touched up the frogs from behind, and the new frog hopped off lively, but Dan'l give a heave, and hysted up his shoulders—so—like a Frenchman, but it warn't no use—he couldn't budge; he was planted as solid as a church, and he couldn't no more stir than if he was anchored out. Smiley was a good deal surprised, and he was disgusted too, but he didn't have no idea what the matter was, of course.

The feller took the money and started away; and when he was going out at the door, he sorter jerked his thumb over his shoulder—so—at Dan'l, and says again, very deliberate, "Well," he says "*I* don't see no p'ints about that frog that's any better'n any other frog."

Smiley he stood scratching his head and looking down at Dan'l a long time, and at last he says, "I do wonder what in the nation that frog throw'd off for—I wonder if there ain't something the matter with him—he 'pears to look mighty baggy, somehow." And he ketched Dan'l by the nap of the neck, and hefted him, and says, "Why blame my cats if he don't weigh five pound!" and turned him upside down and he belched out a double handful of shot. And then he see how it was, and he was the maddest man—he set the frog down and took out after that feller, but he never ketched him. And—"

(Here Simon Wheeler heard his name called from the front yard, and got up to see what was wanted.) And turning to me as he moved away, he said: "Just set where you are, stranger, and rest easy—I ain't going to be gone a second."

But, by your leave, I did not think that a continuation of the history of the enterprising vagabond *Jim* Smiley would be likely to afford me much information concerning the Rev. *Leonidas W.* Smiley, and so I started away.

At the door I met the sociable Wheeler returning, and he button-holed me and re-commenced:

"Well, thish-yer Smiley had a yaller one-eyed cow that didn't have no tail, only jest a short stump like a bannanner, and—"

However, lacking both time and inclination, I did not wait to hear about the afflicted cow, but took my leave.

THE FACTS CONCERNING THE RECENT
RESIGNATION

Washington, Dec. 2, 1867.

I have resigned. The Government appears to go on much the same, but there is a spoke out of its wheel, nevertheless. I was clerk of the Senate Committee on Conchology, and I have thrown up the position. I could see the plainest disposition on the part of the other members of the Government to debar me from having any voice in the counsels of the nation, and so I could no longer hold office and retain my self-respect. If I were to detail all the outrages that were heaped upon me during the six days that I was connected with the Government in an official capacity, the narrative would fill a volume. They appointed me clerk of that Committee on Conchology, and then allowed me no amanuensis to play billiards with. I would have borne that, lonesome as it was, if I had met with that courtesy from the other members of the Cabinet which was my due. But I did not. Whenever I observed that the head of a department was pursuing a wrong course, I laid down everything and went and tried to set him right, as it was my duty to do; and I never was thanked for it in a single instance. I went, with the best intentions in the world, to the Secretary of the Navy, and said—

"Sir, I cannot see that Admiral Farragut is doing anything but skirmishing around there in Europe, having a sort of pic-nic. Now, that may be all very well, but it does not exhibit itself to me in that light. If there is no fighting for him to do, let him come home. There is no use in a man having a whole fleet for a pleasure excursion. It is too expensive. Mind, I do not object to pleasure excursions for the naval officers—pleasure excursions that are in reason—pleasure excursions that are economical. Now, they might go down the Mississippi on a raft"—

You ought to have heard him storm! One would have supposed I had committed a crime of some kind. But I didn't mind. I said it was cheap, and full of republican simplicity, and perfectly safe. I said that, for a tranquil pleasure excursion, there was nothing equal to a raft.

Then the Secretary of the Navy asked me who I was; and when I told him I was connected with the Government, he wanted

522

to know in what capacity. I said that, without remarking upon the singularity of such a question, coming, as it did, from a member of that same Government, I would inform him that I was clerk of the Senate Committee on Conchology. Then there was a fine storm! He finished by ordering me to leave the premises, and give my attention strictly to my own business in future. My first impulse was to get him removed. However, that would harm others beside himself, and do me no real good, and so I let him stay.

I went next to the Secretary of War, who was not inclined to see me at all until he learned that I was connected with the Government. If I had not been on important business, I suppose I could not have got in. I asked him for a light (he was smoking at the time), and then I told him I had no fault to find with his defending the parole stipulations of General Lee and his comrades in arms, but that I could not approve of his method of fighting the Indians on the Plains. I said he fought too scattering. He ought to get the Indians more together—get them together in some convenient place, where he could have provisions enough for both parties, and then have a general massacre. I said there was nothing so convincing to an Indian as a general massacre. If he could not approve of the massacre, I said the next surest thing for an Indian was soap and education. Soap and education are not as sudden as a massacre, but they are more deadly in the long run; because a half-massacred Indian may recover, but if you educate him and wash him, it is bound to finish him sometime or other. It undermines his constitution; it strikes at the foundation of his being. "Sir," I said, "the time has come when blood-curdling cruelty has become necessary. Inflict soap and a spelling-book on every Indian that ravages the Plains, and let them die!"

The Secretary of War asked me if I was a member of the Cabinet, and I said I was. He inquired what position I held, and I said I was clerk of the Senate Committee on Conchology. I was then ordered under arrest for contempt of court, and restrained of my liberty for the best part of the day.

I almost resolved to be silent thenceforward, and let the Government get along the best way it could. But duty called, and I obeyed. I called on the Secretary of the Treasury. He said—

"What will *you* have?"

The question threw me off my guard. I said, "Rum punch."

He said, "If you have got any business here, sir, state it—and in as few words as possible."

I then said that I was sorry he had seen fit to change the subject so abruptly, because such conduct was very offensive to me; but under the circumstances I would overlook the matter and come to the point. I now went into an earnest expostulation with him upon the extravagant length of his report. I said it was expensive, unnecessary, and awkwardly constructed; there were no descriptive passages in it, no poetry, no sentiment—no heroes, no plot, no pictures—not even woodcuts. Nobody would read it, that was a clear case. I urged him not to ruin his reputation by getting out a thing like that. If he ever hoped to succeed in literature, he must throw more variety into his writings. He must beware of dry detail. I said that the main popularity of the almanac was derived from its poetry and conundrums, and that a few conundrums distributed around through the Treasury report would help the sale of it more than all the internal revenue he could put into it. I said these things in the kindest spirit, and yet the Secretary of the Treasury fell into a violent passion. He even said that I was an ass. He abused me in the most vindictive manner, and said that if I came there again meddling with his business, he would throw me out of the window. I said I would take my hat and go, if I could not be treated with the respect due to my office, and I did go. It was just like a new author. They always think they know more than anybody else when they are getting out their first book. Nobody can tell *them* anything.

During the whole time that I was connected with the Government it seemed as if I could not do anything in an official capacity without getting myself into trouble. And yet I did nothing, attempted nothing, but what I conceived to be for the good of my country. The sting of my wrongs may have driven me to unjust and harmful conclusions, but it surely seemed to me that the Secretary of State, the Secretary of War, the Secretary of the Treasury, and others of my *confrères*, had conspired from the very beginning to drive me from the Administration. I never attended but one Cabinet meeting while I was connected with the Government. That was sufficient for me. The servant at the White House door did not seem disposed to make way for me until I asked if the other members of the Cabinet had arrived. He said they had, and I entered. They were all there; but nobody offered me a seat. They stared at me as if I had been an intruder. The President said—

"Well, sir, who are *you?*"

I handed him my card, and he read—"The HON. MARK

TWAIN, Clerk of the Senate Committee on Conchology." Then he looked at me from head to foot, as if he had never heard of me before. The Secretary of the Treasury said—

"This is the meddlesome ass that came to recommend me to put poetry and conundrums in my report, as if it were an almanac."

The Secretary of War said—"It is the same visionary that came to me yesterday with a scheme to educate a portion of the Indians to death, and massacre the balance."

The Secretary of the Navy said—"I recognize this youth as the person who has been interfering with my business time and again during the week. He is distressed about Admiral Farragut's using a whole fleet for a pleasure excursion, as he terms it. His proposition about some insane pleasure excursion on a raft is too absurd to repeat."

I said—"Gentlemen, I perceive here a disposition to throw discredit upon every act of my official career; I perceive, also, a disposition to debar me from all voice in the counsels of the nation. No notice whatever was sent to me to-day. It was only by the merest chance that I learned that there was going to be a Cabinet meeting. But let these things pass. All I wish to know is, is this a Cabinet meeting, or is it not?"

The President said it was.

"Then," I said, "let us proceed to business at once, and not fritter away valuable time in unbecoming fault-findings with each other's official conduct."

The Secretary of State now spoke up, in his benignant way, and said, "Young man, you are laboring under a mistake. The clerks of the Congressional committees are not members of the Cabinet. Neither are the doorkeepers of the Capitol, strange as it may seem. Therefore, much as we could desire your more than human wisdom in our deliberations, we cannot lawfully avail ourselves of it. The counsels of the nation must proceed without you; if disaster follows, as follow full well it may, be it balm to your sorrowing spirit, that by deed and voice you did what in you lay to avert it. You have my blessing. Farewell."

These gentle words soothed my troubled breast, and I went away. But the servants of a nation can know no peace. I had hardly reached my den in the capitol, and disposed my feet on the table like a representative, when one of the Senators on the Conchological Committee came in in a passion and said—

"Where have you been all day?"

I observed that, if that was anybody's affair but my own, I had been to a Cabinet meeting.

"To a Cabinet meeting? I would like to know what business you had at a Cabinet meeting?"

I said I went there to consult—allowing for the sake of argument, that he was in anywise concerned in the matter. He grew insolent then, and ended by saying he had wanted me for three days past to copy a report on bomb-shells, egg-shells, clam-shells, and I don't know what all, connected with conchology, and nobody had been able to find me.

This was too much. This was the feather that broke the clerical camel's back. I said, "Sir, do you suppose that I am going to *work* for six dollars a day? If that is the idea, let me recommend the Senate Committee on Conchology to hire somebody else. I am the slave of *no* faction! Take back your degrading commission. Give me liberty, or give me death!"

From that hour I was no longer connected with the Government. Snubbed by the department, snubbed by the Cabinet, snubbed at last by the chairman of the committee I was endeavoring to adorn, I yielded to persecution, cast far from me the perils and seductions of my great office, and forsook my bleeding country in the hour of her peril.

But I had done the State some service, and I sent in my bill:—

The United States of America in account with the Hon. Clerk of the Senate Committee on Conchology, Dr.

To consultation with Secretary of War	$ 50
To consultation with Secretary of Navy	50
To consultation with Secretary of Treasury	50
Cabinet consultation . . . . No charge.	
To mileage to and from Jerusalem,* *via* Egypt, Algiers, Gibraltar, and Cadiz, 14,000 miles at 20c. a mile . . .	2800
To salary as Clerk of Senate Committee on Conchology, six days, at $6 per day	36
Total	$2986

Not an item of this bill has been paid, except that trifle of 36 dollars for clerkship salary. The Secretary of the Treasury, pur-

* Territorial delegates charge mileage both ways, although they never go back when they get here once. Why my mileage is denied me is more than I can understand.

suing me to the last, drew his pen through all the other items, and simply marked in the margin "Not allowed." So, the dread alternative is embraced at last. Repudiation has begun! The nation is lost.

I am done with official life for the present. Let those clerks who are willing to be imposed on remain. I know numbers of them, in the Departments, who are never informed when there is to be a Cabinet meeting, whose advice is never asked about war, or finance, or commerce, by the heads of the nation, any more than if they were not connected with Government, and who actually stay in their offices day after day and work! They know their importance to the nation, and they unconsciously show it in their bearing, and the way they order their sustenance at the restaurant—but they work. I know one who has to paste all sorts of little scraps from the newspaper into a scrap-book—sometimes as many as eight or ten scraps a day. He doesn't do it well, but he does it as well as he can. It is very fatiguing. It is exhausting to the intellect. Yet he only gets 1800 dollars a year. With a brain like his, that young man could amass thousands and thousands of dollars in some other pursuit, if he chose to do it. But no—his heart is with his country, and he will serve her as long as she has got a scrap-book left. And I know clerks that don't know how to write very well, but such knowledge as they possess they nobly lay at the feet of their country, and toil on and suffer for 2500 dollars a year. What they write has to be written over again by other clerks, sometimes; but when a man has done his best for his country, should his country complain? Then there are clerks that have no clerkships, and are waiting, and waiting, and waiting, for a vacancy—waiting patiently for a chance to help their country out—and while they are waiting, they only get barely, 2000 dollars a year for it. It is sad—it is very, very sad. When a member of Congress has a friend who is gifted, but has no employment wherein his great powers may be brought to bear, he confers him upon his country, and gives him a clerkship in a Department. And there that man has to slave his life out, fighting documents for the benefit of a nation that never thinks of him, never sympathizes with him—and all for 2000 or 3000 dollars a year. When I shall have completed my list of all the clerks in the several departments, with my statement of what they have to do, and what they get for it, you will see that there are not half enough clerks, and that what there are do not get half enough pay.

EUROPEAN GUIDES

But we have taken it out of this guide. He has marched us through miles of pictures and sculpture in the vast corridors of the Vatican; and through miles of pictures and sculpture in twenty other palaces; he has shown us the great picture in the Sistine Chapel, and frescoes enough to fresco the heavens—pretty much all done by Michael Angelo. So with him we have played that game which has vanquished so many guides for us—imbecility and idiotic questions. These creatures never suspect—they have no idea of a sarcasm.

He shows us a figure and says: "Statoo brunzo." (Bronze statue.)

We look at it indifferently and the doctor asks: "By Michael Angelo?"

"No—not know who."

Then he shows us the ancient Roman Forum. The doctor asks: "Michael Angelo?"

A stare from the guide. "No—a thousan' year before he is born."

Then an Egyptian obelisk. Again: "Michael Angelo?"

"Oh, *mon dieu*, genteelmen! Zis is *two* thousan' year before he is born!"

He grows so tired of that unceasing question sometimes, that he dreads to show us any thing at all. The wretch has tried all the ways he can think of to make us comprehend that Michael Angelo is only responsible for the creation of a *part* of the world, but somehow he has not succeeded yet. Relief for overtasked eyes and brain from study and sight-seeing is necessary, or we shall become idiotic sure enough. Therefore this guide must continue to suffer. If he does not enjoy it, so much the worse for him. We do.

In this place I may as well jot down a chapter concerning those necessary nuisances, European guides. Many a man has wished in his heart he could do without his guide; but knowing he could not, has wished he could get some amusement out of him as a remuneration for the affliction of his society. We accomplished this latter matter, and if our experience can be made useful to others they are welcome to it.

Guides know about enough English to tangle everything up

so that a man can make neither head nor tail of it. They know their story by heart—the history of every statue, painting, cathedral, or other wonder they show you. They know it and tell it as a parrot would—and if you interrupt, and throw them off the track, they have to go back and begin over again. All their lives long, they are employed in showing strange things to foreigners and listening to their bursts of admiration. It is human nature to take delight in exciting admiration. It is what prompts children to say "smart" things, and do absurd ones, and in other ways "show off" when company is present. It is what makes gossips turn out in rain and storm to go and be the first to tell a startling bit of news. Think, then, what a passion it becomes with a guide, whose privilege it is, every day, to show to strangers wonders that throw them into perfect ecstasies of admiration! He gets so that he could not by any possibility live in a soberer atmosphere. After we discovered this, we *never* went into ecstasies any more— we never admired anything—we never showed any but impassible faces and stupid indifference in the presence of the sublimest wonders a guide had to display. We had found their weak point. We have made good use of it ever since. We have made some of those people savage, at times, but we have never lost our own serenity.

The doctor asks the questions, generally, because he can keep his countenance, and look more like an inspired idiot, and throw more imbecility into the tone of his voice than any man that lives. It comes natural to him.

The guides in Genoa are delighted to secure an American party, because Americans so much wonder, and deal so much in sentiment and emotion before any relic of Columbus. Our guide there fidgeted about as if he had swallowed a spring mattress. He was full of animation—full of impatience. He said:

"Come wis me, genteelmen!—come! I show you ze letter writing by Christopher Colombo!—write it himself!—write it wis his own hand!—come!"

He took us to the municipal palace. After much impressive fumbling of keys and opening of locks, the stained and aged document was spread before us. The guide's eyes sparkled. He danced about us and tapped the parchment with his finger:

"What I tell you, genteelmen! Is it not so? See! handwriting Christopher Colombo!—write it himself!"

We looked indifferent—unconcerned. The doctor examined

the document very deliberately, during a painful pause. Then he said, without any show of interest:

"Ah—Furguson—what—what did you say was the name of the party who wrote this?"

"Christopher Colombo! ze great Christopher Colombo!"

Another deliberate examination.

"Ah—did he write it himself, or—or how?"

"He write it himself!—Christopher Colombo! he's own handwriting, write by himself!"

Then the doctor laid the document down and said:

"Why, I have seen boys in America only fourteen years old that could write better than that."

"But zis is ze great Christo—"

"I don't care who it is! It's the worst writing I ever saw. Now you musn't think you can impose on us because we are strangers. We are not fools, by a good deal. If you have got any specimens of penmanship of real merit, trot them out!—and if you haven't, drive on!"

We drove on. The guide was considerably shaken up, but he made one more venture. He had something which he thought would overcome us. He said:

"Ah, genteelmen, you come wis me! I show you beautiful, O, magnificent bust Christopher Colombo!—splendid, grand, magnificent!"

He brought us before the beautiful bust—for it *was* beautiful —and sprang back and struck an attitude:

"Ah, look, genteelmen!—beautiful, grand,—bust Christopher Colombo!—beautiful bust, beautiful pedestal!"

The doctor put up his eyeglass—procured for such occasions:

"Ah—what did you say this gentleman's name was?"

"Christopher Colombo!—ze great Christopher Colombo!"

"Christopher Colombo! ze great Christopher Colombo!" Well, what did *he* do?"

"Discover America!—discover America, oh, ze devil!"

"Discover America. No—that statement will hardly wash. We are just from America ourselves. We heard nothing about it. Christopher Colombo—pleasant name—is—is he dead?"

"Oh, corpo di Baccho!—three hundred year!"

"What did he die of?"

"I do not know!—I cannot tell."

"Smallpox, think?"

"I do not know, genteelmen!—I do not know *what* he die of!"

"Measles, likely?"

"May be—may be—I do *not* know—I think he die of some-things."

"Parents living?"

"Im-posseeble!"

"Ah—which is the bust and which is the pedestal?"

"Santa Maria!—*zis* ze bust!—*zis* ze pedestal!"

"Ah, I see, I see—happy combination—very happy combina-tion, indeed. Is—is this the first time this gentleman was ever on a bust?"

That joke was lost on the foreigner—guides cannot master the subtleties of the American joke.

We have made it interesting for this Roman guide. Yesterday we spent three or four hours in the Vatican again, that wonderful world of curiosities. We came very near expressing interest, some-times—even admiration—it was very hard to keep from it. We succeeded though. Nobody else ever did, in the Vatican museums. The guide was bewildered—non-plussed. He walked his legs off, nearly, hunting up extraordinary things, and exhausted all his ingenuity on us, but it was a failure; we never showed any inter-est in any thing. He had reserved what he considered to be his greatest wonder till the last—a royal Egyptian mummy, the best-preserved in the world, perhaps. He took us there. He felt so sure, this time, that some of his old enthusiasm came back to him:

"See, genteelmen!—Mummy! Mummy!"

The eye-glass came up as calmly, as deliberately as ever.

"Ah,—Furguson—what did I understand you to say the gen-tleman's name was?"

"Name?—he got no name!—Mummy!—'Gyptian mummy!"

"Yes, yes. Born here?"

"No! '*Gyptian* mummy!"

"Ah, just so. Frenchman, I presume?"

"No!—*not* Frenchman, not Roman!—born in Egypta!"

"Born in Egypta. Never heard of Egypta before. Foreign lo-cality, likely. Mummy—mummy. How calm he is—how self-possessed. Is, ah—is he dead?"

"Oh, *sacré bleu*, been dead three thousan' year!"

The doctor turned on him savagely:

"Here, now, what do you mean by such conduct as this? Playing us for Chinamen because we are strangers and trying to learn! Trying to impose your vile second-hand carcasses on *us!* —thunder and lightning, I've a notion to—to—if you've got a nice *fresh* corpse, fetch him out!—or by George we'll brain you!"

We make it exceedingly interesting for this Frenchman. However, he has paid us back, partly, without knowing it. He came to the hotel this morning to ask if we were up, and he endeavored as well as he could to describe us, so that the landlord would know which persons he meant. He finished with the casual remark that we were lunatics. The observation was so innocent and so honest that it amounted to a very good thing for a guide to say.

There is one remark (already mentioned) which never yet has failed to disgust these guides. We use it always, when we can think of nothing else to say. After they have exhausted their enthusiasm pointing out to us and praising the beauties of some ancient bronze image or broken-legged statue, we look at it stupidly and in silence for five, ten, fifteen minutes—as long as we can hold out, in fact—and then ask:

"Is—is he dead?"

That conquers the serenest of them. It is not what they are looking for—especially a new guide. Our Roman Furguson is the most patient, unsuspecting, long-suffering subject we have had yet. We shall be sorry to part with him. We have enjoyed his society very much. We trust he has enjoyed ours, but we are harassed with doubts.

BAKER'S BLUE–JAY YARN

Animals talk to each other, of course. There can be no question about that; but I suppose there are very few people who can understand them. I never knew but one man who could. I knew he could, however, because he told me so himself. He was a middle-aged, simple-hearted miner who had lived in a lonely corner of California, among the woods and mountains, a good many years, and had studied the ways of his only neighbors, the beasts and the birds, until he believed he could accurately translate any remark which they made. This was Jim Baker. According to Jim Baker, some animals have only a limited education, and use only very simple words, and scarcely ever a comparison or a flowery figure; whereas, certain other animals have a large vocabulary, a fine command of language and a ready and fluent delivery; consequently these latter talk a great deal; they like it; they are conscious of their talent, and they enjoy "showing off." Baker said, that after long and careful observation, he had come to the conclusion that the blue-jays were the best talkers he had found among birds and beasts. Said he:—

"There's more *to* a blue-jay than any other creature. He has got more moods, and more different kinds of feelings than other creatures and mind you, whatever a blue-jay feels, he can put into language. And no mere commonplace language, either, but rattling, out-and-out book-talk—and bristling with metaphor, too—just bristling! And as for command of language—why *you* never see a blue-jay get stuck for a word. No man ever did. They just boil out of him! And another thing: I've noticed a good deal, and there's no bird, or cow, or anything that uses as good grammar as a blue-jay. You may say a cat uses good grammar. Well, a cat does—but you let a cat get excited, once; you let a cat get to pulling fur with another cat on a shed, nights, and you'll hear grammar that will give you the lockjaw. Ignorant people think it's the *noise* which fighting cats make that is so aggravating, but it ain't so; it's the sickening grammar they use. Now I've never heard a jay use bad grammar but very seldom; and when they do, they are as ashamed as a human; they shut right down and leave.

"You may call a jay a bird. Well, so he is, in a measure—

533

because he's got feathers on him, and don't belong to no church, perhaps; but otherwise he is just as much a human as you be. And I'll tell you for why. A jay's gifts, and instincts, and feelings, and interests, cover the whole ground. A jay hasn't got any more principle than a Congressman. A jay will lie, a jay will steal, a jay will deceive, a jay will betray; and four times out of five, a jay will go back on his solemnest promise. The sacredness of an obligation is a thing which you can't cram into no blue-jay's head. Now on top of all this, there's another thing: a jay can out-swear any gentleman in the mines. You think a cat can swear. Well, a cat can; but you give a blue-jay a subject that calls for his reserve powers, and where is your cat? Don't talk to *me*—I know too much about this thing. And there's yet another thing: in the one little particular of scolding—just good, clean, out-and-out scolding—a blue-jay can lay over anything, human or divine. Yes, sir, a jay is everything that a man is. A jay can cry, a jay can laugh, a jay can feel shame, a jay can reason and plan and dis-cuss, a jay likes gossip and scandal, a jay has got a sense of humor, a jay knows when he is an ass as well as you do—maybe better. If a jay ain't human, he better take in his sign, that's all. Now I'm going to tell you a perfectly true fact about some blue-jays.

* * *

"When I first begun to understand jay language correctly, there was a little incident happened here. Seven years ago, the last man in this region but me, moved away. There stands his house,—been empty ever since; a log house, with a plank roof—just one big room, and no more; no ceiling—nothing between the rafters and the floor. Well, one Sunday morning I was sitting out here in front of my cabin, with my cat, taking the sun, and looking at the blue hills, and listening to the leaves rustling so lonely in the trees, and thinking of the home away yonder in the States, that I hadn't heard from in thirteen years, when a jay lit on that house, with an acorn in his mouth, and says, 'Hello, I reckon I've struck something.' When he spoke, the acorn dropped out of his mouth and rolled down the roof, of course, but he didn't care; his mind was all on the thing he had struck. It was a knot-hole in the roof. He cocked his head to one side, shut one eye and put the other one to the hole, like a 'possum looking down a jug; then he glanced up with his bright eyes, gave a wink or two with his wings—which signifies gratification, you understand,—and says, 'It looks like a hole, it's located like a hole,—blamed if I don't believe it *is* a hole!'

"Then he cocked his head down and took another look; he glances up perfectly joyful, this time; winks his wings and his tail both, and says, 'O, no, this ain't no fat thing, I reckon! If I ain't in luck!—why it's a perfectly elegant hole!' So he flew down and got that acorn, and fetched it up and dropped it in, and was just tilting his head back, with the heavenliest smile on his face, when all of a sudden he was paralyzed into a listening attitude and that smile faded gradually out of his countenance like breath off'n a razor, and the queerest look of surprise took its place. Then he says, 'Why I didn't hear it fall!' He cocked his eye at the hole again, and took a long look; raised up and shook his head; stepped around to the other side of the hole and took another look from that side; shook his head again. He studied a while, then he just went into the *de*tails—walked round and round the hole and spied into it from every point of the compass. No use. Now he took a thinking attitude on the comb of the roof and scratched the back of his head with his right foot a minute, and finally says, 'Well, it's too many for *me*, that's certain; must be a mighty long hole; however, I ain't got no time to fool around here, I got to 'tend to business; I reckon it's all right—chance it, anyway.'

"So he flew off and fetched another acorn and dropped it in, and tried to flirt his eye to the hole quick enough to see what become of it, but he was too late. He held his eye there as much as a minute; then he raised up and sighed, and says, 'Consound it, I don't seem to understand this thing, no way; however, I'll tackle her again.' He fetched another acorn, and done his level best to see what become of it, but he couldn't. He says, 'Well, *I* never struck no such a hole as this, before; I'm of the opinion it's a totally new kind of a hole.' Then he begun to get mad. He held in for a spell, walking up and down the comb of the roof and shaking his head and muttering to himself; but his feelings got the upper hand of him, presently, and he broke loose and cussed himself black in the face. I never see a bird take on so about a little thing. When he got through he walks to the hole and looks in again for half a minute; then he says, 'Well, you're a long hole, and a deep hole, and a mighty singular hole altogether—but I've started in to fill you, and I'm d——d if I don't fill you, if it takes a hundred years!'

"And with that, away he went. You never see a bird work so

since you was born. He laid into his work like a nigger, and the way he hove acorns into that hole for about two hours and a half was one of the most exciting and astonishing spectacles I ever struck. He never stopped to take a look any more—he just hove 'em in and went for more. Well at last he could hardly flop his wings, he was so tuckered out. He comes a-drooping down, once more, sweating like an ice-pitcher, drops his acorn in and says, '*Now* I guess I've got the bulge on you by this time!' So he bent down for a look. If you'll believe me, when his head come up again he was just pale with rage. He says, 'I've shoveled acorns enough in there to keep the family thirty years, and if I can see a sign of one of 'em I wish I may land in a museum with a belly full of sawdust in two minutes!'

"He just had strength enough to crawl up on to the comb and lean his back agin the chimbly, and then he collected his impressions and begun to free his mind. I see in a second that what I had mistook for profanity in the mines was only just the rudiments, as you may say.

"Another jay was going by, and heard him doing his devotions, and stops to inquire what was up. The sufferer told him the whole circumstance, and says, 'Now yonder's the hole, and if you don't believe me, go and look for yourself.' So this fellow went and looked, and comes back and says, 'How many did you say you put in there?' 'Not any less than two tons,' says the sufferer. The other jay went and looked again. He couldn't seem to make it out, so he raised a yell, and three more jays come. They all examined the hole, they all made the sufferer tell it over again, then they all discussed it, and got off as many leather-headed opinions about it as an average crowd of humans could have done.

"They called in more jays; then more and more, till pretty soon this whole region 'peared to have a blue flush about it. There must have been five thousand of them; and such another jawing and disputing and ripping and cussing, you never heard. Every jay in the whole lot put his eye to the hole and delivered a more chuckle-headed opinion about the mystery than the jay that went there before him. They examined the house all over, too. The door was standing half open, and at last one old jay happened to go and light on it and look in. Of course that knocked the mystery galley-west in a second. There lay the acorns, scattered all over the floor. He flopped his wings and raised a whoop. 'Come here!' he says, 'Come here, everybody; hang'd if this fool hasn't been trying to fill up a house with acorns!' They all came a-swooping down like a blue cloud, and as each fellow lit on the door and took a glance, the whole absurdity of the contract that that first jay had tackled hit him home and he fell over backwards suffocating with laughter, and the next jay took his place and done the same.

"Well, sir, they roosted around here on the house-top and the trees for an hour, and guffawed over that thing like human beings. It ain't any use to tell me a blue-jay hasn't got a sense of humor, because I know better. And memory, too. They brought jays here from all over the United States to look down that hole, every summer for three years. Other birds too. And they could all see the point, except an owl that come from Nova Scotia to visit the Yo Semite, and he took this thing in on his way back. He said he couldn't see anything funny in it. But then he was a good deal disappointed about Yo Semite, too."

[HUCK'S VISIT TO THE RAFT][1]

By way of illustrating keelboat talk and manners, and that now departed and hardly-remembered raft-life, I will throw in, in this place, a chapter from a book which I have been working at, by fits and starts, during the past five or six years, and may possibly finish in the course of five or six more. The book is a story which details some passages in the life of an ignorant village boy, Huck Finn, son of the town drunkard of my time out West, there. He has run away from his persecuting father, and from a persecuting good widow who wishes to make a nice, truth-telling, respectable boy of him; and with him a slave of the widow's has also escaped. They have found a fragment of a lumber-raft (it is high water and dead summer-time), and are floating down the river by night, and hiding in the willows by day—bound for Cairo, whence the negro will seek freedom in the heart of the free states. But, in a fog, they pass Cairo without knowing it. By and by they begin to suspect the truth, and Huck Finn is persuaded to end the dismal suspense by swimming down to a huge raft which they have seen in the distance ahead of them, creeping aboard under cover of the darkness, and gathering the needed information by eavesdropping:

But you know a young person can't wait very well when he is impatient to find a thing out. We talked it over, and by and by Jim said it was such a black night, now, that it wouldn't be no risk to swim down to the big raft and crawl aboard and listen— they would talk about Cairo, because they would be calculating to go ashore there for a spree, maybe; or anyway they would send boats ashore to buy whisky or fresh meat or something. Jim had a wonderful level head, for a nigger: he could most always start a good plan when you wanted one.

I stood up and shook my rags off and jumped into the river, and struck out for the raft's light. By and by, when I got down nearly to her, I eased up and went slow and cautious. But everything was all right—nobody at the sweeps. So I swum down along the raft till I was most abreast the camp-fire in the middle, then I crawled aboard and inched along and got in among some bun-

[1] From *Life on the Mississippi* by Mark Twain. Reprinted by permission of the publisher, Harper and Brothers, New York.

dles of shingles on the weather side of the fire. There was thirteen men there—they was the watch on deck of course. And a mighty rough-looking lot, too. They had a jug, and tin cups, and they kept the jug moving. One man was singing—roaring, you may say; and it wasn't a nice song—for a parlor, anyway. He roared through his nose, and strung out the last word of every line very long. When he was done they all fetched a kind of Injun war-whoop, and then another was sung. It begun:

> "There was a woman in our towdn,
> In our towdn did dwed'l [dwell],
> She loved her husband dear-i-lee,
> But another man twyste as wed'l.
>
> "Singing too, riloo, riloo, riloo,
> Ri-too, riloo, rilay - - - e,
> She loved her husband dear-i-lee,
> But another man twyste as wed'l."

And so on—fourteen verses. It was kind of poor, and when he was going to start on the next verse one of them said it was the tune the old cow died on; and another one said: "Oh, give us a rest!" And another one told him to take a walk. They made fun of him till he got mad and jumped up and begun to cuss the crowd, and said he could lam any thief in the lot.

They was all about to make a break for him, but the biggest man there jumped up and says:

"Set whar you are, gentlemen. Leave him to me; he's my meat."

Then he jumped up in the air three times, and cracked his heels together every time. He flung off a buckskin coat that was all hung with fringes, and says, "You lay thar tell the chawin-up's done"; and flung his hat down, which was all over ribbons, and says, "You lay thar tell his sufferin's is over."

Then he jumped up in the air and cracked his heels together again, and shouted out:

"Whoo-oop! I'm the old original iron-jawed, brass-mounted, copper-bellied corpse-maker from the wilds of Arkansaw! Look at me! I'm the man they call Sudden Death and General Desolation! Sired by a hurricane, dam'd by an earthquake, half-brother to the cholera, nearly related to the smallpox on the mother's side! Look at me! I take nineteen alligators and a bar'l of whisky for breakfast when I'm in robust health, and a bushel of rattlesnakes and a dead body when I'm ailing. I split the everlasting rocks with my glance, and I squench the thunder when I speak! Whoo-oop! Stand back and give me room according to my strength! Blood's my natural drink, and the wails of the dying is music to my ear. Cast your eye on me, gentlemen! and lay low and hold your breath, for I'm 'bout to turn myself loose!"

All the time he was getting this off, he was shaking his head and looking fierce, and kind of swelling around in a little circle, tucking up his wristbands, and now and then straightening up and beating his breast with his fist, saying, "Look at me, gentlemen!" When he got through, he jumped up and cracked his heels together three times, and let off a roaring "Whoo-oop! I'm the bloodiest son of a wildcat that lives!"

Then the man that had started the row tilted his old slouch hat down over his right eye; then he bent stooping forward, with his back sagged and his south end sticking out far, and his fists a-shoving out and drawing in in front of him, and so went around in a little circle about three times, swelling himself up and breathing hard. Then he straightened, and jumped up and cracked his heels together three times before he lit again (that made them cheer), and he began to shout like this:

"Whoo-oop! bow your neck and spread, for the kingdom of sorrow's a-coming! Hold me down to the earth, for I feel my powers a-working! whoo-oop! I'm a child of sin, *don't* let me get a start! Smoked glass, here, for all! Don't attempt to look at me with the naked eye, gentlemen! When I'm playful I use the meridians of longitude and parallels of latitude for a seine, and drag the Atlantic Ocean for whales! I scratch my head with the lightning and purr myself to sleep with the thunder! When I'm cold, I bile the Gulf of Mexico and bathe in it; when I'm hot I fan myself with an equinoctial storm; when I'm thirsty I reach up and suck a cloud dry like a sponge; when I range the earth hungry, famine follows in my tracks! Whoo-oop! Bow your neck and spread! I put my hand on the sun's face and make it night in the earth; I bite a piece out of the moon and hurry the seasons; I shake myself and crumble the mountains! Contemplate me through leather—*don't* use the naked eye! I'm the man with a petrified heart and biler-iron bowels! The massacre of isolated communities is the pastime of my idle moments, the destruction of nationalities the serious business of my life! The boundless vastness of the great American desert is my enclosed property, and I bury my dead on my own premises!" He jumped up and cracked his heels together three times before he lit (they cheered him again), and as he come down he shouted out: "Whoo-oop! bow your neck and spread, for the Pet Child of Calamity's a-coming!"

Then the other one went to swelling around and blowing again—the first one—the one they called Bob; next, the Child of Calamity chipped in again, bigger than ever; then they both got at it at the same time, swelling round and round each other and punching their fists most into each other's faces, and whooping and jawing like Injuns; then Bob called the Child names, and the Child called him names back again; next, Bob called him a heap rougher names, and the Child come back at him with the very worst kind of language; next, Bob knocked the Child's hat off, and the Child picked it up and kicked Bob's ribbony hat about six foot; Bob went and got it and said never mind, this warn't going to be the last of this thing, because he was a man that never forgot and never forgive, and so the Child better look out, for there was a time a-coming, just as sure as he was a living man, that he would have to answer to him with the best blood in his body. The Child said no man was willinger than he for that time to come, and he would give Bob fair warning, *now*, never to cross his path again, for he could never rest till he had waded in his blood, for such was his nature, though he was sparing him now on account of his family, if he had one.

Both of them was edging away in different directions, growling and shaking their heads and going on about what they was going to do; but a little black-whiskered chap skipped up and says:

"Come back here, you couple of chicken-livered cowards, and I'll thrash the two of ye!"

And he done it, too. He snatched them, he jerked them this way and that, he booted them around, he knocked them sprawling faster than they could get up. Why, it warn't two minutes till they begged like dogs—and how the other lot did yell and laugh and clap their hands all the way through, and shout, "Sail in, Corpse-Maker!" "Hi! at him again, Child of Calamity!" "Bully for you, little Davy!" Well, it was a perfect pow-wow for a while. Bob and the Child had red noses and black eyes when they got through. Little Davy made them own up that they was sneaks and cowards and not fit to eat with a dog or drink with a nigger; then Bob and the Child shook hands with each other, very solemn, and said they had always respected each other and was willing to let bygones be bygones. So then they washed their faces in the river; and just then there was a loud order to stand by for a crossing, and some of them went forward to man the sweeps there, and the rest went aft to handle the after sweeps.

I lay still and waited for fifteen minutes, and had a smoke out of a pipe that one of them left in reach; then the crossing was finished, and they stumped back and had a drink around and went to talking and singing again. Next they got out an old fiddle, and one played, and another patted juba, and the rest turned themselves loose on a regular old-fashioned keelboat breakdown. They couldn't keep that up very long without getting winded, so by and by they settled around the jug again.

They sung "Jolly, Jolly Raftsman's the Life for Me," with a rousing chorus, and then they got to talking about differences betwixt hogs, and their different kind of habits; and next about women and their different ways; and next about the best ways to put out houses that was afire; and next about what ought to be done with the Injuns; and next about what a king had to do, and how much he got; and next about how to make cats fight; and next about what to do when a man has fits; and next about differences betwixt clear-water rivers and muddy-water ones. The man they called Ed said the muddy Mississippi water was wholesomer to drink than the clear water of the Ohio; he said if you let a pint of this yaller Mississippi water settle, you would have about a half to three-quarters of an inch of mud in the bottom, according to the stage of the river, and then it warn't no better than Ohio water—what you wanted to do was to keep it stirred up—and when the river was low, keep mud on hand to put in and thicken the water up the way it ought to be.

The Child of Calamity said that was so; he said there was nutritiousness in the mud, and a man that drunk Mississippi water could grow corn in his stomach if he wanted to. He says:

"You look at the graveyards; that tells the tale. Trees won't grow worth shucks in a Cincinnati graveyard, but in a Sent Louis graveyard they grow upwards of eight hundred foot high. It's all on account of the water the people drunk before they laid up. A Cincinnati corpse don't richen a soil any."

And they talked about how Ohio water didn't like to mix with Mississippi water. Ed said if you take the Mississippi on a rise when the Ohio is low, you'll find a wide band of clear water all the way down the east side of the Mississippi for a hundred mile or more, and the minute you get out a quarter of a mile from shore and pass the line, it is all thick and yaller the rest of the way across. Then they talked about how to keep tobacco from getting mouldy, and from that they went into ghosts and told about a lot that other folks had seen; but Ed says:

"Why don't you tell something that you've seen yourselves? Now let me have a say. Five years ago I was on a raft as big as this, and right along here it was a bright moonshiny night, and I was on watch and boss of the stabboard oar forrard, and one of my pards was a man named Dick Allbright, and he come along to where I was sitting, forrard—gaping and stretching, he was— and stooped down on the edge of the raft and washed his face in the river, and come and set down by me and got out his pipe, and had just got it filled, when he looks up and says:

"'Why looky-here,' he says, 'ain't that Buck Miller's place, over yander in the bend?'

"'Yes,' says I, 'it is—why?' He laid his pipe down and leaned his head on his hand, and says:

"'I thought we'd be furder down.' I says:

"'I thought it, too, when I went off watch'—we was standing six hours on and six off—'but the boys told me,' I says, 'that the raft didn't seem to hardly move, for the last hour,' says I, 'though she's a-slipping along all right now,' says I. He give a kind of a groan, and says:

"'I've seed a raft act so before, along here,' he says, ''pears to me the current has most quit above the head of this bend durin' the last two years,' he says.

"Well, he raised up two or three times, and looked away off and around on the water. That started me at it, too. A body is always doing what he sees somebody else doing, though there mayn't be no sense in it. Pretty soon I see a black something floating on the water away off to stabboard and quartering behind us. I see he was looking at it, too. I says:

"'What's that?' He says, sort of pettish:

"''Tain't nothing but an old empty bar'l.'

"'An empty bar'l!' says I, 'why,' says I, 'a spy-glass is a fool to *your* eyes. How can you tell it's an empty bar'l?' He says:

"'I don't know; I reckon it ain't a bar'l, but I thought it might be,' says he.

"'Yes,' I says, 'so it might be, and it might be anything else, too; a body can't tell nothing about it, such a distance as that,' I says.

"We hadn't nothing else to do, so we kept on watching it. By and by I says:

"'Why, looky-here, Dick Allbright, that thing's a-gaining on us, I believe.'

"He never said nothing. The thing gained and gained, and I judged it must be a dog that was about tired out. Well, we swung down into the crossing, and the thing floated across the bright streak of the moonshine, and by George, it *was* a bar'l, Says I:

"'Dick Allbright, what made you think that thing was a bar'l, when it was half a mile off?' says I. Says he:

"'I don't know.' Says I:

"'You tell me, Dick Allbright.' Says he:

"'Well, I knowed it was a bar'l; I've seen it before; lots has seen it; they says it's a ha'nted bar'l.'

"I called the rest of the watch, and they come and stood there, and I told them what Dick said. It floated right along abreast, now, and didn't gain any more. It was about twenty foot off. Some was for having it aboard, but the rest didn't want to. Dick Allbright said rafts that had fooled with it had got bad luck by it. The captain of the watch said he didn't believe in it. He said he reckoned the bar'l gained on us because it was in a little better current than what we was. He said it would leave by and by.

"So then we went to talking about other things, and we had a song, and then a breakdown; and after that the captain of the watch called for another song; but it was clouding up now, and the bar'l stuck right thar in the same place, and the song didn't seem to have much warm-up to it, somehow, and so they didn't finish it, and there warn't any cheers, but it sort of dropped flat, and nobody said anything for a minute. Then everybody tried to talk at once, and one chap got off a joke, but it warn't no use, they didn't laugh, and even the chap that made the joke didn't laugh at it, which ain't usual. We all just settled down glum, and watched the bar'l, and was oneasy and oncomfortable. Well, sir, it shut down black and still, and then the wind began to moan around, and next the lightning began to play and the thunder to grumble. And pretty soon there was a regular storm, and in the middle of it a man that was running aft stumbled

and fell and sprained his ankle so that he had to lay up. This
made the boys shake their heads. And every time the lightning
come, there was that bar'l, with the blue lights winking around
it. We was always on the lookout for it. But by and by, toward
dawn, she was gone. When the day come we couldn't see her anywhere, and we warn't sorry, either.

"But next night about half past nine, when there was songs
and high jinks going on, here she comes again, and took her old
roost on the stabboard side. There warn't no more high jinks.
Everybody got solemn; nobody talked; you couldn't get anybody
to do anything but set around moody and look at the bar'l. It
begun to cloud up again. When the watch changed, the off watch
stayed up, 'stead of turning in. The storm ripped and roared
around all night, and in the middle of it another man tripped and
sprained his ankle, and had to knock off. The bar'l left toward day,
and nobody see it go.

"Everybody was sober and down in the mouth all day. I
don't mean the kind of sober that comes of leaving liquor alone
—not that. They was quiet, but they all drunk more than usual
—not together, but each man sidled off and took it private, by
himself.

"After dark the off watch didn't turn in; nobody sung, nobody
talked; the boys didn't scatter around, neither; they sort of
huddled together, forrard; and for two hours they set there,
perfectly still, looking steady in the one direction, and heaving a
sigh once in a while. And then, here comes the bar'l again. She
took up her old place. She stayed there all night; nobody turned
in. The storm come on again, after midnight. It got awful dark;
the rain poured down; hail, too; the thunder boomed and roared
and bellowed; the wind blowed a hurricane; and the lightning
spread over everything in big sheets of glare, and showed the
whole raft as plain as day; and the river lashed up white as milk
as far as you could see for miles, and there was that bar'l jiggering
along, same as ever. The captain ordered the watch to man the
after sweeps for a crossing, and nobody would go—no more
sprained ankles for them, they said. They wouldn't even *walk* aft.
Well, then, just then the sky split wide open, with a crash, and the
lightning killed two men of the after watch, and crippled two
more. Crippled them how, say you? Why, *sprained their ankles!*

"The bar'l left in the dark betwixt lightnings, toward dawn.
Well, not a body eat a bite at breakfast that morning. After that

the men loafed around, in twos and threes, and talked low together. But none of them herded with Dick Allbright. They all
give him the cold shake. If he come around where any of the men
was, they split up and sidled away. They wouldn't man the
sweeps with him. The captain had all the skiffs hauled up on the
raft, alongside of his wigwam, and wouldn't let the dead men be
took ashore to be planted; he didn't believe a man that got ashore
would come back; and he was right.

"After night come, you could see pretty plain that there was
going to be trouble if that bar'l come again; there was such a
muttering going on. A good many wanted to kill Dick Allbright,
because he'd seen the bar'l on other trips, and that had an ugly
look. Some wanted to put him ashore. Some said: 'Let's all go
ashore in a pile, if the bar'l comes again.'

"This kind of whispers was still going on, the men being
bunched together forrard watching for the bar'l, when lo and
behold you! here she comes again. Down she comes, slow and
steady, and settles into her old tracks. You could 'a' heard a pin
drop. Then up comes the captain, and says:

"'Boys, don't be a pack of children and fools; I don't want
this bar'l to be dogging us all the way to Orleans, and *you* don't:
Well, then, how's the best way to stop it? Burn it up—that's the
way. I'm going to fetch it aboard,' he says. And before anybody
could say a word, in he went.

"He swum to it, and as he come pushing it to the raft, the men
spread to one side. But the old man got it aboard and busted in
the head, and there was a baby in it! Yes, sir; a stark-naked baby.
It was Dick Allbright's baby; he owned up and said so.

"'Yes,' he says, a-leaning over it, 'yes, it is my own lamented
darling, my poor lost Charles William Allbright deceased,' says
he—for he could curl his tongue around the bulliest words in
the language when he was a mind to, and lay them before you
without a jint started anywheres. Yes, he said, he used to live up
at the head of this bend, and one night he choked his child,
which was crying, not intending to kill it—which was prob'ly
a lie—and then he was scared, and buried it in a bar'l, before his
wife got home, and off he went, and struck the northern trail
and went to rafting; and this was the third year that the bar'l
had chased him. He said the bad luck always begun light, and
lasted till four men was killed, and then the bar'l didn't come any
more after that. He said if the men would stand it one more

night—and was a-going on like that—but the men had got enough. They started to get out a boat to take him ashore and lynch him, but he grabbed the little child all of a sudden and jumped overboard with it, hugged up to his breast and shedding tears, and we never see him again in this life, poor old suffering soul, nor Charles William neither."

"*Who* was shedding tears?" says Bob; "was it Allbright or the baby?"

"Why, Allbright, of course; didn't I tell you the baby was dead? Been dead three years—how could it cry?"

"Well, never mind how it could cry—how could it *keep* all that time?" says Davy. "You answer me that."

"I don't know how it done it," says Ed. "It done it, though —that's all I know about it."

"Say—what did they do with the bar'l?" says the Child of Calamity.

"Why, they hove it overboard, and it sunk like a chunk of lead."

"Edward, did the child look like it was choked?" says one.

"Did it have its hair parted?" says another.

"What was the brand on that bar'l, Eddy?" says a fellow they called Bill.

"Have you got the papers for them statistics, Edmund?" says Jimmy.

"Say, Edwin, was you one of the men that was killed by the lightning?" says Davy.

"Him? Oh, no! he was both of 'em," says Bob. Then they all haw-hawed.

"Say, Edward, don't you reckon you'd better take a pill? You look bad—don't you feel pale?" says the Child of Calamity.

"Oh, come, now, Eddy," says Jimmy, "show up; you must 'a' kept part of that bar'l to prove the thing by. Show us the bung-hole—*do*—and we'll all believe you."

"Say, boys," says Bill, "less divide it up. Thar's thirteen of us. I can swaller a thirteenth of the yarn, if you can worry down the rest."

Ed got up mad and said they could all go to some place which he ripped out pretty savage, and then walked off aft, cussing to himself, and they yelling and jeering at him, and roaring and laughing so you could hear them a mile.

"Boys, we'll split a watermelon on that," says the Child of

Calamity; and he came rummaging around in the dark amongst the shingle bundles where I was, and put his hand on me. I was warm and soft and naked; so he says "Ouch!" and jumped back.

"Fetch a lantern or a chunk of fire here, boys—there's a snake here as big as a cow!"

So they run there with a lantern, and crowded up and looked in on me.

"Come out of that, you beggar!" says one.

"Who are you?" says another.

"What are you after here? Speak up prompt, or overboard you go."

"Snake him out, boys. Snatch him out by the heels."

I began to beg, and crept out amongst them trembling. They looked me over, wondering, and the Child of Calamity says:

"A cussed thief! Lend a hand and less heave him overboard!"

"No," says Big Bob, "less get out the paint-pot and paint him a sky-blue all over from head to heel, and *then* heave him over."

"Good! that's it. Go for the paint, Jimmy."

When the paint come, and Bob took the brush and was just going to begin, the others laughing and rubbing their hands, I begun to cry, and that sort of worked on Davy, and he says:

"'Vast there. He's nothing but a cub. I'll paint the man that teches him!"

So I looked around on them, and some of them grumbled and growled, and Bob put down the paint, and the others didn't take it up.

"Come here to the fire, and less see what you're up to here," says Davy. "Now set down there and give an account of yourself. How long have you been aboard here?"

"Not over a quarter of a minute, sir," says I.

"How did you get dry so quick?"

"I don't know, sir. I'm always that way, mostly."

"Oh, you are, are you? What's your name?"

I warn't going to tell my name. I didn't know what to say, so I just says:

"Charles William Allbright, sir."

Then they roared—the whole crowd; and I was mighty glad I said that, because, maybe, laughing would get them in a better humor.

When they got done laughing, Davy says:

"It won't hardly do, Charles William. You couldn't have

growed this much in five year, and you was a baby when you come out of the bar'l, you know, and dead at that. Come, now, tell a straight story, and nobody'll hurt you, if you ain't up to anything wrong. What *is* your name?"

"Aleck Hopkins, sir. Aleck James Hopkins."

"Well, Aleck, where did you come from, here?"

"From a trading-scow. She lays up the bend yonder. I was born on her. Pap has traded up and down here all his life; and he told me to swim off here, because when you went by he said he would like to get some of you to speak to a Mr. Jonas Turner, in Cairo, and tell him—"

"Oh, come!"

"Yes, sir, it's as true as the world. Pap he says—"

"Oh, your grandmother!"

They all laughed, and I tried again to talk, but they broke in on me and stopped me.

"Now, looky-here," says Davy; "you're scared, and so you talk wild. Honest, now, do you live in a scow, or is it a lie?"

"Yes, sir, in a trading-scow. She lays up at the head of the bend. But I warn't born in her. It's our first trip."

"Now you're talking! What did you come aboard here for? To steal?"

"No, sir, I didn't. It was only to get a ride on the raft. All boys does that."

"Well, I know that. But what did you hide for?"

"Sometimes they drive the boys off."

"So they do. They might steal. Looky-here; if we let you off this time, will you keep out of these kind of scrapes hereafter?"

"'Deed I will, boss. You try me."

"All right, then. You ain't but little ways from shore. Overboard with you, and don't you make a fool of yourself another time this way. Blast it, boy, some raftsmen would rawhide you till you were black and blue!"

I didn't wait to kiss good-by, but went overboard and broke for shore. When Jim come along by and by, the big raft was away out of sight around the point. I swum out and got aboard, and was mighty glad to see home again.

The boy did not get the information he was after, but his adventure has furnished the glimpse of the departed raftsman and keelboatman which I desire to offer in this place.

NOTES

The number following each title below indicates the page on which the selection begins.

DOWN EAST HUMOR

THE HUMOR OF *The Farmer's Almanac* (199)

The passages are by Robert Thomas, editor of *The Farmer's Almanac*, or his correspondents. "Amusing," in the 1809 *Almanac*, is the Yankee tall tale which, in two changed versions, later appeared in *The Spirit of the Times* (see p. 84). "My Neighbor Freeport," from the 1813 issue, shows how Thomas, in his allegorical writing, advanced comic native portraiture. The other sketches, "Old Betty Blab," "The Scrape," and "The Baker," appeared, respectively, in issues for 1817, 1836, and 1837.

JACK DOWNING'S LETTERS AND OTHER DOCKYMENTS (203)

"Jack's Grandfather" is part of Jack's autobiography, which appeared as the introduction to *The Life and Writings of Major Jack Downing* (1834), from which this version is taken. Later, minor changes, most of them for the worse, were made in this passage. This is an early example of the framework structure of narrative later very useful to various humorists. The first two letters had their first book publication in this same volume; the third appeared in a somewhat different form in *John Smith's Letters* (1839), and the fourth was first printed, in the pages of a book, in *My Thirty Years Out of the Senate* (1859). All were originally written for newspapers or magazines. The texts of letters used here are from the 1859 volume. "How They Drafted the Militia Company in Downingville" was first composed after the letter from Cousin Nabby, which here precedes it.

THE SAYINGS OF SAM SLICK (229)

"The Clockmaker," from Haliburton's *The Clockmaker* (1837) depicts the Yankee peddler of general tradition. The passage is highly reminiscent of a passage in James S. French, *The Sketches and Eccentricities of Colonel David Crockett* (1833), from which it may have been derived. "Natur'," from *The Attaché; or Sam Slick in England* (1843), displays an interesting theory of aesthetics and, in addition, shows Sam, by his own description, garbed alternately as a Yankee peddler and Western backwoodsman.

PASSAGES FROM *The Biglow Papers* (237)

"What Mr. Robinson Thinks," Number III of the First Series (1847), is presented complete, with the framework of Parson Wilbur's remarks. John P. Robinson, here celebrated, was a prominent Whig who, in 1847, deserted his party to support General Cushing. Cushing was the commander of the Massachusetts troops in Mexico and a Democratic candidate for governor. Parson Wilbur's prefatory remarks to Number V, "The Debate in the Sennit," are not included. The poem is Hosea's versification of a speech by Calhoun, with comments of other senators. "A Second Letter from B. Sawin," Number VIII of the same series, is Hosea's translation into verse of an epistle from Birdofredum Sawin, who reports on what the war did to him.

"The Courtin'" appeared in its complete form when the second series appeared (1866). Lowell's account of its writing was as follows: "While the introduction to the First Series was going through the press, I received word from the printer that there was a blank page left which must be filled. I sat down at once and improvised another fictitious 'notice of the press,' in which, because verse would fill up space more cheaply than prose, I inserted an extract from a supposed ballad of Mr. Biglow. I kept no copy of it, and the printer, as directed, cut it off when the gap was filled. Presently I began to receive letters asking for the rest of it . . . Afterward, being asked to write it out as an autograph for the Baltimore Sanitary Commission Fair, I added other ·verses . . . sketching in the characters and making a connected story."

MRS. PARTINGTON (258)

The passages are all from *Life and Sayings of Mrs. Partington* (1854). "The Biography" is merely a part of the introductory section of the book. The passages show the typical form of the Partington sketches. "The Cat and the Kittens" is referred to in the introduction to this volume.

WIDOW BEDOTT'S MONOLOGUES (271)

Both sketches are taken from *Widow Bedott Papers* (1855). The first of these was tremendously popular, appearing again and again in the newspapers and in anthologies of American humor. As late as the eighties, Widow Bedott was a popular figure on the American stage. The Rev. Mrs. Sniffles is the Widow Bedott following a second marriage, having acquired a husband after a long pursuit, filled with disappointments, of various potential candidates of her own selection.

THE HUMOR OF THE OLD SOUTHWEST

TALL TALK (281)

"Theatrical Performance" is reprinted from Lunenberg C. Abernathy's *Laughable Anecdotes* (Frankfort, 1832), a compilation of newspaper and almanac humor which not only contains this sample of frontier boasting but also contains the first printing I have found of the famous sketch, "Cousin Sally Dillard." The remarks here printed are ascribed to either Nimrod Wildfire or Davy Crockett in subsequent reprintings.

"Crockett's Coon Story" appeared in *Sketches and Eccentricities of Colonel David Crockett* (1833), probably written by James S. French. In other versions of the tale, other frontier heroes achieved the same end by grinning at a coon.

"Mike Fink Beats Davy Crockett at a Shooting Match," from *The Crockett Almanac* (1840), interestingly links two frontier heroes together. Probably this acquaintance is legendary. The speaker is supposed to be Davy Crockett. The concluding passage derives from the widespread literature portraying Southwesterners as prodigious drinkers.

"Sal Fink, the Mississippi Screamer," is from *The Crockett Almanac* for 1854. Sal is probably an entirely legendary creation, the daughter of Mike.

"Sunrise in His Pocket" is a tale told by Davy Crockett, one of the most poetic of the imaginative flights of almanac writers. It was discovered by Miss Constance Rourke in *The Crockett Almanac*. Mr. Max Eastman comments interestingly on the passage in his essay on American humor.

GEORGIA SCENES (287)

"Georgia Theatrics" and "The Fight" are both taken from *Georgia Scenes* (1835). The former story became useful as a political allegory and as such was recited in the halls of Congress and was repeated by the compiler of one of the Davy Crockett books. The latter is notable not only for its characterization but also for various naturalistic touches which carry the humor of physical discomfiture to extraordinary extremes. Ransy Sniffle is a well depicted biological and sociological phenomenon.

A TIGHT RACE CONSIDERIN' (299)

This sketch, by the unidentified author who signed himself "Madison Tensas," taking his pen name from two adjoining counties in

Louisiana, is from *Odd Leaves from the Life of a Louisiana Swamp Doctor* (Philadelphia, 1843). It offers an example of a moderately effective use of the framework structure. The comic literature about inefficient doctors in the Southwest was large, probably because these gentlemen were effective agents of physical discomfort.

SIMON SUGGS (308)

Both selections are from *Some Adventures of Captain Simon Suggs* (1845). The second provides an interesting parallel for the camp-meeting scene in *Huckleberry Finn*. See De Voto, *Mark Twain's America*, p. 255.

GEORGIA COMEDY (326)

"Major Jones Pops the Question" is from *Major Jones's Courtship* (1843). This version and the two mock oral tales which follow are taken from the 1872 edition. In 1937, an abbreviated version of "The Hoosier and the Salt Pile" won hearty laughter when presented by the comedian, Bob Burns, on a radio program broadcast nationally.

THE BIG BEAR OF ARKANSAS (337)

T. B. Thorpe's masterpiece appeared in *The Spirit of the Times* in 1841. It was later printed by Porter in his collection of humorous stories with the same title in 1845, and in Thorpe's *The Hive of the Bee-Hunter* (1854). It is one of the most famous as well as one of the finest of Southwestern tall tales. The shouts which precede the character's appearance are phrases of a frontier boast, and the passage on page 340, about the fear of the bears, is reminiscent of the stories of the way coons feared Davy Crockett.

THE STANDING CANDIDATE (349)

From *Streaks of Squatter Life* (1846), this sketch by Robb is typical of many in the literature of the Southwest which celebrated political gatherings and the speeches made there.

OVID BOLUS, ESQ. (356)

This is a characteristic essay from *Flush Times in Alabama and Mississippi* (1853).

COMIC HAPPENINGS IN TENNESSEE (368)

"The Knob Dance" appeared in *The Spirit of the Times*, XV, 267 (August, 1845) and was reprinted by Porter in his collection called *A Quarter Race in Kentucky* (1846). As the first sentence indicates, it was one of a series of tales in which authors vied with one another in *The Spirit*.

"Sicily Burns's Wedding" and "Rare Ripe Garden Seed" are from *Sut Lovingood's Yarns* (1867). The latter episode, in the book, continues for a few more pages to prepare the way for the next chapter. The "sody" (soda) mentioned on page 376 had been used by Sicily when she played a mean trick on Sut.

The Harp of a Thousand Strings (388)

This mock sermon, which circulated widely in the newspapers and comic journals in the fifties and sixties, has been attributed, on the basis of a newspaper article published in the Louisville *Courier-Journal* in 1881, to Henry Taliaferro Lewis. (See *Harp of a Thousand Strings with Waifs of Wit and Pathos* [(n.p.): 1907], pp. 19–20.) If he was the author, which I rather doubt, he showed little of the skill in his other writings. The piece was printed in *The Spirit of the Times* in 1855, having been picked up from a New Orleans exchange. It is the best representative of huge numbers of similar burlesques.

LITERARY COMEDIANS

Phoenixiana (393)

Both sketches are from *Phoenixiana* (1855). An introductory note which accompanied "Musical Review Extraordinary" when it appeared in *The Pioneer* in 1854 indicated that it was a burlesque on San Francisco musical criticisms. The passage is interesting for its introduction of "the Pike" into widely known humor. "Interview between the Editor and Phoenix" tells what happened to Phoenix when the editor, whose place the humorist had taken for a time, sought revenge for what had happened to his paper. It furnishes an excellent example of what Professor Leacock called "the humor of discomfiture written in the first person."

The Writings of Artemus Ward (400)

"One of Artemus Ward's Business Letters" and "Interview with President Lincoln" are from *Artemus Ward: His Book* (1862). "The Tower of London," from *Artemus Ward in London* (1867), was one of Browne's contributions to *Punch*. The version here used is the one which appeared in that magazine, differing slightly from the version published in the book. The other selections, "I am Here" and "A Romance—William Barker, the Young Patriot," are from *Artemus Ward: His Travels* (1865). The first three selections are written by the illiterate showman created by Browne; the other two are by an Artemus Ward who more nearly approaches the character and outlook of Browne. "I am Here," a part of Ward's account of his trip to California, Nevada, and Utah, contains an amusing story of the totally depraved Yankee bargainer of comic tradition. "A Romance" is representative of a number of burlesques written by Ward, representative, too, of a large body of similar passages in the works of the Literary Comedians. Fortunately, for purposes of comedy, if not of literature, the pattern taken off is still quite recognizable.

LETTERS OF PETROLEUM V. NASBY (410)

"Shows Why He Should Not Be Drafted" originally appeared in *The Nasby Papers* (1864). The bitterly satirical "The Assassination" appeared in *Divers Opinions and Prophecies* (1865). "The Reward of Virtue" is from *Swingin Round the Cirkle* (1867). The last selection was illustrated with the picture reproduced on page 416.

ORPHEUS C. KERR'S CHILDHOOD (418)

This, the first of the *Orpheus C. Kerr Papers* (1862), reveals Newell's tendency to pun whenever he has a chance.

BILL ARP'S CORRESPONDENCE (421)

Bill Arp, in the selections printed here, adopts two rather inconsistent attitudes. In the letter to Lincoln, written during the early stages of the Civil War, he is a Southerner who sympathizes with the North—a Georgia prototype of Nasby. In the letter to Ward, Bill is a Southerner, sympathizing with the people of his section. Like Artemus Ward, the comic character thus merges with the character of his creator. The selections are from *Bill Arp's Peace Papers* (1872). In other versions, the spelling was more orthodox.

JOSH BILLINGS' MEDITATIONS (427)

The two essays, from *Josh Billings on Ice* (1868), are characteristic collections of quaintly worded aphorisms. In a recent article, "Humor and America," *Scribner's*, C, 12 (July, 1936), Mr. Max Eastman called Billings "the father of imagism." "For," says the critic, "he was the first man in English literature to set down on his page . . . a series of verbal pictures, and leave them there for what they might be worth." The opening sentences of "Amerikans" and many sentences in "Live Yankees" illustrate the point, though such imagery is not entirely unknown in American humor before Billings. "Amerikans" offers an interesting comparison between American and English humor.

THE HAUNTED MAN (430)

In *Condensed Novels* (1867), Bret Harte, like many a literary comedian, wrote very effective parody. In this field of humor, he was one of the best, and this passage from his parody on Dickens is one of his most effective. For a time, plans were made to include in the volume containing Harte's parodies some of Mark Twain's early humorous writings.

New Year's Calls (433)

This passage, taken from *Saratoga in 1901* (1872), was much reprinted in anthologies and is highly reminiscent of "Doesticks on a Bender" in *Doesticks What He Says* (1855). Said Doesticks: " . . . went into an eating-house, called for a plate of beans, when the plate brought the waiter in his hand. I took it, hung up my beef and beans on a nail, ate my hat, paid the dollar a nigger, and sided out on the step-walk . . ." Cleverly both authors made use of mangled language and incongruous association.

Life in Danbury (436)

The sketches are typical of many domestic sketches by the literary comedians. They are taken from *They All Do It; or Mr. Miggs of Danbury and His Neighbors* (1877).

Life in an Odd Corner (439)

Both passages are from *Out of the Hurly-Burly* (1874). "The Morning Argus Creates a Sensation" is somewhat abbreviated, and "My First Political Speech" is only a part of the chapter dealing with Pitman's election. The former sketch makes much use of parody—of which obituary poems were a chief target. Compare the Ode in *Huckleberry Finn* with Clark's poems. "My First Political Speech" is an example of the discomfiture of the genial idiot, told in the first person. Paragraphs preceding the selection tell of Adeler's woe as he prepared his speech, made the trip to the near-by town, and heard others say the things he had planned to say.

The Brakeman at Church (449)

Published in the Burlington *Hawk-Eye* in 1879, this sketch quickly won wide fame. Says Mrs. Burdette: "Its popularity was immediate, and after its publication in the newspaper letter, it was republished . . . as a pamphlet, and was distributed by tens of thousands. It was copied by every newspaper of more than the slightest importance in the country . . ."—*Robert J. Burdette: His Message*, p. 127. Here the combination of railroad jargon with theological discussion proved highly amusing.

Bill Nye's Adventures in Politics (452)

"Accepting the Laramie Postoffice" and "A Resign" are from *Remarks* (1887). Both, published in the Laramie *Boomerang*, were widely republished. The first won comment in the London *Daily News,* and the latter, Nye asserted, with less exaggeration than one might suppose, was copied "from Japan to South Africa, and from Beersheba to a given point." "He Sees the Navy" is from *Bill Nye's Thinks* (1888), later republished as *Sparks* (1891). Though Nye wrote humor of every sort fashionable—tall tales, parodies, essays, accounts of domestic vicissitudes, anecdotes, and paragraphs, the passages reveal the qualities of most of his writings. Their relationship with the sort of humor in Seba Smith's writings will be quite evident.

MR. DOOLEY TO MR. HENNESY (460)

The two excerpts are from *Mr. Dooley in Peace and War* (1898). The second reveals the distrust for "book larnin' " cherished by American humorous apostles of common sense since the beginning of native humor.

LOCAL COLORISTS

IN CALIFORNIA (467)

"The Society upon the Stanislaus" was collected in *The Heathen Chinee* (1871). Stanislaus is a river southeast of San Francisco. The satire was directed at a local scientific society.

"The Luck of Roaring Camp" appeared in the *Overland Monthly,* August, 1868. This story won wide acclaim for Harte in the East, and brought flattering offers for Eastern publication of similar stories.

IN THE MIDDLE WEST (478)

The passage, Chapter VII of *The Circuit Rider* (1878), deals with two figures beloved by the humorists of the old Southwest, the "standing candidate" and the discomforted preacher.

SAM LAWSON'S NEW ENGLAND STORIES (482)

The two tales are taken from the volume *Sam Lawson's Fireside Stories* (1871). The first excellently displays Mrs. Stowe's highly effective use of the framework.

UNCLE REMUS'S SOUTHERN NEGRO STORIES (503)

The selections are from *Uncle Remus: His Songs and Sayings* (1880).

MARK TWAIN

THE NOTORIOUS JUMPING FROG OF CALAVERAS COUNTY (515)

This famous tale was sent East to appear in *Artemus Ward's Travels.* Arriving too late for inclusion in the volume, it was printed, instead, in Henry Clapp's *Saturday Press,* November 18, 1865. It was collected in *The Celebrated Frog of Calaveras County, and Other Sketches* (1867). Lowell called it "the finest piece of humorous literature yet produced in America."

THE FACTS CONCERNING THE RECENT RESIGNATION (522)

The passage is from *Mark Twain's Sketches, New and Old* (1875). It continues the tradition of political satire, and displays Mark in the role of a genial numbskull.

EUROPEAN GUIDES (528)

One of the most famous episodes in *Innocents Abroad* (1869). Here, maliciously, the doctor acts the sort of role consistently enacted, for purposes of comedy, by humorous lecturers.

BAKER'S BLUE-JAY YARN (533)

The blue-jay story is contained in Chapters II and III of *A Tramp Abroad* (1879). The asterisks indicate the end of Chapter II. For appreciative comment, see De Voto, *Mark Twain's America*, pp. 247–251. Says Mr. De Voto, in conclusion: "The story exhibits a good many aspects of Mark Twain's humor. It is a narrative interlude . . . in which the argument of the book halts while Mark Twain is over-hearing the talk of men who are leisurely and entertained. Its material comes from the Negro's bestiary, interstitial with his boyhood in Hannibal; and in this way the humor rises from fantasy, from the imaginative mythmaking of the slaves on the frontier. But also, Jim Baker, the narrator, exists; he is a creation from the world of reality. He lives, and no fantasy has gone into his creation, but only the sharp perception of an individual. His patient, explanatory mind actually works before our eyes and no one can doubt him. His speech has been caught so cunningly that its rhythms produce complete conviction. Fantasy is thus an instrument of realism and the humor of Mark Twain merges into the fiction that is his highest reach."

HUCK'S VISIT TO THE RAFT (538)

This passage, intended for use in *Huckleberry Finn*, appeared only in *Life on the Mississippi* (1883). The chapter from which it was omitted was probably Chapter XVI of Huck's story, since the opening paragraph of this chapter tells how Huck and Jim saw "a monstrous long raft" and then wondered when they would get to Cairo. The passage contains some of the finest tall talk and tall tales in American humor.

IDENTIFIABLE PSEUDONYMS OF
AUTHORS MENTIONED

Addums, Mozis (George William Bagby)

Adeler, Max (Charles Heber Clark)

Aesop, G. Washington (George T. Lanigan)

Allen — Josiah Allen's Wife (Marrietta Holley)

Arp, Bill (Charles Henry Smith)

Aunt Maguire (Frances M. Whitcher)

Aunt Patty (Caroline Lee Hentz)

Baldwin (Augustus Baldwin Longstreet)

Bedott, Widow (Frances M. Whitcher)

Beedle, Johnny (J. W. McClintock)

Biglow, Hosea (James Russell Lowell)

Billings, Josh (Henry Wheeler Shaw)

Breitmann, Hans (Charles G. Leland)

Brown, Vandyke (William P. Brannan)

Browne, Dunn (Samuel Fiske)

Burlington Hawkeye Man (Robert J. Burdette)

Bushwhacker, Dr. (Frederic S. Cozzens)

Chip (F. P. W. Bellew)

Col. Vanderbomb (J. B. Jones)

Commodore Rollingpin (John H. Carter)

Contributor, Fat (A. Miner Griswold)

Cox, Sunset (S. S. Cox)

Crabshaw, Timothy (Oliver H. Prince)

Dadd, B. (John H. Williams)

Danbury News Man (James M. Bailey)

Doesticks, Q. Philander (Mortimer Thomson)

Dooley, Mr. (Finley Peter Dunne)

Dow, Jr. (Joseph F. Paige)

Downing, J., Major (Charles Augustus Davis)

Downing, Major Jack (Seba Smith)

Dr. Bushwhacker (F. S. Cozzens)

Duckworth, Dodemus (Asa Greene)

Elmwood, Elnathan (Asa Greene)

Erratic Enrique (Henry Clay Lukens)

Falconbridge (Jonathan F. Kelley)

Fat Contributor (A. Miner Griswold)

Fibbleton, George (Asa Greene)

Fumble, Fudge (Marcus L. Byrne)

Gath (G. A. Townsend)

Gilhooley (W. W. Clark)

Green, Hiram (William Albert Wilkins)

Hall (Augustus Baldwin Longstreet)

Hannibal, Professor Julius Caesar (W. H. Levinson)

559

Hawkeye Man, Burlington (Robert J. Burdette)

Haywarde, Richard (Frederic S. Cozzens)

Hill, Yankee (George H. Hill)

Hoffenstein, Rube (Joseph C. Aby)

Hornet, Bolivar (Marcus L. Byrne)

Jolthead, Jonathan (Thomas Green Fessenden)

Jones, Major (William T. Thompson)

Josh (Samuel L. Clemens)

Josiah Allen's Wife (Marrietta Holley)

Kerr, Orpheus C. (Robert H. Newell)

Knickerbocker, Diedrich (Washington Irving)

Letter H. (Charles Graham Halpine)

Lovingood, Sut (George W. Harris)

McArone (George W. Arnold)

Major Jones (William T. Thompson)

Maurice, Jaques (James W. Morris)

Muldoon, Dennis (George B. Goodwin)

Nasby, Petroleum Vesuvius (David Ross Locke)

Nye, Bill (Edgar Wilson Nye)

O'Lanus, Corry (J. Stanton)

Old Si (Samuel W. Small)

Old Un (Francis A. Durivage)

Oldstyle, Jonathan (Washington Irving)

O'Reilley, Miles (Charles G. Halpine)

Otis, Herod (Willis Hazard)

Partington, Mrs. (Samuel P. Avery)

Partington, Mrs. Ruth (B. P. Shillaber)

Patty, Aunt (Caroline Lee Hentz)

Paul, John (Charles H. Webb)

Paxton, Philip (Samuel A. Hammett)

Pepper, K. N. (James W. Morris)

Perkins, Cyrus D. (James M. Bailey)

Perkins, Eli (Melville D. Landon)

Phoenix, John (George Horatio Derby)

P. I. Man, The (Jay C. Goldsmith)

Pipes, Jeems (Stephen C. Massett)

Pomeroy, Brick (Marcus M. Pomeroy)

Poor Richard (Benjamin Franklin)

Quad, M. (Charles B. Lewis)

Rattlehead (Marcus L. Byrne)

Rollingpin, Commodore (John H. Carter)

S——l (G. W. Harris)

Sage of Rocky Creek (Francis B. Lloyd)

Sanders, Billy (Joel Chandler Harris)

Sass, Job (George E. Foxcraft)

Sawin, Birdofredum (James Russell Lowell)

Short-and-Fat, Sampson (Samuel Kettell)

Shuttle, Job (Thomas Small Weaver)

Singularity, Thomas (Junius Nott)

Skinflint, Obediah (Joel Chandler Harris)

Skitt (H. E. Taliaferro)

Slick, Jonathan (Anna S. Stephens)

Slick, Samuel (Thomas Chandler Haliburton)

Slick, Sam Jr. (Samuel P. Avery)

Smith, John (Seba Smith)

Snodgrass, Thomas Jefferson (Samuel L. Clemens)

Solitaire (John S. Robb)

Spike, Ethan (Matthew F. Whittier)

Spoopendyke (Stanley Huntley)

Spriggins, Widow (Frances M. Whitcher)

Squibob (George Horatio Derby)

Stahl (G. M. Wharton)

Strauss, Yawcob (Charles F. Adams)

Strickland, Joe (Arnold)

Sugartail (G. W. Harris)

Sunset Cox (S. S. Cox)

Topnoody and Waxem (W. J. Lampton)

Tribune Man, The (Henry Ten Eyck White)

Twain, Mark (Samuel L. Clemens)

Uncle Ben (John S. Draper)

Uncle Remus (Joel Chandler Harris)

Uncle Solon (Roland E. Robinson)

Uncle Toby (Tobias H. Miller)

Vanderbomb, Col. (P. B. Jones)

Ward, A. (George M. Baker)

Ward, Artemus (Charles Farrar Browne)

Ward, Betsey Jane (William Comstock)

Waxem, Topnoody and (W. J. Lampton)

Widow Bedott (Frances M. Whitcher)

Widow Spriggins (Frances M. Whitcher)

Wife, Josiah Allen's (Marrietta Holley)

Wilbur, Homer (James Russell Lowell)

Wink, Josh (W. D. Nesbit)

Yankee Hill (George H. Hill)

York's Tall Son (William T. Porter)

Young Un (George P. Burnham)

INDEX OF HUMOROUS WRITERS

(Italicized numbers refer to selections in the text. References to notes on selections are not included.)